Brewing Science

Volume 2

FOOD SCIENCE AND TECHNOLOGY

A SERIES OF MONOGRAPHS

Maynard A. Amerine, Rose Marie Pangborn, and Edward B. Roessler, PRINCIPLES OF SENSORY EVALUATION OF FOOD. 1965.

S. M. Herschdoerfer, QUALITY CONTROL IN THE FOOD INDUSTRY. Volume I – 1967. Volume II – 1968. Volume III – 1972.

Hans Riemann, FOOD-BORNE INFECTIONS AND INTOXICATIONS. 1969.

Irvin E. Liener, TOXIC CONSTITUENTS OF PLANT FOODSTUFFS. 1969.

Martin Glicksman, GUM TECHNOLOGY IN THE FOOD INDUSTRY. 1970.

L. A. Goldblatt, AFLATOXIN. 1970.

Maynard A. Joslyn, METHODS IN FOOD ANALYSIS, second edition. 1970.

A. C. Hulme (ed.), THE BIOCHEMISTRY OF FRUITS AND THEIR PRODUCTS. Volume 1 – 1970. Volume 2 – 1971.

G. Ohloff and A. F. Thomas, GUSTATION AND OLFACTION. 1971.

George F. Stewart and Maynard A. Amerine, INTRODUCTION TO FOOD SCIENCE AND TECHNOLOGY. 1973.

C. R. Stumbo, THERMOBACTERIOLOGY IN FOOD PROCESSING, second edition. 1973.

Irvin E. Liener (ed.), TOXIC CONSTITUENTS OF ANIMAL FOODSTUFFS, second edition. 1974.

Aaron M. Altschul (ed.), NEW PROTEIN FOODS: Volume 1, TECHNOLOGY, PART A – 1974. Volume 2, TECHNOLOGY, PART B — 1976. Volume 3, ANIMAL PROTEIN SUPPLIES, PART A — 1978.

S. A. Goldblith, L. Rey, and W. W. Rothmayr, FREEZE DRYING AND ADVANCED FOOD TECHNOLOGY. 1975.

R. B. Duckworth (ed.), WATER RELATIONS OF FOOD. 1975.

Gerald Reed (ed.), ENZYMES IN FOOD PROCESSING, second edition. 1975.

A. G. Ward and A. Courts (eds.), THE SCIENCE AND TECHNOLOGY OF GELATIN. 1976.

John A. Troller and J. H. B. Christian, WATER ACTIVITY AND FOOD. 1978.

A. E. Bender, FOOD PROCESSING AND NUTRITION. 1978.

D. R. Osborne and P. Voogt, THE ANALYSIS OF NUTRIENTS IN FOODS. 1978.

Marcel Loncin and R. L. Merson, FOOD ENGINEERING: PRINCIPLES AND SELECTED APPLICATIONS. 1979.

Hans Riemann and Frank L. Bryan (eds.), FOOD-BORNE INFECTIONS AND INTOXICATIONS, Second Edition. 1979.

N. A. Michael Eskin, PLANT PIGMENTS, FLAVORS AND TEXTURES: THE CHEMISTRY AND BIOCHEMISTRY OF SELECTED COMPOUNDS. 1979.

J. G. Vaughan (ed.), FOOD MICROSCOPY. 1979.

J. R. A. Pollock (ed.), BREWING SCIENCE, Volume 1, 1979. Volume 2 — 1981.

Irvin E. Liener (ed.), TOXIC CONSTITUENTS OF PLANT FOODSTUFFS, Second Edition. 1979.

In preparation

Jack C. Bauernfeind (ed.), CAROTENOIDS AS COLORANTS AND VITAMIN A PRECURSORS: TECHNOLOGICAL AND NUTRITIONAL APPLICATIONS.

Brewing Science

Volume 2

Edited by

J.R.A. Pollock

Pollock and Pool Limited
Reading, England

1981

ACADEMIC PRESS

London · New York · Toronto
Sydney · San Francisco

A Subsidiary of Harcourt Brace Jovanovich, Publishers

ACADEMIC PRESS INC. (LONDON) LTD.
24–28 Oval Road
London NW1

United States Edition published by
ACADEMIC PRESS INC.
111 Fifth Avenue
New York, New York 10003

British Library Cataloguing in Publication Data

Brewing Science. — (Food Science and technology). Vol. 2
  1. Brewing
  I. Pollock, James Richard Allan
  II. Series
  663'.3'015   TP570

  ISBN 0-12-561002-5   LCCCN 78-72546

Printed in Great Britain by
John Wright and Sons Ltd., at the Stonebridge Press, Bristol

List of Contributors

M. AMAHA, *Asahi Breweries Ltd., 1 Kyobashi, 3—Chome, Chuo-ku, Tokyo, Japan*

J. D. G. ARMITT, *Castlemaine Perkins, G.P.O. Box 44, Brisbane, Queensland 4001, Australia*

L. CHAPON, *Laboratoire de Chimie Biologique II 2ᵉ Cycle—Boulevard des Aiguillettes, Case Officielle 140, 54037 Nancy Cedex, France*

G. CHARALAMBOUS, *Technical Center, Anheuser-Busch Inc., 721 Pestalozzi St., St. Louis, MO 63118, U.S.A.*

S. ENGAN, *A/S Hansa Bryggeri, Post boks 300, N-5001 Bergen, Norway*

R. B. GILLILAND, *Arthur Guinness Son and Co. (Dublin) Ltd., St. James Gate, Dublin, Ireland*

J. V. HARVEY, *The South Australian Brewing Co. Ltd., 224–230 Hindley Street, Adelaide, South Australia*

N. HASHIMOTO, *The Research Laboratories of Kirin Brewery Co. Ltd., Miyahara-Cho, Takasaki, Gumma Pref., Japan*

K. KITABATAKE, *Asaki Breweries Ltd., 1 Kyobashi, 3—Chome, Chuo-ku, Tokyo, Japan*

J. R. A. POLLOCK, *Pollock and Pool Ltd., Ladbroke Close, Woodley, Reading RG5 4DX, England*

C. RAINBOW, *51 Tower Road, Burton upon Trent, Staffordshire ED15 0NY, England*

I. RUSSELL, *Beverage Research Department, Labatt Brewing Company Ltd., London, Ontario, Canada N6A 4M3.*

G. G. STEWART, *Beverage Research Department, Labatt Brewing Company Ltd., London, Ontario, Canada N6A 4M3*

Preface

The continuation of the collaborative effort to produce, in one place, as complete as possible a description of where brewing science is today leads to this second volume of the resulting work.

In this volume the emphasis is on beer, its composition, its analysis and some of its properties; and on the microbiology of the process and by-product handling. Progress in all these fields, perhaps especially on the analytical front, has been striking during the past two decades and the authors' contributions reflect this. The theoretical aspects of how the composition of beer is related to its organoleptic qualities (which will also be treated in Volume 3) and to the staling processes which occur in it are much less clear, and there are many lines of thought on this, as, it is hoped, will be clear from some of the discussions.

It is a sorrow to record the deaths of Dr. Mikio Amaha and of Dr. C. Rainbow, whose distinguished contributions to brewing science and practice enriched the brewing world. Dr. Mikio's elegant contribution in the present volume to the subject of the origins of gushing provides a definitive description of this subject, and Dr. Rainbow's summary of the present state of knowledge on the subject of beer spoilage organisms deals with a subject which was for so many years one of his great interests.

December 1980   J. R. A. POLLOCK

Contents

1. Brewing Yeast

R. B. Gilliland

2. Yeast Flocculation
G. G. Stewart and I. Russell

3. Beer Composition: Volatile Substances
Sigmund Engan

4. Involatile Constituents of Beer
George Charalambous

5. Analysis of Beers
John V. Harvey

6. Flavour Stability of Packaged Beers
Naoki Hashimoto

7. Oxygen and Beer
Lucien Chapon

9. Beer Spoilage Microorganisms
C. Rainbow

10. Brewery and Malthouse Effluents and their Management
J. D. G. Armitt

Contents of Volume 1

1. Analysis and Composition of Barley and Malt
M. Moll

2. The Physiology of Malting
Anna M. MacLeod

3. Unmalted Grains in Brewing

A. M. Canales

4. The Chemistry of Hops
M. Verzele

5. Manufactured Products from Hops and Their Use in Brewing
R. P. Hildebrand

6. Composition and Analysis of Hops and Derived Products
H. Pfenninger, F. Schur and P. Anderegg

7. Water in Malting and Brewing
M. Moll

To the memory of Philippe Kreiss

1. Brewing Yeast

R. B. GILLILAND

Arthur Guinness Son and Co. Ltd., Dublin, Ireland

I. INTRODUCTION

Yeasts are larger than bacteria and are, therefore, easier to observe and count microscopically. They are single-celled and so are easier to deal with experimentally than fungi which form mycelia and frequently grow in mats or clumps. They grow rapidly in defined media and they have a well defined genetic cycle. For these and other reasons yeasts have been selected as test organisms for thousands of scientific studies of the biology, biochemistry and genetics of living organisms. There is, therefore, a wealth of information about the life of yeasts which would never have become available if they had been studied only from the industrial viewpoint. There have been a number of valuable and extensive studies of yeast starting with Alfred Jörgensen's (1886) book followed by that of Guilliermond (1912) and including in more recent years books by Skinner *et al.* (1947), White (1954), Ingram (1955) and Reed and Peppler (1973) and texts edited by Roman (1957), Cook (1958), Reiff *et al.* (1960, 1962), Lodder (1970), Rose and Harrison (1969, 1971, 1970) and Prescott (1975). There are also chapters on yeasts in the more specialized brewing texts by Hough, Briggs and Stevens (1971) and by Findlay (1971). These should be consulted for more extensive coverage of yeast science than can be given in this chapter which has as its object the presentation of the present state of knowledge of the biology of yeast which is of direct interest to the brewery microbiologist.

II. THE NATURE OF BREWING YEAST CELLS

A. Origins

Ripening fruits, particularly grapes, normally harbour on their skins various microorganisms including yeasts. If the ripe fruit falls to the ground the yeasts reproduce on the decaying fruit and survive the winter in the soil. In spring or summer yeasts are blown into the air with dust and recolonize the fruit. Insects also play a part in distributing yeasts on fruit. It is a small step from this natural process to collecting the fruit, squeezing it and allowing the yeasts on the skin to act on the sugars of the fruit. In this way wine and cider are formed.

The production of beer requires two further steps: first, the conversion of cereal starch into sugar, by malting and mashing, and secondly the introduction of yeast from an outside source. It is not known where brewing yeast originated, perhaps from fruit, or perhaps by chance infection, but for thousands of years yeasts have been collected from one brew and passed on to another. During this time yeasts from good fermentations were carefully preserved, while the yeasts from poor fermentations were thrown out. The result of this process of selection is that all modern brewing yeasts belong to one of two species and even these two species are very similar to one another. The two species are *Saccharomyces cerevisiae*, which is used in ale and stout fermentation, and *Saccharomyces carlsbergensis*, which is the yeast used in lager brewing. *Saccharomyces carlsbergensis* has recently been renamed *Saccharomyces uvarum* by van der Walt (1970) and it is maintained by Windisch and Neumann (1972) that these two yeasts should be combined under a single name, *Saccharomyces cerevisiae*. Here we shall retain the names *Saccharomyces cerevisiae* and *Saccharomyces carlsbergensis*.

B. The Microscopical Examination of Brewing Yeasts

Brewing yeasts are round or ovoid, non-motile cells measuring from 5×10^{-6} m (5 μm) to 10×10^{-6} m (10 μm) in diameter. Individual cells cannot be distinguished with the naked eye but are comfortably observed with a dry lens objective on an ordinary microscope. Considerable information about a sample of yeast can be obtained by examining a water suspension of the yeast on a plain slide at a magnification of 450 with either normal or phase-contrast illumination.

The cells of brewing yeast are generally ovoid and of very regular shape and size. If the yeast is fresh the interior of the cell is relatively clear and the cell wall is thin. As yeasts become older the cell wall becomes thicker and darker, and granulations appear within the cell. Normally a vacuole can be seen within the cell. Sometimes very small highly refractile particles, which are in continuous movement (Brownian motion) may be seen within the vacuole; these are polymetaphosphate or volutin granules. It is possible to distinguish between a culture of *S. cerevisiae* and one of *S. carlsbergensis* by the fact that in the latter a proportion of cells can be observed which have a small flat edge at one part of the cell wall, whereas this is never observed in *S. cerevisiae*.

Electron micrographs of thin sections of brewery yeasts reveal much more of the internal organization of the cell than can be observed with the optical microscope. The following structures can be seen under the electron microscope (see Plates I and II).

C. Cell Wall

The cell wall is somewhat elastic but is rigid enough to retain the shape which the cell assumes. It is 100–300 nm thick and it accounts for 18–25% of the dry weight of the cell (Northcote and Horne 1952, Nurminen *et al.* 1970). The cell wall may double its weight as the cell ages (Griffin and MacWilliam 1969). If the cell wall has not been treated before sectioning it appears to have a smooth outline. If the cell is first disintegrated and the cell walls are washed and then boiled in dilute sodium hydroxide before electron microscopy, or if they are pre-treated with glucanase or pronase, then the cell wall appears as a fibrillar mat (Kopécka *et al.* 1974). On disintegration of the complex molecules of the cell wall it is found to consist of 35–45% glucan, 40–45% mannan, 5–10% protein, 1–2% chitin, 3–8% lipid, and 1–3% of inorganic substances such as phosphate (Nurminen 1976).

Yeast glucan is a highly branched carbohydrate or polyglucose structure in which the units are mainly β-1,3 with β-1,6 linkages; it forms the inner layers of the cell wall (Peat *et al.*1958, Tanaka and Phaff 1965, Fleet and Manners 1976). Yeast mannan consists of an α-1,6 linked chain with α-1,2 and α-1,3 linked side chains (Haworth *et al.* 1941, Phaff 1963, Ballou *et al.* 1974). It is linked with enzymes, protein and phosphate in the outer layer of the cell wall and exhibits antigenic properties. Glucan–protein, mannan–protein and glucoman-nan–protein complexes have been separated from yeast cell walls by mild alkali treatment. These polysaccharide–protein complexes contain varying amounts of glucan, mannan and protein and also glucosamine which can form a link between polysaccharide and protein (Falcone and Nickerson 1956, Kessler and Nickerson 1959, Korn and Northcote 1960). The phosphate in the cell wall is bound in mannan–protein complexes. The protein has a high content of aspartic and glutamic acids and contains relatively large amounts of sulphur. Chitin is a straight-chain compound of *N*-acetylglucosamine units joined by β-1,4 linkages; glucosamine also appears in cell constituents other than chitin. Most of the chitin is localized in the region of bud scars.

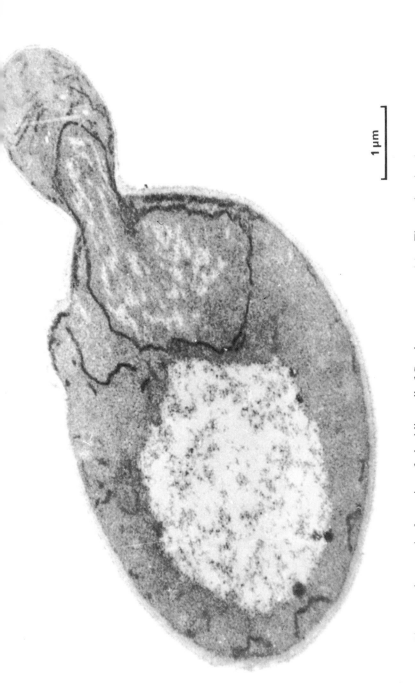

1 μm

PLATE I. Electron micrograph of a section of a budding cell of *Saccharomyces cerevisiae.* The nucleus is migrating into the bud before nuclear division.

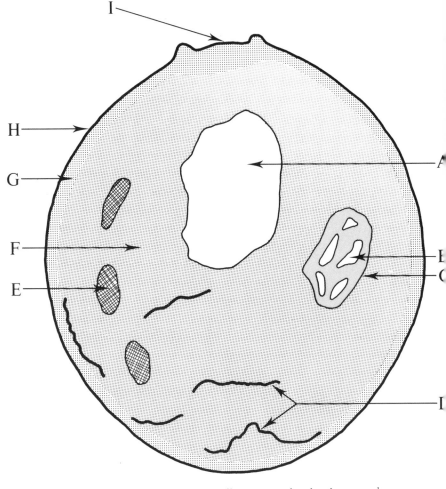

PLATE II. Diagram of a section of a yeast cell as seen under the electron microscope.

A: Vacuole
B: Chromosomal material
C: Nucleus
D: Endoplasmic reticulum
E: Mitochondrion
F: Cytoplasmic fluid
G: Cytoplasmic membrane
H: Cell wall
I: Birth scar

D. Birth and Bud Scars

A birth scar is found on the cell wall where the cell has separated from its mother cell. Birth scars generally occur at the end of the long axis of the cell. Bud scars may be found on the cell wall where buds have formed and then separated as daughter cells. Bud scars have a characteristic shape of a hill surrounded by a low wall formed by the edges of the cell walls. The ability of a cell to produce buds is limited. One cell of *Saccharomyces cerevisiae* may produce as many as 40 buds but a limit of about 20 is more normal. This has been established by isolating a yeast cell in a droplet of a complete medium and removing each daughter cell with a micromanipulator soon after it is formed. The size of the parent cell increases with each bud produced whereas newly formed daughter cells are uniform and small (Hayashibe *et al.* 1973).

E. The Cytoplasmic Membrane

The cytoplasmic membrane, or plasmalemma, is a thin elastic balloon lying directly behind the cell wall and following its shape. In electron micrographs with good resolution the cytoplasmic membrane is seen to consist of a double or triple layer 8–10 nm in cross-section. Chemically it contains mannan, protein and lipids. In some cases the cytoplasmic membrane may be seen to form intrusions or invaginations into the cytoplasm. The cell wall can be dissolved off by treatment with snail-gut juice which does not affect the cytoplasmic membrane. If this is done in a solution with osmotic pressure equal to that within the cell then the cell contents will be retained by the cytoplasmic membrane and the protoplast thus formed will become spherical. If the osmotic pressure of the surrounding liquid is lowered the membrane will burst, releasing the cell contents. Carefully treated protoplasts placed in a weak agar medium can regenerate new cell walls and return to normal vegetative growth (Nečas 1971). The cytoplasmic membrane is semipermeable and it regulates the flow of nutrients into the cell and flow of by-products out of the cell; this it does according to their lipid solubility and degree of dissociation (Suomalainen and Nurminen 1976). It also permits passage of some enzymes or enzyme precursors out of the cell into the cell wall.

F. The Endoplasmic Reticulum

In electron micrographs a double membrane system may frequently be seen lying along the inside wall of the cell or randomly located within the cell; this is the endoplasmic reticulum. The endoplasmic reticulum produces spherical vesicles which contain enzymes which assist in softening the cell wall and allowing bud formation.

G. The Vacuole

The vacuole in electron micrographs is a lightly staining round or oval body of about one-third the diameter of the cell. It is bounded by a single membrane and may contain denser staining volutin granules. The vacuole splits up into smaller bodies at budding and several of these enter the bud.

H. The Nucleus

In electron micrographs the nucleus is readily distinguished as a large body with an irregular outline which is enclosed in a single nuclear membrane. The literature describing the search for chromosomes within the nucleus is voluminous but inconclusive. A narrow bundle of microtubules can be demonstrated traversing the nucleus between pores in the nuclear membrane (Matile *et al.* 1969). The resting nucleus contains a nucleolus which stains deeply with acid fuchsin. During cell reproduction the nucleus elongates and extrudes into the newly formed bud; it is then constricted and divides into two halves, one half being retained in the parent cell and one half being in the newly formed bud. Each half contains a nucleolus.

I. Mitochondria

Mitochondria are not easily seen in electron micrographs of brewing yeasts unless the cells have been grown under very aerobic conditions. Mitochondria may then be seen as double-walled structures with internal membranes or christae. Under anaerobic conditions or when grown in the presence of high concentrations of glucose, the mitochondria degenerate and are difficult to recognize. Mitochondria have a high lipid content; they also contain ribonucleic acid and a lesser amount of deoxyribonucleic acid together with protein material.

J. Cytoplasmic Fluid

The liquid within the cell which is not differentiated into organelles visible with the optical or electron microscope is the cytoplasmic fluid. It contains, in addition to water, the carbohydrates glycogen and trehalose and also ribosomes, enzymes and mineral salts. Yeast glycogen is a high molecular weight, branched, polymer of glucopyranose. It may separate from the cytoplasmic fluid in transparent spheres up to 40 nm in diameter. Trehalose is a non-reducing disaccharide consisting of two glucopyranosyl units. Ribosomes are extremely small particles consisting of ribonucleic acid and protein.

III. THE NAMING OF YEASTS

A. How Yeasts are Named

A pure culture of yeast normally does not readily change its appearance, growth characteristics, method of sporing, ability to ferment certain sugars, or requirement for specific nutrients or growth factors. It is, therefore, of great value to have a recognized name for the yeast. For example if we say *Kluyveromyces fragilis* it implies a yeast which is rather small and oval in shape, which forms reniform spores, which is able to ferment glucose, galactose, sucrose, lactose and raffinose, which can grow at high temperatures and which has many other specific characters. The name associated with a set of characteristics also means we can recognize the same yeast if we come across it again.

As yeasts belong to the plant family the rules of the International Code of Botanical Nomenclature apply to them. Each yeast is therefore known by a binomial combination, the first name is the genus (e.g. *Saccharomyces*), the second the species (e.g. *cerevisiae*) and this may be followed by the name of the person who first described the species. When the species has been transferred to another genus the name of the discoverer is put in brackets and is followed by the reviser's name, e.g. *Kluyveromyces fragilis* (Jörgensen) van der Walt was first described by Jörgensen and named *Saccharomyces fragilis*; it was transferred to the genus *Kluyveromyces* by van der Walt.

The family or genus to which yeast belongs is determined by its mode of growth and by its method of sexual and asexual reproduction. These may be difficult for the inexperienced taxonomist to distinguish. Once the genus has been established the species is determined mainly on physiological differences which are comparatively easy to examine. The species is however a nebulous concept and it depends on individual decision as to what distinguishing features are sufficient to establish a separate species. It is open to informed opinion as to whether a suggested new species name is justified and should be accepted, or is unwarranted and should be ignored or referred to as a variety of another species. Fortunately one school of yeast taxonomy located in Delft is pre-eminent and publications of Lodder, Kreger van Rij and Stelling Dekkar are accepted generally as reflecting the best opinion available. Alternative systems of classification have however been evolved by Kudriavzev (1960) and by Novák and Zsolt (1961). There have been many attempts to improve the meaning of the species concept for yeast. One of these is Numerical Taxonomy in which a very large number of characters of the yeasts are determined and groups of yeasts which have a high percentage of common characters are reckoned to be of the same species. One difficulty is that often there is no clear-cut dividing line at any particular "percentage similarity" above which we can say yeasts are in the same species and below which it is justifiable to call them different species. Numerical Taxonomy, which requires a computer to deal with the necessary calculations, has been energetically followed by Kocková-Kratochvílová and her colleagues (1966, 1969, 1976) in Czechoslovakia for the genus *Saccharomyces* and has been applied to the genus *Pichia* by Poncet (1967). New analytical techniques have recently been used in yeast taxonomy. These include the application of proton magnetic resonance to determine the structure of cell wall mannans (Spencer and Gorin 1968, Gorin and Spencer 1970) and the determination of the base composition of the deoxyribonucleic acid expressed as the ratio of guanine + cytosine to the total bases in the DNA (Meyer and Phaff 1969, Nakase and Komagata, 1971). Immunology has also been applied to distinguish between yeasts, or to demonstrate similarity between species, by Campbell (1967, 1970, 1973). Callejas *et al.* (1977) have recommended the more sensitive technique of immuno-diffusion as giving superior differentiation between species of yeast. Tsuchiya *et al.* (1965) have based a system of classification on serology. These methods are not however used in the more classical taxonomy described by Lodder (1970).

B. Yeast Taxonomy

The yeasts belong to a rather ill defined group in the true fungi (Eumycophyta). Yeasts are unicellular or at least spend part of their vegetative cycle as single cells. They are spherical, ovoid, pear-shaped or sausage-shaped and are larger than the bacteria. Yeasts lack chlorophyll. They possess well defined, tough but not rigid, cell walls. They have a well organized nucleus. They are non-motile. Most yeasts reproduce vegetatively by budding but some form cross-walls and divide by fission; conidia are not produced. Within this rather loose definition yeasts do not all fall into one sub-division of the true fungi but, depending on their ability to sporulate and the nature and method of sporulation, they may be put into one of the three sub-divisions or classes, *Ascomycetes*, *Basidiomycetes* or *Fungi imperfecti*. The yeasts in these classes are discussed in a simplified form in the following paragraphs. For fuller information Lodder (1970) should be consulted.

Beech *et al.* (1968) have compiled a useful key to the yeasts which relies on physiological tests. These are relatively easy to carry out so that it does not require an intimate knowledge of the biology of yeasts to apply this system. Barnett and Pankhurst (1974) have produced a computer-made key for identifying yeasts which is also based on physiological tests only, and Wiles (1953) has given practical details of the way in which a laboratory can identify yeasts in batches of twenty at a time.

C. Ascomycetes

Yeasts which form spores within an ascus are placed in the order *Endomycetales* in which they are divided between three families, *Saccharomycetaceae, Spermophthoraceae* and *Endomycetaciae.*

Saccharomyceteceae have round or oval spores and are divided into the following four sub-families:

(1) *Schizosaccharomycoideae* divide by fission and contain one genus *Schizosaccharomyces* with five species.

(2) *Saccharomycoideae* divide by multilateral budding and contain the following twelve genera. The number of species in each genus is given in brackets after the genus name:
Saccharomyces (41), *Hansenula* (28), *Dekkera* (2), *Pichia* (45), *Pachysolen* (1), *Citeromyces* (1), *Debaromyces* (10), *Schwanniomyces* (4), *Wingea* (1), *Kluyveromyces* (19), *Saccharomycopsis* (1) and *Lodderomyces* (1).
The total number of species in this group is about 154. The brewing and baking yeasts are included in the genus *Saccharomyces.*

(3) *Lipomycetoideae* form an ascus by conjugation of parent and bud. The cell is capsulated. There is one genus, *Lipomyces*, containing two species.

(4) *Nadsonoideae* reproduce by bud-fission at opposite poles of the cell and have an intricate mechanism of zygote formation. There are four genera, *Nadsonia, Saccharomycodes, Hanseniaspora* and *Wickerhamia*, with a total of seven species.

Spermophthoraceae have needle shaped spores. The family includes yeasts in three genera, *Nematospora, Metchnikowia* and *Coccidiasci* with a total of seven species.

Endomycetaceae contains yeasts which produce abundant mycelium as well as *pseudomycelium*. There is one genus, *Endomycopsis*, with ten species.

D. Basidiomycetes

Yeasts which discharge a spore by a drop-excretion mechanism from the end of a sterigma (ballistosporogeneous yeasts) are placed in the class *Basidiomycetes* in which there is one family, *Sporobolomycetaceae*, containing three genera, *Sporidiobolus, Sporobolomyces* and *Bullera*, with a total of 16 species.

E. Fungi Imperfecti

Yeasts which do not form spores are placed in the Fungi imperfecti. They are included in one family, *Cryptococcaceae*, which includes the genera *Rhodotorula* (10 species) *Cryptococcus* (19), *Torulopsis* (51), *Candida* (104),

Trigonopsis (1), *Schizoblastosporion* (1), *Kloeckera* (4), *Pityrosporum* (3), *Brettanomyces* (8), *Trichosporon* (12) and *Sterigmatomyces* (4), with a total of about 186 species. Species in the genus *Brettanyomyces* may be encountered in brewing. Some species in the genera *Pichia, Candida, Torulopsis, Rhodotorula* and *Hansenula* may be found in samples from the brewery or from trade, but these are aerobic yeasts and are generally of little importance in brewing (Hemmons 1954, Windisch 1954, Brady 1958, Gilliland 1961, Wiles 1949, 1950, 1952 and 1953).

F. The Genus *Saccharomyces*

Yeasts in the genus *Saccharomyces* ferment glucose vigorously. They form round or oval spores which are not easily liberated from the ascus and they do not form pellicles on liquid media. The *Saccharomyces* may be divided into three groups. In the first group (the former Zygosaccharomyces) conjugation precedes ascus formation. Many of this group are osmophilic. In the second group no conjugation occurs before ascus formation; the cells are diploid or of a higher ploidy. The spores are normally haploid and conjugation occurs between spores, or between spore cultures, to regenerate the diploid state. The third group contains yeasts which were formerly in the genus *Torulaspora*; they are haploid and conjugate before sporing, often by means of pro-tuberances which develop on some cells.

The different species in these three groups are differentiated mainly by their ability to assimilate and to ferment the carbohydrates galactose, maltose, sucrose, melibiose, lactose, raffinose and starch. Fermentative ability can be assessed by seeding the yeast culture into sugar broth in a test tube containing a small submerged tube, incubating and observing gas produced and trapped in the small tube. This method may give misleading results, especially with slow-fermenting yeasts. It is preferable to use the sugar broth in 1 oz. screw-capped McCartney bottles in which the aluminium cap contains a number of holes and the cap liner is of good rubber. Gas produced can then be detected and measured daily by inserting the needle of a well oiled hypodermic syringe through one of the holes in the cap into the bottle and observing the movement of the plunger (Gilliland 1962). The interpretation of assimilation tests has been criticized by Barnett (1977) who has recommended aerobic tests in liquid media with some quantification of the growth obtained.

Where more than one species share the same sugar fermentation pattern they may be distinguished by their method of spore formation, by their ability to ferment or assimilate other carbohydrates and by their ability to grow on media containing 100 p.p.m. of the antibiotic Actidione (cycloheximide). The characteristics of the species in the genus *Saccharomyces* are summarized in Table 1.

TABLE 1. Characteristics of species in the genus *Saccharomyces*

Ferments	Species	Conjugation before sporing	Ability to grow on actidione medium	Further distinguishing features
Glucose only	S. inconspicuus	+	−	Grows in vitamin-free media; lactate utilized
	S. bisporus	+	−	Cells small
	S. bailii	+	−	Cells large
	S. telluris	−	−	1 or 2 ascospores per ascus
	S. aceti	−	−	1 to 4 ascospores per ascus
Glucose + galactose	S. unisporus	−	+	
	S. delbrueckii	+	−	
	S. dairensis	−	−	1 or 2 spores per ascus, cells small
	S. globosus	−	−	1 to 4 spores per ascus, cells small
	S. transvalensis	−	−	1 or 2 spores per ascus, cells large
	S. saitoanus	−	−	Sucrose assimilated
Glucose + maltose	S. rouxii	−	−	Growth in 60% glucose medium
	S. prostoserdovii	−	−	No growth in 60% glucose
Glucose + sucrose + 1/3 raffinose	S. rosei	+	−	Inulin fermented
	S. kloeckerianus	+	+	
	S. capensis	−	−	
Glucose + melibiose	S. norbensis	−	−	
Glucose + maltose + melibiose	S. hienipiensis	−	−	
Glucose + galactose + melibiose + 1/3 raffinose	S. oleaceus	−	−	
Glucose + galactose + sucrose + 1/3 raffinose	S. chevalieri	−	−	
	S. exiguus	+	+	No growth on 50% glucose medium
	S. vafer	+	−	Growth on 50% glucose medium
Glucose + galactose + sucrose + melibiose + raffinose	S. kluyverii	+	−	
	S. microellipsoides	+	−	Trehalose assimilated, xylose not assimilated
	S. mrakii	+	+	Does not assimilate trehalose or zylose

(*continued p. 12*)

TABLE 1. (*cont.*)

Ferments	Species	Conjugation before sporing	Ability to grow on actidione medium	Further distinguishing features
	S. amurcae	+	+	Assimilates trehalose and xylose
	S. coreanus	–	–	
Glucose + sucrose + maltose	*S. heterogenicus*	–	–	
Glucose + sucrose + maltose + 1/3 raffinose	*S. bayanus*	–	–	
	S. fermentati	+	–	
Glucose + sucrose + maltose + 2/3 raffinose	*S. eupagycus*	+	+	Ethylamine hydrochloride utilized
	S. inusitatus	–	–	Ethylamine hydrochloride not utilized
Glucose + galactose + maltose + melibiose + 1/3 raffinose	*S. oleaginosus*	–	–	
Glucose + galactose + sucrose + maltose	*S. italicus*	–	–	
Glucose + galactose + sucrose + maltose + 1/3 raffinose	*S. pretoriensis*	+	–	Arbutin not split
	S. montanus	+	+	Arbutin split
	S. cerevisiae	–	–	
Glucose + galactose + sucrose + maltose + raffinose + melibiose	*S. florentinus*	+	+	Xylose not assimilated; ethylamine hydrochloride utilized
	S. cedri	+	+	Xylose assimilated; ethylamine hydrochloride utilized
	(*S. uvarum*) (*S. carlsbergenesis*)	–	–	Ethylamine hydrochloride not utilized
Glucose + galactose + sucrose + maltose + 1/3 raffinose + starch	*S. diastaticus*	–	–	

G. The Genus *Brettanomyces*

The *Brettanomyces* are interesting to brewers because they take part in the fermentation of lambic beer and were used in completing the fermentation of high-gravity export beers (Custers 1940, Gilliland 1961). They are also the most potent yeasts in producing off-flavours in bottled beer. They are small slow-growing yeasts frequently ogive in shape, which reproduce by budding and normally do not form spores, though sporulation has been found in two species (van der Walt and van Kerken 1960). They produce more esters than other yeasts and give a characteristic fruity aroma to the growth medium. They produce acetic acid when grown aerobically and have a negative Pasteur effect (Wiken *et al.* 1961). They are resistant to cycloheximide. The seven species are distinguished as follows:

Ferments	*Species*	*Further distinguishing features*
Glucose only	Br. custersianus	Assimilates trehalose but not cellobiose
	Br. abstinens	Assimilates cellobiose but not trehalose
Glucose, sucrose and maltose	Br. bruxellensis	Does not assimilate galactose
	Br. lambicus	Assimilates galactose latently
Glucose, galactose, sucrose maltose and cellobiose	Br. custersii	Ferments galactose slowly, lactose assimilated latently
	Br. intermedius	Ferments galactose quickly lactose not assimilated
Glucose, galactose, sucrose, maltose, cellobiose and lactose	Br. claussenii	No filament formation
	Br. anomalus	Abundant filament formation

Observation of sporulation in two species of *Brettanomyces* necessitated that the sporing strains be transferred to a genus in the *Ascomycetes* and the genus *Dekkera* was formed by van der Walt (1964) with the two species *Dekkera bruxellensis* and *Dekkera intermedius* which, apart from their ability to sporulate, are identical with the corresponding *Brettanomyces* species. The reasons why sporulation in these yeasts was unobserved for so many years are that sporulation is sparse and slow, it requires media enriched with vitamins, the spores are released from the ascus so that it is often difficult to recognize that sporulation has occurred and the ability to sporulate is readily lost in laboratory-maintained cultures.

IV. YEAST VIABILITY

In any yeast culture, half of the cells will not have produced any buds; they will have a birth scar but no bud scar. One quarter of the cells will have produced one daughter cell and so will have a birth scar and one bud scar; one eighth of the cells will have two bud scars, and so on. Only one in 2000 cells will have produced 10 buds and one in 2 million will have produced 20 buds. A yeast cell which has died of old age after producing 20–40 buds is therefore extremely rare. Cells may however die from other causes, for example by subjection to high temperature, by poison, by a mutation which is lethal to the cell or by starvation and autolysis.

It is important for the brewer that the yeast he uses to start a fermentation is alive and active. It should normally contain less than 5% dead cells. By examination of a water suspension of the yeast on a plain slide an experienced observer can obtain a fair idea of the condition of the yeast and by counting the apparently living and dead cells in a haemacytometer slide the percentage of dead cells can be estimated. A more objective dead cell count can be obtained by suspending the cells in a solution containing 0·01 % Methylene Blue and 2% sodium citrate, as recommended by Burns (1957). In this solution dead cells can readily be distinguished as they are stained blue; living cells do not stain as the plasma membrane is impermeable to the dye. The Methylene Blue technique gives excellent results with a healthy yeast culture but it has limitations if the culture is in poor condition or has been maltreated.

Various other dyes have been recommended from time to time for distinguishing between living and dead cells. These include methyl green, eosin, acridine orange, rhodamine B, neutral red and erythrosine. Parkkinen *et al.* (1976) compared Methylene Blue staining with a fluorochrome technique using primuline, acridine orange or acriflavine. They found the fluorochrome technique gave results similar to methylene blue with samples in which the dead cell count was low but that when the dead cell count was over 40% then the fluorochrome method was much more reliable.

The standard method of determining viability of microorganisms is to do a haemacytometer count on a suspension of the cells, to plate a measured quantity of this suspension on a wort gelatin medium and to incubate the plate and count the resultant colonies. This method may give highly erroneous results with brewing yeast which often gives inexplicably low plate counts. This is not due only to clumping of cells but also to death of the cells during preparation of the plate (Mills 1941, Gilliland 1959).

The most accurate estimation of the percentage of dead cells in a yeast sample can be obtained by a Slide Viability technique (Gilliland 1959). In this method the cells are suspended in a growth medium containing 6% gelatine and the suspension is placed in a haemacytometer slide. The edges of the coverslip are sealed with melted petroleum jelly to prevent the slide from drying out and the slide is incubated for 20 hours at 18 °C before examination. Slides of a series of different dilutions of the cell suspension should be made so that a convenient number will occur in some slides. After incubation for 20 hours living cells will have formed microcolonies of 4–20 cells while those that are dead remain unchanged single cells. When Slide Viability was compared with Methylene Blue viability the agreement was very good at viabilities over 85% but at lower viabilities the Methylene Blue method underestimated the percentage of dead cells. The reason for this is that the loss of the impermeability of the membrane to the dye may not be the first vital component of the cell to disappear. If the yeast is first treated with Methylene Blue and then used in a Slide Viability test it can be seen that no cell which stains with Methylene Blue is ever capable of producing a bud but some unstained cells also fail to reproduce and are apparently dead (Gilliland 1959). Similar results have been observed with rhodamine staining (Takahaski 1968).

A suspension of brewer's yeast was subjected to gradually increasing temperatures and after each increase the viability was determined by Methylene Blue staining and by Slide Culture. The results were as follows:

Yeast heated to 43°C for	Viability by Methylene Blue	Viability by Slide Culture	Viability by Plate Culture
0 min	97%	97%	25%
1 min	97%	97%	2%
2 min	97%	24%	0·4%
3 min	97%	0%	0·1%
5 min	97%	0%	0%
10 min	10%	0%	0%
20 min	0%	0%	0%

It is clear that the cells lost ability to reproduce long before they lost their ability to resist staining with Methylene Blue. Counts of colonies on a gelatine plate always underestimated the viability when it was high, as has been observed by other workers.

A limitation of the Slide Viability technique was observed in that when applied to brewer's yeast it gave false results if the number of cells on the slide was low. Thus a slide containing 119 cells in the counting area gave 97% viability; that is 115 of these cells produced a micro colony. On the contrary a slide containing 90 or fewer cells in the counting area gave viability of 0–1% as only one or none of the cells budded or produced a colony (Gilliland 1959). This extraordinary behaviour, which was called the "lethal dilution effect", could also be observed in liquid cultures. If a series of decreasing seeding rates of brewer's yeast was added to wort and incubated it was found that if the seeding was less than 0·05 g per litre or $0·3 \times 10^6$ cells per ml, then most of the cells died and only a very few reproduced normally. This phenomenon has never been satisfactorily explained but the observation of Van Engel (1969) that yeast needs zinc for reproduction may have some relevance, as when 1 p.p.m. of a zinc salt was added to the wort medium the lethal effect was reduced but was still very noticeable. The effect was observed only with brewery yeast but not with the same yeast after it had been regrown in laboratory culture.

V. GROWTH RATE OF BREWER'S YEAST

A. Effect of Temperature on Growth Rate

The rate of reproduction of brewer's yeast in wort depends on the temperature and reaches a maximum at about 30 °C. Reproduction rate varies between strains. *Saccharomyces cerevisiae* grows more quickly than *Saccharomyces carlsbergensis* at high temperatures but more slowly than *S. carlsbergensis* at low temperatures. The following reproduction times were observed in a comparison of one strain of each of the two species.

Temperature	S. cerevisiae	S. carlsbergensis
39 °C	4·0 hr	No growth
36 °C	2·0 hr	4·8 hr
33 °C	1·4 hr	1·8 hr
28 °C	1·6 hr	2·0 hr
18 °C	3·2 hr	3·7 hr
10 °C	11·0 hr	9·0 hr
8 °C	42·0 hr	24·0 hr

Webb (1977) found that the maximum growth temperature of *S. cerevisiae* was 37·5–39·8 °C while that of brewing strains of *S. carlsbergensis* was 31·6–34 °C Some non-brewing strains, which Walsh and Martin (1977) suggested should be called *S. uvarum*, had a higher maximum temperature of 38·2–40 °C. Lewis and Enevoldsen (1973) found that a temperature increase of 10 °C doubled the growth rate and that the amount of nitrogenous materials in the wort did not affect the growth rate but limited the extent of growth.

B. Growth of Yeast in Brewery Fermentations

When yeast is added to wort and its reproduction is monitored by careful cell counts, the usual growth curve of a single-celled organism is observed. This consists of a lag phase during which the cell becomes larger but does not produce any buds, followed by a logarithmic phase in which the yeast count doubles in regular time increments and this merges into a stationary phase in which the yeast count remains constant.

The lag phase of brewer's yeast is relatively short if the yeast has been properly harvested, rapidly cooled and stored cool for up to three days before pitching into aerated wort. In fact the duration of the lag phase is generally less than one reproduction time. The brewer may refer to the relatively long period which elapses before the specific gravity of the fermentation begins to fall rapidly as a lag phase but this is incorrect as far as the yeast is concerned. During this period the yeast is reproducing rapidly and in top fermentations the maximum count will be reached soon after rapid fermentation begins. In lager fermentations yeast reproduction is much slower but continues for about three days after the yeast has been added to the wort.

If cell size is monitored during a brewery fermentation it is found that the cell increases in size during the lag phase before budding starts. The average cell size decreases during active growth but increases again after budding has stopped and cell count has become stationary. As a consequence of these changes in size the total cell mass increases before cell count begins to rise and continues increasing after maximum cell count has been reached.

The original gravity of the wort has little effect on the lag time or on the reproduction time of brewing yeasts as is shown by the following results obtained with *Saccharomyces cerevisiae* at 25 °C.

Original gravity* of wort	Lag time	Reproduction time
1010	2·1 hr	2·2 hr
1020	1.6 hr	2·0 hr
1040	1·6 hr	2·0 hr
1070	1·6 hr	2·0 hr
1100	4·0 hr	2·8 hr

* Specific gravity × 1000.

Reproduction of yeast in a brewery fermentation is limited primarily by the availability of oxygen. The yeast reproduces until the oxygen in the wort is all used up and it then can go through one or two more divisions but after that further growth is very slow. The amount of yeast produced in a fermentation depends on the yeast strain; it is increased with increased available oxygen, with increased wort strength and with increased temperature of fermentation. In lager fermentations a maximum count of $30–50 \times 10^6$ cells per ml might be expected. In ale or stout fermentations the maximum count may be $60–100 \times 10^6$ cells per ml.

The time required to complete a brewery fermentation depends on the extent of exponential growth of the yeast. Kirsop and Brown (1972) have shown that if the concentration of all the non-carbohydrate constituents of a wort were halved yeast growth was reduced but was completely restored on addition of amino acids. Nitrogenous compounds are therefore the only ones which are near critical concentration in the wort for maximum yeast growth. Jones (1972) has reported on the effect of wort composition on yeast behaviour and beer quality.

C. Growth of Yeast in Bottled Beer

Beer which is to be naturally conditioned in bottle must contain adequate fermentable residue and a sufficient number of healthy yeasts. A suitable amount of fermentable residue is about 4°, or 1% of sugar, and a suitable number of yeast cells is about 0·5–1 million cells per ml. After bottling and during storage the cells reproduce about three times so that the cell count increases by about eight times to reach a maximum of 4–5 million cells per ml. Reproduction under these conditions is not so rapid as in wort. The doubling time in beer at 18 °C for one strain of *Saccharomyces cerevisiae* was 13 hours compared with a doubling time of 3·2 hours in wort at the same temperature.

Wild yeast can reproduce in bottled beer more rapidly than brewer's yeast. For example a strain of *Saccharomyces diastaticus* isolated as a contaminant in draught ale had a reproduction time of 5·5 hours at 18 °C as compared with 13 hours for brewer's yeast. Yeasts in bottled beer may be killed by the presence of certain strains of *Acetobacter rancens* in the beer with consequent prevention of natural conditioning (Gilliland and Lacey 1966).

D. Death of Yeast due to Extremes of Temperature

Brewer's yeasts are relatively sensitive to heat. Most strains are killed by exposure to 52 °C for 10 minutes, suspended in wort, but some strains may be slightly more resistant. In practice it is unwise to allow the brewing yeasts to reach a temperature over 38 °C and a lengthy period at a temperature over 25 °C results in death of the cells followed by autolysis. Wild yeasts are generally more heat resistant than brewer's yeast and a heat test for the detection of wild yeasts has been used as a method for monitoring the purity of the brewing yeast (Gilliland 1955, Lund and Thygesen 1957).

Yeast spores are more resistant to high temperatures than the parent cells but the difference is relatively small (Ingram 1955). The resistance of sporing and vegetative cells to high temperatures had been used for distinguishing between different yeasts, but this method has fallen out of use as it is unreliable because of strain variation.

There are some psychrophilic species of yeast which grow at low temperatures and have relatively little resistance to high temperatures. These are found in polar areas and include the species *Candida scottii* and various species in the genera *Cryptococcus* and *Rhodotorula*. Other species which may be isolated from warm-blooded animals are psychrophobic and may grow at temperatures up to 45 °C and have correspondingly high death temperatures;

among these species are *Candida sloofii, Saccharomycopsis guttalata, Saccharomyces telluster* and *Kluyveromyces fragilis.*

Moist brewer's yeast, or yeast cultures grown on agar slopes, are sensitive to freezing which may cause the death of a large proportion of the cells. In practice it is advisable to aim at a temperature of 4 °C for storage of the brewing yeast and also for storage of yeast cultures. Yeast cultures which have been freeze-dried will withstand temperatures below zero without injury to the cells.

VI. FLOCCULATION

A. Mechanism of Flocculation

Many brewer's yeasts aggregate into clumps towards the end of a fermentation. This flocculation is reversible in that the clumps disperse again into single cells if they are washed with distilled water or if a fermentable sugar is added to the liquid in which they are suspended. The mechanism which causes flocculation is still not completely understood, in spite of considerable study. The subject has been reviewed by Jansen (1958) and by Rainbow (1966).

The major factor controlling the stage of the fermentation at which flocculation occurs is the concentration of sugar remaining in the fermenting wort. When this falls below a certain level flocculation begins. Divalent ions of calcium, magnesium or manganese are necessary for flocculation and, of these, calcium is much the most effective. Nishihara *et al.* (1976) found magnesium to be an absolute requirement for flocculation of yeast grown in a magnesium-deficient medium. Harris (1959) and Mill (1964) suggested that the calcium ions form a bridge between carboxyl groups on the cell surface of adjacent cells. The bridge was strengthened by hydrogen bonding between hydroxyl and hydrogen groups on carbohydrate molecules. Lyons and Hough (1970) suggested that the bridge was formed by calcium or magnesium ions between phospho-mannan-protein molecules on the cell wall. Mill (1964) found that sodium ions were antagonistic to flocculation and that flocculated yeast was dispersed by 1,2-epoxypropane which esterifies carboxyl groups. Stewart and Goring (1976), on the other hand, found that with some strains of yeast low concentrations of sodium (10 p.p.m.) caused flocculation but stronger concentrations of sodium ions dispersed the flocs. In very flocculent strains, with strongly negative charges on the cells, the sodium ion may act as a "counter ion" to neutralize the repellant forces of these negative charges. Stewart *et al.* (1975) found further evidence for the implication of calcium–carbonyl complexes in flocculation and they suggest that the carbonyl groups are those in acidic wall proteins. Jayatissa and Rose (1976) used treatment of yeast cells with 60% hydrofluoric acid to remove most of the phosphorus but little carbohydrate or protein. This treatment did not remove the ability to flocculate so that apparently phospho-diester links are not involved in bridge formation but calcium and carboxyl groups may be responsible for floc formation.

Patel and Ingledew (1975b) found that an increase in acid-soluble glycogen in the yeast cell corresponded with an increase in capability to flocculate. Masschelein and Devreux (1957) showed that isolated cell walls showed the same flocculation characteristics as whole cells so that flocculation was definitely a cell wall phenomenon. They also showed that the mannan content of flocculent cells decreased as the cells approached the flocculation point and they suggest that mannan controlled flocculation by masking active flocculation sites. Eddy and Rudin (1958) found that treatment with papain released a protein–mannan complex from yeast cell walls and at the same time destroyed their flocculence, so that it appeared likely that this protein had a role in flocculation.

The medium in which the yeast is growing may play a part in flocculation. Stewart and Goring (1976) found that some strains which flocculated in wort did not flocculate in a synthetic medium and Morimoto et al. (1975) found a high-molecular weight fraction of wort which promoted flocculation.

B. Genetics of Flocculation

Flocculation ability in yeast is controlled genetically by one homozygous gene pair (Gilliland 1951) or by up to three gene pairs (Thorne 1951). Lewis et al. (1976) reviewed work on genetic control of flocculation and reported that in one brewing yeast flocculation was controlled by a single pair of dominant genes; in another yeast a second dominant flocculence gene was identified. They also reported very high spontaneous mutation rates from flocculence to non-flocculence, as had previously been observed by other workers. Mutation is generally in the direction of loss of ability to flocculate, and this is important in the quality control of brewing yeast. Stewart et al. (1975) found that, in the yeast they were studying, there was a multiple gene system controlling flocculence and both dominant and recessive flocculation genes were present.

C. Classification and Measurement of Flocculation

The flocculation characteristics of brewing yeast are of great technical importance. Traditionally, in ale and stout fermentations, the yeast crop was collected as top yeast by skimming or by some system such as the Burton Union which depends on naturally formed flocs rising to the top. In lager fermentation yeast was cropped as bottom yeast and more recently ale fermentations have been carried out in cylindro-conical fermenters with a yeast which flocculates intensely towards the end of the fermentation so that most of the yeast can be withdrawn as a plug from the bottom of the vessel. In many breweries yeast is now separated from the beer by centrifuge which makes the flocculation characteristics of the yeast of less importance so long as it remains in suspension for most of the fermentation. Numerous systems of classification of flocculation and numerous ways of measuring the flocculating ability of yeast have been described.

Yeasts can be divided into non-flocculent types, which do not form clumps under any conditions, and flocculent types which may form clumps under certain conditions. The flocculent group has been subdivided in a number of ways. There is general agreement that chain-forming yeasts, in which the bud does not separate from the parent, form a separate group. These chain-forming yeasts behave technically very similarly to a head-forming yeast which flocculates towards the end of a fermentation (Gilliland 1957). Most writers, however, regard true flocculence as reversible, which flocculence caused by chain formation is not. A test has been described (Lewis and Johnston 1974) which distinguishes between chain-forming yeasts and truly flocculent yeasts. In this test the yeast is harvested at the end of a fermentation, transferred to distilled water and sonicated for 15 seconds which will break up both chains and flocs. It is then suspended in a pH 4·5 acetate buffer containing a calcium salt. The true flocculent yeast will then re-aggregate but the chain-forming yeast will remain dispersed.

Yeasts which show true flocculation have been further subdivided into two classes by Gilliland (1957) who called the non-flocculent yeasts Class I, those which flocculated into loose clumps and formed a yeast head at the end of fermentation were called Class II and strains which flocculated intensely into large clumps which fell to the bottom of the fermentation and did not form a yeast head were called Class III; the chain-forming type was called Class IV. Stewart et al. (1975) divided yeasts showing true flocculation into those which flocculated in wort fermentations but not in a glucose–ammonium salts medium and those which flocculated in both media; he also used, as a distinction, their ability to exhibit co-flocculation with another strain. Co-flocculation with two reference strains had previously been used as a distinguishing character by Hough (1957), who also distinguished different classes by suspending the yeast in a calcium chloride solution at pH 5 and at pH 3·5 and observing both floc formation and ability to form a climbing film of yeast at the liquid–air interface. In addition, the dispersion of clumps by 10% maltose and also floc formation which occurred only on addition of 3% ethyl alcohol were used as distinguishing tests.

In addition to these qualitative tests the intensity of flocculation can be measured by various methods generally dependent on the rate of sedimentation of flocs in a buffered solution containing calcium ions. Burns (1937, 1941) suspended 0·5 g of twice-washed yeast in 10 ml of pH 4·6 buffer in a 15 ml graduated tapered tube and measured the amount of yeast sedimented after 10 minutes. Strongly flocculent yeasts gave 1 ml or more of sediment while weakly flocculent or non-flocculent yeasts gave 0–0·5 ml of sediment. Helm *et al.* (1953) refined the Burns test and used 500 p.p.m. of calcium sulphate in the water used for washing and suspension. Kato and Nishikawa (1957) used a similar test but measured the yeast photometrically in the top 8 ml of the tube and also in the bottom 2 ml after standing for 10 minutes. The ratio of these two measurements gave a measure of sedimentation intensity. Chester (1963) grew the yeast in a synthetic medium, resuspended the yeast by shaking and read the optical density photometrically at intervals. The sedimentation time was taken as the time required for the optical density to fall by a standard amount and varied with different yeasts from 1 to 100 minutes. Woof (1962) measured photometrically the yeast in suspension just below the liquid surface at intervals over a period of two hours and typified the yeast by two parameters, the "terminal count" and the "terminal time". Greenshields *et al.* (1972) found the existing methods to be impracticable in dealing with highly flocculent yeasts from a tower continuous fermenter, and an adaptation of Burns' method using an automatic recording spectrophotometer was recommended.

VII. VARIANT YEASTS IN THE BREWING YEAST

A. Variation within the Species

A single species of yeast such as *Saccharomyces cerevisiae* can include strains which exhibit considerable differences in character. These differences may be insufficient to justify a different botanical name but may still be of great technical importance in industry. Some of these strains have been described as separate species but the separation has not been considered justified, for example species described as *Saccharomyces ellipsoideus*, *Saccharomyces turbidans*, *Saccharomyces intermedius* and *Saccharomyces anamensis* are now all included in the species *S. cerevisiae*. Thorne (1975) has reviewed this problem and distinguishes between "classification" depending on qualitative (all or none) characters of the yeast and "typing" depending on quantitative characters. He points out that any system of distinguishing between strains involves the compromise of striking a reasonable balance between differentiation and simplicity, so that the problem has no clear-cut solution. For the brewer this means that most weight should be given to those characters which affect either the process or the product and relatively little weight should be given to distinguishing characters which have no effect on the process or product.

B. Mutants of the Brewing Yeast

It is essential to maintain the purity of the brewing yeast and to detect variants before they reach such proportions that they could affect the process. These variants may arise by mutation of the brewing yeast. In some cases where a single gene is concerned, the difference is qualitative and the acquired character, or the loss of character, may be quite stable. For example the ability to ferment maltotriose is governed by a single gene, so mutation can cause loss of the gene function and inability to ferment this sugar. The mutant is stable in that it is most unlikely to regain the ability to ferment maltotriose. In other cases the character may be governed by many genes and there may be an almost continuous variation in the intensity of expression of the character from strain to strain. This is the case with a character such as fermentation rate. With variants of this type it is possible, by repeated selection, to move towards one extreme of the character. However, reversion towards the original norm is likely to occur on repeated use of the selected strain.

C. Detection of Mutants in the Brewing Yeast

The following tests have been found useful for the detection of mutants in the brewing yeast.

1. Low Concentration Actidione Plates

Harris and Watson (1968) recommend the use of accurately measured small concentrations of Actidione for distinguishing aberrant strains or species of *Saccharomyces*. The actidione susceptibility of the brewing yeast must first be established and a concentration just above this should be used in the test. The Actidione must be added at the time of plating as it is unstable on heating. Gilliland (1971a) has given examples of the reaction of various yeast strains in this test and commented on its value for the detection of maltotriose non-fermenting yeasts.

2. Crystal Violet Plates

Katò (1967) recommended the use of crystal violet for suppressing colony formation of brewing yeast and allowing the detection of other yeasts. The concentration of crystal violet required to inhibit the brewing yeast must first be established and this may range from 20 p.p.m. to 80 p.p.m. (Gilliland 1971a).

3. Attenuation Limit

The attenuation limit, or lowest specific gravity attainable in a particular wort by fermenting with a strain of yeast, is an important characteristic of the strain. The attenuation limit depends on the number of the individual carbohydrates in the wort which the yeast can ferment. Normal brewing yeasts ferment glucose, sucrose, maltose and maltotriose. Some strains of *S. cerevisiae* and of *S. carlsbergensis* cannot ferment maltotriose and so have abnormally high attenuation limits. Other strains can ferment some of the minor sugars such as isomaltose, panose, isopanose or maltotretraose (Gilliland 1969). These strains will have attenuation limits below the normal. Strains of *S. diastaticus* can ferment longer chain maltodextrins and so have very low attenuation limits.

The attenuation limit can be determined as follows:

Add 0·25 g of a pure culture of the yeast under test to 5 ml of sterilized wort in a 25 ml Erlenmeyer flask; close the flask with a water trap, incubate for 24 hours at 25 °C, filter off the yeast and determine the specific gravity by the drop method (Williams and Stringer 1955). If necessary the determination can be completed within 6 hours if the flask is shaken during incubation. If an abnormal attenuation limit is recorded and confirmed then a sugar analysis of the fully attenuated beer may be carried out by paper chromatography or by gas liquid chromatography of silylated sugars in order to find which sugars are left unfermented. The attenuation limit of the brewing yeast is of value in process control to indicate the limiting specific gravity which can be attained in the brewery fermentation but it does not indicate the presence of small numbers of wild or variant yeasts. This can only be done after isolation of pure cultures, by plating out the yeast, and determining the attenuation limit of each isolate.

4. Flocculation Tests

Any of the tests described in section VI.C may be used to typify a pure strain of yeast or to distinguish one strain from another. They can also be applied to the brewing yeast in the hope of determining whether any change has taken place in its ability to flocculate, but they generally fail for two reasons. The first reason is that differences in intensity of flocculation may arise from changes in the wort, changes in aeration, age of the sample or stage of the fermentation at which the yeast was collected. The second reason is that whereas these tests may detect gross admixture with a yeast of different flocculation characteristics they cannot detect the presence of small proportions of such yeasts.

The best way to monitor the composition of the brewing yeast in order to detect small proportions of yeast with differing flocculation properties is to plate out the yeast and determine the flocculation characteristics of 50 individual colonies. This can be done by picking off colonies and adding them to 5 ml quantities of sterilized wort in 10 ml clear glass bottles and incubating them for four days at 24 °C. The sediments are then examined. A loose sandy deposit indicates a chain-forming yeast (Class IV). If the sediment is solid the liquid is poured off and the yeast shaken up in the last few drops so that the appearance of the suspension can be examined under a strong light as the bottle is slowly rotated on its side. If granulation is completely absent the yeast is non-flocculent (Class I). If small clumps can be seen giving a regular granular appearance the yeast is a head-forming flocculent yeast (Class II). If the yeast has formed large flaky clumps, from which the liquid readily drains leaving a pattern of yeast clumps on the glass wall then the yeast is a non-head forming flocculent yeast (Class III). The percentage of chain-forming strains may also be determined by slide culture (Gilliland 1959), or by a direct microscopic method (Curtis and Wenham 1958) Slide culture cannot distinguish between flocculent and non-flocculent yeasts.

The flocculence classification test as described above was developed for top fermentation yeasts and is not particularly good at distinguishing differences between strains of *Saccharomyces carlsbergensis* (Watson 1964) and adaptations for lager yeasts have been described by Yoshida (1962) and by Patel and Ingledew (1975a). We have found that it is possible to distinguish between flocculent (Class II) and non-flocculent (Class I) lager yeasts by taking single colonies direct from the wort-gelatine plate and dispersing each colony with a platinum needle in a drop of 0·1% aqueous calcium chloride solution. Class I colonies give a milky dispersion in the droplet, whereas Class II colonies show aggregation; the difference can readily be observed with a low power stereo-microscope.

D. Wild Yeasts

Wild yeasts may gain access to the brewing yeast by aerial contamination, by contamination by insects, or by contact with unsterilized plant. Generally the numbers of these wild yeasts are very small and they cause little concern. Wild yeasts may cause trouble if they are difficult to remove from the beer by fining or if they are carried forward to beer which is naturally conditioned. If wild yeasts are allowed to increase in numbers they can cause flavour problems and it is prudent to put a limit of, say, 10 wild yeast cells per million brewing yeast cells as the maximum which can be tolerated.

E. Tests for the Detection of Wild Yeasts

Many tests have been described for the detection of wild yeasts. Some of these tests are designed to detect specific wild yeasts while others are of more general application; they include the following tests.

Spore formation (Bourgeois 1968)
Resistance to 10 p.p.m. Actidione (Lee and Wilkie 1965)
Resistance to 0·1–0·4 p.p.m. Actidione (Harris and Watson 1968)
Growth in lysine medium (Morris and Eddy 1957)
Heat test (Gilliland 1955)

Growth in maltotriose (Gilliland 1969)
Fining characteristics (Ellison and Doran 1961)
Giant colony appearance (Richards 1967)
Growth factor requirements (Schultz and Atkin 1947)
Growth in crystal violet medium (Katò 1967)
Growth in fuchsin sulphite medium (Brenner *et al.* 1970)
Growth in crystal violet–fuchsin sulphite medium (Lin 1975)
Colony colour on brom-cresol green medium (Hall 1971)
Immuno-fluorescence serology (Richards 1968).

It is of course impractical to apply all of these tests regularly to the brewing yeast so a selection must be made of tests which will adequately detect impurity in the yeast and which are reasonably simple to perform. No one test is adequate so a combination of tests is required. The following tests appear to be most useful.

1. 10 p.p.m. Actidione Plate

A 0·1 g sample of the washed yeast is plated on wort agar containing 10 p.p.m. of Actidione. This completely suppresses the growth of brewing yeasts but permits the growth of many other species. Many genera of yeast appear to be immune to Actidione and the following genera were found to be able to grow on a solid medium containing 1000 p.p.m. Actidione: *Hansenula, Candida, Pichia, Cryptococcus, Torulopsis, Endomycopsis, Lipomyces, Trigonopsis, Sporobolomyces, Trichosporan* and *Brettanomyces*. A number of species of Saccharomyces can grow on plates containing 10 p.p.m. Actidione; these include *S. chevalieri, S. lactis, S. validus, S. dairensis, S. florentinus, S. exiguus, S. pastori, S. muciparus, S. bisporus, S. microellipsodes* and *S. pombe*. A plating method in which the sole source of nitrogen is lysine has also been used extensively (Morris and Eddy 1957). The lysine plate and the Actidione plate detect similar wild yeasts and we have found the latter to give more clear-cut distinction and so to be preferable. Some species of *Saccharomyces*, e.g. *S. fermentati, S. vafer, S. rosei, S. rouxii* and *S. microellipsodes* also can grow on lysine agar, as can the *Kluyveromyces*.

2. Heat Resistance

A suspension of the yeast containing a known concentration of cells is sealed in a glass ampoule which is placed in a water bath at 54 °C for 10 minutes. The ampoule is then shaken, broken open and 1 ml of the suspension is used to seed a wort-gelatine plate which is incubated at 21 °C for four days. Colonies appearing on the plate are those of heat-resistant wild yeasts. An isolated test of this kind is of little value but if it is applied regularly to the brewing yeast any trend towards an increase of wild yeast can be detected.

3. Fining Test

Yeasts which carry a very low negative charge may resist removal by finings. Ellison and Doran (1961) have described a test in which the brewing yeast was used to carry out miniature fermentations which were examined for the presence of persistant haze at the end of fermentation and during 18 days storage of the beer. Haze was produced in this test by as little as one cell of *Saccharomyces cerevisiae* var. *turbidans* in 100 million culture cells.

4. Selective Media

Brenner *et al.* (1970) used 0·30–0·35% fuchsin sulphite to suppress the growth of brewing yeasts while permitting the growth of *S. cerevisiae* var. *ellipsoideus*, *S. diastaticus* and genera such as *Hansenula* and *Candida*. Katò (1967) and Scherrer *et al.* (1969) investigated the use of a medium containing crystal violet to suppress the growth of brewing yeast and to allow other *Saccharomyces* to grow, and Richards (1970) recommended a medium containing 20 p.p.m. of crystal violet. Lin (1974, 1975) used a medium containing 4 p.p.m. crystal violet and 0·35% fuchsin sulphite which inhibited ale or lager yeasts but allowed 13 out of 15 strains of wild yeast to form colonies. The two wild yeast strains which failed to give colonies grew on the lysine medium, which Lin suggested should be used as a complementary test. Green and Gray (1950) described "WLN medium" containing bromcresol green and Hall (1971) found that this medium could be used to distinguish respiratory mutants and wild yeasts from ale yeasts by means of observations on the colony form and colour. This medium was not suitable for distinguishing between lager yeasts and wild yeasts as *S. carlsbergensis* gave colonies similar in colour to many wild yeasts.

5. Serology

An antiserum can be prepared by giving a rabbit a series of injections with a suspension of wild yeast. The purified rabbit serum is treated with a pure culture of brewery yeast to absorb all antibodies reactive to the brewing yeast. The yeast for test is spread on a plain slide, fixed with acetone, treated with non-reactive horse serum for 30 minutes to cover the non-specific sites, washed, treated with the wild yeast serum for 30 minutes, washed and then treated with fluorescein-conjugated goat antirabbit serum for 30 minutes to label the absorbed rabbit anti-serum. When the slide is examined under ultraviolet illumination wild yeasts are readily distinguished from the mass of culture yeasts by their green-blue fluorescence. By this method one wild yeast in many thousands of culture yeasts can be detected (Richards and Cowland 1967, Richards 1968). This immuno-fluorescent method has the great advantage that a result can be obtained on the day of the test and that it is very sensitive. It has the disadvantage that it gives no indication of the nature of the wild yeast present and that it is possible for the culture yeast to produce variants which fluoresce in this test but which are otherwise indistinguishable. Haikara and Enari (1975) used a mixture of sera prepared against four wild yeasts and found it much more effective in detecting contaminants in yeasts from various breweries than any of the selective media. The serum detected 80% of a wide range of wild yeasts tested and was recommended for routine quality control.

VIII. PURE CULTURES OF BREWING YEASTS

A. Maintenance

Where the number of yeast strains to be stored is not too large, they can be maintained on slopes of a solid medium in 28 ml screw-capped McCartney bottles. The medium contains 3 g malt extract, 3 g yeast extract, 10 g glucose, 5 g peptone, and 20 g agar in 1 litre of water (MYGP). Brewery wort solidified with 2% agar may also be used. The inoculated slopes are kept at 25 °C for 1 or 2 days until growth is visible and are then placed in a cabinet accurately maintained at 4 °C. These cultures will survive for several years but they should be subcultured twice a year to guard against possible loss.

Kirsop (1974) made a detailed study of the properties of 600 stock cultures of yeasts in 25 genera after they had been maintained in this way for a number of years. She found substantial variation from the original descriptions in biochemical and morphological properties. Variation was very much lower in freeze-dried cultures than in cultures maintained on slopes and the former technique was recommended.

The freeze-dry, or lyophil, culture technique has much to recommend it where large numbers of strains must be maintained. Progressive improvements have been made for many yeast strains so that criticisms of the low survival rates obtained are no longer justified. In the standard application of this method the yeast is suspended in "mist. desiccans" (3 parts of 20% glucose, 4·5 parts of horse serum) and freeze-dried and sealed under vacuum in a glass ampoule. The culture is reconstituted by breaking the ampoule and suspending the pellet in 0·5 ml of sterile yeast extract, peptone, medium. Richards and Elliot (1968) found that viability of *S. carlsbergensis* in lyophilized cultures was increased by pre-treatment of the yeasts with β-mercaptoethanol and by incorporation of ascorbic acid in the "mist. desiccans" system. Richards (1975) found the serum component of "mist. desiccans" affected survival adversely and that 20% sucrose was a better suspending medium. He found no loss of brewing characters in freeze-dried cultures. Hall and Webb (1975) question the value of treatment with β-mercaptoethanol and recommended a menstruum of 10% glucose plus 10% sodium glutamate. Using this method a survival rate of 60% was obtained after three year's storage of an ale yeast. Even under the best conditions the percentage viability of some strains of yeast after lyophilization is low but the method is recommended for maintenance of brewing characters (Kirsop 1974, Barney and Helbert 1976). Death of cells occurs mainly during the preparative process and the rate of death during storage over a number of years is very low so that if a small percentage of the cells survives the preparation the method is successful.

Other methods such as storing yeasts on solid media under mineral oil, or storing in strong sugar solutions, have little to recommend them. Preparation of cultures by liquid nitrogen freezing has been recommended by Burrows (1970) and by Wellman and Stewart (1973).

B. Transport

Lyophil cultures are ideal for sending through the post with suitable packing to protect the glass ampoule. Slope cultures in screw-capped McCartney bottles packed in a wooden box or in a stiff cardboard cylinder generally travel safely but occasionally may be killed during transport, presumably due to exposure to extremes of temperatures. It may be necessary to send larger quantities of yeast to a brewery which lacks facilities for propagation of a culture. In this case the yeast is propagated to give the required amount, it is then separated from the growth medium, washed with sterile water and again separated by filtration or by centrifuging. The resultant yeast cake is placed in a plastic bag which is packed in an insulated container surrounded by a number of sealed plastic bags containing ice. The bag containing the yeast must be fitted with a safety vent to release pressure should the package be delayed and the yeast begin autofermentation.

Baker's yeast is prepared commercially on the large scale in an active dried form which is ideal for transport and has excellent keeping qualities. In this process pressed yeast from a culture grown in a low nitrogen medium is extruded through a perforated metal plate to form cylinders of 0.2 cm diameter and 3 cm long. These are then slowly dried by a warm air stream so that the temperature of the yeast does not exceed 40 °C at any time. The various commercially used processes for yeast drying are described by Reed and Pepler (1973). Unfortunately it has not been found possible to use a similar drying process for brewing yeast and retain viability.

C. Propagation

Hansen first devised a method for the propagation of yeast from laboratory culture to give amounts sufficient to start a brewery fermentation. He recommended that the volume increment between cultures should be 10 or less so that a 10 ml culture was used to seed 100 ml; this was used to seed 1 litre with succeeding fermentations of 5 l, 20 l, 150 l, 600 l and 2400 l. He also recommended minimum aeration and a fermentation temperature similar to that used in the brewery. This system worked well but was very slow, particularly for lager yeasts cultured at low temperatures. Curtis and Clark (1957, 1960) found that the volume increment between successive cultures could be raised from 10 to 100 or higher without any disadvantage and that the propagation temperature could be higher than brewing temperature. Increased aeration and harvesting of the yeast before the fermentation was completed also helped to increase the crop and reduce production time. We have found the following system of producing cultures for brewery use to work satisfactorily. The source of any culture is the "master culture" which is fully tested for purity twice a year and then subcultured onto 12 wort-agar slopes in screw-capped McCartney bottles. These are incubated at 25 °C for two days and then stored at 4 °C. Surface growth of yeast from one of the slopes is washed with sterile wort into 100 ml of wort in a 250 ml Erlenmeyer. After two days' incubation at 25 °C this culture is used to inoculate 1 l of wort in a 2 l Erlenmeyer which is incubated at 25 °C for one day and then kept at 4 °C. This forms the "reserve culture" for the brewery and it is replaced every three weeks, each time going back to a slope culture. When a new culture is required for the brewery the yeast from a "reserve culture" is added to 10 l of wort in a 20 l vessel which is incubated at 25 °C and oxygenated for 24 hours. After 24 hours 120 g of yeast has been produced and the 10 l of fermenting wort is then added to a propagation vessel containing 5000 l of wort which has been heat sterilized and cooled to 24 °C. This propagation is oxygenated at 30 l of oxygen per minute for the first 6 hours. The propagation is completed in 36 hours, when about 100 kg of yeast should have been formed. The contents of the propagator is then run into 80 000 l of wort for the first brewery fermentation. In this way a yeast may be propagated up to the brewery stage within three days of request. Samples of the yeast are examined at each stage of the propagation to ensure that purity is maintained and that viability is high. In the first brewery fermentation some abnormalities may be observed but these disappear in succeeding brewery fermentations.

"Continuous batch" propagation of yeast, each time starting off from an intermediate stage, has also been advocated and this is particularly attractive for lager brewers who replace their brewing yeast after 6–10 brewery fermentations and so require fresh cultures very regularly (Thorne 1970). It is, however, a more dangerous process, both from the point of view of possible infection and also because of the possibility of mutation of the yeast in the propagator, and consequent replacement of the brewery yeast by a mutant. It is safer to start each propagation with an authenticated culture.

Strandskov et al. (1965) described a process in which the yeast culture was seeded into a small volume of wort in the propagation vessel and allowed to reproduce till the count had doubled; then an equal volume of sterile wort was added. This process was repeated until the maximum capacity of the vessel was reached. This has the advantage of minimizing the number of vessels and number of transfers required.

IX. FERMENTATION SYSTEMS AND COLLECTION OF BREWING YEAST

A. Methods of Yeast Collection

Different methods of separating the bewing yeast from the beer have evolved from the properties of different strains of yeast. The traditional distinction is between top (ale or stout) yeasts and bottom (lager) yeasts. This distinction by type of beer is no longer valid as bottom yeast is now used in some ale fermentations and lager yeast may be collected by centrifuging the beer. Some of the most common methods used for yeast collection are as follows.

B. Bottom Yeast

1. Lager Fermentation

Towards the end of a lager fermentation the yeast sediments to the floor of the fermentation vessel. The beer is then run off to lagering tanks and the sedimented yeast is pushed off the floor into a yeast collecting vessel situated below the fermentation vessel.

2. Plug Collection

A strongly flocculent yeast is used for ale fermentation in a cylindro-conical vessel. When fermentation is completed the fermentation is chilled. The yeast falls to the bottom and forms a dense plug of yeast which can be withdrawn and stored for use. This system was described nearly fifty years ago (Nathan 1930) but has become popular only in recent years.

C. Top Yeast

1. Ale Fermentation

A yeast which flocculates towards the end of the fermentation is used. Shortly after flocculation has begun the fermenting liquid may be run from the fermenting vessel into a "skimmer", or alternatively fermentation and skimming may take place in the same vessel. The yeast rises to the top of the fermentation and is then skimmed off mechanically or by suction into a yeast collecting vessel. The yeast is then chilled and stored for further use. Usually the middle skimmings alone are used for pitching.

2. Burton Union

Fermenting wort is discharged from the fermentation vessel towards the end of fermentation into Union vessels of 4 brls capacity. The yeast purges itself off through a swan-necked pipe at the apex of the Union vessel and is collected in a yeast trough and then chilled and stored. Excess beer is drained off the yeast in the collecting vessels and returned to the Union vessels.

D. Non-flocculating Yeast

1. Centrifuge Collection

Yeast separation formerly depended on flocculation and if a brewing yeast became non-flocculent it had disastrous effects both on the crop recovered (either as skimmed yeast or as bottom yeast) and also on the clarity of the beer going on to storage vessel. It is now possible to separate non-flocculent yeasts very efficiently by centrifuging the beer at the end of fermentation. A self-dicharging centrifuge should be used and the discharged yeast should be immediately chilled and stored. The yeast gains heat during centrifuging and if the fermentation temperature has been allowed to rise to, say, 27 °C, the further temperature increase during centrifuging may damage the yeast. If a secondary fermentation, or conditioning, is required then either the centrifuge is adjusted to allow sufficient yeast to remain in the beer going to storage vat, or else a portion of the beer is allowed to by-pass the centrifuge.

2. Proportional Pitching

In proportional pitching a portion of the fermenting wort is withdrawn from the fermentation vessel at the time of maximum yeast count; this may be as early as 24 hours after the yeast has been added to the wort. This portion of the fermenting wort is then added to the worts for the next fermentation at a suitable rate which is normally about 10%. If it is desired to hold the fermenting wort for any length of time it should be chilled immediately after collection to about 4 °C and it can then be safely held for a number of days. Either centrifuging or proportional pitching can equally well be applied to lager, ale or stout fermentations and both methods can also be used with yeasts which flocculate late in the fermentation.

E. Continuous Fermentations

If a stirred fermentation of wort is allowed to proceed almost to completion and if wort is then added slowly and continuously while beer is drawn off at the same rate, then an equilibrium will be reached and continuous fermentation will proceed. Continuous fermentation has a number of obvious advantages over batch fermentations and since the beginning of the century attempts have been made to use it for beer production. It was, however, only in 1957 that continuous fermentation to produce beer was put into commercial practice using a system of two or more stirred fermentation vessels in series. The yeast was separated by centrifuge and a portion of the recovered yeast could be fed back to the first fermenter. These systems had turnover times of about 16 hours for ale and 30 hours for lager. The continuous tower fermenter has also been used commercially for ale production using a highly flocculent yeast. In this method wort is fed in through the centre of the cone shaped bottom of the vessel and beer is drawn off the top of the vessel. A very heavy concentration of the flocculent yeast builds up at the bottom of the fermenter and fermentations are very rapid. An even more rapid method, the "Bioreactor" system, involves the forcing of wort by pressure through a plug of yeast mixed with an inert support (Celite). In this method fermentation times as low as 2 hours could be obtained. Narziss and Hellich (1972), Pollock and Weir (1975) and Grinbergs et al. (1977) describe the use of this system for the fermentation of beer and of sugar adjuncts. A conditioning period in contact with yeast was necessary to reduce the high diacetyl content of beer produced by this process. Portno (1973) has reviewed continuous fermentation and suggested improvements which might be made.

Continuous fermentation is used by a few breweries but its use is not spreading rapidly. To many brewers, the disadvantages of continuous fermentation, as compared with batch fermentation, outweigh its advantages. A higher standard of sterility of wort and plant is required for continuous fermentation than for batch fermentations in which the plant can be sterilized between each fermentation. It is more difficult to change the production rate of a continuous fermentation by a large factor than it is to change the amount produced in a batch fermentation in which one or more sets of vessels may be added or subtracted at each batch. Yeast is more likely to cause trouble by mutation in continuous fermentations than in batch fermentation. Thorne (1968, 1970) found alarming numbers of mutants in laboratory continuous fermentations which he had kept going for 6–9 months. Infection with either wild yeasts or lactobacilli can also be a very serious hazard in continuous fermentations. Flavour differences caused by higher concentrations of esters, or of diacetyl, have been associated with continuous fermentations. Continuous fermentation would be more attractive from the process point of view if it could be coupled with continuous wort production but in spite of a number of serious attempts to produce wort continuously this has not yet been found commercially attractive.

F. Yeast Storage

The liquid yeast collected at the end of fermentation by skimming, or as bottom yeast, or by centrifuging, may vary widely in yeast content but should contain about 50% beer and 50% yeast measured as pressed yeast. Liquid yeast may be stored in this form for pitching later brews or it may be concentrated by pressing in a chilled yeast press. Yeast may be left in the chilled press until required for use or the press may be emptied into suitable containers and the yeast kept in a cold room. Pressed yeast normally contains 75–76% moisture, 46% of which is within the cells and 29% is present as interstitial liquid (White 1954). Liquid yeast has the advantage over pressed yeast in that it gives more vigorous fermentation so that lower pitching rates can be used; it is easy to collect and to store free of infection and it is easier to add and to mix with the fresh wort of the next fermentation. Liquid yeast has the disadvantage that it contains much more fermented beer than pressed yeast; if excise duty is assessed in the fermenting vessel after pitching then duty is in effect paid twice on this barm beer. Liquid yeast during storage should be circulated through a pump and cooler to keep the temperature at 2–4 °C and a similar temperature should be aimed at for storage of pressed yeast.

G. Treatment of Brewing Yeast

In lager breweries it is usual to treat the yeast collected for repitching by mixing it with 2 volumes of chilled water and passing it through a vibrating screen which retains some of the bitter sediment precipitated with the yeast (Roessler 1968). Pasteur suggested disinfection of yeast by washing with dilute solutions of tartaric acid. Since then washing the brewing yeast with tartaric acid, phosphoric acid or a mixture of phosphoric acid and ammonium persulphate has been recommended (Bah and McKeen 1965, Bruch et al. 1964). We have found that yeast washed with acid gave a more active fermentation and lower final pH in the beer than was given by unwashed yeast. Acid washing readily eliminates *Obesum-bacterium proteus* from the yeast but to eliminate lactobacilli a pH of 2·7 must be attained unless persulphate is included in the wash when a pH 3·5 is sufficient.

X. YEAST PRODUCTION DURING BREWERY FERMENTATIONS

During a brewery fermentation the yeast reproduces until it reaches a maximum yeast count which depends on the fermentation conditions and on the yeast strain. The total crop of yeast from a fermentation will increase somewhat with increased pitching rates but by no means in proportion to the pitching rate (Griffin 1970b). The "times reproduction" has little meaning as a characteristic, either of the fermentation or of the yeast, as it depends on the pitching rate. If the pitching rate is 0·5 g/l the times reproduction may be 30 (total crop 15 g/l), whereas with 2 g/l pitching rate, but otherwise identical fermentations, it may be only 9 (total crop 18 g/l). In brewery lager fermentations the "times reproduction" is normally 3–8 but in stout fermentations, where a much lower pitching rate and a higher temperature is used so that the fermentation is more vigorous, the times reproduction may be 10–40. The total amount of yeast produced in standard laboratory fermentations varied considerably with different yeast strains and crops varying from 5 g/l to 22 g/l (as pressed yeast at 75% moisture) were recorded (Gilliland 1962). The yeast crop was a constant characteristic of strains over a period of nine months so it appears to be a stable characteristic of yeast. The difference between strains was reduced when the fermentations were aerated more intensively and the difference in yeast crop practically disappeared in shaken flask cultures. Griffin (1970a) also found wide strain variation in yeast crop, one strain giving three times the crop given by another strain. Yeast crop is increased with increasing aeration, with increasing temperature of fermentation and also with increasing strength of wort. A wort of OG 1040 may give 6 lbs/brl (17 g/l) when under similar conditions a wort of OG 1070 will give 10 lbs/brl (28 g/l) as pressed yeast.

Surplus yeast can never be economically produced if it has grown at the expense of duty paid wort. Savings on brewing loss could, therefore, be made by restricting yeast growth. Methods by which this can be done, as for example reduction of wort aeration, would also reduce the vigour of the fermentation, increase the fermentation time and raise the final pH of the beer. It is, therefore, normal to concentrate on obtaining the desired fermentation time and tolerate what surplus yeast this produces.

XI. USE OF SURPLUS YEAST

Yeast is a saleable by-product which is used in making yeast extract and as a constituent in animal feeds. Where there is easy access to yeast processing plants, liquid yeast may be collected from the brewery in tanker and sent direct to the plant, or it may first be pressed in plate presses to recover the valuable barm beer, and then sent to the processing plant. Alternatively the yeast may be separated from the barm beer on rotary drum vacuum filters or by centrifuging, then liquefied by heating to 90 °C and dried on rotary drum driers. This produces a crisp autolysed yeast flake and powder which can be sold to yeast processors.

XII. OXYGEN REQUIREMENTS OF BREWING YEAST

It has already been mentioned that available oxygen in the wort is an essential for good yeast reproduction and fast fermentation in the brewery. The effect of oxygen in brewery fermentations has been reviewed by Kirsop (1974) who states that the primary effect of oxygen deficiency is reduced yeast reproduction; secondary effects are reduced fermentation rate, reduced formation of pyruvate, fusel oil and acetoin, reduced nitrogen absorption and yeast viability and increased pH ester formation. David and Kirsop (1972, 1973a) found that the amounts of oxygen required in the wort by different strains of brewing yeast varied from 2 p.p.m. to 30 p.p.m. which corresponds to 30% saturation of wort with air to 100% saturation with oxygen at 20 °C. It is worth noting that air saturation of water at 20 °C gives 9 p.p.m. oxygen but that in wort of OG 1030 the corresponding figure is 7·5 p.p.m., at OG 1040 it is 6·2 p.p.m. and at OG 1080 it is 4·9 p.p.m. The amount of air or oxygen injected into the wort may bear little relationship to that going into solution so that it is necessary to measure the oxygen in solution in the wort in order to know how much is available to the yeast. The position is further complicated by the fact that oxygen determinations in wort which has been pitched with yeast mean little as the yeast rapidly removes oxygen from solution; additions of aerated or oxygenated wort to a fermentation containing yeast may be very valuable to the yeast but may give only transient increases in the oxygen in solution. Further, as soon as carbon dioxide evolution commences, this will tend to wash any remaining oxygen out of solution.

David and Kirsop (1973a) showed that the oxygen requirement of yeast could be satisfied by addition of sterols to the wort, so that oxygen was required because it was essential for biosynthesis of sterols. Wort contains very small quantities of sterols or substances which can act as substitutes for sterols, so that some growth can take place when yeast is added to de-aerated wort. Yeast grown aerobically has a carry-over of sterols within the cells which allows it to grow under anaerobic conditions (David and Kirsop 1973b). Wilson and McLeod (1976) found that the greatest analytical difference between aerobically and anaerobically grown S. cerevisiae cells was in their sterol contents, which differed by a factor of 10. They also noted that aerobically grown cells retained viability during storage under starvation conditions while anaerobically grown cells showed a rapid decline in viability; this corresponds with our observations. Markham (1969) related original oxygen saturation of brewery wort to yeast yield, growth rate, fermentation rate and viability of yeast crop. His work indicated that for the yeast and conditions he used 20% oxygen saturation of wort gave optimum results. This does not necessarily apply to other yeasts or other conditions (David and Kirsop 1972, 1973a).

XIII. NUTRIENT REQUIREMENTS OF BREWING YEAST

Yeast requires oxygen for growth, together with sources of carbon, nitrogen, phosphorus, sulphur, various minerals and certain vitamins. The growth requirements of yeast have been reviewed by Suomalainen and Oura (1971).

As a source of carbon, brewer's yeast can use glucose, galactose, fructose, sucrose, maltose, maltotriose, maltulose and maltotriulose. Some strains of *S. cerevisiae* can use various other sugars such as trehalose, melezitose or inulin and some strains can utilize some of the minor constituents of wort such as isomaltose, panose, isopanose or maltotetraose (Gilliland 1969).

Brewer's yeast can use ammonium salts, amino acids and small peptides as sources of nitrogen. A mixture of amino acids gives more rapid and more complete growth of yeast than ammonium salt but the ammonium salt is better than any single amino acid. Brewer's yeast uses the amino acids in wort in a preferential sequence in which glutamic acid, aspartic acid, asparagine, glutamine, serine, threonine, lysine and arginine, are most rapidly absorbed and the amino acid proline is largely untouched so that it is the major amino acid remaining in the beer (Jones and Pierce 1964, 1969).

Brewer's yeasts require phosphate for continued growth though they are capable of minimal growth in a phosphate-free medium while they use their cellular reserves of phosphate (Markham *et al.* 1966). Yeasts take up phosphate as $H_2PO_4^-$ from solutions containing phosphate ions and they store it as metaphosphate in the volutin granules. Growth of brewer's yeast increases with increasing phosphate in the medium to a maximum at 60 µg per l (Markham and Byrne 1967).

Brewer's yeasts can use inorganic sulphate or sulphite, thiosulphate, methionine or glutathione as a source of sulphur for growth (Maw 1960, 1963, Schultz and McManus 1950).

Potassium and magnesium are necessary for yeast growth and calcium stimulates growth though it is not a growth requirement. Yeast also requires very small amounts of copper, iron, zinc, manganese and perhaps traces of other elements. Cadmium, copper and silver are poisonous to yeast if present above 0·2 p.p.m. in the medium (White 1954). Copper is the most likely to occur, especially on the first use of newly cleaned copper vessels or plant (Hoggan and Compson 1963).

Different species of yeast have different requirements for growth factors and even within one species there may be a difference in requirement between different strains. The brewing yeasts normally require biotin, pantothenic acid and inositol for growth. A deficiency of pantothenic acid will cause excessive production of H_2S by the yeast (Wainwright 1970). Some strains may also require thiamin, *p*-amino benzoic acid, nicotinic acid and pyridoxine; these strains may grow in the absence of these growth factors but show improved growth in their presence. Brewer's yeasts do not need riboflavin or folic acid.

All the nutrients required for yeast growth are normally in adequate supply in aerated malt wort. Kirsop and Brown (1972) have shown that if the concentration of all the non-carbohydrate constituents of malt wort were halved the rate of fermentation was reduced but it could be completely restored by the addition of serine or arginine. Thus the constituent which was nearest to inadequacy was nitrogen and, where the adjunct rate in the grist is high, nitrogen in the wort may be a limiting factor for yeast growth. It has also been suggested that there may be a deficiency of zinc in some worts (Densky *et al*. 1966, Helin and Slaughter 1977).

For laboratory media, malt wort, either as a liquid or solidified with agar, is suitable for yeast growth. Synthetic media are available commercially, for example Yeast Nitrogen Base which can be used for nitrogen assimilation experiments and Yeast Carbon Base which can be used for carbon assimilation tests. In the latter medium the source of nitrogen is ammonium sulphate and more rapid growth of yeasts can be obtained if amino acids are added. "MYGP" medium is widely used for yeast growth and for culture maintenance. It contains 3 g malt extract, 3 g yeast extract, 10 g glucose and 5 g peptone in 1 l of water. Cutts and Rainbow (1950) have defined a medium containing only pure chemicals for nutritional studies on yeasts.

XIV. YEAST DEGENERATION

If a series of increasingly sluggish fermentations occurs in a brewery, or if yeast crops become progressively smaller, this is often said to be due to yeast degeneration. The term yeast degeneration is, however, not specific and the effect may be due to a number of different causes.

Insufficient dissolved oxygen in the wort can lead to poor yeast reproduction and slower fermentations (Hudson 1967, Thompson and Ralph 1967). The deterioration may be progressive as the yeast crop from a poorly aerated fermentation is liable to contain a greater percentage of dead cells than yeast from a normal fermentation. A useful first action if fermentations are sluggish is therefore to increase the intensity or duration of wort aeration, or to change from aeration to oxygenation of the wort. The composition of the wort may be unsuitable for the yeast either through insufficiency of some factor required for yeast growth or through presence of some agent inhibitory to yeast growth. As discussed in the previous section, these wort deficiencies are unlikely to occur although in some cases there may be nitrogen insufficiency, zinc insufficiency or an inhibitory amount of copper in the wort. Apparent yeast degeneration could also be due to bad yeast management. If yeast is left too long in contact with completed fermentations, particularly if the temperature is relatively high, autolysis and death of some of the yeast cells will occur and if the yeast is inadequately chilled during storage, death of the cells may occur. In either case a high proportion of dead cells in the pitching yeast would lead to sluggish fermentations and perpetuation of the adverse conditions.

By far the most likely cause of yeast degeneration is none of the above possibilities, but mutation of the culture yeast. If the yeast collection system depends on the flocculent character of the yeast then mutation to non-flocculence will cause decreased crops. Curtis and Wenham (1958) found a change from 100% flocculent to 90% non-flocculent yeast during 14 successive fermentations. This change was accompanied by the high racking gravities typical of yeast degeneration. In this case the yeast composition was regularly monitored so the cause was known to be a change in flocculation characteristics. Gilliland (1957) has also described progressive change in yeast character over a series of successive brewings which led to demonstration of all the signs of yeast weakness. In lager fermentations mutation to non-flocculence leads to progressively lower crops and may lead to insufficient yeast recovery to give adequate yeast for pitching to the next brewing.

A second type of mutation which can give the effects of yeast degeneration is loss of the ability to ferment maltotriose, a sugar which constitutes 15% of the fermentable carbohydrate of wort. Mutants of this type can occur spontaneously in most brewing yeasts and they have been described by Blom and Schwarz (1947), Green and Stone (1952) Gilliland (1956, 1969) and Yamamoto and Inoue (1962). Brightwell (1973) described a non-maltotriose fermenting strain of *S. cerevisiae* which was very agglutinative and had a remarkable resistance to heat and to sterilants. Strains unable to ferment maltotriose have been found both in *S. cerevisiae* and in *S. carlsbergensis*. If a mutant of this type increases its proportion in successive brewings then a stage will be reached where sluggish fermentations occur. This may lead to excessively long fermentation times in an attempt to reach the desired racking gravity with consequent high dead cell counts and progressively more difficult fermentations. Gilliland (1969) has described the mechanism of selection of malto-triose non-fermenting yeasts in both a top fermentation and in a lager brewery. In the former the mutant gave a larger crop and better skimmings than the culture yeast. In the latter the mutant grew faster and gave an earlier bottom crop than culture yeast. In both cases the proportion of the mutant increased rapidly in successive brewings and gave the typical symptoms of yeast degeneration. The obvious course when this occurs is to change the yeast by introducing a new pure culture. It is, however, extremely difficult to eliminate a brewing yeast entirely from a brewery so that infection of the new pure culture by the previous yeast may be expected and the necessity for a second and third yeast propagation is probable.

XV. INTERACTION OF STRAINS AND VARIATION IN PROPORTION IN MIXED CULTURE YEASTS

A. Stability of Mixed Cultures

When Hansen isolated single cells of brewing yeasts in 1880 he enabled brewers to produce pure cultures of yeasts for the first time. Up to then, brewer's yeasts had been mixed cultures which by normal processes had evolved into cultures either containing one predominant strain or cultures containing two or three mutally compatible strains. On the Continent of Europe many brewers adopted Hansen's methods for isolation and propagation of pure cultures for brewery use but in Britain these methods were regarded with suspicion and were not brought into general use until many years later. This may have been because of unfortunate experiences due to the use of unsuitable strains of yeast; more likely it was due to the introduction of pure cultures into a non-sterile brewery where the new yeast was rapidly contaminated and taken over by unsuitable strains of culture or wild yeast. This led to the erroneous idea that pure cultures were unstable and rapidly degenerated. In some breweries mixed cultures were preferred even after the use of the pure culture system had become widespread. In one top fermentation brewery a mixture of two strains was established in skimming type fermentations and on regular monitoring it was found that the proportion of the two strains was relatively stable over many years (Gilliland 1971b). In some lager breweries a mixture of a flocculent strain and a non-flocculent strain was found to give more acceptable fermentation and lagering than either strain separately. Mixed cultures always involve a risk that some relatively small change in the fermentation process may upset the previously established stable balance in the proportion of the two strains. Frequent monitoring of the composition of the mixture is necessary and if the proportion changes remedial action must be taken either by adding more of a culture of one strain or by starting from a mixture of the two strains in the desired proportion. It is always more satisfactory to search for a suitable single strain than to replace a mixed culture which is inherently less stable.

B. Interaction of the Brewing Yeast with Mutants or with Wild Yeasts

Brewing yeast strains have been well established over the years by natural selection as the most suitable strains for their purpose. A good brewing yeast strain is consequently resistant to take-over by variant strains or by wild yeasts. There are about 6×10^{15} cells in a 1000 hectolitre brewery fermentation so that with a normal mutation rate of one in 10^7 cells it is obvious that many mutations must occur. Mutation most frequently causes loss of the ability of the cell to produce some protein, generally an enzyme. The brewing yeast is diploid or polyploid; thus, when mutation to the recessive takes place in one gene of an allelic pair the other gene of the pair can still function so that phenotypically the yeast will still behave normally. This means that cells showing a phenotypic change should only be expected in one in 10^{14} cells. Even so phenotypic mutants must occur in every batch fermentation and Thorne (1968) observed very frequent mutation in continuous fermentations which had been kept going over a period of nine months. Mutations are generally deleterious to the yeast. For example the mutant may lose the ability to ferment maltose, or the ability to produce some growth factor required for its metabolism; mutants of the latter kind would disappear without trace as they could not compete with the brewing yeast. A mutant must have some selective advantage which allows it to increase in successive brewings if it is to reach large proportions in the brewing yeast. This advantage might be a greater relative growth rate or a preferential selection during harvesting. The yeast mutants which have most frequently caused trouble in breweries are the two already described involving loss of ability to flocculate and loss of ability to ferment maltotriose. Wild yeasts may cause trouble because they are not removed by fining due to their very low electric charge on the cell. Ellison and Doran (1961) have described detection of one cell of this type in 160 million culture cells by a method involving miniature laboratory fermentations. *S. diastaticus* is another wild yeast which can cause trouble because of its abnormally low attenuation limit and the off-flavour it can give to beer (Gilliland and Harrison 1966). The most potent producers of off-flavours are yeasts in the genus *Brettanomyces*, which are very slowly growing yeasts, but they can be difficult to eliminate from a brewery where they have established themselves (Gilliland 1961). Aerobic yeasts such as *Pichia*, *Candida* and *Torula* are frequent contaminants of brewing yeast (Brady 1958) but these generally do little harm. They can, however, grow as a pellicle on beer which is exposed to the air in a vat and, under these conditions, may produce sufficient esters to alter the beer flavour.

XVI. YEAST GENETICS

A. The Haploid–Diploid System

The study of yeast genetics was pioneered by Winge and his co-workers in the Carlsberg Laboratory in Denmark and by Lindegren in America. Winge

(1935) established that *Saccharomyces* species were normally diploid but that yeast spores were haploid. The ascus could be dissected by means of a micromanipulator and individual spores could be isolated in droplets of growth medium on a coverslip in a moist chamber. The isolated spores could develop into vegetative cultures. It was also found that if two spores were placed together in a droplet they could fuse and would then give rise to a diploid culture (Winge and Laustsen 1937). Because the spores could give rise to haploid cultures whose characteristics could be tested it was easy to study the genetic make-up of the parent diploid yeast. This availability of both haploid and diploid stages for testing makes yeast peculiarly attractive for genetic studies, as in most organisms this is not possible. In a typical investigation, two yeasts, one capable of fermenting maltose and one unable to ferment maltose, were induced to sporulate. Four-spored asci of each were dissected and the four spores from an ascus were isolated and grown into vegetative cultures. On testing these single-spore cultures from the first yeast, every one was able to ferment maltose so the parent yeast was homozygous for this character and thus has the genetic make up MA_1MA_1 (or MA_1MA_1, $MA_2MA_2, MA_3MA_3 \ldots$). Single spores from the second yeast were all unable to ferment maltose so it was completely recessive for this character (ma_1ma_1, $ma_2ma_2 \ldots$). Single spores from each of the two yeasts were placed together and fused to form a diploid hybrid yeast. This hybrid was cultured, induced to form spores and four-spored asci were dissected and the individual spores cultured. The maltose-fermenting abilities of the four single spore cultures from asci of the hybrid were tested and in every case two were found to be able to ferment maltose and two were not. The hybrid had, therefore, the formula MA_1ma_1 and the two parents MA_1MA_1 and ma_1ma_1. This is the simplest case giving a 2 : 2 ratio in the four single-spore cultures from a single ascus of the hybrid. Frequently more complicated ratios were found. Some of these corresponded exactly to the ratios to be expected if one parent were homozygous for two or three dominant genes. There were also occasional deviations from expected ratios where there was either an excess or a deficiency of fermenting spores and the explanation for these deviations was hotly debated between Winge and Lindegren.

Many of the strains used by Winge were homothallic and single-spore cultures readily self-diploidized. Hybrids from such yeasts can only be made by direct spore-to-spore mating. Lindegren, however worked with strains in which single spore cultures did not self-diploidize. Moreover when four single spores were isolated from an ascus and grown on into haploid cultures, two of these cultures had a mating-reaction "*a*" and two had mating reaction "α". When two "*a*" or two "α" cultures were mixed and cultured no hybridization took place. But when "*a*" and "α" cultures were mixed hybridization took place and many of the bizarre shapes of the hybrid cells formed by fusion of two yeasts could be seen in the culture. This "mass-mating" technique made the production of hybrids much simpler and less time consuming (Lindegren and Lindegren 1943). Further improvements in technique were the separation of spores from disrupted asci by selective adsorption by liquid paraffin (Emeis 1958a) and the use of snail enzyme for dissolving the ascus walls (Johnston and Mortimer 1959).

B. Production of Hybrid Yeasts

In order to produce a hybrid yeast it is necessary first to induce sporulation in the two parent yeasts, second to isolate single spores or single-spore cultures from each yeast, and third to cause hybridization by placing either single spores or single spore cultures in contact with one another. These three requisites are relatively easy to satisfy with some *Saccharomyces* but unfortunately not with brewing yeasts which are notoriously difficult to sporulate and whose spores frequently have very low viability.

1. Induction of Sporulation

There has been a very extensive study of methods of inducing yeasts to form spores. These are reviewed by Fowell (1969). The classical method is to place a few drops of a suspension of vegetative cells on the top of a block of plaster-of-paris which is placed in a glass dish containing some water and covered with a ground glass plate. Improvements involved the use of special media for growth of the culture before sporulation (Lindegren 1944, Sando 1956 and Fowell and Moorse 1960), the discovery that for most yeasts a sodium acetate agar gave improved sporulation (Stantial 1935, Adams 1949, Fowell 1952) and the finding that, particularly in liquid cultures, the cell concentration was related to the percentage sporulation achieved (Kirsop 1954, Sando 1960) though it is not so related on an acetate agar medium (Fowell 1967).

A method of sporulation which works well with most yeasts is as follows. Culture the yeast strain at 30 °C in a brewery wort of original gravity 1·050 or a nutrient broth containing 1% yeast extract and 5% glucose. After two or three days' incubation, separate the yeast cells by centrifuging, wash twice with distilled water and resuspend in a few drops of water. Spread this suspension over a slant of a medium containing 0·5 g sodium acetate and 1·0 g potassium chloride per 100 ml of water and solidified with 1·5% agar. Incubate the slant at 25° and examine for spores after three days and daily thereafter. It has been found, however, that no one method is best for all yeasts; for a particular strain one of the many variations recommended may give better results.

2. Isolation of Spores

Having achieved good sporulation, preferably giving rise to many four-spored asci, the next step is to isolate single spores. In the original method, a droplet containing a suspension of the sporing culture was placed on a coverslip together with a pattern of well separated droplets of sterile growth medium. The coverslip was cemented with vaseline onto a moist chamber. A glass needle with a very finely tapered tip was mounted in a micromanipulator and inserted through the side opening of the moist chamber. A single ascus was drawn out of the droplet containing the yeast, excess liquid was removed from the ascus, the needle was placed across the ascus and with pressure and rolling the ascus was broken. The released spores were then each placed in a separate droplet of sterile medium. This method requires considerable training and skill both in the use of the micromanipulator and in the preparation of the needles. Pretreatment of the sporing suspension with snail enzyme greatly reduces the difficulty of dissection and instead of using a very fine tipped needle a broader tipped needle can be used effectively (Johnston and Mortimer 1959). Instead of using droplets of liquid medium on the coverslip to receive the isolated spore a film of malt-agar can be used (Fowell 1955). The use of an electric micro-forge can reduce the difficulty of making needles (Fonbrune 1949), but needles can be made satisfactorily without this equipment by using a dissection microscope and a miniature gas burner formed from a hypodermic needle. A needle tip is roughly formed by drawing out a glass rod first in a normal flame and then with the micro-burner. The tip is then more accurately fashioned by mounting the needle in the micromanipulator and pushing its tip against a loop of platinum wire electrically heated to dull red heat. The needle is drawn out from a droplet of melted glass on the heated wire under observation through a low-power microscope.

Large numbers of single spores can be obtained by grinding a sporulating culture with powdered glass to disrupt the asci so releasing the spores. The suspension of spores, cell debris and some vegetative cells is then shaken with liquid paraffin and the mixture centrifuged. The spores are selectively taken up by the oil which is spread over a malt agar medium. Most of the colonies produced should be haploid cultures derived from single spores. Colonies of diploid yeasts derived from surviving vegetative cells or from fusion of spores or from fusion of haploid cells can generally be distinguished by their larger size (Emeis 1958b, Emeis and Gutz 1958). Treatment of the sporulating culture with snail enzyme makes disruption easier and spores can then be separated by sonication followed by paraffin treatment (Magni 1963). Heat treatment may be used to eliminate vegetative cells which are less heat tolerant than the spores (Fowell 1966) and electrophoresis has also been used to separate spores from vegetative cells (Resnick *et al.* 1967).

3. Hybridization

Single spores from asci of the two parent yeasts can be isolated in a moist chamber and then placed in contact with one another either at the edge of a droplet of liquid medium or at a marked position on a thin layer of an agar medium. The moist chamber is incubated overnight at 15 °C and then examined under the microscope to find if hybridization has taken place. This method is satisfying in that one can be sure that the diploid has been formed by fusion of spores and not by self-diploidization between haploid cells derived from a single spore. It is the only practical method for yeasts whose spores readily self-diploidize as for example *S. chevalieri*.

Vegetative haploid cells can also be hybridized under the microscope. This has the advantage that the single spore culture is not lost (as it is by direct hybridization of spores) and the same single-spore isolate can be used for a number of different matings (Chen 1950).

A less time-consuming method is the "mass-mating" technique introduced by Lindegren and Lindegren (1943). If this is combined with the isolation of single-spore cultures by disruption of the asci by grinding followed by culture after separation of the spores at an oil–water interface, then hybrids can be produced without the use of the micromanipulator. Haploid cultures of opposite mating type are mixed in a small amount of nutrient medium and incubated overnight at 16 °C. The mixture is examined under the microscope and hybridization is easily detected by the presence of zygotes of bizarre shapes. This may be followed by isolation of pure cultures of the new hybrid by plating (Palleroni 1961) or by isolation of diploid cells with the micromanipulator (Fowell 1951).

A modification of the mass-mating technique using solid media for producing the zygotes gave rather better results (Haefner 1965). This method has been simplified by Fowell (1969) who used slant cultures of haploid cells grown on wort-agar to carry out multiple hybridizations. A microspatula was used to transfer a small portion of one culture to droplets of water or a number of marked sites on a slide kept in a moist chamber. Similar portions of a number of different haploid cultures were mixed with the first culture in the droplets; after 3–4 hours at room temperature the droplets were examined and if zygote formation had occurred the droplet was transferred to a liquid culture and, after growth, hybrid cells were isolated by micromanipulator.

C. Genetics of *Saccharomyces*

Since the early demonstration by Winge and Laustsen of regular 2 : 2 segregation of a character in the four spores isolated from the ascus of a hybrid yeast, the study of yeast genetics has come a long way. In many ways Saccharomyces offers a model subject for genetic investigation and there is now a very extensive literature on the subject. This has been reviewed by Mortimer and Hawthorne (1966, 1969) and here only a few of the more important results will be mentioned.

1. Polymeric Genes

It was soon found that segregation ratios other than 2 : 2 frequently occurred in the four spores from a hybrid ascus. Some of these could be explained by a hybrid being able to be heterozygous for more than one gene controlling a particular ability, i.e., having *polymeric genes*. Thus if the hybrid was heterozygous for two maltose genes, either of which conferred the ability to ferment maltose, then segregation of fermenters to non-fermenters of 4 : 0, 3 : 1 and 2 : 2 will be found in four-spored asci in the ratio 1 : 4 : 1 provided linkage of the polymeric genes is not involved. With three polymeric genes, all of which segregate independently, then the ratio is 19 : 16 : 1. If linkage occurs between the polymeric genes this will upset the expected ratios. The genetic composition of spores phenotypically displaying the character is not clear in the case of polymeric genes and can only be determined by analysing hybrids formed by back-crossing the single-spore cultures with haploids of known composition.

2. Complementary Genes

Complementary genes, unlike polymeric genes, must all be functional for the cell containing them to be functional. Two complementary genes may for example be responsible for coding for production of two enzymes required at different stages during a chain of reactions leading to the end product. If either gene is absent then the corresponding enzyme will not be produced and the chain will not function. In the simplest case, with two complementary genes and no linkage, the ratio of functional to non-functional spores in four-spored asci should be 2 : 2, 1 : 3 or 0 : 4 in the ratio 1 : 4 : 1. The genetic composition of non-functional single-spore cultures is not clear where complementary genes are involved and can only be determined by hybridizing them with haploids of known composition.

3. Gene Linkage

Gene linkage occurs when two genes (A and B) are located close together on the same chromosome. Their relative distance apart can be calculated by the frequency of departure from the expected ratio (1 : 1 : 4) of parental ditype (AB, AB, ab, ab), non-parental ditype (Ab, Ab, aB, aB) and tetratype (AB, Ab, aB, ab) in the four spores from single asci of a hybrid between spores with the genetic make-up AB and ab. Genes may also be linked to their centromere; this can be detected in some yeasts by the analysis of tetraploids (Leupold 1956), or in the rather unusual case of linear asci where the spore types appear in a regular order in the ascus (Hawthorne 1955), or by crossing with a yeast containing a known centromere-linked gene (Perkins 1949).

4. Irregular Segregation

Irregular segregation involving an excess of functional phenotypes in the isolated spores may be due to "gene conversion" which was first described in *Saccharomyces* by Lindegren (1955). The effect of gene conversion is to cause a yeast heterozygous for one gene (Mm), which should therefore give four spores in an ascus as M, M, m, m (that is two functional spores), to give four spores M, M, M, m (that is three functional spores). In the parent one recessive (m) gene has been converted to the dominant (M). Conflicting genetic explanations of the mechanism of gene conversion have been offered and the subject has been reviewed by Whitehouse and Hastings (1965) and by Emerson (1967). A deficiency of functional phenotypes in spore isolates may be caused by mutation which normally involves loss of ability of the gene to code for the particular protein. If this protein is an enzyme which is necessary for one of the steps in a biochemical pathway the system will break down and the expected end-product will not be produced. If the pathway concerned has as its end-product an amino acid and this pathway is broken for lack of an enzyme required for one of the steps then this will be expressed as a requirement for this amino acid for growth of the yeast. Very many mutants of this kind have been isolated and studied. Other mutations may involve loss of a permease and if this permease facilitates entrance of a yeast inhibitor or anti-metabolite to the cell then its loss may confer resistance to the inhibitor. Mutants involving resistance or sensitivity to radiation, temperature mutants, morphological mutants and mutants involving suppressor genes have also been studied.

5. Genetic Maps

From extensive studies of inheritance patterns in yeast it has been possible to produce maps of their genetic structure. This was first done by Lindegren (1949) and since then has been greatly extended to include over 175 genes on seventeen chromosomes (Hawthorne and Mortimer 1968, Mortimer and Hawthorne 1975).

6. Cytoplasmic Inheritance

A type of mutation which occurs fairly frequently in yeast is loss of ability to grow on non-fermentable substrates such as glycerol. This is accompanied by the formation, on normal solid media, of smaller than normal colonies. These mutants are called "petites", or respiratory mutants. Inheritance of this characteristic was studied by Ephrussi (1953) and was found to display none of the ratios expected by Mendelian segregation but to be due to cytoplasmic factors. When "petite" mutants were crossed with wild type then wild type diploids were obtained which gave only wild type spores. Later it was found that similar respiratory deficient cells could occur as a result of normal genetic mutation and in these cases Mendelian segregation occurred (Chen et al. 1950). Both Mendelian and cytoplasmic inheritance may also be involved in conferring ability to grow in the presence of antibiotics such as chloramphenicol or erythromycin (Linnane et al. 1968).

7. Killer Character

Some yeasts ("sensitives") can be killed when grown together with other strains ("killer" strains). "Neutral" strains are resistant to the killer action of the killer strain and also they have no killer activity themselves (Somers and Bevan 1969, Bevan and Somers 1969). The killer activity is not governed by a simple gene but is due to a cytoplasmic factor "k" which requires also a gene M for its maintenance. The neutral yeasts have a different cytoplasmic factor "n" which also requires the gene M for maintenance. Cells with neither "k" nor "n" are sensitive; the gene M makes no difference to sensitives. All single-spore cultures from killer strains are killers and all single-spore cultures from sensitive strains are sensitive. If a hybrid is made between killer and sensitive, then if both parents contained the M gene all the spores will be killers; if one of the parents contained the recessive "m" gene then there will be two killer spores in each four-spored ascus of the hybrid.

The killer yeasts carry a double-stranded ribonucleic acid species encapsulated in a virus-like particle (Wickner 1976). The killing agent is an extracellular glycoprotein of high molecular weight which kills sensitive yeast cells but does not affect other cells. Philliskirk and Young (1975) found that the killer character was rare in ale yeasts in the National Collection of Yeast Cultures (3 out of 360) and none of the 58 lager yeasts had killer activity. On the other hand, the majority of these brewing yeasts were sensitives and were killed when cultured in the presence of killer strains. The killer character was found in a number of other genera of yeast, the highest proportion of killer strains being found in the genus Hansenula (41 %) and many killer strains were found in laboratory cultures of Saccharomyces (31%). Kreil et al. (1975) obtained similar results in an examination of German yeasts, that is none of the brewing yeasts were "killers" but very many brewing and baking yeasts were "sensitives". Maule and Thomas (1973) established that production difficulties in a two-stage stirred continuous fermenter system were due to the instrusion of a killer strain. This yeast produced a "herbal/phenolic" flavour and when its concentration in the culture rose to 3–5% it rapidly caused the death of brewing yeast. It was suggested that the killer factor had some similarities to an agent produced by *Acetobacter* which was lethal to yeasts in bottled beer (Gilliland and Lacey 1966).

D. Hybridization of Brewing Yeasts

Improvement of brewing yeasts by hybridization was naturally tried soon after the discovery of the way to produce yeast hybrids but was found to be technically difficult and so far has met with little practical success. Brewing yeasts generally sporulate very poorly, if at all, and even when spores are found and isolated few of them are found to be viable and capable of mating with other isolates. Emeis (1958b) found in 11 strains of *S. carlsbergensis* only 4% sporulation and spore viability of 0·07–2·0%. Thorne (1951) found sporulation in 12 out of 20 top fermentation yeasts and obtained 12% spore germination while Johnston (1965) obtained 7·1% spore viability in studying 33 strains of *S. cerevisiae* and only 25% of the viable spores gave haploid cultures. Anderson and Martin (1975) obtained spores from 11 out of 13 strains of *S. cerevisiae* and from 5 out of 7 strains of *S. carlsbergensis*. Percentage sporulation varied from less than 1% to 82% and was less then 21% in all the strains of *S. carlsbergensis*. The poor sporulation of brewing yeasts may be due to incompetence in the cells through loss of an essential gene involved either in meiotic division or in the generation of spore walls, or it may be due to unusual ploidy of the yeast. Emeis and Windisch (1960) and Johnston (1963) found some brewing yeasts to be triploid, polyploid or aneuploid and such yeasts cannot produce normal spores. Among the spores isolated by Anderson and Martin (1975), ten could mate with either "*a*" or "*α*" tester strains, indicating that they may be aneuploid, carrying genes for both mating types; 314 spores were sterile and unable to mate with either "*a*" or "*α*" tester strains: these must have come from triploid or aneuploid parent yeasts. They also demonstrated that not all pairings of spore cultures of opposite mating type were successful owing to "incompatability".

A second reason for lack of success in producing better brewing yeasts by hybridization is lack of a clear-cut objective. It is not productive to aim simply at "a better yeast" without knowing exactly which character we wish to change. If we wished to change a qualitative character such as ability to ferment a particular sugar this should be possible. Windisch and Emeis (1969) successfully made a hybrid between *S. diastaticus* and *S. carlsbergensis* which had the dextrin-fermenting ability of *S. diastaticus* and the brewing properties of *S. carlsbergensis* and so was suitable for making a highly attenuated beer— "diat pils". Johnston (1963, 1965) produced a yeast hybrid with improved ability for continuous fermentation and Enebo *et al.* (1960) reported the production of a hybrid between top and bottom yeast which gave beer with improved aroma and flavour.

In a similar way, hybrids of brewer's yeast might be made with altered vitamin requirements, flocculation characteristics, antibiotic resistance or any other character amenable to simple genetic control.

If alteration in a quantitative character is required then the procedure is much more difficult but not impossible. Fowell (1958) has described the very long series of hybrids and back-crosses and selections which was required to produce a baker's yeast with improved maltase activity and better baking performance. The work was made more difficult by the fact that the "best" hybrid yeasts did not necessarily come from mating the "best" mating strains. Lodder and Loggers (1968) tested 2000 hybrids to find a baker's yeast with higher than normal maltose-fermenting ability and hybrids have also been produced with improved alcohol yield for whiskey fermentations. Mosiashvili and Shalutashvili (1971) produced wine yeast hybrids of high pectolytic activity. Thornton and Eschenbruch (1976) found wine yeast to be homothallic which makes hybridization difficult but not impossible and they hoped to produce hybrids with improved properties. Clayton *et al.* (1972) and Anderson and Martin (1975) produced hybrids of brewing yeast with increased fermentation rate. With brewer's yeast it has therefore been shown that hybridization is possible and if improvement in some character were very desirable then a programme of genetic research should have a good chance of success.†

XVII. STRAIN SELECTION AMONG BREWING YEASTS

There is a wide variation in suitability of different strains of brewing yeast for use in a particular brewery. A yeast which performs admirably in one brewery may be quite unsuitable for use in another brewery which uses a different fermentation procedure. It is essential to be able to carry out laboratory tests which will assess the suitability for brewing of different strains of yeast. In deciding which tests have value for this assessment we must first decide the relative importance of the various characteristics of the yeast. The characteristics which might be considered are fermentation rate, attenuation limit, total amount of yeast produced during fermentation, loss of bittering substances during fermentation, flocculation behaviour, cropping as skimmings or as bottom yeast, fining characteristics, oxygen requirement, sulphide produced, fusel oils and other volatiles produced, flavour of beer and stability of the yeast. Many of these characters can be assessed in laboratory fermentations.

The use of various vessels for carrying out small-scale fermentations was compared by the E.B.C. Yeast Group in collaborative tests (Cook 1963). It was found that a minimum depth of fermenting liquid of 50 cm was required. In

† Recently, very significant advances have been made in the production of new yeasts by the techniques of rare mating, protoplast fusion and transformation. These have been reviewed by Tubb (1979) and Stewart (1978).

shallower vessels insufficient circulation took place and the yeast fell to the bottom of the vessel. A tube 120 cm long by 5 cm in diameter was recommended for 0·5 l fermentations. A tube 6·8 cm in diameter and 91 cm long has been found satisfactory for 21 fermentations (Gilliland 1962). When the latter was used it could be followed by pouring the fermenting liquid, late in the fermentation, into a tube 4·5 cm in diameter and 120 cm long for observation of head formation and for collection and estimation of the amount of yeast formed on skimming. The partition of the yeast in this system between skimmings, yeast in suspension and sedimented yeast was very similar to that occurring with the same yeast in the brewery. It was found most important in using these miniature fermenting vats to ensure sufficient aeration or oxygenation of the wort. Best results were obtained by aeration of the wort at the start of fermentation and again after 18 hours and then closing the fermenting tubes with a water-trap. Fermentations should be carried out at a temperature similar to that obtaining in the brewery. Thus top fermentations should either be maintained at the temperature of the brewery fermentation, if this is controlled at a constant level, or should be put through a series of increasing temperatures if the brewery fermentation temperature is allowed to rise during the fermentation. Lager fermentations are carried out at 4–9 °C, again similar to the temperature in the brewery fermentation. The base of the tube used for lager fermentations should be a calibrated tube 1·5 cm in diameter so that the amount of deposited yeast can be recorded at intervals during the fermentation. The wort used should be the same as that used in the brewery.

A collection of yeast strains is selected for test. These may be single-cell cultures isolated from the brewing yeast, isolates from other brewer's yeasts, or strains recommended for the particular fermentation by a yeast culture collection such as the National Collection of Yeast Cultures held by the Ministry of Agriculture, Fisheries and Food at Norwich, England. These strains are first examined for microscopical appearance, flocculation characteristics and attenuation limit. Some strains may be eliminated at this stage as being unsuitable. The strains surviving this test are then subjected to E.B.C. tube fermentations. It is convenient to test strains in batches of ten, each strain being tested in duplicate fermentations. In every set of ten either one or two standard strains should be included to serve as a reference and to ensure that the wort or conditions were not abnormal. The fermentations are monitored for those characterists which are of interest and the final beers are subjected to analysis and tasting.

In one search for an improved brewing yeast, 600 strains were tested in this way. Most of the strains could be eliminated from further testing after this test because they were clearly less suitable than the standard strain in some character or because they were identical either with the standard strain or with other test strains. Strains which showed promise were then tested in five successive fermentations where the crop from one fermentation was used to pitch the next fermentation. The ten best strains were then used for 10-litre fermentations and the resulting beers subjected to more extensive tests including flavour, head retention and volatiles by gas–liquid chromatography. The best strains were then taken to the pilot plant stage and eventually to the full commercial scale (Gilliland 1962). A by-product of this programme was the acquisition of a set of yeasts with known differences from the standard brewery yeast which were retained and could be called upon if any characteristic of the brewing yeast was required. Similar successful programmes of yeast selection have been described by Stevens (1966) and Richards (1973) and by Thorne (1973) for a lager yeast.

Yeasts produced by hybridization or by treatment of brewing yeast cultures with mutagens could be tested in a similar way. If an alteration in the fermentation system is required then a new yeast selection programme should be used as there is a no reason to suppose that the best yeast for a skimming type fermentation would also be the best yeast for continuous fermentation or for a sedimentation system. It is of course unnecessary to use a selection programme if it is simply required to replace the brewing yeast by an exactly similar yeast which can be obtained from a laboratory-maintained pure culture of the brewing yeast or from a culture of the same yeast maintained by an outside laboratory.

XVIII. YEAST AUTOLYSIS AND AUTOFERMENTATION

Autolysis is the break-down of the constituents of an organism by its own enzymes. There have been many publications on yeast autolysis, which have been reviewed by Joslyn (1955) and Thorne (1971) but the mechanism and sequence of events which occurs during yeast autolysis are still not fully understood.

In the living cell there are, within the cell membrane, available substrates (carbohydrates and proteins) and also active enzymes (carbohydrases and proteases) but the enzymes do not act in an uncontrolled way on the substrates. This is presumably because enzymes and substrates are isolated from one another by the internal organization of the cellular organelles. It is thought, for example, that the proteases are located within the vacuoles, which are therefore lysosomes, and that the extra-vacuolar cytoplasm contains inhibitors for each protease. If the cell and vacuole are disrupted at pH 7, the enzyme-inhibitor complexes are fairly stable but if the pH is reduced the complexes are dissociated and the proteases are activated (Pringle 1975).

Yeast autolysis should be avoided in brewing although it has been suggested that release of nitrogenous substances from the yeast which occurs during lager maturation may contribute to beer flavour (Masschelein et al. 1973). If autolysed cells are observed in a brewing yeast it is probable that a large proportion of the cells are dead so that if this yeast is used in the brewery it will give an extended lag phase and a sluggish fermentation. If autolysis takes place in contact with beer, deterioration of flavour can occur with production of "yeasty" flavours and a bitter astringency (Thorne 1971). Yeast autolysis may also cause colloidal problems in beer (Woollmer 1935). Yeast autolysis is also dangerous in that it can lower the biological stability of the beer against growth of lactobacilli. This it does both by raising the pH of the beer and also by providing nutrients for the lactobacilli in the form of amino acids and vitamins.

The rate of autolysis of yeast increases with temperature so it is essential to prevent the temperature of the brewing yeast rising above 35 °C. Brewing yeast is more likely to autolyse if it has received inadequate aeration during growth; this tendency can be corrected by the addition of "Tween 80" or lecithin to the fermentation as well as by increasing the oxygenation (Thompson and Ralph 1967). Different strains of yeast grown under the same conditions can have very different susceptibilities to autolysis (Kulka 1953). It would be unwise to choose a strain for brewing which was very prone to autolysis.

Autofermentation is different from autolysis in that it can take place in the living cell whereas autolysis follows death of the cell. If liquid brewer's yeast is stored at moderate temperatures of 10–20 °C autofermentation takes place during which some of the reserve carbohydrates stored in the cell are fermented and alcohol is produced. At the same time some nitrogenous compounds are excreted. If autofermentation is allowed to continue the proportion of nitrogenous compounds to alcohol excreted increases and eventually the cell dies and autolysis takes over. Masschelein et al. (1973) studied the compounds released from yeast during maturation of lager beer and found that they consisted mainly of amino acids and small peptides; nucleotides also increased during maturation.

Complete autolysis of yeast is encouraged for the commercial production of yeast extract. In this process the yeast is held at 45 °C and is usually mixed with sodium chloride which acts as a plasmolysing agent and increases the rate of autolysis. When autolysis is complete the cell walls are separated from the soluble material by centrifugation. Flavouring materials may be added to the solution which is then concentrated to a paste for culinary purposes. Surplus brewery yeast can be used for making yeast extract but hop bitter substances absorbed on the yeast cell walls must first be removed. The compounds released from yeast during autolysis include alcohol, amino acids, peptides, vitamins, ergosterol, lipids, nucleic acid components, and the enzymes invertase, peptidase and protease. Yeast autolysis has been used as a commercial source of the enzyme invertase, either in the soluble form or concentrated on the cell residue after partial hydrolysis (Meister 1965). Invertase is present in the outer cell wall of yeast and is released into the medium during fermentation. It is destroyed by pasteurization and its absence can be used as a test of pasteurization efficiency (Owades *et al.* 1960).

Another phenomenon connected with excretion from yeast cells is "shock excretion" which has been studied by Delisle and Phaff (1961), Lewis and Phaff (1963, 1964, 1965) and by Lewis and Stephanopoulos (1967). If washed yeast cells are suspended in a glucose solution they rapidly release amino acids into the medium. This process is independent of osmotic pressure but is dependent on the presence of a fermentable sugar. "Shock excretion" is not autolysis as the cells are still healthy and when added to a suitable medium they can reproduce. It is suggested that "shock excretion" is due to a change in the permeability of the cell membrane during glucose transport into the cell. Calcium ions strongly inhibit the leakage. A similar leakage of nitrogenous substances from the cell takes place to a lesser extent during normal brewery fermentations.

REFERENCES

Adams, A. M. (1949). *Can. J. Res., Sect. C.* **27**, 179.
Anderson, E. and Martin, P. A. (1975). *J. Inst. Brew.* **81**, 242.
Bah, S. and McKeen, W. E. (1965). *Can. J. Microbiol.* **11**, 309.
Ballou, C. E., Lipke, P. N. and Raschke, W. C. (1974). *J. Bacteriol.* **117**, 461.
Barnett, J. A. (1977). *J. Gen. Microbiol.* **99**, 183.
Barnett, J. A. and Pankhurst, R. J. (1974). "A New Key to the Yeasts". North-Holland, Amsterdam and London.
Barney, M. C. and Helbert, J. R. (1976). *J. Am. Soc. Brew. Chem.* **34**, 61.
Beech, F. W., Davenport, R. R., Goswell, R. W. and Burnett, J. K. (1968). *In* "Identification Methods for Microbiologists" (B. M. Gibbs and D. A. Shapton, eds.), Part B, p. 151. Academic Press, London and New York.
Bevan, E. A. and Somers, J. M. (1969). *Genet. Res.* **14**, 71.
Blom, J. and Schwarz, B. (1947). *J. Inst. Brew.* **53**, 302.
Bourgeois, C. (1968). *Biotechnique*, p. 2.
Brady, B. L. (1958). *J. Inst. Brew.* **64**, 304.
Brenner, M. W., Karpiscak, M., Stern, H. and Hsu, W. P. (1970). *Proc. Ann. Meet. Am. Soc. Brew. Chem.*, 79.
Brightwell, R. W. (1973). *J. Inst. Brew.* **79**, 15.
Bruch, C. W., Hoffman, A., Gosine, R. M. and Brenner, M. W. (1964). *J. Inst. Brew.* **70**, 242.
Burns, J. A. (1937). *J. Inst. Brew.* **43**, 31.

Burns, J. A. (1941). *J. Inst. Brew.* **47**, 10.

Burns, J. A. (1957). *Brewers' Guardian* **86** (March 81) and **86** (4) (April 17).

Burrows, S. (1970). *In* "The Yeasts" (A. H. Rose and J. S. Harrison, eds.), Vol. III, p. 349. Academic Press, London and New York.

Callejas, C., Rodriguez, M. A. and Canales, A. M. (1977). *J. Am. Soc. Brew. Chem.* **35**, 12.

Campbell, I. (1967). *Proc. E.B.C. Congr.*, *Madrid* p. 145.

Campbell, I. (1970). *J. Gen. Microbiol.* **63**, 189.

Campbell, I. (1973). *J. Gen. Microbiol.* **77**, 127.

Chen, S. Y. (1950). *C.R.H. Acad. Sci.* **230**, 1897.

Chen, S. Y., Ephrussi, B. and Hottinger, H. (1950). *Heredity* **4**, 337.

Chester, V. E. (1963). *Proc. R. Soc.*, *Ser. B.* **157**, 223.

Clayton, E., Howard, G. A. and Martin, P. A. (1972). *Proc. Ann. Meet. Am. Soc. Brew. Chem.* p. 78.

Cook, A. H. (ed.) (1958). "The Chemistry and Biology of Yeasts". Academic Press, New York and London.

Cook, A. H. (1963). *Proc. E.B.C. Congr.*, *Bruxelles* p. 477.

Curtis, N. S. and Clark, A. G. (1957). *Proc. E.B.C. Congr.*, *Copenhagen*, p. 249.

Curtis, N. S. and Clark, A. G. (1960). *J. Inst. Brew.* **66**, 287.

Curtis, N. S. and Wenham, S. (1958). *J. Inst. Brew.* **64**, 421.

Custers, M.Th. J. (1940). "Onderzoekingen over het Gistgeslacht *Brettanomyces*". Thesis: W. D. Meinema, Delft.

Cutts, N. S. and Rainbow, C. (1950). *J. Gen. Microbiol.* **4**, 150.

David, M. H. and Kirsop, B. H. (1972). *Proc. Ann. Meet. Am. Soc. Brew. Chem.* p. 14.

David, M. H. and Kirsop, B. H. (1973a). *J. Inst. Brew.* **79**, 20.

David, M. H. and Kirsop, B. H. (1973b). *J. Gen. Microbiol.* **77**, 529.

Delisle, A. L. and Phaff, H. J. (1961). *Proc. Ann. Meet. Am. Soc. Brew. Chem.* p. 103.

Densky, H., Gray, P. J. and Buday, A. (1966). *Proc. Ann. Meet. Am. Soc. Brew. Chem.* p. 93.

Eddy, A. A. and Rudin, A. D. (1958). *J. Inst. Brew.* **64**, 19.

Ellison, J. and Doran, A. H. (1961). *Proc. E.B.C. Congr.*, *Vienna*, p. 224.

Emeis, C. C. (1958a). *Brau. Wiss. Beil.* **11**, 160.

Emeis, C. C. (1958b). *Naturwiss.* **45**, 441.

Emeis, C. C. and Gutz, H. (1958). *Z. Naturforsch. B.* **13**, 647.

Emeis, C. C. and Windisch, S. (1960). *Z. Naturforsch. B.* **15**, 702.

Emerson, S. (1967). *Annu. Rev. Genet.* **1**, 201.

Enebo, L., Johnsson, E., Nordström, K. and Möller, A. (1960). *Sv. Bryggeritidskr.* **75**, 273.

Ephrussi, B. (1953). "Nucleo-Cytoplasmic Relations in Micro-organisms". Clarendon Press, Oxford.

Falcone, G. and Nickerson, W. J. (1956). *Science* **124**, 272.

Findlay, W. P. K. (ed.) (1971). "Modern Brewing Technology". Macmillan, London and Basingstoke.

Fleet, G. H. and Manners, D. J. (1976). *J. Gen. Microbiol.* **94**, 180.

Fonbrune, P. de (1949). "Technique de Micromanipulation". Masson, Paris.

Fowell, R. R. (1951). *J. Inst. Brew.* **57**, 180.

Fowell, R. R. (1952). *Nature, London* **170**, 578.

Fowell, R. R. (1955). *J. Appl. Bacteriol.* **18**, 149.

Fowell, R. R. (1958). *In* "Recent Studies in Yeast and Their Significance in Industry" (Proc. Symp., Dublin, 1956, S.C.I. Monograph No. 3), p. 116. Society of Chemical Industry, London.

Fowell, R. R. (1966). *Process Biochem.* **1**, 25.
Fowell, R. R. (1967). *J. Appl. Bacteriol.* **30**, 450.
Fowell, R. R. (1969). *In* "The Yeasts" (A. H. Rose and J. S. Harrison, eds.), Vol. 1, p. 303. Academic Press, London and New York.
Fowell, R. R. and Moorse, M. E. (1960). *J. Appl. Bacteriol.* **23**, 53.
Gilliland, R. B. (1951). *Proc. E.B.C. Congr.*, Brighton p. 35.
Gilliland, R. B. (1955). *J. Appl. Bacteriol.* **18**, 161.
Gilliland, R. B. (1956). *C.R. Trav. Lab. Carlsberg, Ser Physiol.* **26**, 139.
Gilliland, R. B. (1957). *Wallerstein Lab. Commun.* **20**, 41.
Gilliland, R. B. (1959). *J. Inst. Brew.* **65**, 424.
Gilliland, R. B. (1961). *J. Inst. Brew.* **67**, 257.
Gilliland, R. B. (1962). *J. Inst. Brew.* **68**, 271.
Gilliland, R. B. (1969). *Proc. E.B.C. Congr.*, Interlaken p. 303.
Gilliland, R. B. (1971a). *J. Inst. Brew.* **77**, 276.
Gilliland, R. B. (1971b). *Brewers' Guardian* (Oct. 29).
Gilliland, R. B. and Lacey, J. P. (1966). *J. Inst. Brew.* **72**, 291.
Gilliland, R. B. and Harrison, G. A. F. (1966). *J. Appl. Bacteriol.* **29**, 244.
Gorin, P. A. J. and Spencer, J. F. T. (1970). *Adv. Appl. Microbiol.* **13**, 25.
Green, S. R. and Gray, P. P. (1950). *Wallerstein Lab. Commun.* **13**, 357.
Green, S. R. and Stone, I. (1952). *Wallerstein Lab. Commun.* **15**, 347.
Greenshields, R. N., Yates, J., Sharp, P. and Davies, T. M. C. (1972). *J. Inst. Brew.* **78**, 236.
Griffin, S. R. (1970a). *J. Inst. Brew.* **76**, 41.
Griffin, S. R. (1970b). *J. Inst. Brew.* **76**, 357.
Griffin, S. R. and MacWilliam, I. C. (1969). *J. Inst. Brew.* **75**, 355.
Grinbergs, M., Hildebrand, R. P. and Clarke, B. J. (1977). *J. Inst. Brew.* **83**, 25.
Guilliermond, A. (1912). "Les Levures" (translated and revised by F. W. Tanner (1920) "The Yeasts"). Wiley, New York.
Haefner, K. (1965). *Z. Allg. Mikrobiol.* **5**, 77.
Haikara, A. and Enari, T-M. (1975). *Proc. E.B.C. Congr., Nice* p. 363.
Hall, J. F. (1971). *J. Inst. Brew.* **77**, 513.
Hall, J. F. and Webb, T. J. B. (1975). *J. Inst. Brew.* **81**, 471.
Harris, J. O. (1959). *J. Inst. Brew.* **65**, 5.
Harris, J. O. and Watson, W. (1968). *J. Inst. Brew.* **74**, 286.
Haworth, W. N., Heath, R. L. and Peat, S. (1941). *J. Chem. Soc., London* p. 833.
Hawthorne, D. C. (1955). *Genetics* **40**, 511.
Hawthorne, D. C. and Mortimer, R. K. (1968). *Genetics* **60**, 735.
Hayashibe, M., Sando, N. and Abe, N. (1973). *J. Gen. Appl. Microbiol.* **19**, 287.
Helin, T. R. M. and Slaughter, J. C. (1977). *J. Inst. Brew.* **83**, 15.
Helm, E., Nøhr, B. and Thorne, R. S. W. (1953). *Wallerstein Lab. Commun.* **16**, 315.
Hemmons, L. M. (1954). *J. Inst. Brew.* **60**, 288.
Hoggan, J. and Compson, D. G. (1963). *Proc. E.B.C. Congr., Bruxelles* p. 370.
Hough, J. S. (1957). *J. Inst. Brew.* **63**, 483.
Hough, J. S., Briggs, D. E. and Stevens, R. (1971). "Malting and Brewing Science". Chapman and Hall, London.
Hudson, J. R. (1967). *Proc. E.B.C. Congr., Madrid* p. 187.
Ingram, M. (1955). "An Introduction to the Biology of Yeasts". Pitman, London.
Jansen, H. E. (1958). *In* "The Chemistry and Biology of Yeasts" (A. H. Cook, ed.), p. 635. Academic Press, New York and London.
Jayatissa, P. M. and Rose, A. H. (1976). *J. Gen. Microbiol.* **96**, 165.

Johnston, J. R. (1963). *Proc. E.B.C. Congr., Bruxelles* p. 412.
Johnston, J. R. (1965). *J. Inst. Brew.* **71**, 130.
Johnston, J. R. and Mortimer, R. K. (1959). *J. Bacteriol.* **78**, 292.
Jones, M. (1972). *Wallerstein Lab. Commun.* **35**, 131.
Jones, M. and Pierce, J. S. (1964). *J. Inst. Brew.* **70**, 307.
Jones, M. and Pierce, J. S. (1969). *Proc. E.B.C. Congr., Interlaken* p. 151.
Jörgensen, A. (1886). "Die Mikroorganismen der Gärungsindustrie". 15th edition translated and edited by A. Hansen (1948). "Micro-organisms and Fermentation". Griffin & Co. Ltd., London.
Joslyn, M. A. (1955). *Wallerstein Lab. Commun.* **18**, 107.
Katò, S. (1967). *Bull. Brew. Sci.* **13**, 19.
Katò, S. and Nishikawa, N. (1957). *Bull. Brew. Sci.* **3**, 39.
Kessler, G. and Nickerson, W. J. (1959). *J. Biol. Chem.* **234**, 2281.
Kirsop, B. (1974). *J. Inst. Brew.* **80**, 565.
Kirsop, B. H. (1954). *J. Inst. Brew.* **60**, 393.
Kirsop, B. H. and Brown, M. L. (1972). *J. Inst. Brew.* **78**, 51.
Kockovà-Kratochvílová, A., Vojtková-Lepšíková, A., Šandula, J. and Pokorna, M. (1966). *Folia Microbiol., Prague* **11**, 200.
Kockovà-Kratochvílová, Anna (1976). Biologické Práce XXII/6, Bratislava, Publ. House Slav. Acad. Sci.
Kockovà-Kratochvílová, A., Šandula, J., Vojtková-Lepšíková, A. and Kasmanová, M. (1969). "Taxometric Study of the Genus *Saccharomyces*/Meyen/Rees". Part I. Vydavatelstvo Slovenskej Akadémie Vied, Bratislava.
Kopécka, M., Phaff, H. J. and Fleet, G. H. (1974). *J. Cell Biol.* **62**, 66.
Korn, E. D. and Northcote, D. H. (1960). *Biochem. J.* **75**, 12.
Kreil, H., Kleber, W. and Teuber, M. (1975). *Proc. E.B.C. Congr., Nice* p. 323.
Kudriavzev, W. I. (1960). "Die Systematik der Hefen". Akademie Verlag, Berlin.
Kulka, D. (1953). *J. Inst. Brew.* **59**, 285.
Lee, B. K. and Wilkie, D. (1965). *Nature, London* **206**, 90.
Leupold, U. (1956). *C.R. Trav. Lab. Carlsberg, Ser. Physiol.* **26**, 221.
Lewis, C. W. and Johnston, J. R. (1974). *Proc. J. Gen. Microbiol.* **1**, 73.
Lewis, M. J. and Enevoldsen, B. S. (1973). *Tech. Quart. Master Brewers Ass. Am.* **10**, 20.
Lewis, M. J. and Phaff, H. J. (1963). *Proc. Ann. Meet. Am. Soc. Brew. Chem.* p. 114.
Lewis, M. J. and Phaff, H. J. (1964). *J. Bacteriol.* **87**, 1389.
Lewis, M. J. and Phaff, H. J. (1965). *J. Bacteriol.* **89**, 960.
Lewis, M. J. and Stephanopoulos, D. (1967). *J. Bacteriol.* **93**, 976.
Lewis, C. W., Johnston, J. R. and Martin, P. A. (1976). *J. Inst. Brew* **82**, 158.
Lin, Y. (1974). *Proc. Ann. Meet. Am. Soc. Brew. Chem.* **32**, 69.
Lin, Y. (1975). *J. Inst. Brew.* **81**, 410.
Lindegren, C. C. (1944). *Wallerstein Lab Commun.* **7**, 153.
Lindegren, C. C. (1949). "The Yeast Cell, Its Genetics and Cytology", 1st edn. Educational Publishers Inc., St. Louis, Mo.
Lindegren, C. C. (1955). *Science* **121**, 605.
Lindegren, C. C. and Lindegren, G. (1943). *Proc. Nat. Acad. Sci. U.S.A.* **29**, 306.
Linnane, A. W., Lamb, A. J., Christodoulou, C. and Lukins, H. B. (1968). *Proc. Nat. Acad. Sci. U.S.A.* **59**, 1288.
Lodder, J. (ed.) (1970). "The Yeasts—A Taxonomic Study". North-Holland Publishing Co., Amsterdam and London.
Lodder, J. and Loggers, G. (1968). U.S. Patent 3 394 008. 23 July.
Lund, A. and Thygesen, P. (1957). *Proc. E.B.C. Congr., Copenhagen* p. 241.

Lyons, T. P. and Hough, J. S. (1970). *J. Inst. Brew.*, *London* **76**, 564.
Magni, G. E. (1963). *Proc. Nat. Acad. Sci. U.S.A.* **50**, 975.
Markham, E. (1969). *Wallerstein Lab Commun.* **32** (107), 5.
Markham, E. and Byrne, W. J. (1967). *J. Inst. Brew.* **73**, 271.
Markham, E., Mills, A. K. and Byrne, W. J. (1966). *Proc. Ann. Meet. Am. Soc. Brew. Chem.* 76.
Masschelein, Ch. and Devreux, A. (1957). *Proc. E.B.C. Congr.*, *Copenhagen* p. 194.
Masschelein, Ch. A., Meerssche, J. van de, Haboucha, J. and Devreux, A. (1973). *Proc. Ann. Meet. Am. Soc. Brew. Chem.* p. 114.
Matile, Ph., Moor, H. and Robinow, C. F. (1969). *In* "The Yeasts" (A. H. Rose and J. S. Harrison, eds.), Vol. I, p. 219. Academic Press, London and New York.
Maule, A. P. and Thomas, P. D. (1973). *J. Inst. Brew.* **79**, 137.
Maw, G. A. (1960). *J. Inst. Brew.* **66**, 162.
Maw, G. A. (1963). *J. Gen. Microbiol.* **31**, 247.
Meister, H. (1965). *Wallerstein Lab. Commun.* **28**, 7.
Meyer, S. A. and Phaff, H. J. (1969). *J. Bacteriol.* **97**, 52.
Mill, P. J. (1964). *J. Gen. Microbiol.* **35**, 53, 61.
Mills, D. R. (1941). *Food Res.* **6**, 361.
Morimoto, K., Shimazu, T., Fujii, T. and Horie, Y. (1975). *Rep. Res. Lab. Kirin Brewing Co.*, *Yokahama* **18**, 63.
Morris, E. O. and Eddy, A. A. (1957). *J. Inst. Brew.* **63**, 34.
Mortimer, R. K. and Hawthorne, D. C. (1966). *Annu. Rev. Microbiol.* **20**, 151.
Mortimer, R. K. and Hawthorne, D. C. (1969). *In* "The Yeasts" (A. H. Rose and J. S. Harrison, eds.), Vol. I, p. 385. Academic Press, London and New York.
Mortimer, R. K. and Hawthorne, D. C. (1975). *In* "Methods in Cell Biology" (David M. Prescott, ed.), Vol. XI, p. 221. Academic Press, New York and London.
Mosiashvili, G. I. and Shalutashvili, I. D. (1971). *Vinodel. Vinograd. SSSR* **31**, No. 3, 19. via *Chem. Abstr.* 75, 62146j.
Nakase, T. and Komagata, T. (1971). *J. Gen. Appl. Microbiol.* **17**, 227, 259.
Narziss, L. and Hellich, P. (1972). *Brewers' Digest* **47** (9), 106.
Nathan, L. (1930). *J. Inst. Brew.* **36**, 538.
Nečas, O. (1971). *Bacteriol. Rev.* **35**, 149.
Nishihara, H., Toraya, T. and Fukui, S. (1976). *J. Ferment. Technol.* **54**, 356.
Northcote, D. H. and Horne, R. W. (1952). *Biochem. J.* **51**, 232.
Novák, E. K. and Zsolt, J. (1961). *Acta Bot.* **7**, 93.
Nurminen, T. (1976). "On the Isolation, Enzymes and Lipid Composition of the Plasma Membrane and Cell Wall of Baker's Yeast". Thesis: Helsinki University of Technology, Finland.
Nurminen, T., Oura, E. and Suomalainen, H. (1970). *Biochem. J.* **116**, 61.
Owades, J. L., Jakovac, J. and Vigilante, C. (1960). *Proc. Ann. Meet. Am. Soc. Brew. Chem.* p. 63.
Palleroni, N. J. (1961). *Phyton, Buenos Aires* **16**, 117.
Parkkinen, E., Oura, E. and Suomalainen, H. (1976). *J. Inst. Brew.* **82**, 283.
Patel, G. B. and Ingledew, W. M. (1975a). *J. Inst. Brew* **81**, 123.
Patel, G. B. and Ingledew, W. M. (1975b). *Can. J. Microbiol.* **21**, 1608, 1614.
Peat, S., Whelan, W. J. and Edwards, T. E. (1958). *J. Chem. Soc.*, *London* 3862.
Perkins, D. D. (1949). *Genetics* **34**, 607.
Phaff, H. J. (1963). *Annu. Rev. Microbiol.* **17**, 15.
Philliskirk, G. and Young, T. W. (1975). *Antonie van Leeuwenhoek; J. Microbiol. Serol.* **41**, 147.

Pollock, J. R. A. and Weir, M. J. (1975). *J. Inst. Brew.* **81**, 375.
Poncet, S. (1967). *Antonie van Leeuwenhoek; J. Microbiol. Serol.* **33**, 345.
Portno, A. D. (1973). *Brewers' Guardian* (July) p. 33.
Prescott, D. M. (ed.) (1975). "Methods in Cell Biology", Vols. XI and XII "Yeast Cells". Academic Press, New York and London.
Pringle, J. R. (1975). *In* "Methods in Cell Biology" (David N. Prescott, ed.), Vol. XII, p. 149. Academic Press, New York and London.
Rainbow, C. (1966). *Process Biochem.* **1**, 489.
Reed, G. and Peppler, H. J. (1973). "Yeast Technology". A.V.I. Publishing Company Inc., Westport, Ct.
Reiff, F., Kautzmann, R., Lüers, H. and Lindemann, M. (1960 and 1962) "Die Hefen", Vols. 1 and 2. Verlag Hans Carl, Nürnburg.
Resnick, M. A., Tippetts, R. D. and Mortimer, R. K. (1967). *Science* **158**, 803.
Richards, M. (1967). *J. Inst. Brew.* **73**, 162.
Richards, M. (1968). *J. Inst. Brew.* **74**, 433.
Richards, M. (1970). *Wallerstein Lab. Commun.* **33**, 11.
Richards, M. (1973). *Brewers' Digest* **48** (12), 48.
Richards, M. (1975). *Proc. Ann. Meet. Am. Soc. Brew. Chem.* **33**, 1.
Richards, M. and Cowland, T. W. (1967). *J. Inst. Brew.* **73**, 552.
Richards, M. and Elliott, F. R. (1968). *Antonie van Leeuwenhoek; J. Microbiol. Serol.* **34**, 227.
Roessler, J. G. (1968). *Brewers' Digest* **43**, (8), 94.
Roman, W. (ed.) (1957). "Yeasts". W. Junk, The Hague.
Rose, A. H. and Harrison, J. S. (eds.) (1969, 1971 and 1970). "The Yeasts", Vols. I, II and III. Academic Press, London and New York.
Sando, N. (1956). *Sci. Rep. Res. Inst. Tohoku Univ. Ser. IV* **22**, 99.
Sando, N. (1960). *Sci. Rep. Res. Inst. Tohoku. Univ. Ser. IV* **26**, 139.
Scherrer, A. Sommer, A. and Pfenninger, H. (1969). *Brauwissenschaft* **22**, 191.
Schultz, A. S. and Atkin, L. (1947). *Arch. Biochem.* **14**, 369.
Schultz, A. S. and McManus, D. K. (1950). *Arch. Biochem.* **25**, 401.
Skinner, C. E., Emmons, C. W. and Tsuchiya, H. M. (1947). "*Henricis* Molds Yeasts, and Actinomycetes", 2nd edn. John Wiley, New York; Chapman and Hall, London.
Somers, J. M. and Bevan, E. A. (1969). *Genet. Res.* **13**, 71.
Suomalainen, H. and Nurminen, T. (1976). *J. Inst. Brew.* **82**, 218.
Suomalainen, H. and Oura, E. (1971). *In* "The Yeasts" (A. H. Rose and J. S. Harrison, eds.), Vol. II, p. 3. Academic Press, London and New York.
Spencer, J. F. T. and Gorin, P. A. J. (1968). *J. Bacteriol.* **96**, 180.
Stantial, H. (1935). *Trans. R. Soc. Can., Sect.* 3. **29**, 175.
Stevens, T. J. (1966). *J. Inst. Brew.* **72**, 369.
Stewart, G. G. (1978). *J. Am. Soc. Brew. Chem.* **36**, 175.
Stewart, G. G. and Goring, T. E. (1976). *J. Inst. Brew.* **82**, 341.
Stewart, G. G., Russell, I. and Garrison, I. F. (1975). *J. Inst. Brew.* **81**, 248.
Strandskov, F. B., Ziliotto, H. L., Brescia, J. A. and Bockelmann, J. B. (1965). *Proc. Ann. Meet. Am. Soc. Brew. Chem.* p. 129.
Takahaski, T. (1968). *Bull. Brew. Sci.* **14**, 11.
Tanaka, H. and Phaff, H. J. (1965). *J. Bacteriol.* **89**, 1570.
Thompson, C. C. and Ralph, D. J. (1967). *Proc. E.B.C. Congr., Madrid* p. 177.
Thorn, J. A. (1971). *Brewers' Digest* **46** (Oct.), 110.
Thorne, R. S. W. (1951). *Proc. E.B.C. Congr., Brighton* p. 21.
Thorne, R. S. W. (1968). *J. Inst. Brew.* **74**, 516.

Thorne, R. S. W. (1970). *J. Inst. Brew.* **76**, 555.

Thorne, R. S. W. (1973). *Brewers' Guardian* **102**, 39.

Thorne, R. S. W. (1975). *Process Biochem.* **10** (7), 17.

Thornton, R. J. and Eschenbruch, R. (1976). *Antonie van Leeuwenhoek; J. Microbiol. Serol.* **42**, 503.

Tsuchiya, T., Fukazawa, Y. and Kawakita, S. (1965). *Mycopathol. Mycol. Appl.* **26**, 1.

Tubb, R. S. (1979). *J. Inst. Brew.* **85**, 286.

Van Engel, E. L. (1969). *Proc. Ann. Meet. Am. Soc. Brew. Chem.* p. 35.

Wainwright, T. (1970). *J. Gen. Microbiol.* **61**, 107.

Walsh, R. M. and Martin, P. A. (1977). *J. Inst. Brew.* **83**, 169.

Walt, J. P. van der (1964). *Antonie van Leeuwenhoek; J. Microbiol. Serol.* **30**, 273.

Walt, J. P. van der (1970). *In* "The Yeasts" (J. Lodder, ed.), p. 555. North-Holland, Amsterdam and London.

Walt, J. P. van der and Kerken, A. E. van (1960). *Antonie van Leeuwenhoek; J. Microbiol. Serol.* **26**, 292.

Watson, D. H. (1964). *Brewer's Guardian* **93** (12), 17.

Webb, T. J. B. (1977). *J. Inst. Brew.* **83**, 4.

Wellman, A. M. and Stewart, G. G. (1973). *Appl. Microbiol.* **26**, 577.

White, J. (1954). "Yeast Technology". Chapman and Hall, London.

Whitehouse, H. L. K. and Hastings, P. J. (1965). *Genet. Res.* **6**, 27.

Wickner, R. B. (1976). *Bacteriol. Rev.* **40**, 757.

Wikén, T., Scheffers, W. A. and Verhaar, A. J. M. (1961). *Antonie van Leeuwenhoek; J. Microbiol. Serol.* **27**, 401.

Wiles, A. E. (1949). *J. Inst. Brew* **55**, 165, 172.

Wiles, A. E. (1950). *J. Inst. Brew.* **56**, 183.

Wiles, A. E. (1952). *J. Inst. Brew* **58**, 252.

Wiles, A. E. (1953). *J. Inst. Brew* **59**, 265.

Williams, D. O. and Stringer, W. J. (1955). *Amer. Brew.* **88** (May), 39.

Wilson K. and McLeod, B. J. (1976). *Antonie van Leeuwenhoek; J. Microbiol. Serol.* **42**, 397.

Windisch, S. (1954). *Brau. Wiss. Beil.* **7**, 135.

Windisch, S. and Emeis, C. C. (1969). W. German Patent 1 442 311.

Windisch, S. E. and Neuman, I. (1972). *In* "Fermentation Technology Today" (G. Terui, ed.), Proc. 4th Int. Ferment. Symp., p. 877. Soc. Ferment., Japan.

Winge, Ö. (1935). *C.R. Trav. Lab. Carlsberg, Ser. Physiol.* **21**, 77.

Winge, Ö. and Laustsen, O. (1937). *C.R. Trav. Lab. Carlsberg* **22**, 99.

Wollmer, W. (1935). *Tagesz. Brau., Wiss. Beil.* **33**, 711.

Woof, J. B. (1962). *J. Inst. Brew.* **68**, 315.

Yamamoto, Y. and Inoue, T. (1962). *Rep. Res. Lab. Kirin Brewing Co., Yokohama* No. 5, 11, 17.

Yoshida, S. (1962). *Bull. Brew. Sci., Tokyo* **8**, 37.

2. Yeast Flocculation

G. G. STEWART AND I. RUSSELL

*Brewing Research Department, Labbatt Brewing Company Ltd.,
London, Ontario, Canada*

I. INTRODUCTION

In order to achieve a beer of high quality, it is axiomatic that not only must the culture effectively remove the required nutrients from the growth and fermentation medium (that is the wort) and impart the desired flavour to the beer, but in addition the microorganisms themselves must be removed from the fermented wort after they have fulfilled their metabolic role. Yeast flocculation is quite simply the agglomeration of otherwise discrete microorganisms into flocs such that under quiescent conditions they reach sufficient mass as to settle out of suspension; under certain other circumstances, some yeast strains are carried to the surface of the fermenting medium adsorbed by the rising carbon dioxide bubbles. If the fermented wort is to be filtered or centrifuged, it is also important that the yeast flocs possess sufficient rigidity and associated porosity so that separation of the beer can be easily achieved.

Freely suspended microorganisms, yeast cells included, often occur in groups or flocs of a characteristic size many orders of magnitude greater than that of a single cell. It is reasonable to suggest that microorganisms can occur either as single cells or as multicellular groups; however, some microorganisms have a tendency to form larger flocs than others, under what are apparently identical environmental conditions. The occurrence of flocs has been found in many biological systems, for example, the reaction between antibody and antigen (Shawn and Lis 1972), the cohesion of tissue cells (Moscona 1962), the aggregation of sponge cells (Moscona 1967), biological waste sewage treatment systems (Pavoni *et al.* 1972), citric acid production (Steel *et al.* 1955) and mushroom mycelium production (Block *et al.* 1953) as well as the flocculation of yeast cells (for reviews, see Windisch 1968, Rainbow 1970, Geilenkotton and Nyns 1971, Stewart 1975). The aggregation of microorganisms is effected by an interaction of polymers excreted by the microbial cell or exposed at the cell surface; the process is not merely one whereby polymers bridge between adjacent cell surfaces. Although the mechanism of cell aggregation has yet to be fully elucidated, the factors involved and the manner in which they influence aggregation seem to be common to nearly all cell flocculation systems. This observation suggests that there may be similar or identical mechanisms involved in the flocculation of many different cell types.

Flocculation involves the formation of an open agglomeration, the mechanism of which depends upon molecules acting as bridges between separate particles; this open structure is indeed implicit in the word "flocculation" which derives from the Latin *flocculus* meaning "a tuft of wool". The term flocculation has in fact been used as a general description for all aggregation processes by which an originally stable colloid forms larger particles which no longer remain suspended due to Brownian motion. There are many definitions of yeast flocculation but the one preferred by Stewart (1975) is that: *Flocculation is the phenomenon wherein yeast cells adhere in clumps and sediment rapidly from the medium in which they are suspended.*

There exists little or no consistency regarding the terminology used in describing or defining flocculation, but for those studying the aggregation of microorganisms conformity and the utmost precision of observations are prerequisites for meaningful interpretation of results. Terms such as clumping, aggregation, coagulation and flocculation, while used synonymously by some investigators, are nevertheless used to describe very different phenomena by other workers. However measured, in this chapter the terms aggregation or flocculation will be used synonymously and will be meant to describe the adhesion of yeast cells into groups forming discrete three-dimensional matrices.

Aggregation of cells may be actively or passively obtained. For example, it would be passive whenever cells simply fail to effect complete separation after cell division (a phenomenon known as chain formation in yeast). On the other hand, it would be active whenever free cells form stable aggregates as a consequence of random collision. The flocculation to be discussed in this chapter is almost exclusively of the active type, since it occurs in the absence of cell division (i.e. in the non-growing or stationary phase) and only under rather circumscribed environmental conditions. However, some reference will be made to chain formation in yeast.

Because of the importance of antibody/antigen reactions and sewage bacteria and micro-algae, a considerable volume of literature has accumulated. By comparison, work reported on the flocculation and agglutination of yeast is sparse. The flocculation of yeast has, nevertheless, been studied by many investigators, using a variety of methods, with the result that numerous agents and conditions have been advocated as the cause of or as able to increase flocculation.

The flocculation characteristics of a particular yeast culture is one of its most important properties when considering the selection of a yeast strain for brewing purposes; other characteristics under this heading are an adequate level of reproduction, and a medium to high rate of fermentation prolonged and sufficient enough to complete attenuation. Fulfillment of these conditions must be accompanied by the production of a palatable beer. It is however difficult to be dogmatic about such generalized specifications since requirements will vary from brewery to brewery depnding upon the type of beer required and the fermentation conditions used. For example, a yeast strain with a very different type of flocculation would be required for a top-fermenting ale system than would be necessary if the yeast was to be removed with a centrifuge at the completion of fermentation.

A most important aspect of the flocculation characteristics of a brewing yeast strain is the period during the fermentation cycle that the yeast culture flocculates. One of the most troublesome problems encountered by the brewer is "hung" or "stuck" fermentations, i.e. incomplete attenuation of the wort. Hung fermentations are invariably caused by one of two factors: (1) premature flocculation of the yeast culture in the fermenting wort (Curtis 1956, 1963), and (2) failure of the yeast, although still in suspension, to utilize all of the fermentable wort sugars; this is usually due to the inability of the yeast to take up and metabolize maltotriose. It is also possible that the yeast may fail to flocculate, thus making its removal from the fermented wort very troublesome; this in turn often causes some difficulty in obtaining a bright sparkling beer: under such circumstances, off-flavours, due to yeast autolysis, can often result. Indisputably, knowledge of the mechanisms that control flocculation at the biochemical, molecular and genetic level are of paramount importance to both the brewer and the brewing microbiologist.

Over the last few years a detailed study of yeast flocculation has been conducted in the author's laboratory in an attempt to elucidate the various mechanisms and controls that influence the flocculation characteristics of brewer's yeast strains. Strains of both *Saccharomyces cerevisiae* (i.e. ale strains) and *Sacch. carlsbergensis* (*uvarum*) (i.e. lager strains) have been studied and interesting differences between the flocculation characteristics of strains within each species have been found. This chapter is a review of this laboratory's investigations and a survey of the "state of the art" generally speaking. The purpose is not to provide a comprehensive citing of the literature, but rather to attempt an integration of those studies that have led to new insights concerning the title subject. Unpublished material presently in the process of publication together with a discussion of the current literature is included and the coverage is intended to be contemporary and representative rather than complete.

II. HISTORICAL REVIEW

Historical developments in yeast flocculation are extremely disjointed but nevertheless have been well documented by Jansen (1958). Consequently, only investigations that are pertinent to a modern conceptual view will be discussed. Pasteur (1876) described the presence of a flocculating yeast in an ordinary top fermentation but conducted no investigation of the phenomenon. The first investigations on yeast flocculation were conducted in Germany during the final decade of the last century (Kusserow 1897, Lange 1899, Delbruck 1901, Lindner 1901). These early investigations clearly pointed to a relationship between wort composition and the flocculence of the yeast, a concept which, as will be described later, finds credibility with current theories of flocculation. This work however, suffered from the fact that it was too empirical in nature, a criticism that indeed could be directed at more contemporary studies; since these experiments were carried out with different types of yeasts propagated under different conditions, the results were hardly comparable.

At the turn of the century, flocculation of top fermentation yeast was attributed to the action of several types of bacteria on yeast—the so-called symbiotic theory. Barendrecht (1901) was the first to describe a bacterium which caused agglutination of industrial yeast grown under aerated conditions. He also demonstrated the influence of hydrogen ion concentration on the flocculation of a pure yeast culture in some preliminary tests with acidified suspensions of yeast. Beyerinck (1908) was of the opinion that although bottom yeasts in breweries may flocculate on their own (i.e. show autoagglutination or autoflocculation), this certainly was not the case with top fermentation yeasts. Flocculation of this latter type of yeast could only be caused by symbiosis of the yeast with different types of bacteria. It was assumed that the yeast cell became enveloped in mucilage produced by these bacteria and consequently flocculated. If under special conditions, the formation of mucilage by such bacteria was suppressed, the agglutination of the yeast was less complete. With infected yeasts this mechanism may still hold and indeed aggregation of yeast caused by *Lactobacilli* has recently been reported (Momose *et al.* 1969a, b); this however certainly does not explain the flocculation of top fermentation yeasts in ordinary practice (White and Kidney, 1979).

An engaging theory of flocculation, developed by Lange (1907), was based on the premise that flocculation is caused by an adsorbed layer of protein on the cell wall, which in the case of a powdery yeast is absent, having been dissolved by the proteolytic action of certain secreted enzymes (proteases). In the case of a flocculent yeast, insufficient protease is secreted and the protein layer on the cell wall remains intact. As stated, Lange's theory cannot be upheld although many aspects of it are interesting and, as will become evident later, find their place in modern concepts of flocculation.

The effect of salts on yeast flocculation has been widely studied and the influence of lime and magnesia in the brewing liquor has aroused considerable debate. Seyffert (1896) described a pure culture of yeast that lost its flocculation by reason of the softness of the brewing liquor and acquired it again after addition of lime to the liquor. Schonfeld and Krumhaar (1918) stated that calcium salts of strong acids were the cause of the behaviour of powdery (non-flocculent) yeasts, flocculence being caused by a layer of insoluble calcium phosphate deposited on the wall. The theory continued to exist until Burns (1937) proved the opposite, i.e. that calcium ions and certain other salts have a direct and positive influence upon yeast flocculation.

Schonfeld (1909, 1910) attempted to distinguish flocculent and powdery types of yeast by suspending them in water—the flocculent yeast settled in flocs, while the powdery yeast formed a milky suspension. He further maintained that a flocculent yeast could be transformed into a powdery yeast by propagating a flocculent culture at high temperatures (25–30 °C). This finding confirmed the work of Hayduck (1905) who was of the opinion that non-flocculence in brewery yeast is enhanced by the action of strong aeration and higher temperatures during fermentation.

The influence of wort proteins and metabolic products on yeast flocculation was described many years ago but, with the development of colloid chemistry, efforts were made to bring yeast flocculation into the domain of this branch of chemistry. Luers and Heusz (1921) determined the viscosity of yeast suspensions in buffer solutions at different pH values and they found that maximum viscosity corresponded to maximum flocculation. This phenomenon was explained by assuming that large flocs of yeast possess a high resistance because bulky conglomerates retard the flow more than small ones. Luers' work was continued by Geys (1922) who was the first to measure the charge on the yeast cell by means of microelectrophoresis. According to Geys, yeast cells have a positive charge when suspended in water but this charge becomes neutral during the initial stages of fermentation and during the later stages the yeast cell became negative and finally positive once again. Since Geys' method of microelectrophoresis was not free of serious errors, the results were inconclusive.

Yeast flocculation was extensively discussed by Stockhausen (1927) who considered it to be brought about by the flocculation of proteins at pH 4·7–4·8; the flocculated protein adsorbed by the yeast cells in turn caused the cells to settle out. In later papers (Stockhausen and Silbereisen 1933, 1935) it was assumed that yeast flocculation is mainly caused by the presence of yeast gum. However, by determining the compound secreted by yeast cells suspended in distilled water, it was shown that an increase in such gum substances was not accompanied by an increase in flocculation.

In 1937, Burns introduced a new method for measuring yeast flocculation in which the amount of yeast which settles from a yeast suspension in a graduated tube after standing for 10 minutes is determined. Burns, working with English top fermentation yeast, showed that the flocculence of the pitching yeast is closely related to the yeast content of the beer at dropping, to the attenuation and to the progress of fermentation in the fermentation vessel. Most of Burns' views on yeast flocculation have since been confirmed and his method for determining yeast flocculation is still in general use.

A survey of literature published in the *Journal of the Institute of Brewing* prior to 1945 has revealed that no attempt was made to explain the mechanism of yeast separation in British brewing systems. In the pre-1940 period, except for the studies of Burns and Bishop, research on yeast flocculation was mainly concerned with lager yeast. Jansen (1958) has succinctly summarized this period: "Factors influencing yeast flocculation present in the fermenting medium had been investigated and some slight agreement on the influence of electrolytes on flocculation established. Racial differences in flocculation were known, but had not been subjected to genetical research while the complexity of the whole phenomenon of yeast flocculation was generally recognized."

III. THIRD EUROPEAN BREWING CONVENTION CONGRESS, 1951

Chronologically speaking it is often an arbitrary and difficult decision to say exactly at what date a survey of a particular topic ceases to be historical and a discussion of modern concepts begins. In the case of yeast flocculation however, the year 1951 is clearly a turning point in time because in that year a major theme of the Third European Brewing Convention Congress held in Brighton, England, was the subject of yeast flocculation. At this conference new concepts were discussed and a revival of interest in yeast flocculation research occurred. The papers presented at Brighton have been reviewed by Comrie (1952) and much of the following is based on this review together with summaries of the actual papers. Furthermore, since the research discussed in 1951 forms the basis of more recent studies, these too are discussed as "logical" consequences thereof.

IV. CLASSIFICATION OF FLOCCULATION

The degree of intensity of flocculation is a specific characteristic of a yeast strain and a number of attempts have therefore been made to measure flocculation and to classify strains according to this parameter. Gilliland (1951) isolated different brewing ale strains and studied their behaviour during fermentation; he was particularly interested in the quantity of yeast in suspension and by this measure differentiated between four major classes of yeast.

Class I: Yeast in this group is completely dispersed at all stages of fermentation: these are non-flocculent strains.

Class II: Yeast strains herein are, initially, completely dispersed but form loose clumps towards the end of fermentation.

Class III: Yeasts of this class are, initially, completely dispersed but flocculate towards the end of fermentation into "caseous" masses.

Class IV: These yeasts are highly flocculent; the clumps may settle out during the early stages of fermentation because the newly formed cells do not separate from the parent cells.

The yeast strains in Class I present technical difficulties in their separation at the end of fermentation which renders them unsuitable for brewing unless the yeast is to be mechanically removed at dropping. According to Gilliland (1951, 1957) the yeasts of Class II are the standard yeasts of top fermentation; they possess good fermenting power, bring about a rapid fermentation, and produce consistent attenuation; and little of the yeast remains dispersed at the end of the fermentation. The yeasts of Class III are less suitable than those of Class II since their flocculation properties are so pronounced that they fail to attain an adequate degree of attenuation. Windisch (1968) has stated that strains corresponding to Class I–III are also found among lager yeasts. Lager strains with such an intense a flocculation characteristic as to be placed in Gilliland's Class IV have not been reported—the author confirms this fact from his own experiences. The ale yeasts of Class IV are unsuitable for conventional brewing. However, yeast strains from this class have been found to be of use in certain continuous processes and stirred batch systems (Smith and Greenshields 1974).

Hough (1957) has devised a more complex scheme of differentiating categories of ale yeast based upon flocculation characteristics; isolates from pitching yeasts were tested for their ability to form:

(a) A film of cells at the air–liquid interface of an aqueous suspension of yeast (head formation).
(b) Aggregates in calcium chloride solution at pH 3·5.
  (i) Some strains aggregating in this test disperse on addition of maltose.
  (ii) Other strains not aggregating in this test precipitate when ethanol is added.
(c) Aggregates in calcium chloride solution buffered at pH 5·0.
(d) Aggregates in calcium chloride solution buffered at pH 5·0 when an appropriate second strain is added (mutual flocculation or co-flocculation).
(e) Chains of cells in malt extract liquid medium (chain formation).

Studies in the author's laboratory (Stewart *et al.* 1975a) have led to the proposal of a classification of brewer's yeast strains according to their flocculation characteristics based on the growth media in which the strain was cultured. In ale strains (i.e. *Saccharomyces cerevisiae*) five categories have been recognized:

(1) *Non-flocculent strains.* These are strains of ale yeast that, with the exception of the budding stage, exist as single cells and have no ability to clump or flocculate.

(2) *Co-flocculent strains.* There have been a number of publications from the author's laboratory (Stewart *et al.* 1972, 1973) describing the flocculation characteristics of co-flocculent strains. Although it has been stated that both strains participating in this type of flocculation are non-flocculent on their own, this is not exactly the case. It would appear, on further study, that the cells of one of the strains (the B type), in the presence of Ca^{2+} ions, have a diffusive type of agglutination although they do not flocculate out of suspension. On addition of the co-flocculent partner (the A type), which is completely non-flocculent, the diffusive agglutination of the B type cells becomes firm and much more distinct and the whole culture quickly sediments. Despite reports in the literature (Eddy 1955, 1958) indicating that a number of strains with either A or B type co-flocculation properties exist, research in this laboratory has revealed only one strain with A type co-flocculent properties, whereas a number of strains with B type co-flocculation properties have been found.

(3) *Strains flocculent on their own after growth in wort* (*i.e. pure strain flocculation*). These are strains which are flocculent when cultured in wort but non-flocculent when cultured in a defined medium consisting of glucose, maltose, ammonium ion, vitamins and ions. There appears to be an inducer peptide present in wort that stimulates flocculation; this is the same material as that reported previously to induce co-flocculation (Stewart *et al.* 1973, 1974, 1975a). Wort is not the sole source of such peptides; gelatin, yeast extract and peptone, when added to the defined medium, have also been found to induce flocculation in all of the strains in this category. Furthermore, as with co-flocculation, amino acids such as glutamic and aspartic acids, when present in excess in the growth medium, induce flocculation in ale strains of this category. This ability is not restricted to the L-isomers since the non-metabolizable D-isomers of aspartic and glutamic acids are also capable of inducing floccu-lation among strains of this category. The type of flocculation being primarily discussed in this chapter requires that the yeast strain be *grown* in the presence of the inducer before flocculation will occur. There are instances reported (Kudo 1960, Kudo and Kijima 1960) where certain compounds (e.g. humic acid) will induce floc formation when added to a non-growing suspension of the yeast culture, this is not the case in wort nor any of the literature being cited here.

(4) *Strains flocculent on their own after growth in either wort or the glucose–ammonium salts medium.* These are strains which when cultured in wort or the defined medium become flocculent, i.e. no wort inducer is necessary. It would appear that strains in this category are able to synthesize their own flocculation-inducing material.

(5) *Chain-forming yeast strains.* When some strains bud, the daughter cell does not separate cleanly from the mother cell so that in time clumps of cells form which are visible to the naked eye and, if large enough, tend to settle from the medium. If a yeast strain has this tendency to form chains it will do so in any growth medium. However, a comparison of wort and the defined medium has shown that all such strains display a greater tendency to chain formation in the latter medium. It is possible that nutritional variations between the two media may result in differences in the degree of chain formation. This phenomenon is discussed in greater detail later in this chapter.

In lager, (i.e. *Sacch. uvarum* (*carlsbergensis*) strains examined to date, only two subdivisions have been recognized:

(1) *Non-flocculent strains.* These strains display characteristics similar to those of non-flocculent ale strains.

(2) *Strains flocculent on their own.* Even when grown in a defined medium, all flocculent lager strains will become flocculent; no wort inducer appears necessary in the growth medium. Flocculent lager strains would seem to be able to synthesize their own flocculation-inducing material; to date no strain of lager yeast has been found that requires an exogenous supply of such peptide material in the growth medium. Further, it is interesting to note that lager strains have a much reduced tendency towards chain formation than ale strains.

This general classification of yeast strains according to their flocculation characteristics is, as with all classifications, a grouping of strains that have a number of basic similarities. Since all yeast strains are independent living entities however, a number of differences within each category can be expected to occur. One example of such a difference is the apparent requirement for Ca^{2+} ion (or certain other ions) in the flocculation medium before flocculation will take place. All truly flocculent yeasts (excluding chain formers) require the presence of Ca^{2+} ions (or certain other ions) before they are able to flocculate. However, a superficial examination of a number of yeast strains would leave the impression that some strains, even after considerable washing with deionized water, nevertheless flocculate in deionized water at pH 4·0 with no apparent requirement for an ion such as calcium. If these strains, however, are first washed with EDTA solution (or another chelating agent), centrifuged, and subsequently washed a number of times with deionized water to remove all traces of EDTA and then resuspended in deionized water at pH 4·0 they are found to be unable to flocculate. These EDTA-washed cells, however, become flocculent immediately upon addition of Ca^{2+} ions to the yeast suspension. It would therefore appear that some strains retain their adsorbed cell wall metal ions (Ca^{2+} ions in particular) with far greater affinity than do other strains that are easily de-flocculated with water. For simplicity's sake, however, both types of strains, assuming that they have other flocculation characteristics in common have been placed in the same flocculation category.

V. EVALUATION OF YEAST FLOCCULATION

While considerable effort has been made to elucidate the mechanism of yeast flocculation, there has been a great deal of variability amongst the numerous techniques for measuring the state or intensity of aggregation. The measurement of yeast flocculation is a topic which provokes considerable discussion and debate; suffice to say that it is imperative that there exists some degree of standardization in such tests. Due to the plethora of various flocculation tests and the fact that every laboratory involved in this area of study appears to have its own "pet" method, it is difficult to interpret and apply results from one laboratory to another. In general, the measurement techniques have been somewhat arbitrary and subjective and have represented qualitative rather than quantitative evidence of aggregate formation. Over the years diverse methods for measuring flocculation have been tried and published. In a majority of the methods, the yeast cells are removed from the growth medium, washed and then allowed to sediment in a standard medium of known pH and defined composition (Helm *et al.* 1953). A small number of flocculation measurements have been carried out in the actual growth medium as distinct from a sedimentation medium (Gilliland 1951). This latter method appears to offer certain advantages, and can be considered as an *in vivo* test in contrast to the more artifical *in vitro* test.

Most methods used to measure yeast flocculation have been based upon the sedimentation properties of yeast flocs suspended in a liquid "milieu". As early as 1910 Schonfeld determined the quantity of sedimented yeast following fermentations performed in cylindrical vessels. In 1937 Nielsen evaporated the yeast suspensions to dryness and evaluated the dry weight of the culture, the rate of sedimentation being estimated by a value representing the proportion of yeast originally present in the upper 75% of suspension which passed into the lower 25% per minute. As discussed in the historical review, Burns (1937) described the first method in which precise experimental conditions were devised whereby a known quantity of pressed yeast (0·5 g in a sodium acetate–acetic acid buffer at pH 4·6) was measured into a graduated tapered centrifuge tube. After vigorously shaking and subsequent standing for 10 minutes, the volume of the settled flocculated cells was determined.

The Burns test has been modified by Helm *et al.* (1953) who studied the effect of altering the test conditions and confirmed that calcium ion was necessary for the expression of the flocculence character. Kato and Nishikawa (1957) further modified the method by advocating that, after standing for a set period of time at 20 °C, an aliquot of the suspension should be drawn off the top and the cell concentration measured photometrically at 800 nm; the sedimented cells were also suitably diluted and their optical density determined. The ratio of these two readings gave a measure of sedimentation rate which was translated into a "sedimentation percentage".

Woof (1962) produced sedimentation curves (cell count plotted against time) of a number of different yeasts in beer. The curves consisted of two straight portions linked by a short elbow. It has been suggested that the flocculating power of a yeast could be expressed in terms of the coordinates of the intersection of the extrapolated straight portions of the curve.

In the author's laboratory, three methods are used routinely to measure yeast flocculence.

1. Sedimentation Method (e.g. Helm Sedimentation Test)

In this test, the yeast culture is removed from the growth medium and washed a number of times with deionized water. The culture is then resuspended in deionized water containing 80 µg/ml of calcium ion as calcium chloride at pH 4·0 and, depending on the scale of the test, the suspension placed in a test tube (10 ml scale) or measuring cylinder (100 ml scale). Figure 1 illustrates the flocculation of a number of yeast strains with varying degrees of flocculence, under the conditions of this test.

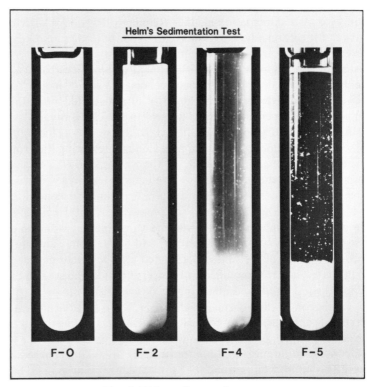

FIG. 1. Helm sedimentation test.

2. Direct Observation of Floc Formation in the Growth Medium

This test is a modification of that originally employed very effectively by Gilliland (1951). In this method, a small inoculum of the yeast strain is seeded into 20 ml screw-capped glass bottles containing 15 ml of medium. After three days of incubation at 25 °C, the flocculation characteristics of the culture are determined by the nature of the flocs subsequent to the sediment being brought back into suspension by shaking the bottle (Fig. 2). This method

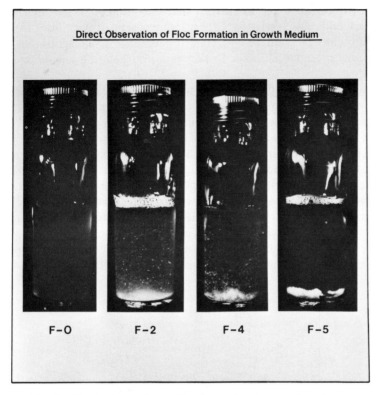

FIG. 2. Direct observation of floc formation in growth medium.

allows for routine flocculence determinations of a large number of cultures and has been used extensively in the genetic studies that will be discussed later in this chapter.

To express the flocculation results from the above flocculation tests, a subjective gradation of flocculation has been devised:

>5—Extremely flocculent
>4—Very flocculent
>3—Moderately flocculent
>2—Weakly flocculent
>1—Rough
>0—Non-flocculent

3. Static Fermentation Method

In this method, the concentration of yeast in suspension is determined during the course of the fermentation (Stewart *et al.* 1975b). Although the first two methods for measuring yeast flocculence can be viewed as artificial *in vitro* tests for flocculence due to the fact that they are conducted under rather artificial conditions in relation to the brewing process, this method of assay for yeast flocculence is an *in vivo* style test because it is carried out under conditions more closely akin to the static fermentation encountered in a brewery.

Two methods of graphically presenting the results of the static fermentation experiments have been employed. In the first instance, the gravity of the fermenting wort is plotted against incubation time and compared on an adjacent graph to the concentration of yeast in suspension using a similar time axis. The example in Fig. 3 considers the effect of wort oxygen level at pitching on the flocculation properties of a bottom-cropping strain of *Sacch. cerevisiae*. One fermentation vessel was oxygenated to a level of 8 p.p.m. whereas the other was treated for a similar period with oxygen-free nitrogen to give a wort oxygen level less than 1 p.p.m. Treatment of results in this manner fails to give a direct visual impression of the culture's flocculation characteristics. In an attempt to overcome this problem, the concentration of yeast in suspension has been plotted against the precentage attenuation of the wort (Fig. 4). One

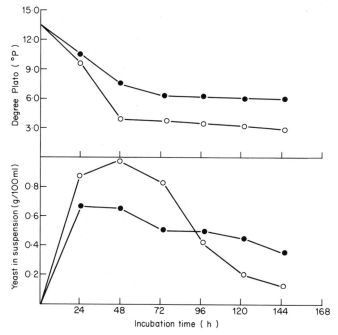

FIG. 3. Static fermentation test for flocculation, comparing fermentation rate with yeast in suspension. ——, wort O_2 level; ● nitrogen (O_2 p.p.m. <1); ○, oxygen (O_2 p.p.m. = 8).

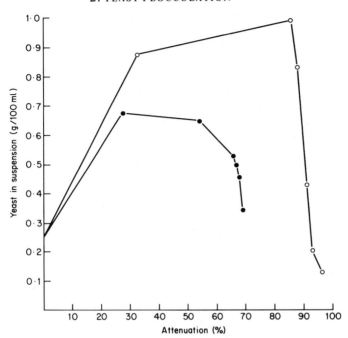

FIG. 4. Static fermentation test for flocculation, comparing yeast in suspension with percentage wort attenuation. ——, wort O_2 level; ●, nitrogen (O_2 p.p.m. <1); ○, oxygen (O_2 p.p.m. = 8).

hundred per cent attenuation of the wort has been taken as that wort gravity achieved when the yeast's flocculation characteristic is ignored, by agitation in the same wort as that being used for static fermentation. In this manner, the influence of a culture's flocculation can be directly related to its ability to attenuate a wort.

In a recent publication Calleja and Johnson (1977) have compared quantitative methods for measuring yeast flocculation. Studying the sex-directed flocculation in the fission yeast *Schizosaccharomyces pombe* they have developed some quantitative methods which may be useful in other cell-aggregating systems. Two quantitative objective methods for measuring flocculation were compared and correlated with subjective estimation by eye. One method involved counting in a haemocytometer the number of free cells (i.e. cells not found in flocs) and then the total number of cells after complete deflocculation by protease. The number of cells in flocs was then derived by subtracting the number of free cells from the total number of cells. The other method made use of the decrease in turbidity of a flocculated culture on standing. The difference in turbidity readings between 0 and 5 minutes was assumed to represent the turbidity component due to cells in flocs. Both methods were found applicable to monitoring the flocculation of a yeast culture containing 500 gross flocs per ml.

VI. FLOCCULATION INDUCERS

It has been previously stated that some ale yeast strains are flocculent after growth in wort but non-flocculent after growth in a defined medium consisting of glucose, maltose, ammonium ion, vitamins and ions. One of the major differences between wort and the defined medium is the presence of protein and polypeptide in the former. The effect of such materials on the flocculation of certain yeast strains has been investigated by precipitating the proteins and peptides from wort and adding this precipitate to the defined medium (Stewart et al. 1973). When ale strains which are non-flocculent in the defined medium, but flocculent in wort, were cultured in this protein-enriched medium, stationary phase cells once more exhibited flocculence. When the wort precipitate was treated with protease (i.e. papain, trypsin, etc.), thus hydrolysing all protein and peptide material to free amino acids, such treated material failed to induce flocculation. Wort proteins and/or polypeptides have therefore been shown to play a vital role in the phenomenon of flocculation in certain ale yeast strains.

A specific peptide fraction with the ability to induce flocculation in appropriate ale strains has been isolated. The fractionation was performed using ion-exchange chromatography and a number of peptide fractions have been isolated. The only fraction capable of inducing flocculation was that eluted from an anionic resin with acetic acid. Furthermore, amino acid analysis, after hydrolysis, revealed that this fraction was high in acidic amino acid residues when compared to other wort peptide fractions. It therefore appears that one of the mechanisms by which cells are linked in flocs is through divalent ion bridges involving carboxyl groups contained in acidic peptides which are situated on the surface of the yeast cell wall.

The fact that peptides will induce flocculation in certain yeast strains has been indicated in a number of publications which were not involved directly in the brewing process. Calleja and Johnson (1971) have investigated the flocculation properties of a haploid strain of the fission yeast Schizosaccharomyces pombe. As stated previously, flocculation in this species of yeast is regarded as the initial phase of the sexual process because it is always followed by sexual conjugation. For flocculation to occur in this yeast, it was found that the cultural conditions were important since flocculation did not take place in a mineral salts medium which presumably was deficient in peptide and amino acid material. A further publication in this area (Duntze et *al.* 1970) deals with the agglutination of haploid cells of *Saccharomyces cerevisiae* during mating. It has been found that this agglutination is induced by a heat stable, dialysable material which is destroyed as a result of protease treatment. There would therefore appear to be a number of similarities between these situations and the flocculation of brewer's yeast strains.

In the context of flocculation inducers, the Kirin Laboratory (Morimoto *et al.* 1975, Fujii and Horie 1975) has studied factors that induce early flocculation (i.e. flocculation before the end of primary fermentation although sufficient nutrient still remains in the fermenting medium). A substance has been found in wort that induces early flocculation. Upon purification the substance (EP) was inactivated by pronase treatment. EP consisted of α-glucan, β-glucan, araboxylan and glycoprotein. The α-glucan and β-glucan appeared to have no early flocculating inducing activity but the araboxylan moiety with protein appeared to be the cause of the induction of early flocculation. This early flocculating factor would appear to be of similar structure to the acidic peptide previously described.

VII. YEAST CELL WALL STRUCTURE AND FLOCCULATION

There is little doubt that differences in the flocculation characteristics of various yeast cultures, grown under a variety of conditions, are primarily manifestations of the yeast culture's cell wall structure. The structure of the yeast cell is subject to considerable discussion (Lyons and Hough 1970b, Phaff 1971). However, it is thought to consist essentially of two layers (Fig. 5), the mannan-phosphate-protein layer, which is the outer layer, connected to a structural glucan layer.

The ability to confer flocculation on a yeast strain resides in the mannan layer of the cell wall. This fact has been illustrated in two ways. Firstly, cells treated with a proteolytic enzyme (Lyons and Hough 1970a, 1971, Russell *et al.* 1973) led to almost complete removal of the mannan together with a large proportion of the cell wall protein and phosphorous; flocculent cultures were rendered non-flocculent. The glucan of the cell wall however, was untouched as a result of treatment with proteolytic enzyme. Secondly, inhibition of mannan synthesis (e.g. with cycloheximide) results in potentially flocculent strains remaining non-flocculent (Baker and Kirsop 1972). Masschelein (1962) has reported that the period of deflocculation coincides with mannan synthesis and has stated that this polysaccharide appears as a regulator of the intensity of flocculation. It is considered that in strains that require an inducer in the growth medium to become flocculent, the inducer can only be

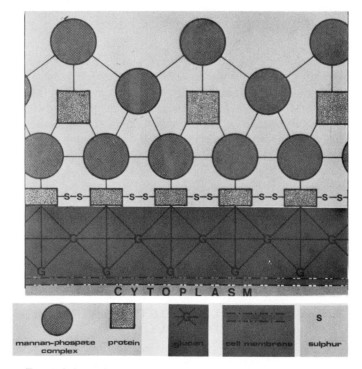

FIG. 5. Schematic structure of the cell wall of *Saccharomyces sp.*

incorporated into the cell wall when the mannan is of a suitable complexity of structure.

Gross analysis (Table 1) of isolated cell walls has revealed some interesting differences between flocculent (which includes co-flocculent and flocculent) and non-flocculent cultures in both ale and lager yeast strains. In the walls of all flocculent cultures examined there was a much higher content of total carbohydrate than in the walls of non-flocculent cultures. The increased carbohydrate content was found to be due to an elevated level of mannan; the glucan level of flocculent and non-flocculent cells appeared to be very similar. Although there is some controversy concerning the levels of mannan in flocculent and non-flocculent cell walls, recent studies by a number of investigators (Griffin and McWilliam 1969, Jayatissa and Rose 1976) would appear to support the findings detailed above, namely, that there is a higher mannan content in flocculent cell walls than in non-flocculent walls.

Lyons and Hough (1970a, 1971) have reported that the mannan-protein-phosphate layer of the walls of flocculent cells contains a higher level of phosphorous than that of the walls of non-flocculent cells. However, the

TABLE 1. Gross composition of flocculent and non-flocculent cell walls[a]

	Ale strain LAB B/69 (CF[b])	Ale strain LAB 11/69 (F[b])	Ale strain LAB 3/69 (NF[b])	Lager strain LAB 21/69 (F[b])	Lager strain LAB 27/69 (NF[b])
Carbohydrate (%)	79	80	68	77	68
Glucan (%)	49	42	45	47	46
Mannan (%)	30	38	23	30	22
Mannan : glucan ratio	0·6	0·9	0·5	0·5	0·5
Protein (%) (N × 6·25)	15·1	13·8	18·1	11·6	17·9
Phosphorus (%)	0·2	0·2	0·4	0·3	0·4

[a] All cultures were grown in wort at 21 °C and harvested in early stationary phase.
[b] CF, co-flocculent; F, flocculent; NF, non-flocculent.

involvement of phosphorus in yeast flocculation has become a rather controversial subject as a result of the studies of Ballou and his co-workers (Cawley and Ballou 1972). During their studies on yeast mannan structure, they have isolated a number of mutants of *Sacch. cerevisiae* which have altered mannan structure. One such mutant has a lower phosphate content than its parental wild type but it exhibits a much higher degree of flocculence. Further, studies by Griffin and McWilliam (1969) and by Jayatissa and Rose (1976) have confirmed the studies cited from the author's laboratory in that they too failed to detect any differences between the cell wall phosphate level of flocculent and non-flocculent cell walls.

It has been stated on many occasions that only when the yeast cell surface is examined with the electron microscope will any meaningful differences between the microstructures of flocculent and non-flocculent cultures be revealed. However, until recently, with the exception of the investigations of Lyons and Hough (1970a, 1971) with the scanning electron microscope, no detailed study of this nature had been reported. In the author's laboratory (Day *et al.* 1975), a number of flocculent and non-flocculent cultures were shadow-cast with tungsten oxide and examined under the electron microscope. Differences between flocculent and non-flocculent cultures were immediately apparent and such differences were accentuated after the cells had undergone a brief ether wash (Fig. 6). The cells of non-flocculent cultures appeared to possess no extracellular projections, whereas cells from flocculent cultures are covered with an extensive layer of fimbriae or hairlike protuberances.

The surface hairs, associated with the flocculent culture, can be removed with little difficulty. For example, a suspension of a flocculent yeast was placed in a blender and blended at maximum speed for approximately 30 seconds. The hairs were removed from the cell wall and at the same time the yeast

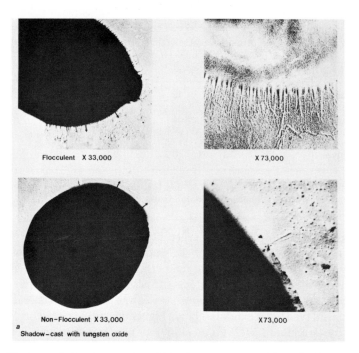

Fig. 6. Electron photomicrographs of *Saccharomyces cerevisiae*; shadow-cast with tungsten oxide.

culture lost its ability to flocculate. This result would cast some doubt upon analytical data and conclusions obtained from experiments with isolated cell walls since the isolation of such cell walls involves considerable abrasion during which the hairs would probably be dislodged from the cell surface.

No studies on the composition of cell wall hairs from flocculent cultures have been conducted, but it would seem reasonable to speculate that they may be glyco-peptide or phospho-mannan in nature. If this is the case, the elevated mannan content of isolated flocculent cell walls could conceivably be due to the presence of dislodged hairs.

VIII. ROLE OF METAL IONS IN FLOCCULATION

Mill (1964a, b, 1966) was the first to suggest that flocculated cells are linked by salt bridges, namely calcium ions joining two carboxyl (or possibly phosphate) groups at the surface of two cells. The structures thus formed are stabilized by hydrogen bonds between complementary carbohydrate hydroxy groups at the cell surface. Studies in the author's and other laboratories have confirmed these findings, and have shown that other divalent ions, such as magnesium and manganese, are apparently able to replace calcium in the bridging function. Larger divalent ions such as uranyl, barium and strontium (Taylor and Orton 1975) have been observed to inhibit floc formation. While these ions may compete for certain specific sites on the cell surface and therefore behave as competitive inhibitors to such flocculation-inducing ions as calcium, it is considered that their larger radii may prevent the effective stabilization normally imparted by the formation of hydrogen bonds.

A number of publications have indicated that flocculent yeast strains can adsorb considerably more calcium ion on to their cell surfaces than can non-flocculent strains (Masschelein 1957). It has also been proposed (Lyons and Hough 1970a, 1971) that isolated cell walls prepared from flocculent cultures will bind more calcium ion than walls prepared from non-flocculent cultures. Recently, the calcium-binding of flocculent and non-flocculent cultures has been investigated further (Stewart et al. 1975a, b). In this study, the calcium-binding ability of whole yeast cells was considered as opposed to cell wall preparations because it was felt that cell walls present two surfaces for calcium binding; consequently, the results obtained using such preparations might be difficult to interpret.

It was found that there is strain-to-strain variation in calcium adsorption onto the cell surface, which is in all likelihood a reflection of the differences in structure of the cell walls from strain to strain. In addition, this strain to strain variation in calcium adsorption *per se* does not correlate with flocculence when one strain is compared with another. The only meaningful measure of calcium binding behaviour which correlates with flocculation is the ease with which calcium is washed off the cell, in that flocculent cells adsorb calcium ion more firmly than non-flocculent cells, so that the calcium adsorbed by the non-flocculent cells is easily removed by washing. The fimbriate or "hairy" nature of flocculent yeast cell surfaces as shown in the electron micrographs (Fig. 6) suggests speculation as to why flocculent cells bind their calcium more strongly than their smooth-surfaced non-flocculent counterparts: it would seem reasonable to postulate that the calcium might be held in the interstices of such projections and would therefore be more firmly adsorbed to the cell surface.

Porter and Macauley (1965) have shown that the effect of calcium depends largely upon the pH and that this dependence varies from one yeast strain to another. On the basis of this observation, they classified yeast strains into the following "well defined" groups:

Group A: Strongly flocculent strains, whose flocculation is much more dependent on the actual pH value of the medium than on its calcium content. Only traces of calcium are necessary in order to produce marked flocculence.

Group B: Moderately flocculent strains that show only limited response to either calcium or pH.

Group C: Potentially very flocculent strains at higher pH levels but which require considerable amounts of calcium for the development of their flocculation.

A number of reports in the literature have stated that flocculation is antagonized by monovalent ions such as sodium and potassium. However, a recent report (Stewart and Goring 1976) looks at the problem from a new perspective. Low concentrations (1–10 mg ion/litre) of sodium or potassium ion are able to induce flocculation in those strains displaying intense flocculation in the presence of calcium ion. However, high concentrations of either sodium or potassium ion (50–100 mg ion/litre) have been found to antagonize floc formation. It has been suggested that, whereas divalent ions such as calcium act by bridging cells through negative charges on the cell surface, monovalent ions induce flocculation by a "counter-ion" effect wherein repellent forces of the negative charges on the cell surface are neutralized, thus allowing some floc formation due to hydrogen-bonding or other types of non-ionic bonding between cells. The antagonism of high concentrations of monovalent ions towards flocculation may be due to the fact that all available cell surface charges are neutralized, resulting in insulation of the cells and thus preventing cell to cell hydrogen bonding.

Although calcium, magnesium and manganese play an important function in intercellular cross-linking between yeast cells (Stewart and Goring 1976, Stewart and Russell 1976), magnesium has been reported to be the only metal capable of inducing floc-forming ability (Nishihara *et al.* 1976a, b); magnesium ion is absolutely required in the growth medium before a yeast culture will become flocculent. It seems plausible to suggest that a factor responsible for flocculation is induced by magnesium ions. It is noteworthy that studies of floc-forming bacteria belonging to *Flavobacterium* (Endo *et al.* 1976) have indicated that calcium is required in the growth medium in order to induce the synthesis of some component(s) of the cell surface which is essential for flocculation. However, intercellular cross-linking between bacterial cells, previously induced to be flocculent, can be brought about in a medium containing appropriate concentrations of calcium, barium or manganese.

IX. RELATIONSHIP BETWEEN THE CELL SURFACE CHARGE AND FLOCCULATION

The electric charge on the yeast cell surface clearly must be an important factor in any contact phenomenon among single-cell organisms. This was realized many years ago, and numerous studies were carried out with the aim of discovering a relationship between flocculating ability and cell surface charge with, on the whole, considerable disagreement among investigators. During fermentation in wort, there is always a net negative charge on the yeast cell surface (Wiles 1951). This is due partly to the inorganic surface groups but also to the adsorption of anions from the surrounding medium. Until recently, little was known of the precise relationship between surface charge and cell wall structure although in the 1950s Eddy and Rudin (1958a, b, c), from the results of studies on the effect of pH value on the electrophoretic mobility of yeasts, concluded that the negative charge is attributable partly to phosphate groups and partly to protein. In addition, Eddy and Rudin (1958b) attempted to find a possible relationship between the surface charge on a yeast cell and its flocculating ability. Such studies, however, proved disappointing because, as fermentation proceeded, no sudden change in the density of the charge on the cells either with flocculent or non-flocculent yeasts could be detected.

Recently, Jayatissa and Rose (1976) have assessed the relative contributions from acidic amino acid residues and phosphodiester linkages in the flocculation of Sacch. cerevisiae. In their studies they could not correlate the wall phosphorus level with the sedimentation rate of cultures. Further, measuring the electrophoretic mobility at pH 4·0, which indicates the density of phosphate groups in the outer layers of the wall to a depth of 4·2 nm with buffer of ionic strength 0·005 M (Richmond and Fisher 1973) did not indicate any correlation to exist between the phosphate contents of the outer layers of walls and the flocculation rate of the organisms. Jayatissa and Rose (1976) reported on the use of hydrofluoric acid (HF), which under carefully controlled conditions specifically excises the phosphodiester linkages from the cell wall mannan. Such treatment, surprisingly, increased flocculation rates and the electrophoretic mobility due to phosphorus was completely absent. The results indicate that phosphodiester linkages in yeast cell wall mannan are not involved in bridge formation with calcium ion during floc formation and that bridges arise principally through carboxyl groups.

X. GENETIC CONTROL OF YEAST FLOCCULATION

Genetic studies on yeast flocculation began 30 years ago. The first reference found on the subject was by Pomper and Burkholder (1949) who crossed a haploid that possessed a "disperse" character (non-flocculent) with a haploid possessing a "non-disperse" character (flocculent). The "disperse" character was reported to be dominant over the "non-disperse" character. No reference as to the type of flocculation was made; very likely chain formation was being considered rather than the type induced by calcium ion.

During the early 1950s Gilliland and Thorne independently carried out extensive studies of the genetics of yeast flocculation. Gilliland (1951) studied two non-brewing strains of *Sacch. cerevisiae* which differed only in their flocculation properties. From the results of a number of crosses, it was proposed that a single gene was responsible for the expression of the flocculence phenotype, but it was not possible to deduce whether the gene was dominant or recessive. Thorne (1951, 1952) performed matings between one flocculent and four non-flocculent brewing strains and, confirming Gilliland's studies, demonstrated that flocculence was an inherited characteristic with flocculence considered dominant over non-flocculence. Thorne further proposed that control over flocculation was exercised by at least three pairs of polymeric genes, together with a gene that appeared to have an inhibitory effect upon the expression of the flocculation gene. The degree of flocculation exhibited by the yeast was unaffected by the number of dominant genes present and the presence of only one was adequate to confer complete flocculation on the strain.

Subsequent to the early pioneer work of Gilliland and Thorne, there were no significant investigations on this subject until quite recently. In the past three years Johnson and his colleagues (Lewis and Johnson 1974, Lewis *et al.* 1976) published accounts of an in-depth study on the genetics of flocculence, and Anderson (née Clayton) (Clayton *et al.* 1972, Anderson and Martin 1975) made considerable reference to the topic during her wide-ranging investigations into the hybridization of industrial strains of *Sacch. cerevisiae* and *Sacch. uvarum* (*carlsbergensis*). Both studies arrived at similar conclusions, namely, that flocculation is under the genetic control of a multiple gene system and that flocculence is modified by the influence of additional modifier (suppressor) genes or cytoplasmic genetic factors. Lewis *et al.* (1976) identified two dominant (FLO 1 and FLO 2) and one recessive gene (flo 3) for flocculence, the presence of only one of which is necessary for the flocculation phenotype to be expressed. Quantitatively, the presence of each gene separately resulted in approximately the same intensity of flocculation; there was no observable additive effect of the genes in combination with each other. In a study of the effects of different mutagens on brewing yeast Molzahn (1977) found the flocculation of a moderately flocculent strain was increased. In this case, the mutation had probably removed a modifier (or suppressor) gene and promoted an increase in flocculation.

Genetic work involving brewer's yeast strains is fraught with difficulties due to their frequent triploid, polyploid or aneuploid nature (Johnston 1965, Windisch 1961). In line with many workers who have attempted genetic studies on brewer's yeast strains (Anderson and Martin 1975, Fowell 1969), the author's laboratory has found that such strains sporulate poorly, rarely form spores in fours in the ascus and that many of the spores that do form are non-viable (Stewart *et al.* 1975b). As a result of these problems, it was decided to commence a study of the genetic control of flocculation with a flocculent haploid strain (coded 169) which contained a single flocculation gene. This strain (169) was then crossed with strains previously reported to contain either FLO 1 or FLO 2. All three genes were found to be allelic and thus were consolidated into the single gene locus FLO 1 (Russell *et al.* 1980). The map distance between FLO 1 and ade 1 was calculated at 37 cM (Stewart and Russell 1977). FLO 1 was located on the right arm of Chromosome I (Rothstein and Sherman 1980).

XI. INSTABILITY OF FLOCCULATION

One of the least understood aspects of flocculation is the phenomenon by which the flocculation characteristics of a particular yeast strain change spontaneously. In many breweries, the behaviour of the yeast is by no means constant. A flocculent yeast can, without any apparent reason, gradually lose its clumping characteristics and become more and more powdery. Sometimes the reverse occurs, i.e. a non-flocculent yeast can become progressively flocculent after a number of generations in the fermentation cellar. At the same time, it often loses its ability to attenuate the wort and the fermentation becomes sluggish.

The flocculation characteristics of a particular yeast strain is the sum of the flocculation characteristics of the individual cells that make up that strain. It has been found possible to isolate, from a particular strain, a culture similar in every respect to the parent, except that it has different flocculation characteristics. For example, Chester (1963) was able to isolate a number of less flocculent variants from a flocculent yeast strain. Thompson (1970) reported the isolation of a bottom-cropping mutant from a top-fermenting ale strain. The bottom-cropping strain was found to be stable, although a number of others were found to revert and were less resistant to autolysis than their parent. Thompson (1970) considers that the frequency of such a mutation is characteristic of the strain, although on the basis of his experience, a mutation rate of one in every 500 cells would not be uncommon. Studies in the author's laboratory (Stewart *et al.* 1975) would confirm that, in many cases, the flocculation properties of certain strains are somewhat unstable. For example, a number of non-flocculent cultures of the co-flocculent ale strain B have been isolated; such isolates are unable to participate in co-flocculation under normal conditions.

Norstedt and his co-workers (Norstedt and Bengtsson 1969, Gyllang and Martinson 1971) have studied the properties of a lager yeast strain that has an increased sedimentation rate after a number of consecutive fermentations. For this particular strain, the attenuation rate is decreased when the yeast which falls to the bottom of the fermentation vessel is selected and used as pitching yeast during a number of consecutive fermentations. The reduced attenuation rate has been attributed to the selection of respiratory deficient mutants that have increased sedimentation; many had lost their ability to ferment maltotriose, whereas no reduction was found in their ability to ferment glucose, fructose or maltose. The induction of respiratory deficient mutants of ale yeast strains by formaldehyde in the mash has been described by Cowan *et al.* (1974). Some respiratory deficient mutants showed slower growth rates than the parent, and sedimented rapidly; the latter produced a rapid fermentation, but the beer flavour was distinctly different. It should not be assumed, however, that all respiratory deficient mutants are more flocculent than their parents because Silhankova *et al.* (1970) would tend to argue the opposite, i.e. that respiratory deficient mutants are less flocculent than their parents. Although, at the present time, no biochemical or morphological studies of such mutant cultures have been carried out, it is most likely that flocculation changes are manifestations of an altered cell surface structure which are in turn reflections of the biosynthetic activity of the culture.

XII. METABOLIC CONTROL OF FLOCCULATION

Research on yeast flocculation has concentrated on the structure of the cell surface and the genetic control of the phenomenon. However, little has been published on the metabolic differences between flocculent and non-flocculent strains. Although a gene(s) has been identified that codes for flocculation, the available information concerning the mode of expression of such a gene(s) is meagre. The metabolic consequences of the gene expression must result in the cell wall being organized in such a manner that the cell will be able to become flocculent. Further, any overall theory of flocculation must explain the nature and origin of the forces that cause the yeast cells to begin clumping at a certain stage during the fermentation (i.e. early stationary growth phase).

In a flocculent strain, a protein (almost certainly an enzyme) is synthesized at a greater or possibly a lesser rate than in a non-flocculent strain, resulting in an alteration of cell wall structure. The differences in the structure of flocculent cell walls when compared with non-flocculent cell walls, which were revealed on observation of the culture with an electron microscope (Fig. 5), could be manifestations of such a gene action. The physiological state of the cell is an important criterion due to the fact that flocculation is only manifested during stationary growth phase. It could very well be that only at a particular stage in the growth cycle (e.g. when a specific nutrient is exhausted or at a point of overproduction of a specific cell component) are the flocculence genes able to synthesize a particular enzyme which, in turn, will influence the structure of the yeast cell wall.

Another interesting facet of the problem is the situation with respect to yeast strains that can flocculate after growth in a single defined medium, as compared with those strains that require inducer material (e.g. peptide) in the growth medium before they are able to flocculate. To date, no genetic comparison of these two types of yeast strain has been conducted. It could very well be, however, that strains able to flocculate in the defined medium have additional genes and are therefore more biosynthetically competent than the strains that require the flocculation inducer material in the growth medium.

Any consideration of yeast flocculation must, in the final analysis, ask the question: "Why do yeast strains flocculate at all; of what use to the yeast is the ability to flocculate; in what way does flocculation bequeath to the cell an adaptive advantage?" Yeast strains most certainly do not flocculate for the convenience (or inconvenience) of the brewer! While it is difficult to give a definite answer, one might speculate that it might be a vestigial manifestation of the sexual phase wherein the agglutination of cells that precedes copulation has been shown to be induced by peptide material in a number of different yeast species, i.e. *Sacch. cerevisiae* (Sakurai *et al.* 1976, Yoshida *et al.* 1976), *Schizosacch. pombe* (Calleja 1970, Calleja and Johnson 1971) and *Hansenula wingei* (Crandall and Brock 1968, Crandall and Caulton 1975).

Johnson (personal communication) has evolved an intriguing and novel theory, namely that flocculation is a means of protection during adverse environmental conditions. Yeast has always, even before domestication by Man, been a dweller in solutions of complex composition. Such solutions have waxed and waned in nutrient concentration due to the drying by the sun, to rainfall and to the metabolic activities of the yeasts themselves. In a yeast clump there would be a negative gradient in terms of nutrient concentration towards the centre of the clump. Consequently, the cells in the centre would live in a less enriched medium than those on the periphery and hence would have a longer generation time. Cells which do not flocculate would therefore have a selective advantage over those which do but will disadvantage some of their own kind because from an evolutionary and selective adaptation point of view numbers of progeny is the all important factor. During conditions of starvation a portion of the cells in the centre of a clump will be protected due to the fact that some of the cells autolyse and therefore release their proteins, nucleic acids, carbohydrates and vitamins. Under such conditions, if all but one of the cells starve to death, that survivor should be one which has evolved the genetic mechanism for flocculation.

XIII. CHAIN FORMATION IN BREWER'S YEAST

Previous reference has been made in this chapter to the fact that when some ale yeast strains bud, the daughter cell does not separate cleanly from the mother cell, so that in time, clumps of cells form that are visible to the naked eye and, if large enough, tend to settle from the medium (chain formation does not appear to occur to any extent in lager yeasts). This is a separate phenomenon not to be confused with flocculation: in the case of chain formation, as a result of incomplete cell division, the cells are not bridged together but are physically joined at their cell walls.

The process whereby a bud disconnects from its mother cell is known as bud abscission. The phenomenon has been explained (Barton 1950) in physical terms based on the idea that the independent increase in volume of the daughter cell results in a stretching of the birth scar. The shearing action between the two scars causes the mechanical connection to break. Physical forces would appear to be only a part of the mechanism and the processes are in all probability facilitated by the participation of cell-wall-splitting enzymes. Lok and Rose (personal communication) have studied this aspect and have treated chain-forming yeast cultures with trypsin and glucanase singly and together. Only when a mixture of the two enzymes was used was there a marked effect on the separation of the cells from the chain, an indication that the linkage between the attached cells consists of both peptide bonds and glucan material.

Four genes have been identified which are necessary for cell separation, cdc 3, cdc 10, cdc 11 and cdc 12 (Hartwell 1974). Mutation of any of these genes gives strains which have lost their ability to complete the process of cell division and their cells therefore form multiple elongated buds that do not separate from the parent cell.

XIV. FOAMING OF SAKÉ AND WINE YEASTS

During the course of saké fermentations, most saké mashes develop a high froth head at an early stage of fermentation. The high froth is maintained for a week or so and then breaks down at a later stage of fermentation. As a large number of yeast cells is included in the froth, it appears that most common saké yeast strains tend to adhere to the surface of gas bubbles. A similar situation prevails in wine-making where froth-head formation is evident at an early stage of grape juice fermentation. Up to 5% of the capacity of a fermentation tank is normally reserved to prevent such froth from spilling over and, from a practical point of view, frothless strains are advantageous since a tank can be used to its full capacity.

Ouchi and his colleagues (Nunokawa *et al.* 1971, Ouchi *et al.* 1973) have isolated mutants of saké yeast which do not form a froth head during fermentation and similar non-foaming mutants have been obtained from wine yeasts by Eschenbruch and Rassell (1975). Ouchi has compared the gross cell wall composition of the parent strain and two strains of the mutant. They showed, "that there were no marked differences in cell wall composition between the parent and mutant strains" and concluded, "that changes in the physicochemical properties which occurred in the cells of the mutant strains are due to structural alterations of the outermost layer of the cell wall, the demonstration of which will require special techniques." One can only speculate at this juncture, but an examination of shadow-cast foaming and non-foaming strains with an electron microscope might prove to be revealing.

XV. CONCLUDING REMARKS

There are two determining factors that influence the flocculence of a particular yeast culture, one being internal and the other external. The internal factors refer to the genotype, namely, the genetic determinants of flocculation, because, for example, whatever the environmental conditions, a genotypically non-flocculent yeast will always be non-flocculent. The external factors refer essentially to the growth medium; studies to date have made significant progress towards elucidating these environmental factors that influence the development of flocculation, particularly in relation to yeast cell wall structure. In recent years a far greater understanding of the genetic control of flocculation has been obtained; however, factors which modify the expression of the flocculence genes require additional comprehension.† Further, the mode of expression, in a metabolic sense, of the flocculence gene(s) remains largely unknown. The next decade should see significant developments in this field and the advent of brewing yeast strains bred to specified criteria (e.g. so as to have the exact flocculation characteristics for the fermentation conditions in use) is not too far away.

† *Note added in proof*

A flocculent haploid strain of *Sacch. cerevisiae*, containing FLO 1, was mutagenized with *N*-methyl-*N'*-nitro-*N*-nitrosoguanidine. Non-flocculent mutants were isolated with a selection procedure based on the slower sedimentation of non-flocculent cells. On closer study one of the non-flocculent mutants was found to contain an unlinked nuclear suppressor for FLO 1; this suppressor has been designated fsu 1. The gene fsu 1 is neither centromere linked nor linked to his 4 or the mating type locus (Chromosome III). The gene fsu 1 behaves as a recessive gene in some diploids and as a dominant gene in others, illustrating the genetic complexity of the flocculation phenomenon.

REFERENCES

Anderson, E. and Martin, P. A. (1975). *J. Inst. Brew.* **81**, 242.

Baker, D. A. and Kirsop, B. (1972). *J. Inst. Brew.* **78**, 454.

Barendrecht, H. P. (1901). *Centr. Bakteriol. Parasitenk* **7**, 623.

Barton, A. A. (1950). *J. Gen. Microbiol.* **4**, 84.

Beyerinck, M. W. (1908). *Centr. Bakteriol. Parasitenk.* **20**, 137.

Block, S. S., Stearns, T. W., Stephens, R. L. and McCandless, R. F. J. (1953). *Agric. Food Chem.* **1**, 890.

Burns, J. A. (1937). *J. Inst. Brew.* **43**, 31.

Calleja, G. B. (1970). *J. Gen. Microbiol.* **64**, 247.

Calleja, G. B. and Johnson, B. F. (1971). *Can. J. Microbiol.* **17**, 1175.

Calleja, G. B. and Johnson, B. F. (1977). *Can. J. Microbiol.* **23**, 68.

Cawley, T. N. and Ballou, C. E. (1972). *J. Bacteriol.* **111**, 690.

Chester, V. E. (1963). *Proc. R. Soc. B* **157**, 223.

Clayton, E., Howard, G. A. and Martin, P. A. (1972). *Proc. Ann. Meet. Am. Soc. Brew. Chem.* p. 78.

Comrie, A. A. D. (1952). *Wallerstein Lab. Commun.* **15**, 339.

Cowan, W. D., Hoggan, J. and Smith, J. E. (1974). *Proc. IV Int. Yeast Symposium, Vienna,* p. B39.

Crandall, M. and Brock, T. D. (1968). *Bacteriol. Rev.* **32**, 139.

Crandall, M. and Caulton, J. H. (1975). *In* "Methods in Cell Biology" (D. M. Prescott, ed.), Vol. XII, pp. 186, Academic Press, New York and London.

Curtis, N. S. (1956). *Brewer's Guild J.* **42**, 175.

Curtis, N. S. (1963). *Brewers' Digest* **38** (3), 42.

Day, A. W., Poon, N. H. and Stewart, G. G. (1975). *Can. J. Microbiol.* **21**, 558.

Delbruck, M. (1901). *Jahrb. Versuchs-u Lehranstalt Brauerei, Berlin* **4**, 305.

Duntze, W., MacKay, V. and Manney, T. R. (1970). *Science* **168**, 1472.

Eddy, A. A. (1955). *J. Inst. Brew.* **61**, 307.

Eddy, A. A. (1958). *J. Inst. Brew.* **64**, 143.

Eddy, A. A. and Rudin, A. D. (1958a). *Proc. R. Soc. B* **148**, 419.

Eddy, A. A. and Rudin, A. D. (1958b). *J. Inst. Brew.* **64**, 19.

Eddy, A. A. and Rudin, A. D. (1958c). *J. Inst. Brew.* **64**, 139.

Endo, Y., Nakamure, K. and Tagahashi, H. (1976). *Agric. Biol. Chem.* **40**, 2289.

Eschenbruch, R. and Rassell, J. M. (1975). *Vitis* **14**, 43.

Fowell (1969). *In* "The Yeasts" (A. H. Rose and J. S. Harrison, eds), Vol. 1, p. 303. Academic Press, London and New York.

Fujii, G. and Horie, Y. (1975). *Rep. Res. Lab. Kirin Brewery Co., Yokohama* **18**, 75.

Geilenkotton, I. and Nyns, E. J. (1971). *Brewers' Digest* **46** (4), 64.

Geys, K. (1922). *Z. Brauw.* **45**, 51.

Gilliland, R. B. (1951). *Proc. E.B.C. Congr., Brighton* p. 35.

Gilliland, R. B. (1957). *Wallerstein Lab. Commun.* **20**, 41.

Griffin, S. R. and McWilliam, I. C. (1969) *J. Inst. Brew.* **75**, 355.

Gyllang, H. and Martinson, E. (1971) *Prog. E.B.C. Congr., Estoril* p. 265.

Hartwell, L. H. (1974). *Bacteriol. Rev.* **38**, 164.

Hayduck, F. (1905). *Wschr. Brau.* **22**, 661.
Helm, E., Nohr, B. and Thorne, R. S. W. (1953). *Wallerstein Lab. Commun.* **16**, 315.
Holmberg, S. and Kielland-Brandt, M. C. (1978). *C.R. Trav. Lab. Carlsberg* **25**, 37.
Hough, J. S. (1957). *J. Inst. Brew.* **63**, 483.
Jansen, H. E. (1958). *In* "The Chemistry and Biology of Yeasts" (A. H. Cook, ed.), p. 635. Academic Press, New York and London.
Jayatissa, P. M. and Rose, A. H. (1976). *J. Gen. Microbiol.* **96**, 165.
Johnston, J. R. (1965). *J. Inst. Brew.* **71**, 130.
Kato, S. and Nishikawa, N. (1957). *Bull. Brew. Sci., Tokyo* **3**, 39051.
Kudo, S. (1960). *Rep. Res. Lab. Kirin Brewing Co., Yokohama* **3**, 25.
Kudo, S. and Kijima, M. (1960). *Rep. Res. Lab. Kirin Brewing Co., Yokohama* **3**, 33.
Kusserow, R. (1897). *Brennerei Ztg.* **14**, 318.
Lange, H. (1899). *Wschr. Brau.* **16**, 49.
Lange, H. (1907). *Wschr. Brau.* **24**, 445.
Lewis, C. W. and Johnston, J. R. (1974). *Soc. Gen. Microbiol. Proc.* **1**, 73.
Lewis, C. W., Johnston, J. R. and Martin, P. A. (1976). *J. Inst. Brew.* **82**, 158.
Lindner, P. (1901). *Johrb Versuchs-u Lehramstalt Brauerei, Berlin* **4**, 309.
Luers, A. and Heusz, R. (1921). *Z. Brauw.* **44**, 18.
Lyons, T. P. and Hough, J. S. (1970a). *J. Inst. Brew.* **76**, 564.
Lyons, T. P. and Hough, J. S. (1970b). *Brewers' Digest* **45** (8), 52.
Lyons, T. P. and Hough, J. S. (1971). *J. Inst. Brew.* **77**, 300.
Masschelein, C. A. (1957). *Rev. Ferment. Ind. Aliment.* **12**, 283.
Masschelein, C. A. (1962). *Petit J. Brass.* **71**, 203.
Masschelein, C. A., Jeunehomme-Ramos, C., Castiau, C. and Devreux, A. (1963). *J. Inst. Brew.* **69**, 332.
Mill, P. J. (1964a). *J. Gen. Microbiol.* **35**, 53.
Mill, P. J. (1964b). *J. Gen. Microbiol.* **35**, 61.
Mill, P. J. (1966). *J. Gen. Microbiol.* **44**, 329.
Molzahn, S. H. (1977). *Proc. Ann. Meet. Am. Soc. Brew. Chem.* p. 54.
Momose, H., Iwano, K. and Tonoike, R. (1969a). *J. Agric. Chem. Soc., Japan* **43**, 119.
Momose, H., Iwano, K. and Tonoike, R. (1969b). *J. Gen. Appl. Microbiol.* **15**, 19.
Morimoto, K., Shimazu, T., Fujii, T. and Horie, Y. (1975). *Rep. Res. Lab. Kirin Brewing Co., Yokohama* **18**, 63.
Moscona, A. A. (1962). *J. Cell. Comp. Physiol.* **60**, 65.
Moscona, A. A. (1967). *In Vitro* **3**, 13.
Nielsen, N. (1937). *C.R. Trav. Lab., Carlsberg* **19**, 17.
Nishihara, H., Toraya, T. and Fukui, S. (1976a). *J. Ferment. Technol.* **54**, 351.
Nishihara, H., Toraya, T. and Fukui, S. (1976b). *J. Ferment. Technol.* **54**, 356.
Norstedt, C. and Bengtsson, A. (1969). *Proc. E.B.C. Congr., Interlaken,* p. 263.
Nunokawa, Y., Toba, H. and Ouchi, K. (1971). *J. Ferment. Technol.* **49**, 959.
Ouchi, K., Takahashi, K., Suzuki, S. and Nunokawa, Y. (1973). *J. Gen. Appl. Microbiol.* **19**, 429.
Pasteur, L. (1876). *In* "Etudes sur la Biere", p. 196. Gauthier Villars, Paris.
Pavoni, J. L., Tenney, M. W. and Echelberger, W. F. (1972). *J. Water Poll. Control. Fedn.* **44**, 414.
Phaff, H. J. (1971). *In* "The Yeasts" (A. H. Rose and J. S. Harrison, eds), Vol. 2, p. 135, Academic Press, New York and London.
Pomper, S. and Burkholder, P. R. (1949). *Proc. Nat. Acad. Sci. U.S.A.* **35**, 456.
Porter, A. M. and Macauley, R. J. (1965). *J. Inst. Brew.* **71**, 175.

Rainbow, C. (1970). *In* "The Yeasts" (A. H. Rose and J. S. Harrison, eds), Vol. 3, p. 147. Academic Press, New York and London.
Richmond, D. V. and Fisher, D. J. (1973). *In* "Advances in Microbiology and Physiology" (A. H. Rose and D. W. Tempest, eds), Vol. 3, p. 1. Academic Press, London and New York.
Rothstein, R. and Sherman, F. (1980). *Genetics* (in press).
Russell, I., Stewart, G. G. and Garrison, I. F. (1973). *J. Inst. Brew.* **79**, 48.
Russell, I., Stewart, G. G., Reader, H. P., Johnston, J. R. and Martin, P. A. (1980). *J. Inst. Brew.* **86**, 120.
Sakurai, A., Sakata, K., Tamura, S., Aizawa, K., Yanagishima, N. and Shimode, C. (1976). *Agric. Biol. Chem.* **40**, 1451.
Schonfeld, F. (1909). *Wschr. Brau.* **36**, 521.
Schonfeld, F. (1910). *Wschr. Brau.* **27**, 541.
Schonfeld, F. and Krumhaar, H. (1918). *Wschr. Brau.* **35**, 302.
Seyffert, H. (1896), *Z. Brauw.* **19**, 318.
Shawn, M. A. and Lis, A. K. (1972). *J. Immunol.* **36**, 256.
Silhankova, L., Savel, J. and Mostek, J. (1970). *J. Inst. Brew.* **76**, 280.
Smith, E. L. and Greenshields, R. N. (1974). *Chem. Engr.* **281**, 28.
Steel, R., Lantz, C. P. and Martin, S. M. (1955). *Can. J. Microbiol.* **1**, 299.
Stewart, G. G. (1975). *Brewers' Digest* **50** (3). 42.
Stewart, G. G. and Garrison, I. F. (1972). *Proc. Ann. Meet, Am. Soc. Brew. Chem.* p. 118.
Stewart, G. G., Russell, I. and Garrison, I. F. (1973). *Proc. Ann. Meet. Am. Soc. Brew. Chem.* p. 100.
Stewart, G. G., Russell, I. and Garrison, I. F. (1974). *Tech. Quart. Master Brewers Ass. Am.* **11**, p. xiii.
Stewart, G. G., Russell, I. and Garrison, I. F. (1975a). *J. Inst. Brew.* **81**, 248.
Stewart, G. G., Russell, I. and Goring, T. E. (1975b). *Proc. Ann. Meet. Am. Soc. Brew. Chem.* p. 137.
Stewart, G. G. and Goring, T. E. (1976). *J. Inst. Brew.* **82**, 341.
Stewart, G. G. and Russell, I. (1976). *Proc. V Inst. Ferm. Symp.*, Berlin pp. 187.
Stewart, G. G. and Russell, I. (1977). *Can. J. Microbiol.* **23, 441.**
Stockhausen, F. (1927). *Wschr. Brau.* **44**, 121.
Stockhausen, F. and Silbereisen, K. (1933). *Wschr. Brau.* **50**, 349.
Stockhausen, F. and Silbereisen, K. (1935). *Wschr. Brau.* **52**, 257.
Taylor, N. W. and Orton, W. L. (1975). *J. Inst. Brew.* **81**, 53.
Thompson, J. W., Shovers, J., Sandine, W. E. and Elliker, P. R. (1970). *Appl. Microbiol.* **19**, 883.
Thorne, R. S. W. (1951). *Proc. E.B.C. Congr.*, Brighton p. 21.
Thorne, R. S. W. (1952). *C.R. Trav. Lab.*, Carlsberg **25**, 101.
White, F. H. and Kidney, E. (1979). *Proc. E.B.C. Congr.*, West Berlin, p. 801.
Wiles, A. E. (1951). *Proc. E.B.C. Congr.*, Brighton p. 84.
Windisch, S. E. (1961). *Wallerstein Lab. Commun.* **24**, 316.
Windisch, S. E. (1968). *Brewers' Digest* **43** (11), 62.
Woof, J. B. (1962). *J. Inst. Brew.* **68**, 315.
Yoshida, K., Hagiya, M. and Yanagishima, N. (1976). *Biochem. Biophys. Res. Commun.* **71**, 1085.

3. Beer Composition: Volatile Substances

SIGMUND ENGAN

A/S Hansa Bryggeri N-5001 Bergen, Norway

INTRODUCTION

A great number of volatiles have been identified in beer, and the different substances may influence the aroma and flavour of the product to a very different degree. Some volatiles are present only in extremely small quantities, while others are found in comparatively high concentrations. Some of the volatiles are of great importance and may contribute greatly to the beer flavour, while others are of importance merely in building up the background flavour of the product.

The volatile substances found in beer are of great importance for the quality of the product, and they may be decisive in determining the acceptability of the beer by the consumer. Therefore, it may be of great interest for the brewer to know how different factors in the brewing process may affect the formation of

93

the different volatile flavour components, and in what way, and to what extent, he will be able to influence the formation of these compounds.

All the volatiles found in a normal beer may be regarded as normal beer constituents, and they may all contribute to the optimum flavour of the product. Some substances are often regarded as contaminants, but it is mostly a question of concentration if a compound is to be regarded as a contaminant or not. In fact, in abnormal concentrations all the volatiles of beer may be regarded as contaminants.

The composition and the concentration of beer volatiles will depend on the raw materials used for production of the beer, on the working conditions in the brewery, and on the yeast strain used for fermentation. The different substances may be divided into the following groups, according to their chemical composition:

Alcohols
Esters
Carbonyls
Organic acids
Sulphur compounds
Amines
Phenols
Miscellaneous

Table 1 shows the most important factors influencing the concentration of these volatiles in beer. In what follows the different groups of volatiles will be considered, and more detailed information given on the different factors influencing their concentrations.

In this chapter we will not go into any details regarding the various pathways for the formation of the different volatiles: here we will look only at the factors that, in practical work, may influence the concentration of these components in beer.

I. ALCOHOLS

In addition to ethanol, one of the main products of fermentation, a great number of other alcohols are found in beer, and higher alcohols—or fusel alcohols—constitute an important part of the by-products formed during beer fermentation. Their formation is linked to yeast protein synthesis and they are formed from keto-acids, which in turn may be formed by transamination or deamination of the amino acids in the wort, or synthesized from wort carbohydrates. The keto-acids are converted to higher alcohols by decarboxylation and reduction (Fig. 1). The relationship between some amino acids, the corresponding keto acids and the resulting alcohols is shown in Fig. 2.

TABLE 1. Factors influencing the concentration of volatiles in beer

	Yeast strain	Fermentation	Pitching rate	Lagering (second fermentation)	Storage (staling, ageing)	Amino acids	Carbohydrates	Wort aeration	Wort pH	Barley, malt	Hops	Lautering	Mashing	Wort boiling	Infection
Alcohols	XXX	XXX	X	X	X	XXX	XX	X	(X)	X	X		X		
Esters	XXX	XXX	X	X	X	X	X	XX		X	(X)		X		
Carbonyls															
Acetaldehyde	X	XXX	X	XX	X			X							XXX
Diacetyl	XXX	XXX	X	XXX	X	XXX		XX	XX	X	(X)				XXX
Others		X			XXX					X	X	XXX	X	XX	
Organic acids	XXX	XXX	X			X		X		XX	X			XX	
Sulphur compounds															
Sulphur dioxide	X	XX		X						X	X			X	
Hydrogen sulphide	XX	XX		X		X					X				XXX
Organic S-compounds	X	X		X	X					XXX	X			X	XXX
Amines					X					XX	XX		X	X	
Phenols					X					XX	XX		X	X	
Miscellaneous	X	X									XX			XX	XXX

X = some influence; XX = moderate influence; XXX = great influence.

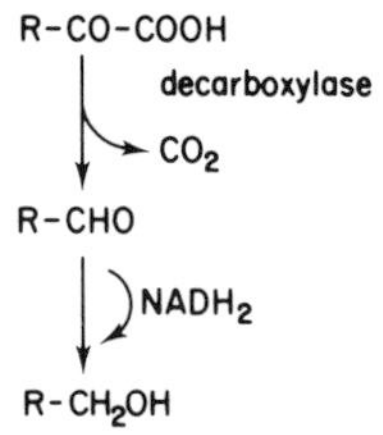

$$R-CO-COOH$$
$$\Big|\, \overset{decarboxylase}{\underset{\searrow\; CO_2}{}}$$
$$R-CHO$$
$$\Big|\, \Big) NADH_2$$
$$R-CH_2OH$$

FIG. 1. Formation of higher alcohols from keto acids.

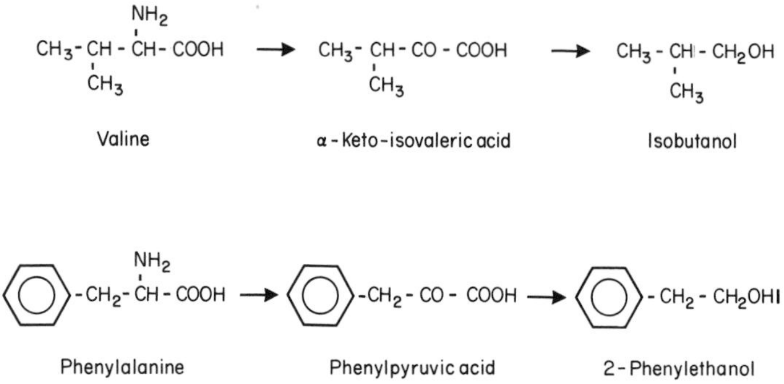

$$\underset{Valine}{CH_3-\underset{\underset{CH_3}{|}}{CH}-\overset{\overset{NH_2}{|}}{CH}-COOH} \longrightarrow \underset{\alpha-Keto-isovaleric\ acid}{CH_3-\underset{\underset{CH_3}{|}}{CH}-CO-COOH} \longrightarrow \underset{Isobutanol}{CH_3-\underset{\underset{CH_3}{|}}{CH}-CH_2OH}$$

$$\underset{Phenylalanine}{\langle\bigcirc\rangle -CH_2-\overset{\overset{NH_2}{|}}{CH}-COOH} \longrightarrow \underset{Phenylpyruvic\ acid}{\langle\bigcirc\rangle -CH_2-CO-COOH} \longrightarrow \underset{2-Phenylethanol}{\langle\bigcirc\rangle -CH_2-CH_2OHI}$$

FIG. 2. The relationship between some amino acids and the corresponding keto acids and higher alcohols.

Table 2 gives a survey of the different alcohols which have thus far been identified in beer. A positive correlation has been found between the concentrations of different higher alcohols, for instance between isoamyl alcohol (2-methylbutanol + 3-methylbutanol) and isobutanol (Engan 1975a, Haukeli *et al.* 1973) and between amyl alcohol and 2-phenylethanol (Engan 1975a). Figure 3 shows the correlation found between amyl alcohol and isobutanol in beer samples from ten different breweries.

A. The Influence of Fermentation and Lagering

1. Yeast Strain

The yeast strain used for fermentation seems to be of great significance in determining the level of higher alcohols in beer. With the other conditions held constant, some brewery yeasts are reported to produce five times as much higher alcohols as others (Thorne 1966). Laboratory and pilot plant fermentations, as well as full scale trials in different breweries, have demonstrated the great importance of the yeast strain (Äyräpää 1968, Drews and Riemann 1967, Drews *et al.* 1964, 1969c, Engan and Aubert 1971, Geiger and Piendl 1975a, Mändl *et al.* 1975, Wellhoener 1966).

TABLE 2. Alcohols in beer

Name	References	Typical concentrations in beer (p.p.m.)	Reference
Methanol	Drawert and Tressl (1969) Van der Kloot and Wilcox (1960)	0·56	Van der Kloot and Wilcox (1960)
Ethanol	Drawert and Tressl (1969)		
1-Propanol	Drawert and Tressl (1969) Enebo (1957)	3·5–13·8 7·5–16·7	Chen and David (1974) Engan (1975a)
2-Propanol (isopropanol)	Drawert and Tressl (1969)	0·2–2·4	Rosculet (1970)
Glycerol	Enebo (1957) Enebo (1957) Lawrence (1964) Piendl (1973)	1510–2190 1090–2120	Enebo (1957) Parker and Richardson (1970)
2-(Methylthio) ethanol	Tressl (1975)		
1-Butanol	Lawrence (1964) Pfenninger (1963)		
2-Butanol (sec.-butanol)	Drawert and Tressl (1969) Rosculet and Rickard (1968) Rosculet (1970)	trace	Rosculet (1970)
Tert-Butanol	Drawert and Tressl (1969)	8·6–56·6	Chen and David (1974)
Isobutanol (2-methylpropanol)	Lawrence (1964) Antoniani (1961)	4·0–23·0 42·5–128	Engan (1975a) Antoniani (1961)
2,3-Butanediol	Drews et al. (1967) Schreier et al. (1974) Szlavko (1973b)	40–282 0·345–3·175	Drews et al. (1967) Schreier et al. (1974)
Methionol (3-(methylthio)-1-propanol)	Drawert and Tressl (1969)		
1-Pentanol	Lawrence (1964)		
2-Pentanol	Drawert and Tressl (1969)	10·2–33·9	Chen and David (1974)
3-Pentanol	Drawert and Tressl (1969)	13–23	Engan (1974a)
2-Methylbutanol (optically active amyl alcohol)	Drawert and Tressl (1969) Lawrence (1964) Pfenninger (1963)	7–20	Meilgaard et al. (1971a)

(continued over page)

TABLE 2 (*cont.*)

Name	References	Typical concentrations in beer	
		(p.p.m.)	Reference
3-Methylbutanol (isoamyl alcohol)	Drawert and Tressl (1969) Lawrence (1964) Pfenninger (1963)	37·8–122·5 27–62 25–68	Chen and David (1974) Engan (1974a) Meilgaard et al. (1971a)
2-Methyl-3-buten-2-ol	Palamand et al. (1971)	trace	Palamand et al. (1971)
Furfuryl alcohol	Harrison (1963) Lawrence (1964)	2·1–8	Tressl et al. (1975c)
5-Methylfurfuryl alcohol	Tressl et al. (1975c)	<0·01	Tressl et al. (1975c)
2,5-(Dihydroxymethyl)furan	Tressl et al. (1975c)	8·2–25	Tressl et al. (1975c)
1-Hexanol	Drawert and Tressl (1969) Lawrence (1964)		
2-Hexanol	Drawert and Tressl (1969)		
trans-2-Hexen-1-ol	Drawert and Tressl (1969, 1972)		
cis-3-Hexen-1-ol	Drawert and Tressl (1969, 1972)		
1-Heptanol	Drawert and Tressl (1969)		
2-Heptanol	Drawert and Tressl (1969)		
1-Hepten-3-ol	Drawert and Tressl (1969)		
Benzyl alcohol	Drawert and Tressl (1969)		
1-Octanol	Strating and Van Eerde (1973)		

The use of adjuncts may influence the amino acid content of the wort and thus the production of higher alcohols. In the literature, data are also found indicating that these conditions are without significant influence (Voerkelius 1966), but the degree of influence may be determined by the type and the quantity of the adjuncts used.

As between one third and one half of the amino acids of wort are produced by proteolysis during mashing (Barrett and Kirsop 1971, Jones 1974, Jones and Pierce 1967), the mashing procedure is supposed to influence the amino acid content of the wort and thus the formation of higher alcohols during fermentation. According to Enari (1975), however, changes in the mashing programme may not have any really significant effect on the free amino acids in the wort, the most important factors being the malt and the grist used.

2. Carbohydrates

The formation of volatiles may depend on the concentration of fermentable sugars in the wort, and a relation has been found between wort strength and the concentration of higher alcohols in the beer, as shown in Fig. 6.

Fermentation of wort, to which was added various amounts of carbohydrate solutions, showed that addition of sugar solutions could enhance the production of higher alcohols (Engan 1972a). Hough and Stevens (1961) found, on the other hand, that the addition of sugar to wort led to diminished production of higher alcohols. Jenard and Devreux (1964) fermented different combinations of wort and a sucrose solution and found that increased sucrose addition gave increased production of higher alcohols. Drews and Riemann (1967) also found an increase in higher alcohols when 50% of the wort was replaced by a sucrose solution. Maule (1967) found that artificial enrichment of wort by glucose led to the production of considerably more isobutanol and isoamyl alcohol, but less 1-propanol than fermentation of a wort brewed at an increased gravity, so as to contain the same amount of fermentable sugar.

However, this effect seems to depend on the yeast strain, and some of the discrepancies found in the literature may be due to different behaviour of differing yeasts. Szlavko (1974) found that with increasing dilution of wort with a glucose solution, an ale yeast gave decreasing levels of amyl alcohols, tyrosol and 2-phenylethanol, while a lager yeast gave increasing levels of the same alcohols.

Figure 7 shows the concentration of isoamyl alcohols at different levels of carbohydrate addition. The results of these experiments (Engan 1972a) showed that, with isoamyl alcohol and 2-phenylethanol, the concentration increased with the addition of sugar solutions at all levels exceeding 5% addtion. Fructose gave somewhat higher values of these alcohols as well as of isobutanol, than did glucose, sucrose or maltose. As also observed by Äyräpää

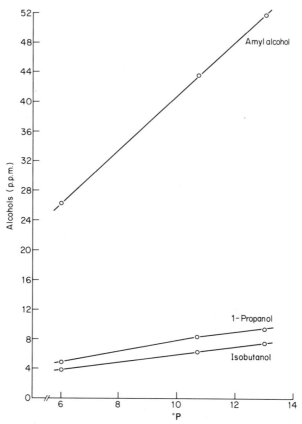

FIG. 6. The relationship between wort strength and the concentration of some higher alcohols.

(1971), sucrose gave more amyl alcohols than maltose at low nitrogen levels (high levels of sugar addition). Pollock and Weir (1976) found, by fermentation of nitrogen-free sugar solutions, that maltose gave less of most of the volatiles than fructose, glucose and sucrose.

3. Wort Aeration

The oxygen content of the wort is of great importance for fermentation and for yeast growth (Markham 1969, Thoss 1966), and may thus be of significance for the formation of higher alcohols. Most results indicate that increased aeration leads to increased production of higher alcohols. (Drews and Riemann 1967, Mandl et al. 1975.) Addition of oxygen after the fermentation has started, that is, aeration during fermentation, may also result in greater production of higher alcohols (Enari et al. 1970).

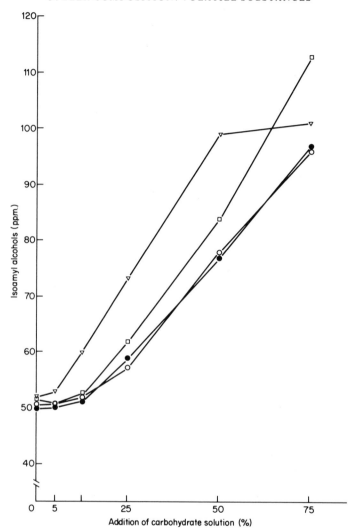

FIG 7. Concentrations of isoamyl alcohols when different amounts of a 10% carbohydrate solution was added to wort (Engan 1972a). ○ = glucose; ▽ = fructose; □ = sucrose; ● = maltose.

Some full scale experiments in three Norwegian breweries indicated that a reduction in the oxygen content of the wort resulted in reduced production of higher alcohols during fermentation (Engan and Aubert 1973). Geiger and Piendl (1975a) found that both "under-aeration" and "over-aeration" gave more 2-phenylethanol than normal aerations of the wort.

4. The Influence of Barley and Malt Quality, and of Hops

Some variations in the higher alcohols of beers have been found to be due to different barley varieties and different growing areas for the barley, resulting in differences in the nitrogen content of the wort (Drews and Riemann 1967, Narziss and Miedaner 1970a). Mandl *et al.* (1972) also found that the malt modification could influence the content of higher alcohols in the resulting beer. According to their results, the use of normally modified and slightly overmodified malts led to higher concentrations of the isoamyl alcohols than were obtained when slightly undermodified malt was used, while undermodified malt gave the highest concentration of 1-propanol.

Hops may also have an influence on the concentration of higher alcohols. Fermentation of sweet wort and addition of isomerized hop extract after fermentation may result in an increased concentration of higher alcohols in beer (Drewett *et al.* 1970). This effect was, however, found to be most pronounced with the top-fermenting yeasts used for ale fermentation.

II. ESTERS

The esters constitute an important group among the beer volatiles, because of their often very strong, penetrating, fruity flavours. Most of the esters found in beer are formed during fermentation, and ester formation appears to be linked to the lipid metabolism of the yeast.

The direct, enzyme-free formation of esters is an equilibrium reaction between an alcohol and an acid, and this reaction is a possible route to the formation of esters in beers. Worts and beers contain a great number of alcohols and acids, and they may all react to form esters, so the theoretical number of esters in beer is, indeed, very large. Direct formation of esters would, however, be too slow to account for the concentration of some of the esters found in beer. Nordström (1964a) suggested that the formation of ethyl acetate during fermentation proceeds according to the following reaction:

$$CH_3CO.SCoA \quad + \quad C_2H_5OH \leftrightharpoons CH_3COOC_2H_5 + CoA\text{-}SH$$

(Acetyl coenzyme A)   (Ethanol)   (Ethyl acetate)   (Coenzyme a)

This was later confirmed by Howard and Anderson (1976), who synthesized ethyl acetate from ethanol and acetyl coenzyme A with cell-free extracts from *Saccharomyces cerevisiae*.

According to Nordström (1964a, 1965a), ester formation is linked to yeast growth, and it is reduced when growth is inhibited. Some recent reports show, however, that the reverse may be the case and that no general correlation seems to exist between yeast cell mass and beer volatiles (Anderson and Kirsop 1974, 1975a, Äyräpää 1973, Lie and Haukeli 1973, Norstedt *et al.* 1975).

Nordström (1964b) predicted a correlation between medium-chain fatty acids and their ethyl esters, and correlations between the concentrations of fatty acids and their corresponding ethyl esters in beer have been established in some cases (Engan 1973a, 1975a). Figure 8 shows the correlation found between hexanoic acid and ethyl hexanoate in beer samples from ten breweries. A positive correlation has also been found between different acetate

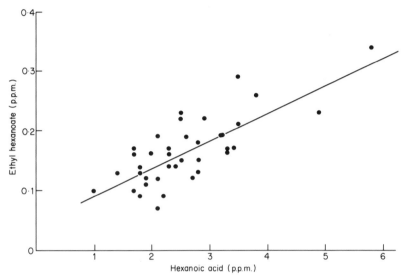

FIG. 8. The correlation between the concentrations of hexanoic acid and ethyl hexanoate in different beer samples.

esters (Engan 1975a, Haukeli *et al.* 1973). Figure 9 shows the correlation between ethyl acetate and isoamyl acetate in different beer samples. Correlations are also found between higher alcohols and the corresponding acetate esters (Engan 1974a, Haukeli *et al.* 1973) which is illustrated in Fig. 10, which shows the correlation between 2-phenylethyl acetate and 2-phenyl-ethanol in a number of beer samples.

Not all the esters which are synthesized during fermentation are necessarily present in the finished beer. According to Nordström (1964a), the ethyl esters of unbranched saturated fatty acids may be bound to the yeast cell, and the strength of this binding increases with increasing molecular weight. Ethyl decanoate was found almost completely in the yeast phase, so that the highest of these esters expected to be found in beer in significant concentration is ethyl octanoate.

Table 3 shows the different esters which have hitherto been identified in beer.

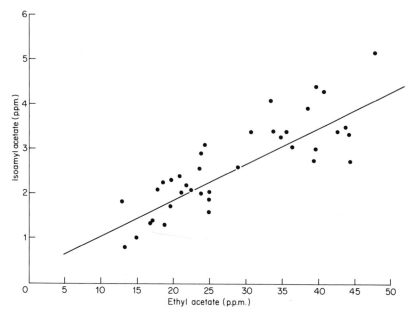

FIG. 9. The correlation between the concentrations of ethyl acetate and isoamyl acetate in different beer samples.

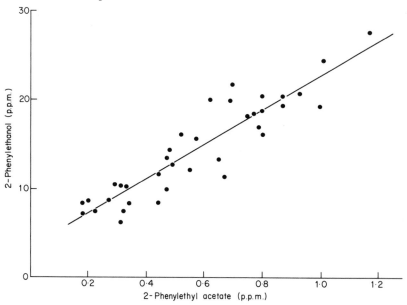

FIG. 10. The correlation between the concentrations of 2-phenylethyl acetate and 2-phenylethanol in different beer samples.

TABLE 3. Esters in beer

Name	References	Typical concentrations in beer (p.p.m.)	Typical concentrations in beer: Reference
Methyl formate	Drews *et al.* (1966b)	0·37	Drews *et al.* (1966b)
Methyl acetate	Drawert and Tressl (1969)	1–22	Bärwald (1967)
	Drews *et al.* (1966b)	0·02	Drews *et al.* (1966b)
Methyl hexanoate (methyl caproate)	Drawert and Tressl (1972)		
Methyl hexenoate	Drawert and Tressl (1972)		
Methyl heptenoate	Drawert and Tressel (1972)		
Methyl octanoate (methyl caprylate)	Drawert and Tressl (1972)		
Methyl-4-decenoate	Silbereisen *et al.* (1970)		
Methyl-4,8-decadienoate	Silbereisen *et al.* (1970)		
Ethyl formate	Drews *et al.* (1966b)	0·02	Drews *et al.* (1966b)
	Lawrence (1964)	0·4–2·2	Postel *et al.* (1972)
Ethyl acetate	Drews *et al.* (1966b)	13·3–47·6	Engan (1975a)
	Lawrence (1964)	8·2–45·8	Postel *et. al.* (1972)
Ethyl propionate	Drawert and Tressl (1972)	0·2	Harrison (1967)
	Harrison (1967)		
Ethyl lactate	Drawert and Tressl (1969)	0·01	Drews *et al.* (1966b)
	Komoda and Yamada (1967)		
	Lawrence (1964)		
Ethyl butyrate	Drawert and Tressl (1969)	0·09	Drews *et al.* (1966b)
	Komoda and Yamada (1967)		
	Lawrence (1964)		
Ethyl isobutyrate	Drews *et al.* (1966b)	0·12	Drews *et al.* (1966b)
	Lawrence (1964)		
Ethyl hydrogen succinate	Palamand *et al.* (1973)	0·22	Tressl *et al.* (1975b)
	Tressl *et al.* (1975b)		
Ethyl isovalerate	Drawert and Tressl (1972)	0·2	Rosculet (1970)
	Harrison (1967)		
Ethyl 2-furoate	Tressl *et al.* (1975c)	0·01–0·05	Tressl *et al.* (1975c)

(*continued over page*)

TABLE 3 (cont.)

Name	References	Typical concentrations in beer	
		(p.p.m.)	Reference
Ethyl hexanoate (ethyl caproate)	Drawert and Tressl (1969) Drews et al. (1966b) Lawrence (1964)	0·07–0·34 0·1–0·5	Engan (1975a) Postel et al. (1972)
Ethyl hexenoate Diethyl succinate	Drawert and Tressl (1972) Palamand et al. (1973) Strating and Van Eerde (1973) Palamand and Grigsby (1974)		
Ethyl nicotinate Ethyl heptanoate	Buttery et al. (1967) Drawert and Tressl (1969) Strating and Van Eerde (1973)	0·03	Drews et al. (1966b)
Ethyl isoheptanoate Ethyl heptenoate Ethyl benzoate	Buttery et al. (1967) Drawert and Tressl (1972) Buttery et al. (1967) Drews et al. (1966b)		
Ethyl octanoate (ethyl caprylate)	Drawert and Tressl (1969) Komoda and Yamada (1967) Lawrence (1964)	0·08–0·61 0·1–0·9	Engan (1975a) Postel et al. (1972)
Ethyl nonanoate (ethyl pelargonate) Ethyl decanoate (ethyl caprate)	Drawert and Tressl (1969) Drawert and Tressl (1969) Drews et al. (1966b) Lawrence (1964)		
Ethyl 4-decenoate	Buttery et al. (1967) Nickerson and Likens (1966) Strating and Van Eerde (1973)		
Ethyl 9-decenoate Ethyl 4,8-decadienoate	Lawrence (1964) Buttery et al. (1967) Nickerson and Likens (1966)		
Ethyl laurate	Drawert and Tressl (1969) Komoda and Yamada (1967)	0·6	Komoda and Yamada (1967)
Ethyl myristate	Drawert and Tressl (1969) Komoda and Yamada (1967)	0·4	Komoda and Yamada (1967)
Ethyl oleate Ethyl linoleate Ethyl linolenate	Visser and Lindsay (1971a) Visser and Lindsay (1971a) Visser and Lindsay (1971a)		

Compound	References	Threshold	
n-Propyl acetate	Komoda and Yamada (1967) Lawrence (1964) Rosculet (1970)		
Isopropyl acetate	Drawert and Tressl (1969)	0·75	Drews et al. (1966b)
Isobutyl formate	Drawert and Tressl (1969) Drews et al. (1966b)		
n-Butyl acetate	Drawert and Tressl (1969) Lawrence (1964)	0·23	Drews et al. (1966b)
Isobutyl acetate	Drews et al. (1966b) Lawrence (1964)	0·03–0·25	Engan (1975a)
sec-Butyl acetate	Drews et al. (1966b) Lawrence (1964)		
n-Butyl hexanoate (butyl caproate)	Drawert and Tressl (1972)		
Isobutyl benzoate	Drawert and Tressl (1972)		
n-Butyl octanoate (butyl caprylate)	Drawert and Tressl (1972)		
Isobutyl laurate	Drawert and Tressl (1972)		
Isoamyl formate	Drawert and Tressl (1969)		
n-Pentyl acetate	Drawert and Tressl (1972) Lawrence (1964)		
Isoamyl acetate	Drews et al. (1966b) Lawrence (1964)	0·8–5·2 0·8–6·6	Engan (1975a) Postel et al. (1972)
Isoamyl propionate	Drawert and Tressl (1972)		
Isoamyl lactate	Lawrence (1964)		
n-Pentyl butyrate	Drawert and Tressl (1969)		
Isoamyl butyrate	Drawert and Tressl (1972)		
2-Methylbutyl isobutyrate	Maule (1967)		
n-Pentyl isovalerate	Drawert and Tressl (1972)		
Isoamyl isovalerate	Drawert and Tressl (1972)		
n-Pentyl hexanoate (amyl caproate)	Drawert and Tressl (1969) Lawrence (1964)		
Isoamyl hexanoate (isoamyl caproate)	Drawert and Tressl (1969) Drews et al. (1966b)	0·05	Drews et al. (1966b)
Pentyl 2-hexanoate	Drawert and Tressl (1969)		
Isoamyl heptanoate	Drawert and Tressl (1969)		
n-Pentyl benzoate	Drawert and Tressl (1969)		
Isoamyl benzoate	Drawert and Tressl (1969)		
Isoamyl octanoate (isoamyl caprylate)	Buttery et al. (1967) Drawert and Tressl (1969)		
Isoamyl nonanoate	Drawert and Tressl (1969)		
Isoamyl decanoate (isoamyl caprate)	Drawert and Tressl (1969)		

(continued over page)

TABLE 3 (cont.)

Name	References	Typical concentrations in beer (p.p.m.)	Reference
n-Hexyl acetate	Drews et al. (1966b) Lawrence (1964)	0·03	Hashimoto (1975)
n-Hexyl butyrate	Drawert and Tressl (1969)		
n-Hexyl isobutyrate	Drawert and Tressl (1969)		
n-Hexyl hexanoate (hexyl caproate)	Drawert and Tressl (1969)		
n-Hexyl octanoate (hexyl caprylate)	Drawert and Tressl (1969)		
n-Hexyl decanoate (hexyl caprate)	Drawert and Tressl (1972)		
n-Heptyl acetate	Buttery et al. (1967)		
	Drawert and Tressl (1969)		
Heptyl 2-butyrate	Drawert and Tressl (1969)		
n-Octyl acetate	Drawert and Tressel (1969)		
n-Octyl butyrate	Drawert and Tressl (1969)		
n-Octyl hexanoate (octyl caproate)	Drawert and Tressl (1969)		
2-Octyl hexanoate (2-octyl caproate)	Drawert and Tressl (1969)		
2-Phenylethyl acetate	Harrison (1963) Lawrence (1964) Drews et al. (1966b)	0·18–1·17 0·1–1·5	Engan (1975a) Postel et al. (1972)
2-Phenylethyl butyrate	Drawert and Tressl (1969)		
2-Phenylethyl isovalerate	Drawert and Tressl (1972)		
2-Phenylethyl hexanoate	Drawert and Tressl (1972)		
2-Phenylethyl hexenoate	Drawert and Tressl (1972)		
2-Phenylethyl octanoate	Drawert and Tressl (1972)		
Tyrosol acetate	Tressl et al. (1975c)	0·2–0·8	Tressl et al. (1975c)
Furfuryl formate	Strating and Van Eerde (1973)		
Furfuryl acetate	Buttery et al. (1967) Tressl et al. (1975c)	0·03–0·04	Tressl et al. (1975c)
3-Indolyl-2-ethyl acetate	Tressl (1975)		

A. The Influence of Fermentation and Lagering

1. Yeast Strain

As with the higher alcohols, the yeast strain is of great significance in determining the amount of esters formed during fermentation (Engan and Aubert 1971, Nordström 1965a, Thorne 1966). Figure 11 shows the concentrations of some esters in beers fermented with three different yeast strains: each strain seems to give its own characteristic pattern (compare Fig. 4). Figure 12 shows the correlation found between the concentrations of 2-phenylethyl acetate in two different kinds of beer from ten different breweries, each brewery using the same yeast strain to ferment the two beers. Similar correlations have also been found between the concentrations of other esters in the same beer samples (Engan 1975a).

2. Fermentation Temperature

The formation of esters during fermentation may be influenced by the fermentation temperature. With a strain of bottom fermenting yeast Engan (1969a) found that an increase of the fermentation temperature from 10 to 25 °C resulted in an increase in the concentration of ethyl acetate from 12·5 to

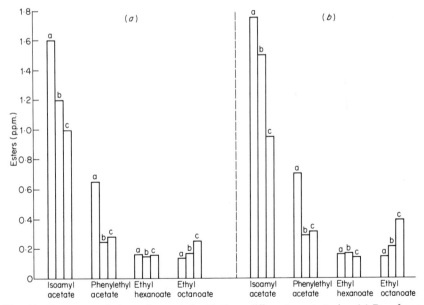

FIG. 11. Some esters in beers fermented with three different yeast strains. (a) Beer from breweries A, B and C, fermented with yeast strain a, b and c, respectively. (b) Beer fermented with yeast a in breweries B and C, yeast b in breweries A and C and yeast c in breweries A and B.

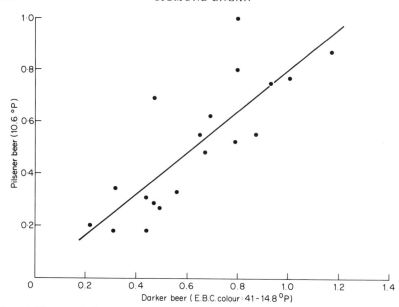

FIG. 12. The correlation between the concentrations (p.p.m.) of 2-phenylethyl acetate in two different kinds of beer from ten breweries, each brewery using the same yeast strain to ferment the two beers.

21·5 p.p.m. and in the concentration of isoamyl acetate from 0·5 to 1·1 p.p.m. Miedaner *et al.* (1974) found with temperatures between 8·5 and 16 °C only very small differences in the concentration of ethyl acetate. However, an increase of the temperature to 20 °C resulted in a marked increase in the formation of this ester. With isoamyl acetate the same authors found great variations, also in the temperature ranges 8·5–12 °C. According to Norstedt *et al.* (1975) different esters show different temperature dependences. Within the temperature range studied, 8–20 °C, they found that only ethyl acetate and 2-phenylethyl acetate increased in concentration over the entire temperature range. The temperature dependency also seems to vary with yeast strain and fermentation conditions (Engan and Aubert 1977).

3. Fermentation Method

Continuous fermentation appears to result in higher levels of esters than conventional batch fermentation, but the difference depends greatly on the yeast strain (Mäkinen and Enari 1969). High concentrations of esters have been found to occur in a stirred continuous fermentation (Portno 1970). Haboucha *et al.* (1967) found that agitation during fermentation reduced the amount of ethyl acetate, and a similar effect was found by Pollock and Weir

(1973) with ethyl acetate and ethyl octanoate. Fermentation under pressure (Miedaner *et al.* 1974) led to reduced formation of esters, in the same way as was found with higher alcohols. Increased pressure during fermentation results in increased concentration of CO_2, and the results of Norstedt *et al.* (1975) indicate that the effect of pressure on ester formation is due to the influence of the CO_2 concentration. They found that reduced pressure stimulated, and increased pressure inhibited, the formation of acetate esters, while the ethyl esters of C_8, C_{10} and C_{12} acids seemed to reach a maximum around atmospheric pressure.

4. Pitching Rate

Maule (1967) found that a four-fold increase in pitching rate resulted in a marked reduction in the formation of ethyl acetate. The formation of other esters was also reduced somewhat. A two-fold increase in pitching rate influenced only the ethyl acetate. Norstedt *et al.* (1975) found that the pitching rate, varying within a very wide range, had only a very moderate influence on the ester level.

5. Lagering and Storage

The esters are formed primarily during the main fermentation, as shown in Fig. 13, and only small changes are in many cases found to take place during

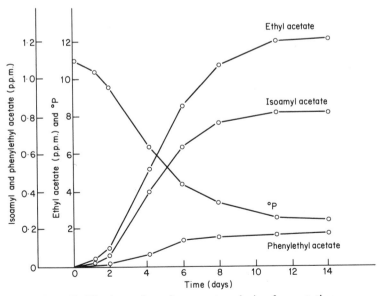

FIG. 13. The formation of some esters during fermentation.

the lagering period (Hashimoto and Kuroiwa 1972, Hashimoto et al. 1969, Nordström 1965b). But increases up to 100% have also been reported (Narziss 1972). Residual extract at racking, and the lagering conditions, will, of course, be of great importance.

In bottled beer during storage, a slow reduction in the ester content may take place, depending on the storage temperature (Engan 1969c, 1972b, Stenroos 1973). Reduction in the levels of ethyl esters of higher unsaturated fatty acids may be connected with the occurrence of stale flavour, as they may be converted to compounds having significance in stale beer flavour (Visser and Lindsay 1971a).

B. The Influence of Raw Materials and Wort Composition

1. Original Gravity

Nordström (1965a) found that ester formation depended on the concentration of the alcohol moiety, and at higher alcohol concentrations proportionally more esters were formed per unit weight of ethanol produced. In accordance with this, it has been found by several authors that comparatively more esters are formed during fermentation of stronger than of weaker beers (Anderson and Kirsop 1974, Anderson et al. 1975, Engan 1973a, Palmer and Rennie 1974). This fact will have consequences for high-gravity brewing, but may be of interest in the brewing of normal beers as well.

Norstedt et al. (1975) found, from analyses of beers from different breweries, that differences in brewery equipment seemed to modify considerably the effect of original gravity on ester fomation. To regulate ester formation in high-gravity brewing, controlled oxygenation of the wort during a short period of the fermentation has proved to be efficient—see section II.B.4.

2. Amino Acids

In contrast to the higher alcohols, whose concentrations may be influenced by the types of amino acids present in wort, the concentration of ethyl acetate seems to be independent of the nitrogen source, while the level of isoamyl acetate increases when the concentration of isoamyl alcohol increases (Engan 1970).

According to Nordström (1964a, c) ester formation may be stimulated if the concentration of nitrogenous nutrients in the wort is increased. Masschelein et al. (1965) found a direct connection between yeast growth rates, influenced by the nitrogen composition of the wort, and the formation of isoamyl acetate. Maule (1967) found an inhibition of ester formation following elevated mashing temperatures, which was thought to be a result of diminished proteolysis in the mash tun.

Norstedt et al. (1975) found little variation in the concentration of most of the esters when the alpha-amino nitrogen content of the wort varied in the range 100–300 mg/l. They found, however, that ethyl hexanoate increased somewhat in concentration with increasing concentrations of amino nitrogen, while this led to a decrease in the concentration of phenylethyl acetate.

It has also been found that a reduction in the nitrogen content of the wort, caused, for instance, by dilution with a sugar solution, may influence the concentration of esters (Anderson and Kirsop 1974, Engan 1972a, Norstedt *et al.* 1975).

3. Carbohydrates

Norstedt *et al.* (1975) found that the use of 15% or 30% sucrose as adjunct slightly increased the level of most esters. The use of varying amounts of different carbohydrate solutions as additions to wort, showed that ethyl acetate was little influenced up to replacement of 50% of the wort (Engan 1972a). No significant difference was observed between different carbohydrates. Isobutyl acetate, isoamyl acetate and 2-phenylethyl acetate increased in concentration up to replacement of 25–50% of the wort. Ethyl hexanoate and ethyl octanoate showed in most cases a maximum at 25% sugar addition. Figure 14 shows the concentration of some esters after fermentation of wort to which was added different amounts of sucrose or fructose.

Different effects of sugar additions have been reported, but this may be due to different sensitivity of the different yeast strains used.

4. Wort Aeration

Wort aeration seems to influence ester production in such a way that low levels of oxygen may give enhanced ester formation. Cowland and Maule (1966) found that ester formation was highest under anaerobic conditions and that even small additions of oxygen during fermentation inhibited their formation. Norstedt *et al.* (1975) found no effect on the rate of oxygenation in the interval 6–30 mg O_2/litre, but found an increase in esters if the wort was deoxygenated, and a reduced ester formation if aeration was continued after pitching and during fermentation.

Full-scale experiments in two different breweries (Engan and Aubert 1973) showed that fermentation of a slightly aerated wort could give a somewhat greater ester production than a normally aerated wort.

As mentioned in section II.B.1 high gravity brewing may result in levels of esters in the beer which are too high. An effective way to reduce ester formation is controlled oxygenation during a short period of the fermentation (Anderson and Kirsop 1975a b, Anderson *et al.* 1975, Palmer and Rennie 1974).

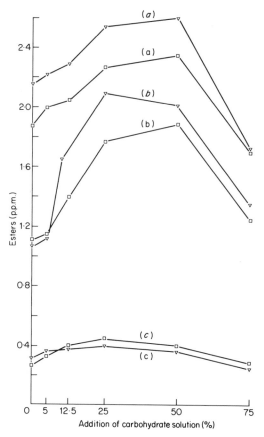

Fɪɢ. 14. Concentrations of some esters when different amounts of a 10% carbohydrate solution was added to wort (after Engan 1972a). ▽ = fructose; □ = sucrose; (a) = isoamyl acetate; (b) = 2-phenylethyl acetate; (c) = ethyl octanoate.

5. Fatty Acids

Äyräpää and Lindström (1973) have demonstrated that unsaturated, long-chain fatty acids may effectively reduce the formation of esters, and this could be a way to control ester production in high-gravity brewing (Anderson and Kirsop 1974, Palmer and Rennie 1974). This effect of the unsaturated fatty acids is related to the effect of oxygen, as oxygen is necessary for the biosynthesis of these acids. The use of fatty acids in ester regulation may, however, negatively influence the flavour stability of the beer, and Norstedt *et al.* (1975) suggest that this probably may be overcome by the use of pure oleic acid rather than fatty acids from cereals.

6. Effect of pH

Nordström (1965a) observed that wort pH had little influence on ester formation, but low pH seemed to favour a somewhat lower ester production. Norstedt *et al.* (1975) found pH to be without any practical influence on the ester level.

7. Barley, Malt, Hops and Adjuncts

Minor variations in the ester content have been found to be due to different barley varieties, growing areas and methods of malting (Narziss and Miedaner 1970a, b). Highly modified malt may result in a more vital fermentation, which was found by Mändl *et al.* (1972) to lead to higher ester concentrations.

Norstedt *et al.* (1975) found that the use of maize as an adjunct did not have much effect on the level of esters. They also studied the influence of the hopping rate, but the variations found in the ester content seemed to be without technical importance.

Two esters, methyl 4-decenoate and methyl 4,8-decadienoate, which have been found in wort and beer in very small concentrations (Nickerson and Likens 1966, Silbereisen *et al.* 1970) originate from the essential oil of hops (Buttery and Ling 1966).

During fermentation these methyl esters may partly be converted to the corresponding ethyl esters (Buttery *et al.* 1967, Nickerson and Likens 1966).

III. CARBONYLS

Many carbonyls have very high flavour potential, which make them an important group of beer volatiles. The beer carbonyls may be divided into different groups, depending on origin, flavour effect or chemical constitution. In the following we will look at acetaldehyde, diacetyl and related compounds, and some other carbonyls of importance.

Table 4 gives the different aldehydes found in beer, and Table 5 the different ketones (including keto acids).

A. Acetaldehyde

The carbonyl found in highest concentration in beer is acetaldehyde. It is formed during fermentation and it is a metabolic branching point in the pathway leading from carbohydrate to ethanol. The acetaldehyde formed may either be reduced to ethanol or oxidized to acetic acid, and in the final step of alcoholic fermentation, acetaldehyde is reduced to ethanol by an enzymatic reaction. A minor portion of the acetaldehyde will be oxidized to acetic acid,

TABLE 4. Aldehydes in beer

Name	References	Typical concentrations in beer (p.p.m.)	Reference
Formaldehyde (methanal)	Drawert and Tressl (1969) Krüger (1969)		
Acetaldehyde (ethanal)	Drawert and Tessl (1969) Lawrence (1964)	2·5–20 1·2–24·4	Engan (1975a, b) Postel et al. (1972)
Glyoxal (oxaldehyde, ethanediol)	Palamand et al. (1970b)		
Glyoxylic acid (oxoacetic, aldehydoformic acid)	Wheeler et al. (1971) Markl and Palamand (1973)	0·23–1·03	Palamand et al. (1970b)
Propionaldehyde (propanal)	Hashimoto (1972) Rosculet and Rickard (1968)		
Acrolein (2-propenal)	Rosculet and Rickard (1968)		
Malonaldehyde (propanedial)	Markl and Palamand (1973)		
Methylglyoxal (pyruvaldehyde)	Palamand et al. (1970a) Wheeler et al. (1971)	0·99–11 0·04–0·293	Palamand et al. (1970a) Wheeler et al. (1971)
Butyraldehyde (n-butanal)	Hashimoto (1972) Rosculet and Rickard (1968)		
Isobutyraldehyde (2-methylpropanal)	Hashimoto (1972) Rosculet and Rickard (1968)	0–0·024	Wheeler et al. (1971)
Crotonaldehyde (2-butenal)	Wheeler et al. (1971)	0–0·036	Wheeler et al. (1971)
Methional (3-methylthio-1-propanal)	Visser and Lindsay (1971b)		
Valeraldehyde (n-pentanal)	Rosculet and Rickard (1968)		
Isovaleraldehyde (3-methylbutanal)	Hashimoto (1972) Rosculet and Rickard (1968)		
2-Methylbutanal	Drawert and Tressl (1969) Hashimoto (1972)		
5-Hydroxypentanal	Markl and Palamand (1973)		
Glutaraldehyde (pentanedial)	Markl and Palamand (1973)		
Furfural (2-furaldehyde)	Harrison (1963)	0·01–0·07	Tressl et al. (1975c)

Compound	Reference	Value	Reference
2-Thiophenecarboxaldehyde	McDougall et al. (1963)	0–0·107	Wheeler et al. (1971)
n-Hexanal (caproic aldehyde)	Rosculet and Rickard (1968); Pickett et al. (1976); Rosculet (1971)		
trans-2-Hexenal	Markl and Palamand (1973)		
2,4-Hexadienal	Markl and Palamand (1973)		
2-Methylpentanal	Markl and Palamand (1973)		
3-Methylpentanal	Markl and Palamand (1973)		
5-Methylfurfural	Drost et al. (1971); Tressl et al. (1974)	<0·01	Tressl et al. (1975c)
5-Methyl-2-thiophenecarboxaldehyde	Pickett et al. (1976)		
5-Hydroxymethylfurfural	McDougall et al. (1963); Tressl et al. (1975c)	<2–<5	Tressl et al. (1975c)
n-Heptanal	Drawert and Tressl (1969); Markl and Palamand (1973)		
4-Heptenal	Wheeler et al. (1971)	0·001–0·009	Wheeler et al. (1971)
Benzaldehyde	Tressl et al. (1975c)	0·01–0·03	Tressl et al. (1975c)
4-Hydroxybenzaldehyde	Palamand et al. (1971)		
Salicylaldehyde (2-hydroxybenzaldehyde)	Markl and Palamand (1973)		
Protocatechuic aldehyde (3,4-dihydroxybenzaldehyde)	Drawert and Tressl (1969)		
Octanal (caprylic aldehyde)	Wheeler et al. (1971)	0·004–0·017	Wheeler et al. (1971)
Octadienal	Meilgaard et al. (1971b)		
Phenylacetaldehyde	Markl and Palamand (1973); Rosculet (1971)		
p-Anisaldehyde (4-methoxybenzaldehyde)	Markl and Palamand (1973)		
p-Tolualdehyde (4-methylbenzaldehyde)	Markl and Palamand (1973)		
Piperonal (3,4-methylenedioxybenzaldehyde)	Markl and Palamand (1973)		
Vanillal (vanillin)	Palamand et al. (1971); Tressl et al. (1975c)	<0·01	Tressl et al. (1975c)
Syringaldehyde	Tressl et al. (1975c)	<0·01	Tressl et al. (1975c)
n-Nonanal	Wheeler et al. (1971)	0·004–0·014	Wheeler et al. (1971)
trans-2-Nonenal	Drost et al. (1971); Jamieson and Van Gheluwe (1970)	0·00003†	Wang and Siebert (1974a)

† In fresh beer.

(continued over page)

TABLE 4 (cont.)

Name	References	Typical concentrations in beer	
		(p.p.m.)	Reference
trans-2-trans-4-Nonadienal	Dominguez and Canales (1974)		
trans-2-cis-6-Nonadienal	Meilgaard (1972)		
Cinnamaldehyde (3-phenylpropenal)	Markl and Palamand (1973)		
Hydrocinnamaldehyde (3-phenylpropanal)	Palamand et al. (1971)		
n-Decanal	Wheeler et al. (1971)	0·006–0·015	Wheeler et al. (1971)
Decadienal	Meilgaard et al. (1971b)		
Citral	Palamand et al. (1971)		
n-Dodecanal	Wheeler et al. (1971)	0·002–0·016	Wheeler et al. (1971)

TABLE 5. Ketones in beer

Name	References	Typical concentrations in beer	
		(p.p.m.)	References
Acetone (2-propanone)	Lawrence (1964) Rosculet and Rickard (1968)	1	Harrison (1970)
Hydroxyacetone (acetol)	Markl and Palamand (1973)		
Pyruvic acid	Enebo (1957) Lawrence (1964)	10–220 21–95	Coote et al. (1973) Mändl et al. (1969, 1970)
Methyl ethyl ketone (2-butanone)	Rosculet and Rickard (1968) Wheeler et al. (1971)	0·005–0·012	Wheeler et al. (1971)
Diacetyl (2,3-butanedione)	Haukeli and Lie (1972) Scherrer (1971) Voerkelius (1961)	0·05–0·20 0·04–0·48 0·02–0·63	Engan and Aubert (1971) Wheeler et al. (1971) White and Wainwright (1975a)
Acetoin (3-hydroxy-2-butanone)	Brenner et al. (1963) Haukeli et al. (1971) Lawrence (1964)	2·9–19·3	Engan and Aubert (1971)
α-Ketobutyric acid (2-oxobutanoic acid)	Harrison and Collins (1968)	0·13–0·88	Harrison and Collins (1968)
Oxaloacetic acid	Rosculet (1971)		
2-Pentanone (methyl propyl ketone)	Drawert and Tressl (1972) Rosculet and Rickard (1968)		
3-Pentanone (diethyl ketone)	Drawert and Tressl (1969)		
3-Methyl-2-butanone (isopropyl methyl ketone)	Rosculet and Rickard (1968)		
2,3-Pentanedione	Harrison (1970)	0·01 0–0·1	Harrison (1970) White and Wainwright (1975a)
Acetonyl acetate	Markl and Palamand (1973)		
α-Ketoisovaleric acid	Harrison and Collins (1968)	0·24–1·35	Harrison and Collins (1968)
γ-Ketovaleric acid (levulinic acid)	Clarke et al. (1962)		
α-Ketoglutaric acid	Coote and Kirsop (1974) Harrison and Collins (1968)	0–20	Coote and Kirsop (1974)
2-Hexanone (methyl n-butyl ketone)	Rosculet (1971)		

(continued over page)

TABLE 5 (*cont.*)

Name	References	Typical concentrations in beer	
		(p.p.m.)	Reference
2,3-Hexanedione	Harrison (1970)	0·01	Harrison (1970)
	Rosculet (1971)		
2,5-Hexanedione	Palamand et al. (1971)		
2-Methyl-1,3-cyclopentanedione	Markl and Palamand (1973)		
2-Acetylfuran	Tressl et al. (1974)	0·03–0·15	Tressl et al. (1975c)
4-Methyl-2-pentanone (isobutylmethyl ketone)	Drawert and Tressl (1972)	0·014–0·037	Wheeler et al. (1971)
	Wheeler et al. (1971)		
α-Ketocaproic acid	Markl and Palamand (1973)		
2-Keto-D-gluconic acid	Markl and Palamand (1973)		
α-Keto-β-methylvaleric acid	Harrison and Collins (1968)	1·01–2·84	Harrison and Collins (1968)
2-Heptanone (methyl amyl ketone)	Drawert and Tressl (1969)		
3-Heptanone (ethyl butyl ketone)	Kahn (1969)		
4-Heptanone (dipropyl ketone)	Drawert and Tressl (1969)		
2,3-Heptanedione	Palamand et al. (1971)		

Compound	Reference	Value	
2-Methyl-1,3-cyclohexanedione	Markl and Palamand (1973)		
ω-Oxoheptanoic acid	Palamand et al. (1971)		
5-Methyl-2-acetylfuran	Tressl et al. (1975c)	<0·01	Tressl et al. (1975c)
2-Octanone (methyl hexyl ketone)	Drawert and Tressl (1972)		
6-Methyl-5-hepten-2-one	Markl and Palamand (1973)		
Phenyl glyoxylic acid	Markl and Palamand (1973)		
o-Aminoacetophenone	Palamand and Grigsby (1974)		
2-Nonanone (methyl heptyl ketone)	Palamand et al. (1971)		
Phenylpyruvic acid	Markl and Palamand (1973)		
Acetovanillone	Tressl et al. (1975c)	<0·01	Tressl et al. (1975c)
2-Decanone (methyl octyl ketone)	Drawert and Tressl (1969)		
3-Decanone (ethyl heptyl ketone)	Drawert and Tressl (1969)		
D-Carvone	Palamand et al. (1971)		
4-Phenyl-2-butanone (benzylacetone)	Kahn (1969)		
2-Undecanone (methyl nonyl ketone)	Rosculet (1971)		
Ionone	Markl and Palamand (1973)		
2,6,6-Trimethyl-1-crotonyl-1,3-cyclohexadiene	Strating and Van Eerde (1973)	0·030–0·070	Shimazu et al. (1975)
Humuladienone	Shimazu et al. (1975)		

but the distribution between oxidation and reduction has been found to be
sensitive to the concentration of ethanol, in such a way that an increased
ethanol concentration reduces the formation of acetic acid (Nordström 1968).

1. Influence of Yeast and Fermentation

The concentration of acetaldehyde varies during fermentation and lagering,
and reaches a maximum during the main fermentation, as illustrated in Fig. 15.
The figure shows the concentration of acetaldehyde during fermentation at
two different temperatures. In some cases, two peaks have been observed
(Bärwald *et al.* 1973). During secondary fermentation, or lagering, the
concentration normally decreases.

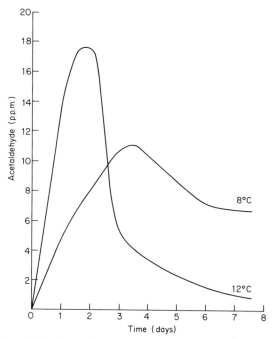

FIG. 15. Acetaldehyde during fermentation at two different temperatures.

The yeast strain used for fermentation has been reported to be of
significance in determining the acetaldehyde level in beer (Drews *et al.* 1969c,
Wellhoener 1966). Otter and Taylor (1971) examined five different strains of
Saccharomyces cerevisiae and two of *Saccharomyces carlsbergensis* and found
no significant differences in the acetaldehyde production. Full-scale experiments with three different strains of *S. carlsbergensis,* carried out at three

different breweries, gave greater variations in acetaldehyde from brewery to brewery than from yeast to yeast (Engan and Aubert 1971).

According to Wellhoener (1966), an increase in fermentation temperature does not increase the acetaldehyde content of the beer. Sommer (1969) used top-fermenting yeasts at 12, 16 and 20 °C and found no differences in the acetaldehyde concentration. Both Drews *et al.* (1969c) and Pessa (1971) found that higher fermentation temperatures gave lower levels of acetaldehyde in the beer (compare Fig. 15). In the experiments carried out by Bärwald *et al.* (1973), an increase in fermentation temperature from 10 to 20 °C resulted in a great increase in acetaldehyde concentration. An increase in pitching rate was also found by Bärwald *et al.* (1973) to increase the acetaldehyde concentration.

2. Influence of Wort Composition and Wort Treatment

Wort aeration may influence the formation of acetaldehyde, and Bärwald *et al.* (1973) found higher concentrations after fermentation of a more highly aerated wort than after fermentation of a wort with less oxygen. Cowland and Maule (1966) showed that high levels of air during fermentation led to the production of high levels of acetaldehyde.

Otter and Taylor (1971) found comparatively high levels of acetaldehyde in some top-fermented, primed beers, i.e. beers sweetened after the main fermentation, and this was found to be due to sulphur dioxide used as a preservative in the commercial sucrose solution used for priming. If sulphur dioxide is present with active yeast, this may lead to elevated concentrations of acetaldehyde in the beer.

A deficiency of vitamins in the fermenting medium, especially a deficiency of pantothenic acid or thiamine, is reported to give increased levels of acetaldehyde (Wucherpfennig and Semmler 1972a, b, c), but this should normally not occur in a beer wort.

3. Influence of Lagering and Pasteurization

During the early stages of lagering, the acetaldehyde content falls (Enebo 1957, Hashimoto 1966, Pessa 1971). Slight increases in the concentration of acetaldehyde from the storage tank to the bottled beer have been observed (Pessa 1971), but these increases were, in some cases, very small.

The use of stabilizing agents, especially anti-oxidants, may influence the acetaldehyde content (Pessa 1971); for instance sulphite may form a complex with acetaldehyde and other carbonyl compounds. The acetaldehyde concentration may increase during pasteurization of bottled beer, especially if there is a high air content in the bottle head-space. During flash pasteurization, however, no increase has been observed (Engan 1973b, 1975b, Pessa 1971).

In bottled beer during storage, the acetaldehyde concentration may change according to oxidation, first increasing and thereafter decreasing (Engan 1969c, Hashimoto 1966, Pessa 1971).

4. Influence of Infection

Infections may influence the concentration of acetaldehyde. Both infection of the wort with bacteria and infection of the yeast may increase the production of acetaldehyde (Niefind and Spath 1971). Very high concentrations have been found after infection with *Zymomonas anaerobia*, but this seems to be important only for English "primed ale" or similar products, to which glucose or fructose are added (Dadds *et al.* 1971).

B. Diacetyl and Related Components

Diacetyl and 2,3-pentanedione occur in all brewery fermentations (White and Wainwright 1975b). Very small amounts may be produced by the yeast, greatly dependent on the yeast strain (Haukeli and Lie 1972), but the absence of vicinal diketones during lager fermentation has been reported (Inoue and Yamamoto 1969).

1. Formation from Acetohydroxy Acids

Different theories have been suggested for the formation of diacetyl and congeners during beer fermentation, and in his comprehensive review, Wainwright (1973) gives the present knowledge of the matter. It now seems to be clearly established that yeast produces acetohydroxy acids, and that diacetyl and 2,3-pentanedione is formed by oxidative decarboxylation of 2-acetolactate and 2-acetohydroxybutyrate, respectively (Inoue and Yamamoto 1970, Inoue *et al.* 1968, Suomalainen and Ronkainen 1968). Decarboxylation of the acetohydroxy acids leads to 3-hydroxy-2-ketones, and oxydative decarboxylation gives the respective vicinal diketones, as shown in Fig. 16.

The diacetyl formed by spontaneous degradation of 2-acetolactate can be reduced by the yeast to acetoin and further to 2,3-butanediol. A diacetyl problem may appear if the degrading of acetolactate takes place at a time where no more yeast is present to reduce the diacetyl formed.

2. Influence of Fermentation and Lagering Conditions

The importance of using a proper yeast strain has been stressed; different yeasts may give rise to different diacetyl levels in the beer (Geiger and Piendl 1975b, Haukeli and Lie 1972, Wellhoener 1966). Inoue (1974) found that more acetohydroxy acids were formed when the fermentation temperature was elevated. One reason for this was found to be that the rate and order

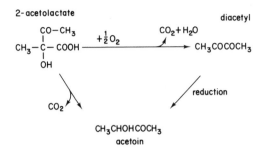

FIG. 16. Formation of diacetyl from 2-acetolactate.

disappearance of amino acids differed with changes in fermentation temperature.

Mandl *et al.* (1974) found that the yeast strains and the fermentation conditions used in their experiments seemed to have no effect on the level of vicinal diketones. However, different yeast strains appear to be influenced to a different degree by the fermentation temperature (Geiger and Piendl 1975b). As a general rule higher fermentation temperatures give greater amounts of vicinal diketones, but the latter will also be more rapidly degraded under the conditions, so that high temperature fermentations may accelerate removal of acetolactate without necessarily giving diacetyl (Wainwright 1974).

Prolonged contact with yeast ensures low levels of diacetyl, and the time required seems to be less at higher temperatures than at lower. Low diacetyl levels may be difficult to achieve with short beer production times, as the acetolactate formed may give diacetyl at a stage when yeast is no longer present to remove it.

Pressure during fermentation reduces the formation of acetolactate and leads to a faster reduction of the diacetyl (Sommer 1975). The faster removal of diacetyl by pressure fermentation has also been observed by Liebs *et al.* (1970).

Geiger and Piendl (1975b) found that pitching rate may influence the formation of acetohydroxy acids, but the influence depended on the yeast strain. According to Sommer (1975), a high pitching rate may also result in faster fermentation and thus in higher concentration of acetolactate, but also to a faster reduction of diacetyl formed. The reduction of diacetyl by the yeast may be added to the process as a special diacetyl reducing phase (Liebs *et al.* 1970). According to Meilgaard (1976), most North American breweries, excluding those where a secondary fermentation is practised, today use a distinct "diacetyl reduction phase" at the end of fermentation.

3. Influence of Wort Composition and Wort Treatment

Trace amounts of diacetyl are found in wort at pitching and are presumed to be a consequence of chemical reactions occurring in the copper (Haukeli and Lie 1971, Inoue and Yamamoto 1970, Inoue *et al.* 1968, White and Wainwright 1975b). White and Wainwright (1975b) found that this level always fell to approximately 0·01 p.p.m. in the first 12–24 hours after pitching.

The levels of the acetohydroxy acids found in under- and over-aerated worts were higher than in normally aerated worts (Geiger and Piendl 1975b, Mändl *et al.* 1974).

The redox-potential in the fermenting wort seems to be an important factor in controlling the decomposition of the 2-acetohydroxy acids (Inoue *et al.* 1968, White and Wainwright 1975b). Addition of a reducing agent such as sodium metabisulphite at pitching may slow down the rate of acetohydroxy acid decomposition during fermentation, resulting in increased concentrations at the end of fermentation (White and Wainwright 1975b).

Access of air during fermentation increases the amount of diacetyl produced, but, given time, the yeast can usually remove it since the amount is limited by the amount of acetolactate present (Wainwright 1974).

The formation of 2-acetohydroxy acids, and thus of diacetyl and pentanedione, is related to the amino acids valine and leucine, and a shortage of amino acids may result in increased formation of the hydroxy acids. According to Latimer *et al.* (1969), brewers may invite diacetyl troubles when they push ratios of adjunct—especially adjuncts with low nitrogen levels—to 50% or more.

The conversion of acetohydroxy acids to vicinal diketones is dependent on pH, and the reaction has an optimum at the pH of beer (Haukeli *et al.* 1971). White and Wainwright (1975b) found that a lowering of the wort pH decreased the peak concentration of 2-acetohydroxy acids, without a corresponding increase in diketone concentration. Low pH, according to Cabane *et al.* (1973), results both in faster degradation of acetolactate and faster removal of the resulting diacetyl by the yeast. Similar results were found by Pajunuen and Makinen (1975), who concluded that a reduction in beer lagering and maturation time can be realized by decreasing the pH value of the wort. Low pH in beer may, however, negatively influence the flavour stability of the product (Grigsby *et al.* 1972).

4. Influence of Infection

Infections with *Pediococcus* or with *Lactobacillus* may result in undesirably high concentration of diacetyl in beer. *Pediococcus cerevisiae* does not reduce diacetyl and pentanedione like the brewery yeasts, so that the concentration remains at peak level (Barwald *et al.* 1969). Some strains of *Lactobacillus* will produce more diacetyl than *Pediococcus cerevisiae* (Scherrer 1971). The lactobacilli produce no 2,3-pentanedione, and *Pediococcus cerevisiae* only traces of this compound (Scherrer, 1971). Analysis of a beer with high levels of vicinal diketones may thus show if this is due to the yeast (high concentrations of both diacetyl and pentanedione), or to an infection (high concentration of diacetyl and low concentrations of pentanedione).

C. Other Carbonyls

Browning reactions lead to the formation of a great number of carbonyls, as reviewed by Hodge (1967). Such reactions take place during malting and during mashing. Carbonyls are found in malt and small concentrations also occur in barley (Damm and Kringstad 1964, Hrdlicka *et al.* 1970, Wagner 1971). Wort boiling results in a decrease in carbonyls and fermentation increases the concentration of some carbonyls and decrease the concentration of others. In the following we will look at some carbonyls which have attracted interest recently.

1. Glyoxal and Methylglyoxal

Both glyoxal and methylglyoxal are found in malt, and methylglyoxal has been found in hops (Palamand *et al.* 1970a, b). Its concentrations in wort increase during wort boiling. During fermentation, lagering and pasteurization the concentration of glyoxal gradually decreases (Palamand *et al.* 1970c), while methylglyoxal may increase somewhat during fermentation and decrease during lagering (Palamand *et al.* 1970b). The increase in methylglyoxal during fermentation is not due to synthesis by the yeast, but methylglyoxal appears to be formed by chemical processes in the wort (Saha and Middelkauff 1970), and the yeast seems to be able to convert or remove some of the methylglyoxal.

2. Furanaldehydes

Furfural, 5-methylfurfural and 5-hydroxymethylfurfural are of some interest in beer. Furfural is found in wort, and the concentration may decrease during fermentation and lagering (Hrdlicka *et al.* 1968). During pasteurization and during storage of bottled beer, the concentration may increase, and this increase has been suggested to be an indication of the deteriorations taking place in the beers (Ahrenst-Larsen and Hansen 1963, Benard and Scriban 1975, Brenner and Khan 1976, Lau and Lindsey 1972, McDougall *et al.* 1963).

Kieninger and Bikova (1975) found a close relationship between the concentration of 5-hydroxymethylfurfural in Congress wort, the effect of gibberellic acid addition during the malting process, and the effect on kilning temperature. They also found that increased wort boiling time increased the concentration of 5-hydroxymethylfurfural, and an increase in concentration was also observed after the Whirlpool stage.

Both pasteurization and storage of bottled beer increase the concentration of 5-hydroxymethylfurfural, and both this compound and 5-methylfurfural may have a connection with the deteriorations taking place during oxidation, or ageing, of beer (Drost et al. 1971, Hashimoto 1972).

3. Stale Flavour Carbonyls

It is a well-known fact that development of off-flavours—referred to as stale flavour, oxidized flavour, aged flavour, cardboard flavour, strawlike flavour, bread flavour, etc.—takes place in bottled beer during storage. A number of carbonyls may participate in this flavour deterioration of beer, but other components also may be of importance.

It has been observed that the oxidized, or aged, beer flavour seems to mask flavours observed in the fresh beer, flavours whose continued presence has been confirmed by analysis (Engan and Aubert 1971). A result of this is that beers from different breweries, after development of an aged beer flavour, may show less flavour differences than before. The deleterious effect of oxygen on beer was recognized early. De Clerk published in 1934 (a, b) his first papers on the redox conditions in the brewing process, and the influence of oxygen on beer. This resulted in the development of methods for reducing the air content in the beer. It was early recognized however that the detrimental effect of air could begin at an early stage in the process, that is in the brewhouse (Emslander 1937).

Carbonyl compounds seem to be of great significance for the stale, or oxidized, flavour of beer as may be established by using a so-called "odour-filter" (Wheeler et al. 1971). The addition of small quantities of a 2,4-dinitrophenylhydrazine solution to stale beer is used to bind the carbonyl compounds which results in a disappearance of the stale flavour. Among the carbonyl compounds, some aldehydes, especially higher, unsaturated aldehydes, may be of significance to stale flavour. Greatest attention has been directed to trans-2-nonenal, which appears to be the main component in the cardboard flavour, or papery flavour, in beer (McFarlane 1973). But the appearance of 2-nonenal is only part of the complex oxidation process taking place in beer, and other components may be of similar, or maybe greater, significance, at least in some phases of the ageing process. In solution in water, 2-nonenal is unstable (Meilgaard and Moya 1970, Wohleb et al. 1972), and in very old beer, or strongly oxidized beer, it may have hardly any significance at all. Analyses of beer stored at 38 °C have shown that the concentration of 2-nonenal increases, reaches a maximum, and thereafter decreases (Wang and Siebert 1974a, b).

A great number of carbonyl compounds may be of importance in the oxidized flavour of beer (Lau and Lindsey 1972, Markl and Palamand 1973, Meilgaard 1972, Palamand and Grigsby 1974, Visser and Lindsey 1971b, Wheeler et al. 1971), and different reactions may be involved in the formation of the stale flavour carbonyls. The melanoidins in beer are able to oxidize higher alcohols to carbonyls, an effect which may depend on the conditions under which the melanoidins are formed (Hashimoto 1972, 1974, Hashimoto and Kuroiwa 1975). Another reaction which may lead to the formation of carbonyls is Strecker degradation of amino acids (Blockmans et al. 1975, Hashimoto and Kuroiwa 1975). The reaction involves a dicarbonyl compound such as may be present in the melanoidins of beer, and the amino acid is degraded to an aldehyde with one C-atom fewer. Oxidative degradation of isohumulone takes place during beer ageing, and this may also lead to the formation of a number of carbonyls (Hashimoto and Kuroiwa 1975).

Greatest importance in relation to the formation of carbonyls during beer staling has been ascribed to the lipid content of the beer, primarily the content of unsaturated fatty acids like linoleic acid and linolenic acid, or oxidation products of these (Dominguez and Canales 1974, Drost et al. 1971, Hashimoto and Kuroiwa 1975, Meilgaard 1972, Visser and Lindsey 1971a).

The most important factor regarding the prevention of the formation of stale flavour carbonyls and other stale flavour components is the avoidance of contact with air at any stage after the main fermentation. It is important also to control the oxidations taking place in the brewhouse, and to get a bright wort after lautering (Barwald 1974, Drost et al. 1971, Gombert 1975, Meilgaard 1972, Van Gheluwe et al. 1970, Van Gheluwe and Valyi 1974).

IV. ORGANIC ACIDS

A great number of volatile, low-volatile and non-volatile organic acids are present in beer. Clarke et al. (1962) detected 81 acids in beer, and today the total number known has exceeded 100.

The concentration of acids in beer is influenced by the raw materials, by the procedure in the brewhouse, and by the yeast and the fermentation conditions. The organic acid metabolism of yeasts during fermentation has recently been reviewed by Whiting (1976). Clarke et al. (1962) found that all the volatile acids they detected in beer also could be found in hopped wort, though in different relative proportions, and Tressel et al. (1975b) also found that most of the acids in beer were already present in wort.

Lower free fatty acids are not present in appreciable concentrations in wort (Arkima 1969), but they increase greatly during fermentation. On the other hand, higher fatty acids are reduced in concentration from wort to beer.

Klopper *et al.* (1975) found that during wort production and wort treatment each purification step brings about a reduction of free fatty acids.

The organic acids reported to be found in beer are tabulated in Table 6 (for keto acids (oxo acids) see Table 5—ketones in beer).

A. The Influence of Yeast and Fermentation

The lower free fatty acids are products of yeast metabolism and they are not found in wort in perceptible concentrations (Äyräpää *et al.* 1961, Arkima 1969). They are formed during fermentation: Fig. 17 shows the formation of some of the fatty acids during the main fermentation. While lower fatty acids

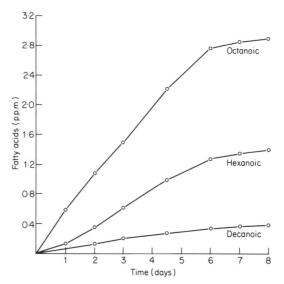

FIG. 17. The formation of some fatty acids during a brewery fermentation.

increase dramatically during fermentation, higher fatty acids show a great decrease. Jones *et al.* (1975) found 0·18 mg/l of the C_6 to C_{12} free fatty acids in a brewery wort, while the concentration in the corresponding beer was 9·65 mg/l. Of the free fatty acids having 14 to 18 carbon atoms in the chain, they found 4·35 mg/l in wort and 0·99 mg/l in the corresponding beer.

Yeast contains a great number of fatty acids from C_2 to C_{18}. Unsaturated fatty acids, like oleic acid and palmitoleic acid, are formed in yeast by desaturation of the corresponding saturated acids, stearic acid and palmitic acid (Suomaleinen and Keranen 1968). The concentration of the fatty acids (free) in beer has been found to depend on the yeast strain (Krauss

TABLE 6. Organic acids in beer†

Name	References	Typical concentrations in beer	
		(p.p.m.)	Reference
Formic	Clarke et al. (1961, 1962) Enebo (1957)	22–43	Zürcher and Krauss (1971)
Acetic	Clarke et al. (1961, 1962) Enebo (1957) Lawrence (1964)	150–280 57–145	Drawert and Hagen (1970) Zürcher and Krauss (1971)
Propionic	Clarke et al. (1961, 1962) Harrison (1963)	5 0·5–3·6	Harrison (1970) Zürcher and Krauss (1971)
Butanoic (n-butyric)	Clarke et al. (1961, 1962) Tressl et al. (1975b)	0·6–3·3	Arkima (1969)
2-Butenoic (crotonic)	Drawert and Tressl (1969)		
Isobutyric	Lawrence (1964) Tressl et al. (1975b)	0·7–3·3	Arkima (1969)
Pentanoic (n-valeric)	Drawert and Tressl (1969) Lawrence (1964)	0·1 0·03	Harrison (1970) Tressl et al. (1975b)
Isovaleric (3-methylbutyric)	Drawert and Tressl (1969) Lawrence (1964)	1·5–3·4 1·17–1·73	Arkima (1969) Tripp et al. (1968)
2-Methylbutyric	Drawert and Tressl (1972)		
2-Pentenoic	Drawert and Tressl (1969)	2·2–5·8	Arkima (1969)
Hexanoic (caproic)	Äyräpää et al. (1961) Clarke et al. (1961)	1·0–5·8	Engan (1975a)
Isohexanoic (4-methylvaleric)	Drawert and Tressl (1972)		
Isohexenoic (4-methyl-3-pentenoic)	Tressl et al. (1975b)	0·32	Tressl et al. (1975b)
2-Hexenoic	Clarke et al. (1961, 1962) Drawert and Tressl (1969)	0·01	Tressl et al. (1975b) (2- + 3-hexenoic)
3-Hexenoic	Clarke et al. (1961, 1962) Drawert and Tressl (1969)		
Heptanoic (enanthic)	Clarke et al. (1961) Harrison (1963)	0·03 0·17–1·03	Tressl et al. (1975b) Tripp et al. (1968)

† Not including keto acids (see Table 5) or amino acids.

(continued over page)

TABLE 6 (*cont.*)

Name	References	Typical concentrations in beer	
		(p.p.m.)	Reference
2-Heptenoic	Drawert and Tressl (1972)	<0·01	Tressel et al. (1975b)
3-Heptenoic	Clarke et al. (1962)		
Octanoic (caprylic)	Äyräpää et al. (1961)	2·7–8·8	Engan (1975a)
	Clarke et al. (1961)	3·3–8·2	MacPherson and Buckee (1974)
		6·8–14·7	Tripp et al. (1968)
2-Octenoic	Drawert and Tressl (1969)	<0·01	Tressl et al. (1975b)
Nonanoic (pelargonic)	Drawert and Tressl (1972)	0·02	Tressl et al. (1975b)
	Clarke et al. (1961, 1962)	0·20–0·43	Tripp et al. (1968)
2-Nonenoic	Drawert and Tressl (1969)	<0·01	Tressl et al. (1975b)
Decanoic (capric)	Tressl et al. (1975b)	0·1–2·0	Engan (1975a)
	Äyräpää et al. (1961)	0·56–3·02	MacPherson and Buckee (1974)
	Clarke et al. (1961, 1962)	0·23	Tressl et al. (1975b)
4-Decenoic	Drawert and Tressl (1972)	0·03	Tressl et al. (1975b)
4,8-Decadienoic	Drawert and Tressl (1972)	<0·01	Tressl et al. (1975b)
Undecanoic	Drawert and Tressl (1969)	0·34–0·49	Tripp et al. (1968)
	Harrison (1963)	0·3–1·9	Zürcher and Krauss (1971)
Isoundecanoic	Krauss and Forch (1975)		
	Zürcher and Krauss (1971)		
Dodecanoic (lauric)	Clarke et al. (1961, 1962)	1·20–2·39	MacPherson and Buckee (1974)
	Harrison (1963)	0·05–0·70	Sandra and Verzele (1975a)
Dodecenoic	Drawert and Tressl (1972)	0·01	Tressl et al. (1975b)
Tridecanoic	Drawert and Tressl (1969)	<0·01	Tressl et al. (1975b)
	Harrison (1963)	0·72–1·18	Tripp et al. (1968)
Isotridecanoic	Drawert and Tressl (1972)		
Tetradecanoic (myristic)	Clarke et al. (1961, 1962)	0·006–0·029	Krauss et al. (1972)
	Drawert and Tressl (1969)	0·33–0·56	MacPherson and Buckee (1974)
		0·95–2·5	Tripp et al. (1968)
Tetradecenoic	Drawert and Tressl (1972)		
Pentadecanoic	Drawert and Tressl (1969)	0·002–0·011	Krauss et al. (1972)
	Harrison (1963)		

Hexadecanoic (palmitic)	Clarke *et al.* (1961, 1962)	0·048-0·122	Krauss *et al.* (1972)
	Harrison (1963)	0·59-1·03	MacPherson and Buckee (1974)
Hexadec-9-enoic	Drawert and Tressl (1972)	0·004-0·024	Krauss *et al.* (1972)
		0·039-0·157	Sandra and Verzele (1975a)
Heptadecanoic	Drawert and Tressl (1972)	<0·01	Tressl *et al.* (1975b)
Octadecanoic (stearic)	Clarke *et al.* (1961, 1962)	0·009-0·063	Krauss *et al.* (1972)
	Harrison (1963)	0·32-0·71	MacPherson and Buckee (1974)
		0·044-0·223	Sandra and Verzele (1975a)
Oleic (*cis*-9-octadecenoic)	Clarke *et al.* (1961, 1962)	0·010-0·051	Krauss *et al.* (1972)
	Harrison (1963)	0·11-0·77	MacPherson and Buckee (1974)
		0·031-0·206	Sandra and Verzele (1975a)
Linoleic (*cis*-9-*cis*-12-octadecadienoic)	Clarke *et al.* (1961, 1962)	0·07-0·76	MacPherson and Buckee (1974)
	Drawert and Tressl (1969)	0·011-0·460	Sandra and Verzele (1975a)
Linolenic (9,12,15-octadecatrienoic)	Clarke *et al.* (1961, 1962)	0·002-0·008	Krauss *et al.* (1972)
	Drawert and Tressl (1969)	0·010-0·138	Sandra and Verzele (1975a)
Dodecosanoic (behenic)	Clarke *et al.* (1961, 1962)		
	Drawert and Tressl (1969)		
Hexacosanoic (cerotic)	Clarke *et al.* (1961, 1962)		
	Drawert and Tressl (1969)		
Hydroxy acetic (glycolic)	Kahn (1969)	25-35	Hashimoto (1975)
2-Hydroxy-3-methylbutyric	Tressl *et al.* (1975b)	0·26	Tressl *et al.* (1975b)
2-Hydroxyglutaric	Coote and Kirsop (1974)	0·17	Coote and Kirsop (1974)
2-Hydroxy-3-methylpentanoic	Tressl *et al.* (1975b)	0·29	Tressl *et al.* (1975b)
2-Hydroxy-4-methylpentanoic	Tressl *et al.* (1975b)	0·33	Tressl *et al.* (1975b)
2-Hydroxyheptanoic	Tressl *et al.* (1975b)	0·06	Tressl *et al.* (1975b)
2-Hydroxyoctanoic	Tressl *et al.* (1975b)	0·04	Tressl *et al.* (1975b)
3-Hydroxyoctanoic	Tressl *et al.* (1975b)	0·07	Tressl *et al.* (1975b)
3-Hydroxydecanoic	Tressl *et al.* (1975b)	0·16	Tressl *et al.* (1975b)
9,10,13-Trihydroxy-11-*trans*-octadecenoic	Drost *et al.* (1971)		
Furan-2-carboxylic	Tressl *et al.* (1975b)	0·3-0·8	Tressl *et al.* (1975b)
Benzoic	Marinelli *et al.* (1968)	0·45	Tressl *et al.* (1975b)
2-Hydroxybenzoic (salicylic)	Tressl *et al.* (1975b)	0·02	Tressl *et al.* (1975b)
4-Hydroxybenzoic	Tressl *et al.* (1975b)	0·13	Tressl *et al.* (1975b)
Protocatechuic (3,4-dihydroxybenzoic)	Tressl *et al.* (1975b)		

(continued over page)

TABLE 6 (*cont.*)

Name	References	Typical concentrations in beer	
		(p.p.m.)	Reference
Gallic (3,4,5-trihydroxybenzoic)	Kitabatake and Amaha (1968)	0·1–13·3	Kitabatake and Amaha (1968)
Phthalic	Clarke et al. (1962)	0·02	Tressl et al. (1975b)
Vanillic	Tressl et al. (1975b)		
2-Phenylacetic	Drawert and Tressl (1969)	0·93	Tressl et al. (1975b)
	Harrison (1963)		
4-Hydroxyphenylacetic	Tressl et al. (1974)	0·04	Tressl et al. (1975b)
Phenylpropionic	Tressl et al. (1975b)	0·01	Tressl et al. (1975b)
4-Hydroxyphenylpropionic	Tressl et al. (1975b)	0·02	Tressl et al. (1975b)
Phenyllactic	Tressl et al. (1975b)	1·2	Tressl et al. (1975b)
trans-Cinnamic	Tressl et al. (1975b)	0·50	Tressl et al. (1975b)
cis-Cinnamic	Tressl et al. (1975b)	<0·01	Tressl et al. (1975b)
trans-p-Coumaric (4-hydroxy-trans-cinnamic)	Tressl et al. (1975b)	1·9	Tressl et al. (1975b)
cis-p-Coumaric (4-hydroxy-cis-cinnamic)	Tressl et al. (1975b)	0·02	Tressl et al. (1975b)
trans-Ferulic	Tressl et al. (1975b)	4·6	Tressl et al. (1975b)
cis-Ferulic	Tressl et al. (1975b)	1·1	Tressl et al. (1975b)
Lactic	Lawrence (1964)	L(+): 2–491	Drawert and Hagen (1970)
	Tressl et al. (1975b)	D(–): 24–200	
		tot.: 28–532	
Malic (hydroxysuccinic)	Lawrence (1964)	4–139	Mändl et al. (1969)
	Marinelli et al. (1968)		
Gluconic	Drawert and Hagen (1970)	8–102	Drawert and Hagen (1970)
Aconitic (1,2,3-propanetricarboxylic)	Rosculet (1971)		
Citric	Lawrence (1964)	141–285	Mändl et al. (1969)
	Marinelli et al. (1968)	90–216	Hashimoto (1975)
Isocitric	Rosculet (1971)	10–52	Hashimoto (1975)
Oxalic	Lawrence (1964)	1·5–4·5	Hashimoto (1975)
Malonic	Marinelli et al. (1968)	0·02	Tressl et al. (1975b)
	Tressl et al. (1975b)		

Compound	Reference	Amount	Reference
Fumaric	Lawrence (1964)	11–23	Hashimoto (1975)
	Marinelli et al. (1968)		
Succinic	Marinelli et al. (1968)	48	Tressl et al. (1975b)
	Tressl et al. (1975b)	80	Palamand et al. (1973)
Tartaric	Lawrence (1964)	13	Hashimoto (1975)
Glutaric (pentanedioic)	Tressl et al. (1975b)	0·01	Tressl et al. (1975b)
Mesaconic	Lawrence (1964)	6–9	Hashimoto (1975)
Citramalic (2-hydroxy-2-methylsuccinic)	Fantozzi (1970)	5·86–15·22	Fantozzi (1970)
Heptanedioic (pimelic)	Tressl et al. (1975b)	0·01	Tressl et al. (1975b)
Octanedioic (suberic)	Tressl et al. (1975b)	0·15	Tressl et al. (1975b)
Nonanedioic (azelaic)	Tressl et al. (1975b)	1·5	Tressl et al. (1975b)
Decanedioic (sebacic)	Tressl et al. (1975b)	0·20	Tressl et al. (1975b)
Undecanedioic	Tressl et al. (1975b)	0·13	Tressl et al. (1975b)
Dodecanedioic	Tressl et al. (1975b)	0·18	Tressl et al. (1975b)
2-Acetolactic	Haukeli and Lie (1971)	0·2–0·5	Haukeli and Lie (1971)
	Wainwright (1973)		
2-Aceto-2-hydroxybutyric	Haukeli and Lie (1971)		
	Wainwright (1973)		

and Forch 1975, Krauss *et al.* 1975). Coote and Kirsop (1974) investigated the concentrations of acetate, pyruvate, lactate, succinate, pyroglutamate, malate, citrate, 2-ketoglutarate and 2-hydroxyglutarate in a number of beers, and found that the yeast strain influenced all these except pyroglutamate. The method of yeast propagation was also found to influence the concentration of these acids.

Krauss and Forch (1975) found that an increase in pitching rate gave a slight reduction in free fatty acids. According to Jost and Piendl (1976) pitching rate has the greatest significance on the formation of acetic acid, followed by the fermentation temperature (lower temperatures gave higher concentrations) and the yeast strain, whereas wort aeration was not important. Engan and Aubert (1973) found that when aeration was reduced, the formation of free fatty acids of C_6 to C_{10} chain length increased. A similar connection between wort aeration and the concentration of free fatty acids was found by Krauss and Forch (1975). They found that all conditions which accelerated fermentation (aeration, higher fermentation temperature, stirring of the substrate) caused a decrease in the free fatty acid concentration in beer.

In continuous fermentations Sandegren and Enebo (1961) reported the formation of higher concentrations of fatty acids than were found in conventional brews, but the contrary effect was found by Makinen and Enari (1969).

B. The Influence of Raw Materials and Wort Composition

Malt is the main source of the free fatty acids present in wort, and the quantities are, for the greater part, determined by the lautering procedure, while grist composition seems to be of less importance (Klopper *et al.* 1975). The role of hops in affecting the fatty acid content of beer is not very clear (Sandra and Verzele 1975a), but Tressl *et al.* (1975b) found unsaturated fatty acids of chain length 6–12 in beer originating from hops.

The concentration of citric acid in beer is found to depend on the content in malt and wort, and under- and over-modified malts give more citrate in beer than normally modified malt (Gehlhoff and Piendl 1974). The germination temperature and the kilning temperature also influence the acid content of the malt.

Wort boiling leads to a drastic reduction in the concentration of various fatty acids, and the whirlpool leads to a great reduction also (Klopper *et al.* 1975).

Forch *et al.* (1975) investigated the effect of the wort content of phosphorus, magnesium, calcium and biotin on the concentration of free fatty acids in beer. They found that calcium had no effect, but that the other components influenced the concentration of fatty acids. An increase in phosphate, up to

150 mg/l, increased the concentration of fatty acids, and magnesium had a similar, but smaller, effect. An increase in free fatty acids from 5·1 mg/l to 16·6 mg/l followed an increase in biotin content from 0 to 10 µg/l. According to Forch et al. (1975) varying concentrations of free fatty acids in beer are, however, not due to differences in the phosphate, magnesium or biotin levels of the wort, but to different contents of amino acids, together with the yeast strain and fermentation conditions.

Adding different amounts of sugar solution, thus reducing the concentration of amino acids in the medium, influenced the concentration of octanoic acid after fermentation as shown in Fig. 18 (Engan 1972a). Decanoic acid was influenced to a lesser extent if less than 50% of the wort was replaced by sugar solutions.

V. SULPHUR COMPOUNDS

The volatile sulphur compounds found in beer are sulphur dioxide, hydrogen sulphide, and a number of organic sulphur compounds, mainly mercaptans (thiols) and organic sulphides. Sulphur compounds may be present in the raw materials, and they may also result from the metabolism or from infecting microorganisms.

A. Sulphur Dioxide

The raw materials used in brewing may contain different amounts of sulphur dioxide but most of it disappears during wort boiling and the sulphur dioxide found in beer is mostly formed during fermentation.

Brenner et al. (1955) found, in a number of malts, concentrations ranging from 28 to 47 p.p.m. of sulphur dioxide, but 21 out of 24 malts investigated by Thalacker and Ihring (1973) were free from the substance. Hops may also contain sulphur dioxide (Brenner et al. 1955), depending on sulphuring (Schild and Zacherl 1965). Hop extracts contain considerably less sulphur dioxide than hop powder (Thalacker and Ihring 1973). More than 94% of the sulphur dioxide found in the raw materials may be lost during wort boiling (Thalacker 1975) and the content in the raw materials seems to have no effect on the sulphur dioxide content of the beer.

The main factors influencing the level of sulphur dioxide in beer are original gravity and type of fermentation (Thalacker et al. 1974), while other influencing factors like yeast strain, fermentation conditions and secondary fermentation seem to be of lesser importance. Strong beers (15·5 °P) have, on average, twice as much sulphur dioxide as 11–14 °P beers (Thalacker et al. 1974, Tressl et al. 1975a), but great variations occur within each group.

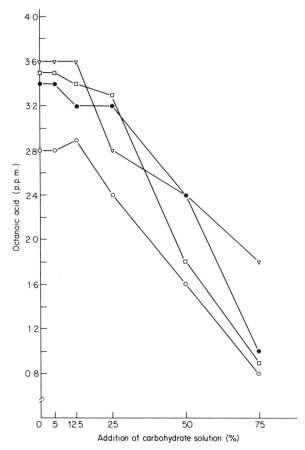

FIG. 18. Concentration of octanoic acid when different amounts of a 10% carbo-hydrate solution was added to wort (Engan 1972a). ○ =glucose; ▽ =fructose; □ =sucrose; ● =maltose.

According to Thalacker *et al.* (1974), top-fermented beers generally have significantly lower sulphur dioxide contents than bottom-fermented beers.

B. Hydrogen Sulphide

Hydrogen sulphide is formed during fermentation and may be smelled in the fermentation gas; small amounts remain in the beer. According to Anderson *et al.* (1971) recent analytical studies have suggested that inorganic volatile compounds containing sulphur, especially hydrogen sulphide, do not make such an important contribution to beer flavour as was originally thought.

Normal beers, when free from infection, contain little, if any, free hydrogen sulphide. As long ago as in 1928, Wanderscheck investigated different factors influencing the amount of hydrogen sulphide evolved during fermentation. Ricketts and Coutts (1951) found this substance to be a normal constituent of the liberated gas during fermentation of both hopped and unhopped malt worts as well as of sugar solutions.

The production of hydrogen sulphide during fermentation is influenced by the yeast strain (Wanderscheck 1928), and Kleber and Lampl (1957) found that its formation runs parallel with the intensity of fermentation. According to Wainwright (1971), more hydrogen sulphide is formed the greater the amount of yeast growth, and faster fermentations give more hydrogen sulphide than do slower fermentations.

The use of elemental sulphur, as a fungicide, on the raw materials has also been shown to increase the possibility of significant formation of hydrogen sulphide during fermentation (Acree et al. 1972).

Messchelein et al. (1961) found that the sulphur content of the wort did not depend on the brewing procedure, but essentially on the raw materials. They also found a certain relationship between the initial amount of hydrogen sulphide in wort and the amount remaining in beer at racking.

The importance of the sulphate in wort as a precursor of hydrogen sulphide has been demonstrated (Wanderscheck 1928, Anderson and Howard 1974a), and most of the free hydrogen sulphide excreted by brewery yeasts appears to be derived from sulphate rather than from other sulphur-containing compounds present (Anderson and Howard 1974a). The importance of sulphate, sulphur dioxide and elemental sulphur has also been pointed out by Brenner et al. (1974). That different results may be obtained with different yeast strains is shown by the results of Jangaard et al. (1973), who found that addition of sodium sulphate or elemental sulphur to wort decreased production of hydrogen sulphide. The same authors found that the acid washing of the yeast markedly increased the production of hydrogen sulphide. Figure 19 shows the different sulphur-containing precursors which may influence production of hydrogen sulphide. According to Wainwright (1970), the yield of hydrogen sulphide in fermentation obviously depend on at least four types of components in the wort: (1) sulphate and sulphite, (2) metal ions, (3) vitamins and (4) amino acids. Deficiency of pantothenate, or vitamin B_6 (for some yeasts), can result in methionine deficiency in the fermenting medium and this may lead to increased production of hydrogen sulphide. Wainwright (1970) found that the production of hydrogen sulphide in normal worts was probably chiefly regulated by the concentration of certain amino acids, which do not themselves contain sulphur, but which inhibit methionine biosynthesis. This control by the detailed amino acid composition of wort may explain the unpredictability of the occurrence of hydrogen sulphide in beer.

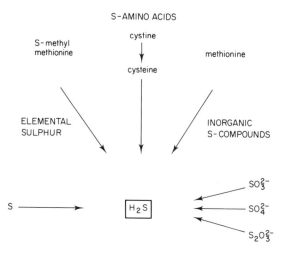

FIG. 19. Formation of hydrogen sulphide from S-containing precursors. (Niefind and Späth 1973, with permission from Elsevier Publishing Co.).

C. Organic Sulphur Compounds

Several organic sulphur compounds have been identified in beer, see Table 7. They may result from yeast metabolism, pure chemical reactions or bacterial contamination. Following the suggestion made by Lüers and Leiss (1933) that thiols are present in fermentation gases, thiols have been presumed to be partly responsible for young bouquet in beer. As a result of this, special attention was paid to thiols, and different methods were suggested for their estimation (Brenner and Laufer 1972, Brenner et al. 1954b, 1955, Jansen et al. 1971). In Japanese beer, however, no thiols could be detected, except in sunstruck, or lightstruck, beer, while thiocarbonyls were found in minute concentrations (Hashimoto and Kuriowa 1966, Hashimoto et al. 1968).

Sunstruck flavour in beer has been ascribed to 3-methyl-2-butene-1-thiol (prenyl mercaptan) formed by reaction of hydrogen sulphide or other sulphur containing compounds with a side chain of the isohumulones under the influence of light (Kuroiwa and Hashimoto 1961). Both Verzele et al. (1970) and Späth et al. (1975) are of the opinion that prenyl mercaptan cannot alone be responsible for sunstruck flavour, and the problem seems to need further investigation.

In addition to thiols and thiocarbonyls, organic sulphides have been detected in beer; among these, that which has attracted most attention and which occurs in the highest concentration is dimethyl sulphide. Dimethyl sulphide has been related to lager flavour and its concentration in lagers seems to be considerably higher than in ales (Anderson *et al.* 1975, Dalgliesh 1974).

Anderson *et al.* (1971) found that yeast did not form detectable amounts of volatile organosulphur compounds in synthetic media, and in wort only traces were produced. They suggested that most of the dimethyl sulphide found in beer was the result of spoilage by bacteria and not due to yeast activity during fermentation. That infections caused by brewery bacteria, particularly wort spoilage organisms, may generate dimethyl sulphide and traces of other sulphur volatiles has also been found by others (Anderson and Howard 1974b, Drews *et al.* 1969). Anderson and Howard (1974b) found a number of volatile sulphur compounds in malt and hops, but most of this material extracted into the wort was driven off during wort boiling.

Dimethyl sulphide is a component of malt aroma (Palamand *et al.* 1970c), and Anderson *et al.* (1971) found that it sometimes is present in sterile boiled wort and that significant amounts from this source may remain in beer after processing. Kavanagh *et al.* (1975) found the levels of dimethyl sulphide in malt to be significantly dependent upon kilning temperature. Important factors were also barley variety, grain sulphur content and extent of modification. Szlavko and Worrall (1975) found more dimethyl sulphide in malt from 6-row barley than in malt from 2-row barley, and suggested that partial control of dimethyl sulphide is possible by a judicious selection of the malt.

Malt contains a precursor of dimethyl sulphide, and if this precursor is carried through to the pitched wort, it may be converted to dimethyl sulphide during fermentation. Niefind and Späth (1975a, b) found this precursor to be S-methylmethionine, which is formed during germination of barley and which is partly destroyed during malt kilning and wort boiling. The amount of S-methylmethionine in malt was found to depend on kilning temperature and the moisture content of the malt. The higher the kilning temperature and the lower the water content of the malt, the less dimethyl sulphide seems to be formed during fermentation. Niefind and Späth (1975a) also suggested that the difference in dimethyl sulphide content of ale and lager may be partly due to differences in the mashing process. In the decoction system, portions of the mash are boiled and this may strongly reduce the enzymic activity. Less S-methylmethionine may then be hydrolysed to dimethyl sulphide and a greater portion will get through to the pitching wort. The very low dimethyl sulphide values in ales may be explained by the higher enzymatic activity during the infusion mashing.

It has also been suggested (Sinclair *et al.* 1970, 1970) that some of the difference between ales and lagers in relation to dimethyl sulphide may be due to the higher temperatures used in top fermentation, which may give a more

TABLE 7. Sulphur compounds in beer

Name	References	Typical concentrations in beer	
		(p.p.m.)	Reference
Hydrogen sulphide	Brenner et al. (1953, 1954a)	0–0·001 (free)	
		0·0007–0·046 (bound)	Sinclair et al. (1969)
			Späth et al. (1972)
Sulphur dioxide	Brenner et al. (1955)	0·0005–0·0224	
	Thalacker et al. (1974)	0–2·3 (free)	
		0·8–23·6 (total)	Klopper (1973)
Methyl mercaptan (methanethiol)	Drews et al. (1969a, b)	0–0·0011	Jansen et al. (1971)
Ethyl mercaptan (ethanethiol)	Drews et al. (1969a, b)	0–0·0006	Jansen et al. (1971)
Allyl mercaptan	Pickett et al. (1976)		
Thioformaldehyde	Kuroiwa and Hashimoto (1970)	0·0001	Kuroiwa and Hashimoto (1970)
Dithioformaldehyde	Kuroiwa and Hashimoto (1970)	0·0001	Kuroiwa and Hashimoto (1970)
Dimethyl sulphide	Drews et al. (1969a, b)	0–0·013 (ale)	

Compound	Reference	Concentration (mg/l)	Reference
Dimethyl disulphide	Drews et al. (1969a, b)	0·018–0·144 (lager)	Sinclair et al. (1970)
		0·017–0·112	Engan (1975a)
		0·0001–0·0003	Jansen et al. (1971)
		0–0·003	Richardson and Mocek (1971)
Thioacetone	Kuroiwa and Hashimoto (1970)	0·00002	Kuroiwa and Hashimoto (1970)
Ethyl methyl sulphide	Pickett et al. (1976)		
Diethyl sulphide	Drews et al. (1969a)	0–0·005	Bärwald et al. (1970)
Diethyl disulphide	Drews et al. (1969a, b)	0–0·010	Bärwald et al. (1970)
Methyl butyl sulphide	Richardson and Mocek (1971)	0–0·001	Richardson and Mocek (1971)
Ethyl butyl sulphide	Pickett et al. (1976)		
3-Methyl-2-butene-1-thiol	Kuroiwa and Hashimoto (1970)	0·030†	Kuroiwa and Hashimoto (1970)
3-Methylthiopropylacetate	Schreier et al. (1974)	0·005–0·180	Schreier et al. (1975)
2-Methyltetrahydrothiophene-3-one	Schreier et al. (1974)		
Ethyl-3-methylthiopropionate	Schreier et al. (1974)		
2-Methylthioacetic acid	Tressl et al. (1975b)	<0·01	Tressl et al. (1975b)
3-Methylthiopropionic acid	Schreier et al. (1974)	0·03	Tressl et al. (1975b)
	Tressl et al. (1975b)		
2-Thiophenic acid	Tressl et al. (1974)	<0·01	Tressl et al. (1975b)
2-Acetylthiophene	Pickett et al. (1976)		

† In lightstruck beer.

efficient carbon dioxide washout of volatiles during fermentation. According to Steffen *et al.* (1971), however, carbon dioxide washing during fermentation does not lead to any great reduction in the concentration of sulphur compounds.

The experiments of White and Parsons (1975) suggest that *S*-methylmethionine may not be the precursor of dimethyl sulphide, but that the precursor is an unknown compound with a high molecular weight. They also found that while different yeast strains varied in their ability to produce dimethyl sulphide during fermentation, no clear distinction could be found between ale and lager yeasts.

Residual dimethyl sulphide precursor may be found in bottled beer (White and Wainwright 1976), and this may lead to increased dimethyl sulphide levels during pasteurization and storage. An increase in dimethyl sulphide concentration during the ageing of beer has also been observed (Ahrenst-Larsen and Hansen 1963, Engan 1972c).

VI. AMINES

A number of different amines have been identified in beer—see Table 8, but by far the largest part of the volatile bases in beer consists of ammonia.

Volatile amines are not formed during fermentation, but originate from the malt and the hops employed, and the conditions during mashing and boiling influence their concentration in beer (Drews *et al.* 1957, Slaughter 1970). Great variations in the concentration and composition of the volatile amine fraction have been found in different beers, and according to Koike *et al.* (1972) this is due to differences in raw materials and brewery processes. In American beers, ethylamine seems to be the major volatile amine (Palamand *et al.* 1969), while dimethylamine seems to be the prevalent amine in European beers (Drews *et al.* 1957, Slaughter and Uvgaard 1971).

Hrdlicka *et al.* (1964) found that amines are formed during germination of barley and they suggested that these compounds may be responsible for the characteristic aroma of germinating barley. They also found that, during the brewing process, the total amine concentration diminished, but a slight increase in diamines was observed. Palamand *et al.* (1969) found no clear pattern in the concentration of amines during production. They also examined the amine content of the raw materials, and found that the concentrations of volatile amines were generally low, being highest in hops and lower in malt, rice, barley and maize, decreasing in that order. Among different hop varieties investigated, Fuggles contained the highest quantities of amines, followed by Alsace, Backa, Hallertau and Sacramento.

TABLE 8. Amines in beer

Name	References	Typical concentrations in beer (p.p.m.)	Typical concentrations in beer: Reference
Ammonia	Drews *et al.* (1957)		
Methylamine	Drews *et al.* (1957)	0·005	Drews *et al.* (1957)
	Hrdlicka *et al.* (1964)	0·02–0·32	Palamand *et al.* (1969)
Ethylamine	Drews *et al.* (1957)	0·010	Drews *et al.* (1957)
	Hrdlicka *et al.* (1964)	0·25–2·12	Palamand *et al.* (1969)
		0·11–0·30	Koike *et al.* (1972)
Propylamine	Hrdlicka *et al.* (1964)	trace–0·17	Palamand *et al.* (1969)
	Palamand *et al.* (1969)		
Isopropylamine	Hrdlicka *et al.* (1964)		
n-Butylamine	Drews *et al.* (1957)	0·005	Drews *et al.* (1957)
	Hrdlicka *et al.* (1964)	0–0·07	Palamand *et al.* (1969)
2-Butylamine	Hashimoto (1975)		
Isobutylamine	Hrdlicka *et al.* (1964)	0·05–0·10	Koike *et al.* (1972)
	Koike *et al.* (1972)	0·004–0·22	Palamand *et al.* (1969)

(*continued over page*)

TABLE 8 (cont.)

Name	References	Typical concentrations in beer (p.p.m.)	Reference
n-Amylamine	Drews et al. (1957)	0·01	Drews et al. (1957)
Isoamylamine	Hrdlicka et al. (1964) Koike et al. (1972)	0–0·16	Palamand et al. (1969)
Hexylamine	Hrdlicka et al. (1964) Palamand et al. (1969)	0·005–0·28	Palamand et al. (1969)
Dimethylamine	Drews et al. (1957) Hrdlicka et al. (1964) Mincione et al. (1973) Koike et al. (1972)	0·37–0·78 0·07–0·69	Koike et al. (1972) Slaughter and Uvgaard (1971)
Diethylamine	Palamand et al. (1969)	trace–0·16	Palamand et al. (1969)
Diisobutylamine	Koike et al. (1972)	0·03–0·06	Koike et al. (1972)
N,N'-Dimethyl-n-butylamine	Koike et al. (1972)		
Trimethylamine	Hrdlicka et al. (1964)		
Tripropylamine	Hrdlicka et al. (1964)		
Ethanolamine	Hrdlicka et al. (1964)		
1,3-Diaminopropane	Hrdlicka et al. (1964)		
1,4-Diaminobutane	Hrdlicka et al. (1964)		
1,5-Diaminopentane	Mincione et al. (1973)		
N,N'-Di-1,4-diaminopentane	Slaughter (1970)		
Pyrrolidine			
p-Hydroxybenzylamine	Slaughter and Uvgaard (1972)	0·16–0·72	Slaughter and Uvgaard (1972)
Histamine	Vogel et al. (1962)	0·0005–0·001	Vogel et al. (1962)

VII. PHENOLS

A great number of phenolic compounds are naturally present in wort and beer (Dadic *et al.* 1970) and the pivotal role of phenols in beer quality has been stressed by Dadic (1974). Most of the phenolic compounds in beer are, however, non-volatile polyphenols. Table 9 shows some phenols reported to be found in beer. A number of phenolic compounds are also tabulated in Table 2 (alcohols), Table 3 (esters), Table 4 (aldehydes), Table 5 (ketones) and Table 6 (acids), the total number of volatile phenolic compounds known in beer being about 60.

TABLE 9. Volatile phenols in beer

Name	References	Typical concentrations in beer	
		(p.p.m.)	Reference
Phenol	Tressl *et al.* (1975c)	<0·01	Tressl *et al.* (1975c)
Guaiacol	Tressl *et al.* (1975c)	0·01–0·02	Tressl *et al.* (1975c)
4-Vinylphenol	Tressl *et al.* (1975c)	0·04–0·15	Tressl *et al.* (1975c)
4-Vinylguaiacol	Dallos *et al.* (1967) Tressl *et al.* (1974)	0·05–0·55	Tressl *et al.* (1975c)
4-Vinylsyringol	Tressl *et al.* (1974)	<0·01	Tressl *et al.* (1975c)
4-Ethylsyringol	Tressl *et al.* (1975c)	<0·01	Tressl *et al.* (1975c)
Isoeugenol	Tressl *et al.* (1975c)	<0·01	Tressl *et al.* (1975c)
4-Propenylsyringol	Tressl *et al.* (1975c)	<0·01	Tressl *et al.* (1975c)

Volatile phenols are normally present in beer in very small quantities. In elevated concentrations they may give beer an off-flavour which has been described as phenolic, medicinal or pharmaceutical. Unacceptably high concentrations of volatile phenols in beer may originate from brewing water, from infection of the wort with bacteria or with wild yeasts, from cleaning compounds, from container coatings, or from crown and can linings (Dadic *et al.* 1971, Engan 1969b, Riemann and Scheibe 1969, Steiner 1968, West *et al.* 1963).

Steiner (1968) found that the normal content of volatile phenols in beer depended on the malt and the hops used as raw materials. Dark beer was found to contain more volatile phenols than pale beer, and more phenols were found in special beers with higher hop rates. The hop variety also played a role, and beer with Saazer hops contained 20% more phenols than beers hopped with other varieties investigated (Woluzacher Elsasser, Steirischer).

Barley and malt contain a number of phenol carboxylic acids (Kringstad 1972, Tressl *et al.* 1974), and during kilning and wort boiling they are partly degraded to give volatile phenols. Figure 20 shows the reactions leading from

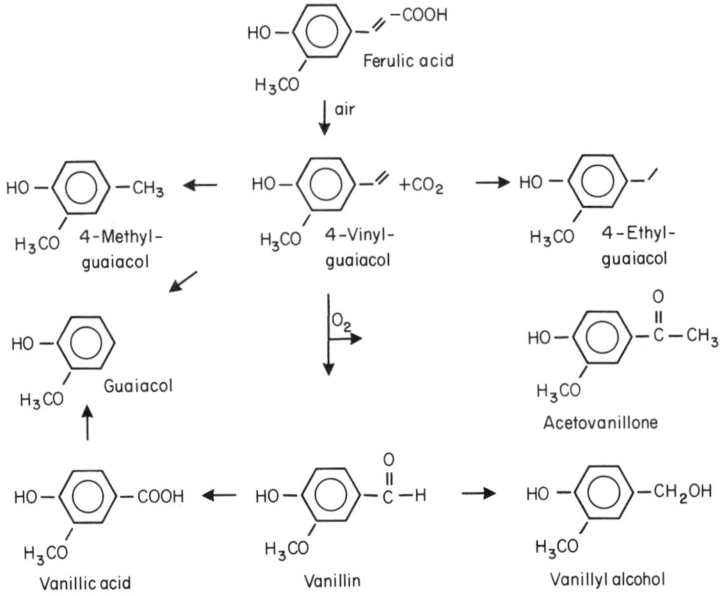

FIG. 20. Reactions leading from ferulic acid to different phenols found to be present in wort and beer. Similar reactions may take place with p-coumaric acid and with sinapic acid (Tressl et al. 1974).

ferulic acid to different phenols found to be present in wort and beer. Tressl et al. (1974) found that all phenols formed by decarboxylation of phenol carboxylic acids and identified in wort, could be identified in beer as well.

The concentration of volatile phenols may change during ageing of beer, and in most cases an increase has been found (Barwald 1970, Engan 1969b). Dadic et al. (1971) have given some suggestions on how to prevent the occurrence of phenolic off-flavours in beer. Most important seems to be the avoidance of chemical and bacterial contamination of water and other brewing raw materials, the pursuit of clean practices throughout the brewing process and particularly in fermentation, and the utilization of appropriate packaging materials.

VIII. MISCELLANEOUS COMPOUNDS

Table 10 shows a number of different components identified in beer and not included in the previous tables. Some of them originate from hops, and some are Maillard reaction products.

TABLE 10. Miscellaneous volatiles in beer

Name	References	Typical concentrations in beer (p.p.m.)	Reference
Diethyl ether	Kunitake (1967)	0·07–0·97	Kunitake (1967)
2-Methyl-2-butene	Lawrence (1964)		
	Zenz (1970)		
Isoprene (2-methyl-1,3-butadiene)	Zenz (1970, 1972)		
3,4-Dimethyl-2-pentene	Hashimoto (1975)		
Myrcene	Harold et al. (1961a, b)	0·0001–0·001	Hashimoto (1975)
	Lawrence (1964)		
Caryophyllene	Howard and Slater (1957)	0·0003–0·001	
	Lawrence (1964)	0·027†	Hashimoto (1975)
Humulene	Lawrence (1964)	0·0007–0·005	
	Palamand et al. (1971)		
	Harold et al. (1961b)		
Farnesene	Howard and Slater (1957)	0·063†	Hashimoto (1975)
	Howard and Slater (1957)		
Ocimene	Palamand et al. (1971)	0·019†	Hashimoto (1975)
α-Pinene	Hashimoto (1975)		
Limonene	Hashimoto (1975)		

(continued over page)

TABLE 10 (*cont.*)

Name	References	Typical concentrations in beer	
		(p.p.m.)	Reference
Indole	Harold *et al.* (1961a)		
	Lawrence (1964)		
γ-Butyrolactone	Spence *et al.* (1973)	2·0	Spence *et al.* (1973)
	Tressl *et al.* (1975c)		
γ-Valerolactone	Spence *et al.* (1973)	1·6	Spence *et al.* (1973)
	Tressl *et al.* (1975c)		
γ-Octalactone	Tressl *et al.* (1975c)	0·02–0·05	Tressl *et al.* (1975c)
γ-Nonalactone	Tressl *et al.* (1975c)	0·1–0·5	Tressl *et al.* (1975c)
γ-Decalactone	Buttery *et al.* (1967)	0·005–0·020	Tressl *et al.* (1975c)
	Tressl *et al.* (1975c)		
4,4-Dimethyl-4-butanolid	Tressl *et al.* (1975c)	0·02–0·05	Tressl *et al.* (1975c)
4,4-Dimethyl-2-butene-4-olid	Tressl *et al.* (1975c)	0·05–0·10	Tressl *et al.* (1975c)
4-Hydroxy-4-methyl-2-pentenolid	Sandra and Verzele (1975b)	0·01–0·05	Sandra and Verzele (1975b)
Maltol	Tressl *et al.* (1974)	8·0‡	Tressl *et al.* (1975c)
5-Hydroxymaltol	Tressl *et al.* (1974)	1·2‡	Tressl *et al.* (1975c)
5-Hydroxy-5,6-dihydromaltol	Tressl *et al.* (1974)	23‡	Tressl *et al.* (1975c)
Isomaltol	Tressl *et al.* (1975c)	0·8‡	Tressl *et al.* (1975c)
Cyclotene	Tressl *et al.* (1975c)	1·3‡	Tressl *et al.* (1975c)
4-Hydroxy-2,5-dimethyl-3-furanone	Tressl *et al.* (1975c)	2·6‡	Tressl *et al.* (1975c)
1-(2,3,6-Trimethylphenyl)-1,3-butadiene	Strating and Van Eerde (1973)		

† In dry-hopped beer.
‡ In dark beer.

Diethyl ether has been identified in some beers (Kunitake 1967) and isoprene may be an indicator of deteriorations taking place in the beer (Zenz 1970, 1972). Drost et al. (1971) found four components which increased in concentration during ageing of beer and which they supposed to be responsible for oxidized flavour. Two of these were identified as 2-*trans*-nonenal and 5-methylfurfural (see section III.C.2 and III.C.3). Later the other two were identified (Strating and Van Earde 1973) and they, or at least one of them, seem to be oxidation products of carotenoids which originate from the barley. One of the compounds has a smell of leather/geranium (1-(2,3,6-trimethylphenyl)-1,3-butadiene) and the other has a lovely odour of black-currant ((2,6,6-trimethyl-1-crotonyl)-1,3-cyclohexadiene).

Lactones which are found in beer may be formed during fermentation (Suomalainen and Nykänen 1972), and they may also originate from hop oil or from the degradation of hop bitter substances (Tressl and Renner, 1975, Tressl et al. 1975c).

The γ-pyrones found in beer may be considered as aroma fortifiers. Maltol has similar antioxidant properties to ascorbic acid, and may contribute to flavour stability (Tressl et al. 1975c).

REFERENCES

Acree, T. E., Sonoff, E. P. and Splittstosser, D. F. (1972). *Am. J. Enol. Viticult.* **23**, 6.
Ahrenst-Larsen, B. and Hansen, H. L. (1963). *Brauwissenschaft* **16**, 393.
Anderson, R. G. and Kirsop, B. H. (1974). *J. Inst. Brew.* **80**, 48.
Anderson, R. G. and Kirsop, B. H. (1975a). *J. Inst. Brew.* **81**, 111.
Anderson, R. G. and Kirsop, B. H. (1975b). *J. Inst. Brew.* **81**, 296.
Anderson, R. G., Kirsop, B. H., Rennie, H. and Wilson, R. J. H. (1975) *Proc. E.B.C. Congr.*, *Nice* p. 243.
Anderson, R. J. and Howard, G. A. (1974a). *J. Inst. Brew.* **80**, 245.
Anderson, R. J. and Howard, G. A. (1974b). *J. Inst. Brew.* **80**, 357.
Anderson, R. J., Howard, G. A. and Hough, J. S. (1971). *Proc. E.B.C. Congr.*, *Estoril* p. 253.
Anderson, R. J., Clapperton, J. F., Crabb, D. and Hudson, J. R. (1975). *J. Inst. Brew.* **81**, 208.
Antoniani, C. (1961). *Proc. E.B.C. Congr.*, *Vienna* p. 216.
Arkima, V. (1969). *Proc. E.B.C. Congr.*, *Interlaken* p. 507.
Arkima, V. and Sihto, E. (1963). *Proc. E.B.C. Congr.*, *Brussels* p. 268.
Äyräpää, T. (1963). *Proc. E.B.C. Congr.*, *Brussels* p. 276.
Äyräpää, T. (1968). *J. Inst. Brew.* **74**, 169.
Äyräpää, T. (1970). *Brauwissenschaft* **23**, 48.
Äyräpää, T. (1971). *J. Inst. Brew.* **77**, 266.
Äyräpää, T. (1973). *Proc.3 Intern. Spec. Symp. Yeasts, Otaniemi/Helsinki*, Part II, p. 31.
Äyräpää, T. and Lindström, I. (1973). *Proc. E.B.C. Congr.*, *Salzburg* p. 271.
Äyräpää, T., Holmberg, J. and Sellmann-Persson, G. (1961). *Proc. E.B.C. Congr.*, *Vienna* p. 286.

Barrett, J. and Kirsop, B. H. (1971). *J. Inst. Brew.* **77**, 39.

Barrett, J., Griffiths, C. M. and Kirsop, B. H. (1967). *J. Inst. Brew.* **73**, 445.

Bärwald, G. (1967). *Brauwelt* **107**, 1560.

Bärwald, G. (1970). *Monats. Brau.* **23**, 248.

Bärwald, G. (1974). *Brauwelt* **114**, 159.

Bärwald, G., Kesselschläger, J. and Dellweg, H. (1969). *Naturwiss.* **56**, 285.

Bärwald, G., Gübel, H.-J., ten Hompel, U., John, M., Miglio, G. and Niefind, H.-J. (1970). "Einsatz der Gaschromatographie in der gärungsgewerblichen Betriebskontrolle". Sonderdruck Tagesz. Brau.

Bärwald, G., Wellhoener, H. J. and Prucha, J. (1973). *Proc. E.B.C. Congr., Salzburg* p. 197.

Bavisotto, V. S. and Roch, L. A. (1959). *Proc. Ann. Meet. Am. Soc. Brew. Chem.* p. 63.

Bavisotto, V. S., Roch, L. A. and Heinisch, B. (1961). *Proc. Ann. Meet. Am. Soc. Brew. Chem.* p. 16.

Benard, M. and Scriban, R. (1975). *Embouteillage* No. 154, 27.

Blockmans, C., Devreux, A. and Masschelein, C. A. (1975). *Proc. E.B.C. Congr., Nice* p. 699.

Brenner, M. W. and Khan, A. A. (1976). *J. Am. Soc. Brew. Chem.* **34**, 14.

Brenner. M. W. and Laufer, L. (1972). *Proc. Ann. Meet. Am. Soc. Brew. Chem.* p. 98.

Brenner, M. W., Owades, J. L. and Golyzniak, R. (1953). *Proc. Ann. Meet. Am. Soc. Brew. Chem.* p. 83.

Brenner, M. W., Owades, J. L. and Golyzniak, R. (1954a). *Proc. Ann. Meet. Am. Soc. Brew. Chem.* p. 81.

Brenner, M. W., Owades, J. L., Gutcho, M. and Golyzniak, R. (1954b). *Proc. Ann. Meet. Am. Soc. Brew. Chem.* p. 88.

Brenner, M. W., Owades, J. L. and Fazio, T. (1955). *Proc. Ann. Meet. Am. Soc. Brew. Chem.* p. 133.

Brenner, M. W., Blick, S. R., Frenkel, G. and Siebenberg, J. (1963). *Proc. E.B.C. Congr., Brussels* p. 233.

Brenner, M. W., Khan, A. A. and Bernstein, L. (1974). *Proc. Am. Soc. Brew. Chem.* **32**, 82.

Buttery, R. G. and Ling, L. (1966). *Brewers' Digest* **41** (8), 71.

Buttery, R. G., Black, D. R., Lewis, M. J. and Ling, L. (1967). *J. Food Sci.* **32**, 414.

Cabane, B., Ramos-Jeunehomme, C., Lapage, N. and Masschelein, C. A. (1973). *Proc. Ann. Meet. Am. Soc. Brew. Chem.* p. 94.

Chen, E. C.-H. and David, J. J. (1974). *J. Sci. Food Agric.* **25**, 1381.

Clarke, B. J., Harold, F. V., Hildebrand, R. P. and Murray, P. J. (1961). *J. Inst. Brew.* **67**, 529.

Clarke, B. J., Harold, F. V., Hildebrand, R. P. and Morieson, A. S. (1962). *J. Inst. Brew.* **68**, 179.

Coors, J. H., Coe, R. W., Schroedl, D. and Jangaard, N. O. (1974). *Tech. Quart., Master Brewers Ass. Am.* **11**, 71.

Coote, N. and Kirsop, B. H. (1974). *J. Inst. Brew.* **80**, 474.

Coote, N., Kirsop, B. H. and Buckee, G. K. (1973). *J. Inst. Brew.* **79**, 298.

Cowland, T. W. and Maule, D. R. (1966). *J. Inst. Brew.* **72**, 480.

Dadds, M. J. S., Macpherson, A. L. and Sinclair, A. (1971). *J. Inst. Brew.* **77**, 453.

Dadic, M. (1974). *Tech. Quart., Master Brewers Ass. Am.* **11**, 140.

Dadic, M. and Belleau, G. (1975). *Proc. Am. Soc. Brew. Chem.* **33**, 159.

Dadic, M., Van Gheluwe, J. E. A. and Valyi, Z. (1970). *J. Inst. Brew.* **76**, 267.

Dadic, M., Van Gheluwe, J. E. A. and Valyi, Z. (1971). *Wallerstein Lab. Commun.* **34**, 5.

Dalgliesh, C. E. (1974) *Proc. 13th Conv. Aust. Sect. Inst. Brew.* p. 5

Dallos, F. C., Lautenbach, A. F. and West, D. B. (1967). *Proc. Ann. Meet. Am. Soc. Brew. Chem.* p. 103.

Damm, E. and Kringstad, H. (1964). *J. Inst. Brew.* **70**, 38.

DeClerck, E. and Delaunoy, A. (1966). *Bull. Ass. Anciens Etud. Brass., Louvain* **62**, 1.

DeClerck, J. (1934a). *Wschr. Brau.* **51**, 196, 204.

DeClerck, J. (1934b). *Wschr. Brau.* **51**, 213.

Dominguez, X. A. and Canales, A. M. (1974). *Brewers' Digest* **49** (7), 40.

Drawert, F. and Hagen, W. (1970). *Brauwissenschaft* **23**, 300.

Drawert, F. and Tressl, R. (1969). *Brauwissenschaft* **22**, 169.

Drawert, F. and Tressl, R. (1972). *Tech. Quart., Master Brewers Ass. Am.* **9**, 72.

Drewett, K. G., Holliday, A. G. and Laws, D. R. J. (1970). *J. Inst. Brew.* **76**, 153.

Drews, B. and Riemann, J. (1967). *Monats. Brau.* **20**, 254.

Drews, B., Just, F. and Drews, H. (1957). *Proc. E.B.C. Congr., Copenhagen* p. 167.

Drews, B., Specht, H. and Bärwald, G. (1964). *Monats. Brau.* **17**, 101.

Drews, B., Specht, H. and Schwartz, E. (1966a). *Monats. Brau.* **19**, 76.

Drews, B., Specht, H. and Gübel, H.-J. (1966b). *Monats. Brau.* **19**, 145.

Drews, B., Specht, H. and Trénel, G. (1967). *Monats. Brau.* **20**, 149.

Drews, B., Bärwald, G. and Niefind, H.-J. (1969a). *Monats. Brau.* **22**, 140.

Drews, B., Bärwald, G. and Niefind, H.-J. (1969b). *Proc. E.B.C. Congr. Interlaken* p. 419.

Drews, B., Bärwald, G. and Niefind, H.-J. (1969c). *Tech. Quart., Master Brewers Ass. Am.* **6**, 193.

Drost, B. W., Van Eerde, P., Hoekstra, S. F. and Strating, J. (1971). *Proc. E.B.C. Congr. Estoril* p. 451.

Emslander, E. (1937). *Wschr. Brau.* **54**, 65.

Enari, T.-M. (1975). *E.B.C.–Barley and Malting symposium, Zeist*, Monograph-II, p. 146.

Enari, T.-M., Mäkinen, V. and Haikara, A. (1970). *Tech. Quart., Master Brewers Ass. Am.* **7**, 11.

Enebo, L. (1957). *Proc. E.B.C. Congr., Copenhagen* p. 370.

Engan, S. (1969a). *Brygmesteren* **26**, 23.

Engan, S. (1969b). *Brygmesteren* **26**, 279.

Engan, S. (1969c). *J. Inst. Brew.* **75**, 371.

Engan, S. (1970). *J. Inst. Brew.* **76**, 254.

Engan, S. (1972a). *J. Inst. Brew.* **78**, 169.

Engan, S. (1972b). *Brygmesteren* **29**, 313.

Engan, S. (1972c). *Beretn. 16. Skandin. Bryggeritekn. Møde, Copenhagen*, p. 169.

Engan, S. (1973a). *Brygmesteren* **30**, 41.

Engan, S. (1973b). *Brygmesteren* **30**, 177.

Engan, S. (1974). *Brewers' Digest* **49** (8), 52.

Engan, S. (1975a). *Brygmesteren* **32**, 107.

Engan, S. (1975b). *Brewers' Digest* **50** (4), 65.

Engan, S. and Aubert, O. (1971). *Proc. E.B.C. Congr., Estoril* p. 407.

Engan, S. and Aubert, O. (1973). *Proc. E.B.C. Congr., Salzburg* p. 209.

Engan, S. and Aubert, O. (1977). *Proc. E.B.C. Congr. Amsterdam*, p. 591.

Fantozzi, P. (1970). *Birra e Malto* **17**, 217 (abstr. *J. Inst. Brew.* (1970). **76**, 578).

Forch, M., Krauss, G. and Proksch, H. (1975). *Proc. Am. Soc. Brew. Chem.* **33**, 148.

Gehlhoff, R. and Piendl, A. (1974). *Brauwissenschaft* **27**, 305.

Geiger, E. and Piendl, A. (1975a). *Proc. Am. Soc. Brew. Chem.* **33**, 48.

Geiger, E. and Piendl, A. (1975b). *Brewers' Digest* **50** (8), 50.

Geiger, E. and Piendl, A. (1976). *Brauerei-J*. p. 13.

Gombert, J. (1975). *Brauwelt* **115**, 598.

Grigsby, J. H., Palamand, S. R., Davis, D. P. and Hardwick, W. A. (1972). *Proc. Ann. Meet. Am. Soc. brew. Chem.* p. 87.

Haboucha, J., Masschelein, C. A. and Devreux, A. (1967). *Proc. E.B.C. Congr., Madrid* p. 197.

Harold, F. V., Hildebrand, R. P., Morrieson, A. S. and Murray, P. J. (1961a). *J. Inst. Brew.* **67**, 161.

Harold, F. V., Hildebrand, R. P. and Morrieson, P. J. (1961b). *J. Inst. Brew.* **67**, 172.

Harrison, G. A. F. (1963). *Proc. E.B.C. Congr., Brussels* p. 247.

Harrison, G. A. F. (1967). *Brewers Digest* **42** (6), 74.

Harrison, G. A. F. (1970). *J. Inst. Brew.* **76**, 486.

Harrison, G. A. F. and Collins, E. (1968). *Proc. Ann. Meet. Am. Soc. Brew. Chem.* p. 101.

Hashimoto, N. (1966). *Rep. Res. Lab. Kirin Brewing Co., Yokahama* **9**, 1.

Hashimoto, N. (1972). *J. Inst. Brew.* **78**, 43.

Hashimoto, N. (1974). *Tech. Quart., Master Brewers Ass. Am.* **11**, 121.

Hashimoto, N. (1975). *Koryo*, No. 112, 23.

Hashimoto, N. and Kuroiwa, Y. (1966). *Proc. Ann. Meet. Am. Soc. Brew. Chem.* p. 121.

Hashimoto, N. and Kuroiwa, Y. (1972). *Brewers' Digest* **47** (8), 64.

Hashimoto, N. and Kuroiwa, Y. (1975). *Proc. Am. Soc. Brew. Chem.* **33**, 104.

Hashimoto, N., Kuroiwa, Y. and Aramaki, K. (1968). *Proc.10th Conv. Aust. Sect. Inst. Brew.* p. 1.

Hashimoto, N., Kuroiwa, Y. and Sogawa, H. (1969). *Rep. Res. Lab. Kirin Brewing Co., Yokahama* **12**, 57.

Haukeli, A. D. and Lie, S. (1971). *J. Inst. Brew.* **77**, 538.

Haukeli, A. D. and Lie, S. (1972). *J. Inst. Brew.* **78**, 229.

Haukeli, A. D., Engan, S. and Lie, S. (1971). *Brygmesteren* **28**, 269.

Haukeli, A. D., Jacobsen, T. and Lie, S. (1973). *Tech. Quart., Master Brewers Ass. Am.* **10**, 47.

Hodge, J. E. (1967). *In* "Chemistry and Physiology of Flavours" (H. W. Schultz, E. A. Day and L. M. Libbey, eds.), p. 465. Avi Publ. Co. Inc., Westport, Conn.

Hough, J. S. and Stevens, R. (1961). *J. Inst. Brew.* **67**, 488.

Hough, J. S., Briggs, D. E. and Stevens, R. (1971). "Malting and Brewing Science", p. 460. Chapman and Hall, London.

Howard, D. and Anderson, R. G. (1976). *J. Inst. Brew.* **82**, 70.

Howard, G. A. and Slater, C. A. (1957). *J. Inst. Brew.* **63**, 126.

Hrdlicka, J., Dyr, J. and Kubicková, K. (1964). *Brauwissenschaft* **17**, 373.

Hrdlicka, J., Dyr, J. and Jely, E. (1968). *Brauwissenschaft* **21**, 333.

Hrdlicka, J., Dyr, J. and Semerád, O. (1970). Scientific Papers Inst Chem Technol. Prague. *Food*, **E28**, 79.

Inoue, T. (1974). *Rep. Res. Lab. Kirin Brewing Co., Yokohama* **17**, 25.

Inoue, T. and Yamamoto, Y. (1969). *Arch. Biochem. Biophys.* **135**, 454.

Inoue, T. and Yamamoto, Y. (1970). *Proc. Ann. Meet. Am. Soc. Brew. Chem.* p. 198.

Inoue, T., Masuyama, K., Yamamoto, Y., Okada, K. and Kuroiwa, Y. (1968). *Proc. Ann. Meet. Am. Soc. Brew. Chem.* p. 158.

Jamieson, A. M. and Van Gheluwe, J. E. A. (1970). *Proc. Ann. Meet. Am. Soc. Brew. Chem.* p. 192.

Jangaard, N. O., Gress, H. S. and Coe, R. W. (1973). *Proc. Ann. Meet. Am. Soc. Brew. Chem.* p. 46.

Jansen, H. E., Strating, J. and Westra, W. M. (1971). *J. Inst. Brew.* **77**, 154.

Jenard, H. and Devreux, A. (1964). *Echo Brass*. **20**, 1119.
Jones, M. (1974). *E.B.C. Wort Symposium, Zeist*, Monograph-I, p. 90.
Jones, M. and Pierce, J. S. (1963). *Proc. E.B.C. Congr., Brussels* p. 101.
Jones, M. and Pierce, J. S. (1967). *J. Inst. Brew.* **73**, 343.
Jones, M. and Pierce, J. S. (1969). *Proc. E.B.C. Congr., Interlaken* p. 151.
Jones, M., Pragnell, M. J. and Pierce, J. S. (1969). *J. Inst. Brew.* **75**, 520.
Jones, M. O., Cope, R. and Rainbow, C. (1975). *Proc. E.B.C. Congr., Nice* p. 669.
Jost, P. and Piendl, A. (1976). *J. Am. Soc. Brew. Chem.* **34**, 31.
Kahn, J. H. (1969). *J. A.O.A.C.* **52**, 1166.
Kamiyama, S. and Nakagawa, A. (1968). *Brewers' Digest* **43** (2), 60.
Kavanagh, T. E., Steward, S. R., Hildebrand, R. P., Clarke, B. J. and Meeker, F. J. (1975). *J. Inst. Brew.* **81**, 322.
Kieninger, H. and Bikova, V. (1975). *Brauwelt* **115**, 1250.
Kirsop, B. H., Griffiths, C. M. and Barrett, J. (1967). *Proc. E.B.C. Congr., Madrid* p. 219.
Kitabatake, K. and Amaha, M. (1968). *Bull. Brew. Sci., Tokyo* **14**, 17.
Kleber, W. and Lampl, P. (1957). *Proc. E.B.C. Congr., Copenhagen* p. 377.
Klopper, W. J. (1973). *Brauwissenschaft* **26**, 109.
Klopper, W. J., Tuning, B. and Vermeire, H. A. (1975). *Proc. E.B.C. Congr., Nice* p. 659.
Koike, K., Hashimoto, N., Kitami, H. and Okada, K. (1972). *Rep. Res. Lab. Kirin Brewing Co., Yokahama* **15**, 25.
Komoda, H. and Yamada, M. (1967). *J. Agric. Chem. Soc. Japan* **41**, 51.
Krauss, G. and Forch, M. (1975). *Proc. Am. Soc. Brew. Chem.* **33**, 37.
Krauss, G., Zürcher, C. and Holstein, H. (1972). *Monats. Brau.* **25**, 113.
Krauss, G., Forch, M. and Holstein, H. (1975). *Monats. Brau.* **28**, 229.
Kringstad, H. (1972). *Brauwissenschaft* **25**, 272.
Krüger, E. (1969). *Monats. Brau.* **21**, 155.
Kunitake, N. (1967). *Bull. Brew. Sci., Tokyo* **13**, 7.
Kuroiwa, Y. and Hashimoto, N. (1961). *Agric. Biol. Chem. Japan* **25**, 257 (abstr. *Wallerstein Lab. Commun.* (1961). **24**, 342).
Kuroiwa, Y. and Hashimoto, N. (1970). *Brewers' Digest* **45** (5), 44.
Latimer, R. A., Glenister, P. R., Koepple, K. G. and Dallos, F. C. (1969). *Tech. Quart., Master Brewers Ass. Am.* **6**, 24.
Lau, V. K. and Lindsay, R. C. (1972). *Tech. Quart., Master Brewers Ass. Am.* **9** (1), xvii.
Lawrence, W. C. (1964). *Wallerstein Lab. Commun.* **27**, 123.
Lie, S. and Haukeli, A. D. (1973). *Proc. E.B.C. Congr., Salzburg*, p. 285.
Liebs, P., Krüger, M. and Wolter, H.-C. (1970). *Nahrung* **14**, 33.
Lüers, H. and Leiss, F. (1933). *Wschr. Brau.* **50**, 373, 381.
MacPherson, J. K. and Buckee, G. K. (1974). *J. Inst. Brew.* **80**, 540.
Mäkinen, V. (1971). Thesis, State Inst. Techn. Res., Helsinki, Publ. no. 162.
Mäkinen, V. and Enari, T.-M. (1969). *Brewers' Digest* **44** (5), 42.
Mändl, B., Wullinger, F., Fischer, A. and Piendl, A. (1969). *Brauwissenschaft* **22**, 278.
Mändl, B., Wullinger, F., Fischer, A. and Piendl, A. (1970). *Brauwissenschaft* **23**, 11.
Mändl, B., Wullinger, F., Wagner, D., Binder, W. and Piendl, A. (1972). *Brewers' Digest* **47** (1), 74.
Mändl, B., Geiger, E. and Piendl, A. (1974). *Brauwissenschaft* **27**, 57.
Mändl, B., Geiger, E. and Piendl, A. (1975). *Proc. E.B.C. Congr., Nice* p. 539.
Marinelli, L., Feil, M. F. and Schait, A. (1968). *Proc. Ann. Meet. Am. Soc. Brew. Chem.* p. 113.
Markham, E. (1969). *Wallerstein Lab. Commun.* **32**, 5.
Markl, K. S. and Palamand, S. R. (1973). *Tech. Quart., Master Brewers Ass. Am.* **10**, 184.

Masschelein, C. A., Ramos-Jeunehomme, C. and Devreux, A. (1961). *Proc. E.B.C. Congr., Vienna* p. 148.

Masschelein, C. A., Jenard, H., Jeunehomme-Ramos, C. and Devreux, A. (1965). *Proc. E.B.C. Congr., Stockholm* p. 209.

Maule, D. R. (1967). *J. Inst. Brew.* **73**, 351.

McDougall, J., Shada, J. D. and Dakin, P. E. (1963). *Proc. Ann. Meet. Am. Soc. Brew. Chem.* p. 48.

McFarlane, W. D. (1973). *Tech. Quart., Master Brewers Ass. Am.* **10** (3), xxix.

McFarlane, W. D. and Thompson, K. D. (1964). *J. Inst. Brew.* **70**, 497.

Meilgaard, M. (1972). *Brewers' Digest* **47** (4), 48.

Meilgaard, M. C. (1976). *Tech. Quart., Master Brewers Ass. Am.* **13**, 78.

Meilgaard, M. and Moya, E. (1970). *Tech. Quart., Master Brewers Ass. Am.* **7**, 135.

Meilgaard, M., Elizondo, A. and Mackinney, A. (1971a). *Wallerstein Lab. Commun.* **34**, 95.

Meilgaard, M., Aymá, M. and Ruano, J. I. (1971b). *Proc. Ann. Meet. Am. Soc. Brew. Chem.* p. 219.

Miedaner, H., Narziss, L. and Wörner, G. (1974). *Brauwissenschaft* **27**, 208.

Mincione, B., Di Fiore, R., Di Matteo, M., Scudiero, A. and Musso, S. S. (1973). *Industrie Agrarie* **11**, 387 (abstr. *J. Inst. Brew.* (1975). **81**, 138).

Narziss, L. (1972). "Abriss der Bierbrauerei", 3 Aufl. Ferdinand Enke Verlag, Stuttgart.

Narziss, L. and Miedaner, H. (1970a). *Brauwissenschaft* **23**, 121.

Narziss, L. and Miedaner, H. (1970b). *Brauwissenschaft* **23**, 185.

Nickerson, G. B. and Likens, S. T. (1966). *J. Chromatogr.* **21**, 1.

Niefind, H. J. and Späth, G. (1971). *Proc. E.B.C. Congr., Estoril* p. 459.

Niefind, H. J. and Späth, G. (1973). *Proc. E.B.C. Congr., Salzburg* p. 297.

Niefind, H. J. and Späth, G. (1975a). *Proc. Am. Soc. Brew. Chem.* **33**, 54.

Niefind, H. J. and Späth, G. (1975b). *Proc. E.B.C. Congr., Nice* p. 97.

Nordström, K. (1964a). *Svensk Kem. Tidskr.* **76**, 510.

Nordström, K. (1964b). *J. Inst. Brew.* **70**, 42.

Nordström, K. (1964c). *J. Inst. Brew.* **70**, 209.

Nordström, K. (1965a). *Proc. E.B.C. Congr., Stockholm* p. 195.

Nordström, K. (1965b). *Brewers' Digest* **40** (11), 60.

Nordström, K. (1968). *J. Inst. Brew.* **74**, 192.

Norstedt, C., Bengtsson, A., Bennet, P., Lindström, I. and Äyräpää, T. (1975). *Proc. E.B.C. Congr., Nice* p. 581.

Nykänen, L., Puputti, E. and Suomalainen, H. (1966). *J. Inst. Brew.* **72**, 24.

Otter, G. E. and Taylor, L. (1971). *J. Inst. Brew.* **77**, 467.

Pajunen, E. and Mäkinen, V. (1975). *Proc. E.B.C. Congr., Nice* p. 525.

Palamand, S. R. and Grigsby, J. H. (1974). *Brewers' Digest* **49** (9), 58.

Palamand, S. R., Hardwick, W. A. and Markl, K. S. (1969). *Proc. Ann. Meet. Am. Soc. Brew. Chem.* p. 54.

Palamand, S. R., Nelson, G. D. and Hardwick, W. A. (1970a). *Tech. Quart., Master Brewers Ass. Am.* **7**, 111.

Palamand, S. R., Nelson, G. D. and Hardwick, W. A. (1970b). *Proc. Ann. Meet. Am. Soc. Brew. Chem.* p. 186.

Palamand, S. R., Davis, D. P. and Hardwick, W. A. (1970c). *Tech. Quart., Master Brewers Ass. Am.* **7** (4), xv.

Palamand, S. R., Markl, K. S. and Hardwick, W. A. (1971). *Proc. Ann. Meet. Am. Soc. Brew. Chem.* p. 211.

Palamand, S. R., Grigsby, J. H., Davis, D. P. and Hardwick, W. A. (1973). *Proc. Ann. Meet. Am. Soc. Brew. Chem.* p. 132.

Palmer, A. K. and Rennie, H. (1974). *J. Inst. Brew.* **80**, 447.

Parker, W. E. and Richardson, P. J. (1970). *J. Inst. Brew.* **76**, 191.

Pessa, E. (1971). *Proc. E.B.C. Congr., Estoril* p. 333.

Pfenninger, H. B. (1963). *Proc. E.B.C. Congr., Brussels* p. 257.

Pickett, J. A., Coates, J., Peppard, T. L. and Sharpe, F. R. (1976). *J. Inst. Brew.* **82**, 233.

Piendl, A. (1973). *Brauwissenschaft* **26**, 141.

Pierce, J. S. (1966). *Process Biochem.* **2**, 412.

Pollock, J. R. A. and Weir, M. J. (1973). *Proc. Ann. Meet. Am. Soc. Brew. Chem.* p. 1.

Pollock, J. R. A. and Weir, M. J. (1976). *J. Am. Soc. Brew. Chem.* **34**, 70.

Portno, A. D. (1970). *Wallerstein Lab. Commun.* **33**, 149.

Postel, W., Drawert, F. and Adam, L. (1972). *Chem. Mikrobiol. Technol. Lebensm.* **1**, 169.

Rapp, A., Steffan, H., Hastrich, H. and Ullemeyer, H. (1975). Mitteilungsbl. GDCh-Fachgr. *Lebensm. Chem. Gerichtl. Chem.* **29**, 33.

Richardson, P. J. and Mocek, M. (1971). *Proc. Ann. Meet. Am. Soc. Brew. Chem.* p. 128.

Ricketts, J. and Coutts, M. W. (1951). *Am. Brewer* **84** (8), 7; (9) 27; (10) 33.

Riemann, J. and Scheibe, E. (1969). *Brauwelt* **109**, 1074.

Rosculet, G. (1969). *Proc. Ann. Meet. Am. Soc. Brew. Chem.* p. 127.

Rosculet, G. (1970). *Brewers' Digest* **45** (4), 64.

Rosculet, G. (1971). *Brewers' Digest* **46** (6), 68.

Rosculet, G. and Rickard, M. (1968). *Proc. Ann. Meet. Am. Soc. Brew. Chem.* p. 203.

Saha, R. B. and Middelkauff, J. E. (1970). *Proc. Ann. Meet. Am. Soc. Brew. Chem.* p. 176.

Sandegren, E. and Enebo, L. (1961). *Wallerstein Lab. Commun.* **24**, 269.

Sandra, P. and Verzele, M. (1975a). *J. Inst. Brew.* **81**, 302.

Sandra, P. and Verzele, M. (1975b). *Proc. E.B.C. Congr., Nice* p. 107.

Scherrer, A. (1971). *Schweiz. Brau-Runds.* **82**, 21.

Schild, E. and Zacherl, R. (1965). *Brauwissenschaft* **18**, 321.

Schreier, P., Drawert, F. and Junker, A. (1974). *Brauwissenschaft* **27**, 205.

Schreier, P., Drawert, F. and Junker, A. (1975). *Brauwissenschaft* **28**, 73.

Shimazu, T., Hashimoto, N. and Kuroiwa, Y. (1975). *Proc. Am. Soc. Brew. Chem.* **33**, 7.

Silbereisen, K., Krüger, E. and Baron, G. (1970). *Monats. Brau.* **23**, 93.

Sinclair, A., Hall, R. D. and Burns, D. T. (1969). *Proc. E.B.C. Congr. Interlaken* p. 427.

Sinclair, A., Hall, R. D., Burns, D. T. and Hayes, W. P. (1970). *J. Sci. Food Agric.* **21**, 468.

Slaughter, J. C. (1970). *J. Inst. Brew.* **76**, 22.

Slaughter, J. C. and Uvgaard, A. R. A. (1971). *J. Inst. Brew.* **77**, 446.

Slaughter, J. C. and Uvgaard, A. R. A. (1972). *J. Inst. Brew.* **78**, 322.

Sommer, G. (1969). *Monats. Brau.* **22**, 183.

Sommer, G. (1975). *Tagesz. Brau.* **72**, 468.

Späth, G., Niefind, H. J. and Martina, M. (1972). *Monats. Brau.* **25**, 91.

Späth, G., Niefind, H. J. and Martina, M. (1975). *Monats. Brau.* **28**, 73.

Spence, L. R., Palamand, S. R. and Hardwick, W. A. (1973). *Tech. Quart., Master Brewers Ass. Am.* **10**, 127.

Steffen, P., Beubler, A. and Dickscheit, R. (1971). *Nahrung* **15**, 71.

Steiner, K. (1968). *Schweiz. Brau.-Runds.* **79**, 176.

Stenroos, L. E. (1973). *Proc. Ann. Meet. Am. Soc. Brew. Chem.* p. 50.

Strating, J. and Van Eerde, P. (1973). *J. Inst. Brew.* **79**, 414.

Suomalainen, H. and Keränen, A. J. A. (1968). *Chem. Phys. Lipids* **2**, 296.

Suomalainen, H. and Nykänen, L. (1972). *Wallerstein Lab. Commun.* **35**, 185.

Suomalainen, H. and Ronkainen, P. (1968). *Nature, London* **220**, 792.

Szlavko, C. M. (1973a). *J. Inst. Brew.* **79**, 283.

Szlavko, C. M. (1973b). *J. Inst. Brew.* **79**, 450.

Szlavko, C. M. (1974). *J. Inst. Brew.* **80**, 534.

Szlavko, C. M. and Worrall, R. J. (1975). *J. Inst. Brew.* **81**, 438.

Thalacker, R. (1975). Mitteilungsbl. GDCh-Fachgr. *Lebensm. Chem. Gerichtl. Chem.* **29**, 129.

Thalacker, R. and Ihring, H. H. (1973). *Monats. Brau.* **26**, 62.

Thalacker, R., Ihring, H. H., Muskat, E. and Wagner, B. (1974). *Monats. Brau.* **27**, 166.

Thorne, R. S. W. (1950). *Wallerstein Lab. Commun.* **13**, 319.

Thorne, R. S. W. (1966). *Tech. Quart., Master Brewers Ass. Am.* **3**, 160.

Thoss, G. (1966). *Brauwelt* **106**, 1777.

Trachman, H. and Saletan, L. T. (1969). *Proc. Ann. Meet. Am. Soc. Brew. Chem.* p. 19.

Tressl, R. (1975). *Brauwelt* **115**, 404.

Tressl, R. and Renner, R. (1975). *Monats. Brau.* **28**, 195.

Tressl, R. and Friese, L. (1976). *5th Intern. Ferm. Symp., Berlin, Abstr. of Papers* p. 381.

Tressl, R., Kossa, T. and Renner, R. (1974). *Monats. Brau.* **27**, 98.

Tressl, R., Holzer, M. and Neumann, L. (1975a). *Monats. Brau.* **28**, 45.

Tressl, R., Kossa, T., Renner, R. and Köppler, H. (1975b). *Monats. Brau.* **28**, 109.

Tressl, R., Kossa, T. and Renner, R. (1975c). *Proc. E.B.C. Congr., Nice* p. 737.

Tripp, R. C., Timm, B., Iyer, M., Richardson, T. and Amundson, C. H. (1968). *Proc. Ann. Meet. Am. Soc. Brew. Chem.* p. 65.

Van der Kloot, A. P. and Wilcox, F. A. (1960). *Proc. Ann. Meet. Am. Soc. Brew. Chem.* p. 113.

Van Gheluwe, J. E. A. and Valyi, Z. (1974). *Tech. Quart., Master Brewers Ass. Am.* **11**, 184.

Van Gheluwe, J. E. A., Valyi, Z. and Dadic, M. (1970). *Brewers' Digest* **45** (11), 70.

Verzele, M., Jansen, H. E. and Ferdinandus, A. (1970). *J. Inst. Brew.* **76**, 25.

Visser, M. K. and Lindsay, R. C. (1971a). *Tech. Quart., Master Brewers Ass. Am.* **8**, 123.

Visser, M. K. and Lindsay, R. C. (1971b). *Proc. Ann. Meet. Am. Soc. Brew. Chem.* p. 230.

Voerkelius, G. A. (1961). *Brauwissenschaft* **14**, 389.

Voerkelius, G. A. (1966). *Brauwissenschaft* **19**, 434.

Vogel, R., Schievelbein, H. and Eckert, T. (1962). *Brauwissenschaft* **15**, 242.

Wackerbauer, K. (1969). *Monats. Brau.* **22**, 211.

Wagner, B. (1971). *Monats. Brau.* **24**, 285.

Wainwright, T. (1970). *Proc. Ann. Meet. Am. Soc. Brew. Chem.* p. 127.

Wainwright, T. (1971). *J. Appl. Bact.* **34**, 161.

Wainwright, T. (1973). *J. Inst. Brew.* **79**, 451.

Wainwright, T. (1974). *The Brewer* **60**, 638.

Wanderscheck, H. (1928). *Wschr. Brau.* **15**, 441, 463.

Wang, P. S. and Siebert, K. J. (1974a). *Tech. Quart., Master Brewers Ass. Am.* **11**, 110.

Wang, P. S. and Siebart, K. J. (1974b). *Proc. Am. Soc. Brew. Chem.* **32**, 47.

Weinfurtner, F., Wullinger, F., Piendl, A. and Wagner, D. (1967). *Brauwelt* **107**, 671.

Wellhoener, H. J. (1966). *Brauwelt* **106**, 813.

West, D. B., Lautenbach, A. F. and Brumsted, D. D. (1963). *Proc. Ann. Meet. Am. Soc. Brew. Chem.* p. 194.

Wheeler, R. E., Pragnell, M. J. and Pierce, J. S. (1971). *Proc. E.B.C. Congr. Estoril* p. 423.

White, F. H. and Parsons, R. (1975). *Proc. E.B.C. Congr., Nice* p. 721.

White, F. H. and Wainwright, T. (1975a). *J. Inst. Brew.* **81**, 37.

White, F. H. and Wainwright, T. (1975b). *J. Inst. Brew.* **81**, 46.
White, F. H. and Wainwright, T. (1976). *J. Inst. Brew.* **82**, 46.
Whiting, G. C. (1976). *J. Inst. Brew.* **82**, 84.
Wohleb, R., Jennings, W. G. and Lewis, M. J. (1972). *Proc. Ann. Meet. Soc. Brew. Chem.* p. 1.
Wucherpfennig, K. and Semmler, G. (1972a). *Z. Lebensm. Unters. Forsch.* **148**, 77.
Wucherpfennig, K. and Semmler, G. (1972b). *Z. Lebensm. Unters. Forsch.* **148**, 137.
Wucherpfennig, K. and Semmler, G. (1972c). *Weinwissenschaft* **27**, 193.
Zenz, H. (1970). *Mitt. Versuchsst. Gärungsgew., Wien* **24**, 47.
Zenz, H. (1972). *Mitt. Versuchsst. Gärungsgew., Wien* **26**, 188.
Zürcher, C. and Krauss, G. (1971). *Monats. Brau.* **24**, 230.

4. Involatile Constituents of Beer

GEORGE CHARALAMBOUS

Technical Center, Anheuser-Busch Inc., St. Louis, Missouri, U.S.A.

I. INORGANIC COMPOUNDS OF BEER

A. General Introduction

The range of inorganic compounds in beer can vary from half a gram to two grams per litre of beer (500–2000 p.p.m.) and it has been established that these minerals, which include major cations, trace metals and anions, influence both the taste and the clarity of the finished beer. For example, the taste and flavour of the beer is dependent upon the quantity of chloride (fullness of flavour); of sulphate (dryness of flavour); of carbonate (a variety of flavour effects); sodium (important in overall beer flavour); magnesium (disagreeable flavour); as for iron, lead, copper, zinc, tin—all may potentiate haze formation in beer. Moll (1972) has reviewed comprehensively the influence of various ions on beer taste. On the positive side, beer minerals comprise a well-equilibrated mixture from the nutritional point of view. All of them, and especially phosphorus, are present in a readily available form and at a useful level of concentration. The high potassium to sodium ratio (10 to 1) leads to a desirable body tissue dehydration, and makes beer the preferred beverage in low-sodium diets, according to Saletan (1959).

It is axiomatic that, as with any other constituents of beer, the inorganic compounds in it must originate from the materials used in its brewing. Also, under certain conditions, brewing plant construction materials can make a contribution. Processing and packaging are, in addition, responsible for modifying the final content of inorganic compounds in the finished product.

B. Factors affecting the Inorganic Compounds Content of Beer

Mändl (1974) enumerates the factors influencing the mineral content of wort as follows: barley variety, climate, fertilizers, malting facilities, mashing procedure and pesticides in respect to barley. In regard to the mineral content of beer, the following factors will be discussed.

1. Raw Materials

(a) *Grains*

A knowledge of the mineral composition of cereals is important because it makes possible an estimate of the contributions of such soluble components as chloride to the wort and beer. According to Piendl (1973), however, malt is a minor contributor; also, it should be remembered that much variation exists in the proportion of the various types of adjuncts employed in brewing. Table 1 shows detailed mineral compositions of certain cereals, including the man-made cereal triticale (a hybrid of rye and wheat).

TABLE 1. Mineral composition, cereal grains

	Calcium	Phosphorus	Potassium	Magnesium	Iron	Copper	Manganese	Sodium	Sulphur	Chlorine	Cobalt	Zinc	Iodine (µg/kg)	Ash (%)
Barley grain	300–4100	2000–9200	4900–9900	100–2300	40–100	1.3–20.0	2.4–30.0	100–600	1000–3500	900–1700	0.000–0.32	11.9–20.9		2.7
Corn grain	100–3500	300–13 000	300–9200	200–9200	10–100	0.9–9.0	0.0–14.0	0–1300	100–1900	200–1000	0.002–0.3	11.4–26.9	0.06–0.7	1.2
Millet grain	100–1300	2000–3900	4800	1800	40–50	24.0	9.0–92.7	400	1400	1600	0.048	12.0–19.1		
Oats grain	400–4800	2900–5300	2200–8900	300–2900	20–80	2.4–13.0	20.0–203.7	100–1600	1500–3100	500–1900	0.000–0.32	11.9–18.9		3.4
Sorghum grain	100–3700	1000–5200	2800–5000	200–2500	20–180	2.0–19.1	7.9–27.31	100–900	1500–2100	700–1400	0.04–0.73	11.9–18.9		2.2
Rice grain, brewers without hulls	100–500	1200–2600	1000–2000	400–800	10–100	4.4–5.1	4.4–5.3	300–600	100–1100	200–900		2.0		0.6
Wheat grain	100–4100	800–6800	3100–7900	1000–3500	10–120	1.1–16.7	3.9–85.9	0–2200	1200–3200	300–1800	0.05–0.15	11.9–18.9		1.8
Rye grain	100–1200	1800–5300	3700–6400	900–1700	40–120	5.9–11.0	29–156.8	0–500	1300–2100	100–700		11.9–46.9		2.5
Triticale 72-S, 1975 Crop	<500	4020	5430	1370	50	7.5	59.7	<100			0.005	46.0		2.0

Sources: (1) "Composition of Cereal Grains and Forages", 1958 National Academy of Sciences, National Research Council, Washington, D.C. Publication No. 585. (2) "Atlas of Nutritional Data on United States and Canadian Feeds", 1971 National Academy of Sciences, Washington, D.C. (3) Triticale Analysis: G. Charalambous, unpublished.

Note: All values are on a moisture-free basis and expressed in milligrams per kilogram.

(b) *Water*

Potable water, suitable for brewing liquor, is subject to strict controls to ensure its acceptability (see Chapter 7, Vol. 1.). Willey (1976) mentions that sparkling clear, pure water is perhaps the most bland, essentially tasteless beverage known to man. However, the geology of water supplies and the pollutionary changes resulting from domestic and industrial discharges have led to the necessity of careful treatment of the raw water sources available.

Water purity depends on biological and non-biological factors. The concern here is with the latter, that is the inorganic compounds which end up in the finished beer. Except for a minor contribution from malt, their main derivation is from the original brewing water (ground or well waters versus surface water) and from its subsequent treatment. The latter includes deionization or softening procedures, other treatments to check scale formation, and the addition of acid or lime for alkalinity control. The range of 500–2000 mg of inorganic compounds that may be found in a litre of beer of various origins reflects the wide variety of brewing waters employed in different parts of the world.

Table 2 provides a general mineral analysis of water in the U.S.A. (1976). Table 3 provides a general mineral analysis of water in Canada (1976). Table 4 provides a general mineral analysis of water in p.p.m. in South America, South Africa, Mexico and Australia (1976). Table 5 provides an analysis of water supplies for a Tokyo brewery (January–October 1976).

(c) *Deliberate additions*

(i) *"Burtonization"*. This process involves the addition to water by many brewers of salts (usually calcium or magnesium sulphate and sodium or calcium chloride). The addition of calcium sulphate to the brewing water results, among other things, in the precipitation of phosphates during mashing. Phosphates precipitate assisting in lowering the wort pH.

The presence of calcium carried through to beer aids yeast flocculation and causes oxalate to separate in the form of crystalline calcium oxalate. (The aim is a final concentration of 60–80 mg calcium per litre of beer.)

Since there is much variability in both raw materials and in brewing methods, some special interest attaches to the calcium content of beer, as shown in Table 6. A considerable number of U.S.A. beers analysed over a period of ten years showed a high of 110 p.p.m., a low of 26 p.p.m., the average being 66 p.p.m. The distribution of values was as follows:

> 0– 30 p.p.m. calcium: 4·3%
> 31– 60 p.p.m. calcium: 35·8%
> 61– 90 p.p.m. calcium: 47·6%
> 91–120 p.p.m. calcium: 12·3%

TABLE 2. General mineral analysis of water, U.S.A.

	East		West	
	A	B	A	B
Sodium	2–38	6–10	10–165	16–44
Potassium	0·3–3·3	0·1–0·5	1·3–4·0	1–2
Calcium	7–56	4–13	2–84	5–22
Magnesium	0·5–22	1–5	1–28	3–10
Iron	0·02–0·05	0–0·03	0·02–0·06	0–0·04
Manganese	0·01–0·02	0–0·01	0·01–0·02	0–0·01
Aluminium	0·4–3·2	1–3	0·4–3·2	2–3
Nitrate	Trace–5·4	1–5	Trace–5·4	2·4
Chloride	14–82	6–16	20–47	4–8
Sulphate	9–80	3–17	20–181	7–113
Phosphate	<0·05–5·0	0–4	<0·05–4·0	0–3·95
Silica	2–29	3–12	5–23	8–14
Total dissolved solids	89–400	10–37	195–260	40–182
Total hardness	36–230	6–26	8–314	24–76
Total alkalinity	17–141	5–20	37–250	21–39

Sources: G. Charalambous, unpublished; Schlitz Brewing Company; Industrial Utility of Public Water Supplies in the United States.

Notes: (1) All values are in mg/l for city waters. (2) Figures under East represent ranges for the calendar year 1975 from six representative brewing centres east of the Mississippi. (3) Figures under West are same as for East except west of the Mississippi. (4) *A* figures are ranges from twelve-monthly composite samples made up of equal portions taken each working day. *B* figures are minimum and maximum variations over the calendar year 1975 for all six cities.

In addition, a variety of market-fresh beers from the last quarter of 1976 were found by atomic absorption spectrophotometry (Anheuser-Busch files) to contain the following amounts of calcium in mg/litre.

U.S.A. beers: 13·0; 24·5; 26·0; 26·5; 26·5; 30·0; 33·0; 36·0; 38·0; 39·0
Canadian beers: 35·0; 36·5
German beers: 8·0; 8·0; 9·0
(all light specials)
Danish beers: 16·5
Japanese beers: 5·0

Additional values are quoted in Table 6, which summarizes salient data of ions in finished beer.

A recent publication by Pomeranz (1976) presents a survey of the sequential changes in, and the fate of minerals during, the transformation of brewing raw materials into beer.

TABLE 3. General mineral analysis of water, Canada

	East		West	
	A	B	A	B
Sodium	5–15	1–2	1–3	1–2
Potassium	0–2	0·5–1	0–2	0–2
Calcium	0–42	1–4	0–26	2–6
Magnesium	0–9	0·5–2	0–8	0–1
Iron	0–0·15	0·01–0·09	0·02–0·26	0·01–0·09
Copper	0	—	0–0·08	0–0·08
Nitrate	0–1·70	0·10–0·70	0–1·50	0·05–1·10
Nitrite	0–0·01	0·01	0–0·03	0·01–0·02
Chloride	10–41	1·0–10·0	0–14·0	1·0–7·0
Sulphate	0–35	2–12	0–2·0	0–2·0
pH	6·45–8·60	0·15–1·50	6·15–8·00	0·02–1·60
Total hardness	0–142	2–20	2–93	2–21

Sources: Molson Breweries of Canada Limited; Moosehead Breweries Limited.
Notes: (1) All values are in mg/l for city waters. (2) Figures under East indicate ranges for the calendar year 1975 from representative brewing centres in the provinces of Ontario, Quebec and Newfoundland. (3) Figures under West indicate ranges for the calendar year 1975 from representative brewing centres in the provinces of Manitoba and British Columbia. (4) Same as note (4) in Table 2 for U.S.A. water analyses. (5) Newfoundland water; total hardness, zero p.p.m.
In summary, Newfoundland water: zero p.p.m.—total hardness ($CaCO_3$), zero p.p.m.—SO_4^{2-}, zero p.p.m.—K^+, 7 p.p.m.—Na^+, 12 p.p.m.—Cl^-, and 7·0 p.p.m.—pH.

(ii) *Addition of metabisulphite.* When yeast ferments wort, undesirable acetaldehyde produced by the decarboxylation of pyruvic acid may be removed by adding bisulphite ions, which form an aldehyde–bisulphite complex. Elimination of acetaldehyde prevents its acting as a hydrogen acceptor for NADH. Potassium metabisulphite is sometimes added after fermentation as an antioxidant.

2. Metal Vessels, Packaging in Metal Containers

Metal vessels and mains, especially burnished surfaces, may contribute trace elements such as lead, zinc, copper, tin, aluminium. Packaging in steel cans may contribute traces of iron over a period of time; four samples of canned beer (tinplate cans) showed the following increase in iron content analysed by the ICAP method (see under Methods of Determination, section C) over twelve months:

0·10   0·15   0·18   0·35

TABLE 4. General mineral analyses

	Two brewing centres in Venezuela, Jan–Dec 1976		Three brewing centres in Mexico, Dec 1976	Four brewing centres in South Africa Sept–Nov 1976	Two brewing centres in Australia, Dec 1976
Sodium	12	40	6–35	16–38	2–6
Potassium	5	15	NA	1·1–2·2	0–1
Aluminium	0·10–0·20	0·05–0·20			
Calcium	15–38	26–35	27–41	2·3–37	1–3
Magnesium	6·8–15·1	8·3–17	4–8	2·2–25	0–1
Iron	0–0·21	0·03–0·49	0	0·02–0·38	0–0·05
Manganese	0	0–Tr.	NA	0·005–0·013	NA
Zinc	NA	NA	NA	0·008–0·019	0–0·05
Copper	NA	NA	NA	NA	0–0·01
Nitrate	0·02–1·66	0–0·63	3–19	0·05–0·30	NA
Nitrite	0·0–0·01	0·001–0·008	Trace	0–0·1	NA
Chloride	14–28	80–112	3–4	13–31	0–10
Sulphate	13–38	26–43	18–55	7–33	5
Phosphate	NA	NA	NA	NA	NA
Silica	2–28	2·7–27	8–56	2·6–5·9	NA
Total solids	91–233	279–365	178–216	81–167	NA
Total hardness	68–130	118–152	94–102	15–46	NA
pH	6·9–7·7	7–8·1	7·5–7·9	5·4–7·4	6·5–7·5

Note: NA = Not available.

3. Fermentation

The fate of the inorganic compounds during brewing is summarized in Table 6. The main points of interest are:

Potassium   Most of the potassium in the wort is derived from the malt and adjuncts. A certain quantity is absorbed by the yeast and is therefore lost during fermentation.

Sodium   Comes mostly from the brewing materials. There is little loss during fermentation.

Calcium   Mostly from brewing materials, also water. Virtually no loss during fermentation.

Magnesium   Mostly from the malt and adjuncts, also from the water. Some is lost during fermentation.

Chloride   Mostly from brewing water. Little loss during brewing.

Phosphate   Mostly from the malt and adjuncts. During brewing, mostly organic phosphate is lost. An appreciable amount is absorbed by the yeast.

Nitrate   From the brewing water and hops with little contribution from the malt and adjuncts. Fate during brewing is obscure with an indication of little change in nitrate level from wort to beer.

TABLE 5. Analysis of 1976 water supplies for a brewery in Tokyo

	Jan	Feb	Mar	Apr	May	June	July	Aug	Sept	Oct	Nov	Dec
Colour Units†			0	0	0	0	0	0	0	0		
Turbidity Units‡			0·1	0	0·1	0·1	0·1	0	0	0		
pH Value	6·7	6·8	6·8	6·8	6·7	6·9	6·9	6·9	7	7		
Conductance μ 75 cm^{-1}, 25 °C	256	262	222	187	173	191	236	230	212	247		
Dissolved residue (evap.) (p.p.m.)	182	211	186	176	115	—	—	224	—	—		
Total hardness, $CaCO_3$ (p.p.m.)	73	76	62	55	38	55	81	61	59	70		
Ca—hardness, $CaCO_3$ (p.p.m.)	—	54	—	—	30	—	—	56	—	—		
Mg—hardness, $CaCO_3$ (p.p.m.)	—	22	—	—	8	—	—	5	—	—		
Total alkalinity, $CaCO_3$ (p.p.m.)	29	29·5	24·5	19·5	18·0	21·5	29·0	28·0	25·5	27·5		
Total Fe (p.p.m.)	0·15	0·13	0·04	0·03	0	0	0	0·01	0·01	0		
SO_4^{2-} (p.p.m.)	44	48	42	42	30	32	42	48	41	45		
Cl^- (p.p.m.)	27·5	28·2	22·2	19·2	17·6	17·7	21·7	20·1	16·7	21·1		
SiO_2 (colorimetric) (p.p.m.)	23	23	22	20	16	18	22	23	20	25		
NH_3—N (p.p.m.)	0	0	0	0	1·1	1·6	0	0	0	0		
NO_3—N (p.p.m.)	2·2	1·9	2·1	1·6	1·1	1·3	2·2	2	1·7	3·2		
Chlorine residual (p.p.m.)	1·4	1·3	1·2	1·3	1·1	1·3	1·2	1·2	1·3	1·4		
Oxygen consumed, $KMnO_4$ (p.p.m.)	1·6	1·9	1·4	1·6	1·7	1·5	1·8	1·6	1·3	1·3		

† pt–Co method.
‡ Kaolin p.p.m.

TABLE 6. Summary of salient data on ions in beer

	Range (mg/l)	Reference number	Source and fate during brewing	Effect on the physical properties of beer-flavour, clarity, head retention
Major cations				
Potassium	196–427	1	Mostly from malt and adjuncts. Some is lost during fermentation.	Imparts salty taste (21)
Sodium	18–363	1	Mostly from brewing materials and water. Little loss during fermentation. Required to maintain potassium uptake.	Imparts mawkish flavour (15)
Calcium	26–110	2	From brewing materials and water. Levels in water, wort, and beer do not change.	Has favourable effect on flavour (16); also oxalate removal by precipitation (22)
Magnesium	51–85	3	Mostly from malt and adjuncts, also water. Some is lost during fermentation	As the sulphate, imparts disagreeable taste (17); in general, less favourable effect on taste than calcium (16)
Trace Elements				
Zinc	0·064–2·40	4	Mainly from metal mains and vessels. Also, in canned beer, from end sealing compound used (13)	Contributes to haze
Nickel	0·010–0·056	5	Mostly from metal vessels and equipment	Promotes hazes and gushing
Chromium	0·011–0·021	5	Mainly from metal mains and vessels	
Tin	0·08–0·24	5	Mostly from metal mains and vessels	Promotes hazes and gushing
Aluminium	0·10–0·50	6	From aluminium vessels and containers	
Copper	0·02–0·78	7	From metal mains and vessels, also from certain herbicides on hops	Promotes oxidative haze formation
Iron	0·02–0·34	8	From water and containers	Causes wort darkening; promotes oxidative hazes in the finished beer. Sometimes gushing and foam deterioration are caused by high levels of ferrous ions (19, 20)

(continued p. 176)

TABLE 6 (*cont.*)

	Range (mg/l)	Reference number	Source and fate during brewing	Effect on the physical properties of beer-flavour, clarity, head retention
Anions				
Chloride	122–439	9	Mostly from brewing water; from certain starch hydrolysates and crude sugars; also from salt addition to beer. Little loss during brewing	Imparts fullness and sweetness (18). Confers mild flavour (17)
Sulphate	109–429	3	Mostly from brewing water	Imparts a dry flavour (15, 16)
Oxalate	6–27	10	Mostly from malt; a little from hops. Calcium oxalate tends to precipitate during brewing	Produces hazes and gushing
Phosphate	175–587	11	Mostly from malt and adjuncts; much is absorbed by yeast. During brewing, most phosphate lost is organic	
Nitrate	0·5–20	12	From brewing water and hops (14). Fate during brewing is obscure	Imparts off flavours (16) and a high colour (12)

Sources: All values are on U.S.A. beers (1966–1976) courtesy of J. E. Siebel Sons' Company, Chicago, Illinois, except for nitrate (12).
Methods employed, references:

(1) Flame photometric. (2) A.S.B.C. Methods of Analysis, 1976. (3) Adaptation of APHA method for magnesium in water. (4) In *Proc. Ann. Meet. A.S.B.C.* (1962), p. 64. (5) Atomic absorption. (6) In *Proc. Ann. Meet. A.S.B.C.* (1963), p. 149. (7) A.S.B.C. Methods of Analysis, 1976. (8) A.S.B.C. Methods of Analysis, 1976. (9) In *Proc. Ann. Meet. A.S.B.C.* (1959), p. 102. (11) A.S.B.C. Methods of Analysis, 1976, Beer-15. (12) Stone *et al.* (1968). (13) Weiner and Taylor (1968). (14) Postel (1976).

Effect on physical properties of beer:

(15) Rudin (1974). (16) Narziss (1972). (17) Hough *et al.* (1971). (18) Mändl (1974). (19) Voerkelius (1970). (20) Ulloa *et al.* (1976). (21) Moll *et al.* (1972). (22) Latimer and Glenister (1968).

C. Methods for the Determination of Inorganic Ions in Beer

1. Atomic Absorption Spectrophometry; Photometry, Coulometry; Microcoulometric Analysis

Atomic absorption spectroscopy is the modern method of choice for the routine control analysis of metallic ions in beers: iron, copper, zinc, calcium and aluminium in beer are all determinable by this method with an accuracy and precision, as well as rapidity and moderate cost, which have rendered older chemical methods obsolete.

The technique involves the aspiration of a sample in solution or fine suspension and its heating in a flame to a high temperature. The chemical bonds between molecules are broken by the flame, with the production of atoms which absorb either ultraviolet or visible radiation. Light from a hollow cathode tube, which contains the element under examination, is passed simultaneously through the flame. A proportion of the light striking the flame will be absorbed at the resonance wavelength by the unexcited atoms of the element. The degree of absorption depends on the concentration of metal atoms in the sample.

Early applications of atomic absorption spectrometry to beer by Frey *et al.* (1967) and Weiner and Taylor (1969) have been consolidated by improved methodology and a comparison of results by this method with those obtained by standard, older methods was made by Saletan (1970), summarized in Table 7. Full details concerning current work on the application of atomic absorption spectrophotometry to analytical problems in brewing chemistry

TABLE 7. Comparison of results by AAS and other methods

	Parts per million			
	AAS	Colorimetry	Flame Photometry	Argon plasma atomic emission spectroscopy
Iron	0·05–0·59	0·06–0·59[a]		0·05–1·01
Copper	0·03–0·41	0·03–0·39[b]		0·03–0·13
Calcium	38–85		36–86[c]	29·8–69·9
Zinc	0·05–0·11	0·06–0·10[d]		0·05–0·17
Aluminium	0·12–1·09	0–1·3[e]		0·12–1·86

Notes: Figures quoted are ranges for about 20 beers in each case (Saletan 1970), except for atomic emission spectroscopy by which 15 beers were analysed (George Charalambous, 1976, unpublished), included in above table for comparison purposes.

[a] Bipyridine international method (A.S.B.C. 1958, Beer—18). [b] Zinc dibenzyldithiocarbamate international method (A.S.B.C., 1958, Beer—19). [c] A.S.B.C. procedures (1951), p. 8. [d] Dithizone, A.S.B.C. procedures (1962), p. 64. [e] Pyrocatecholsulphonephthalein, A.S.B.C. procedures (1963), p. 149.

may be found in the annual reports of the relevant A.S.B.C. Subcommittees and in succeeding reports of the relevant subcommittees of the Analysis Committee of the Institute of Brewing (London).

Lead in beer was found by Weissler using dithizone complexing and extraction to be at a concentration of 0·03–0·05 mg per ml. Weiner (1969) also applied atomic absorption to the determination of traces of copper, iron, zinc and lead. A microcoulometric method for chloride used by Schait (1970) gave a range of 88–226 p.p.m. in the beers tested. A colorimetric method for total, inorganic, and organic phosphorus in brewing products and materials was applied by Van Gheluwe *et al.* (1970) leading to the following results:

Inorganic phosphorus (mg per 100 ml)

	Average	High	Low
Canadian lagers	20·3	27·5	15·0
U.S. lagers	13·3	16·2	8·9
European lagers	17·8	19·5	16·2
Canadian ales	13·4	17·0	7·7

This comprehensive report by Van Gheluwe *et al.* on the determination of phosphorus also comments on the fate of phosphorus during fermentation. In all-malt beers and syrup adjunct beers with up to 50% syrup, the phosphorus content drops to one-third of its original amount during fermentation. Van Gheluwe *et al.* found the phosphorus uptake by the yeast to be 12–13 mg per 100 ml, representing 40% for an all-malt beer. Increased syrup adjunct use was seen to lead to an increasing uptake of phosphorus by yeast.

The effect of sulphites on beer foam quality is discussed by Brenner and Bernstein (1976). It is reported that the presence in the kettle of about 25 mg of sulphur dioxide per litre of wort results in a substantial loss of foam properties from beer. It is claimed that the foam destruction results from the sulphite-induced cleavage of disulphide groups in the wort proteins which, in turn, reduces the quantity of higher-molecular-weight proteinacous materials thought necessary for sustaining good foam.

The determination of ammonia in beer by means of an ammonia-specific ion electrode has been reported by Wisk and Siebert (1973) to be about 2 p.p.m. Their data indicate a ready assimilation of ammonia by yeast, which results in a low level at the end of fermentation, remaining approximately constant from that point on.

The iron content of beer has been exhaustively reviewed (52 references) in the context of iron's adverse effects on physical stability and often on beer foam quality, by Voerkelius (1970). An improved method for determination of iron in beer using ferrozine has been reported by Canales *et al.* (1975) giving results in the range of 0·08–0·65 p.p.m. (in good agreement with methods in A.S.B.C. Methods of Analysis, Beer—18).

A comprehensive report on nitrates in worts, beers, and brewing by Saletan *et al.* (1968) traces the fate of the nitrate ion in the brewing process; shows the beer nitrate content to be due not only to the brewing water, but also to hops, while malt and adjuncts do not contribute any significant amounts; and states that of the 41 U.S.A. and 20 other beers examined, 95% of the former and 75% of the latter contained less than 20 p.p.m. of nitrate. The method employed is colorimetric and based on the American Public Health Association method for nitrates in water. The nitrate content of wort and beer was found to be essentially the same except when nitrate was present at high levels.

2. Inductively Coupled Argon Plasma–Atomic Emission Spectroscopy (ICAP)

A recently (1975) developed analytical system, comprising a computer-controlled spectrometer with inductively coupled argon plasma excitation, has been applied to the simultaneous multielement determination of up to 50 ions in water and beer. Trace metals can be determined in the sub-p.p.m. level, quickly, precisely and reproducibly.

Briefly, the basis of the method is atomic emission promoted by coupling the sample, nebulized to form an aerosol, with high-temperature argon gas produced by passage of argon through a powerful radio-frequency field. The system used for this work is the inductively coupled argon plasma-atomic emission spectrograph,† ATOMCOMP,® comprising three modules: a radio-frequency generator; the plasma torch and associated sample nebulizer system; and a spectrometer along with a read-out system that is operated under control of a dedicated minicomputer. Radiation from the argon plasma, defined by an entrance slit to the spectrometer, is dispersed by a grating, and selected wavelengths that fingerprint elements of interest are transduced by photomultipliers, a separate one for each element. The electronic energy thus produced is treated by the computer and reported on the teletypewriter directly as concentration of each element.

The beer samples were treated as follows. After being degassed, 50 ml samples were made up exactly to 50 ml with distilled, deionized water and analysed against aqueous calibration standards. Water samples were analysed directly. Differences of $\pm 5\%$, or 5 times the detection limit (whichever is the larger value) were considered to be significant. Table 8 shows the range in parts-per-million of metallic ions in 20 beers, both U.S.A. and others.

† Manufactured by Jarrell Ash Division of Fisher Scientific Company, Waltham, Massachusetts, U.S.A.

TABLE 8. Metallic ions in beer by ICAP

	Concn. (mg/l)	Detection limits (mg/l)
Silver	<0·006	0·006
Aluminium	<0·02–1·57	0·02
Boron	0·11–3·55	0·005
Barium	0·015–0·043	0·001
Beryllium	<0·001	0·001
Calcium	23·0–61·2	0·02
Cadmium	<0·002–0·008	0·002
Cobalt	<0·005–0·005	0·005
Chromium	0·009–0·041	0·005
Copper	0·036–0·100	0·003
Iron	0·056–0·68	0·004
Potassium	170·0–326·0	0·2
Lithium	<0·005	0·005
Magnesium	67·9–90·8	0·001
Manganese	0·078–0·17	0·001
Sodium	21·0–62·0	0·05
Nickel	<0·008	0·008
Lead	<0·03	0·03
Phosphorus	202–207 (2 beers only)	0·05
Silicon	11·2–46·7	0·02
Strontium	0·08–0·83	0·001
Titanium	<0·002–0·009	0·002
Vanadium	<0·02	0·02
Zinc	0·01–2·94	0·004
Zirconium	<0·002	0·002

The above analytical results are courtesy of Jarrell-Ash Division of Fisher Scientific Company, Waltham, Massachusetts, and Monsanto International, St. Louis, Mo., U.S.A.

II. BEER CARBOHYDRATES

A. General Composition

According to a recent review (Anon. 1975) the composition of an average North American beer includes 3·3–4·4 % carbohydrates, composed of: 75–80% dextrins (>G4), 20–30% mono- and oligosaccharides (<G4), and 5–8% pentosans.

1. Mono-, Di- and Trisaccharides

The saccharides, containing fewer than four glucose units, which remain in beer after fermentation, include monosaccharides (D-ribose, L-arabinose, D-xylose, D-glucose, D-fructose, D-galactose) along with glycerol and myo-inositol; disaccharides (maltose, isomaltose, kojibiose, nigerose, maltulose);

and trisaccharides (panose and isopanose in addition to varying amounts of maltotriose). Several of these low-molecular-weight carbohydrates have been characterized in special cases only (e.g. in beers produced with super-attenuating or non-attenuating yeast strains) and are found in bare traces; the possibility exists that they arose from enzymatic degradation and possible rearrangement of the parent carbohydrates (Hay and Smith 1962).

2. Dextrins (Alpha-glucans)

The saccharides of dextrins with more than three glucose units per molecule have been thoroughly reviewed by Enevoldsen (1974) as part of an account dealing with the amount, the distribution, and the structure of individual components or groups of dextrins present in wort and in beer. Since the dextrins in beer are generally produced during mashing and conserved during fermentation, they are probably best dealt with in section II and only certain points, specifically beer-orientated, will be mentioned here.

The mashing process results in the gelatinization of the starch granules and in the depolymerization of amylose and amylopectin. From this follows the formation of fermentable sugars as well as of dextrins. These higher dextrins are intermediates leading to the formation of lower molecular weight dextrins (with a degree of polymerization of 4–6) along with fermentable sugars. As early as 1955, Gjertsen established the fact that the level of dextrins is not altered during fermentation, also that the same amount of dextrins end up in beer whether brewing from malt and adjuncts or from malt alone. The dextrins have been catalogued into distinct groups according to their content of linear and singly branched oligosaccharides on the one hand, and multiply branched megalosaccharides on the other.

Dextrins are believed to be pure glucose polymers; in the literature up to the end of 1976, there is no mention of dextrins containing traces of impurities such as phosphate or sulphate groups. Their main contribution probably is the nutritional value they give to beer. Although devoid of flavour themselves (Otter *et al.* 1970), they may act as flavour carriers. Dextrins may also act as protective colloids and, in addition, they have the potential to bind carbon dioxide and promote head formation of beer (Pfenninger 1974).

3. Beta-Glucans

Beta-glucan is the generic name for all compounds of two or more glucose molecules linked together in the β-1,3 or β-1,4 configuration. This polysaccharide may either consist of long chains of high molecular weight (200 000), being then of a white fibrous nature, or be of low molecular weight (50 000) and of a more powdery texture. Two β-glucans from beer had molecular weights of 70 000 (Gjertsen 1966) and 114 000 (Igarashi 1965). Beta-glucan is derived from cereal grains and exerts a major influence on wort and beer viscosity also (indirectly) on beer flavour by contributing to palate fullness. According to Narziss (1974) the beer content of β-glucan can vary in the range of 70–510 mg/l. its normal amount being 200–250 mg/l. In wort, the β-glucan range is 90–670 mg/l; 400 mg/l being a typical value for ale malt wort (Bathgate 1974). Enevoldsen (1974) states that, while the importance of β-glucans to wort and beer is undeniable, their contribution by weight is not great: β-glucans at the level of 100–300 mg/l amount to only 0·3–1·0% of the "dextrins" in beer.

Pierce et al. (1972, 1976) have reviewed the nature and the role of β-glucan and β-glucanases in brewing, collating earlier reports by Preece at Edinburgh (1948, 1957, 1964); by Meredith et al. at Winnipeg (1951, 1953, 1955); by Luchsinger et al. (1958, 1960, 1962, 1964, 1965, 1967, 1970) in West Virginia; and by Bathgate (1974, 1975) in Nutfield.

Beta-glucans play an important part in determing viscosity at all stages in the brewing process, contributing 40–45% of the viscosity of the finished beer. Several workers (Luchsinger 1958, Dahlstrom 1959, Pierce 1970) have stated that there is very little change in β-glucan content between wort and beer. Pierce, on the other hand, reports finding a 100% increase of a high-molecular-weight β-glucan during fermentation (from 0·15 to 0·32 mg/l over 44 hours of fermentation). In addition to viscosity, the effects of β-glucan on the finished beer include: formation of voluminous precipitates, especially in high-gravity beers (Gjertsen 1966) and separation of material which blocks beer filters (Leedham et al. 1975). Non-biological hazes produced during storage were found by Gjertsen (1966) to consist of β-glucan; palate fullness and foam stability were both favourable aspects of the presence of β-glucan in beer (Krauss 1970, Schild 1968, Narziss 1973). It may thus be concluded (Pierce 1976) that effects of β-glucans on beer and the brewing process can be both desirable and troublesome. A compromise must be reached through an improvement of the quality of malt and adjunct; a change of the physical conditions of brewing and of brewing equipment; and the use of exogenous enzymes: all of these play a part in regulating the β-glucan levels during brewing and, therefore the attendant effects on the finished beer. If the level of high-molecular weight β-glucan is kept as low as possible in the hopped wort, there should be less chance of a dangerously high increase of the level of this type of β-glucan in beer (Pierce 1976).

According to Pfenninger et al. (1974), assessment of the effect of β-glucans on wort and beer is problematical because of analytical difficulties: different methods of isolation and estimation lead to widely divergent results. Pierce (1970) also acknowledges the necessity of discounting early results in view of confusion between α- and β-glucans. Further, presently used extraction methods provide no information on the chain length of the β-glucans. Since all workers in this field agree that the β-glucan fractions of high molecular weight exert the greatest influence on viscosity, little conclusive information is to be gained from estimation of total beer β-glucan. For these reasons, Pfenninger *et al.* (1974) insist that β-glucan estimations seldom correlate with viscosity measurements. Finally, Bathgate (1974) stresses the absence of correlation between the β-glucan content of barley and its malting potential.

4. Pentosans

Pentosans are non-starchy polysaccharides comprising chiefly xylose and arabinose units. Together with β-glucan they form the cementing material in the barley endosperm (see Chapter 2, Vol. 1) and comprise the water-soluble gums (about 2% of the grain). Barley contains about 10% pentosan in its dry matter; of this about 75% is in the husk and the balance in the endosperm cell walls. The molecular weight of barley pentosans lies between 50 000 and 200 000. The amount of pentosan passing into the wort on mashing depends on the modification degree of the malt. Somewhat higher pentosan values are found in decoction worts as compared with worts prepared by the infusion method (Steiner 1968).

Four different enzymes are thought to be involved in the degradation of pentosans, leading to the traces of D-xylose and L-arabinose reported at various times in wort and beer (Hay and Smith 1962); also a beer chill haze was found by de Clerck *et al.* (1953) to contain 32–36% pentose sugars. The total contribution of complex polysaccharides, such as β-glucans and pentosans, to the quality of beer is difficult to define. In terms of the flavour and texture of the finished beer, some workers (Luchsinger 1967, Scriban 1973) have suggested that worts with high β-glucan content give rise to beers with a mellow mouth feel and with good head retention. According to Bathgate (1974) it is unlikely that β-glucans and pentosans promote better beer head retention by a simple increase in viscosity. However, β-glucans and pentosans may enhance the foaming properties of the finished beer by a synergistic association with such other beer components as dextrins and protein. More recently, Kirsop (1976) found a haze present in a processed commercial ale to consist principally (88%) of pentosan (arabinoxylan). Analysis of a hydrolysed sample for individual sugars gave a xylose:arabinose ratio of 6 : 1; other sugars present were glucose (1·5%) and mannose (0·5%). Since a microbiological origin could be excluded, it is surmised that the pentosan found in this haze was derived from the arabinoxylan in the grain after degradation during malting or mashing.

B. Fate of Carbohydrates during Fermentation

In fermentation, the carbohydrates are the major source of energy for the yeast, being degraded to the alcohol and carbon dioxide found in beer.

Carbohydrate composition, as a major factor affecting the fermentability of worts, has been recently discussed by Enari (1975). The fate of some individual sugar components of the carbohydrates available for fermentation in a North American lager wort has been reported by Ingledew (1975). The wort investigated was 11·7° Plato and made with corn adjunct, containing 80% fermentable sugars. The major sugars (glucose, maltose and maltotriose) amounted to over 96% of the fermentable moiety. A five-day fermentation with lager yeast (*Saccharomyces carlsbergensis*) was carried out and the beer was analysed (by gas–liquid chromatography following silylation) just prior to brine cooling. Table 9 (Ingledew 1975) lists the sugar levels before and after primary brewery fermentation. As can be seen, all fructose, sucrose and glucose were utilized by the yeast; the non-fermentables included all sugars containing more than three glucose units. It is noteworthy that, after bottling, this beer contained merely traces of maltotriose in spite of only 95% of the maltose and 80% of the maltotriose having been metabolized by that time. This would point to the residual maltose and maltotriose being attacked during cooling in the primary fermentation tank and in subsequent fermentation or ageing stages. The percentage of sugar utilized was 75, close to 80% in the finished beer: a normal lager beer fermentation level. Clapperton and McWilliam (1971) report that, from all-malt grits containing 0·2–0·7% maltotetraose, fast-fermenting strains of *Saccharomyces cerevisiae* remove some maltotetraose while slow-fermenting strains of this yeast fail to utilize it. It is stressed that some yeast strain *are* able to use both the panoses and maltotetraose. In the case of the latter, the amounts fermented are, in general, 900 mg/l or less at the end of the main fermentation.

TABLE 9. Carbohydrate content of corn adjunct wort before and after primary fermentation

Sugars	Fermentable carbohydrate (%)	mg carbohydrate/100 ml wort		% of each utilized
		Before fermentation	After fermentation	
Fructose	1·34	126	0	100
Glucose	15·71	1473	0	100
Sucrose	1·89	177	0	100
Maltose	66·95	6278	275	95·6
Maltotriose	14·10	1322	270	79·6
Fermentable carbohydrate		9376	545	94·2
Non-fermentable carbohydrate		2374	2355	0·8
Total carbohydrate		11 750	2900	75·3

The rate and order of disappearance of each carbohydrate are also of interest. In this particular fermentation, sucrose rapidly decreased in the first five hours of fermentation while maltose was not significantly attacked during that time, being rapidly utilized, along with maltotriose, between 10 and 50 hours of fermentation. Glucose and fructose were utilized after sucrose and before maltose. Differences in the rate and order of sugar metabolism between the above quoted and other, older fermentations can best be accounted for by variations in the method of wort preparation and the yeast strain.

C. Effect of Carbohydrates on the Properties of Beer

1. Physical Properties

The residual carbohydrates in beer account for its sweetness. Table 10 shows the relative sweetness of some beer sugars and other constituents; some other, including synthetic sweeteners have been included for comparison. The tabulation is based on a method involving duplication of the sweetness of a fresh 5% aqueous sucrose solution. The sugars having 4–9 glucose residues were compared to maltose and found to fall well below the threshold of taste detection of the latter (G. Charalambous, unpublished).

TABLE 10. Relative sweetness of certain beer constituents and some synthetic sweeteners

	Sweetness (sucrose = 1)
Sucrose	1
Dextrin	0
Maltose	0·5
Galactose	0·6
Glucose, Xylose	0·7
Glycerol	0·8
Fructose	1·1
Glycyrrhizin	50
Cyclamate	30–80
Sodium saccharin	200–700

The contribution of the dextrin fraction to beer flavour is debatable. Though without any special flavour themselves, dextrins are generally assumed to impart fullness or body to the beer. However, Otter et al. (1970) who examined the contribution of the oligosaccharides to the palate of beer, concluded that dextrins have little or no effect on it; possibly they may act as flavour carriers (Pfenninger 1974). On the other hand, dextrins (α-glucans, rather than the β-glucans) have been implicated by Letters (1969) as leading to beer hazes through their association with polyphenolic and protein beer material. It is not certain whether dextrins affect head retention of beer. As for the β-glucans, they contribute to palate and viscosity of the finished beer.

2. Nutritional, Physiological and Caloric Properties

Although beer is not strictly classified as a food, many beneficial properties have been claimed for it. The presence of a wide range of vitamins in beer may have nutritional significance; the nutritional and physiological properties of beer have been reviewed by Saletan (1959) and in an anonymous *Brewers Digest* article (1975). Further, Buday and Denis (1974) have reported on the diuretic effect of the major constituents of beer; it was found that the diuretic effect is partly due to its solids content, especially that part formed during fermentation, rather than to the beer's volatile components.

In addition, Vanbelle *et al.* (1972) conclude that 1 litre of beer per day will supply 1/7 to 1/10 of human protein requirement and a still better proportion of essential amino acids (e.g. 15% of daily requirement of lysine and over 20% of the methionine is supplied by 1 litre of beer of original extract over 11%). For additional nutritional data on beer, see section V.D. on vitamin content of beer.

The residual carbohydrates in beer, along with the alcohol, account for the greater part of its caloric value, which is relatively low: 400–500 cal/1000 ml in regular (non-dietetic) beer, compared with 600–700 cal/1000 ml in milk and 500–700 cal/1000 ml in regular (non-dietetic) soft drinks. The caloric content of beer can be readily calculated where the alcohol by weight, per cent of real extract and specific gravity of a beer are known. Depending on alcohol content, 3·9 to 4·9% by volume, a twelve-fluid-ounce or 335 ml container of U.S.A. regular (non-dietetic) beer will provide 132–167 calories. The apportioning of calories between alcohol and carbohydrates in a 12-oz. beer container is as follows. Of the 135 calories in a 12-oz. container of 3·9% (by volume) alcohol regular U.S. beer, 75 calories are due to the alcohol and approximately 56 calories to the carbohydrates. Of the 156 calories in a 12-oz. container of 4·9% (by volume) alcohol regular U.S. beer, 95 calories are due to the alcohol and approximately 57 calories to the carbohydrates. Of the 96 calories in a 12-oz. container of 4·0% (by volume) alcohol light U.S. beer, approximately 77 calories are due to the alcohol and 16 calories to the carbohydrates. Table 11 summarizes carbohydrate and calories contents of some North American beers.

3. Low-calorie Beers

Low-calorie beers currently on the U.S.A. market contain 2·25–3·42% (by weight) alcohol, 70–97 calories, 2·0–5·5 g carbohydrates, 0·7–1·2 g protein,

TABLE 11. Carbohydrates and calories in beer (12-oz.)

Beer	Original extract (%)	Residual extract (%)	Carbohydrate (%)	Protein (%)	Alcohol by vol (%)	Alcohol by wt (%)	12-oz. container Carbohydrate (g)	12-oz. container Calories
A	11·80	4·0	3·7	0·3	4·9	3·9	13·1	156
B	10·60	3·8	3·5	0·3	3·9	3·15	12·4	135
C	11·60	3·8	3·5	0·3	4·9	3·9	12·4	153
D	10·40	3·6	3·3	0·3	3·9	3·15	11·6	132
E	12·50	4·75	4·4	0·35	5·0	3·9	15·58	167

and 0 g fat per 12-oz. can, as compared with 3·2–3·9% (by weight) alcohol, 130–170 calories, 12–16 g carbohydrates, 0·82–1·11 g protein, and 0 g fat per 12-oz. can of regular beer. Since the caloric content of a particular beer depends only on its extract and alcohol content, a significant decrease of caloric content can be achieved only by lowering the beer's original gravity.

One main approach taken in the production of low-calorie beer is the reduction of the residual carbohydrates in beer by using limit dextrinase or amyloglucosidase, followed by the most complete removal possible by fermentation of the resulting sugars. A number of patents describe this approach for the production of a beer with low alcoholic content, low carbohydrate content, and low caloric value: U.S. Patent 3 852 495; Canadian Patent 2 052 963. Most of these patents have been assigned to A.G. für Brauerei Ind. A modification of this first main process leads to highly fermented beer through the fermentation of wort with yeast obtained by crossing different species which directly ferment the wort dextrins (German Patent 1 442 311 assigned to Versuchs- und Lehranstalt für Brauerei Berlin).

The second main approach in the production of low-calorie beers is represented by U.S. Patent 3 717 471 (M. R. Sfat and B. J. Morton assigned to Bio-Techical Resources, Inc.) and is also described in British Patent 1 355 698. To produce a low-carbohydrate beer, barley malt is extracted with water

TABLE 12. Oligosaccharide composition of some light beers by acrylamide gel permeation chromatography

Beer	G-1	G-2	G-3	G-4	G-5	G-6	G-7	G-8	G-9
Regular	0·024	0·114	0·219	0·418	0·138	0·188	0·194	0·295	0·285
Light 1	0·029	0·076	0·095	0·044	0·027	0·031	0·029	NR	NR
Light 2	0·034	0·151	0·131	0·050	0·054	0·048	0·051	0·059	0·056
Light 3	0·039	0·114	0·112	0·048	0·052	0·040	0·039	0·042	
Light 4	0·125	0·070	0·068	0·023	0·015	0·015	NR	NR	NR
Light 5	0·157	0·042	0·049	0·020	0·014	NR	NR	NR	NR
Light 6	0·239	0·063	0·051	0·021	0·016	0·010	NR	NR	NR
Light 7	0·064	0·080	0·071	0·024	0·019	0·033	NR	NR	NR
Light 8	0·063	0·059	0·046	0·011	0·006	NR	NR	NR	NR
Light 9	0·027	0·100	0·480		0·196	0·188	0·162	0·213	0·216
Light 10	0·285	0·084	0·098	0·037	0·040	0·060	0·024	NR	NR
Light 11	0·046	0·108	0·130	0·065	0·073	0·051	0·051	0·055	
Light 12	0·041	0·132	0·122	0·061	0·064	0·056	0·061	0·070	
Light 13	0·034	0·165	0·135	0·057	0·060	0·053	0·065	0·070	0·069
Light 14	0·015	0·077	0·115		0·048	0·058	0·063	0·067	0·064

Notes: (1) NR = Not resolved, (2) Regular beer for comparison.

under conditions leading to the extraction of proteins but not of carbohydrates. The resulting extract contains about 20% protein and a highly fermentable sugar is added to it, producing a wort which is low in non-fermentable carbohydrates. This wort is then fermented.

Another approach in producing low-calorie beers involves the removal of alcohol by an evaporation process. The popularity of this approach has fluctuated over the last hundred years; recently, however, there has been a renewed interest in the production of low-calorie, alcohol-free beers and German Patent 1 442 238 (to Henninger-Brau A.G.) is a modern representative of this approach. British Patent 1 204 160 (to Allied Breweries Ltd.) involves a yeast fermentation in a wort containing a carbohydrate and a source of nitrogen, until about one-half of the total attenuation is reached. Following removal of the yeast, the residual liquor is subjected to a secondary fermentation and further processing (addition of flavouring and sweetening materials) leading to a beer with less than 1% alcohol content.

Table 12 presents the carbohydrate composition of several 1976 U.S.A. and non-U.S. low-gravity or "light" beers by the Dellweg polyacrylamide gel fractionation method (G. Charalambous, unpublished).

4. Primed Beers

Residual carbohydrates in beer include the components of "primings", that is, materials added in the cellars for palate, flavour, colouring and conditioning purposes. These materials usually are a boiled solution of cane or brewing sugar and liquor as priming and a boiled solution of burnt or caramelized cane sugar and liquor as colouring. This practice is mainly encountered in British, Canadian, Australian and New Zealand beers (ales, stouts, lagers, pilsener-type). British usage is a solution of priming sugars of about S.G. 1150 at the level of 0·35–1·75 l/hl. Otter (1967) lists the sugar content of a few primed British ales and stouts. Little, if any, published information is available concerning the carbohydrate composition of Australian and New Zealand primed beers. Table 13 presents such data (South Australian Brewing Company Ltd., Adelaide, S.A., private communication).

As mentioned, primings are usually a boiled solution of cane or brewing sugar. The old-type priming syrups contained a large percentage of blackstrap and, with pasteurization, the beer assumed a bready character such as in an over-pasteurized beer. Non-pasteurized draft beer was not affected. Present day brewing syrups, being highly refined, have led to considerabler improvement in the final beer stability of flavour. However, it is recommended (Panelist 1973) that a tasteless and odourless ion-exchange brewing syrup, of very low ash content, be used for priming purposes.

TABLE 13. Carbohydrate composition of primed Australian and New Zealand beers

Beer no.	Original extract (°P)	Apparent extract (°P)	Total carbohydrate	Fructose	Glucose	Maltose	Triose	Tetraose
					g per 100 ml beer			
1	10·25	2·24	2·92	0·28	0·31	0·70	0·33	0·25
2	10·28	2·26	2·86	0·36	0·43	0·48	0·26	0·22
3	8·77	3·02	3·33	0·52	0·52	0·53	0·34	0·39
4	10·30	—	—	0·30	0·83	0·02	0·08	0·02
5	9·73	0·93	1·90	0·23	0·23	—	0·11	0·26
6	10·63	1·99	2·98	0·30	0·29	0·30	0·47	0·26
7	10·68	2·28	3·17	0·16	0·10	0·73	0·32	0·47
8	12·35	3·10	3·92	0·11	0·07	1·05	0·54	0·54

Notes: Beers 1–6 are Australian; 7 and 8, New Zealand. All were sampled and analysed (GLC, see **Methodology**) in 1975 and 1976. All were primed with varying amounts of sucrose (maximum in beer number 3, equivalent to 0·90 kg/hl).

D. Methods used in the Separation and Estimation of Beer Carbohydrates

1. Separation and Estimation of the Oligosaccharides (G1–G15)

The modern era in the study of beer sugars is barely a quarter of a century old and was ushered in by the development of the various chromatographic techniques. In general, these techniques permit the separation of the mono-, di-, tri- and oligosaccharides in wort, beer, adjunct and barley and malt syrups, according to their molecular weight or number of glucose units, whenever possible followed by quantitative determinations.

The pioneer studies, extending roughly over a fifteen-year period since 1950, involved separation of the sugars on a variety of columns (carbon-celite: Whistler and Durso 1950, Barton-Wright 1953, Gjertsen 1955; charcoal: Hay and Smith 1962; cellulose: Otter *et al.* 1969) and by paper chromatography (Barton-Wright *et al.* 1951, Gjertsen 1953, MacFarlane and Held 1953, Held and MacFarlane 1957, Hall *et al.* 1956, Enevoldsen and Bathgate 1969, Enevoldsen 1970). Thin-layer chromatography was briefly used in the next few years (Franken-Luykx and Klopper 1967, Schur *et al.* 1973) while gas–liquid chromatographic (GLC) separation using the volatile trimethylsilyl (TMS) derivatives (Sweeley *et al.* 1963) has been widely applied to the study of wort and beer carbohydrates (Brobst and Lott 1966, Marinelli and Whitney 1967, Otter and Taylor 1967, Clapperton and Holliday 1968, Tuning 1971). Brobst (1974) improved on the GLC of TMS ethers by a modification involving the treatment of sugars with hydroxylamine hydrochloride to form their oximes prior to silylation. As reported by Jamieson (1976), this modification eliminates the multiple peaks resulting from the tautomeric forms of the sugars, leading to a more precise determination of fermentable sugars in beer and brewing materials.

Gel filtration on "Sephadex" had been applied early to the estimation of sugars (Djurtoft 1961) but it is gel filtration chromatography on the polyacrylamide gel "Bio-Gel P-2" that has been a major breakthrough in the analysis of beer carbohydrates. A series of papers by Dellweg *et al.* (1969, 1970, 1971) and by Trénel and John (1969, 1970) has shown chromatography on polyacrylamide gel to be the method of choice for the fractionation and quantitative evaluation of beer oligosaccharides with a chain length of 1 to about 15 glucose units. Table 14 gives the oligosaccharide content of a number of beers (1975, 1976) obtained by this method.

The proponents of polyacrylamide gel for the chromatography of beer fermentable sugars indicate the advantage of "Bio-Gel P-2" over "Sephadex", inasmuch as there exists a danger with dextran gels that traces of carbohydrates may be set free from the matrix. It should be noted, however, that in our experience, the admittedly excellent results obtained with "Bio-Gel P-2"

TABLE 14. Oligosaccharide composition of some beers and malt liquors by acrylamide gel permeation chromatography (author's laboratory) (g/100 cc)

Origin/nature	Specific gravity	G-1	G-2	G-3	G-4	G-5	G-6	G-7	G-8	G-9
U.S.A.										
Beer	1·0059	0·026	0·186	0·282	0·381	0·168	0·234	0·260	0·327	0·290
	1·0075	0·031	0·224	0·455	0·423	0·230	0·291	0·250	0·298	0·274
	1·0092	0·029	0·135	0·278	0·566	0·328	0·364	0·321	0·323	0·303
	1·0071	0·020	0·143	0·260	0·539	0·265	0·302	0·269	0·309	0·301
	1·0058	0·030	0·185	0·297	0·295	0·169	0·251	0·278	0·355	0·315
	1·0036	0·029	0·139	NR	0·630	0·409	0·340	0·297	0·370	0·394
	1·0038	0·030	0·096	0·215	0·254	0·118	0·156	0·154	0·227	0·225
	1·0040	0·030	0·100	0·220	0·280	0·120	0·170	0·160	0·250	0·240
	1·0061	0·042	0·116	0·204	0·490	0·185	0·225	0·185	0·262	0·322
Malt beverage	1·0546	3·256	12·274	1·750	0·450	0·150	0·328	0·322	0·328	0·336
Dietetic beer	—	0·07	0·05	0·06	0·04	ND	ND	ND	DN	ND
Malt liquor	1·0073	0·044	0·124	0·215	0·264	0·103	0·156	0·142	0·236	0·145
Malt liquor	1·0082	0·356	0·265	0·488	0·394	0·364	0·328	0·310	0·294	0·238
Canadian										
Lager	1·0083	0·039	0·070	NR	0·631	0·278	0·295	0·240	0·239	0·220
Ale	1·0093	0·085	0·087	0·172	0·713	0·287	0·276	0·301	0·303	0·290
Lager	1·0074	0·077	0·174	NR	0·602	0·292	0·266	0·235	0·223	0·193

Canadian										
Ale	1·0087	0·096	0·176	0·350	0·431	0·213	0·295	0·218	0·238	0·197
Lager	1·0081	0·092	0·206	NR	0·535	0·228	0·256	0·211	0·271	0·237
Ale	1·0084	0·205	NR	0·553	0·543	0·286	0·268	0·195	0·198	0·173
European										
	1·0094	0·473	0·195	0·481	0·258	0·197	0·189	0·258	0·283	0·220
	1·0066	0·047	0·248	0·320	0·231	0·171	0·233	0·231	0·272	0·214
	1·0053	0·029	0·104	NR	0·600	0·239	0·273	0·256	0·286	0·277
A	1·0119	0·048	0·280	0·579	0·678	0·332	0·351	0·251	0·295	0·320
B	1·0064	0·090	0·524	0·726	0·406	0·175	0·164	0·162	0·166	0·143
	1·0081	0·056	0·162	NR	0·559	0·226	0·308	0·207	0·211	0·185
	1·0088	0·042	0·174	0·353	0·261	0·176	0·196	0·157	0·161	0·123
	0·9998	NR	NR	0·017	0·037	0·029	NR	NR	NR	NR
Japanese	1·0061	0·056	0·370	0·265	0·221	0·131	0·182	0·211	0·286	0·238
Chinese (Peking)	1·0116	0·079	0·509	1·118	0·166	0·104	0·172	0·197	0·291	0·257

NR = Not resolved; ND = not determined.

Notes: A and B refer to a Czech beer's two versions. A is the beer exported to the U.S.A., while B is the beer brewed in Czechoslovakia and exported to the U.K. As can be seen, there is a sizeable difference in these two beers' oligosaccharide content.

depend greatly on the particular lot of this gel supplied by the manufacturer. Kainuma *et al.* (1976) have recently developed a multicolumn system of "Bio-Gel P-2" and "Bio-Gel P-6" at elevated temperatures for the fractionation of maltosaccharides of various structures.

Finally, Brobst *et al.* (1973) have described a moderate pressure liquid chromatographic system for the analysis of carbohydrate mixtures with cation-exchange resins and polyacrylamide gels at elevated temperatures in an all-aqueous system and a practical operating time of 1–2 hours.

2. Determination of Dextrins

The methods used in studying the beer dextrins are based on their separation according to molecular weight or degree of polymerization. Structural determinations of the beer dextrins have been achieved through specific enzymatic methods combined with chromatographic techniques. These techniques are basically the same as those outlined above for the separation and estimation of beer mono-, di-, tri- and oligosaccharides.

TABLE 15. Residual dextrins in adjunct lager beer

	Composition	Percentage
DP ⩾ 35	Higher dextrins	15·2
DP 28–DP 34		4·0
DP 22–DP 27		6·2
DP 17–DP 21		9·7
DP 16	Megalosaccharides	1·6
DP 15		2·6
DP 14		3·8
DP 13		3·9
DP 12		2·8
DP 11		2·0
DP 10		2·5
DP 9	Oligosaccharides	6·1
DP 8		5·5
DP 7		4·7
DP 6		5·0
DP 5		3·9
DP 4		13·1
DP 3 (non-fermentable)		3·9
DP 2 (non-fermentable)		2·4
DP 1 (non-fermentable)		1·1
Total carbohydrate		100·0
Dextrins of DP ⩾ 10		54·4
Dextrins of DP 4–9		38–3
Total dextrins (DP ⩾ 4)		92·7

Again, as for the beer oligosaccharides, gel permeation chromatography on "Bio-Gel P-2" has proven the method of choice for the determination of beer dextrins in the megalosaccharide region (degree of polymerization greater than 10). Enevoldsen and Schmidt (1973) have obtained residual carbo-hydrate values in 22 domestic and foreign beers. These data, since the amount of dextrins does not change during fermentation, can be used to back-calculate the amount of dextrins in wort. Table 15 (Enevoldsen and Schmidt 1973) lists residual dextrins (degree of polymerization $DP = 1$ to $DP \geqslant 35$) in a Danish lager (made with the use of 70% barley malt and 30% maize grits). The determination of the dextrin content of beer may be carried out by the American Chemical Society Brewing Chemists method BEER-17 according to the formula:

$$\text{Dextrin } \% = 0.9 \times (D - 1.053M)$$

in which $M = \%$ maltose in beer before hydrolysis, $D = \%$ dextrose in beer after hydrolysis. This calculation gives, for example, the values of 1.4% dextrin in a light beer and 2.2% dextrin in a regular beer.

3. Determination of Beta-glucans

A very common method for assessing the content of β-glucan in a beer is to precipitate the latter with 30% ammonium sulphate. This method, however, allows the determination in an extract of precipitable β-glucans only, it does not measure an important category of β-glucans. Klopper (1975) recently summarized the methods available for determination of β-glucan determi-nation in beer as follows:

Total β-glucans 1. α-*plus* β-glucans (acid hydrolysis) *minus* α-glucans
              (enzymatic hydrolysis)
           2. β-glucans (enzymatic hydrolysis)
Soluble β-glucans Ammonium sulphate precipitation

Two other approaches exist. One is enzymatic hydrolysis using a specific β-glucan hydrolase—if available: no perfectly pure β-glucan hydrolase has been found to date and correction must be made for the α-glucan hydrolase impurities these "specific" enzymes contain. A rather different method of precipitation of β-glucan from beer is the freeze-thaw procedure described by Amaha *et al.* (1969). According to Pierce (1972), the reproducibility of results by this method depends critically on very precise conditions of temperature and pressure; only part of the total β-glucan is precipitated by this means, depending on its physicochemical condition.

The fractionation of β-glucans into fractions of different molecular weight has been effected using gel permeation chromatography (Klopper 1975). This author also states that a convenient, simple and cheap method to determine qualitatively the presence or absence of β-glucan has yet to be found. To date, best results are obtained by the differentiation between glucose found by acid hydrolysis and glucose formed after enzymatic hydrolysis using α-glucan hydrolases (cf. Table 15). Not only does the reproducibility of this method need further improvement, but by consensus (Enari *et al.* 1975) it is agreed that good analytical methods for both β-glucans and β-glucanases are urgently needed.

4. Determination of Pentosans

Methods for estimation of soluble pentosan in the literature (Luers 1939, Luchsinger *et al.* 1958, Narziss *et al.* 1967, Bathgate and Dalgleish 1975) lead to a wide variety of results, indicating the difficulty in a precise determination of these polysaccharides.

Currently, the best analytical method involves the acid hydrolysis of the isolated pentosan fraction and, following chromatographic separation, the estimation of the individual sugars. This approach is exemplified by Kirsop (1976) in an analysis of a beer haze consisting largely of pentosan (see section I.D.).

III. NITROGENOUS CONSTITUENTS OF BEER

A. Introduction

The importance of nitrogenous compounds in beer has long been recognized and their role in flavour, foam stability, colour, haze formation, yeast nutrition and biological stability is well established. There is about 5% nitrogenous materials in the total beer solids which, in turn, represent 4% by weight of a beer (Chen *et al.* 1973).

According to Narziss (1972), a litre of all-malt beer contains about 700 mg of nitrogenous compounds. These are of considerable complexity and variety in molecular size: about 440 mg/l are of low, 120 mg/l of medium and 140 mg/l of high molecular weight. They include amino acids, peptides, polypeptides, proteins (long, folded chains of amino acids linked together by peptide bonds), nucleic acids (deoxyribonucleic and ribonucleic acids) and their degradation products (phosphorylated fragments or nucleotides which, through the hydrolytic removal of phosphate yield nucleosides, which in turn are hydrolysed to free bases—purines and pyrimidines). These beer nitrogenous compounds are derived from two sources: the grains used in brewing and the fermentation process.

Barley proteins are degraded during malting and mashing into such soluble derivatives as amino acids and peptides of varying molecular size. During wort boiling, a considerable proportion of the soluble proteins of wort is precipitated, leaving very little "true protein" in boiled wort.

In all-malt brewing, there is always sufficient protein and proteolytic enzymes to lead to an adequate amount of amino acids and peptides in the wort. In fact, malt supplies the entire range of nitrogenous constituents from simple amino acids to proteinaceous substances of high molecular weight. On the other hand, as noted by Hudson (1966, 1974), the importance of the production of amino acids in malting and mashing may have been over-emphasized at the expense of the peptides and polypeptides that are formed. It is known that a certain amount of the beer's total nitrogen content is present in compounds not found in wort. The wort amino acids are necessary as yeast nutrients, in order to assure rapid and normal fermentation. The bulk of these amino acids are assimilated during fermentation, so that the finished beer contains only low levels of amino acids; some proteins may, in addition, be precipitated as the pH decreases. Thus, beer contains less nitrogen than the wort from which it is obtained. As an example (Hudson 1974) a comparison of the nitrogen contents of both commercial worts and beers on the one hand, and of pilot scale worts (all-malt; adjunct) and beers on the other, shows that between one-third and one-half of the wort nitrogen is lost during fermentation.

In view of their importance to the brewer, the measurement of the nitrogenous substances in beer has been approached from several viewpoints: total nitrogen; free amino nitrogen; coagulable nitrogen; magnesium sulphate—precipitable nitrogen; formol nitrogen; protein fractionation; individual amino acid determination; individual free base, nucleoside and nucleotide determination.

These are discussed under the respective headings of the beer nitrogenous constituents.

B. Classification

1. Amino acids

The beer amino acids may be classified in four groups in order of decreasing ease of assimilation (50%) by brewer's yeast (Ingledew 1975, Jones and Pierce 1969, Pierce 1966).

Group A	Group B	Group C	Group D
Most readily assimilated	Assimilated less readily than group A	Assimilated less readily than groups A and B	Scarcely assimilated
Glutamic acid	Valine	Glycine	Proline
Aspartic acid	Methionine	Phenylalanine	
Glutamine	Leucine	Tryptophan	
Serine	Isoleucine	Tyrosine	
Threonine	Histidine	Alanine	
Lysine			
Arginine			

Ammonia would fall in Group C.

2. Peptides, Polypeptides, Proteins

These beer nitrogenous compounds form a rather heterogeneous group with molecular weights ranging from 5000 to 100 000 (Enari *et al.* 1974). See sections C.1.a and D.5 for ranges quoted by other authors.

3. Nucleic Acid Derivatives

The following nucleic acid derivatives have been identified in commercial beer:

Free bases	Nucleosides	Nucleotides	Other
Uracil	Adenosine	2'-CMP	Nicotinamide-adenine
Adenine	Uridine	3'-CMP	dinucleotide and its reduced
Guanine	Guanosine	5'-CMP	form; nucleotide triphos-
Hypoxanthine	Inosine	2'-AMP	phate and oligonucleotides
Xanthine	Thymidine	3'-AMP	
Thymine	Cytidine	5'-AMP	
Cytosine		2'-GMP	
Methylcytosine		3'-GMP	
Methyluracil		5'-GMP	
		2'-UMP	
		3'-UMP	
		5'-UMP	
		3'-IMP	

Accepted abbreviations for the names of nucleotides are used throughout (see Chapter 1, Vol. 1).

C. Determination

1. Protein

(a) *General*

Nearly all beer protein is derived from barley. During malting proteolytic enzymes act to degrade the less soluble barley proteins into several degradation products: these range from proteins to polypeptides, low-molecular-weight peptides and amino acids. This degradation continues during kilning (which also results in partial destruction of the enzymatic activities). In the early 1960s (Harris and Cook 1962, Robbins *et al.* 1963) it was thought that malting had more influence than mashing on the composition of the nitrogenous compounds in beer. More recent studies (Barrett and Kirsop 1971), however, have shown that considerable amounts of nitrogen and other forms of amino nitrogen are solubilized during mashing. During fermentation, nitrogenous compounds are assimilated from the wort for yeast growth, including appreciable amounts of peptides (Clapperton 1971a, b). In addition, some protein is also contributed by hops and by autolysed yeast cells. Traces of true protein (apparently over 150 000 in molecular weight) do exist in beer. In addition, the main complex nitrogenous beer constituents are present in compounds of 5000 to 70 000 molecular weight; however, these are not proteins but proteoses in which peptides or proteins are coupled with non-nitrogenous materials.

The above preamble leads to the principal difficulty inherent in any method purporting to determine "beer protein", namely the absence of a strict distinction between "true protein" and low-molecular-weight degradation products. The high-molecular-weight degradation products, the so-called proteoses, albumoses and peptones, are considered to be of particular importance to the foam retention and fullness of body of the beer; Hudson (1974) has discussed the relation of complex nitrogen to physical properties; also, Jones (1974) has discussed the variation in the flavour of beer due to its amino acid composition (q.v.).

In view of the above, it is not surprising that several methods have been proposed over the years for the determination of "beer protein". A critical account of some of these, based on a review by Dellweg *et al.* (1970), may serve to introduce the procedures currently adopted by the Analysis Committees of such bodies as the Association of Official Analytical Chemists (1975), the American Society of Brewing Chemists (1976) and the European Brewery Convention (1975). Evaluation of the following procedures is based on the extent to which they approach the protein content obtained from quantitative amino acid determination of the hydrolysate of lyophilysed beer solids (cf. section C.3.b).

(i) *Spectrophotometric methods.* Proteins have a typical absorption maximum at 280 nm; there is however considerable interference at this wavelength from other compounds. Improvements have been effected by considering absorption at both 280 and 260 nm and by using Kalckar's (1947) formula $1.45OD_{280} - 0.74OD_{260} = mg$ protein/ml. Waddell and Hill's (1956) recommended measurement of absorption at 215 and 225 nm and other variations (Franken-Luykx 1967, Scriban and Fosseux 1969) have been suggested. However, although these spectrophotometric procedures were found useful in the case of unhopped wort, they are of doubtful value with beer.

(ii) *Biuret reaction.* In spite of its recognized insensitivity, this method is claimed by Dellweg *et al.* (1970) to have given the most exact results in the determination of several polypeptidic fractions isolated from beer, as compared with the results from the quantitative determination of the individual amino acids. In its micro-form, however, results by the microbiuret method were not quite so good.

(iii) *The Folin–Ciocalteau method* (1927). This, especially as modified and improved by Lowry *et al.* (1951), is acceptably specific. However, since the individual proteins differ greatly in colour-forming ability, the result obtained from the total sample is a reading which is about 25% too high, again as compared with results from the determination of the individual amino acids.

(iv) *Kjeldahl method.* The Kjeldahl total nitrogen determination multiplied by 6.25 leads to a "protein" result in beer generally at least 25% too high (as compared with individual amino acid analysis).

Several techniques for separation and enrichment of protein in samples have been proposed. Kuno and Kihara (1967) described a membrane filtration method which, however, leads to very approximate results (Dellweg *et al.* 1970). Fractionation of the beer nitrogenous constituents was attempted by Dellweg *et al.* (1970) using trichloroacetic acid precipitation (Hiller and Van Slyke 1922); dialysis (Simmonds 1966); ultrafiltration (which is supposed to separate macromolecules of 10–3300 Å size from small molecules and ions); gel filtration on Sephadex (Djurtoft 1963); and ion-exchange chromatography on DEAE-cellulose. Dellweg *et al.* (1970) concluded that none of the fractions obtained by any of the above techniques for separation and enrichment could be unequivocally defined as beer protein.

These difficulties in separation do not permit a clear determination of the amino acid composition of beer proteins. In turn, variations in this composition cannot, in Dellweg's opinion, as yet be reliably used to detect the utilization in brewing of certain materials such as raw adjuncts.

Dellweg *et al.* (1970) opted for a gas chromatographic procedure, using one capillary and one packed column, which required 12 hours for the determination of 18 beer amino acids following hydrolysis of a sample first subjected to ultrafiltration, dialysis or precipitation with trichloroacetic acid.

(b) *Total nitrogen or "protein" determination*

The improved Kjeldahl method for nitrate-free samples as used by the Association of Official Analytical Chemists (1975) has long been adopted by the American Chemical Society of Brewing Chemists (1976) for the determination of beer protein. Following digestion of the sample according to Kjeldahl's procedure, the ammonia is distilled into standard acid, the excess of which is titrated with sodium hydroxide. Several modifications of the basic Kjeldahl digestion method have been reported in the literature (West and Scocic 1974 is one recent example). They include variations in digestion time, use of copper, mercury, selenium, or most recently titanium dioxide (Klopper 1976) as digestion catalysts, titration with a variety of indicators, and use of boric acid solution to receive the ammonia distillate.

Another development is the use of an Autoanalyzer for the estimation of digest ammonia content following a rapid semi-micro method of Kjeldahl digestion. A typical application is that of Mitcheson and Stowell (1970) who reported considerable savings in labour and materials through the adoption of these methods. However, due to the small quantities involved, a greater degree of precision is required from the operators than is necessary for the standard Kjeldahl technique. See also section C.3(b)(iii).

In all cases the nitrogen determined is converted to protein through multiplication of the result of the factor 6·25, and reported as per cent by weight, to two decimal places. Over a considerable period of years, North American beers were found in the author's laboratory to contain 45–47 mg/100 ml total nitrogen; European beers showed a slightly higher "protein" content of 46–49 mg/100 ml.

A distinction is made between total soluble (TSN) and permanently soluble nitrogen in wort: the latter (PSN) is that remaining in solution after wort boiling and constitutes all of the nitrogen compounds available to the fermentation process and, thus, of direct importance in connection with beer. Following Bishop's (1961) recommendation, the formula PSN = 0·94 × TSN is used to calculate PSN from the determined TSN.

(c) *Protein fractionation*

(i) Fractionation of beer protein according to Lundin (1931, 1961) leads to three fractions:

Fraction A   represents the high molecular weight proteins. Following acidification of the sample, this fraction is precipitated with tannic acid.

Its nitrogen content is obtained by difference between the original beer nitrogen and that remaining in solution and usually amounts to 20–30% of the total.

Fraction B   represents polypeptides of intermediate molecular weight. Obtained through difference between phosphomolybdic acid precipitation and Fraction A.

Fraction C   represents mainly compounds of low molecular weight: amino acids and simple peptides.

(ii) Fractionation of beer protein according to Myrbäck and Myrbäck (1931). This method uses magnesium sulphate to precipitate the protein fraction and uranyl acetate for removal of the intermediate fraction. Davies *et al.* (1956) found results from the Lundin and Myrbäck fractionation procedures to be generally comparable. Narziss *et al.* (1968) have expressed a preference for the magnesium sulphate method. The Lundin fractionation method has been largely superseded by more precise procedures.

(iii) Djurtoft (1963) reviewed other methods available at that time for investigating proteins and their applicability to the study of beer proteins. The following account is an update of such techniques.

Ultracentrifugation may be used to determine the molecular weights and dimensions of proteins (Quensel 1942). The composition of lyophilized beer, the changes in wort composition during fermentation, and several other aspects have been studied using filtration through a gel prepared from dextran cross-linked with *epi*-chlorohydrin: by this means resolution is obtained of substances of intermediate size between protein and amino acids. (Djurtoft 1961). Whitaker (1963) also determined the molecular weights of proteins by gel filtration on columns of Sephadex G-100 and G-200 and Meredith (1963) separated beer proteins by starch gel electrophoresis of trichloroacetic acid precipitate. The beer proteins and those in chill haze have also been studied by means of immunoelectrophoresis: this powerful method combines electrophoresis with the immunological reaction between antigen and antibody (Grabar and Williams 1953). A typical application is the fractionation by immunoelectrophoresis of haze-forming compounds in beer by Nummi *et al.* (1969). These authors used, first, chromatography on DEAE-cellulose to fractionate the beer proteins into basic and acidic fractions (a 40 : 60 ratio). Immunoelectrophoresis was then applied leading to a further subdivision of these basic and acidic protein fractions and to conclusions regarding the identitiy of the main haze-forming proteins in beer. Again, Wenn in 1972 reported his separation of nitrogenous materials extracted from beer, wort, barley and malt by isoelectrophoresis in thin layers of Sephadex gel. The isoelectrophoretic species of beer were well resolved on a preparative scale in quantities sufficient for characterization. The conclusion was reached that substances with typical protein-like physical and chemical properties account for but one-third (by weight) of the total complex nitrogen fraction in beer. More recently, Hejgaard and Sørensen (1974) used quantitative two-dimensional immunoelectrophoretic techniques in order to characterize a protein-rich beer fraction. At least three antigens were shown to be present; the dominant antigen was stated to be derived from barley and was undoubtedly the barley albumin identified in beer and haze by earlier workers. Further, crossed immunoelectrophoresis of freeze-dried samples of beer, foam and haze gave similar patterns to those obtained from the protein-rich fraction of this beer.

2. Peptides

Beer contains a range of peptides with molecular weights between 1500 and 5000. The bulk of these seems to be derived from the malt, with the yeast also making some contribution to the peptide fraction. Clapperton (1971) has studied the peptides of malt, wort and beer using the following typical procedure. Following dialysis, the peptides were desalted on ion-exchange resin and fractionated on diethylaminoethylcellulose. Four fractions were obtained; ten units of combined amino acids was the approximate upper limits in peptides recovered. Polypeptides are therefore in the molecular weight range 1500–5000, the latter figure being the limiting molecular weight of dialysable materials. See under D.5 for further comments on the polypeptide molecular weight range.

Currently available separation methods have not permitted the isolation of the simpler peptides in beer in quantities sufficient for the evaluation of their effect on the flavour and physical properties of beer.

Haworth and Oliver (1971) found an empirical relationship between the chromatographic R_f value of a di- or tri-peptide and the R_f values of the constituent amino acids. Good agreement exists between the calculated R_f and the experimental values.

3. Amino Acids

(a) *Total amino acids*

The simpler nitrogenous constituents of beer comprise mainly alpha-amino acids and the estimation of the latter has been the subject of several studies. Pierce in 1966 claimed that the most satisfactory method for determining the total α-amino nitrogen content of malts, worts and beers still was the Van Slyke procedure (1941). He based his preference on this method's specificity for α-amino acids. The procedure involves a gasometric analysis of the nitrogen produced upon treatment of amino compounds with nitrous acid (or of the carbon dioxide produced through treatment with ninhydrin). Following their absorption on ion-exchange resins, the amino acids were quantitatively eluted using a method of gradient elution originally developed by Moore and Stein (1948). While the specificity of this early approach to α-amino acid determination justified Pierce's choice, it is both time consuming and costly.

The formol nitrogen titration method has also been used to estimate amino acids in beer. This method, first described by Schiff (1900) was reviewed and elaborated by Schneller (1949) who modified it in several respects for use with beer and wort, obtaining results that were both quantitative and in good agreement with the Van Slyke method. The need for a rapid procedure was met by estimating the colour from the reaction of α-amino acids with either ninhydrin (Wylie and Johnson 1962) or with 2,4,6-trinitrobenzenesulphonic acid (TNBS) (Satake et al. 1960). Both methods have been widely investigated. The blue-violet colour produced upon reaction of the amino acids at pH 6·7 with ninhydrin is measured at 570 nm while TNBS produces a yellow colour (at 40 °C and pH 8) which is measured at 340 nm. Ninhydrin reacts with the amino acid proline, the yellow colour that results being measured at 440 nm has been regarded as an aspect of the method (cf. Pierce 1966). TNBS on the other hand does not react with proline (or with ammonia).

Bateson in 1970 exhaustively compared the TNBS method with the ninhydrin procedure, concluding that either technique will serve equally well to distinguish between high, low and medium levels of amino nitrogen in worts and beers. It was further recommended that, for results to be strictly comparable, whichever method is chosen for regular analytical work be strictly adhered to.

Buckee et al. in 1974 estimated free α-amino nitrogen in a selection of eight beers under two sets of temperature conditions. It was found that there is no loss in precision when the more rapid method (involving a higher temperature for a shorter period of time) is used. Thus, the TNBS method would compete in rapidity with the faster ninhydrin procedure. Since mixtures of amino acids, amines and peptides of varying composition are being analysed, it should perhaps be stated (Buckee et al. 1974) that the α-amino nitrogen estimation is, at best, only an empirical result, a fact which accounts for the different values for free α-amino nitrogen obtained depending on the method of assay. This is reminiscent of the analogous situation in the determination of total poly-phenols in beer (q.v.).

The Analysis Committee of the European Brewery Convention (1975) after studying both colorimetric methods, concluded that although both give good reproducibility the ninhydrin procedure (as specified by E.B.C.-Analytica) is more precise. The rationale for this Committee's endorsement of the ninhydrin method is that the results obtained by it correspond to the free α-amino nitrogen on free amino acids, while by TNBS a somewhat higher figure is obtained due to its including free α-amino nitrogen on the more complex

TABLE 16. Comparison of alpha amino nitrogen content values of beer by colorimetric methods

Method	Alpha amino nitrogen (mg/1)	Reference
Ninhydrin (5 beers)	26·8–53·3	Bateson (1970)
TNBS (5 beers)	25·3–48·1	Bateson (1970)
E.B.C. Ninhydrin (3 beers)	84, 68, 93	Lie (1973)
E.B.C. TNBS (3 beers)	99, 84, 108	Lie (1973)
E.B.C. TNBS (40 °C/2 h) (8 beers)	24·8–55·2	Buckee et al. (1974)
TNBS (60 °C/30 min) (8 beers)	27·4–65·6	Buckee et al. (1974)

nitrogen compounds. Proline is not included in either method; it may be determined separately by the colorimetric procedure of Wren and Wigall (1965). In Table 16 the α-amino nitrogen contents of beer determined by colorimetric methods are compared.

(b) *Individual amino acids*

A number of methods are available for the determination of individual amino acids in beer. They include:

(i) Paper and thin-layer chromatography.
(ii) High- and low-voltage electrophoresis.
(iii) Ion- and ligand-exchange chromatography.
(iv) Gas chromatography of suitable derivatives.
(v) High-pressure chromatography.
(vi) Radioactive techniques.

(i) Paper and thin-layer chromatography are older methods which have given yeoman service in this context; however, they are time-consuming and do not easily lead to positive identification and quantitative results.

(ii) High- and low-voltage electrophoresis also suffers from above disadvantages. It has, however, been quite useful: applications of this procedure for the determination of amino acids in beer protein hydrolysates by, for example, Nummi et al. (1969) and Wenn (1972) will be found under (iii).

(iii) Ion- and ligand-exchange chromatography has been extensively used since it affords rapid and precise results. Representative of its many applications is the work of: Nummi et al. (1969) who used the ligand (zinc complex) method for protein hydrolysates analysis (Arikawa 1967); Yoshida et al. (1968a, b, 1971) who determined amino acid concentrations in fermenting liquors; and several others.

In addition, Technicon Instruments Corporation released, in March

1977, a revised method for the colorimetric determination of nitrogen (emerald-green colour formed by the reaction of ammonia, sodium salicylate, sodium nitroprusside and sodium hypochlorite in a buffered alkaline medium at a pH of 12·8–13·0. The ammonia–salicylate complex is read at 660 nm. Also, in March 1977, an improved procedure for the analysis of total Kjeldahl nitrogen using a block digestor was announced by Technicon. Both techniques involve the use of the Technicon AutoAnalyzer® II. One drawback of this approach is that it requires expensive single-purpose, dedicated instrumentation and specially trained personnel for its efficient application.

(iv) Gas–liquid chromatography is claimed to provide a complete analysis of the amino acids throughout the brewing process. However, a literature survey indicates that no single technique encompasses all of the amino acids acceptably. The following selected examples from work carried out over the last decade (1967–1977) are indicative of the status of this method.

Jones and Pierce (1967) tracked the fate of amino acids during mashing and hop boiling, analysing their samples by the methods of Spackman, Moore and Stein using an amino acid analyser designed and built by themselves. Their results are discussed under section E. Heyse and Piendl (1972) reported the behaviour of 19 enzymes of a bottom-fermenting flocculent brewery yeast in the context of three worts of different composition: twenty amino acids were tracked by gas chromatography; differences were shown between lager beer wort, export beer wort and strong beer wort. Chen et al. (1973) investigated the effect of mashing temperature on the nitrogenous constituents of beer and wort by means of gas–liquid chromatography of N-trifluoroacetyl-n-butyl esters following the general method developed by Gehrke et al. (1971), following ultrafiltration of the beer in order to remove macromolecular substances. Otter and Taylor (1976) analysed directly a variety of beers and worts by gas–liquid chromatography following the isolation of amino acids by several techniques. They concluded that the best combination for the complete gas–liquid chromatographic analysis of the beer amino acids is as follows: hisitidine, tryptophan, arginine and cystine should be determined as the N-trifluoroacetyl-n-butyl esters on an OV 17/210 column and the balance of 18 amino acids should be estimated as the heptafluorobutyric esters on an SE 30 column. Through this combination of methods, it is possible to determine all the amino acids along with similar compounds such as 4-aminobutyric and 4-aminobenzoic acids, sarcosine, etc.

(v) High-pressure liquid chromatography has been used recently (Herwig et *al.* 1977). Several advantages are claimed, but no quantitative details are provided.

(vi) Radioactive techniques. Jones and Pierce's tracking in 1969 of individual amino acids and the rate of their uptake by yeast is a good example of the application of radioactive techniques. After spiking with the appropriate ^{14}C-labelled amino acid and following a specified procedure, the individual amino acids are estimated for radioactivity using a scintillation method. Results are derived by calculation from the radioactivity

TABLE 17. Amino acid analyses of beers (mg/l)

	European (German)	Canadian
Glycine	10·8–50·9	59–68
Alpha alanine	28·2–206·1	65–175
Beta Alanine	0·6–2·7	ND
Gamma aminobutyric acid	30·4–78·0	124–163
Valine	21·6–149·6	159–169
Leucine	23·5–159·1	57–89
Isoleucine	11·6–75·0	40–65
Sarcosine	1·9–4·9	ND
Serine	9·3–29·6	59–63
Threonine	7·1–18·6	67–116
Aspartic acid	16·7–82·4	48–68
Asparagine	1·0–15·7	ND
Glutamic acid	17·3–76·3	70–97
Glutamine	5·8–17·5	ND
Pyroglutamic acid	5·1–13·8	ND
Arginine	24·6–292·6	165–185
Lysine	16·4–47·1	77–80
Citrullin	1·1–8·1	ND
Ornithin	0–7·1	51–63
Phenylalanine	9·5–38·0	56–76
Tyrosine	13·9–96·2	38–65
Cysteine	7·7–21·4	94–130
Cystine	2·5–7·8	ND
Methionine	5·0–9·6	29–36
Tryptophane	4·5–19·9	48–61
Hisitidine	16·1–46·3	14–18
Proline	242·2–761·9	45–46
Hydroxyproline	3·2–7·8	25–34
Total amino acids	574·6–2284·5	1882–2192

ND = Not determined.
(1) Drawert *et al.*(1975) "German" analyses are by gas–liquid chromatography. Ranges cited are averages of duplicate analyses of a variety of German beers; the upper levels refer to values in Helles Stark Bier.
(2) Chen *et al.* (1973) "Canadian" analyses are by gas–liquid chromatography of Canadian ales and lagers (mashing at 40 °C).

data and are expressed as micrograms of α-amino nitrogen per ml of medium.

Table 17 shows a compilation (from Drawert *et al.* 1975 and Chen *et al.* 1973) of ranges of amino acids (in mg/l) in a variety of beers, determined by gas–liquid chromatography following TAB and TMS-derivative formation.

4. Nucleic Acid Derivatives

The presence in beer of nucleotidic materials, derived both from the mash and from yeast activity during fermentation, has long been known. The pioneer work of Harris and Parsons (1957, 1958) showed the presence in wort of certain nucleosides and free bases and Reich and Bock (1959) investigated the presence of nucleotides in beer by absorption on resin columns, precipitation of the eluate with uranyl acetate, followed by its hydrolysis and re-chromatography on resin. Identification was based on ultraviolet absorption at 260 nm, a wavelength at which beer has a high optical density.

The same technique of chromatographic separation and identification by further chromatography and spectrophotometry was used by Lee and Lewis (1968) to identify in commercial beer three nucleotides, four free bases (purines and pyrimidines), and three nucleosides, along with nicotinamide-adenine dinucleotide (and its reduced form), nucleotide triphosphate and oligonucleotides. A semi-qualitative estimate was that, of the UV-absorbing substances in beer, 58% was nucleotidic material: this comprised 6·2% nucleotides, 32% nucleoside/free bases, and 6% nucleotide triphosphate and oligonucleotides.

Somers and Ziemelis (1972) attempted a further interpretation of ultraviolet absorption in wort and beer through partial resolution of the ultraviolet-absorbing constituents by direct gel column analysis, with continuous monitoring of the effluent at 280 nm. Identification of fractions from the gel column was effected by cellulose thin-layer chromatography.

As recently as 1973, the identification of beer nucleotidic material was based on R_f values; direct quantitative spectrophotometric measurements on eluates or extracts of "spots" excised from the chromatogram were the only means in use, admittedly both tedious and imprecise. Scanning spectrophotometry in one or other of its forms (reflectance, transmittance or fluorescence) was the next advance. Buday *et al.* (1972) used reflectance spectrodensitometry to determine quantitatively beer and wort nucleic acid derivatives. Sixteen such materials were estimated; several unresolved and some unknown components were also reported. Chen *et al.* (1973) reported additional data on the nucleic acid components of wort and ale by thin-layer chromatography and spectrodensitometry. Optimum quantitation by this method depends upon scanning each separated compound at its maximum and measurement of subtended peak areas with a digital integrator, thus relying on expensive instrumentation.

Steward et al. (1974) isolated beer nucleotidic material by anion exchange chromatography. CMP was the only mononucleotide tentatively identified by ultraviolet spectroscopy and retention volume data. No mononucleotides could be obtained by chromatography of charcoal extracts of beer on diethylaminoethyl Sephadex.

A microbead anion-exchange chromatographic system was employed by Pickett (1974) who identified the eluted materials by measuring their absorption between 230 and 300 nm and comparing the spectra with those quoted for nucleotides in the literature. Concentrations of seven beer nucleotides were calculated: CMP, AMP, UMP, IMP, GMP, 5'-GMP and 5'-XMP.

Charalambous et al. (1974a, b, 1975) have applied high-pressure liquid chromatography (HPLC) to the separation, identification and quantitative determination of free bases and nucleosides (1974a) in wort, beer (26 U.S. and foreign beers), malt liquors and wine; also in a great variety of worts prepared in different ways. Nucleotides were next determined by HPLC in 13 U.S. and foreign beers and malt liquors (1975). Free bases, nucleosides and nucleotides were also determined by Charalambous et al. in a single brew at various points in its brewing (1974a, 1975). An important feature of this method is that it permits the direct injection of straight wort, beer, malt beverage or wine through the liquid chromatography unit: no prior treatment of the sample for isolation of the free bases and nucleosides is required. Sample pretreatment is still necessary in the case of nucleotides.

Table 18 presents a comparison of beer content in free bases, nucleosides and nucleotides by various methods.

D. Effects on Beer Quality

The nitrogenous constituents of beer are essential for yeast reproduction; also, they influence the flavour, the colour, the head retention, the haze formation, and the biological stability of beer.

1. Yeast Nutrition

A considerable body of work (summarized in section E) has long established the importance of amino acids as essential factors for yeast growth during fermentation. The experiments of Jones and Pierce (1964, 1965, 1969, 1974) have established both the sequence and the rate of absorption of α-amino acids from wort by yeasts. Further, they have provided sufficient evidence to conclude that, because of the yeasts's transaminase activities, the overall supply of α-amino nitrogen is of greater significance than the amounts of

TABLE 18. Comparison of beer content in free bases, nucleosides and nucleotides by various methods (mg/l)

	Uri-dine	Ura-cil	Ino-sine	Xan-thine	Guano-sine	Adeno-sine	Cyti-dine	5'-UMP	2',3'-CMP	2',3'-UMP	5'-GMP, 3'-IMP	2'-GMP	3'-AMP	3'-GMP	5'-AMP
Buday et al. (1972) reflectance	16, 16	8, 14	2, 7	8–12	40–46	5, 11	30–29	0·5, 0·3			0·5, 0·3				
Chen et al. (1973) reflectance (40 °C mashing)		8, 19	0·8	13, 22	49–43	7, 5							18		3
Pickett (1974) anion exchange								1·1–4·5	2·7–4·1	1·1–4·5		0·7–1·2			0·5–1·9
Charalambous et al. (1974, 1975) HPLC	29–209	0–3	0–2	1–23	40–157	2–35	21–69	0·1–0·6	0·1–2·1	0·2–3·8	0·1–0·8	0·4–1·0	1·2–17	0·1–4·3	0·1–0·5

Note: The purpose of this tabulation is strictly for qualitative comparison purposes, to indicate the state-of-the-art.

individual amino acids (Klopper 1974). From the practical point of view, this leads to the question of the amount of assimilable nitrogen needed in the wort for adequate yeast nutrition. This range is quoted as being from about 140 mg/l (Yoshida, 1968a, b) to about 180 p.p.m. (Enari 1974a, b). In practice, due to the several factors affecting it, the total amino nitrogen of an 11° Plato wort can vary from 80 to 200 mg/l. Between one-third and one-half of that is lost during fermentation, the total amino nitrogen in beer varying from 25 to 110 mg/l (cf. Table 1).

From Jones and Pierce's (1967) experiments with top-fermenting yeast and those of Palmqvist and Äyräpää (1969) involving bottom-fermenting yeast, it can be seen that not all amino acids are of equal importance (Enari 1974a, b). The amino acids are utilized by yeast in a certain order, with slight variations depending on the particular yeast strain. Jones (1974) also comments that when the wide range in wort amino acid content is considered, a distinction should be made between total amino acid concentration and the relative proportions of the constituent amino acids: these two types of variation may have very different effects on the quality of the finished beer.

2. Flavour

(a) *Amino acids*

Both the total amino nitrogen amount and the spectrum of its constituent amino acids influence the flavour of the finished beer through a variety of complex biochemical pathways, since amino acids are metabolized by yeasts via different nitrogen and carbon skeleton pathways. It is these metabolic reactions, involving carbon skeletons and sulphur-containing moieties, that may result in flavour differences. Jones (1974) has shown the influence of amino acid concentration of wort on yeast growth in the range of 70–290 mg/l in an 11° P wort: the yeast growth, as shown by dry weight in g/l, is linear up to 100 mg/l; it then decreases sharply, reaching a plateau at about 200 mg/l, and levels off above this. This agrees with Yoshida's (1968) finding that about 100 mg/l of α-amino nitrogen is required for a healthy yeast leading to a maximum fermentation rate. It is accepted that the lion's share of the wort amino acid content serves to synthesize new cellular and enzymic yeast proteins. However, a correlation has also been found between the wort amino acid content and the formation of higher alcohols, esters and carbonyl compounds in the resulting beer (Äyräpää 1971). Further, Wainwright (1971) demonstrated that the wort's content of the sulphur-containing amino acid methionine markedly influences the production of volatile sulphur compounds by yeast: a methionine-poor wort leads to higher sulphur dioxide and hydrogen sulphide levels in beer. The latter effect is also brought about on the other hand by *high* amounts of glycine, threonine, serine, lysine and histidine.

Finally, changes in the fermentation rate, resulting from variations in the amino acid composition of wort, can also affect the flavour characteristics of beer. For example, an increase in the amino acid levels of wort can in general accelerate the fermentation and stimulate pyruvate production, leading to acetolactate and hence to diacetyl—an older observation (Portno 1966) that addition of valine to the wort inhibited diacetyl production notwithstanding. Enari's results confirm Jones' finding that higher α-amino nitrogen levels in the wort can cause the production of more diacetyl precursor by certain yeast strains (Jones 1974).

(b) *Nucleotides*

Nucleotides belong to the category of flavour-modifiers or enhancers: though present at levels lower than their taste thresholds, they interact synergistically or antagonistically with other constituents, thereby altering the normal flavour profile.

Flavour-active nucleotides have been reported in beer in amounts up to 30 mg/l. (Charalambous *et al.* 1975, Steiner 1974, Pickett 1974, Chen *et al.* 1973, Clapperton 1971a, b). The flavour changes have been characterized as follows: bitter and grainy notes are enhanced by 5'-cytosine monophosphate, 5'-guanosine monophosphate and 5'-uridine monophosphate, while 5'-cytosine monophosphate enhanced sourness at 2 p.p.m.; the 3'- and 2'-isomers also modified the normal blended character of the beer (U.S.A. lager) especially after storage (Charalambous *et al.* 1975). Steiner (1974) reported the beer as being fuller initially, with a strengthening and lingering of bitterness, also a marked mouthfeel: these flavour changes resulted from addition of 2–4 mg/l 5'-guanosine monophosphate to a low-gravity beer and a pale ale. Pickett (1974) stated that flavour profile analysis did not show consistent alterations of individual flavour notes even with 100 mg/l of 5'-guanosine monophosphate added to an English ale. Clapperton (1971) noted that "fuller flavour" resulted from the addition of 5 mg/l 5'-guanosine monophosphate and 10 mg/l 5'-uridine monophosphate.

3. Colour

The boiling of worts with high amino nitrogen levels results in colour development through the Maillard reaction, a problem particularly in ale brewing. The most important browning reaction is believed to take place between the imino acid proline (principal amino acid in wort and beer) and maltose leading to 3-hydroxy-2-methyl-4-pyrone (maltol). The level of proline in wort (280–340 mg/l; Moll *et al.* 1974) can thus affect colour development in beer; this, however, can be controlled through the use of adjuncts which reduce the proline concentration.

4. Head Retention

The wort nitrogen fraction which is not assimilated by yeast has a function in beer's foam stability. The question then arises whether the use of adjuncts, which leads to a reduction of this nitrogen fraction, might also result in a deterioration of the beer foam stability. Klopper (1974) has reported a comparison of all-malt brews with brews containing 40% adjuncts: the assessment of foam stability and foam cling by means of newly developed automatic instrumentation showed no significant difference. It may thus be concluded that beer contains sufficient proteinaceous matter to ensure adequate head retention. Other findings (Enari 1974a, b) had pointed to an enhancement of the head retention of beer by a relatively high concentration of head-forming peptides, an increase in barley protein content leading to improved foam stability. Again, Bishop (1975) notes that foam enhancement arises also from proteoses (amino acid complexes) which tend to be lower in cystine content and show less combination with phenolic compounds. It is generally agreed that beer complexes of molecular weight 5000–12 000 (or higher) and mainly combined with glucose polymers, are those chiefly involved in foam enhancement.

5. Haze Formation

A survey of recent literature, and particularly of reports of the E.B.C. Haze and Foam Group, over the last several years leads to the following currently held concepts. Most beer hazes have been shown by numerous workers to consist of two-thirds proteoses (amino acid complexes) and one-third polyphenols. About 30 years ago (Sandegren 1947) β-globulin was implicated as the nitrogenous component in beer haze. However, over the last 10 years, the application of immunological specific techniques (cf. section 3(c)) has pinpointed the derivation of the nitrogenous haze moiety to be from albumins and barley hordein. Grabar and Daussant in 1971 claimed to have established the immunological identity of the haze and foam proteoses; this identity, however, is not complete since the haze proteoses are rich in sulphur (due to their high cystine content) while the foam proteoses are poor in sulphur (being low in cystine). Bishop (1975) has discussed the evidence for the reasons for and the processes whereby the association between beer haze and the sulphur-containing amino acid cystine might arise. On the one hand, proteoses and polyphenols weakly joined together, therefore easily dissociated by hydrogen bonding, are the haze precursors acknowledged in the past. On the other hand, oxidation of polyphenols to quinones, which oxidize further and couple through stronger, covalent linkages with several groupings of proteoses (such as the cysteine sulphydryl group) is another distinct possibility, supported by the relatively high cystine content of beer haze. In beer, the very high molecular weight of hazes would be attained through further association of pairs and trios of such polyphenolic or quinolic groupings.

In this context of haze formation due to the beer's complex nitrogenous constituents, a point of terminological order made by Bishop (1975) is worth stressing. Their molecular weight ranges (from over 150 000 to 150 000–2 000 000) as determined by some workers (Woof 1967, ten Hoopen 1973) would place them in the "true protein" category. However, this physical evidence notwithstanding, a host of results from chemical studies (nitrogen percentage, precipitation by trichloroacetic or nitrous acid, direct addition tests and immunoelectrophoretic data) point to the complex nitrogenous beer constituents *not* being true proteins. Since they are much larger than peptides and as "polypeptide" has become a catchall term for a range of ill defined molecular sizes, proteoses (referring to amino acid complexes) might be a better designation.

6. Biological Stability

Jones (1974) reported that increases in the α-amino nitrogen content of wort led to higher residual α-amino nitrogen levels in the finished beers and that their biological stability was impaired: they were stable only for 48 days (142 and 19 mg/ml amino nitrogen in wort and beer, respectively) as compared with 66 days (100 and 2 mg/l, amino nitrogen in wort and the corresponding beer, respectively). In this context, the beer's biological stability related to resistance to lactobacillus infection. The Group C, or less readily assimilable amino acids (cf. section A.2), glycine, phenylalanine, tyrosine and alanine comprised the residual α-amino nitrogen in the beer derived from the wort of high amino acid content.

E. Fate during Fermentation

A considerable amount of information exists in the literature on nitrogen utilization or metabolism, some of it already noted under sections B and C above. The salient points may be summarized as follows.

It is accepted that urea and most ammonium salts (but not nitrates) can serve as the only nitrogen sources for brewer's yeast (Ljungdahl and Sandegren 1953). Most yeasts can utilize L-amino acids (D- and L- in the cases of asparagine, aspartic and glutamic acids) as single nitrogen sources, but proline is scarcely utilized and cysteine, lysine and glycine hardly used. In wort, where the complete amino acid spectrum is available, Pierce in 1966 was able to classify the amino acids according to their speed of absorption at 50% utilization under brewery conditions (see section B.1).

Further experiments by Jones and Pierce (1964, 1965, 1969) have led to the conclusion that the order of amino acid uptake seemingly is not dependent upon the concentration of the individual amino acid: rather, it is dictated by permease enzymes which transport the amino acids into the yeast. Since it has been demonstrated that amino acids are not directly incorporated into new protein, transamination was the mechanism suggested in 1969 by Jones and Pierce for the yeast's utlization of most amino acids and this concept is still currently accepted (Klopper 1974). The absence of deamination might be the reason why lysine and certain other amino acids may be incorporated but not used as sole nitrogen sources.

Regarding nucleic acid nitrogen, Chen *et al.* (1973) indicate 10–12% utilization of wort nucleic acid materials, mostly nucleosides and free bases.

Yeast is also capable of utilizing some small peptides, although growth is considerably slower in cases where peptides are the only source of nitrogen. Polypeptides can also be metabolized, as yeasts elaborate low levels of proteolytic enzymes which eventually produce some nitrogen for the cell. Proteolysis, whether towards the end of the growth phase or earlier, may also be quite significant (Ingledew 1975).

IV. PHENOLIC COMPOUNDS OF BEER

A. Introduction

Beer contains a complex mixture of phenolic compounds, variously estimated as having an approximate average of 150 mg/l (Narziss 1972) to 350 mg/l (Ng and Moček 1973). Of this amount, about two-thirds is malt-derived, with hops supplying the balance. These phenolic compounds are classed mainly as semi-volatile and non-volatile; they comprise (a) simple monophenols and monomeric polyphenols; (b) oligomeric and polymeric polyphenols. All of them are prone to chemical changes under both aerobic and anaerobic conditions. Packaged beer may be conceived as a closed system with its components and the air interlocked in a dynamic and ever-changing equilibrium because of chemical interactions. The brewing industry has become increasingly aware of the significance of these phenolic compounds in relation to the colour, the taste and, particularly, the non-biological stability of beer.

The importance of phenolic compounds for beer flavour is now well recognized. Some authors ascribe to polyphenols direct beneficial effects on the organoleptic properties of beer, while others claim that certain poly-phenols in beer participate in the interactions of flavour potentiators which influence the formation of volatiles. On the other hand, over the last two decades, it has been established that both chill and permanent hazes in beer are due to the gradual polymerization of phenolic compounds with proteins to yield insoluble complexes. The pioneer work of Harris and Ricketts (1956,

1959a, b, c, 1960) in England and of McFarlane in Canada (1957, 1963, 1964, 1965) is well known. The structure, properties (including polymerization) and occurrence of phenolic compounds in hazes have been described in many articles, including the classical reports of Gramshaw (1967, 1969a, b, 1970a, b), and will not be considered in detail here. More recent research (Eastmond 1974a, b) has shown that, in contrast to monomers, it is the dimeric, trimeric and polymeric phenolic compounds which are of greater importance with regard to haze formation in beer. There is evidence that ferulic acid occurs in large polymers (Kringstad 1972), becoming involved in oxidative cross-linking (Geissman 1973), and also that certain natural beer constituents (e.g. pro-cyanidin B3) greatly increase the rate of haze formation (Eastmond 1974a, b). The practical conclusion is that, in determining the shelf-life of beer, the concentration of dimeric and polymeric phenolic compounds is much more important than that of the monomers. Also, that not all polyphenols are equally active in promoting haze formation.

Finally, reactive phenolic compounds of intermediate molecular weight (about 1000) appear to be related to the increase of beer colour through the browning reaction (Maillard reaction).

B. Classification of Phenolic Compounds in Beer

In contrast to their precise and well established classification in plants, the nature of the phenolic compounds in beer has sometimes been shrouded by a certain vagueness. Table 19, loosely based on a classification by Meilgaard (1974), attempts a taxonomy of the phenolic compounds in beer, noting their amounts.

C. Estimation

1. Introduction

Gramshaw, as late as 1970, summed up the results from a considerable body of work over the previous decade with the statement that there was still no reliable method of measuring total polyphenols in beer and brewing materials. The underlying reason for this is the large number of different types of compounds comprising the beer phenolic constituents, and the fact that even compounds of the same basic type exist in a range of molecular sizes—and even these may not be homogeneous with respect to phenolic type. These considerations point to the main difficulty besetting the methods proposed for the quantitative determination of "total polyphenols" in beer, namely the lack of a true representative sample of beer polyphenols for the purpose of calibration: in turn this leads to the procedures available for isolating polyphenols from beer being at best a compromise between efficiency and expediency. They point also, last but not least, to the desirability of agreeing upon exact nomenclature: avoiding terminological confusion by pinpointing "catechins" as flavan-3-ols, "anthocyanogens" as flavan-3,4-diols, and so on.

2. Isolation Procedures

To date, three general procedures exist for the isolation of polyphenols from beer, none of them being quite satisfactory.

(a) *Extraction* with ethyl acetate preceded by isooctane extraction (Owades 1955, 1958). This technique is expedient but not 100% efficient, for two reasons. The purpose of the prior extraction with isooctane is to remove isoalpha acids; however, it will not eliminate other interfering compounds (which will contribute to the final results) such as oxidized hop resin products in beer, those being insoluble in isooctane. Also, ethyl acetate will not extract polyphenols associated with protein.

(b) Adsorption on to some polyamide powder (Nylon; Orlon; Perlon) or on to polyvinylpyrrolidone. First introduced by Harris and Ricketts (1956, 1959, 1960) and subsequently modified (McFarlane and Bayne 1961a, b, Steiner and Stocker 1967, 1969), this is a more selective technique leading to the estimation of anthocyanogens in wort and beer. Elution of polyphenols, however, from the polyamides is neither easy nor quantitative. Steiner and Stocker (1967a, b) have also used adsorption of PVPP to good advantage with aqueous dimethylformamide as eluant.

(c) *Precipitation* with lead acetate: Ng and Moček (1973) adapted the long known ability of lead acetate to precipitate polyphenols, to produce an isolation procedure which allows the complete removal of phenolic acids and polyphenols from beer under relatively mild conditions. Following treatment with acetone, a beer sample is treated with lead acetate and then separated into two fractions, one acid and the other alkaline, by addition of sodium hydroxide. Following treatment with an ion-exchange resin, either ethyl acetate or methanol is used to extract the polyphenols in the acid and alkaline fractions. Both of these fractions were shown to contain predominantly polyphenols; having established that, of the known potential interfering materials, melanoidins exert only a minimal effect, the assumption was made that the total polyphenols in each fraction was equal to the difference between total dry weight and weights of protein and carbohydrate (over-whelming components of beer, also precipitated by lead acetate) and ash, each determined independently.

3. Methods of Determination

(a) *Total polyphenols*

Over the last two decades a number of methods of considerable variety have

TABLE 19. Classification of phenolic compounds in beer

Class	Group	Typical representative	Congeners	Amount of group in beer
Monophenols	Phenolic alcohols	HO—⟨ ⟩—CH₂CH₂OH *tyrosol*		3–40 mg/l
	Phenolic acids	HO—⟨ ⟩—CH=CH—COOH *p-coumaric acid*	ferulic, vanillic, gallic, caffeic, syringic, sinapic acids, etc.	10–30 mg/l including esters and glycosides, e.g. chlorogenic acid, neo-chlorogenic acid
	Phenolic amines and amino acids	HO—⟨ ⟩—CH₂CH₂N(CH₃)(CH₃) *hordenine*	tyramine, N-methyl tyramine, tyrosamine, tyrosine	10–20 p.p.m. (3–8 p.p.m. as tyrosine)
Monomeric Polyphenols	Flavonoids (polyhydroxyflavans) Catechines flavan-3-ols	*(+)-catechin*	(+) catechin (+) epicatechin, possibly other isomers	0·5–13 mg/l 1–10 mg/l
	Anthocyanogens (leucoanthocyanins, flavan-3,4-diols)	*leucocyanidin*	leucocyanidin leucopelargonidin leucodelphinidin	4–80 mg/l 0–5 mg/l 1–10 mg/l
	Flavonols (polyhydroxyflavones) Quercetins	*quercetin*	kaempferol, myricetin (occur as glycosides) iso-quercitin astragalin rutin	less than 10 p.p.m.

Condensed

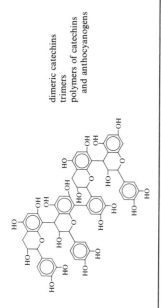

dimeric catechins 5–8 mg/l
trimers 1 mg/l
polymers of catechins uncertain
and anthocyanogens

been proposed for the determination of total polyphenols in beer, brewing materials and beer hazes. These methods include: ultraviolet measurement (Owades 1955); nephelometry (Chapon 1960, 1964); permanganate oxidation (Singleton 1969); and colorimetry (Woof and Pierce 1967, Singleton 1974, de Clerck and Jerumanis 1967, Bishop 1972a, b, Ng and Moček 1973, A.O.A.C. Official methods 1975). Colorimetry appears to be the method of choice; various chromogenic reagents have been suggested. Woof and Pierce (1966) used diazotized p-aminobenzoic acid for colour development. This method has the advantage of not requiring prior isolation of the phenolic compounds but suffers from being too non-specific: for example, humulones contribute to the overall colour.

Singleton and co-workers (1974) favour the Folin–Ciocalteau reagent under specific conditions. The reaction is based on oxidation of the phenolic compounds by the molybdotungstophosphoric acid heteropolyanion in alkaline solution, with the reduction of the original yellow anion to a blue complex heteropolyanion which is measured. This colorimetric method is claimed to work equally well with wine, beer, fruit juices and many biological samples.

The de Clerck and Jerumanis method (1967), after further elaboration by Bishop (1972), has been adopted by the E.B.C. (1975). This procedure involves treatment of the sample with the sodium salt of carboxymethylcellulose of low viscosity and disodium ethylenediaminetetraacetate. The polyphenols are then reacted with ferric iron in alkaline solution and the red colour developed is measured at 600 nm against a blank.

A newer colorimetric procedure, that of Ng and Moček (1973), involves the isolation of polyphenols through lead acetate precipitation (as detailed in

TABLE 20. Total polyphenol content of beer (mg/l)

Origin	No. of beers	Method	Range (mg/l)	References
European	2	Colorimetry $FeCl_3$	182, 195	de Clerck (1947)
American	9	UV	129–271	Owades et al. (1958)
American	14	Colorimetry $FeCl_3$	25–55	Stone and Gray (1961)
American	11	UV	133–214	Nakayama (1961)
American	2	UV	93, 112	Sogawa (1972)
European	3	UV	102–123	Sogawa (1972)
Japanese	37	UV	71–90	Sogawa (1972)
European	3	Colorimetry (E.B.C.) (ammonium ferric citrate)	147–187	Bishop (1972)
Canadian	10	Colorimetry (4-amino antipyrine)	471–786	Ng and Mocek (1973)
American	40	Colorimetry (E.B.C.)	82–205	Charalambous et al. (1972–1977)

section C.2(c)) followed by the use of 4-aminoantipyrine to develop colour which is measured at 550 nm against a blank. This method is unique in this respect: spectrophotometric calibration is carried out using as standards a truly representative sample of polyphenols actually isolated from beer by lead acetate precipitation.

Table 20 presents some estimates of the total polyphenol content of beer by various methods. As will be noted, there is no absolute concordance between these total polyphenol values. This, however, is only to be expected since these values were arrived at by using different methods of isolation of polyphenols, different calibration standards and different reagents for colour development. In view of the diversity of chemical structure and molecular size (cf. Table 19) of the components comprised in the complex mixture of phenolic compounds in beer and possible interference from other beer components in each case (proteins, carbohydrates, α-acids, melanoidins, etc.), the lack of agreement is hardly surprising.

(b) *Specific classes of phenolic compounds*

(i) *Monophenols.* Beer contains a range of 25–60 mg/l of phenolic alcohols, phenolic acids, phenolic amines and phenolic amino acids (cf. Table 19). The phenolic alcohols and phenolic acids of beer have been estimated by various forms of chromatography. Harris (1956), McFarlane and Wye (1957) and Sogawa (1971, 1972, 1973) all identified a host of phenolic acids using paper chromatography coupled with ultraviolet spectrophotometry. This pioneer work led to paper chromatography assuming a dominant position in the field of monophenol analysis; however, it is a technique which has been reviewed extensively and exhaustively in the past (Harborne 1968, Timberlake 1975) and in view of this, and the advent of other forms of chromatography, it will not be discussed here beyond noting the recent work of Charalambous *et al.* (1970–1972) on the phenolic alcohols and phenolic acids of beer and wine using paper chromatography.

Following the above work, thin-layer and gas–liquid chromatography have been applied to the analysis of beer monophenols by several workers. Chapon *et al.* (1961), Bandari (1964), Brumsted *et al.* (1965) and Silbereisen and Kraffczyk (1967) investigated the phenolic acids in beer and brewing materials by thin-layer chromatography on plates coated with starch/polyamide, polyamide and silica gel; developing systems varied from benzene/methanol to ethyl acetate/acetic acid in the first direction and 30% aqueous acid in the second direction (Chapon 1961). Visualization was effected by the usual colour reagents: one per cent ferric chloride, diazotized *p*-nitroaniline and diazotized sulphanilic acid. Gas–liquid chromatography has been used by Dalgliesh *et al.* (1966), and many others all of whom noted this technique's inherent drawback in this context: the non-volatile nature of the beer

monophenols renders their transformation into volatile derivatives mandatory, with the invariably attendant analytical errors arising from poor
quantitation and the formation of artefacts. Most recently, Drawert *et al.*
(1977) have reported on the estimation of phenolic compounds in beer
(including monophenols of all classes) using an all-glass gas chromatograph.
Separation was first carried out by adsorption on polyvinyl polypyrrolidone
and elution with aqueous dimethylformamide, followed by silylation with
hexamethyldisilazan in dimethylformamide.

' Liquid chromatography using columns with different packings has been
used with varying success in the separation and estimation of monophenols.
Hermann and Mosel (1973) were able to determine quantitatively several beer
monophenols by means of a polyamide column. More recently,
Charalambous *et al.* (1973) reported on the successful use of high-pressure
liquid chromatography using a Vydac polar bonded phase as support and
gradient elution solvent systems. The monophenol values obtained by these
workers using HPLC are quoted by Drawert *et al.* (1977) as agreeing well with
their monophenol values in beer analysed by gas–liquid chromatography
following silylation.

The phenolic amines and amino acids of beer account for 10–20 mg/l of the
25–60 mg/l total monophenols present in beer. McFarlane in 1965 devised
methods for the quantitative estimation of the tyrosine-derived amines and
phenols in brewing materials, wort and beer. Separation was effected by
column chromatography (cellulose/alumina), identification of the materials
by thin-layer chromatography (cellulose) and estimation by colorimetry with
Folin's phenol reagent.

In 1964, McFarlane *et al.* had reported on the determination of aromatic
alcohols in beer. Of present interest is his procedure of extracting 2-(*p*-
hydroxyphenyl)ethanol (tyrosol) and 3-β-hydroxyphenylindole (tryptophol)
from beer with ethyl acetate, followed by chromatographic separation of a
chloroform solution on a silicic acid–alumina column. Estimation was by
colorimetry (vanillin–hydrochloric acid reagent for tryptophol and Millon's
reagent for tyrosol). (See also section V.)

In 1971 and 1972, Charalambous *et al.* reported on a column chromatographic method (silicic acid) leading to the separation of several beer-derived
monophenols and quantitation of tyrosol. Identification was carried out by
paper chromatography backed by spectroscopy in the case of tryptophol;
tyrosol was isolated from beer in crystalline form and identified by mass
spectroscopy and nuclear magnetic resonance. The same workers (1976) also
determined tyrosol quantitatively in beer by means of high-pressure liquid
chromatography (Aminex 6 packing; 0·5 M ammonium formate, pH 4·75;
62 °C).

Szlavko (1973) used a gas chromatographic method for determining the aromatic higher alcohols in beer, reporting findings which support the values determined by Charalambous *et al.* (1972). Table 21 summarizes the available data.

(ii) *Monomeric polyphenols.* Beer contains a range of 70–100 mg/l of flavan-3-ols (catechins), flavan-3,4-diols (anthocyanogens) and flavanols (cf. Table 19).

Flavan-3-ols: The pioneer work of McFarlane *et al.* (1961, 1963) set the stage for the modern investigation of catechins in beer and is now mainly of historical interest. Markham (1975) has reviewed developments in this field. More recently, high-pressure liquid chromatography was applied by Charalambous *et al.* (1973) and gas chromatography by Drawert *et al.* (1977) to the determination of catechin in beer. Both authors used the same conditions as in their estimation of the monophenols and their values for D-catechin are in good agreement.

McGuiness *et al.* in 1975 described a gas–liquid chromatographic method for the estimation of monomeric and dimeric catechin in beer. A half-dozen commercial U.K. beers (lagers, ales, stouts) were examined leading to values of 0·5–5·5 mg/l of monomeric and of 0·5–4·0 mg/l proanthocyanidins or dimeric catechins. In an experimental all-malt brew, 8·0 mg/l monomeric and 22·0 mg/l dimeric catechin were determined. A synthetic pentahydroxyflavone (not a normal beer constituent) was used as internal standard.

Flavan-3,4-diols: Harris and Ricketts in 1959 introduced the term "antho-cyanogen" to denote those beer phenolic compounds that are converted by heating with hydrochloric acid from a colourless or "leuco" state to red anthocyanidin pigments. Subsequent research, detailed by Haslam (in Mabry 1975), showed "leucoanthocyanins" actually to comprise flavan-3,4-diols and flavan-3-ol polymers. In order to differentiate between them, Weinges *et al.* in 1969 introduced the trivial names "leucoanthocyanidins" to designate the monomeric flavan-3,4 diols and "proanthocyanidins" to refer to dimeric and oligomeric flavan-3-ols. The latter, first comprising two subdivisions, pro-anthocyanidins A and B, differing in the number of intermonomer covalent bonds, soon had additional proanthocyanidins (C, D, E, F, G) added to the group as more oligomeric flavan-3-ols were discovered (Haslam *et al.* 1972).

The colorimetric method of Harris and Ricketts (1959a, b, c) for the determination of "anthocyanogens" (that is, leucoanthocyanidins or flavan-3,4-diols) and catechins (flavan-3-ols) has been extensively used. It involves precipitation of these compounds with lead acetate, regeneration of their lead salts with hydrogen sulphide, and separation by chromatography on large cellulose columns using aqueous acetic acid as eluant. Two-dimensional paper chromatography was used for further fractionation of these column eluates. This method was modified by Pollock *et al.* (1960) and McFarlane (1961a, b).

TABLE 21. Content of phenolic amines and related compounds in beer (mg/l)

Tyrosol	Tryptophol	Hordenine	N-Methyl tyramine	Origin	Method	Reference
3–18	0·9–2·5	11·7–13·4	6·8–7·9	Canadian	Colorimetry	McFarlane (1964)
10–12				American	Gravimetry	Charalambous (1972)
8–20 (6 beers)				American	HPLC	Charalambous (1976)
6–15 (6 beers)		0·5–12·1		Canadian	GLC	Szlavko (1974)

McFarlane *et al.* (1963) utilized this technique to investigate the selective adsorption of flavan-3,4-diols and flavan-3-ols on other polymers, such as Nylon-66 and Polyclar-AT. Woof *et al.* (1967, 1968) employed first Sephadex (G-10, G-15, G-25 and G-75) and then Bio-Gel (P-2 and P-10) in an attempt to benefit from both the sieving effect of the former and the adsorptivity of the latter, but obtained poor separation. Schmid *et al.* (1961) used Perlon columns while Silbereisen and Kraffczyk (1967) opted for polyamide column chromatography followed by re-chromatography on silica gel, reporting 40–75 mg/l "anthocyanogens" in several beers.

A method for the simultaneous determination of total flavonoids in beer by spectrophotometry (at both 455 nm and 545 nm absorption maxima) was proposed by Dadic in 1971; leucocyanidin and D($\pm$)-catechin were used as representative standards for flavan-3,4-diols and flavan-3-ols, respectively.

Flavanols: This class of flavonoid comprises both flavonols and flavones. Lager beer is stated to contain about 10 p.p.m. of quercetin, kaempferol, myricetin and the glycosides astragalin, *iso*quercitrin and rutin. Their estimation has been carried out by the various forms of chromatography, as described for the flavonoids. McFarlane and Wye (1957) used paper chromatography; Vancraenenbroeck *et al.* (1965, 1969) utilized ion-exchange chromatography and Hermann and Mosel (1973) polyamide column chromatography; Charalambous *et al.* (1973) high-performance liquid chromatography.

(c) *Oligomeric and polymeric polyphenols*

These condensed phenolic dimers, oligomers and polymers amount to 20–60 mg/l in beer. The procedures used to examine these beer components include paper chromatographic analysis using different solvent systems, hydrolysis with acids of varying strength, elution characteristics from columns of Sephadex and polyamide resin, gas–liquid chromatography of trimethylsilyl and trifluoroacetyl derivatives, and comparison of the ultraviolet, nuclear magnetic resonance and mass spectra for each oligomer and polymer.

Gas–liquid chromatography is currently being used for further studies of dimeric flavonoids involved in beer haze formation. Gracey and Barker in 1976 found three unresolved biflavan components in a gas chromatographic profile of beer : Nylon adsorbates. One of these, the major component, had the same structure as Eastmond's beer isolate (1974a, b) namely procyanidin B3 (two (+) catechin units). The other two biflavans were shown to be catechin–gallocatechin pairs, one being a prodelphinidin and the other a procyanidin.

In 1976, McGuiness *et al.* reported on a radio-dilution technique for estimating levels of dimeric catechin in beer and brewing materials. A ^{14}C-labelled dimer of catechin, procyanidin B4, was added to experimental pilot plant brews. Following a specified extraction technique and chromatography on a column of Sephadex LH 20, the level of the labelled dimer in beer was calculated to be in the range of 5–8 mg/l by scintillation counting. Also in 1976, Belleau *et al.* tentatively identified a substance isolated from beer as a catechin trimer.

The above summary of attempts to separate and estimate the flavonoids in beer does point to completely adequate methodology still not being available. For perfect avoidance of artefact formation and other forms of interference due to involved techniques of sample pretreatment, high-performance liquid chromatography might prove the best candidate for this purpose, followed by structural determination by mass spectroscopy and nuclear magnetic resonance spectroscopy.

D. Fate of Phenolic Compounds during the Brewing Process

Progress in the accurate determination of changes in the concentration of phenolic compounds during the brewing and fermentation processes has been relatively slow for the reasons already mentioned in section C.1, namely complexity of the mixture of phenolic compounds in beer due to both their great number and the diversity of their molecular structures. Gramshaw in 1970 summarized the situation and commented on the ambiguity of results obtained using the multiplicity of reagents which lend themselves to the estimation of beer phenolic compounds.

Even at this late date, this point perhaps still needs to be made: each of the several methods proposed for the estimation of phenolic compounds in beer over the last two decades, and outlined under section C.3, applies to a class or group of phenolic compounds sharing certain specific common properties. The results by each individual method refer to a part only of the whole. Their comparison is not always warranted and may even lead to erroneous interpretations of the situations they are meant to define. This is particularly valid as regards efforts geared to establishing the changes in wort polyphenols during fermentation. The following brief survey of representative results from the literature over the period 1947–1967 will bear this out, before discussing findings spanning the following decade 1967–1977.

In 1947 and 1948, de Clerck and Piratzky using the catchall colorimetric method that leads to the determination of coloured ferric ion complexes of polyphenols, reported separately that, during fermentation, the polyphenols decrease roughly by 25%. In 1955, McFarlane *et al.* reported on a small increase of "polyphenols" during fermentation. In this pioneer work, acid hydrolysis of precursors subsequently labelled "anthocyanogens" led to the formation of red-coloured pigments (anthocyanins). In 1960, Pollock and Krauss et al., using a modification of the Harris and Ricketts procedure, separated the precursors on nylon. Following acid hydrolysis, they measured the anthocyanin concentration by measuring the red colour produced. Their conclusion was: little or no change in phenolic compounds during fermentation. In 1961, Chapon developed a nephelometric procedure the application of which led to these results: Chevalier et al. (1961) reported a diminution of polyphenols of about 50% during fermentation and Chollot et al. (1967) found no significant difference in polyphenols after fermentation. In 1965, Haboucha and Devreux concentrated on the anthocyanogens and reported that their affinity for the yeast depended on the physiological state of the latter.

In 1973, Hermann and Mosel reported on an extensive tracking of water-soluble phenolic acids, flavan-3-ols (catechins) and flavonols during the brewing and fermentation process. The changes of their concentrations were determined by quantitative methods leading to the exact determination of the individual phenolic compounds. Thus, flavan-3-ols were extracted from malt, hops, wort, hot and cold trub, and beer; they were then collected on a polyamide column which was extracted with methanol. Following purification, separation was effected on cellulose thin-layer plates and the individual flavan-3-ols were determined colorimetrically (vanillin-hydrochloric acid, 500 nm). This general approach was suitably modified in the case of the phenolic acids and the flavonols. It was found that catechin, epicatechin and gallocatechin (mostly malt-derived) were carried forward through the wort and beer to the end of the primary fermentation but were noticeably diminished during lagering and filtration; only traces of these phenolic compounds were found in the spent grains and in wort deposits.

In 1974, Moll et al. resumed their studies of the effect of fermentation on the fate of the beer phenolic compounds. They investigated such parameters as fermentation temperature, pitching rate, yeast strain, raw materials, etc. The polyphenols were identified by thin-layer chromatography which, followed by photodensitometry, gave qualitative results pointing to minor differences between the polyphenols of wort and beer. Any decrease in polyphenol content was ascribed to adsorption on the yeast cells and a diminution in solubility of some polyphenol–protein complexes due to the decrease in pH. None of the parameters investigated greatly affected this decrease.

In 1976, McGuiness et al. studied the fate of dimeric polyphenols during malting and brewing using a radio-dilution technique reported in section C.3.a(iii). It was found that the higher the level of dimeric polyphenols present in the malt, the greater the amount of these phenolic compounds in the resulting wort. However, when infusion mashing was carried out, less than half of the available dimeric polyphenols were extracted from the malt. Their concentration was in the range of 11–18 mg/l in sweet wort, 6–10 mg/l in boiled wort and 5–8 mg/l in beer. Also, wort boiling led to a substantial loss of dimeric polyphenols: only 20–25% of those originally present in the malt survived in the boiled wort.

E. Influence of Phenolic Compounds on the Non-biological Stability and the Taste of Beer

Biologically stable beers, when stored after packaging, may become cloudy and deposit a haze, becoming unacceptable. The rate of development of this haze determines the shelf-life of packaged beer. Apart from the permanent haze which develops upon storage of packaged beer at room temperature, a transient haze may also form when beer is suddenly cooled to 32 °F (0 °C). Such a haze, called a "chill haze", will disappear when the beer is allowed to reach ambient temperature (70 °F or 20 °C).

Gramshaw (1970b) summarized an extensive body of research on the composition of hazes, regretting the paucity of information on the polyphenolic moiety of hazes and attributing it to the lack of precision of the available methods of measurement. According to the best estimates, the polyphenolic portion of chill and permanent hazes appeared to be in the range of 20–60%; chill hazes from American beers seemed to contain less polyphenol material than those from European beers. However, this difference was found to be ascribable both to differences in brewing practice and to unsatisfactory methods of determination.

Since then, considerable research based on improved methodology has led to the following current concepts concerning non-biological beer hazes. Such hazes are not of constant composition but comprise a variety of materials which are insoluble in the beer, existing in particles small enough to remain in suspension. Large polymers, held together by relatively weak forces, form the major part of these materials, which are mainly polyphenols and polypeptides. Vancraenenbroeck (1974) stated that the properties of the polyphenol–polypeptide complex, which are relevant to beer haze formation, are more important than those of the component parts of the complex.

The characteristics (structure, properties, occurrence and polymerization) of phenolic compounds in hazes have been described in many articles and will not be discussed here in detail beyond noting the following recent findings. Monophenols can also occur in hazes: Kringstad (1972) and Geissman (1973) found evidence that a simple phenolic acid such as ferulic acid occurs in large polymers and may be involved in oxidative cross-linking. On the other hand, Moček (1972) points out that, among the flavan-3-ols and flavan-3,4-diols, not all catechins and leucoanthocyanins polymerize equally readily: the monomeric polyphenols are not equally active in haze formation. Eastmond and Gardner (1974) found that monomeric polyphenols had no significance in beer haze formation whereas dimeric and polymeric polyphenols increase greatly the rate of its formation. Thus, in determinging the shelf-life of beer, the concentration of dimeric and polymeric polyphenols is the more important criterion. McGuinness *et al.* (1975) confirmed that dimeric catechin promotes haze formation; it was also determined that the shelf-lives of beer with high dimer concentrations are very sensitive to the levels of air in the headspace. These observations extend Gramshaw's 1967 report that permanent haze is speedily induced by either a monomeric flavan-3,4-diol or a biflavan isolated from beer.

In general, a large number of different polyphenols and polypeptides can induce beer haze through becoming incorporated into complexes insoluble in beer. Inorganic compounds and carbohydrates can also be complexed chemically with the polyphenol–polypeptide aggregates.

From the practical point of view, improving the beer's shelf-life, through tampering with its polyphenol content, remains a possibility. It is still believed by many workers that all of the polyphenolic constituents of beer participate, to some extent, in haze formation; however, other workers claim that the role of the flavan-3,4-diols has been overemphasized, and it has long been accepted that there is no correlation between the anthocyanogen level and the haze potential of the beer (Silbereisen and Kraffczyk 1967). In fact, Gramshaw (1970) baldly stated that, as far as beer stability is concerned, there seems to be no point in measuring beer polyphenols as such. On the other hand, Vancraenenbroeck (1975) after refuting such doubts, states that the partial removal of polyphenols, and in particular of anthocyanogens, impedes the occurrence of turbidity. Such a removal, he claims (whether by treatment with polyvinylpyrrolidone, or with formaldehyde, or especially by aeration and moderate oxygenation during brewing), will stabilize the taste of the beer: after oxidation, polyphenols can contribute to a harsh taste in the beer.

Charalambous *et al.* (1969) confirmed the observation that formaldehyde treatment of wort (pilot plant brewery worts in this case) did reduce the anthocyanogen content of the finished beer (Macey *et al.* 1964). Since, however, this treatment at the same time reduced the protein content of the finished beer, it is a moot point which of these two decreases is chiefly responsible for the improvement in stability. This observation is in line with Gramshaw's comments (1970) on Whatling's (1968) and Witney's (1966) published data. These showed that formaldehyde addition to the final step of an otherwise conventional malting sequence reduced the wort anthocyanogen value, enhancing the stability of the derived beer, without stating whether some protein may not also have been removed by this procedure.

Charalambous *et al.* (1974) also found that reduced polyphenols added a touch of freshness to the beer taste, while in an oxidized state they contributed to the stale flavour.

The general conclusion from Vancraenenbroeck's (1975) findings is that any modification of the polyphenol composition during production can influence the quality of the finished beer.

V. OTHER BEER CONSTITUENTS OF LOW VOLATILITY

A. Lipids

1. Introduction

Beer contains small amounts of lipids; such fats and fat-like substances are both derived from the brewing raw materials (malt, adjuncts, hops) passing into the finished product, and are also formed by the yeast during fermentation (especially the free, lower fatty acids of chain length 4–10). The importance of lipids for beer quality stems from their effect on foam and flavour stability.

2. Origin

Wort lipids are derived mainly from the malt; when brewed with adjuncts, the lipid composition of the adjunct is directly reflected in that of the wort (Forch and Runkel 1974, Äyräpää 1974). Hops also contain lipids, mainly derived from the waxy surface coating and the seed oil of the hops. These hop lipids are of minor importance so far as normal hopping rates obtain and the hops used do not contain a high proportion of damaged seeds (Hildebrand 1975, Tripp et al. 1968).

The lipid concentration of barley decreases continuously during malting and a similar decrease is also noted during the brewing process. According to Forch (1974) only $0.1-3\%$ of the malt lipids measured in total fatty acid, free higher fatty acids (C_{12} to C_{18}), mono- and di-glyceride fractions end up in the hopped wort. Further, Forch et al. (1974) followed the fate of the barley lipids during fermentation and maturation of beer, arriving at the conclusion that there is no direct correlation between the lipid contents of the hopped wort and the resulting finished beer.

3. Concentration

Table 22 summarizes individual lipid fractions and their concentration in wort and beer (Forch and Runkel 1974). Table 23 shows the ranges of free fatty acids in certain types of beer (Klopper et al. 1975).

According to Klopper (1975 a decrease in free fatty acids can be observed throughout the brewing process: not only do the free fatty acids diminish following each purification step during the production and treatment of the

TABLE 22. Lipids in wort and beer

Lipid fraction	Hopped wort (mg/l)	Beer (mg/l)
Free fatty acids		
C_4–C_{10}	0·3–1	10–18
C_6–C_{12}	1	5–16
C_{12}–C_{18}	1·9–6·4	0·12–0·34
Total fatty acids	2·5–16·4	0·33–0·76
Monoglyceride	0·11–0·68	0·11–0·09
Diglyceride	0·17–0·90	0·03–0·16
Triglyceride	5–8	0·1–0·2
Sterols	0·22–0·34	0·01–0·02
Phospholipids (lysolecithin)	3	0–0·05

TABLE 23. Ranges of free fatty acids in beer (p.p.m.)

Fatty acids	Regular beers	High gravity beers	Low-alcohol beers
C8	3·6–6·4	2·2–4·8	0·1–2·1
C10	0·4–0·6	0·1–1·0	0·0–0·2
C12	0·1–0·3	0·1–0·6	0·0–0·1
C14	0·0–0·4	0·1–2·5	0·0–2·6
C16	0·1–0·3	0·1–0·5	0·1–1·2
C18	0·0	0·0–0·3	0·1–0·6
C18:1	0·0–0·1	0·0–0·8	0·1–0·2
C18:2	0·0–0·1	0·0–0·2	0·0–1·6
C18:3	0·0	0·0	0·0–0·2

wort, but fermentation may also be considered as an additional purification process in so far as, at least, the higher free fatty acids are concerned. Table 24 shows, on the one hand, a considerable increase in C_8 to C_{10} and a considerable decrease in C_{12} to $C_{18:3}$ during fermentation.

As can be seen from Table 23, the concentration of the free, lower fatty acids C_4 to C_{12} increases during fermentation, pointing to the greater importance to beer quality of these metabolic products of yeast as compared with the wort lipids.

The trends regarding increase and decrease of certain groups of free fatty acids shown in Tables 23 and 24 are also consistent with the findings of Rainbow et al. (1975).

TABLE 24. Free fatty acids during fermentation and storage (p.p.m.)

Fatty acids	Days primary 0	Fermentation 7	After 21 days storage	Filtered beer
C8	0·1	3·6	3·5	4·0
C10	0·0	0·5	0·5	0·5
C12	0·2	0·1	0·1	0·1
C14	1·6	0·1	0·2	0·1
C16	3·8	0·3	0·3	·0·2
C18	0·3	0·0	0·0	0·0
C18:1	1·5	0·1	0·0	0·1
C18:2	6·0	0·0	0·0	0·1
C18:3	0·7	0·0	0·0	0·0

4. Effect on Beer Quality

(a) *Wort lipids* (i.e. barley-derived)

Diglycerides have the greatest foam-destroying effect (Krauss *et al* 1972). The foam stability of beer is affected by amounts over 0·25 mg/l of diglycerides; 0·5 mg/l of monoglycerides; 1·5 mg/l of sterols. According to Rainbow *et al.* (1975) malt lipids may be a potential hazard to the head retention of ales, but are present in concentrations too low to influence beer foam. Apart from their foam-inhibiting effect, several wort lipids have also been indicted as precursors of some aroma compounds through oxidative and other processes (Visser and Lindsay 1971).

(b) *Yeast metabolism lipids*

According to Forch and Runkel (1974), in view of the very small proportion of the barley lipids that passes into the finished beer, it is more likely that lipids formed by yeast metabolism have the greater effect on the foam stability and aroma of beer.

Carrington *et al.* (1972) have studied the influence of fatty acids on gushing, determining that saturated fatty acids are weak gushing promoters, while unsaturated fatty acids are weak suppressants.

5. Estimation of Free Fatty Acids and other Lipids

MacPherson and Buckee (1974) have described a gas–liquid chromatographic method for estimating simultaneously from one injection the C_8 to C_{18} free fatty acids in beer, without any interference from other lipid materials such as glycerides and fatty acid esters. The older gas–liquid chromatographic procedure of Tripp *et al.* (1968) is extensively used by most workers in this field. Rainbow *et al.* (1975) mention their having determined free sterols in wort and beer by thin-layer chromatography.

B. Glycerol

1. Introduction; Origin

The glycerol present in beer is of interest because of fermentation relationships between carbohydrate level and yields of glycerol and ethanol: the latter decrease in proportion to the amount of carbohydrate used to produce glycerol and other fermentation by-products. Also, glycerol has been found to modify the flavour of the product. Its derivation is primarily from the alcoholic fermentation process, as a product of yeast carbohydrate metabolism. A smaller contribution comes from the cereal grains; Piendl *et al.* (1972) found a steady increase of the glycerol content of malt during germination, its maximum being reached between the eighth and tenth day. Depending on the barley variety, this maximum has a range of 70–90 mg glycerol/100 g malt (dry weight). About 75 mg/l of glycerol is present in a 12% wort (Mändl 1974) and its range in beer is usually 1000–3000 mg/l; Table 25 is a survey of glycerol levels in beers of different origins.

In their survey of glycerol levels in Canadian beer using gas–liquid chromatography, Parker and Richardson (1970) found no trend traceable to beer type, locality or brand. On the other hand, in a comparable survey of glycerol content of different types of German beer by means of enzymic methods, Mändl and Piendl (1971) found that dark export had the lowest and pale strong beers the highest average contents of glycerol.

The glycerol content of beer has long been known to vary according to the conditions of fermentation and various different mechanisms have been advanced to explain increased yields of glycerol (Neuberg *et al.* 1958). Under one set of fermentation conditions (the presence of bisulphite in the fermentation medium) acetaldehyde can be replaced by dihydroxyacetone phosphate as a substrate for reduced nicotinamide-adenine-dinucleotide (NADH). The alpha glyceryl phosphate that results is then converted into glycerol by glycerokinase or glycerol-3-phosphate dehydrogenase, which is NADH-dependent:

$$
\begin{array}{ccccc}
CH_2OH & & CH_2OH & \alpha\text{-glycero-} & CH_2OH \\
| & \xrightarrow[H^+]{NADH} & | & \xrightarrow{\text{phosphatase}} & | \\
C{=}O & & CHOH & & CHOH \\
| & & | & & | \\
CH_2OPO_3H_2 & & CH_2OPO_3H_2 & & CH_2OH \\
\text{Dihydroxyacetone} & & \alpha\text{-glycerol} & & \text{Glycerol} \\
\text{phosphate} & & \text{phosphate} & &
\end{array}
$$

Other fermentation parameters which influence the glycerol level include pH and temperature: raising the pH or lowering the temperature increases the yield of glycerol.

TABLE 25. Glycerol in beer (g/100 ml)

U.S. beer	0·14–0·18	(Feil and Marinelli 1969)
Canadian beer	0·11–0·25	(Parker and Richardson 1970)
German beer	0·14–0·19	(Mändl and Piendl 1971)
Swedish beer	0·15–0·22	(Enebo 1957)

Nordström (1968) presented redox balance data showing the positive correlation between the formation of glycerol and the growth of yeast during fermentation. He contrasts the biosynthesis of the yeast cell (an oxidative process) with the alcoholic fermentation (an anaerobic process), pointing out that the oxidative process is counterbalanced by the reduction of α-dihydroxyacetone phosphate to glycerol according to the same reaction as shown above.

2. Determination

The estimation of glycerol in beer has been effected by a variety of methods. Of those quoted in the literature, only two need be discussed, the others being non-specific.

(a) Gas–liquid chromatography

This technique has been applied to the quantitative determination of glycerol in beer by Feil and Marinelli (1969), and also by Parker and Richardson (1970). The former workers analysed U.S. beers without any prior sample preparation; the latter surveyed Canadian beers but favoured the technique of trimethylsilylation, determining glycerol in conjunction with carbohydrates containing two, three and four glucose units. This simultaneous determination of sugars and glycerol in beer is particularly interesting since the proportion of carbohydrates diverted to glycerol during the fermentation process changes the yield of ethanol, affecting the redox balance and therefore the growth of the yeast cells (Nordström 1968).

The glycerol levels determined by gas–liquid chromatography in beer are presented in Table 25.

(b) Enzymatic method

This method (Vaughan 1962, Wieland 1963) involves the conversion of glycerol into glycerol-1-phosphate, which is then oxidized by α-glycerophosphate dehydrogenase in the presence of NAD^+. The amount of NADH produced is directly proportional to the concentration of glycerol and is determined by spectrophotometry or fluorometry.

Mändl et al. (1969) determined glycerol in beer by means of the following sequence of enzymatic reactions:

Glycerol is phosphorylated to glycerol-1-phosphate through glycerokinase and adenosine-5'-triphosphate. By means of pyruvate-kinase the adenosine diphosphate formed is again converted into adenosine triphosphate through phosphoenol pyruvate and formation of pyruvate. The pyruvate is then hydrated to the lactate through NADH (reduced nicotinamide-adenosine-dinucleotide) and the enzyme lactate dehydrogenase, whereby NADH is oxidized to NAD.

$$\text{Glycerol} + \text{ATP} \rightleftharpoons \text{Glycerol-1-phosphate} + \text{ADP}$$
$$\text{ADP} + \text{PEP} \rightleftharpoons \text{ATP} + \text{pyruvate}$$
$$\text{Pyruvate} + \text{NADH} + \text{H}^+ \rightleftharpoons \text{lactate} + \text{NAD}^+$$

The amount of NADH used up during the reaction is equivalent to the glycerol concentration. NADH is measured by its absorption at 340 nm.

Although time-consuming, the enzymatic method for the estimation of glycerol in beer is specific and very precise. While the results by gas–liquid chromatography showed an absolute standard deviation of 30 mg/l and a relative standard deviation of 1·83% (Feil and Marinelli 1969) and a coefficient of variation of 8·8% for glycerol in beer (Parker and Richardson 1970), the enzymatic method showed a relative error of the mean and of standard deviation $\pm 0·3\%$ and $\pm 0·9\%$ respectively (Mändl et al. 1971).

3. Effect on Beer Flavour

Triangular taste test results obtained by Parker and Richardson (1970) show the threshold level of glycerol detection in Canadian beer to be 10 mg/ml, with a subthreshold of 5 mg/ml. Higher concentrations of glycerol (up to 20 mg/ml) led to an increase in sweetness of the treated beer. Although the levels of glycerol in beer lie well below the threshold level of its detection by taste, possible synergistic and antagonistic effects of amounts of glycerol below the threshold level cannot be ruled out.

B. Organic Acids

1. Introduction

In spite of the smallness of the amounts in which they are present in beer, organic acids are important constituents for three reasons: their effect on the taste and shelf-life of the beer; as a yardstick of whether fermentation is proceeding normally; and as a means of distinguishing between different types of beer, by giving indications regarding differences in the composition of the raw materials used, also in variations in brewing and fermentation techniques.

The non-volatile organic acids detected or determined, to date, in beer include: citric, fumaric, lactic, malic, pyruvic succinic, glycollic, glutaric (Enebo et al. 1955); oxalic, tartaric (Kuroiwa and Kokubo 1960); glycollic, levulinic/mesaconic (Rosculet 1969); gluconic (Drawert and Hagen 1970); pyroglutamic, α-ketoglutaric and α-hydroxyglutaric acids (Coote and Kirsop 1974). Rosculet (1969), as part of a very thorough study of the metabolic products of yeast fermentation, has covered many aspects of the non-volatile organic acids in beer, including their fate during processing and ageing, their effect on beer flavour, as well as their characterization and estimation.

2. Origin

The organic acids in beer are both malt-derived and the result of the enzymatic activity of yeast. Mändl *et al.* (1975) and Piendl and Gehloff (1974) have stressed the fact that several non-volatile organic acids (citric, malic, gluconic, etc.) are metabolic products of the maturation and germination reactions of barley, being formed or degraded to a very small extent during fermentation.

Different barley varieties and malting conditions (degree of steeping, kilning) have been found to affect directly the quality of beer. Hops do not contribute any significant amounts of organic acids. Kuroiwa and Kokubo (1960) as well as Rosculet (1969) have tracked a number of non-volatile organic acids during fermentation. Thus, α-ketoglutaric and pyruvic acids were found by Kuroiwa and Kokubo (1960) to increase at the earlier fermentation stage, peaking about 100 hours after the beginning, then gradually decreasing to a definite level at the final stage. The fluctuation in the amount of pyruvic acid was more pronounced than that of α-ketoglutaric acid. Rosculet (1969) noted an increase during fermentation in the amounts of lactic and succinic, as well as of pyruvic and α-ketoglutaric acids; this would account for the total amount of non-volatile organic acids being greater in beer than in wort (Enebo *et al.* 1955, Kuroiwa and Kokubo 1960). In summary, malic, citric, isocitric and gluconic acids in beer are chiefly derived from the malt, while succinic, lactic and pyroglutamic acids in beer are formed during wort boiling and fermentation (Ueda *et al.* 1966, Coote and Kirsop 1974). Rudin (1974) reports that only a small amount (about 15 mg/l) of pyruvic acid is found in wort, the main portion of this non-volatile organic acid in beer arising from the fermentation process.

3. Concentration

Table 26 summarizes the wort and beer content of non-volatile organic acids, determined by different methods. Recently, Mändl *et al.* (1969, 1971a, b) estimated pyruvate, D- and L-lactate, citrate and malate by enzymatic methods in some 200 German and other beers of several different types; the results are summarized in Table 27. As can be seen from this table, wheat beers had the lowest and dark export beers the highest average contents of pyruvate. "Alt" beers had the lowest D-lactate and pilsner lager beers the lowest L-lactate

TABLE 26. Non-volatile acids in wort and beer (mg/l)

	Wort		Beer			
	(b)	(c)	(a)	(b)	(c)	(d)
Mesaconic ⎱ Levulinic ⎰	12	12		6–9	9	
Pyruvic	4	5	33·3	6–11	150	10–104
Fumaric	13	17		11–13	21	
Succinic	11	14		41–67	47	36–166
Lactic	7	10		31–51	195	48–292
Glutaric	Nil			0–13		
(Alpha-ketoglutaric)	16	19	6·3	0–4	30	0–20
Oxalic	7	7		Nil	3	
Glycollic	Nil	Nil		0–25	29	
Malic	44	53		42–52	50	14–97
Citric	86	89		88–90	95	56–158
Alpha-hydroxyglutaric						0–7
Pyroglutamic						26–137

(a) Paper partition chromatographic data (Kuroiwa and Kukubo 1960). (b) Silica column and paper partition chromatographic data (Enebo *et al.* 1955). (c) Gas–liquid chromatographic data (Rosculet 1969). (d) Column chromatographic data; organic anion concentration (Coote and Kirsop 1974).

contents, while wheat beers showed the highest D-lactate and Pilsner Dietetic beers the highest L-lactate contents. Citrate was lowest in Pilsner Dietetic beers and highest in dark strong beers. Dark lager and dark export beers had the lowest malate and pale strong beers the highest malate contents.

Gluconate has been determined enzymatically in a variety of worts and beers by Drawert and Hagen (1970b). Pale beers contained an average of 40 mg/l gluconate (range of 27–49 mg/l) while dark beers had an average of 64 mg/l gluconate over a wider range. The highest concentration of gluconate was found in a dark strong beer, 102 mg/l. Dietetic beers were uniformly close to an average of 40 mg/l gluconate. A comparison of the gluconate content of various worts (pale and dark lagers; Pilsner; pale and dark strong; dietetic) with that of the corresponding beers does not show significant variation, leading these authors to the tentative conclusion that the gluconate present in beer is derived from the malt. Mändl *et al.* (1975) have endorsed this conclusion.

4. Determination

Paper partition chromatography, with or without prior separation on a column of the wort and beer non-volatile organic acids, has been used by Enebo *et al.* (1955), Kuroiwa and Kokubo (1960), Hampl and Markova (1969) and Rosculet (1969). Thin-layer chromatography has been applied by

TABLE 27. By-products of fermentation in different beer types

Average values (mg/l)

	Wheat beers	Dark export	Pale export	Pilsner lager	Pilsner dietetic	Pale strong	Dark strong	Pale lager	Dark lager	Mar. beer	"Alt" beer
Pyruvate	42	79	66	59	48	51	66	60	61	60	55
D-Lactate	270	100	48	52	56	98	190	70	110	95	15
L-Lactate	190	155	55	45	325	75	140	65		95	80
Citrate	151	187	203	194	130	266	279	185	174	199	155
Malate	59	54	98	85	78	136	57	80	54	74	100

Suomalainen and Ronkainen (1963), Monties and Bidan (1967), Hampl and Markova (1969) and Roswelt (1969). Column chromatography has been reported by Coote and Kirsop (1974). Gas–liquid chromatography has been used by Harrison and Collins (1968), Marinelli *et al.* (1968), Hampl and Markova (1969) and Rosculet (1969). The enzymatic methods available from Firma Boehringer Mannheim GmbH have been applied by Mändl *et al.* (1969, 1971) in their extensive analyses of a great variety of beers for glycerol, pyruvate, citrate, malate, D- and L-lactate (these last two also by Coote and Kirsop 1974). Similar methods were used by Drawert and Hagen (1970b) for the determination of gluconate in wort and beer. A summary of the reactions involved in these enzymatic methods is given in the section on glycerol (V.B). Mändl *et al.* (1971b) obtained values for relative error of the mean and standard deviation, establishing that these enzymatic methods of analysis for pyruvate, citrate, malate, D- and L-lactate, glycerol (as well as acetate (Drawert and Hagen 1970a)) are as accurate as the various chromatographic techniques enumerated above.

5. Effect on Beer Quality

The various organic acids play a significant part as metabolic products in fermentation. In addition, many of them have intrinsic flavours of their own (e.g. pyruvate—Clapperton 1974). Table 28 lists taste thresholds for some non-volatile organic acids based on some data reported by Engan (1974) and other values quoted by Williams (1974).

From a flavour point of view, lactic acid emerges as the most important non-volatile organic acid in beer, since it is the only one present in beer in the above-theshold amounts.

Coote and Kirsop (1974) examined the influence of several individual acids on the pH by additions to a beer (all-malt wort), concluding that some have a much greater effect than others and that the pH of beer will be affected by the nature as well as by the total amount of non-volatile organic acid present.

TABLE 28. Organic acids.
Organoleptic threshold values (mg/l)

Acid	Thresholds		Amount in beer
Citric	350	85–371	130–279
Lactic	400	47–252	65–450
Tartaric	300		—
Malic	350	87–268	54–136
Malonic	250		—
Succinic	200	65–555	—
Ketoglutaric		500	0–30
Pyruvic		250–300	6–150

D. Vitamins

1. Introduction

Beer contains small amounts of vitamins of the B-Group (B-1 or thiamine; B-2 or riboflavine; B-5 or pantothenic acid; B-6 or pyridoxin; biotin; *meso*-inositol; B-12 or cyanocobalamin); also niacin. For these vitamins of beer, nutritional significance has been alternately claimed (Saletan 1959, Weinfurtner 1964, Anon. 1975, Voss and Piendl 1976) and discounted (Wagner 1967). Their importance to the brewing process lies in their presence in wort in amounts which, although variable, are sufficient to ensure adequate yeast performance in brewing: the B-complex vitamins are highly important as growth factors for yeast during fermentation, especially biotin, inositol and pantothenic acid.

2. Origin

Barley and malt are rich sources of several vitamins; some of these, being concentrated in the embryo and aleurone, are leached out during brewing, while others migrate into the roots during germination, thereby becoming lost to the finished malt. Certain vitamins are known to be present in malt in bound forms, from which they are released during mashing by the action of malt enzymes. Riboflavin, pantothenic acid and pyridoxine increase during malting, as does ascorbic acid which, however, is entirely destroyed during kilning.

3. Concentration

Table 29 sets out the vitamin content of beer along with the percent of the minimum daily requirement of each vitamin supplied by one litre of beer (males, 23–50 years, 154 lbs: see footnote).

A comparison of beer and wort vitamin contents (Table 29; Hough 1971) would indicate a superficial similarity in the ranges of vitamin concentrations to be found in the literature. The following points may be noted: yeast does not use all of the biotin in the wort during fermentation as bottled ale still contains biotin (Lynes and Norris 1948, Schuster 1968); there is, in wort, enough pantothenic acid and riboflavin for yeast growth and the finished beer may contain even more of these vitamins (Hopkins 1945, Weinfurtner *et al.* 1964, 1966); thiamine is taken up from the wort by yeast rapidly and almost quantitatively (Fink and Just 1942a, b; Hopkins 1945, Just 1951, Weinfurtner *et al.* 1964). According to Weinfurtner *et al.* (1964), bottom yeast absorbs from the wort approximately 46% of the inositol and 44% of the pyridoxine. On the other hand, the nicotinic acid content of wort and beer in top fermentation is almost the same (Hopkins 1945) while about 40% of the wort nicotinamide is absorbed by yeast in bottom fermentation (Weinfurtner *et al.* 1964). In

TABLE 29. Vitamin content of beer (mg/l)

Vitamin	(a)	(b)	(c)	% min. daily requirements supplied by one litre beer (e)
Thiamine (B-1)	0·02–0·06	0·01–0·015	0·01	1–40
Riboflavin (B-2)	0·3–1·0	0·31–0·32	0·31	19–63
Pantothenic acid (B-5)	0·4–0·8	0·84–0·98	1·4	No min. daily req.
Pyridoxin (B-6)	0·4–0·9	0·44–0·51	0·71	20–50
Niacin (Nicotinic acid)	5–14	4·6–5·4	8·1	27–83
Biotin			0·007	
Myo-inositol			27·5–31·5 (d)	
Cyanocobalamin (B-12)	0·092–0·14 µg/l (e)			

(a) Saletan (1959). (b) G. Charalambous, unpublished (1976 beers). (c) Voss and Piendl (1976a). (d) Weinfurtner *et al.* (1966). (e) Blondeau, R. (1975).

Note: Based on data in "Recommended Dietary Allowances" (1973), National Research Council, Food and Nutrition Board, Washington D.C. Publication 0–309-02216–9, 8th Edition; also, on data from "Composition of Foods" (1963), United States Department of Agriculture, Agricultural Research Service Handbook No. 8, Washington, D.C. See also paragraph on Nutritional Properties of Beer in chapter on Carbohydrates.

summary: from wort to beer, pantothenic acid and riboflavin increase, while thiamine, inositol and pyridoxine decrease, with nicotinic acid remaining unchanged (top-fermentation).

4. Determination

The vitamin content of brewery raw materials and beer has been determined over the years by a variety of analytical procedures, the advantages and diadvantages of which have been noted by several authors. These methods may be classified as follows:

Biological methods: The oldest and classical procedures, of greatest specificity and notoriously difficult, also quite expensive in time and money since they involve animal experiments.

Chemical and physicochemical methods: For example, paper and thin-layer chromatography, fluorometry, polarography.

Microbiological methods: Carried out with any one of several test organisms.

Schuster and Weinfurtner (1964) have compared and contrasted the first two classes of beer vitamin assays, leaning, on balance, towards the physico-chemical methods. Voss and Piendl more recently (1976b) selected microbio-logical methods for an extensive quantitative determination of the B group vitamins in beer and yeast (1976a), claiming greater sensitivity (10^{-9}–10^{-12} g detection limit) and better specificity as compared with chemical methods. Piendl's assay procedures (1976a) led to results included in Table 29; the coefficient of variation for the six beer vitamins was $\pm 4.2\%$, average recovery of added vitamins to beer was 99%, and general accuracy comparable to that obtained with chemical methods.

E. Non-volatile Aromatic Higher Alcohols: Tyrosol and Tryptophol

1. Introduction

The significance of the non-volatile aromatic higher alcohols tyrosol and tryptophol as beer flavour and aroma components has long been a moot point. Recently however it has become increasingly apparent (a) that these non-volatile higher alcohols are important components of basic beer flavour; and (b) that, beyond a certain point, they exert an adverse effect which can be controlled by varying the composition of the wort through changes in the fermentable sugars available.

2. Origin

Tyrosol and tryptophol are generally recognized as fermentation products and their presence in beer may be considered as part of a normal brewery yeast fermentation. Ehrlich (1916) and Äyräpää (1961, 1963) have demonstrated the fermentation of these alcohols directly from the corresponding amino acids by transamination (keto acid), decarboxylation (aldehyde) and reduction (higher alcohol). Äyräpää (1965) also showed that the keto acid is also formed from carbohydrates through the glycolytic sequence and the pentose phosphate cycle. Interestingly, the decarboxylase involved in the case of indolepyruvic acid (the keto acid intermediate in formation of tryptophol) is not identical with the usual pyruvate decarboxylase, but a separate enzyme.

The formation of tyrosol and tryptophol is dependent on a variety of factors: different yeast strains and fermentation conditions; variations in raw materials; wort composition. The effect of the latter has been thoroughly investigated by Szlavko (1973, 1974). This author reported (1974) that increasing concentration of glucose in the wort led to a decrease of tyrosol with ale yeast and an increase with lager yeast. Tryptophol, on the other hand, both with ale and lager yeasts, increased in concentration to a maximum, decreasing thereafter. The use of adjunct wort resulted in higher amounts of tyrosol and tryptophol and their concentration in beer was seen to be inversely proportional to the nitrogen concentration of the wort (up to a certain level).

3. Determination and Concentration

Colorimetric methods were used by Ehrlich (1916), Drews et al. (1965) and McFarlane et al. (1963, 1964). Nykänen et al. (1966) employed gas–liquid chromatography as did Szlavko (1973). Charalambous and Bruckner (1972) determined tyrosol in beer by column chromatography followed by mass spectroscopic analysis, further estimating it quantitatively in U.S. beers by high-pressure liquid chromatography (1974).

Table 30 lists levels of tyrosol and tryptophol as estimated in a variety of beers by colorimetry, gas chromatography and high-pressure liquid chromatography.

4. Effect on Beer Flavour

Rosculet (1971) ascribed a bitter-fruity character to tryptophol and a bitter "yeast bite" influence to tyrosol, with taste thresholds of 200 and 100 mg/l respectively. Meilgaard (1975) reported thresholds of 414 mg/l for tryptophol (flavour in beer; almonds, solvent) and 200 mg/l for tyrosol (bitter, chemical). Charalambous et al. (1972) and Szlavko (1973) both reported thresholds of 10 and 20 mg/l for tryptophol and tyrosol; these thresholds are, coincidentally, close to levels of these compounds normally found in beer. Above these threshold levels, both alcohols were found by Szlavko (1973) to cause a harsh, lingering bitter aftertaste considered to be undesirable in beers. Charalambous

TABLE 30. Tyrosol and tryptophol in beer (mg/l)

	Tyrosol	Tryptophol
Canadian ales (4)		
(McFarlane 1964, colorimetric data)	8·4–15·5	0·7–2·5
Canadian lagers (2)		
(McFarlane 1964, colorimetric data)	16	0·41–0·42
Finnish lagers (2)		
(Nykanen 1966, GLC data)	5–10	1–4
Canadian ales (10)		
(Szlavko 1973, GLC data)	6·99–21·89	2·1–12·1
Canadian lagers (6)		
(Szlavko 1973, GLC data)	6·19–14·87	0·69–1·36
U.S. beers (6)		
(Charalambous 1974, HPLC data)	8·0–28·0	

The low tryptophol level of Canadian lagers, as opposed to the higher level in Canadian ales, is attributable to the inherent differences between *S. cerevisiae* and *S. carlsbergensis* (*uvarum*).

et al. (1972) reported a slightly sour aftertaste and old fruit aroma for tyrosol and a caramel-like, astringent, harsh taste for tryptophol with an indole-type aroma.

F. Other Minor Beer Components

Tressl *et al.* (1974, 1975) have recently identified several additional minor components of low volatility in beer using chromatographic techniques coupled with mass spectrometry. Over 20 new compounds were identified for the first time in wort and beer, including γ-pyrones, alkylphenols, lactones and furans.

These beer components of low volatility, although not present to any considerable extent in the headspace, might still be expected to contribute to beer flavour, acting as enhancers or "fortifiers" through synergistic effects (Meilgaard 1975).

Pickett *et al.* (1976a) extended the studies of such beer components of low volatility by isolating them through steam distillation of the beer at temperatures below 20 °C under vacuum, followed by extraction of the distillate with highly purified ether under nitrogen. This solvent extraction was deemed satisfactory in view of the very much lower boiling point of the ether compared with the low volatile compounds under examination. Concentrates containing the latter were obtained using conditions precluding thermolysis or oxidation of the components, which were then examined by gas chromatography coupled with mass spectrometry.

The new and improved techniques developed by Pickett *et al.* (1976a) were next applied by these workers in an investigation of the chemical differences between ales and lagers (1976b), involving a series of heterocyclic compounds and their reduction products. Levels of certain reduced heterocyclics, especially 2-acetylfuran, are higher in ales and may prove useful analytically as indicators for ale character, although not, in fact, responsible for ale character: in view of the published flavour threshold of 80 mg/l for 2-acetylfuran (Meilgaard 1975), other heterocyclic compounds with lower thresholds may possibly exert a greater flavour impact either *per se* or through synergism.

Table 31 summarizes the relative amounts of such minor components of low volatility in four lagers and four ales (Pickett *et al.* 1976).

TABLE 31. Minor beer components of low volatility

2-Acetylfuran	Furfuryl alcohol	2-Acetyl-thiophene	Furfural	2-Thiophene carboxaldehyde

	2-Acetylfuran	Furfuryl alcohol	2-Acetyl-thiophene	Furfural	2-Thiophene carboxaldehyde
Ales	+ +	+ + + +	70–97 p.p.b.	+ to + + +	+
Lagers	+	+ + +	4–12 p.p.b.	+ to + +	+

REFERENCES

American Society of Brewing Chemists. (1976). "Methods of Analysis", 7th revised edn. A.S.B.C., St. Paul, Minn.

Anon. (1975). *Brewers' Digest* **50** (10), 38.

Arikawa, Y. (1967). "Accelerated Chromatographic Analysis of Aminoacids by using Metallic Salt Form Ion Exchange". Bulletin, Hitachi Ltd., Tokyo, Japan.

Association of Official Analytical Chemists. (1975). Official Methods of Analysis, 12th edn. A.O.A.C., Washington, D.C.

Äyräpää, T. (1961). *J. Inst. Brew.* **67**, 262.

Äyräpää, T. (1963). *Proc. E.B.C. Congr., Brussels*, p. 276.

Äyräpää, T. (1965). *J. Inst. Brew.* **71**, 341.

Äyräpää, T. (1971). *J. Inst. Brew.* **77**, 266.

Äyräpää, T. (1974). E.B.C. Monograph-I, Zeist, p. 278.

Barrett, J. and Kirsop, B. H. (1971). *J. Inst. Brew.* **77**, 42.

Barton-Wright, E. C. (1953). *Proc. E.B.C. Congr., Nice* p. 98.

Barton-Wright, E. C., Harris, G. and Curtis, N. S. (1951). *J. Inst. Brew.* **57**, 264.

Bass, E. J. and Meredith, W. O. S. (1955a). *Cereal Chem.* **32**, 183.

Bass, E. J. and Meredith, W. O. S. (1955b). *Cereal Chem.* **32**, 374.

Bass, E. J., Meredith, W. O. S. and Anderson, J. A. (1953). *Cereal Chem.* **30**, 313.
Bateson, J. B. (1970). *J. Inst. Brew.* **76**, 150.
Bathgate, G. N. (1974). *E.B.C. Monograph-I, Zeist* p. 198.
Bathgate, G. N. and Dalgleish, C. E. (1975). *Proc. Ann. Meet. Am. Soc. Brew. Chem.* p. 33.
Bathgate, G. N., Palmer, G. H. and Wilson, G. (1974). J. Inst. Brew. **80**, 278.
Belleau, G. and Dadic,, M. (1976). *Proc. Ann. Meet. Am. Soc. Brew. Chem.* p. 158.
Belleau, G., Buday, A. Z. and Van Gheluwe, J. E. A. (1970). *Proc. Ann. Meet. Am. Soc. Brew. Chem.*, **27**, 22.
Bhandari, P. R. (1964). *J. Chromatogr.* **16**, 130.
Bishop, L. R. (1961). *J. Inst. Brew.* **67**, 328.
Bishop, L. R. (1972). *J. Inst. Brew.* **78**, 37.
Bishop, L. R. (1975). *J. Inst. Brew.* **81**, 444.
Blondeau, R. (1975). *Cahiers de Nutrition et de Dietetique* **10**, 59.
Boehringer Mannheim GmbH. (1971). Boehringer Mannheim Food Analysis Manual.
Bourne, D. T. and Pierce, J. S. (1970). *J. Inst. Brew.* **76**, 328.
Bourne, D. T. and Pierce, J. S. (1972). *Tech. Quart., Master Brewers Ass. Am.* **9**, 151.
Bourne, D. T., Jones, M. and Pierce, J. S. (1976). *Tech. Quart., Masters Brewers Ass. Am.* **13**, 3.
Brenner, M. W. and Bernstein, L. (1976). *Proc. Ann. Meet. Am. Soc. Brew. Chem.* **33**, 171.
Brobst, K. M. (1974). "Previews". Pierce Chemical Co., Rockford, Ill.
Brobst, K. M. and Lott, C. E. (1966). *Cereal Chem.* **43**, 35.
Brobst, K. M., Scobell, H. D. and Steele, E. M. (1973). *Proc. Ann. Meet. Am. Soc. Brew. Chem.* p. 4, 43.
Brumsted, D. D., Lautenbach, A. F. and West, D. B. (1965). *Proc. Ann. Meet. Am. Soc. Brew. Chem.* p. 142.
Buckee, G. K., Hickman, E. and Brown, D. G. W. (1974). *J. Inst. Brew.*, **80**, 379.
Buday, A. Z. and Denis, G. (1974). *Brewers' Digest* **49** (6), 56.
Buday, A. Z., Belleau, G. and Van Gheluwe, G. (1972). *Proc. Ann. Meet. Am. Soc. Brew. Chem.* p. 56.
Bugler, L. (1974). *Brauwelt* p. 1610.
Carrington, R., Collett, R. C., Dunkin, I. R. and Halek, G. (1972). *J. Inst. Brew.* **78**, 243.
Chapon, L. (1960). *Brasserie* **15**, 73.
Chapon, L. (1964). *Proc. Ann. Meet. Am. Soc. Brew. Chem.* p. 244.
Chapon, L., Chollot, B. and Urion, E. (1961). *Proc. E.B.C. Congr. Vienna* p. 319.
Charalambous, G. and Bruckner, K. J. (1976). Unpublished.
Charalambous, G. (1974). *Tech. Quart., Master Brewers Ass. Am.* **11** (2), 146.
Charalambous, G. and Bruckner, K. J. (1969). Unpublished.
Charalambous, G. and Weatherby, T. J. (1977). Unpublished.
Charalambous, G., Bruckner, K. J. and Hardwick, W. A. (1971). *Tech. Quart., Master Brewers Ass. Am.* XXXI, 8.
Charalambous, G., Bruckner, K. J., Hardwick, W. A. and Weatherby, T. J. (1972). *Tech. Quart., Master Brewers Ass. Am.* **9** (3), 131.
Charalambous, G., Bruckner, K. J., Hardwick, W. A. and Weatherby, T. J. (1974b). *Tech. Quart., Master Brewers Ass. Am.* **11** (3), 193.
Charalambous, G., Bruckner, K. J., Hardwick, W. A. and Weatherby, T. J. (1975). *Tech. Quart., Master Brewers Ass. Am.* **12** (4), 203.
Charalambous, G., Bruckner, K. J., Linnebach, A. and Hardwick, W. A. (1973) *Tech. Quart., Master Brewers Ass. Am.* **10** (2), 74.

Charalambous, G., Bruckner, K. J., Linnebach, A. and Hardwick, W. A. (1974a). *Tech. Quart., Master Brewers Ass. Am.* **11** (2), 150.
Chen, E. C.-H. and Van Gheluwe, G. (1976). *Proc. Ann. Meet. Am. Soc. Brew. Chem.* **34** (1), 6.
Chen, E. C. -H., Van Gheluwe, G. and Buday, A. Z. (1973). *Proc. Ann. Meet. Am. Soc. Brew. Chem.* p. 4. 6.
Chen, S. C. and Luchsinger, W. W. (1964). *Arch. Biochem. Biophys.* **101**, 71.
Chevalier, P., Chollot, B., Chapon, L. and Urion, E. (1961). *Proc. E.B.C. Congr., Vienna* p. 246.
Chollot, B., Blondot, Ph, Deymie, B. and Urion, E. (1967). *Proc. E.B.C. Congr., Madrid* p. 433.
Clapperton, J. F. (1971a). *J. Inst. Brew.* **77**, 42.
Clapperton, J. F. (1971b). *J. Inst. Brew.* **77**, 177.
Clapperton, J. F. (1974). *J. Inst. Brew.* **80**, 164.
Clapperton, J. F. and Holliday, A. G. (1968) *J. Inst. Brew.* **74**, 164.
Clapperton, J. F. and McWilliam, J. C. (1971). *J. Inst. Brew.* **77**, 519.
Coote, N. and Kirsop, B. H. (1974). *J. Inst. Brew.* **80**, 474.
Coote, N. and Kirsop, B. H. (1976). *J. Inst. Brew.* **82**, 34.
Dahlstrom, R. V. and Morton, B. J. (1952). *Proc. Ann. Meet. Am. Soc. Brew. Chem.*, 142.
Dalgleish, C. E., Horning, E. C., Horning, M. S., Knox, K. L. and Yorger, K. (1966). *Biochem. J.* **101**, 792.
Davies, J. W., Harris, G. and Parsons, R. (1956). *J. Inst. Brew.* **62**, 31.
De Clerck, J. (1957). "A Textbook of Brewing", Vol. 1, p. 548. Chapman and Hall, London.
De Clerck, J. and Jerumanis, J. (1967). *Bull. Ass. Ec. Brass., Louvain* **63**, 137.
Dellweg, H., John, M. and Trenel, G. (1969). *J. Chromatogr.* **42**, 476.
Dellweg, H., John, M. and Trenel, G. (1970). *Proc. Ann. Meet. Am. Soc. Brew. Chem.* p. 154.
Dellweg, H., John, M. and Trenel, G. (1971). *J. Chromatogr.* **57**, 89.
Dellweg, H., Schlanderer, G. and Drews, B. (1970). *Monats. Brau.* **23** (8), 209.
Devreux, A. (1965). *Brass. Malt. Belg.* 131.
Djurtoft, R. (1961). *Proc. E.B.C. Congr., Vienna* p. 298.
Djurtoft, R. (1963). *Wallerstein Lab. Commun.* **26**, 83.
Drawert, F. and Hagen, W. (1970a). *Brauwissenschaft* (8), 300.
Drawert, F. and Hagen, W. (1970b). *Brauwissenschaft* (12), 463.
Drawert, F., Leupold, G. and Lessing, V. (1975). *Proc. E.B.C. Congr., Nice* p. 791.
Drawert, F., Leupold, G. and Lessing, V. (1977). *Brauwissenschaft* (1), 13.
Drews, B., Specht, H. and Schwartz, E. (1965). *Monats Brau.* **18**, 240.
Drews, B., Specht, H. and Schwartz, E. (1966). *Monats Brau.* **19**, 76.
Eastmond, R. (1974). *J. Inst. Brew.* **80**, 188.
Eastmond, R. and Gardner, R. J. (1974). *J. Inst. Brew.* **80**, 192.
Ehrlich, F. (1911). *Ber. Deutsche Chem. Ges.* **44**, 139.
Ehrlich, F. (1916). *Biochem. Z.* **73**, 232.
Enari, T.-M. (1974b). *E.B.C. Monograph, Zeist* p. 73.
Enari, T.-M. (1975). *E.B.C. Monograph-II, Zeist.* p. 146.
Enebo, L. (1957). *Proc. E.B.C. Congr., Copenhagen*, p. 370.
Enebo, L., Blomgren, G. and Johnsson, E. (1955). *J. Inst. Brew.* **61**, 408.
Enevoldsen, B. S. (1970). *Proc. E.B.C. Congr., Interlaken* p. 205.
Enevoldsen, B. S. (1974). *E.B.C. Monograph-I, Zeist* p. 158.
Enevoldsen, B. S. and Bathgate, G. N. (1969). *J. Inst. Brew.* **75**, 433.

Enevoldsen, B. S. and Schmidt, F. (1973). *Proc. E.B.C. Congr., Salzburg* p. 135.
Enevoldsen, B. S. and Schmidt, F. (1974). *J. Inst. Brew.* **80**, 520.
Engan, S. (1974). *J. Inst. Brew.* **80**, 162.
Erdal, K. and Gjertsen, P. (1967). *Proc. E.B.C. Congr., Madrid* p. 295.
European Brewery Convention (1975). *Analytica-III*, 3rd edn. Schweizer Brauerei Rundschau, Zurich, Switzerland
Feil, M. F. and Martinelli, L. (1969). *Proc. Ann. Meet. Am. Soc. Brew. Chem.* p. 29.
Fink, H. and Just, F. (1942a). *Biochem. Z.* **311**, 61.
Fink, H. and Just, F. (1942b). *Biochem. Z.* **311**, 287.
Folin, O. and Ciocalteau, V. (1927). *J. Biol. Chem.* **73**, 627.
Forch, M. and Runkel, U.-D. (1974). *E.B.C. Monograph-I, Zeist* p. 269.
Franken-Luykx, J. M. M. (1967). *J. Inst. Brew.* **73**, 187.
Franken-Luykx, J. M. M. and Klopper, W. J. (1967). *Brauwissenschaft*, **20**, 173.
Frey, S. W., DeWitt, W. G. and Bellomy, B. R. (1967). *Proc. Ann. Meet. Am. Soc. Brew. Chem.* **24**, 199.
Gehloff, G., Schlosser, A. and Piendl, A. (1972). *Tech. Quart., Master Brewers Ass. Am.* **9**, 144.
Gehrke, C. W., Kao, K. and Zumwalt, R. W. (1971). *J. Chromatogr.* **57**, 209.
Geissmann, T. and Neukom, H. (1973). *Cereal Chem.* **50**, 414.
Gjertsen, P. (1953). *J. Inst. Brew.* **59**, 296.
Gjertsen, P. (1955). *Proc. E.B.C. Congr., Baden-Baden*, p. 37.
Gjertsen, P. (1966). *Proc. Ann. Meet. Am. Soc. Brew. Chem.* p. 113.
Grabar, P. and Daussant, J. (1971). *J. Inst. Brew.* **77**, 544.
Grabar, P., Daussant, J., Enari, T.-M. and Nummi, M. (1969). *Proc. E.B.C. Congr. Interlaken* p. 349.
Gracey, D. E. F. and Barker, R. L. (1976a). *J. Inst. Brew.* **82**, 72.
Gracey, D. E. F. and Barker, R. L. (1976b). *J. Inst. Brew.* **82**, 78.
Gramshaw, J. W. (1967). *J. Inst. Brew.* **73**, 258.
Gramshaw, J. W. (1968). *J. Inst. Brew.* **74**, 20.
Gramshaw, J. W. (1969a). *J. Inst. Brew.* **75**, 61.
Gramshaw, J. W. (1969b). *Tech. Quart., Master Brewers Ass. Am.* **6** (4), 239.
Gramshaw, J. W. (1970a). *Tech. Quart., Master Brewers Ass. Am.* **7** (3), 167.
Gramshaw, J. W. (1970b). *Tech. Quart., Master Brewers Ass. Am.* **7** (2), 122.
Haboucha, J. (1965). *Brass. Malt. Belg.* p. 108.
Hall, R. D., Harris, G. and MacWilliam, I. C. (1956). *J. Inst. Brew.* **62**, 232.
Hampl, J. and Markova, J. (1969). *Sci. Paper Inst. Chem. Technol., Prague Fd.* **E25**, 61.
Harborne, J. B. (1968). "Biochemistry of Phenolic Compounds". Academic Press, New York and London.
Harris, G. (1956). *J. Inst. Brew.* **62**, 390.
Harris, G. (1962). *In* "Barley and Malt" (A. H. Cook, ed.), p. 666. Academic Press, New York and London.
Harris, G. and Parsons, R. J. (1957). *J. Inst. Brew.* **63**, 227.
Harris, G. and Parsons, R. J. (1958). *J. Inst. Brew.* **64**, 308.
Harris, G. and Ricketts, R. W. (1959a). *J. Inst. Brew.* **65**, 331.
Harris, G. and Ricketts, R. W. (1959b). *Proc. E.B.C. Congr., Rome* p. 290.
Harris, G. and Ricketts, R. W. (1959c). *J. Inst. Brew.* **65**, 256.
Harris, G. and Ricketts, R. W. (1960). *J. Inst. Brew.* **66**, 313.
Harrison, G. A. F. and Collins, E. (1968). *Proc. Ann. Meet. Am. Soc. Brew. Chem.* p. 101.
Haslam, E. (1975). *In* "Flavonoids" (J. B. Harborne, T. J. Mabry and H. Mabry, eds.). Academic Press, New York and London.

Haworth, C. and Oliver, R. W. A. (1971). *Biochem. J.* **124**, 255.
Hay, G. W. and Smith, F. (1962). *Proc. Ann. Meet. Am. Soc. Brew. Chem.* p. 127.
Hejgaard, J. and Sorensen, S. B. (1974). *C.R. Trav. Lab., Carlsberg* **40**, 187.
Held, H. R. and McFarlane, W. D. (1957). *Proc. Ann. Meet. Am. Soc. Brew. Chem.* p. 116.
Hermann, K. and Mosel, H.-D. (1973). *Brauwissenschaft* **26**, 267.
Herwig, W. C., Wagener, R. E., Cieslak, M. E., Chicoye, E. and Helbert, J. R. (1977). Paper presented at Pittsburg Conference, Cleveland, Ohio, U.S.A.
Heyse, K.-U. and Piendl, A. (1972). *Wallerstein Lab. Commun.* **16**, 35.
Hildebrand, R. P., Kavanagh, T. E. and Clarke, B. J. (1975). *Brewers' Digest* **50** (4), 58.
Hiller, A. and Van Slyke, D. D. (1922). *J. Biol. Chem.* **53**, 253.
Hopkins, R. H. (1945a). *Wallerstein Lab. Commun.* **8**, 110.
Hough, J. S., Briggs, D. E. and Stevens, R. (1971a). "Malting and Brewing Science". Chapman and Hall, London.
Hough, J. S., Briggs, D. E. and Stevens, R. (1971b). "Malting and Brewing Science", p. 206. Chapman and Hall, London.
Hudson, J. R. and Birtwistle, S. E. (1966). *J. Inst. Brew.* **72**, 46.
Igarashi, O. and Sakurai, Y. (1965). *Agric. Biol. Chem.* **29**, 678.
Ingledew, W. M. (1975). *Tech. Quart., Master Brewers Ass. Am.* **12** (3), 146.
Jamieson, A. M. (1976). *Proc. Ann. Meet. Am. Soc. Brew. Chem.* p. 34, 44.
Jerumanis, J. (1968). *Bull. Ass. Ec. Brass., Louvain* **64**, 22.
John, M. (1969). *Tagesz. Brau.* **66**, 782.
Jones, M. (1974). *E.B.C. Monograph, Zeist* p. 90.
Jones, M. and Pierce, J. S. (1964). *J. Inst. Brew.* **70**, 307.
Jones, M. and Pierce, J. S. (1967). *J. Inst. Brew.* **73**, 342.
Jones, M. and Pierce, J. S. (1969). *Proc. E.B.C. Congr., Interlaken* p. 151.
Jones, M., Power, D. M. and Pierce, J. S. (1965). *Proc. E.B.C. Congr., Stockholm* p. 182.
Jones, M. O., Cope, R. and Rainbow, C. (1975). *Proc. E.B.C. Congr., Nice* p. 669.
Kainuma, K., Nogami, A. and Mercier, C. (1976). *J. Chromatogr.* **121**, 361.
Kaltkar, H. M. (1947). *J. Biol. Chem.* **167**, 461.
Klopper, W. J. (1974). *E.B.C. Monograph, Zeist,* p. 12.
Klopper, W. J. (1976). *J. Inst. Brew.* **82**, 353.
Klopper, W. K., Tuning, B. and Vermeire, H. A. (1975). *Proc. E.B.C. Congr. Nice* p. 6659.
Krauss, G. (1970). *Brewers' Digest* **46**, 66.
Krauss, G., Zurcher, Ch. and Holstein, H. (1972). *Monats. Brau.* **25**, 113.
Krauss, G. L. and Enger, H. (1960). *Brauwissenschaft* **13**, 6, 178.
Kringstad, H. (1972). *Brauwissenschaft* **25**, 272.
Kringstad, H. and Damm, E. (1965). *Proc. E.B.C. Congr., Stockholm* p. 129.
Kuno, H. and Kihara, H. K. (1967). *Nature, London* **215**, 974.
Kuroiwa, Y. and Kokubo, E. (1960). *Rep. Res. Lab. Kirin Brewing Co., Yokahama* **2**, 49.
Latimer, R. A. and Glenister, P. (1968). *Proc. Inst. Brewing Austr. New Zealand Sect.* p. 83.
Lee, T. C. and Lewis, M. J. (1968). *J. Food Sci.* **33**, 119.
Letters, R. J. (1969). *J. Inst. Brew.* **75**, 54.
Li, K. C. and Woodruff, J. C. (1968). *J. Agric. Food Chem* **16**, 535.
Lie, S. (1973). *J. Inst. Brew.* **79**, 37.
Ljungdahl, L. and Sandegren, E. (1953). *Proc. E.B.C. Congr., Nice* p. 85.
Lowry, O. H., Rosebrough, N. J., Farr, A. L. and Randall, R. J. (1951). *J. Biol. Chem.* **193**, 265.

Luchsinger, W. W. (1967). *Brewers' Digest* **42** (2), 56.

Luchsinger, W. W., Chen, S. C. and Richards (1956a). *Arch. Biochem. Biophys.* **112**, 524.

Luchsinger, W. W., Chen, S. C. and Richards (1956b). *Arch. Biochem. Biophys.* **112**, 531.

Luchsinger, W. W., Cochrane, D. G. and Kneen, E. (1960). *Cereal Chem.* **37**, 525.

Luchsinger, W. W., English, H., Cochrane, D. G. and Kneen, E. (1958). *Proc. Ann. Meet. Am. Soc. Brew. Chem.* p. 40.

Luchsinger, W. W., Hous, E. F. and Schneberger, G. L. (1962). *Proc. W. Virginia Acad. Sci.* **34**, 51.

Luers, H. and Collignon, E. (1939). *Wschr. Brau.* **56**, 305.

Lundin, H. (1961). *In* "Die Brautechnischen Untersuchungsmethoden", Pawlowski-Schild, 8th edn. Hans Carl, Nurnberg.

Lundin, H. and Schroderheim, J. (1931). *Wschr. Brau.* **48**, 139.

Lynes, K. J. and Norris, F. W. (1948). *J. Inst. Brew.* **54**, 153.

McFarlane, W. D. (1961). *J. Inst. Brew.* **67**, 102.

McFarlane, W. D. (1965). *Proc. E.B.C. Congr., Stockholm* p. 387.

McFarlane, W. D. and Bayne, P. D. (1961). *Proc. E.B.C. Congr., Vienna* p. 278.

McFarlane, W. D. and Held, H. R. (1953). *Proc. E.B.C. Congr., Nice* p. 110.

McFarlane, W. D. and Millingen, M. B. (1964). *Proc. Ann. Meet. Am. Soc. Brew. Chem.* p. 41.

McFarlane, W. D. and Thompson, K. D. (1964). *J. Inst. Brew.* **70**, 497.

McFarlane, W. D. and Wye, E. (1957). *Proc. E.B.C. Congr., Copenhagen* p. 299.

McFarlane, W. D., Sword, P. F. and Blinoff, G. (1963). *Proc. E.B.C. Congr., Brussels* p. 177.

McFarlane, W. D., Thompson, K. D. and Garrat, R. H. (1963). *Proc. Ann. Meet. Am. Soc. Brew. Chem.* p. 98.

McFarlane, W. D., Wye, E. and Grant, H. L. (1955). *Proc. E.B.C. Congr., Baden-Baden* p. 298.

McGuiness, J. D., Laws, D. R. J., Eastmond, R. and Gardner, R. J. (1975). *J. Inst. Brew.* **81**, 237.

McGuinness, J. D., Laws, D. R. J. and Bath, N. A. (1976). *Proc. Ann. Meet. Am. Soc. Brew. Chem.* **34**, 170.

MacPherson, J. K. and Buckee, G. K. (1974). *J. Inst. Brew.* **80**, 540.

Macey, A., Stowell, K. C. and White, H. B. (1964). *Proc. Ann. Meet. Am. Soc. Brew. Chem.* p. 22.

Macey, A., Stowell, K. C. and White, H. B. (1966). *J. Inst. Brew.* **72**, 29.

Mändl, B. (1974). *E.B.C. Monograph-I, Zeist* p. 237.

Mändl, B. and Piendl, A. (1971). *Proc. E.B.C. Congr., Estoril* p. 343.

Mändl, B., Gehloff, R. and Piendl, A. (1975). *Brewers' Digest* **50** (1), 40.

Mändl, B., Wullinger, F., Fischer, A. and Piendl, A. (1969). *Brauwissenschaft* **22** (7), 278.

Mändl, B., Wullinger, F., Schneider, K. and Piendl, A. (1971). *Brauwissenschaft* **24** (2), 43.

Marinelli, Feil, M. F. and Schait, A. (1968). *Proc. Ann. Meet. Am. Soc. Brew. Chem.* p. 113.

Marinelli, L. and Whitney, D. (1966). *J. Inst. Brew.* **72**, 252.

Markham, K. R. (1975). *In* "The Flavonoids" (J. B. Harborne, T. J. Mabry and H. Mabry, eds.), Chapter 1. Academic Press, New York and London.

Martin, P. A. (1973). *J. Inst. Brew.* **79**, 289.

Meilgaard, M. (1974). *Tech. Quart., Master Brewers Ass. Am.* **11** (2), 118.

Meilgaard, M. C. (1975a). *Tech. Quart., Master Brewers Ass. Am.* **12**, 107.

Meilgaard, M. C. (1975b). *Tech. Quart., Master Brewers Ass. Am.* **12**, 151.

Meredith, W. O. S. (1963). *Proc. Ann. Meet. Am. Soc. Brew. Chem.* p. 5.
Meredith, W. O. S., Bass, E. J. and Anderson, J. A. (1951). *Cereal Chem.* **228**, 177.
Mitcheson, R. C. and Stowell, K. C. (1970). *J. Inst. Brew.* **76**, 335.
Mocek, M. and Richardson, P. J. (1972). *J. Inst. Brew.* **78**, 459.
Moffa, D. J. and Luchsinger, W. W. (1970). *Cereal Chem.* **47**, 74.
Moll, M., Duteurtre, B., Scion, G., Chapon, L. and Chapon, S. (1974). *Tech. Quart., Master Brewers Ass. Am.* **11** (4), 250.
Moll, M., Flayeux, R. and That, V. (1972). *Bios* 520.
Monties, B. and Bidan, P. (1967). *Ind. Agric. Aliment.* p. 347.
Moore, S. and Stein, W. H. (1948). *J. Biol. Chem.* **176**, 367.
Myrback, K. and Myrback, S. (1931). *Wschr. Brau.* **48**, 43.
Nakayama, T. (1961). *Proc. Ann. Meet. Am. Soc. Brew. Chem.* p. 61.
Narziss, L. (1972a). "Abriss der Brauerei", p. 264. Enke Verlag, Stuttgart.
Narziss, L. (1972b). "Abriss der Brauerei", p. 269. Enke Verlag, Stuttgart.
Narziss, L. (1972c). "Abriss der Brauerei", p. 64. Enke Verlag, Stuttgart.
Narziss, L. (1973). *Brauwelt* **113**, 3.
Narziss, L. (1974). *E.B.C. Monograph-I, Zeist* p. 188.
Narziss, L., Reicheneder, E. and Nordhoff, R. (1968). *Brauwissenschaft* **21**, 4, 123.
National Research Council, Food and Nutrition Board (1973). "Recommended Dietary Allowances", Publication 0–309–02216–9, 8th edn. Washington, D.C.
Neuberg, J. (1958). *In* "The Chemistry and Biology of Yeasts" (A. H. Cook, ed.), pp. 323–362. Academic Press, New York and London.
Ng, E. and Mocek, M. (1973). *J. Inst. Brew.* **79**, 165.
Nordstrom, K. (1968). *J. Inst. Brew.* **74**, 429.
Norris, F. W. (1945). *J. Inst. Brew.* **51**, 178.
Nummi, M., Loisa, M. and Enari, T.-M. (1969). *Proc. E.B.C. Congr., Interlaken* p. 349.
Nykänen, L., Puputti, E. and Suomalainen, H. (1966). *J. Inst. Brew.* **72**, 24.
Otter, G. E. and Taylor, L. (1976). *J. Inst. Brew.* **82**, 264.
Otter, G. E. and Taylor, L. J. (1967). *J. Inst. Brew.* **73**, 570.
Otter, G. E., Popplewell, J. A. and Taylor, L. J. (1969). *Proc. E.B.C. Congr., Interlaken* p. 481.
Owades, J. L. (1955). *Proc. Ann. Meet. Am. Soc. Brew. Chem.* p. 68.
Owades, J. L., Rubin, G. and Brenner, M. (1958). *Proc. Ann. Meet. Am. Soc. Brew. Chem.* p. 66.
Palmqvist, U. and Äyräpää, T. (1969). *J. Inst. Brew.* **75**, 181.
Panelist (1973). *Tech. Quart., Master Brewers Ass. Am.* **10**, 104.
Parker, W. E. and Richardson, P. J. (1970). *J. Inst. Brew.* **76**, 191.
Pickett, J. A. (1974). *J. Inst. Brew.* **80**, 42.
Pickett, J. A., Coates, J. and Sharpe, F. R. (1976a). *J. Inst. Brew.* **82**, 228.
Pickett, J. A., Coates, J., Peppard, T. L. and Sharpe, F. R. (1976b). *J. Inst. Brew.* **82**, 233.
Piendl, A. and Gehloff, R. (1973). *Process Biochem.* **8** (4), 22.
Piendl, A. and Hopulele, T. (1973). *Proc. Ann. Meet. Am. Soc. Brew. Chem.* **4**, 75.
Pierce, J. S. (1966). *Tech. Quart., Master Brewers Ass. Am.* **3** (4), 231.
Piratzky, W. (1947). *Brauerei* **9**, 10.
Pollock, J. R. A. (1962). *In* "Barley and Malt" (A. H. Cook, ed.). Academic Press, London and New York.
Pollock, J. R. A., Pool, A. A. and Reynolds, T. (1960). *J. Inst. Brew.* **66**, 389.
Pomeranz, Y. and Dikeman, E. (1976). *Brewers' Digest* **51** (7), 30.
Portno, A. D. (1966). *J. Inst. Brew.* **72**, 193.
Preece, I. A. (1948). *Wallerstein Lab. Commun.* **11**, 179.

Preece, I. A. (1957). *Wallerstein Lab. Commun.* **20**, 147.
Preece, I. A. (1964). *Tech. Quart., Master Brewers Ass. Am.* (1), 127.
Quesnel, O. (1942). "Untersuchungen über die Gerstenglobuline". Almqvist and Wiksell, Uppsala, Sweden.
Reich, H. and Bock, R. M. (1958). *Wallerstein Lab. Commun.* **21**, 5.
Robbins, G. S., Farley, M. and Burkhart, B. A. (1963). *Proc. Ann. Meet. Am. Soc. Brew. Chem.* p. 124.
Rosculet, G. (1969). *Proc. Ann. Meet. Am. Soc. Brew. Chem.* p. 127.
Rosculet, G. (1971). *Brewers' Digest* **46**, 68.
Rudin, A. D. (1974). *E.B.C. Monograph-I, Zeist* p. 239.
Saletan, L. T. (1959a). *Wallerstein Lab. Commun.* **22**, 125.
Saletan, L. T. (1959b). *Wallerstein Lab. Commun.* **22**, 131.
Sandegren, E. (1947). *Proc. E.B.C. Congr., Scheveningen* p. 28.
Satake, K., Okayuma, T., Ohashi, M. and Shinada, T. (1960). *J. Biochem., Tokyo* **47**, 654.
Schait, A. and Cuzner, J. (1970). *Proc. Ann. Meet. Am. Soc. Brew. Chem.* **27**, 33.
Schiff, H. (1900). *Liebig's Ann.* **310**, 25.
Schild, von E. and Lempart, K. (1968). *Brauwissenschaft* **21**, 63.
Schmid, P. and Kleber, W. (1961). *Proc. E.B.C. Congr., Vienna* p. 260.
Schneller, M. A. (1949). *Proc. Ann. Meet. Am. Soc. Brew. Chem.* p. 74.
Schulze, W. G., Herwig, W. C., Fly, W. H., and Chicoye, E. (1976). *Proc. Ann. Meet. Am. Soc. Brew. Chem.* **34** (4), 181.
Schur, F., Hug, H. and Pfenninger, H. (1974). *E.B.C. Monograph-I, Zeist.*
Schur, F., Pfenninger, H. and Narziss, L. (1973). *Schweiz. Brau-Runds.* **84** (5), 93.
Schuster, K. (1968). *In* "Handbuch der Lebensmittelschemie" (J. Schormuller, ed.), Book 7, pp. 45–171. Springer Verlag, Berlin.
Schuster, K. and Weinfurtner, F. (1964). *Brauwissenschaft* **17**, 42.
Schuster, K., Narziss, L. and Kumada, J. (1967). *Brauwissenschaft* **20**, 185.
Scriban, R. and Fosseux, P.-Y. (1969). *Brasserie* **24**, 429.
Scriban, S. and Benard, M. (1973). *Bios* **4**, 512.
Silbereisen, K. and Kraffczyk, F. (1967). *Monats. Brau.* **20**, 332.
Silbereisen, K. and Kraffczyk, F. (1968). *Tech. Quart., Master Brewers Ass. Am.* (2), 135.
Simmonds, D. H. (1966). *J. Inst. Brew.* **72**, 573.
Singleton, V. L. (1974). *Tech. Quart., Master Brewers Ass. Am.* **11**, 135.
Singleton, V. L. and Esau, P. (1969). "Phenolic Substances in Grapes and their Significance", Chap. III. Academic Press, New York and London.
Singleton, V. L. and Noble, A. (1976). *In* "Phenolic, Sulfur and Nitrogen Compounds in Food Flavors" (G. Charalambous, ed.). American Chemical Society, Washington, D.C.
Slavko, C. M. (1974). *J. Inst. Brew.* **80**, 534.
Sogawa, H. (1971). *Rep. Res. Lab. Kirin Brewing Co., Yokahama* **14**, 21.
Sogawa, H. (1972). *Rep. Res. Lab. Kirin Brewing Co., Yokahama* **15**, 17.
Sogawa, H. (1973). *Rep. Res. Lab. Kirin Brewing Co., Yokahama* **16**, 29.
Somers, T. C. and Ziemelis, G. (1972). *J. Inst. Brew.* **78**, 233.
Spackman, D. H., Moore, S. and Stein, W. H. (1958). *Anal. Chem.* **30**, 1190.
Steiner, K. (1974). *Schweiz. Brau-Runds.* **85**, 109.
Steiner, K. and Stocker, H. R. (1967a). *Schweiz. Brau-Runds.* 217.
Steiner, K. and Stocker, H. R. (1969). *Proc. E.B.C. Congr., Interlaken* p. 327.
Steiner, K. and Stocker, H. R. (1976b). *J. Inst. Brew.* **65**, 256.

Steward, S. R., Smith, J. L., Kavanagh, T. E., Hildebrand, R. P. and Clarke, B. J. (1974). *J. Inst. Brew.* **80**, 34.

Stone, I. and Gray, P. P. (1961). *Wallerstein Lab. Commun.* 93.

Stone, I. M., Laschiver, C. and Saletan, L. T. (1968). *Wallerstein Lab. Commun.* 193.

Suomalainen, H. and Ronkainen, P. J. (1963). *J. Inst. Brew.* **69**, 478.

Sweeley, C. C., Bentley, R., Makita, M. and Wells, W. W. (1963). *J. Am. Chem. Soc.* **85**, 2497.

Szlavko, C. M. (1973). *J. Inst. Brew.* **79**, 283.

Takayanagi, S., Amaha, M., Sataka, K., Kuroiwa, Y., Igarashi, H. and Murata, A. (1969). *J. Inst. Brew.* **75**, 284.

Technicon Industrial Systems (1977a). Technicon Industrial Method No. 329–75 W–B.

Technicon Industrial Systems (1977b). Technicon Industrial Method No. 376–75 W–B.

Ten Hoopen, H. J. G. (1973). *J. Inst. Brew.* **79**, 29.

Timberlake, C. F. and Bridle, P. (1975). *In* "The Flavonoids" (J. B. Harborne, T. J. Mabry and H. Mabry, eds.) Chapter 5, Academic Press, New York and London.

Trachman, H., Gantz, C. S. and Saletan, L. T. (1970). *Wallerstein Lab. Commun.* **33**, 177.

Trenel, G. and John, M. (1970). *Monats. Brau.* **23**, 6.

Tressl, R., Kossa, T. and Renner, R. (1974). *Monats. Brau.* **27**, 98.

Tressl, R., Kossa, T. and Renner, R. (1975). *Proc. E.B.C. Congr.*, Nice p. 737.

Tripp, R. C., Timm, B., Iyer, M., Richardson, I. and Amundson, C. H. (1968). *Proc. Ann. Meet. Am. Soc. Brew. Chem.* p. 65.

Tuning, B. (1971). *Proc. E.B.C. Congr.*, Estoril, p. 191.

Ueda, R., Hayashida, M. and Termoto, S. (1964) *Hakko Kogaku Zasshi* **42**, 22 (via *Chem. Abstr.* (1966). **64** (9), 13353g).

Ulloa, G. H., Canales, A. M. and Zapata, B. D. (1976). *Proc. Ann. Meet. Am. Soc. Brew. Chem.* p. 33, 167.

United States Department of Agriculture, Agricultural Research Service (1963). *In* "Composition of Foods" Handbook No. 8. Washington D.C.

Van Slyke, D. D., MacFadyen, D. A. and Hamilton, P. (1941). *J. Biol. Chem.* **141**, 671.

Vanbelle, M., De Clerck, E. and Vervack, W. (1972). *Bull. Ass. Anciens Etud. Brass., Louvain* **68**, 81.

Vancraenenbroeck, R. (1974). *E.B.C. Monograph-I, Zeist* p. 19.

Vancraenenbroeck, R., Vanclef, A. and Lontie, R. (1965). *Proc. E.B.C. Congr., Stockholm* p. 360.

Vaughan, N. J. (1962). *J. Biol. Chem.* **234**, 3354.

Visser, M. K. and Lindsay, R. C. (1971). *Tech. Quart., Master Brewers Ass. Am.* **8**, 123.

Voerkelius, G. (1970). *Brauwissenschaft* **23**, 458.

Voss, H. and Piendl, A. (1976a). *Brewers' Digest* **51** (10), 56.

Voss, H. and Piendl, A. (1976b). *Brewers' Digest* **51** (11), 34.

Waddell, W. J. and Hill, C. (1956). *J. Lab. Clin. Med.* **48**, 311.

Wagner, G. M. (1967). *Tech. Quart., Master Brewers Ass. Am.* (4), 260.

Wainwright, T. (1971). *Proc. E.B.C. Congr.*, Estoril p. 437.

Weiner, J. P. (1974). *J. Inst. Brew.* **80**, 486.

Weiner, J. P. and Taylor, L. (1969). *J. Inst. Brew.* **75**, 195.

Weinfurtner, F., Eschenbecher, F. and Heltmann, K. H. (1966). *Brauwissenschaft* 174.

Weinfurtner, F., Eschenbecher, F. and Thoss, G. (1964). *Brauwissenschaft* 27, 121.

Weinges, K., Bahr, W., Goritz, K. and Marx, H.-D. (1969). *Fortscr. Chem. Org. Naturstoffe* **27**, 158.

Weissler, H. E. and Yadav, K. P. (1969). *Proc. Ann. Meet. Am. Soc. Brew. Chem.* p. 53.
West, D. B. and Skocic, G. P. (1974). *Proc. Ann. Meet. Am. Soc. Brew. Chem.* p. 21.
Whatling, A. J., Pasfield, J. and Briggs, D. E. (1968). *J. Inst. Brew.* **74**, 525.
Whistler, R. L. and Durso, D. F. (1950). *J. Am. Chem. Soc.* **72**, 677.
Whitaker, R. (1963). *Anal. Chem.* **35**, 1950.
Wieland, O. (1963). *In* "Methods of Enzymatic Analysis" (H. Burgmeyer, ed.), p. 211. Academic Press, New York and London.
Willey, B. F. (1976). "Phenolic, Sulphur, and Nitrogen Compounds in Food Flavours" (G. Charalambous and I. Katz, eds.), pp. 71–72. Amer. Chem. Soc. Symposium Series 26, Washington, D.C.
Williams, A. A., (1974). *J. Inst. Brew.* **80**, 455.
Wisk, T. J. and Siebert, K. J. (1973). *Proc. Ann. Meet. Am. Soc. Brew. Chem.* **4**, 29.
Witney, J. S. and Briggs, D. E. (1966). *J. Inst. Brew.* **72**, 474.
Woof, J. B. and Pierce, J. S. (1967). *Proc. E.B.C. Congr., Madrid* p. 365.
Woof, J. B. and Pierce, J. S. (1967). *Proc. E.B.C. Congr., Stockholm* p. 387.
Woof, J. B. and Pierce, J. S. (1968). *J. Inst. Brew.* **74**, 264.
Wren, J. J. and Wigall, P. M. (1965). *Biochem. J.* **94**, 216.
Wylie, E. B. and Johnson, M. J. (1962). *Biochim. Biophys. Acta* **59**, 450.
Yoshida, T. (1968). *Rep. Res. Lab. Kirin Brewing Co., Yokahama* **11**, 77.
Yoshida, T. (1971). *Rep. Res. Lab. Kirin Brewing Co., Yokahama* **14**, 37.
Yoshida, T., Hattan, M. and Morimoto, K. (1968). *Rep. Res. Lab. Kirin Brewing Co. Yokahama* **11**, 63.

5. Analysis of Beers

JOHN V. HARVEY

The South Australian Brewing Co. Ltd.,
Adelaide, South Australia

I. INTRODUCTION

The analysis of beers by means of physical, chemical, organoleptic and microbiological methods forms an important part of any system of quality control of the brewing process. In this chapter, selected methods available for various physical and chemical techniques are reviewed and reference made to some organoleptic procedures used for quality control. Some methods relating to control of packaging operations and packaging materials are also mentioned. Routine microbiological methods are described elsewhere.

Reference is made to several collections of standard methods in common use in the industry throughout the world. These include those of the European Brewery Convention (known as Analytica—E.B.C. 1975); of the American Society of Brewing Chemists (A.S.B.C. Methods of Analysis 1975); and of The Institute of Brewing Analysis Committee (Recommended Methods of Analysis 1971). They are referred to in the text simply as E.B.C. (1975), A.S.B.C. (1975) and I of B (1971); some amendments and additions to the latter methods are noted, where applicable, with references given as I of B (1973), etc. At the time of writing, six methods have been adopted by E.B.C. and A.S.B.C. as "International Methods" and it is noted by E.B.C. (1975) that many more methods will be so designated in the years to come.

A. Sampling and Sample Preparation

The data obtained from analysis of a sample of beer can only be reliable if the sample is truly representative of the brew, batch, tank or package of beer under examination. Sampling procedures will obviously vary, with many different sampling devices in use on brewing plant, but it is essential that, whatever means are used, the sample is as representative as possible and is collected in a suitable, clean container.

For some determinations, it is necessary that the beer be fully or partially de-carbonated. This can be accomplished by pouring, stirring or shaking as described, for example, in A.S.B.C. (1975). Suspended matter is removed by filtration if necessary and it is desirable that the sample is attempered to approximately 20 °C before analysis. Bicking (1969) discusses sampling of liquids and gives details of some sampling devices.

When sampling for packaging control the use of standard sampling plans such as those FAO/WHO Codex Alimentarius Commission (1969) or U.S.A. Military Standard 105A (1950) may be considered but for many applications such plans are not feasible because of the large numbers of samples required and the need to employ destructive testing for many procedures. Modifications of standard sampling plans and other methods, discussed by

Harvey (1976), Miller (1975), Singh (1969) and others, are more applicable to the control of packaging materials and to the packaging operation itself.

Storage and handling of samples are obviously important as beer is a labile material. Consequently, if analysis cannot be undertaken within a reasonable time samples must be refrigerated until work can be commenced. Samples for analyses in which the level of carbonation is important must be handled in a manner such that no carbon dioxide is lost; similarly, handling techniques must be adapted as necessary to avoid loss of volatile components where this is important.

B. Recording and Reporting

Every laboratory will have its own systems of recording and reporting analytical results but whatever procedures are used it is essential to record results as soon as they are obtained. Reporting of results is likewise important and the methods used will depend on the type of data to be reported and the use to which they will be put. Results should always be given to a number of significant figures consistent with the errors inherent in the sampling and analytical procedures. Many standard methods state how the results are to be given and it is common for analytical procedures to include an estimate of the standard deviation or some other expression of possible error.

Where alternative methods are available and in common use within the industry, it is advisable to state which method has been employed. There are opportunities, in some parts of the world, to take part in collaborative studies in connection with various analytical procedures. When possible, advantage should be taken of such opportunities and also of the provision of check samples of beer such as those provided by A.S.B.C. Many procedures in general use for the analysis of beer are of an empirical nature and as such their precision will be improved by frequent exchange of samples with other laboratories or participation in collaborative surveys and the use of check samples.

C. Control Schedules

Again, sampling and analytical schedules for the purposes of quality control are a matter of choice and will depend on many factors. Schedules will be different for the examination of "green" beer from fermenting vessels, for checking maturing beer from storage vessels and for bright or finished beer. Further differences will occur in schedules designed for beer from bright beer tanks and for pasteurized beers sampled from packages. As a guide only and for purposes of comparison, Table 1 gives an outline of the control schedules used for two types of lager beer by an Australian brewing organization. The

TABLE 1. Analytical control schedules for bulk and packaged lagers

Sample	Determination	Frequency
Beer ex fermenting vessels	Apparent extract	Daily all vessels
	pH value	As required
	Colour	As required
	Diacetyl	At end of fermentation
	Dissolved oxygen	As required
	Alcohol	As required
	Bitterness	As required
Beer ex maturation vessels	Apparent extract	All vessels at filling and prior to filtration
	pH value	Random check at filling
	Colour	Random check at filling
	Dissolved oxygen	All vessels at filling
	Alchol	As required
	Bitterness	All vessels at filling
	Diacetyl	Random check prior to filtration
	Total nitrogen ⎫ A fraction nitrogen ⎬ Turbidity (haze) ⎭	Random check prior to filtration. All vessels prior to filtration
Beer ex bright beer vessels	Apparent extract ⎫ pH value ⎪ Colour ⎪ Haze ⎬ Carbon dioxide ⎪ Dissolved oxygen ⎭	All vessels at filling
	Alcohol ⎫ Diacetyl ⎪ Bitterness ⎪ Total nitrogen ⎬ A fraction nitrogen ⎪ Head retention ⎭	Selected vessels at filling

determinations listed and the frequencies of application have been evolved over a number of years and naturally are subject to amendment as considered necessary. Numerous schedules have been suggested in the general brewing literature, always with the concept in mind that schedules must be designed to fit the application.

A dynamic process such as brewing presents significant problems of control and it is of utmost importance that any system of control is flexible and dynamic within itself. New production techniques frequently require new, or at least modified, analytical procedures, new sampling methods and sometimes a completely different approach to control of the process. The

TABLE 1 (*cont.*)

Sample	Determination	Frequency
Beer ex bottles and cans	Apparent extract Haze Dissolved oxygen Carbon dioxide Total oxygen Volume of contents Air in head space (cans)	Random samples at 2-hour intervals from each line
	Initial chill haze Stability predicition Chill haze at 2, 4 and 8 months Shelf haze at 8 months	Random samples at 4-hour intervals from each line
	Bitterness Diacetyl Head retention Total nitrogen	Random samples daily from each line
	Original extract Residual extract Alcohol Total carbohydrate Total nitrogen Trace elements—Na, K, Ca, Mg, Cu, Fe, As Anions—Cl, SO_4 Calorific (energy) value	Random samples monthly all packs
Beer ex casks	Apparent extract Haze Carbon dioxide Dissolved oxygen "Keeping" quality Head fermation Head retention	Random samples daily

introduction of in-line or on-site control equipment and other forms of automated process control should only be undertaken after a thorough examination of the factors involved. Integration of existing manual or semi-automatic procedures with newer forms of process control is imperative as is the involvement, at the planning stage, of the personnel responsible for the maintenance, design, operation and interpretation of the existing systems.

Williams *et al.* (1967) give good reasons for the use of a number of determinations for bringing about stronger control of product quality and Hudson (1976) discusses the impact of automated methods on control measures. Many other references will be found to be of value when considering this aspect. Martin (1971) gives a good account of the role of the brewery laboratory in times of change and Robinson (1976) gives guidelines for control schedules and laboratory operations in medium and small breweries.

A useful evaluation of quality control policy and management in a modern brewing organization is given by Wren (1976) who stresses the need for adequate communications in all areas of quality control.

II. PHYSICAL AND CHEMICAL METHODS

A. Introduction

The measurement of a number of physical and chemical characteristics of beer is essential in the achievement of adequate quality control and in some cases is mandatory because of legal requirements. Included in the latter category are the determinations of alcohol, original extract and apparent extract. Methods for these are prescribed by excise and similar regulations in most countries and detailed descriptions of some suitable methods, together with the tables to be used with them, are given in the official methods of the E.B.C. (1975), A.S.B.C. (1975) and I of B (1971).

B. Alcohol

For official purposes, alcohol is usually determined by distillation procedures such as those described in the methods listed above and more recently by I of B (1975). However, for the purposes of in-plant control, other simpler methods can be used. These include the determination by refractometry and by gas–liquid chromatography (GLC), both techniques being capable of providing rapid measurement of large numbers of samples. Other rapid methods include those utilizing the oxidation of ethanol to acetaldehyde by alcohol dehydrogenase, as described by Goldberg and Rydberg (1966), and colorimetric estimation by means of ammonium hexanitrocerate, after dialysis of the beer, as described by Ashurst (1963). Both these procedures can be adapted to automated analysis; with the latter very good agreement with results from manual distillation are claimed.

An automatic distillation procedure is described in detail by Sawyer and Dixon (1968b) and Sawyer et al. (1969). The continuous distillation technique used is adapted from one proposed originally for the determination of volatile aldehydes and ketones. Vapour resulting from the flash distillation of the sample is condensed and an aliquot of the condensate passed through a manifold and mixed with acidified potassium dichromate for determination of alcohol by colorimetry. In practice, a manifold in which the determination of residual carbohydrate is combined with that of alcohol is used and the two resultant parameters are summed to give the original extract (original gravity) of the sample.

The determination of alcohol by colorimetry with vanadium 8-hydroxy-quinolate, as described by Tanaka (1960) and van Gent and Kerrick (1965) for the measurement of alcohol in blood, has been investigated by Sawyer and Dixon (1968b) and found unsuitable for use in an automated procedure for beer.

Refractometry provides a ready means for routine determination of alcohol in process and finished beers, providing that the beers have not been primed after fermentation. An instrument capable of reading to 0·0001 refractive index with a heatable prism with temperature control to $\pm 0·1$ °C is required, as is the compilation of tables or nomographs to provide a ready means of converting refractive indices to alcohol for the beer concerned. Once established, such conversions should be checked occasionally by means of distillation and pycnometer; a separate conversion table, curve or nomograph is required for each type of beer. A description of the technique is given by A.S.B.C. (1975), but most laboratories find it convenient to devise techniques, graphs, tables, etc. most suited to their own needs. Weyh (1971) and (1973) discusses the sources of possible error in refractometric methods and suggests that differences between values obtained by refractometry and distillation can be minimized by treating the beer identically for degassing and by following the procedures exactly for each method. It is particularly important that adequate temperature control is maintained and that a suitable light source is used for illuminating the prism of the instrument. Clarity of the sample must be adequate and degassing carried out efficiently. Alcohol can be determined readily by means of gas–liquid chromatography (GLC), using an electron capture detector and a column packed with a phase such as PEG operating at 100 °C with nitrogen, hydrogen and air. n-Propanol is used as an internal standard and for routine use direct measurement of peak heights is satisfactory. A 4% ethanol solution, accurately standardized by pycnometer, is used to determine a suitable factor. Details of a slightly different technique are given by Trachman (1969).

C. Apparent Extract

The determination of apparent extract (specific gravity) of a beer is one of the most common determinations carried out in any brewery or brewing laboratory. For extreme accuracy, required frequently for legal and similar purposes, determination by pycnometer is recommended. Two main types of pycnometer are in general use, i.e. Reischauer type and Boots (vacuum) type, both of approx. 50 ml capacity. It is essential that all pycnometers are kept scrupulously clean by means of suitable cleaning solutions and rinsed and dried immediately after use, employing 95% ethanol and pure ethyl ether as drying agents. A.S.B.C. (1975) give full details of the use and care of pycnometers of both types.

For most routine control purposes, the determination of apparent extract can be accomplished with sufficient accuracy by means of a suitable hydrometer (saccharometer). Many types are available, some with integral thermometers to cover the ranges of values necessary. In Continental Europe, the Balling or Plato scales, based on standard tables for densities of sucrose in water at 20 ° C, are in general use for extract whilst in Great Britain and some other countries the specific gravity or degress of gravity (the excess over) 1000 for water) are quoted. Plato is used in North and South America and most other countries outside Europe although the British brewers lbs per barrel scale is occacionally employed.

An A.S.B.C. Sub-Committee (1976) reports that "although the Plato tables probably overestimate the solids content of wort by 2–3%, they represent a convenient method of expressing extract and have served the industry well over the years". Retention of the use of the Plato tables is recommended.

However, in a recent statement by the I of B Analysis Committee (1976), a recommendation is made that measurement of specific gravity should be at 20 °C/20 °C and that total extract of a brew should be expressed as "hectolitre-degrees", brewers degrees being defined as the excess specific gravity of the sample over that of water × 1000.

Whatever scale is used, it is essential that all saccharometers are constructed to appropriate specifications and are standardized and handled with care. It is important that bubbles of carbon dioxide gas do not adhere to the bulb or stem of the instrument when a reading is made and that care is taken to read at the highest point of the meniscus as seen in profile at the line of sight. Standardization (calibration) of all saccharometers before use by means of suitable test fluids, the specific gravity of which has been determined by pycnometer, is essential.

Regular calibration of all saccharometers in constant use in laboratory or plant is recommended. Procedures for handling, calibration and care of saccharometers are given by A.S.B.C. (1975) and in some texts dealing with sugars and similar products.

A number of other methods, involving refractometry, falling drop techniques and the use of specific gravity balances have been preferred in some laboratories for many years. A falling-drop technique, described by Thorne and Svendsen (1971), has the advantage of employing very small samples. A procedure developed by Leach et al. (1974), which utilizes an Archimedean plummet, gives results slightly faster than by a pycnometer method.

D. Real Extract and Original Extract

In the calculation of original extract (original gravity) of a beer from its alcohol content and apparent extract, the real or residual extract must be known. This is the extract of the de-alcoholized beer and is found by restoring, to its original volume, the residue in the distillation flask after removal of alcohol and determining the extract by pycnometer. The original extract is then determined from formulae such as

(1) $O = 2A + E -$ correction factor

or

(2) $O = 100 \times \dfrac{(2 \cdot 0665\ A + E)}{100 + 1 \cdot 0665\ A}$

where $O =$ original extract in ° Plato; $A =$ alcohol, % by weight; $E =$ real extract in ° Plato A.S.B.C. (1975); or similar formulae given by E.B.C. (1975).

I of B (1975a) gives details of the calculations employed in Great Britain using the spirit indication and also describes some useful checks for the accuracy of determination of alcohol residue gravity and original gravity. The importance of correcting for the acidity of certain beers is noted by Sawyer *et al.* (1970) whilst descriptions of automated techniques are given by Sawyer and Dixon (1968a) and (1968b) and Sawyer *et al.* (1969) for original gravity and residue gravity.

E. Colour

The colour of beer is a very important characteristic, particularly to the consumer, and its measurement is common to most brewery laboratories. Instrumental (spectrophotometric, photometric) methods and visual methods are both in use but there is a tendency to adopt the former. A.S.B.C. (1975) gives two instrumental procedures and whilst I of B (1971) gives a choice between visual matching and spectrophotometric methods, a later recommendation of I of B (1975b) permits only the latter.

Samples for the determination of colour should be clarified by filtration or centrifugation as necessary and if visual comparison is used it is essential that all operators are checked for colour blindness by means of the Ishihara charts (Tests for Colour Blindness).† Similarly, for visual matching, best results are obtained if a standard white light source, such as the European Standard Artificial north light is used, as described by E.B.C. (1975). The E.B.C. colour

† Ishihara (Tests for Colour Blindness); published by H. K. Lewis and Co., 136 Gower Street, London W.C.1, England.

units, adopted by that body, and also for many years by the Institute of Brewing, were originally based on the older Lovibond 52 Series and refer to a 25 mm (originally 1 in.) light path. Thus, E.B.C. values are approximately twice those obtained by the A.S.B.C. procedure, which employs a path of 0·5 in. of light at 430 nm and defines beer colour as 10 × the optical density obtained. Correction can be made for slight turbidity by determining the optical density at 700 nm; if this is equal to or less than 0·39 × the optical density at 430 nm no correction is made; if it is greater the difference is subtracted from the value at 430 nm. Clydesdale (1973) summarizes attempts to reach more definitive means of measurement of colour.

Standardization of spectrophotometers and care of them is discussed by A.S.B.C. (1975) and E.B.C. (1975).

F. pH Value (Hydrogen Ion Concentration)

The measurement of pH value is a simple task with modern instruments and where a number of determinations are to be made use of a flow through cell can be an advantage. Care must be taken to ensure that cells and electrodes are kept scrupulously clean and that accurately standardized and freshly prepared buffer solutions are used. With the narrow range of pH values normally encountered for a given beer it is desirable to use an instrument which is capable of reading to 0·02 or 0·01 pH unit. Samples should be decarbonated and attempered before the pH value is determined.

G. Total Acidity

A knowledge of the total acidity can be of value in assessing the quality of a beer and may be determined by potentiometric titration, using a good quality glass/calomel electrode pH meter, standardized at pH 7·0 with a suitable buffer solution. Normal precautions for shielding electrode systems and other precautions, important when operating pH meters in the range pH 7–8, should be taken as described by A.S.B.C. (1975). Total acidity can be expressed as the quantity of 1·0 N alkali/100 g beer or as % lactic acid or as % acetic acid.

A.S.B.C. (1975) also gives a method involving the titration of boiled and diluted beer with 0·1 N sodium hydroxide, using 0·5% phenolphthalein as indicator. This procedure is not as accurate as that of potentiometric titration and is not recommended for dark beers and stouts.

Some workers recommend that air should be gently bubbled through the sample for a few minutes before undertaking the titration. Kaczor (1968) compares several methods of decarbonating beer before the determination of total acidity and concludes that decarbonation by shaking and filtering does not remove the carbon dioxide sufficiently for determination by potentiometric titration. He recommends the boiling procedure, as described by A.S.B.C. (1975), for the visual titration method and also for the potentiometric method. Alternative decarbonation procedures which give comparable results include the application of a vacuum for 30 minutes or exposing the sample to atmosphere for up to 3 days.

Volatile acidity, an analysis required only on "acid" beers, is determined by steam distilling 100 ml of the sample until about 250 ml of distillate is available. This is then titrated as for total acidity with 0·1 N alkali and the volatile acidity expressed as acetic acid.

H. Turbidity (Haze)

Most lager beers are filtered bright before packaging and thus the measurement of turbidity (haze) is of great importance to brewers. All three standard methods mentioned earlier define Formazin Turbidity Units (Formazin Haze Units) which are used to give a scale providing broad agreement between the various instruments and methods in use for determining haze.

Formazin standards can be used for visual comparison and also as a means of standardizing instruments although some instruments in common use have their own standards, e.g. Coleman Nephelometer with °Nephelos (°N). Standardization of instruments measuring light scattered at different angles or those relying solely on transmitted light is essential if comparisons are to be made. However, conversion from one scale to another based on published conversion factors may not always be reliable and its is preferable to establish conversion factors for any one instrument or series of beers. Thorne and Nannestad (1959) have stressed that discrepancies between different means of measurement can be as great as 50%. Later (1962), they reported that there are significant differences in particle size and shape between formazin hazes and beer turbidigens and that these differences mitigate against direct conversion of scales of various instruments standardized with formazin.

The effect of beer colour on turbidity is marked in instruments measuring transmitted rather than scattered light. The effect can be reduced by the use of selected filters as suggested by Pope et al. (1966). Clydesdale (1973) discusses the effect of colour which is also dealt with in earlier papers by Jansen (1957) and Thorne and Beckley (1958).

The determination of haze is essential in the measurement of the physical stability of beer and in the determination of the resistance to chillhaze formation in trade and many other prediction and forcing tests, some of which are described in the following section.

I. Haze Formation and Physical Stability

Both A.S.B.C. and E.B.C. methods give procedures for accelerated ageing tests and a number of analytical techniques have been proposed for use in predicting the physical stability of beer, e.g. Challot *et al.* (1967), Thompson and Forward (1969), Chapon and Chemardin (1967), Whatling *et al.* (1968), Moll *et al.* (1971) and Steiner (1972). Of these, the sensitive protein technique proposed by Chapon and Chemardin (1967) has been found to give useful information as have procedures involving the addition of formaldehyde to the sample, e.g. Whatling *et al.* (1968) and Steiner (1972).

Advantages of the analytical techniques include their ability to give predictions within a few hours rather than the days, or even weeks, required by some of the suggested or standard ageing or forcing tests. In the author's laboratory, storage (in water) at 55 °C for 6 days followed by chilling (in water) to 0 °C for 1 day gives haze values which are correlated significantly with those obtained by chilling for 1 day after 2 months at 20 °C. On the other hand, Moll (1971) suggests that a test involving 7 days at 40 °C, followed by a day at 0 °C, may be preferable for beers stabilized with proteolytic enzymes.

Reliable and consistent predicition data can be provided only by use of a rigorously standardized method; the choice of method depends largely upon the facilities available and the degree of correlation obtained between the method used and the performance of the beer in trade. Investigation and trial use of a number of methods seems essential in order to establish that best suited for the beer and market conditions concerned.

J. Foam Characteristics

1. General

The foam or head of a beer has long been considered, for most products, to be one of the most important characteristics. Numerous methods have been described for the evaluation of foam formation, retention and adhesion. It is convenient, however, to consider each of the attributes separately. Some of the earlier procedures employed have been reviewed by Helm and Richardt (1936), Klopper (1954). In more recent years, the E.B.C. Haze and Foam Group (1968, 1970, 1975) has surveyed the field in some detail, and the difficulties associated with the assessment of head retention have been emphasized by Curtis (1966) and (1975). Bishop *et al.* (1975) discuss the sources of error of some methods employed for the measurement of foam stability and Hohn and Issing (1971) examine the correlation between foam retention and other physical properties of beers.

2. Foam Formation

The volume of foam formed depends largely upon the carbon dioxide content of the beer but other factors are significant in relation to retention of the foam and its character. Consequently, most methods giving quantitative results for foam formation are of little consequence, although useful information can be gained from observations made during standard pouring tests and other tests for foam retention. Klopper (1972) compares several methods of forming foam and points out that retention times can differ significantly depending on the means by which the foam is formed.

However, in the author's company a method has been developed for the measurement of foam formation of bulk draught beers and the values attained are found to be significantly correlated with the performance of the beers with regard to foam formation in trade. The procedure uses a standard instantaneous beer cooler with a quick-acting tap with a bracket which holds a standard beer glass, such that the top surface of the glass is level with the tap outlet. The glass is filled, but not overflowed, and the depth of foam measured after a short interval (designed to allow most of the bubbles of carbon dioxide to rise to the head). A number of subsequent pours are made and a mean expressed to 0·1 cm.

Experience with this method indicates that there may be some correlation between foam formation and foam retention but only within a relatively narrow range of CO_2 contents.

3. Foam Retention

Pouring tests have long been utilized to characterize foam or head retention. A number of techniques have been described, for example, by Harvey and Pope (1962) and doubtless many others are in use in breweries throughout the world. Both single-glass and multiple-glass methods give useful information for quality control purposes, providing that the glasses are scrupulously clean and the the procedures are rigidly standardized. It has been found in the author's laboratory that reliable and consistent detection of the "end-point", i.e. the appearance of beer colour through the foam, requires considerable experience and thus errors between operators can be significant. In the latter regard, refinements suggested by de Clerck and de Djicker (1957a), Klopper (1972), Klose and Schmitt (1972) are of interest.

Numerous methods in which foam is formed by "artificial" means, i.e. other than by pouring, have been published. Many of these methods measure the rate at which beer drains from foam produced under standard conditions. Methods due to Blom (1937) and (1957), Ross and Clark (1939), Rudin (1957) and others fall into this category.

Methods for the measurement of foam retention have been the subject of intensive investigation in many laboratories throughout the world. Notwithstanding this, most methods are considered to give, under some circumstances, anomalous results and care should be used in inter-laboratory comparisons, even of the same method.

However, within a single laboratory these methods can give reliable and useful results. In the author's experience, the Blom method has provided reliable data for purposes of quality control over a period of many years for a wide range of products. In addition, it gives, with fully carbonated beers, results that are significantly correlated with measurements obtained with the single-glass pouring technique as described by Harvey and Pope (1962).

The method originally proposed by Rudin (1957) has been modified by Bishop et al. (1975). A procedure based on this modification is proposed for adoption as the official I of B method for head retention, replacing the modified carborundum-addition method previously used by I of B (1971). The standard deviation of the modified Rudin procedure is given by Bishop et al. (1975) as $\pm 3 \cdot 2$ sec compared with $\pm 7 \cdot 1$ sec for the I of B method, the precision of which is given as about ± 12 sec.

In the modified method, a jacketed foam tube is maintained at $20 \pm 0 \cdot 2$ °C and pure CO_2 is supplied at $2 \cdot 7$ kg/cm^2 through a porosity No. 3 sintered glass disc.

Advantage is also taken of modern equipment for stabilizing gas pressure and flow rate. The method stresses the need to use very pure CO_2 for foaming the beer; the errors incurred by using impure CO_2 have been known for some years and its use has been blamed for some of the anomalous results reported in the past. The occurrence of non-linear logarithmic foam collapse rates as reported by, for example, Brenner et al. (1951) and Klopper (1955), is known to be due to the use of impure CO_2.

Some of the more recent methods, such as that described by Klopper (1973), are designed to give measurements for foam retention (stability) and foam cling (adhesion). Klopper's technique uses the NIBEM foam meter which gives automatic measurement of the rate of foam collapse as determined by the de Clerck and de Djicker method (1957b). The beer is poured into a cylindrical glass in a manner to form a head of about 5 cm and the disc and needles of the foam meter placed in contact with the foam. After the measurement of the collapse rate (foam retention) the glass can be transferred to the NIBEM-cling meter for measurement of cling (Klopper 1974).

A.S.B.C. (1975) gives details of two methods for foam retention (referred to as foam collapse rate in the methods) and states that "satisfactory methods for measurement of properties of beer foam other than those involving foam collapse rate have not yet been found". The methods detailed are (a) one for a sigma (Σ) value and (b) one utilizing a foam flashing procedure. The former is a modification of the Carlsberg method and involves measuring both the volume of beer produced from collapsed foam formed when a container of beer is poured into a special foam funnel and the volume of beer from residual foam at a stated time.

In the foam flashing method, which gives foam value units (FVU), a special fitting is attached to a bottle of beer, previously attempered to room temperature, and a quantity of beer is flashed to foam by applying a controlled pressure of CO_2 to the bottle. The foam fills a 200 ml measuring cylinder and the volume of beer resulting from the amount of foam collapsing in 90 seconds is measured and also the volume of beer resulting from the residual foam. These volumes are then used to calculate the FVU.

It is sometimes useful to determine the potential foam retention of beers during processing and for this purpose methods in which the foam is formed by means of the introduction of CO_2 must be used. The Blom method has been found to give reliable results with beers from the fermentation and maturation stages of the process and also with worts. Doubtless other methods, e.g. modified Rudin, will also yield results of value. With such samples, it should be remembered that the size of the bubbles formed can have a greater effect on foam stability than the character of the beer itself, as discussed by de Clerck and de Djicker (1957b) and thus conditions of foam formation must be rigidly standardized.

A more thorough understanding of foam properties could well follow the work of Hemmens (1975), involving tensiolaminometry, which measures the hysteresis in mechanical work performed on a thin film of beer under expansion and compression.

4. Foam Adhesion

Many attempts have been made over a number of years to measure the adhesion of beer foam, also known as cling or lace. That good adhesion or cling is an important character of a beer in the eyes of consumers cannot be denied and consequently this attribute is one for which reliable measurement would be desirable. The NIBEM-Clingmeter described by Klopper (1973, 1974) is stated to give useful data. It has also been found, in a number of laboratories, that photographs taken of glasses after successive amounts of beer have been removed show the degree of adhesion and stability of the adhering foam.

Foam adhesion, like foam formation, can, in general, be said to be difficult to measure. It is little wonder then, that the greater part of the considerable effort that has been undertaken in the study of beer foam has been directed towards the measurement of foam retention or stability.

K. Carbon Dioxide

Numerous methods are available for the determination of carbon dioxide in beer. They include those based on gravimetric, titrimetric and volumetric procedures and on manometric and other pressure measuring devices. A detailed survey of a selection of methods of all the above types is given by de Clerck (1958).

The methods most favoured utilize manometric or other forms of pressure measurement. The latter are based on Henry's Law of Partial Pressures, which relates the partial pressure of a gas in equilibrium with a liquid to the amount of gas dissolved in that liquid. Such methods, in use particularly in the U.S.A. for many years, have been the subject of extensive investigation. Details of methods for beer in tanks and in bottles and cans are given by A.S.B.C. (1975) which includes descriptions of one type (Zahm Nagel) of suitable apparatus and its mode of use. When direct-reading pressure methods are used for cans and bottles, it is important to make allowance for the partial pressure of the air in the headspace of the container and thus the amount of the air in headspace must be known (see section L). The correction necessary for air content is given by A.S.B.C. (1975) where it is stated that such correction is unnecessary if the "headspace air" (gases not soluble in 15% sodium hydroxide) does not exceed about 1·5 ml per 340 ml bottle or its equivalent.

The accuracy of the partial pressure procedure depends, to a large extent, on the standardization of conditions of agitation. Automation of the operation, as described by Takahashi and Sasaki (1970), is reported to improve the accuracy and also the speed of the determination.

Other methods used include some adapted from those evolved for the estimation of CO_2 for other purposes. For example, methods employing a Warburg respirometer or the Van Slyke apparatus are capable of giving accurate values with small samples and have been used for purposes of routine control.

In the manometric method used in the author's company for some 30 years, with continuing modification and improvement, the sample is drawn into a saturated potassium hydroxide or 30% w/v sodium hydroxide solution, and then transferred to a Büchner flask, fitted with a tap funnel, and connected to a vacuum source and a manometer. After evacuation of the system to a standard level, the CO_2 is released from the beer by adding an excess of acid and agitating the flask until a constant reading is obtained on the manometer. Standardization is carried out by means of accurately prepared sodium bicarbonate solutions and a gravimetric method used as an ultimate reference.

Other manometric procedure are given by I of B (1971) and by Bayles et al. (1968). A combined volumetric/manometric method is described by Heard (1973). All can be used by unskilled personnel and are capable of greater accuracy than the normal partial pressure method; in the author's experience precision of 0·005% w/w can be obtained.

A simple manometric procedure, described by Shah (1976), has the advantage of not requiring a vacuum source.

A titrimetric method is described by Postel and Drawert (1970) and others are noted by de Clerck (1958); potentiometric titration is recommended for dark beers and stouts and is more rapid than visual titration, although the latter can be simplified by use of a comparator, as described by de Clerck. A useful gravimetric method is that of Clark (1942) which combines some of the features of volumetric methods with the accuracy normally expected from a gravimetric procedure.

In-line instrumentation and automatic devices are available for the control of the carbonation of beer. One such instrument, described by de Brune *et al.* (1974), includes both differential pressure and temperature transmitters and is capable of controlling and measuring CO_2 to 0·01% w/w over a range from 0·32 to 0·67%. In an instrument described by Gamache (1968), an infrared analyser is employed to measure and indicate the amount of CO_2 swept from a stream of beer by a carrier gas. Rohner and Tomkins (1970) give details of an analyser which withdraws a sample of beer from a stream, creates a predetermined void and agitates the sample to establish the balance of partial pressure. A direct relationship between CO_2 found by chemical means and that found by the void volume method, is then used to indicate carbonation in volumes and to adjust the addition rate accordingly.

Instruments based on the latter technique give accurate results and trouble-free performance, particularly when the flow system is balanced so that sudden changes of pressure and temperature are avoided.

L. Dissolved Oxygen, Total Oxygen and Air Content

1. Dissolved Oxygen

(a) *Introduction*

The importance of protecting beer from oxygen at all stages of processing subsequent to fermentation has long been recognized. Consequently, the need for frequent and accurate determination of the amount of oxygen dissolved in beer at various points in production is well known. For this determination, it is important that the sample be taken in such a manner that atmospheric oxygen is excluded. So-called hypodermic sampling devices, the use of which has been developed in a number of beverage industries in recent years, are of value in taking samples for determination by chemical means.

Special fittings are required for some of the dissolved oxygen meters available. These and fittings for hypodermic sampling are available from

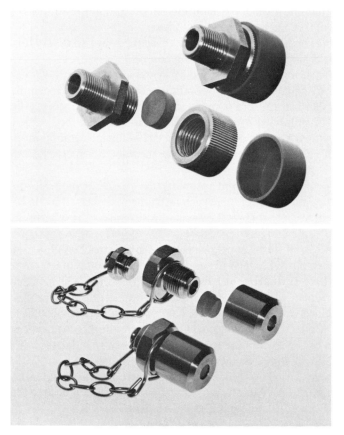

FIG. 1. Types of hypodermic sampling fittings.

regular sources of supply or equipment or can be made for specific applications. Two types are shown in Fig. 1.

(b) *Instrumental methods*

The use of instrumental techniques for the measurement of dissolved oxygen has increased rapidly in recent times in many industrial situations, in particular for water and effluent treatment. Several of the instruments available have been adapted for use with beer or are suitable for such application without modification.

Instrumental electrochemical methods are currently under review by both E.B.C. and A.S.B.C. and it is assumed that recommendations will shortly be made to assist in the selection and use of dissolved oxygen meters for in-line, on-site and laboratory purposes. Electrochemical meters are of two broad types, viz. those with exposed electrode systems, in which the sample comes in contact with the electrode, and those with protected electrode systems. In the latter, the electrodes are separated from the sample by an oxygen-permeable membrane.

The Hays Dissolved Oxygen meter, described by Klimovitz (1972), is a widely used example of the galvanic cell, exposed electrode type meter. It suffers from some disadvantages in routine use as noted below. Another galvanic cell meter, the couloximeter, described by Hersch (1973) and Brenner *et al.* (1974), is used for in-line application and also for the determination of oxygen in the headspace of packaged beer.

Dropping-mercury polarography has been used successfully for the measurement of oxygen in water, wort and beer, as discussed by Brenner *et al.* (1967), who used a Delta-Schwarz Dissolved Oxygen Analyzer. Little interference from oxygen pick-up and other factors is reported with this instrument, for which a low standard error is claimed.

The protected electrode meters, of which there are many, may be divided into the galvanic type (Mackereth) and the polarographic type (Clark), so called from the work of Mackereth (1964) and Clark (1953). Examples of the latter type include the Instrumentation Laboratory Ltd. models and those from Beckman Instruments Inc. and Yellow Springs Instruments Co.

In the author's experience, two, at least, of the meters currently available are best treated as laboratory instruments and are not really suitable for continuous in-line or field use. The Beckman Model 715, as discussed by Reynolds (1972) and the Hays Meter, have been found to give reliable results when used as laboratory instruments and taken to the sampling site on each occasion.

Some other instruments, in general, would appear to be more suitable for laboratory type applications; for example, that employed by Brenner *et al.* (1967). A later instrument, using an electrochemical–potentiometric device, as described by Wackerbauer *et al.* (1975) could be better suited for continuous in-line monitoring. This unit can also be used for the determination of dissolved oxygen in bottles and cans and can be adapted for the determination of air or oxygen in the headspace of a container.

In an extensive survey for the E.B.C. Analysis Committee, made by Howard and Mawer (1976), the advantages and disadvantages of a wide range of meters of several types are tabulated. The choice of meter will obviously depend on many factors and the recommendations made by E.B.C. and A.S.B.C. and others can be taken only as a guide. Perusal of a selection of the many references in the brewing literature, covering the past 20 years, will indicate that the measurement of this important constituent of beer by instrumental means is not simple nor is the use of some of the meters.

(c) *Chemical methods*

Due to the limitations of the available instrumentation and to other factors, many laboratories still rely on a classical chemical technique, using reduced indigo carmine as a colorimetric agent. This method, originally proposed by Rothchild and Stone (1938), has been described in various forms by Van Cauwenberge and de Clerck (1955), Jenkinson and Compton (1959) and others. Doubtless many modifications, in use in various parts of the world, have been produced in attempts to increase the efficiency of this simple technique. Measurement of optical density in a spectrophotometer, as suggested by several workers, is useful.

Both the E.B.C. and A.S.B.C. are considering adopting, as a standard procedure, a technique based on the modifications proposed by Jenkinson and Compton. In this, the indigo carmine solution is converted to the leuco form by heating with glucose and strong potassium hydroxide. An excess of the leuco dyestuff is then added, anaerobically, to the sample. Reaction with the oxygen dissolved in the beer regenerates a proportion of the dye and the colour is matched against standards at 640–700 nm. Regular, fresh preparation of the standard dye solution is important as is the standardization of the solid indigo carmine itself. The method is suitable for use with pale beers with up to 2 mg/litre dissolved oxygen.

The indigo carmine method is accepted as a reference method for the calibration of some of the instruments discussed in (b) above. Some meters can be calibrated against air and some reports, e.g. A.S.B.C. Sub-Committee (1975) suggest that calibration against water, as in the classical Winkler procedure, can give lower results than calibration with indigo carmine. It is stated that, in a survey involving a number of laboratories employing Hays meters, the main problem reported with them was the lack of a simple and reliable method of calibration. However, progress towards a relatively simple and yet accurate calibration procedure, based on the Winkler reaction, is reported. If close agreement between Winkler and indigo carmine procedures can be reached, either can be used for calibration purposes.

2. Air in Headspace and Total Air

The determination of the amounts of air in the headspace of packages has been a popular control measure for many years. Several methods have found favour, one in particular, that of Larsen and Sorenson (1957), is used with success in numerous laboratories. This procedure requires a special gas burette, a large (10 cm) funnel, a source of vacuum and a sink of water of appropriate depth.

In operation, the burette, funnel and sink are filled with water and the package to be checked is inverted under water in the sink, opened carefully and rotated so that any air in the headspace collects in the funnel and is replaced in the container by water. The gases in the burette are absorbed in 10% sodium hydroxide and the residual air is measured.

Garza and Bavisotto (1972) devised an analyser which gives a combination method for dissolved oxygen, headspace oxygen and CO_2 in packaged beers. There are other semi-automated procedures available and several headspace analysers, designed in the main for control of canned foods, may be purchased. GLC may be used for the ready determination of the residual gases in packages. Stutler and Dakin (1964) describe an early automated procedure employing GLC which is mentioned in more detail in section 4.2.A.

Brandon *et al.* (1972) used a Hasch cell in apparatus designed for the determination of oxygen in headspace and found that it gave slightly higher results than the Zahm-Nagel test.

The Zahm-Nagel apparatus can be used to ascertain the total air in a package and this procedure is widely used. Much has been written about the advantages and disadvantages of the shake-out method for total air. Some standardization of conditions can be achieved by using an ultrasonic water bath.

3. Total Oxygen

The total oxygen content of bottled or canned beers is useful in control of the packaging operation. A theoretical value can be obtained by calculation from known dissolved oxygen contents and air in headspace values. However, in this calculation it is assumed that the oxygen content of the air in headspace is 20% thereof, an assumption that is usually not warranted.

Total oxygen can be determined by injecting indigo carmine indicator into a package and mixing thoroughly, preferably by slow mechanical rotation before determination by the normal dissolved oxygen technique. For bottles, an additional crown seal shell with a hole punched therein and containing a soft rubber wad is forced over the original crown. A hole, large enough to permit the entry of a hypodermic needle, is then made in the original crown. Excess indigo carmine in reduced form is then forced into the bottle which is tested for leaks. If no leakage is apparent, the package is then rotated for 1 hour and a sample withdrawn for determination of oxygen.

Specially designed clamps and rubber wads enable a similar procedure to be carried out with cans. Results are normally expressed as ml oxygen per container, e.g.

$$\text{ml/740 ml bottle} = \frac{\text{mg/l dissolved oxygen}}{1 \cdot 8}$$

or

$$\text{ml/500 ml container} = \frac{\text{mg/l dissolved oxygen}}{2 \cdot 67}$$

M. Oxidation State and Oxidation and Reduction Potential

As early as 1934 de Clerck drew attention to the importance of the oxidation–reduction potential in brewing. The concept of rH value was critically examined in relation to beer by a number of workers in the years that followed. As a result, it was concluded that "static" electrometric methods for the measurement of rH were, in general, not satisfactory for beer.

Gray and Stone (1939) proposed a "dynamic" method for the determination of the oxidation state of beer, making use of velocity of reduction of a suitable indicator (dyestuff), in this case 2,6-dichlorophenolindophenol. The time taken, in seconds, for a sample of beer to decolorize a standard amount of indicator to 80% is quoted as the Indicator-Time Test or I.T.T. value. For samples with low reducing power decolorizing to 50% only is taken as the value, cited accordingly, in order to shorten the time taken.

Modifications of the original method, such as that described by de Clerck and Van Cauwenberge (1957), have been numerous as the procedure is one that lends itself to "local" amendments.

An A.S.B.C. Sub-Committee (1967) surveyed three methods—those of Gray and Stone and de Clerck and Van Cauwenberge and also one proposed by Williams et al. (1967) using ceric sulphate as an oxidizing agent. Later, the Sub-Committee recommended (1970) that as the I.T.T. method was satisfactory only for in-plant control it should not be recommended as a standard method. However, the study indicated that the method was valuable for application in individual breweries and should not be discarded entirely.

In many laboratories techniques based closely on the original method of Gray and Stone are used with refinements such as spectrophotometry. A typical method as used in Australia stresses that all operations should be carried out at 20 °C as I.T.T. values are affected by slight changes in temperature. In this method, the dyestuff is made up in dioxane and standardized daily. Twenty ml of attemperated beer is added to 0·5 ml of standardized dye solution and immediately mixed; an aliquot is then transferred to a glass spectrophotometer cell and the time taken to reach various optical densities at 525 nm against beer in the reference cell is recorded. A curve giving optical density against time is prepared for the sample and a standard blank line also derived. In practice, most beers are found to have similar blank lines and as the dye at 80% decoloration has an optical density of 0·220 the standard increase due to the blank (0·015) can be added. Thus, the I.T.T. value is obtained by noting the time taken for an optical density of 0·235 to be reached.

Another method, designed to estimate the oxidizable substances in beer, was proposed by Owades and Zientara (1960). This procedure employs diphenylpicrylhydrazyl (DPH) which reacts with many of the oxidizable substances normally present in beer but not with sugars, purines, amino acids or pyrimidines.

A later method for the estimation of the degree of oxidation is that of Grigsley and Palamand (1975) in which 2-thiobarbituric acid (TBA) is used. This reagent, widely used in measuring oxidative changes in milk and meat products and other foods, reacts with some of the compounds produced in beer by staling. Correlation of TBA values with the extent of staling is reported to be significant.

Chapon *et al.* (1971) describe a technique in which an iron–dipyridyl complex is used to estimate the reducing power of beer. A general relationship exists between values obtained by this method and I.T.T. value.

N. Trace Elements

1. Introduction

The importance of trace elements, particularly small amounts of the "heavy" metals, has been recognized for many years. Methods for some details, e.g. lead and arsenic, have likewise been well documented and procedures for the determination of other metals such as iron, copper and zinc have been reviewed on many occasions. However, most earlier techniques for the determination of small quantities of trace metals could be described as tedious and time-consuming, involving, as they do, wet or dry ashing and extraction procedures.

Legal requirements exist in most countries regarding the maximum levels of some metals permitted in foods and beverages. In many regulations, limits for known toxic metals, including arsenic, lead and antimony, are specified. In other countries, additional metals are listed; for example, in a recommended revision of an Australian Standard for Trace Metals, set by the National Health and Medical Research Council of that country (1974), the limits are as in Table 2.

The need for quicker methods has promoted the introduction of the so-called direct colorimetric methods for metals such as iron, copper, zinc and others. Some of these have been designated as international methods, e.g. those for iron and copper as given by A.S.B.C. (1975) and have found wide application for light coloured beers.

A revolution in the determination of trace metals in foods and beverages followed the introduction in the 1950s of atomic absorption spectroscopy (AAS) and this extremely useful technique has been the subject of several exhaustive studies by industry groups, e.g. Trachman *et al.* (1970), I of B (1973), A.S.B.C. (1972), (1973) and (1974).

The accuracy of AAS is improved significantly with the application of thermal atomization using a carbon rod atomizer; with this technique

Table 2. Limits for trace metals in beverages (as proposed by the Food Standards Committee of the Australian National Health and Medical Research Council—NH and MRC—March 1975)

Metal	Upper limit (mg/l as element)
Antimony	0·10
Arsenic	0·01
Barium†	0·20
Cadmium†	0·05
Copper	1·0
Mercury	0·03
Selenium	2·0
Strontium†	0·75
Tin	0·50
Zinc	1·0

N.B. The limit for all metals not listed, other than aluminium, calcium, iron, lithium, magnesium, manganese, potassium and sodium, is 0·15 mg/l.

† As proposed by The Australian Associated Brewers, at the request of NH and MRC as suitable upper limits for beer.

detection of quantities as low as 1 ng/litre is possible. Other refinements, such as vapour generation equipment, enable elements such as arsenic and mercury to be determined at low levels in beer.

Many elements can be determined by direct aspiration, into the AAS flame, of the de-carbonated beer. Calcium, cobalt, copper, iron, magnesium, manganese, nickel, potassium, sodium, tin and zinc are included in this group, but with some a concentration step is required for low levels.

Table 3 gives operating details as specified by Varian Techtron (1972) for the elements dealt with in this section; similar data are given by other manufacturers of instruments and in texts on AAS.

Specific methods, colorimetric and AAS, follow. For general background information relative to the determination of trace elements in beer the analyst is referred to texts such as that of Rowe (1973) or one of several symposia published in recent years.

Refinements of techniques of AAS are described frequently in the general literature of analytical chemistry. With these, and with attention being paid to new techniques such as anodic stripping polarography and inductively coupled argon plasma excitation (ICAP), it is possible that trace element analysis will undergo further dramatic changes in the near future.

Table 3. Standard operating conditions—atomic absorption spectroscopy

Element	Fuel	Support	Flame	Wavelength (nm)	Detection limit† (mg/l)	Remarks
Aluminium	Acetylene	Nitrous oxide	Reducing	309·5	0·04	
Antimony	Acetylene	Air	Oxidizing	217·6	0·07	
Arsenic	Hydrogen	Nitrogen	—	193·7	0·01	Vapour generation technique
Barium	Acetylene	Nitrous oxide	Reducing	553·6	0·01	
Cadmium	Acetylene	Air	Oxidizing	228·8	0·0006	
Calcium	Acetylene	Nitrous oxide	Reducing	422·7	0·0005	Release agent desirable
Chromium	Acetylene	Air	Reducing	357·9	0·005	
Cobalt	Acetylene	Air	Oxidizing	240·7	0·007	
Copper	Acetylene	Air	Oxidizing	324·7	0·003	
Iron	Acetylene	Air	Oxidizing	248·3	0·005	
Lead	Acetylene	Air	Oxidizing	217·0	0·02	
Magnesium	Acetylene	Air	Oxidizing	285·2	0·0003	Release agent desirable
Manganese	Acetylene	Air	Oxidizing	279·5	0·0003	
Mercury	Acetylene	Air	—	253·7	0·04	Cold vapour technique
Nickel	Acetylene	Air	Oxidizing	232·0	0·008	
Potassium (1)	Propane	Air	Oxidizing	766·5	0·003	Ionization supressant desirable
(2)	Acetylene	Air	Oxidizing	769·9		
Selenium	Hydrogen	Air	Highly reducing	196·0	1·0	Vapour generation technique
Sodium (1)	Acetylene	Air	Oxidizing	330·2		Ionization depressant desirable
(2)	Propane	Air	Oxidizing	589·0	0·0003	
Strontium	Acetylene	Nitrous oxide	Strongly oxidizing	460·7	0·004	Ionization depressant desirable
Tin	Acetylene	Nitrous oxide	Oxidizing	224·6	0·07	
Zinc	Acetylene	Air	Oxidizing	213·9	0·002	

The data in the above table are reproduced by permission of Varian Techtron Pty. Ltd.
† Defined as that concentration in solution of an element which can be detected with 95% certainty.

2. Aluminium

A direct colorimetric method, first proposed by Stone *et al.* (1963), in which catechol violet is used as the reagent, gives reliable results up to 2 mg Al/litre. The presence of iron above 0·25 mg Fe/litre may, however, give rise to erroneous results.

AAS may be used with beer addition standards and a complexing stage employing 8-hydroxyquinoline and methylisobutylketone (MIBK) as described by Trachman *et al.* (1970). Direct aspiration of beer into the nitrous oxide/acetylene flame is possible for concentrations over 1 mg Al/litre.

3. Antimony

Although considered a toxic "heavy" metal, antimony is rarely encountered in foods and beverages. Legal limits, however, exist in many countries for antimony in beverages which may be determined by AAS as described by Rowe (1973). Extraction with hydrochloric acid and MIBK or ammonium pyrrolidine dithiocarbamate (APDC) is used and the extract aspirated directly into an oxidizing air/acetylene flame and read at 217·6 nm.

4. Arsenic

Modifications of the classical Gutzeit method, such as that of Case (1938), have been used for many years for the determination of arsenic in beer, wort and brewing materials. To obviate the need to prepare standard stains on all occasions, permanent water colour copies can be made of stains produced by a suitable range of standard arsenic solutions made from arsenic trioxide in 5% w/w sucrose.

Arsenic can be determined by AAS with the spectrophotometer fitted with vapour generation equipment. In this, the arsenic is evolved as arsine which is atomized in a nitrogen/hydrogen flame; a detection limit of 0·002 mg As/l in a 20 ml sample is reported by Rowe (1973). Standards are prepared by adding arsenic to a matrix similar to beer, e.g. sucrose, and not by the method of standard addition.

A colorimetric method using silver diethyldithiocarbamate, described by the British Standards Institution (1968), has been suggested for beer but a collaborative survey conducted by Institute of Brewing Analysis Committee (1971) suggests that this method is less reliable than the Gutzeit technique. As a result of the survey, the Analysis Committee recommends that the British Pharmacopoeia (1968) modification of the Gutzeit procedure be used; the details are given by I of B (1971) in which precision of approximately ±0·02 mg As/litre is quoted. The Analytical Methods Committee of The

Chemical Society (1975) recommends a molybdenum-blue procedure in preference to one using silver diethyldithiocarbamate.

Pierce and Brown (1976) give details of an automated AAS technique for arsenic in which reduction to the hydride is accomplished with sodium borohydride and combustion occurs in a tube furnace situated in the light path of the spectrophotometer. Data relevant to interfering anions and cations are shown.

5. Barium

A request for information regarding the barium contents of Australian beers led to the investigation of techniques suitable for the determination of this element in beer by AAS. A carbon rod atomizer gives satisfactory results with beers ranging from 0·01 to 0·2 mg Ba/litre and a limit of 0·2 has been suggested for statutory purposes. It was found that calcium in beer causes severe interference with the determination of barium by means of flame emission and consequently flameless AAS (carbon rod atomization) was chosen. A precision of ±0·03 mg Ba/litre is quoted by Hildebrand (1975) for this technique.

6. Cadmium

A method for cadmium in foods, employing ion-exchange concentration, is described by Baetz and Kenner (1975). For AAS extraction with APDC and MIBK is usually advisable for the low levels found in beer; direct aspiration, however, can be used for a limit test at 228·8 nm with carefully adjusted air–acetylene oxidizing flame. Experience in Australia has been that beers contain significantly less than the permitted limit of 0·05 mg/litre.

7. Calcium

Numerous methods have been proposed for the determination of calcium in beer. They include two EDTA titrimetric procedures as given by ASBC (1975); one of these, using Chrome Black T (also known as Eriochrome Black T or Pontochrome Black T), also determines magnesium. The other method in which calcien is used as an indicator, is a direct procedure for calcium only.

In many laboratories, titrimetric methods have been replaced by flame photometry or AAS. The level of calcium in beer requires 1 : 10 dilution of the sample for AAS and a nitrous oxide/acetylene flame is used. A.S.B.C. (1975) gives a method for calcium in which lanthanum chloride is used as a release agent and the standard addition technique is employed; a strontium salt can also be employed as a release agent.

A detailed study of the determination of calcium in beer by AAS undertaken by Trachman (1970) substantiates the need for precautions if results comparable with those obtained by flame photometry or EDTA titration are to be attained. Postel *et al.* (1974) state that AAS with nitrous oxide/acetylene flame gives a standard deviation of ± 0.3 mg Ca/litre.

Calcium in beer can also be measured by means of an ion selective electrode, as described by Buckee (1975). A known addition technique is employed.

8. Chromium

Chromium in beer may be determined by AAS after separation and preconcentration with hydrochloric acid and MIBK. The carbon rod atomizer is preferred for its improved sensitivity and a reducing air/acetylene or nitrous oxide/acetylene flame is used at 357·9 nm.

A number of foods, including beer, have been stated to be significant sources of traces of chromium of dietary importance and the determination of this element by AAS has received attention in recent years. The atomic absorption spectroscopy of chromium is reviewed by Feldman and Purdy (1965).

Colorimetric procedures, such as that of Sultzman (1952), are well known but most have disadvantages when used for low concentrations of the metal. A technique using diphenylcarbazone is available for the detection and determination of traces of chromium in beer, arising from contamination by refrigerant brine containing a dichromate as an inhibitor.

9. Cobalt

Harold and Szobolotzky (1963) reviewed a number of methods for cobalt in beer and concluded that one using 3-methoxy-2-nitrosophenol gave the best results of several colorimetric procedures. An accuracy of ± 0.002 mg Co/litre is claimed for the method. Direct aspiration of beer for AAS is satisfactory for cobalt using an air/acetylene oxidizing flame at 240·7 nm, although extraction of the APDC complex into MIBK at pH 2–4 may be advisable for low concentrations. A detection limit of 0·007 mg/litre is quoted for flame AAS.

10. Copper

Copper in dark beers and stouts may be determined by wet oxidation with nitric, sulphuric and perchloric acids, followed by extraction into amyl alcohol and colour development with sodium diethyldithiocarbamate, as described by Andrews and Stringer (1953) and Webber *et al.* (1955).

For pale beers, a direct procedure, such as that given by A.S.B.C. (1975) is recommended. The precision of direct methods has been improved significantly throughout the years since their introduction and the A.S.B.C. procedure employing zinc dibenzyldithiocarbamate (ZDBT) gives very satisfactory results as does the alternative A.S.B.C. method using cuprethol.

Laboratories equipped for AAS have the choice of several basically similar procedures, such as given by A.S.B.C. (1975). A wavelength of 324·8 nm is employed with an oxidizing air/acetylene flame.

A standard copper solution, containing 1000 mg/litre is prepared from copper metal or copper sulphate. A working solution of 50 mg/litre is made daily and from this, quantities of the beer under examination with 0, 0·1, 0·2, 0·4 and 0·6 mg/litre of added copper are also prepared.

A standard addition curve is produced from the readings obtained by the direct aspiration of the standards into the spectrophotometer. The curve has concentration on the x-axis and absorbance on the y-axis; the amount of copper in the sample is given by the negative intercept on the x-axis (see Fig. 2).

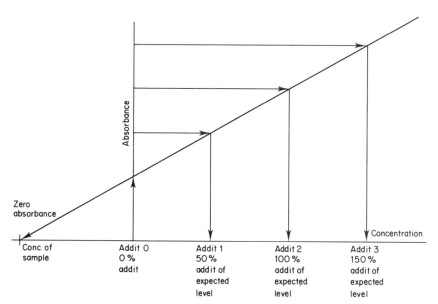

Fig. 2. Atomic absorption spectroscopy: example of standard additive curve.

Determinations should be made in duplicate and all precautions considered normal for the analysis of trace metals should be taken. Postel *et al.* (1972b) gives a detection limit of 0·02 mg/litre and a standard deviation of 4·7%; a limit 0·0005 mg/litre is quoted for the carbon rod technique.

The importance of using de-carbonated beer for preparation of standards is shown by Trachman *et al.* (1970) who also indicate that combined copper and iron standards can be used for these two most frequently determined elements.

11. Iron

Iron may be determined directly by an international method as defined in A.S.B.C. (1975) and E.B.C. (1975) which employs either 2,2'-dipyridyl or *o*-phenanthroline as the colorimetric reagent. A method employing the former reagent, described by I of B (1971), is stated to be suitable for concentrations of iron in beer from 0 to 5 mg/litre. The standard deviation of the international method is given by E.B.C. (1975) as approximately 0·2 mg/litre but experience in the author's laboratory indicates that this value can be reduced with careful attention.

The heating or boiling step, described in the international and I of B methods, may be eliminated but 30 minutes must be allowed for the colour to develop at room temperature. Results in this case may be slightly lower.

Iron in dark beers and stouts can be determined by means of wet ashing, followed by solvent extraction and development of colour with potassium thiocyanate.

A new colorimetric procedure for iron is described by Ulloa et al. (1975) who employ ferrozine, the disodium salt of 3-(2-pyridyl)-5,6-bis(4-phenylsulphonic acid)-1,2,4-triazine, as a reagent giving a sensitivity three times higher than that given by o-phenanthroline or dipyridyl.

AAS techniques for iron, similar to that described by A.S.B.C. (1975), are in use in many laboratories. The procedure is simple and uses direct aspiration of a diluted sample with a wavelength of 248·3 nm for the concentration normally encountered in beer. Postel et al. (1972a) state that the lowest estimable amount of iron is 0·03 mg/litre and the standard deviation of the method employed by them is 1%.

Dilution of the sample 1 : 1 is recommended by Varian Techtron (1972), who describe a single standard addition technique.

12. Lead

Methods for the estimation of lead have, with those for arsenic, copper and iron, long attracted attention. The Institute of Brewing Analysis Committee recommended a standard procedure (1953) in which suspensions of lead sulphide were compared; other convenient methods are described by Bennet and Hudson (1953), Bishop and Kloss (1953) and St. Johnston and Taylor (1953). All these methods employ diphenyldithiocarbazone as the colorimetric reagent. No standard method, however, appears in the current methods of I of B, E.B.C. or A.S.B.C.

AAS is suitable for the reliable determination of the small amounts of lead normally found in beer only after treatment of the sample with a colorimetric reagent and extraction into an organic solvent.

APDC and MIBK are used and standards treated in the same manner; n-butyl acetate has also been used as the organic solvent and an alternative extraction procedure is described by Baetz and Kenner (1975).

Direct aspiration of beverages (but not beer) for the determination of lead is described by Gegiou and Botsivali (1975) who claim that levels down to 0·1 mg/litre can be determined. The standard deviation of the method in the range 0·5–2·0 mg/litre is given as ±0·04 and minimal interference from other metals is reported. The technique has the advantages of rapidity and in most cases the limits set for lead by regulation are within the range of detection.

13. Lithium

This element has been determined in Australian beers by means of flame emission at 670·8 nm and levels below 0·01 mg Li/litre were reported. Some interest in the lithium content of beer has been expressed in relation to the role of beer in a low-sodium diet.

14. Magnesium

Titrimetric methods involving the use of EDTA with Chrome Black T as indicator are available for the determination of magnesium together with calcium, as described by A.S.B.C. (1975).

AAS is also used with an air/acetylene flame and dilution of the sample to give workable concentrations of magnesium. Direct aspiration of the diluted, decarbonated beer and a standard addition procedure are employed. Flame emission has also been used for magnesium.

15. Manganese

AAS is used for manganese, employing direct aspiration. Postel et al. (1973) gives the limit of detection as 0·02 mg Mn/litre and a standard deviation of ±0·01 mg/litre. A modified extraction procedure with APDC and MIBK is described by Rowe (1973) who prefers the use of an air/acetylene flame.

16. Mercury

This metal has been given little attention as a contaminant in beer. Ancillary equipment for AAS spectrophotometers, which will permit the determination of mercury by the cold vapour technique, is suitable for use with a wide range of samples. A concentration step is normally necessary for all methods of determination by AAS, although the cold vapour method can detect as little as 2 ng. A method for the estimation of mercury in water, given by Varian Techtron (1972), has been used for beer.

17. Nickel

A standard colorimetric procedure for nickel, given by E.B.C. (1971), employs the classical reagent dimethylglyoxime; a standard deviation of ±0·11 mg Ni/litre is reported. Descriptions of other colorimetric methods are given by Andrews and Harrison (1954) and Kenigsberg and Stone (1955). These employ α-furildoxime and dimethylglyoxime respectively as the colorimetric reagents.

Nickel can be determined by AAS with direct aspiration but, in general, at the concentrations normally encountered in beer an extraction step is preferred. An oxidizing air/acetylene flame is used at a wavelength of 352·4 nm and a detection limit of 0·008 mg/litre is quoted.

18. Potassium

One of the metals most abundant in beer, potassium is best determined by AAS but flame photometry (flame emission) can also be used. Canales *et al.* (1970) describe a turbidimetric method employing the reagent tetraphenyl-borosodium which precipitates the potassium in a fine state in highly alkaline conditions. The turbidity produced is measured at 589 nm and the method gives results which correlate well with those obtained by flame emission and AAS.

For AAS a 1 : 100 or 1 : 500 dilution is used with a multiple standard addition and an air/acetylene flame and wavelength of 769·9 nm. Cesium nitrate or chloride is added to all solutions, including the blank, in order to suppress ionization in the air/acetylene flame. An air/propane flame is recommended by Varian Techtron (1972) for potassium alone but air/acetylene is preferred when the element is determined jointly with sodium using a dual lamp.

19. Selenium

Little information is available of the occurrence of this element in beer but it has been suggested that many common foods should be screened for selenium. However, as a commonly recommended upper limit is 2 mg Se/litre it is unlikely that beer would exceed the legal requirement. Selenium is another element which can be determined by the vapour generation method and AAS. The selenium in the sample is reduced to free selenium by means of stannous chloride and potassium iodide and further to hydrogen selenide by the action of nascent hydrogen. The procedure is similar to that for arsenic but more care must be exercised; details are given by Rowe (1973) and Varian Techtron (1972).

20. Silicon

There is no general agreement on the desirable limit for silicon (silica) in beer and few figures are available. Katayana and Horie (1971), using a colorimetric method dependent on the formation of molybdenum blue, found a range of 65–143 mg/litre in Japanese domestic and other beers.

AAS could be utilized for the determination of silicon in beer at the concentrations found. A combined method for silica and phosphate in water, given by Parker (1972), involves the sequential separation of the two elements as the heteropoly acids with ammonium molybdate followed by the determination of molybdenum by AAS. An acetylene/nitrous oxide flame is used at a wavelength of 251·6 nm and a detection limit of 0·3 mg/litre is quoted.

21. Sodium

The determination of sodium in beer has assumed greater importance in recent years with the recognition of the significance of low-sodium diets in the treatment of certain medical conditions. Several classical precipitation or colorimetric procedures have been superseded by flame emission and latterly AAS techniques.

Flame emission is carried out at a wavelength of 589·0 nm and AAS at 589·5 or 330·2 nm with an air/acetylene flame which gives a better signal than an air/propane flame. Dilution of the sample 1 : 100 or more or less, depending on the level of sodium, is necessary and a multiple standard addition technique is used. Sodium and potassium are frequently determined together by AAS and lamps combining the two elements are available. For dual determination, standard solutions containing both elements are used for addition. As with potassium, a cesium salt is added as an ion depressant.

22. Strontium

Interest in the level of strontium in beer is connected with the possibility of increased Sr levels due to fall-out of Sr^{90}. The element can be determined in beer by AAS using direct aspiration. A strongly oxidizing acetylene/nitrous oxide flame is used at 460·7 nm and a detection limit of 0·004 mg/litre is quoted. Strontium can also be conveniently determined by flame emission and a lower detection limit (0·001) is quoted. Potassium nitrate or chloride is used as an ion suppressant and the method of standard addition employed. A precision of ± 0.02 mg/l is noted from Australian experience. Work carried out in 1975 for the National Health and Medical Research Council in Australia by the brewing industry indicates that strontium in Australian beers ranges from 0·02 to 0·50 mg Sr/litre; an upper limit for legal purposes of 0·75 mg/litre has been proposed.

23. Tin

Colorimetric methods for the determination of tin in beer have been known for many years and some, e.g. those employing the reagent dithiol, give reliable results. The volatility of many tin compounds makes ashing and digestion procedures somewhat unreliable and other methods have been introduced. Neutron activation analysis, as described by Bowen (1972), gives reasonably reproducible results but is cumbersome and the equipment is expensive.

Hydrolysis of samples with hydrochloric acid, as noted by Szarski (1971), is preferred for treatment of samples for analysis by AAS. Flame conditions are important for determination of this metal but an acetylene/nitrous oxide flame minimizes interference. Standardization is simpler with the latter flame and a detection limit of 0·07 mg/litre is quoted. Because of the low levels of tin normally found in beer and the relatively high detection limit, preconcentration of the hydrochloric acid extract, using APDC into MIBK, is necessary.

Some details are given by Rowe (1973) and Varian Techtron (1972).

24. Zinc

The Institute of Brewing Analysis Committee (1974) recommends a method for zinc using AAS. Reliable results are obtained, particularly when the standard addition procedure is used. Sodium chloride, present in beer, absorbs strongly at the wavelength used (213·9 nm) and thus it is important to maintain the same concentration of NaCl in both standards and unknowns; this is achieved by the method of standard addition. Concentrations down to 0·01 mg/litre can be estimated satisfactorily.

Details of an AAS method are given also by Trachman *et al.* (1970) who state that treatment with APDC and MIBK may be necessary for low concentrations of zinc but that complete recovery is not always obtained.

Colorimetric procedures, including those of Andrews and Lloyd (1951) and Stone (1952), are found to give results that correlate well with those obtained by AAS.

25. Anions

Of the anions present in beer, chloride, nitrate, phosphate and sulphate appear to be those for which analysis is most frequently required. A variety of methods exist for these and a selection only is referred to in the following. Methods for other anions are mentioned briefly.

(a) *Chloride*

A simple titrimetric method, using standardized mecuric nitrate and diphenylcarbazone as an indicator, as described by Owades *et al.* (1961), is satisfactory for chlorides in beer. However, potentiometric titration, employing an ion-selective electrode as proposed by Preen and Woodward (1975), is a simpler procedure.

In the latter method, a silver billet electrode and a mercurous sulphate reference electrode are used with a suitable pH meter. Standard silver nitrate solution is added incrementally to a 25 ml sample of decarbonated beer. Meter readings, in mV, are plotted against the volume of silver nitrate added and the equivalence point is indicated by the inflexion in the curve so plotted.

Chloride can be determined by AAS after quantitative precipitation of silver chloride by the addition of a known amount of silver nitrate. Excess silver in the solution is then determined by AAS. The method, however, would not be preferred, under normal circumstances, to a titrimetric method.

(b) *Nitrate*

Weiner *et al.* (1975) investigated a number of procedures for the determination of nitrate and concluded that a modification of the AOAC method (1970) gave the best results. In this, nitrate is reduced on a cadmium column to nitrite which is then determined using colorimetry with *N*-1-naphthylethylenediamine dihydrochloride and sulphanilimide. Recovery of added nitrate is reported at 98% and levels of up to 30 mg NO_3/litre found in studies with English beers.

An earlier procedure, described by Stone *et al.* (1968), also depends on the reduction of nitrate to nitrite, in this case by zinc in ammoniacal solution. The nitrite is then determined colorimetrically with 1-naphthylamine hydrochloride and sulphanilic acid.

Weiner *et al.* (1975) also reported that nitrite may be readily determined semi-quantitatively, with a prepared nitrite test strip.

(c) *Phosphate*

Colorimetric methods for the estimation of phosphorus in brewing materials and beer have been studied for many years. More recent techniques include those of Hurst (1964) and Belleau *et al.* (1970) which have been used to determine total inorganic and organic phosphorus in raw materials, wort and beer. Sodium molybdate is used as a complexing agent and stannous chloride with hydrazine as a reducing agent. Full details of the method are given by Belleau *et al.* (1970) who found values ranging from 5 to 325 mg P/100 ml for total phosphorus quoted in the literature. A.S.B.C. (1975) gives an ammonium molybdate precipitation method.

AAS can be used for the indirect determination of phosphorus by the estimation of the molybdenum content of a molybdate complex. The determination is normally made in conjunction with that for silicon and the method is suitable for a sample range of 0·01–0·13 mg P (or 0·03–0·4 mg PO_4). The technique is described by Varian Techtron (1972) and Kirkbright *et al.* (1967).

Neutron activation analysis has also been used but obviously must be confined to the few laboratories equipped with this apparatus.

(d) *Sulphate*

For the measurement of sulphate in beer variations of the classical barium sulphate precipitation technique are frequently employed. The precipitate can be filtered, ignited or dried and weighed; or turbidimetry can be used to estimate the amount of bariun sulphate formed. A description of the latter technique is given by Shah (1975) who employs a conditioning agent consisting of glycerol, hydrochloric acid, alcohol and sodium chloride. The sample is suitably diluted and placed in a nephelometer cuvette with a portion of the conditioning agent and stirred at constant speed by means of a magnetic stirrer. Five ml of 20% barium chloride solution is added and stirring continued for a further $2\frac{1}{2}$ minutes at constant speed. The cuvette is then placed in a turbidimeter, standardized against E.B.C. Formazin standards, and the haze read. Standards prepared from sulphate solutions are used to prepare a calibration curve.

(e) Other anions

Fluoride can be estimated in beer with an ion-selective electrode and little interference is suffered within the range of F encountered in beers prepared from fluoridated water. Postel et al. (1976) give details of an electrode method for fluoride.

An ion-selective electrode is also available for bromide and has been used for this element in beer, as described by Buckee (1975). The presence of this anion in beer in a significant amount may indicate that a bromate has been used as a malting additive.

The determination of oxalate in beer has been the subject of numerous studies. Methods depending on the slow precipitation of the oxalate with calcium have been criticized and attempts made to procure more rapid procedures. One such is that of Bernstein and Khan (1973) in which the decrease in absorbance, related to oxalate concentration, of a red 4-(2-pyridilazo)-resorcinol complex is measured. Studies by an A.S.B.C. Sub-Committee (1976) show that, in general, the precipitation method of Burger and Becker (1949) gives more accurate results and that improvements to the rapid method are required.

O. Bitterness

1. Rapid Solvent Extraction Methods

The establishment, in the 1950s, of a significant correlation between the organoleptic impression of bitterness and the spectrophotometric measurement of an isooctane extract of beer gave brewers a ready means of quantitative evaluation of bitterness. Many methods have been proposed utilizing this extraction in which the bitter components, mainly isoacids, are extracted from acidified beer with isooctane (2,2,4-trimethylpentane) and determined by UV spectrophotometry.

Methods proposed by Rigby and Bethune (1955) and Brenner et al. (1956) form the basis of an international method adopted by E.B.C. (1975) A.S.B.C. (1975). I of B (1971) describes a very similar technique.

The international method employs centrifugation for cloudy beers and for all three techniques samples are decarbonated and attemperated to 20 °C before analysis. A sample size of 10 ml is used with 0·5 ml 6 N hydrochloric acid and 20 ml isooctane and extraction performed by shaking on a rotary or wrist-action shaker for a standard period. E.B.C. (1975) uses 15 minutes on a rotary shaker at 130 ± 5 r.p.m. whilst A.S.B.C. (1975) specifies 15 minutes on a wrist-action or platform shaker. However, I of B (1971) gives only 2 minutes shaking (wrist action), a period found to be sufficient for similar shaking in the author's laboratory. The absorbance of the extract, freed from any emulsion by centrifugation or settling, is read at 275 nm in a 1 cm cell, using isooctane as a reference.

Bitterness units (BU or EBU) are calculated thus BU = absorbance at 275 × 50 and reported to the nearest integer.

A modified calculation (absorbance × 70) has been established for beers hopped by means of isomerized extracts.

The method lends itself to automation and several such procedures have been published. Cooper and Hudson (1961), Jamieson and Mackinnon (1965) and Pinnegar (1966) all discuss fully automated procedures for which some difficulties are enumerated. Fisher (1972) outlines a semi-automated procedure which does not suffer from the difficulties inherent with the pumping of an organic solvent (isooctane) through the peristaltic manifold tubing. In the latter technique, the standard I of B method is scaled down, reagents added automatically but shaking is manual. Transfer of the solvent extract, its measurement and recording, however, are automatic.

Hudson (1976) compares typical manual, semi-automatic and fully automatic procedures and quotes the respective throughputs as 10, 50 and 100 per hour. In the author's laboratory a fully automated method has been used successfully for several years employing a Technicon "Auto-Analyzer" and Beckman DB-G recording spectrophotometer.

The method gives excellent correlation with a standard manual method and in addition, internal standards (a range of beers with known bitterness values) are used throughout each run. Throughput is approximately 30 samples per hour and the disadvantages enumerated by Hudson in general have not become evident.

E.B.C. (1975) states the standard deviation of the international method to be ± 2·4 for values around 30 BU. However, Fisher (1972) gives ± 0·37 at 19 BU for the I of B method and also for his semi-automated procedure.

Standard deviations of this order are obtained in the range 20–30 BU by automated and manual procedures in the author's laboratory.

A.S.B.C. (1975) also gives, apart from the international method already discussed, a method for iso-α-acids (IAA) which can return lower values for some beers, particularly those brewed with old hops or isomerized hop extracts. The IAA method involves a second extraction, that of the isooctane extract with alkaline methanol and differs from the international method in that absorbance is read at 255 nm against an isooctane/alkaline methanol reference. The calculation is IAA = (absorbance at $255 \times 96 \cdot 15$) + 0·4 and the value is expressed to the nearest 0·5 mg/litre.

All procedures using absorbance in the region 255–275 nm give erroneous results with beers containing some preservatives and additives, e.g. benzoates, sorbates, n-heptyl-p-hydroxybenzoate, saccharin. The effect of the presence of such materials should be checked.

2. Other Methods

In spite of the extensive work carried out with solvent extraction methods, investigation of other methods has continued in recent years. Mussche (1974) lists some of these and describes in detail a thin-layer chromatographic (TLC) procedure which permits the estimation of iso-α-acids, allo- and hydrated iso-α-acids, hulupones and some of the bitter degradation products of iso-α-acids. The procedure is relatively lengthy, occupying $2\frac{1}{2}$ hours, but a total analysis is obtained and much useful information can be derived from the amounts of iso-α-acids and their degradation products and other components found.

Counter-current distribution, used by Rigby and Bethune (1955) and Wood et al. (1968), estimates the iso-α-acids but, as reported by Mussche (1974), gives high values when compared with those obtained by TLC.

Ion-exchange chromatography, as used by Kowaka et al. (1971), gave some 90 distinct peaks for the substances derived from α-acids and β-acids. Gas chromatography is said to give qualitative data only; liquid chromatography techniques, discussed by Hansen and Ramos (1971) and Otter et al. (1972) are capable of producing selective data on iso-α-acids.

P. Polyphenols, Anthocyanogens, Catechins and Gallotannins

1. Polyphenols

Many workers in the past 20 years have illustrated the importance of the polyphenols and other non-volatile components of beer in relation to its general quality. Dadic and Van Gheluwe (1973) review some of the earlier work and give experimental data confirming the important role played by polyphenols in the flavour, colour and general stability of beer. Gramshaw (1969) divides the simple polyphenols of beer into four main classes; (a) polyhydroxyflavans, (b) flavanols and their glycosides, (c) phenolic and hydroxycinnamic acids, and (d) esters and glycosides of class (c).

Other workers have remarked upon the complexity of the situation of the polyphenolic components of beer. Ng and Mocek (1973) point out that most of the published methods suffer from the very significant disadvantage that a representivative sample of beer polyphenols is difficult to obtain for the purpose of calibration. They describe a procedure in which the polyphenols are extracted under acid and alkaline conditions and the extracted fractions used as standards for calibration of a colorimetric method employing 4-aminoantipyrine as the reagent. The extraction procedure gives values higher than those reported in the literature generally as most other methods neglect the alkaline fraction.

A number of other methods have been evolved for the determination of the total polyphenols of beer. E.B.C. (1975) gives a method in which the polyphenols are reacted with ferric iron in alkaline solution and the resultant red colour measured. This technique, based on a method of de Clerck and Jerumanis (1967), is discussed by Bishop (1972). (In the latter paper it should be noted that the calculation should be $OD \times 820$, not $OD \times 850$ as printed.) Bishop notes that the within-laboratories error is about ± 1.5 and the between-laboratories error is ± 5; E.B.C. gives the standard deviation of individual estimations as ± 9.3.

Sogawa (1971), after reviewing the available methods, used a technique of Owades et al. (1958) in which polyphenols are extracted with ethyl acetate after the removal of isohumulones with isooctane. The solid material, after evaporation of the solvent, is dissolved in acidified methanol and absorbance read at 283 nm; the absorption peak is at 270 nm but ethyl acetate absorbs strongly at this wavelength. Sogawa (1972) also used this procedure as preliminary treatment of beer prior to the identification, by thin-layer chromatography, of phenolic monomers. Belleau and Dadic (1974) describe a technique employing high vacuum separation to separate and purify phenolic monomers and their oxidation products. Charalambous et al. (1973) give details of the use of high-pressure liquid chromatography (HPLC) for the detection of monomeric phenols in beer and the technique has been used for the separation of phenolic components.

2. Anthocyanogens and Catechins

The confusion accompanying the classification and nomenclature of the anthocyanogens and catechins (tanninogens) is discussed by Dadic (1976) who recommends that the terms anthocyanogens and catechins refer to flavan-3, 4-diols and flavan-3-ols respectively. He also describes a procedure for the simultaneous determination of anthocyanogens and catechins by spectrophotometry and uses the terms anthocyanogen value (AV) and catechin value (CV). The sum of these values is the tanninogen value $(TV = AV + CV)$.

Dadic's procedure involves the treatment of 60 ml degassed beer, diluted 1 : 1 with water, with 6 g Nylon-66 resin. The resin is air-dried, washed with water and then refluxed with 5 : 1 propanol/hydrochloric acid. The cooled extract is read at 445 nm and 545 nm against a propanol/hydrochloric acid blank. The AV and CV are calculated thus:

$$CV = 1{\cdot}6 \ (491{\cdot}6A_{455} - 91{\cdot}8A_{545})$$

$$AV = 8{\cdot}8 \ (21{\cdot}0A_{545} - 5{\cdot}9A_{455})$$

It is suggested that no method using only one wavelength, e.g. 550 nm, will give accurate AV's or CV's or an estimate of the distribution of the two components. Notwithstanding this, considerable use has been made of earlier methods such as those given by Harris and Ricketts (1959) and McFarlane (1961) and modifications thereof. In the former procedure, the anthocyanogens are adsorbed by Nylon-66 and eluted therefrom by heating at 100 °C with n-butanol/hydrochloric acid mixture (5 : 1) for 30 min; after cooling, the clear red-purple solution is diluted with the butanol/acid reagent and the adsorbance read, against a blank of treated fresh resin, at 550 nm. A standard curve is prepared by treating leucoanthocyanidin with Nylon-66 in the same manner.

McFarlane pointed out the errors that could be caused by the presence of small amounts of iron or copper in the beers or reagents in the Harris and Ricketts method. He proposed a modification of their method to include the addition of iron to the butanol/acid reagent. As a further modification he also describes a procedure in which polyvinylpyrrolidone (PVP or Agent AT 496) is employed in place of Nylon-66. In this method, degassed beer is shaken with Agent AT for 30 min and the AT residue is centrifuged and washed with water. The residue is then taken up with N-methyl-2-pyrrolidone (freshly distilled) and heated at 100 °C for 30 min. After filtration or centrifugation, the absorbance of the clear red solution is measured at 550 nm. The method gives similar results to the Nylon method and is claimed to be simpler and more convenient.

Other modifications of the Nylon method include reading the absorbance at 525 nm (as used in the author's laboratory) and the use of cyanidin chloride as a standard. Colorimetric methods specifically for catechins, as proposed by Dadic (1971) and McFarlane et al. (1963), are stated by McGuinness et al. (1975) to give widely divergent results. As a consequence, they describe a GLC method for estimating polyphenols, with particular reference to monomeric and dimeric catechins. Their technique utilizes the trimethylsilyl derivatives of the catechins, the separation of which from interfering substances is achieved by treatment with Nylon.

3. Gallotannins

It is only in the past few years that interest has been shown in the gallotannin content of beer, in particular the measurement of the gallotannin that might be present from the addition of tannic acid during processing. Kitabatake and Amaha (1968) demonstrated the presence of free gallic acid in beer and concluded that it was due to the addition of tannic acid. Their work showed that samples of commercial tannic acid contained from 4 to 7% free gallic acid. A Sub-Committee of A.S.B.C. reported (1971) that an iron colorimetric method under consideration gave unreliable results as iron colour develops, to varying amounts, with all polyphenols.

Trachman and Saletan (1971) describe a GLC method for the determination of gallotannins in beer. By definition, they consider gallotannins to be molecules composed of a number of galloyl residues combined with glucose; the various ratios of galloyl residues to glucose as proposed by several workers are discussed in the paper, and a factor for calculating gallotannin from gallic acid is given. The method involves hydrolysis of the beer with acid, a step which converts the gallotannins to gallic acid, followed by extraction of the hydrolysate with ethyl acetate. The dried extract is silylated with N,O-bis(trimethylsilyl)acetamide (BSA) and the silyl derivative is chromatographed on a column packed with Chromasorb W.DMCS coated with Silicone Rubber UC W 98%. n-Octyl gallate and 2,7-naphthalendiol are used as internal standards. The method has also been the subject of collaborative study by the A.S.B.C. Sub-Committee (1973) who recommended that the procedure be adopted tentatively.

An earlier GLC procedure for the determination of a group of phenolic acids extracted from beer with ether is described by Dallos et al. (1967). They used vanillic, p-coumaric, ferulic and sinapic acids as internal standards and reported that BSA gave products which were more convenient to use than those of some other silylation procedures.

Q. Carbohydrates

1. Introduction

Providing, as they do, the substrate for fermentation, a knowledge of the quantities and types of carbohydrate present in wort and beer is important. A.S.B.C. (1975) gives two methods for total reducing sugars and determinations of total carbohydrates after inversion of "free" carbohydrate are made in many laboratories.

Methods for the determination of fermentable sugars are also useful and many of varying complexity are available. Procedures for both total carbohydrate and fermentable sugars have been automated.

2. Total Carbohydrate

Total (hydrolysable) carbohydrate can be determined by several means following hydrolysis of the sample by boiling with hydrochloric acid or by simple heating in the case of automated procedures. In a classical manual technique, hydrolysis is carried out by refluxing 50 ml beer with 15 ml 70% v/v hydrochloric acid and 155 ml water in a boiling water bath for 2 hours. After cooling, the excess acidity is neutralized with potassium hydroxide and the hydrolysed beer is filtered and made up to 250 ml with water. This solution is then titrated against standard Fehling's solution and the total carbohydrate expressed as glucose, using the technique and factors expressed in the original Lane-Eynon volumetric method summarized by A.O.A.C. (1975).

Alternatively, the sugars may be determined by means of the Munson and Walker method for reducing sugars as given by A.S.B.C. (1975).

The Fehling and Munson and Walker techniques are time-consuming and cumbersome and considerable attention has been given to the determination of total carbohydrates by colorimetric, and latterly, by automated colorimetric and potentiometric methods.

Hall (1956) proposed a manual colorimetric method employing anthrone and an automatic procedure is given by Pinnegar and Whitear (1965). Buckee (1972) describes an automatic method employing a Technicon "Auto-Analyzer" in which hydrolysis with hydrochloric acid is followed by determination of the reducing sugars so formed by means of a redox electrode system. The need to pump solutions of anthrone in concentrated sulphuric acid and its requirement for special tubing is obviated. Reproducibility is good as is agreement with the manual anthrone colorimetric method.

3. Fermentable Sugars

The fermentable sugars remaining in beer consist principally of glucose, fructose, maltose and possibly maltotriose; and estimation of the total reducing sugars by one of the methods noted in section 2 above can be used as a guide to the amounts present. A.S.B.C. (1975) expresses the value as anhydrous maltose in per cent by weight; the expression "apparent maltose" is sometimes used but more commonly in connection with wort analysis.

Cooper et al. (1961) described an early "Auto-Analyzer" technique for fermentable sugars in worts and beers and predicted that such a procedure could be of use in control of continuous and batch brewing processes.

Buckee (1973) gives a rapid method in which the fermentable sugars are separated on a charcoal–kieselguhr column and eluted with 15% ethanol. The procedure is combined with the automated oxidation reduction procedure described in his earlier paper (1972).

Chromatography on polyacrylamide gel, used by Dellweg et al. (1970), has also been combined with an automatic procedure using orcinol in sulphuric acid as the colorimetric agent. The same reagent is used by Havlicek and Samuelson (1975) who separate the monosaccharides in beer by partition chromatography on anion exchange resins. A number of other chromatographic methods have been used for the study of carbohydrates in beer; included are paper adsorption chromatography, gel permeation chromatography and gas–liquid chromatography (GLC).

A technique employing GLC of the trimethylsilyl derivatives of carbohydrates in beer is described by Marinelli and Whitney (1967) and this has been found to give reliable and reproducible results. The preparation of the derivatives is based on an earlier technique of Brobst and Lolt (1965) and is suitable for the study of a number of other compounds of interest in beer and brewing materials. A similar GLC procedure is given by Otter and Taylor (1967).

Small amounts of other sugars, e.g. maltotetrose, maltopentose, maltohexose and higher oligosaccharides, may be found in beer and traces of ribose, arabinose, xylose and galactose have been reported, as stated by Hough *et al.* (1971). Column chromatography is required for the resolution of the higher sugars; a suitable technique is described by Gjertsen (1955).

R. Nitrogen Compounds: Total Nitrogen and Nitrogen Fractions; α-Amino Nitrogen

1. Introduction

Determinations of total nitrogen or of the various nitrogen components are some of those most frequently made on beer and yield valuable information. For many purposes, a knowledge of the total nitrogen (total protein) is sufficient and this value is included in most regular routine schedules of analysis.

However, details of some of the components comprising the total nitrogen content are often of value and considerable effort has been expended in deriving analytical methods for them. Included in this category are α-amino nitrogen (free α-amino nitrogen), a knowledge of which is desirable when considering fermentation characteristics, and some form of classification of nitrogen compounds into ranges of molecular weight. Quantitative data relative to the latter aspect are useful when physical stability and head characteristics are considered.

2. Total Nitrogen

A.S.B.C. (1975) gives a standard classical Kjeldahl technique and mentions that many modifications are known. It seems redundant to repeat details of this method which was devised originally in a brewing laboratory and has been well known for so long.

Careful standardization of solutions is obviously necessary and it is important that the recovery of nitrogen from known material is checked at regular intervals. In the author's laboratory, acetanilide of high purity is used for this purpose and a catalyst mixture of potassium sulphate, copper sulphate and titanium dioxide is employed in the ratio 100 : 3 : 3.

Many attempts have been made to automate the Kjeldahl technique for total nitrogen and some are reviewed by Buckee and Hickman (1975) and Buckee (1974). The latter author employs an ammonia probe (ion-selective electrode) to measure the ammonia produced. This method produces faster results with an automated or semi-automated procedure than colorimetric measurement employing sodium phenate and sodium hypochlorite as described by Mitcheson and Stowell (1970) and Moll *et al.* (1975a). The ammonia probe method also has the advantage that only one reagent (1%) sodium hydroxide) is required. Good correlations with the Kjeldahl method are claimed for both procedures.

3. Free α-Amino Nitrogen

The estimation of free α-amino nitrogen is useful as it gives a quick assessment of the amounts of nitrogen compounds assimilable by yeast. Two principal methods are available, one using ninhydrin and the other, trinitrobenzene sulphonic acid (TNBS). Both methods are cited by E.B.C (1975) where it is stressed that the method used must be stated as the TNBS procedure tends to give higher values.

An A.S.B.C. Sub-Committee on Free Amino Nitrogen recommended (1975b) that a ninhydrin method be adopted; this reagent is also used in an automated procedure given by Moll *et al.* (1975b) and an earlier one described by Ashurst and MacWilliam (1963). The non-specificity of this reagent under the conditions of automated techniques led Pinnegar (1966) to develop a method employing TNBS. Buckee *et al.* (1974) give details of a semi-automatic procedure, using TNBS and Hudson (1976) indicates a preference for this procedure over a fully automated technique. In the semi-automatic method, automatic diluting and dispensing equipment are used and the reaction with TNBS is confined to 30 minutes at 60 °C, compared with 2 hours at 40 °C as specified by E.B.C. (1975).

4. Nitrogen Fractions

Various procedures for fractionation of the nitrogen compounds of beer into classes or ranges, based on their complexity or molecular weight, have been proposed. One classical procedure in regular use in many laboratories is that due to Lundin (1931) in which tannic acid is used to separate a high-molecular-weight fraction (the A fraction) and sodium molybdate precipitates a low-molecular-weight fraction (the C fraction). The difference between the total nitrogen of the beer and the A + C gives an intermediate (B) fraction. The procedure is useful for the control of stabilization of packaged and export beers and for the assessment of trends in physical stability and other parameters where correlation with nitrogen values is important.

Conditions for the precipitation of the high (tannin) and low (molybdate) factions are critical and good results can be obtained only if they are constant. For routine control purposes, determination of total and A fraction nitrogen values for a given beer and the expression of the latter as a proportion of the total is often sufficient; a knowledge of the level of C fraction nitrogen may be useful, however, in situations where lack of yeast assimilable nitrogen is suspected.

Other precipitation procedures are described by de Clerck (1958) who states that the figures obtained by precipitation with magnesium sulphate are very close to those of the Lundin A fraction. True protein nitrogen, the determination of which is of minor importance in beer, can be estimated by means of a method described by Bishop (1944) in which the protein is precipitated with acetic acid and sodium nitrite. Trichloracetic acid is also used as an alternative precipitating agent.

Protein profiles of beer can be obtained by means of gel chromatography and disc-electrofocusing, as described by ten Hoopen (1973), who states that disc-electrofocusing in a polyacrylamide gel is less time-consuming and gives better resolution than electrofocusing in a density gradient as described by Bateson and Leach (1969). Savage and Thompson (1973) also give details of gel-electrofocusing of beer proteins.

Frequently, these modern techniques are used as an extension to the characterization of proteins by determination of total and α-amino nitrogen and the Lundin fractions. In particular, as noted by ten Hoopen (1973), further characterization is valuable when dealing with beers prepared from mashes with raw barley or other significant amounts of unmalted carbohydrates.

Another modern technique, immunology, is used together with gel electrophoresis by Loisa et al. (1971) for the quantitative determination of beer proteins.

S. Diacetyl and Related Compounds

Of the many flavour components of beer to have received attention in the past 20 years, diacetyl is one of the most important. Numerous methods have been proposed and the advantages and disadvantages of them discussed thoroughly in the brewing literature. Diacetyl ($CH_3COCOCH_3$) and 2,3-pentanedione ($CH_3COCOC_2H_5$) are important contributors to beer character and many papers have been written about the formation of these and related compounds during fermentation and the changes in levels of them during subsequent maturation and finishing operations. Some workers and methods refer to the compounds as a group, vicinal diketones (VDK), but as the compounds exist primarily as diacetyl in finished beer the term diacetyl is used here; it is, in fact, used by E.B.C. (1975) and A.S.B.C. (1975) although I of B (1971) prefers VDK.

In a detailed review, Wainwright (1973) gives analytical and biochemical considerations of diacetyl and 2,3-pentanedione. He indicates the difficulties inherent in their measurement by analytical and organoleptic means and summarizes, in tabular form, details of nearly 20 methods. Of these, one is a polarographic procedure whilst the others are mainly methods dependent on the displacement of the volatile diketones into a "trapping solution" or gas–liquid chromatography (GLC) techniques.

Early methods for diacetyl as applied to beer were based on the formation of the red nickel complex of its dioxime (dimethylglyoxime) and the determination of the dimethylglyoxine formed from diacetyl is utilized in several later methods, such as two of the four given by A.S.B.C. A survey of methods based on this reaction is reported by Kijima (1966) who states that one such method gives a recovery of 97% in the range of 0·08–0·7 mg diacetyl per litre.

E.B.C. and I of B give single methods only; both employ a Markham or Parras type still in which 100 ml of beer (not decarbonated) is distilled under controlled conditions to yield 25 ml of distillate in 5–10 min. Supply of steam to the still is accomplished by means of a boiling flask or, if a large number of samples are handled, more conveniently by an automatic steam generator. The E.B.C. and I of B methods differ in that in the former colour development is achieved with o-phenylenediamine and the absorbance is measured at 335 nm whilst the I of B method employs α-naphthol and alkaline creatine with absorbance measured at 530 nm.

A.S.B.C. (1975) also gives a distillation method utilizing α-naphthol and creatine at 530 nm and warns that this method is not specific for diacetyl and should be used only for finished beer. Both this method and the I of B technique are based on the earlier procedure of Owades et al. (1960).

Rice et al. (1973) recommend a method which combines the isolation step of the micro method of Owades and Jakovac (1963) with some of the advantages of the UV method of A.S.B.C (1975). The procedure is considerably more sensitive than the micro method.

Gas–liquid chromatography (GLC) is employed in several published methods for diacetyl and this technique is utilized in numerous laboratories equipped with the necessary apparatus. Harrison et al. (1965), Scherrer (1972) and others describe GLC methods. Electron capture detectors are used and various column packings and carrier gases are described, e.g. Spaeth et al. list "Carbowax 1540" on "Chromosorb W-AW60" and 9 : 1 argon–methane as the carrier gas whilst in the author's laboratory "Porapak Q" is used as packing without a liquid phase in a technique based on that of Latimer et al. (1969). Internal standards such as chloroform and acetone are used and the method calibrated by adding diacetyl of known purity to beer. The purity of diacetyl can be determined by formation and measurement of dimethyl-glyoxime as described by Gjertsen *et al.* (1964) or by Brenner *et al.* (1963), as cited in the I of B colorimetric method.

GLC methods are capable of estimating 2,3-pentanedione, acetoin and 2,3-butanediol in beer, as stated by Scherrer and Spaeth *et al.* Inoue and Yamamoto (1970) maintain that GLC methods, together with some of the colorimetric methods, give erroneous results due to the formation of VDK by decarboxylation of α-acetohydroxy acids during analysis. This fact is noted by other workers, particularly in relation to the non-specific colorimetric procedures.

In an attempt to obtain greater accuracy, Inoue and Yamamoto modified the micro method of Owades and Jakovac (1963) to achieve a determination of both diacetyl and 2,3-pentanedione, expressed as diacetyl. They also describe a GLC technique for the two diketones and methods for α-acetohydroxy acids in both beer and fermenting wort.

Automated and semi-automated procedures are described by Brandon (1964, 1967 and 1968) for diacetyl and acetoin and good agreement with manual methods is claimed.

In summary, it should be remembered that the choice of method for estimation of diacetyl in finished, particularly pasteurized, beer is not as vital as that for the choice for determination in fermenting wort or beer during maturation. Many methods can give rise to misleading results when used for the latter and consequently should be employed with their short-comings in mind. With qualification, the Markham still I of B method performs well for the purpose of routine control of levels in beer after fermentation. As a general purpose procedure a GLC technique would probably be preferred.

An A.S.B.C. Sub-Committee (1976) found that most laboratories in North America use the standard A.S.B.C. methods; the micro method and the broad spectrum VDK procedure being the most popular. A detailed comparison of the four A.S.B.C. methods is given by Gales (1976) who also recommends a modified broad spectrum method which measures all of the precursors.

A report of the E.B.C. Analysis Committee (1976) expresses concern that the E.B.C. method gives a low recovery (50%) of diacetyl added to beer. On the other hand, A.S.B.C. reference method A and the I of B method give good recoveries. The latter method however, has a high replication error.

Table 4 gives a comparison of the operating conditions of various methods for diacetyl.

T. Fatty Acids and Lipids

Non-volatile constituents of beer such as free fatty acids (C_4 to C_{10}) have

Table 4. Comparison of conditions for methods for diacetyl

Method/reference	Sample treatment	Reagents	Absorbance measured at (nm)	Remarks
A.S.B.C. A	Distillation	Iron/dimethyl glyoxime	520	Reference method
A.S.B.C. B	Distillation	α-naphthol/creatine	530	Broad spectrum method (VDK)
A.S.B.C. C	Heat to 65 °C—sparge with CO_2	Iron/hydroxylamine HCl	530	Micro method
A.S.B.C. D	Distillation	Hydroxylamine	230	Rapid method (UV)
E.B.C.	Distillation	o-phenylene diamine	335	—
I of B	Distillation	α-naphthol/creatine	530	Broad spectrum (VDK)
Rice et al.	Heat to 100 °C—sparge with N_2	Hydroxylamine	230	—
Owades and Jakovac (1963)	Heat to 65 °C—sparge with CO_2	Hydroxylamine HCl	530	—

received considerable attention in the last few years, particularly since Drost *et al.* (1971) postulated that they may contribute to the staling of beer. Consequently, several methods for their determination have been proposed and are noted below.

Klopper *et al.* (1975) and Sandra and Verzele (1975) describe GLC procedures using flame ionization systems; in both cases several preparatory steps are necessary. In the former method the beer is freeze-dried before solution in methanol and treatment with boron trifluoride and extraction into heptane. The heptane extract is evaporated under nitrogen and injected into the chromatograph. The extraction process given by Sandra and Verzele is simpler and chromatography on packed and open tubular columns is used.

Jones *et al.* (1975) separate the fatty acids and neutral lipids and phospholipids on silcic acid. Determination of the separated components is by GLC employing the method of Tripp *et al.* (1968).

MacPherson and Buckee (1974) give details of another GLC procedure in which a chloroform–methanol mixture is used to isolate the lipid fraction at pH 1·0 and the free fatty acids are separated as potassium salts. The acids are then liberated by acidification and converted to their methyl esters for injection into the chromatograph. The method permits the estimation of free fatty acids from C_8 to C_{18} with one injection; for acids below C_8 a procedure such as that described by Arkima (1973) is suggested.

The MacPherson and Buckee procedure is fairly rapid and is considered suitable for routine analysis. Other lipid materials, e.g. glycerides and fatty acid esters, do not interfere. Reproducibility and precision are satisfactory.

U. Sulphur Compounds

1. Introduction

The importance of the numerous volatile sulphur compounds in the overall flavour characteristics of beer and in control of processing operations has long been recognized. The occurrence of hydrogen sulphide in fermentation gas led to many surveys of the mechanisms of the formation of this compound and of mercaptans. Ricketts and Coutts (1951) summarized much of the earlier work and described a simple lead acetate strip technique for the semi-quantitative determination of hydrogen sulphide.

Several methods for hydrogen sulphide, mercaptans and other volatile sulphur compounds have been published in the past two decades. However, these compounds (with the exception of sulphur dioxide, also mentioned in this section) have, in general, proved to be difficult to determine with acceptable accuracy. The availability recently of specialized gas chromatographic equipment provides a ready means for their determination in beer. However, of necessity, many brewery laboratories must rely on other methods for the estimation of this group of compounds. Both GLC and chemical methods are briefly discussed in the following.

2. Sulphur Dioxide

Sulphur dioxide (SO_2) is probably the sulphur compound most frequently determined in beer. An international method, using p-rosaniline hydrochloride as the colour reagent, has been adopted and is described by A.S.B.C. (1975). Accurately standardized sodium sulphite solutions are used for calibration employing a beer addition technique and the colour developed is read at 550 nm after 30 min at 25 °C. The procedure is quicker than methods employing distillation, based on the classical Monier Williams technique (1927) and is preferred over other published methods.

For purposes of routine control a more rapid method is of value, particularly when total sulphur dioxide content is over 10–15 mg/l. In this method, 50 ml beer is added to 10 ml 40% w/w NaOH with a little octyl alcohol to prevent foaming. After standing for 20 min, some starch indicator is added followed by 50 ml 20% H_2SO_4 and titration is carried out immediately with N/50 iodine.

I of B (1971) gives two distillation methods, one for general use and one as a rapid quality control. In the former, acidified beer is boiled under reflux with a carrier gas (carbon dioxide or nitrogen) and the residual SO_2 collected in a receiver containing 10-vol. hydrogen peroxide. The sulphuric acid so formed is titrated with 0·02N NaOH using bromophenol blue as indicator. In the rapid procedure 250 ml beer and 10 ml concentrated HCl are distilled and the distillate passed into 15 ml water with some starch indicator added. Standard iodine solution (0·1N iodine) is run in from a burette during the distillation until the blue colour is maintained; persistance of the colour for 1 min is taken as the end point.

Buckee and Hargitt (1976) compare the above distillation procedures with another, ascribed to Tanner (1963), in which the sample is boiled with phosphoric acid and methanol and a more dilute titrating solution (0·01N NaOH) is used with a different indicator. The Tanner procedure, which is favoured for estimating sulphur dioxide in a variety of foodstuffs within the European Economic Community, gives significantly lower results than the E.B.C. or I of B distillation procedures.

The determination of sulphur dioxide in beer by means of an ion-selective electrode has not proved entirely satisfactory (Buckee 1975) but the technique has been found to be suitable for glucose and other syrups and in isinglass finings. In spite of encouraging reports from some quarters, the ion-selective electrode can give misleading results with beer and also with wine.

A number of studies have been made of the relationship between free, bound and total SO_2. In a recent one, Tressl *et al.* (1975), used GLC with a sulphur-selective detector for free SO_2 and converted the bound SO_2 to H_2S by reduction with stannous chloride in HCl. The H_2S was then also measured by GLC.

3. Hydrogen Sulphide

As stated by Brenner et al. (1953), the work of Ricketts and Coutts (1951), mentioned above, re-awakened interest in the estimation of hydrogen sulphide and other volatile sulphur compounds in beer.

Brenner et al. concluded that a colorimetric procedure, involving the production of methylene blue from p-aminodimethylaniline and ferric chloride, was the most specific and sensitive. Initially, the method included a step whereby the hydrogen sulphide was swept out of the sample of acidified beer at 85 °C; a later modification of Brenner et al. (1954) specifies room temperature. Sainsbury and Maw (1967) and Lawrence (1968) both employ a temperature of 75 °C and sweep the H_2S from a large, acidified sample of beer by means of oxygen-free nitrogen.

However, conflicting results were obtained in many laboratories with these and similar methods, a fact acknowledged by Brenner and Laufer (1972) in a survey of the methods for hydrogen sulphide and volatile thiols. In many cases, significant correlations between analytical and organoleptic assessments of beers were not found and the earlier concept of free and total H_2S was considered to be invalid.

All workers in the field have faced the considerable difficulties inherent in the accurate determination of very small amounts of reactive compounds which have very low odour, and possibly, taste thresholds. The advent of the flame photometric detector (FPD) for a specific GLC procedure has enabled the accurate determination of hydrogen sulphide and other sulphur volatiles in trace amounts. Jansen et al. (1971), Richardson and Mocek (1971, 1973) and McCowen et al. (1971) all describe procedures, using the FPD, for hydrogen sulphide and a number of other sulphur volatiles.

Beer headspace analysis in conjunction with GLC with FPD was first described by Drews (1969). In general, in finished beer only hydrogen sulphide and dimethyl sulphide are present in amounts over the sensitivity limit of the FPD. Various procedures for the concentration of sulphur volatiles are given by McCowen et al. (1971) who report that adsorption of the compounds on a molecular sieve and replacement with water prior to injection in the chromatograph gives satisfactory results.

Another approach to the determination of hydrogen sulphide, introduced by Brenner and Khan (1974), involves sweeping the H_2S and volatile thiols from a sample of beer at 37 °C into a trap containing triethyl lead chloride which binds H_2S and SH compounds. Micro-titration with tetraacetoxymercurifluorescein (TMF) of a single portion of the triethyl lead chloride solution gives two end points, one for sulphide and the other for SH compounds. The procedure is based on an earlier and more lengthy method of Brenner and Laufer (1972) which also utilizes fluorometric titration. For laboratories with the necessary apparatus the method should be useful for purposes of routine control.

An ion-selective electrode, sensitive only to the sulphide ion, is described by Owades et al. (1967) for the determination of H_2S in beer. They obtained values considerably less than those reported by various chemical methods and considered that, as the sample is not changed during analysis, the absence of artefacts gave more accurate results. However, the technique does not seem to have found favour in brewery laboratories, possibly due to reports of inconsistent results.

A chemical odour filter, first described by Brenner et al. (1955) and later modified by Brenner and Laufer (1972), is useful for differentiating between the olfactory effects of H_2S and volatile thiols. Zinc sulphate is used to remove H_2S from the sample and zinc and copper sulphate to remove both H_2S and thiols. Even if H_2S is present at a sub-threshold level its removal may alter the "nose" of the beer.

4. Volatile Thiols and Organic Sulphides

Early methods for the determination of volatile thiols, such as that of Brenner et al. (1954), relied on heating or distillation to separate the compounds from the sample, a process which probably created more thiols. Later, flash exchange GLC was employed by Hashimoto and Kuroiwa (1966) and by Lawrence (1968). Sainsbury and Maw (1967) used a colorimetric procedure with a heating step.

Drews (1969), Jansen et al. (1970) and McCowen et al. (1971) describe techniques using GLC with FPD; the sensitivity and accuracy of the procedure are reviewed by McCowen et al.

In the past few years, dimethyl sulphide (DMS) has been recognized as an important flavour component and its determination, by means of GLC with FPD, is described by Kavanagh et al. (1975) and White and Parsons (1975). Richardson and Mocek (1971) give a method for a number of sulphides including DMS diethyl sulphide, diethyl disulphide and methyl-n-butyl sulphide and also describe triangular tasting assessments of the imbalance of these compounds.

Brenner and Khan (1974) devised a method for the fluorometric determination of volatile thiols together with H_2S as described earlier in this section.

The sulphur alcohol, methionol, was first reported in beer as a flavour component by Szlavko (1973a, b) who used GLC with FPD for its detection. Schreier et al. (1975) describe a method for the isolation and estimation of methionol and related compounds.

V. Volatile Components

1. Introduction

The importance of the volatile components of beer has long been recognized and their identification by organoleptic means has been a prime aim of brewers and brewing chemists for many years.

Rapid advances in analytical techniques in the past 20 years have provided accurate and diverse tools for the isolation, identification and estimation of a wide range of volatile components. Rosculet (1970, 1971) lists a number of procedures for use in connection with volatile components and his survey, which contains over 1500 references, is extremely comprehensive. In the following brief summary, only a broad outline of some of the methods available for the more important components is given. Methods for alcohols, esters, organic acids, aldehydes and ketones, amines and several other groups are noted. Method for sulphur compounds are given in Section U.

Modern analytical techniques, such as gas–liquid chromatography (GLC), provide many options with regard to methodology and major and ancillary equipment. The choice of procedure depends on many factors and thus provision of definitive detail in a short survey is difficult and has not been attempted. However, remarks made in relation to the determination of alcohols and esters by GLC apply, in many instances, to the determination of other volatile components.

Newer techniques, such as high-pressure liquid chromatography (HPLC), referred to elsewhere in this chapter for the estimation of non-volatile components, could also well be used in the future for volatile components.

2. Alcohols and Esters

The determination of ethyl alcohol is dealt with in another section and will not be considered here. Detection and estimation of the aliphatic and aromatic alcohols present in beer were made easier by the introduction of commercial GLC equipment some 20 years ago and many papers have been published since. A.S.B.C. (1975) recommends the use of a direct injection method for lower boiling volatiles, particularly the alcohols. In this procedure GLC with flame ionization detection is employed and an internal standard solution comprising n-propyl alcohol, isobutyl alcohol and isoamyl alcohol with some esters is used. The adoption of this procedure in preference to other techniques, such as headspace and extraction methods, followed a survey made by an A.S.B.C. Sub-Committee formed in 1969 to report on the applications of GLC to problems in brewing chemistry.

A successful application of an extraction procedure for low and medium boiling fractions, described initially by Powell and Brown (1966), has been modified by Trachman and Saletan (1969). This technique, in which beer is extracted with carbon disulphide to give a concentrate which is then subjected to GLC, has found wide application in brewing laboratories for the determination of alcohols, esters and some acids. Powell and Brown reported some 14 identified components including β-phenylethanol and β-phenylethyl acetate. Trachman and Saletan note the occurrence of at least another 15 components while Rosculet (1970) lists some 30 esters and alcohols found in beer and Lawrence (1964), in another detailed review, names 11 alcohols, 21 esters, 40 acids and some 15 carbonyl compounds.

Another extraction procedure, using ethyl acetate as the extractant, is described by Szlavko (1973) for the determination of the aromatic higher alcohols β-phenylethanol, tryptophol and tyrosol.

Extraction procedures have been combined with distillation and one such, described by Gruss *et al.* (1975), gives better reproducibility than headspace techniques and permits the determination of a wide range of alcohols and esters. Examples of the use of combined procedures are also given by Whitear (1974); a comparison of GLC methods, made by Lindsay *et al.* (1972), favours a carbon disulphide extraction and gives details of improvements obtained by employing porous polymers to trap volatile flavour compounds. A later evaluation of some of the polymers available for this purpose is given by Micketts and Lindsay (1974).

Improvements in extraction methods using carbon disulphide, designed to give increased reproducibility, are noted by Stenroos *et al.* (1976) who also gives details of data handling and interpretation.

The technique in which the headpspace vapour of beer is injected into the chromatograph, introduced by Kepner *et al.* (1963), has found favour in many laboratories. Hurst (1974) describes an improved procedure for collecting and concentrating headspace volatiles.

Engan (1971, 1975) describes a headspace method for esters and alcohols and discusses the relationships between these flavour components.

Hoff and Herwig (1976) gives details of a rapid GLC procedure for headspace volatiles and illustrate the reproducibility for 12 components. Correlations between data so gained and triangular taste panel results are shown and the concept of aromagrams using per cent of total peak areas is introduced.

A colorimetric method for total esters using a reaction with hydroxamic acid is given by Steiner and Lanzlinger (1975).

3. Aldehydes and Ketones

Methods for volatile carbonyls in beer have been described by Hashimoto (1966), Jamieson and Chen (1972) and Jamieson and Van Gheluwe (1974). All workers use a flash-exchange technique in which the volatile carbonyl compounds are swept from the sample, converted to dinitrophenylhydrazones, reacted with α-ketoglutaric acid and subjected to GLC. A number of volatile carbonyls, including acetaldehyde and acetone, have been determined by this technique.

A simple colorimetric method, largely specific for acetaldehyde in beer, is described by Otter and Taylor (1971). In this procedure, the sample is distilled and the distillate collected in an ice-cooled flask; quantities of fructose and resorcinol (the colorimetric reagent) are added and following heating and cooling under standard conditions, absorbance is read at 555 nm.

Pessa (1971) used a headspace GLC procedure for acetaldehyde when following variations in this component during fermentation, maturation and storage in container.

Micro-diffusion techniques for volatile aldehydes, described by Harold et al. (1962) and modified by Hashimoto (1968), and Steiner (1971) have been used for the determination of these compounds in wort and beer.

Steffen et al. (1970) describe a colorimetric procedure for ethyl acetate by which acetaldehyde can also be determined. Other colorimetric procedures include that of Enebo (1957).

One carbonyl compound to attract a considerable amount of attention in recent years is trans-2-nonenal. It was suggested several years ago that this compound is responsible for the characteristic cardboard papery flavour of stale beer and since 1971 a number of papers relative to its occurrence and estimation have appeared. Wang and Siebert (1974) describe an extraction procedure using methylene chloride; dinitrophenylhydrazone derivatives are prepared from the extract and HPLC used for the resolution of these. Wohlele et al. (1972) give details of a procedure in which GLC is preceded by a concentration step using a porous polymer. Meilgaard et al. (1971) describe an involved procedure for the identification of carbonyl compounds.

4. Organic Acids, Amines and other Compounds

Many organic acids have been detected in beer and their estimation assumes some importance in the overall flavour of the product. Methods noted by Rosculet (1971) include titrimetric, colorimetric, GLC, paper and column chromatography and those utilizing enzyme reactions. Routine determination can be automated, using an organic acid analyser which employs partition chromatography on silica gel followed by titration. A semi-automatic procedure, described by Coote and Kirsop (1974), uses a column packed with acidified silicic acid and eluted with mixtures of chloroform and tertiary amyl alcohol. The effluent from the column is mixed with an indicator (sodium salt of o-nitrophenol) and the absorbance read at 350 nm.

Several volatile amines have been reported in beer and GLC and paper and thin-layer chromatography procedures have been used for their estimation

(Rosculet 1970). Koike *et al.* (1972) give a method using flash-exchange GLC which they used to determine eight volatile amines. Steiner and Lanzlinger (1975), in a series of methods for volatile compounds in beer, use treatment with copper sulphate and carbon disulphide for amines. An amine of some physiological importance, *p*-hydroxybenzylamine, is determined by a method described by Slaughter and Uvgard (1972) who previously had described a procedure (1971) for other amines.

The volatile components arising from hops and hop preparations form an important group of flavour components and numerous references to their estimation occur in the brewing literature. The majority of these techniques involve GLC; for example, the detailed methods described by Harold *et al.* (1961) in which the separation and estimation of many fusel oil components and volatile compounds arising from malt and hops are given. Kavanagh *et al.* (1975) used GLC of silyl derivatives of extracted hop seed oil components in a survey to determine the role of fatty acids therein in beer.

W. Preservatives, Additives and Contaminants

1. Preservatives and Cold Sterilants

Whilst the number of preservatives permitted for use in beer has been reduced in most parts of the world in recent years, a few are still employed, particularly in the role of cold sterilants. Of the time-tested preservatives sulphur dioxide is probably the most common; methods for its determination are given in section U.

Other compounds which have found considerable use, particularly in the past, are benzoic acid and sodium benzoate. To an extent, these have been replaced more recently by sorbic acid and potassium sorbate. Methods for the determination of this group are well documented for many foods and beverages and will not be discussed in detail here. However, it must be remembered that the presence of this group can interfere with the determination of isohumulones in beer as they absorb strongly at the wavelength used (275 nm) in the determination of bitterness following extraction with iso-octane. Use is made of this in a method noted later for an ester of hydroxybenzoic acid and it is possible also to estimate benzoates and sorbates in this manner.

Smyly *et al.* (1976) give details of a method for sodium benzoate using high-pressure liquid chromatography (HPLC). This method requires less sample preparation and analysis time than the official procedure of the A.O.A.C. (1975). A modification of the latter method suitable for beer and wine is given by Amerine and Ough (1974) who also describe two methods for potassium sorbate. These involve steam distillation of the sample followed by a colorimetric procedure (using thiobarbituric acid) or measuring the absorbance of the distillate at 250 nm.

In the past decade esters of hydroxybenzoic acid have found favour in some countries as cold sterilants. Their use is not universally permitted, however, and some doubt exists in relation to their efficacy in beer. Several methods for their determination are available, in particular for n-heptyl *p*-hydroxybenzoate. A.S.B.C. (1975) gives two methods for this ester, a specific GLC procedure and a non-specific method in which absorbances at 245 and 275 nm of an isooctane extract are measured.

The GLC procedure employs a flame ionization detector, a single column and isothermal operation; n-hexyl *p*-hydroxybenzoate is used as an internal standard. The UV absorption method is recommended for control purposes and has the advantage that the same isooctane extract can also be used for the determination of bitterness (isohumulones). n-Heptyl *p*-hydroxybenzoate is known to reduce the surface tension of beer, a fact utilized by Weissler and Eigel (1967) in a method in which the decrease in surface tension of a treated beer from a norm of 45–50 dynes/cm is measured under accurately standardized conditions and the decrease equated against that caused by the addition of known amounts of the additive. The procedure is rapid but requires a precision tensionometer and great care in manipulation.

Another cold sterilant, n-octyl gallate, has been used for some years and several methods for its estimation are available. Cuzner *et al.* (1970), comparing spectrofluorometric, spectrophotometric and GLC methods, concluded that the GLC procedure was the most precise, particularly when *N*,*O*-bis(trimethylsilyl)acetamide was used as the silylation agent.

Diethylpyrocarbonate (DEPC) is a sterilant which has found favour in some countries for use with a number of beverages. In recent years, however, it has been suggested that its use can produce undesirable amounts of urethane, a known carcinogen. DEPC is also referred to as diethyldicarbonate (DEDC) and can be determined in beer by a titrimetric method described by Cuzner *et al.* (1971). In this procedure, beer is extracted with chloroform and the extract is reacted with an excess of morpholine which is back-titrated with acid. A method for residual diethylcarbonate (DEC) in beer, employing GLC is also described and others are surveyed by Ough (1976).

2. Additives: Antioxidants, Fining Agents, Enzymes and Stabilizers

There are, of course, many compounds which are added to beer during processing for various purposes. Those used depend to an extent on the legislation relating to food additives in the country concerned but, in general, the use of additives or processing aids is kept to a minimum and is controlled by recognized good manufacturing practices. A few only of the major additives and aids are dealt with here.

Antioxidants form an important class of compounds used in beer and well-defined methods are available for ascorbic acid and erythorbic acid and their salts. Bisulphites, dithionites and other sources of sulphur dioxide are also used as antioxidants and methods for these are described elsewhere.

Alginates and similar compounds, e.g. carrageenan, are used as protein precipitants (kettle finings) and residues can persist in beer. Buckee *et al.* (1976) give details of an electrophoretic method, using a polyacrylamide gel, for carrageenan and furcellaran in beer. They describe chemical methods for sodium alginate and carrageenan; for the former orcinol–hydrochloric acid is used as a colorimetric reagent, measuring absorbance at 620 nm.

Residual tannic acid in beer, following treatment with this substance in a stabilizing procedure, can be determined by means of methods for gallotannins as given in section P. Small quantities of proteolytic enzymes remaining after treatment have been determined by a number of methods; A.S.B.C. (1975) gives a qualitative procedure which can be made semi-quantitative. A substrate of buffered skim milk powder (as a casein source) is used and changes in appearance of the substrate suspension, following the addition of beer, are observed; other empirical methods employ different substrates.

A satisfactory quantitative method used in the author's laboratory is one utilizing hide powder azure as a substrate, as described by Savage and Thomson (1970). Hide powder azure is a protein with the dyestuff Remazo-Brilliant Blue covalently bound to it. In the estimation, hydrolysis of the protein is catalysed by the enzyme and amino acids with blue dyestuff attached are liberated in proportion to the activity of the enzyme. A high purity papain preparation is used as a reference standard. The method can be used for the estimation of enzyme concentration in beer during process and in bright beer before and after pasteurization and has been found to be more reliable than some other procedures. It can also be utilized as a "go/no-go" check for the presence of enzyme.

Another stabilizing agent, polyvinyl pyrrolidone (PVP), can be determined by column chromatography on silica gel as in a method given by Postel (1973). This technique can also be used as a qualitative check for the presence of PVP.

Artificial sweeteners, such as saccharin, are permitted in beers in some countries and methods for their determination are necessary for legal purposes. Eeckhaut (1971) gives details of a procedure for saccharin based on the purification of an ether extract of the beer and conversion of the saccharin to salicylic acid. The procedure is lengthy and involves several extraction and distillation stages. Qualitative checks for the presence of saccharin are numerous; one in which an ether extract is heated with resorcinol and sulphuric acid and then cooled and neutralized with NaOH, whereupon saccharin produces a deep green fluorescence, is preferred.

3. Contaminants

The non-microbiological contaminants of beer are many and brewery laboratories should be equipped for "screening" suspect samples as thoroughly as possible. The presence of toxic metals, if suspected can be checked by chemical means or atomic absorption spectroscopy. The classical Reinsch test for arsenic is useful for this element and a wide range of simple spot tests is available for many elements.

Many foreign objects and particles can be found in packaged beers; of these some are readily seen and identified but in other cases only minute amounts of the contaminants are present. A detailed work by Glenister (1975) on deposits found in beer is very valuable as an aid to the identification of particulate foreign matter in beer. Flakes of paint and lacquer, particles of asbestos, diatomaceous earth, starch and many other possible contaminant substances can be separated by centrifugation and identified microscopically, with or without staining. An ammoniacal wash followed by staining with Eosin Y and Saffranin O is used by Glenister (1974) for separation and identification of adsorbent stabilizers such as prepared clays, silica gel preparations, polyamides and activated carbons.

The detection of asbestos is dealt with by Bernstein (1974).

Contamination by grease, oil, etc., can be detected by diminution in head retention and the presence of chemical contaminants can often be confirmed by changes in pH value, colour, acidity or other similar parameters.

X. Miscellaneous Determinations

In a survey of this nature it is obvious that many analytical procedures must be omitted and that detailed bench instructions can be given for only a few methods. The methods covered are considered to represent a reasonable cross-section of those that may be required, either as routine or as occasional methods, in a typical brewery laboratory.

Some determinations not noted in the preceding sections are tabulated in Table 5 with details of published references.

III. ORGANOLEPTIC METHODS

A. Introduction

The literature relating to the assessment of beer by organoleptic means is considerable and grows significantly each year. In this section, a few of the

Table 5. Miscellaneous determinations and references

Determinations	Reference
Amino acids	(1) Marinelli *et al.* (1967)
	(2) Olsen (1970)
	(3) Barwald and Pruchu (1971)
	(4) Otter and Taylor (1976)
Analysis check service	Lom (1975)
Apparent dextrin	A.S.B.C. (1975)
Ash	A.S.B.C. (1975)
Automated analysis	Buckee and Hickman (1975)
Caloric content (energy value)	(1) Saletan (1959)
	(2) A.S.B.C. (1975 Supp.)
End fermentation (yeast fermentable extract)	A.S.B.C. (1975)
Furfural	Brenner and Khan (1976)
Interpretation of results	Whitear (1974b)
In-line instrumentation	Royston (1971)
Nucleotides and nucleic acid derivatives	(1) Saha *et al.* (1971)
	(2) Buday *et al.* (1972)
	(3) Somers and Ziemelis (1972)
	(4) Steward *et al.* (1974)
Polarimetry	Dadic (1975)
Viscosity	(1) I of B (1971)
	(2) A.S.B.C. (1975)

procedures available for routine use are discussed and suggestions made regarding training tasters.

As the requirements for organoleptic testing vary with circumstances the techniques discussed herein will not necessarily be applicable in all cases. However, where inter-brewery comparisons are made or the measurement of flavour trends over long periods is important it is advisable to employ standardized procedures. An excellent information guide to sensory evaluation methods is given by Prell (1976).

With regard to flavour profile or similar techniques, it is encouraging to know that work is in hand, on an international basis, to derive a standard system of nomenclature. This work, being conducted jointly by the E.B.C., A.S.B.C. and M.B.A.A., commenced in 1975; progress is summarized by Clapperton *et al.* (1976) and in later reports issued by the bodies concerned.

B. Difference or Discrimination Tasting

The well-known triangular technique, described by Bengsston (1953) and other earlier workers, has found extensive use in breweries for many years. A.S.B.C. (1975) gives some simple instructions for the conduct of the test which include advice regarding presentation of the samples and the advisability of smelling all three glasses before and after swirling the contents. E.B.C. (1975) also give procedures for triangular and two glass difference tastings.

In the test each taster is presented with three glasses, two of which contain one beer and one the other beer. It is important that the room in which tasting is conducted is quiet and free from extraneous odours. Goodall and Colquhoun (1967) discuss in some detail the requirements of a tasting room.

Beers should be presented at a reasonable drinking temperature (in the author's opinion between 6 and 10 °C) and in coloured glasses. With regard to colour, ruby red is specified by E.B.C. (1975) and preferred by A.S.B.C.; glasses of amber or similar colour are also satisfactory.

Goodall and Colquhoun also discuss methods of selecting and training panels, the effect of fatigue and the sources of bias and ways and means of overcoming same.

A detailed summary of methods of difference tasting and procedures available for selection of panel members is given by Dawson et al. (1963). The reader is also referred to the relevant sections of the work of Amerine et al. (1965).

Bengsston's or similar probability tables are used to determine the significance levels of the results. A panel of at least 10 members is desirable for difference tasting and the author prefers panels with 16–20 members. In order to achieve satisfactory attendances at meetings a panel of 24 is used in the author's Company. Panel members should be screened at intervals with regard to their ability to detect known differences of, say, bitterness, sweetness or carbonation, and regular training sessions, using beers to which type substances have been added at levels near established thresholds, are used for checking and maintaining the interest and ability of the panel.

Other difference tests, e.g. two glass paired comparison and duo–trio procedures, are employed for some applications but are not used as widely in the brewing world as the triangular tests. Byer and Gray (1953), however, found that two-sample comparison tests give better results than triangular tests.

Hoff and Herwig (1976) describe a procedure employing routine GLC of 12 headspace volatile components and give correlations between triangular difference results and the levels of those components. A useful discussion on the interpretation of the results of triangular taste test results is that given by Young (1971), whilst Wren (1971) also warns of some of the pitfalls encountered in discrimination tests.

C. Profile Tasting and Rating Procedures

In the natural endeavour of every brewery to produce products of consistent flavour characteristics beers, are constantly checked or rated for flavour. In many cases, in the course of daily routine, such tasting is performed by various members of production and technical staffs without resort to elaborate recording or scoring procedures. It is wise, however, to record in a simple fashion the results of all such checks during processing and at the time of release for sale in order that trends may be observed.

Since the concept of the flavour profile was introduced by Cairncross and Sjostrom (1950) numerous and varied methods have been published and thus the efforts of the joint E.B.C.–A.S.B.C.–M.B.A.A. working party are most welcome. In an initial step the working party has proposed a list of 40 "first tier" terms shown in tabular form on a pro-forma tasting sheet in Fig. 3. It is acknowledged that it is unnecessary to have all 40 terms for any one beer or series of beers but trials with this form in the author's experience have shown that all of the terms were used at least once in the assessment of a series of some 40 different beers.

Access to computer facilities can greatly assist the collation and interpretation of data from profile taste testing and several references occur in the recent literature to such applications, e.g. Brown *et al.* (1974) and Soltoft (1974).

As with difference tasting, training of those taking part in profile or rating panels is essential. It is advisable to recognize and to note that some tasters have particular abilities to detect individual flavour components at levels below those normally considered as threshold. Similarly, others may be "taste-blind" to the same, or other, components. Valuable information about a panel can be built up by making such observations and the value of the panel, particularly when dealing with pilot plant or other experimental beers, is greatly increased. Profile panels of at least 10 members are often preferred although a smaller expert panel selected from the main group can be used for specific work.

With routine profile tasting it is advisable, as recommended by Wren (1976), to have some tasters who are not part of the regular production team of the beers concerned.

Undesirable off-tastes and trends in flavour may not always be detected by those close to the production of the product. Zürcher (1971) gives details of a scheme for training tasters to recognize flavour faults in beers. Training is also discussed by Mercredy *et al.* (1975) who trained a panel to discriminate, at the 95% confidence level, between some 15 flavour characteristics.

The suggestions made by E.B.C.–A.S.B.C.–M.B.A.A. group regarding standard type substances for estimation of thresholds, contained in the report of an A.S.B.C. Sub-Committee (1976) are valuable and should lead to some interesting and valid work at an international level.

Detailed surveys of profile tasting have been made in recent years by Clapperton (1973, 1974) and Soltoft (1974). The former papers stress that

Identity	Beer 1	Beer 2	Beer 3	Beer 4
32. Sweet	. . . . .	. . . . .	. . . . .	. . . . .
33. Salty	. . . . .	. . . . .	. . . . .	. . . . .
34. Acidic	. . . . .	. . . . .	. . . . .	. . . . .
35. Bitter	. . . . .	. . . . .	. . . . .	. . . . .
36. Metallic	. . . . .	. . . . .	. . . . .	. . . . .
37. Astringent	. . . . .	. . . . .	. . . . .	. . . . .
38. Powdery	. . . . .	. . . . .	. . . . .	. . . . .
39. Carbonation	. . . . .	. . . . .	. . . . .	. . . . .
40. Body	. . . . .	. . . . .	. . . . .	. . . . .
1. Spicy	. . . . .	. . . . .	. . . . .	. . . . .
2. Alcoholic	. . . . .	. . . . .	. . . . .	. . . . .
3. Solvent-like	. . . . .	. . . . .	. . . . .	. . . . .
4. Estery	. . . . .	. . . . .	. . . . .	. . . . .
5. Fruity	. . . . .	. . . . .	. . . . .	. . . . .
6. Floral	. . . . .	. . . . .	. . . . .	. . . . .
7. Acetaldehyde	. . . . .	. . . . .	. . . . .	. . . . .
8. Nutty	. . . . .	. . . . .	. . . . .	. . . . .
9. Resinous	. . . . .	. . . . .	. . . . .	. . . . .
10. Hoppy	. . . . .	. . . . .	. . . . .	. . . . .
11. Grassy	. . . . .	. . . . .	. . . . .	. . . . .
12. Straw-like	. . . . .	. . . . .	. . . . .	. . . . .
13. Grainy	. . . . .	. . . . .	. . . . .	. . . . .
14. Malty	. . . . .	. . . . .	. . . . .	. . . . .
15. Worty	. . . . .	. . . . .	. . . . .	. . . . .
16. Caramel	. . . . .	. . . . .	. . . . .	. . . . .
17. Burnt	. . . . .	. . . . .	. . . . .	. . . . .
18. Medicinal	. . . . .	. . . . .	. . . . .	. . . . .
19. Diacetyl	. . . . .	. . . . .	. . . . .	. . . . .
20. Fatty acid	. . . . .	. . . . .	. . . . .	. . . . .
21. Oily	. . . . .	. . . . .	. . . . .	. . . . .
22. Rancid	. . . . .	. . . . .	. . . . .	. . . . .
23. Fishy	. . . . .	. . . . .	. . . . .	. . . . .
24. Sulphitic	. . . . .	. . . . .	. . . . .	. . . . .
25. Sulphidic	. . . . .	. . . . .	. . . . .	. . . . .
26. Cooked vegetable	. . . . .	. . . . .	. . . . .	. . . . .
27. Yeasty	. . . . .	. . . . .	. . . . .	. . . . .
28. Ribes	. . . . .	. . . . .	. . . . .	. . . . .
29. Papery	. . . . .	. . . . .	. . . . .	. . . . .
30. Leathery	. . . . .	. . . . .	. . . . .	. . . . .
31. Mouldy	. . . . .	. . . . .	. . . . .	. . . . .

Notes:
1. Intensity units
   - 1 × . . . . Fleeting impression.
   - 2 . × . . . Slight but distinctly noticeable impression.
   - 3 . . × . . Moderate impression.
   - 4 . . . × . Strong impression.
   - 5 . . . . × Intense impression.
2. Numbers on left-hand side taken from table in paper by Clapperton *et al.* (1976).

FIG. 3. Profile Rating Taste Testing: experimental form.

profile systems cannot remain static but must be in a state of continuous evolution. It is important that as many people as possible be involved in the evolutionary process; as mentioned earlier, access to computer facilities is of considerable advantage in handling data from profile studies.

Lewis *et al.* (1974), in a paper presented in a M.B.A.A. Workshop on Beer Flavour, describe sensory analysis of beer flavour in the perception of bitterness. Palamand (1974) gives an account of descriptive flavour terminology in which the properties of some concentration-dependent compounds are discussed.

Canales and Cantu (1974) give a detailed description of a procedure used to select the members of an expert panel for profile purposes and list some 35 compounds which can be aded to beer for training and selection purposes. Cloninger *et al.* (1976) discuss a number of rating scales for sensory evaluation technique and give some detailed theoretical considerations.

Siegel *et al.* (1974), in a practical programme for flavour testing, indicate that the profile method is efficient and lends itself to computer handling in an overall system of quality control. It is also useful in detection of flavour trends in single or multiple plants with single or multiple brands; comparisons with competitive products are also simplified by this technique.

D. Tasting for Routine Quality Control

Many systems, all tailored for the needs of individual breweries and situations, exist for routine control of the vital quality attribute of taste. The system used in the author's Company in summarized in Table 6. In addition to the daily tastings noted, regular meetings of a select panel including production, technical, laboratory, marketing, distribution and other personnel handle many difference and profile samples. Flavour stability studies of

Table 6. Summary of tasting procedures for quality control

Sample	Frequency	Personnel involved
Mains water	Daily	Central laboratory staff
Brewing liquor	Daily	Central laboratory staff
Wort	Spot check	Production and central laboratory staff
Beer ex maturation tanks	(1) All tanks	Production staff
	(2) Spot checks	Central laboratory staff
Beer ex bright beer tanks	All tanks	Production and central laboratory staff
Finished beer ex packages and casks	All production runs	Senior production and technical staff

representative samples of all packaged products are continuous and normally extend to 12 months in the container. Bulk draught beers are studied after storage and "keeping quality" tests. Samples of both packaged and bulk draught beers are withdrawn from trade at random and also presented to the panel.

Competitive beers are also subjected to limited flavour stability studies and an attempt is made to obtain profiles of fresh samples of such beers at regular intervals.

An independent evaluation of some the Company's packaged products is obtained by submitting samples monthly to a consulting laboratory. The profiles and flavour stability data, received therefrom, are compared with the results returned by the Company's own select panel on similar samples.

Wren (1971) divides the types of tasting tests available for quality control into three groups, viz. discrimination (difference) tests, and descriptive tests; which includes flavour profile tests and preference tests. The last group really have a place only when outside consumer tasting is considered and cannot be used as a "within" brewery test. Wren describes methods used for training tasters for quality control purposes and also gives a simplified flavour profile procedure for use by production personnel. After suitable training such personnel were able to produce flavour judgements well correlated with, and rated equally with, routine chemical and physical measurements.

Einstein (1974) discusses briefly some examples of panel methods and points out that flavour testing cannot be an isolated technique. Results from a wide range of procedures must be used to obtain balanced decisions regarding flavour. Panels involving participation by outside consumers, e.g. visitors to a brewery, are particularly useful in the evaluation of new or modified products.

Experiences with an outside consumer panel under Australian conditions are described by Williams (1972) who concludes that home tasting trials can provide useful information for preference and paired-sample differential tastings. If properly designed, such trials give results which are capable of statistical analysis and can be checked by evaluation by an expert select panel within the brewery.

IV. CONTROL OF PACKAGING OPERATIONS AND MATERIALS

A. Introduction

In this section, a brief description is given of a system for control of packaging operations and also of some methods available for the quality control of major packaging materials.

With greater emphasis on the production and quality of packaged beers, interest in the efficient control of the packaging operation has increased with the speeds of packaging lines. Sampling plans and schedules are necessary in order that a satisfactory degree of control can be effected over a particular operation or series of operations.

Experience with packaging plant quickly indicates where and when the "danger points" of the operation occur. For example, air and oxygen contents are more likely to be high and CO_2 levels low at the commencement of filling than at other times.

With packaged beers it is important to remember that the beer is only part of the package to which quality control must be applied. The customer is exposed to the complete pack: bottle or can, seal, label, carton, etc., and the overall picture is the one that he or she retains.

In this situation of overall quality assessment and control, the roles of those responsible for the control of the packaging operation are very important. As Wren (1976) states, it is much easier to divert defective beer and/or packages or packaging materials before they are combined than after packaging is completed. At the latter stage remedial action is far more difficult and inevitably very costly. As a consequence, in many organizations an apparently disproportionate amount of quality control effort is directed towards packaging operations and packaging materials.

That this effort is warranted is an indication of the complexity of the control measures required in a modern packaging operation utilizing high-speed equipment.

B. Control of Packaging Operations

1. CO_2, Air and Oxygen

On-site testing, particularly for CO_2, dissolved oxygen and air contents, is essential for efficient packaging control. Many plants have packaging quality control laboratories within, or adjacent to, packaging departments. Work carried out in such laboratories must be integrated with the overall situation regarding quality control in the organization; ideally however, someone within, or responsible for, the control function should have authority to stop a packaging line upon the occurrence of out of control or abnormal results.

Quality control limits and product specifications are of considerable value in determining the mode and degree of action to be taken. Limits and specifications must not be too tight as, if they are, there is a tendency for them to be ignored.

Carbonation and general air and oxygen control are of paramount importance. The relevant determinations are dealt with in sections K and L respectively. For packaging control, CO_2 can be measured by a direct-reading pressure method, e.g. with the Zahm-Nagel apparatus or by manometric means. It is possible to remove several bottles or cans from a packaging line, add saturated potassium hydroxide to each and mix the contents in a large container and remove an aliquot for determination of CO_2 by a manometric method.

Garza and Bavisotto (1972) describe an elegant analyser by means of which dissolved oxygen, headspace oxygen and CO_2 can be rapidly and accurately determined. The system, which employs a Hersch oxygen detector, makes use of a modified Zahm-Nagel piercing device.

Another instrument using a Hersch cell is that described by Brandon *et al.* (1972) who state that it gives slightly higher air values than the Zahm-Nagel apparatus.

An earlier automated device, known as "Robair", for determination of headspace gases in carbonated beverages is described by Stutler and Dakin (1963). This apparatus samples packages from a conveyor at predetermined intervals and samples the headspace gases by means of specialized piercing devices and syringes operated by solenoid valves. The gases are transferred automatically to a gas chromatograph for analysis. High air contents can be shown rapidly and corrective action taken.

Headspace samplers of various types and with differing levels of automation have been available from manufacturers for some years. Depending on type they can be coupled to gas chromatographs or to oxygen analysers employing polarographic and galvanic techniques. Sampling chambers of these instruments are usually of low volume, e.g. $0 \cdot 2$ ml and thus sampling is accomplished at pressures which are essentially identical with the headspace pressures in the containers.

2. Total Package Evaluation

A useful control procedure involves sampling, at regular intervals, complete cartons of packages and evaluating all components, including the beer. In this manner, the condition of bottles, crowns, labels, cans, cartons, etc., can be checked and the efficiencies of gluing, coding or dating and general packaging operations noted. A check form for a typical evaluation is given in Fig. 4; such a form can be expanded to include CO_2, air, oxygen figures and other data relative to the beer itself.

3. Volumes and Clarity

In the operation of high-speed packaging lines it is important to have systematic and regular checks of the volume of contents. A range of automatic weighing devices is available, particularly for cans, but these are of limited use for bottles where container weights vary considerably. Equipment for measuring filling height is likewise available but, with the variations normally encountered with bottles, cannot give a completely reliable guide to the

Production date: Time: Type: Size:

Inspection parameter	Results
Carton: Total weight (g) Printing Manufacturing date Date marking Damage Forming Gluing Number correct Extraneous matter Bottles: Type Physical condition Extraneous matter Label placement Label condition Label coding/marking Fill height, mm Crown seals: Manufacturer Shell type Physical condition Crimp diameter Liner type Total volume of 1 doz. bottles (ml) Weight of carton less beer (g) Mean volume of one bottle (ml)	

FIG. 4. Total package evaluation: form for assessing bottles in cartons.

contents of containers. Consequently, measurement of contents by weight or volume is usually necessary to maintain efficient checks.

A schedule involving the sampling from each packaging line of one or two dozen containers at least twice and preferably three or four times per shift has been found to give satisfactory results. Measuring by weighing bottles full and then emptying them, draining and reweighing is used and allowance made for the density of the product in calculating the volume. With aluminium cans a constant weight for the can is assumed and volume calculated. Brimfull volumes can also be ascertained at the same time and the amount of headspace, i.e. brimfull volume − fill volume calculated and expressed as a percentage of the brimfull volume. Again, with cans a constant brimfull or lidded volume can be assumed but not, under normal conditions, with bottles.

The clarity and taste of products ex package should be checked at regular, say hourly, intervals and the results recorded in order that they can be correlated with those from examination of other samples taken before and after packaging. Whilst turbidity meters can be used, inspection in a suitable glass under standard lighting conditions is simple and generally satisfactory.

4. Bottle Washing

Control of the alkalinity of bottle washing solutions is essential and checks should be carried out at least twice daily for efficient operation. Simple titrimetric methods are quick and accurate and can be supplemented by instrumental means if desired. Instruments employing conductivity are common but are subject to varying degrees of interference; some automated sampling devices are also available for automatic or semi-automatic titration methods.

Where additives, such as phosphates and chelating agents, are used it is important to control the concentrations by full analysis of the various washer solutions at least weekly so that the amounts of the additives, as well as the alkalinities of the solutions, may be maintained at optimum levels. Chelating agents based on EDTA or similar compounds can be determined by incremental titration with a standard calcium solution in the presence of ammonium oxalate. Determination of the end-point of the titration by nephelometry is convenient. Washer solutions should be filtered bright, preferably after standing and chilling.

The concentration of phosphate in solutions can be found by application of a modified molybdate procedure following digestion with sulphuric acid and hydrogen peroxide to destroy organic matter. The absorbance of the molybdate complex is read at 650 nm and results expressed in terms of the particular phosphate compound employed. Additives containing sodium gluconate or sodium heptonate are more difficult to assay as methods suited for routine control are not available.

Efficient control of the bottle washing operation, particularly where large proportions of heavily soiled returnable bottles are used, is important and experience has shown that maintenance of total alkalinity alone is not sufficient where additives are employed. The diminution of the concentrations of additives is not always at the same rate as of alkalinity and thus ideal control can frequently be achieved only by control of the individual components of the solution.

The freedom of bottles from caustic "carryover" on leaving a bottle washer can be readily checked by the use of indicator papers or by collecting the wash water drained from a bottle and spotting on a tile with a suitable indicator. Whilst a considerable amount of washer solution must be carried over from the rinse section before any deleterious effect on beer is apparent, any carryover at all is indicative of poor rinsing.

The levels of free chlorine in the final rinse water (if this is chlorinated) should be checked at regular intervals by means of test papers or a simple colorimetric method.

5. Pasteurizing

Tunnel pasteurizers are examples of plant in the operation of which ideal conditions for corrosion exist. It is necessary in most applications to add chemicals to control this and also to control microbiological and algae growth in sprays and elsewhere. Control of corrosion is normally achieved by the addition of corrosion inhibitors such as chromates or phosphates and by maintenance of the pH value of the recirculated water between pH 9 and pH 10. Modern pasteurizers frequently have cathodic protection devices fitted to combat corrosion by introducing a sacrificial component.

It is advisable to check the pH values of pasteurizer waters at regular intervals and adjust additions of chemicals for control of pH accordingly. The levels of corrosion inhibitors can be checked by rapid methods for the analysis of the anions concerned. Quaternary ammonium compounds are often used as algicides in pasteurizers and a suitable method for their determination in pasteurizer waters is one involving titration with a standard solution of an anionic substance (e.g. dioctyl sodium sulphosuccinate) using tetrabromo-fluorescein as an indicator. The basic method is described in A.O.A.C. Methods (1975).

A knowledge of the amount of pasteurization a beer has received is essential in the control of the operations. Some years ago, the concept of pasteurization units (PU) was promoted by Baselt et al. (1954) who defined a PU as the amount of heat received by beer during one minute at 140 °F (60 °C). Other workers, e.g. Scruggs and Baselt (1955) and Powell and Brown (1962), have surveyed the methods for the evaluation of pasteurization and the concept of PU as a means of evaluating pasteurization is well recognized. These workers determined that the mean slope of the thermal death time curve for beer spoilage organisms is 12·5 °F (7 °C). The efficiency of the pasteurization process, carried out at any temperature or range of temperatures, is expressed as the equivalent time at the selected reference point, i.e. at 140 °F (60 °C).

In practice, the effectiveness of treatment at temperatures other than 140 °F is given by the equation

$$\log_{10} t = \frac{140 - T}{12 \cdot 5}$$

where t = time, in minutes, at temperature T in °F equivalent to 1 minute at 140 °F, i.e. 1 PU.

For handling charts from travelling or other recorders the formula can be used to produce a table giving equivalent PU values/minute at all working temperatures and the values thus obtained are summed to obtain the total pasteurization received by the package. In the author's Company, readings in the range 130–150 °F are used; at the lower temperature each minute is equivalent to 0·16 PU and at the upper end of the scale to 6·31 PU. Planimeters and similar devices can also be used to determine the total area under the pasteurization curve and thus arrive at the total PU value.

It is important that all thermometers and recorders are checked regularly for calibration and general performance and that measurements are made at intervals during each production period.

A number of biochemical and biological methods for the evaluation of pasteurization have been described in the past and some of these are reviewed by Haas and Fleischman (1956) who also give details of a method dependent upon the determination of the enzyme invertase. These workers correlated the destruction of invertase with the PUs received by the beer and concluded that an appreciable amount of enzyme was destroyed at the same levels of pasteurization necessary for the destruction of microorganisms. For example, 100% destruction of the enzyme occurred at between 5·5 and 6 PU, a level found to be adequate for complete pasteurization and one corresponding to the level of 5·6 PU stated by Scruggs and Baselt (1955) to be sufficient for beers with extremely high bacterial populations.

The procedure of Haas and Fleischman depends upon the measurement of the amount of sucrose split into fructose and glucose by the enzyme. The concentration of reducing sugar is determined by the Somogyi–Nelson technique as described by Somogyi (1945). Degassed beer is used and the complete determination takes less than 2 hours.

The invertase test is the basis of a number of "go/no-go" procedures for checking the efficiency of pasteurization. One such method, based on a procedure described by Stutzel (1953), involves mixing 20 ml beer with 20 ml of 20% sucrose solution and heating to 55 °C for 60 minutes. A blank in which beer is heated above 55 °C before mixing with the sucrose solution serves as a comparison. After holding at 55 °C both assay and blank are cooled and 1 ml aliquots mixed with 5 ml Fehling's solution. No decolorization of the Fehling's solution in either indicates that the invertase has been inactivated and pasteurization achieved.

The introduction of membrane filtration as a laboratory technique has greatly increased the sensitivity of microbiological methods for pasteurization control. It is usual to pass 100 ml beer through a suitable membrane and to incubate the membrane on selective media. Growth of viable yeasts will be indicated in 36–48 hours but that of some bacteria, e.g. lactobacilli will not show in this time. As staining of microorganisms on the membrane is not always satisfactory, the technique depends on incubation to achieve reliable results. Thus rapid results are not readily obtained but the procedure, in various forms, is widely used in the monitoring of aseptic filling operations in particular.

6. Miscellaneous

Obviously many other checks and analytical procedures are used in control of packaging operations and the range and scope of such will depend on the packages produced and other circumstances. Checks that may be necessary include the detection and determination of various trace metals, grease, oil or other contaminants and the presence of foregin materials such as paint flakes, glass particles, paper fibres and similar matter. Methods for some of the latter are mentioned in section II.W.3.

C. Control of Packaging Materials

1. Bottles

Much has been written on the necessity for rigid quality control as applied to beer bottles and several well recognized industry specifications, which include details of methods, are in existence. One of these, published by the United States Brewers Association Inc. (1972a) gives considerable detail and is valuable for in-brewery control. Various sampling plans for control of incoming bottles are in use; one found to be useful depends upon the receipt of advance samples representative of the production from a particular plant, a shift or some other period. It is convenient to take a portion of the advance sample for various physical tests and measurements and to use the remainder for in-plant evaluation, particularly the assessment of breakage.

Table 7 lists the test method recommended in the U.S. Brewers Association specification and some additional useful checks. A report of the A.S.B.C. Sub-Committee on Bottle Testing (1950) recommends a range of procedures and discusses many in detail.

Apart from physical measurements, such as height, body diameter, crown ring diameter, and weight and capacity, it is usually sufficient to check glass colour and thickness, hydrostatic bursting pressure and thermal shock.

The two latter determinations are best made by standard procedures such as those of the American Society for Testing Materials (1965); methods C-147-69 and C-147-65 deal with these parameters. Method C-147-65 for thermal shock specifies a differential of 75 °F from cold to hot for the first immersion. However, experience in the author's Company has shown that a differential of 85 °F sometimes gives better correlation with performance in the plant.

A suitable rapid-weighing balance is used for bottle weight and dial or other gauges employed for physical measurements. Capacities at fill-point and

Table 7. Bottle test methods

Parameter	Method or reference
Dimensions:	
Height	Standard gauge
Outside diameter	Calipers or comparator
Locking (crown) ring diameter	Dial or go/no-go gauges
Reinforcing ring diameter	Dial or go/no-go gauges
Width of locking ring	Dial gauge
Throat diameter	Plug go/no-go gauges
Weight	Balance to 0·1 g
Capacity:	
Overflow (brimfull)	Balance to 0·1 g
Fill point (fill height)	Balance to 0·5 g
Internal pressure (hydrostatic bursting pressure)	ASTM C-147-69 (1969)
Thermal shock	ASTM C-149-65 (1965)
Colour	A.S.B.C. (1950, 1964)
Out of perpendicular	Gauge
Quality	Gauge
Glass distribution (wall thickness)	Micrometer
Surface protective coatings	
Lubricity	USBA (1972a)
Coating strength	USBA (1972a)
Annealing	ASTM C-148-65 (1965)

brimfull (overflow) can be determined by weighing with water or, less accurately, by volumetric means. Glass colour is determined by measuring the absorbance of a piece of suitable size which can be selected from pieces obtained from the hydrostatic bursting pressure test. The thickness of the piece of glass used for the measurement of colour is measured at two or three places and the absorbance measured at 550 nm and calculated to a thickness of 0·125 in. (3·2 mm). The absorbance at 0·125 in. is then converted to per cent transmission as this parameter is usually quoted in specifications.

Details of non-destructive procedures for colour are given by Nissen and Ulbricht (1950) and Gamer et al. (1964). For rapid "go/no-go" checks standard bottles representing the upper and lower limits of the agreed colour range can be used and are frequently available from manufacturers. Bottles should be viewed by transmitted light.

An example of a report for bottle testing data is given in Fig. 5. Acceptable quality levels (AQL) are frequently agreed between bottle manufacturer and bottler and exchange of data and good liaison between the two parties are desirable. The control of bottles, and of all other packaging materials, has become of increasing importance as speeds of packaging have increased; this aspect of quality control and quality assurance in brewing operations is now

Type..   Date manufactured..............................
Physical testing .... doz.   Date received.......................................
Thermal testing .... doz.   Code no...
Total quantity received .... doz.

QUALITY CONTROL TESTING STATISTICS

Variate	No. tested	Range	Mean	Over limits	Under limits	Control limits
Weight (g)						611–645
Height (cm)						27·71–28·02
Body diameter (cm)						8·090–8·412
Crown ring diameter (cm)						2·636–2·700
Volume at S.F.H.† (ml)						740 min.
Brimful volume (ml)						760·9–778·6
Bursting pressure (kPa)						1200
Colour (%T)						22–32
Thermal shock (%)						2 max.
Wall thickness (mm)						

† Standard fill height.

FIG. 5. Quality control of bottles: advance sample report.

well recognized and must obviously occupy an important place in any scheme of overall control, as mentioned earlier.

2. Cans and Can Ends

The purchase specifications for cans, used by the U.S. Brewers Association (1969), include several test methods and the specifications given by various manufacturers frequently contain details of additional tests. Liaison between can manufacturers and users has resulted in the acceptance of procedures for examining all aspects of can quality.

Advance samples of both can bodies and can ends are often requested by the canner and subjected to routine examination. Checks for physical dimensions, lithography, metal exposure and damage are obviously important but in recent years considerable emphasis has been placed on the detection of traces of solvents remaining from the can lining process. A simple sniff test of bodies and ends is valuable as a screening procedure, but more complicated techniques are sometimes necessary to ensure that adequate quality control is maintained.

Beer can linings are discussed in general by Glasen (1971) who describes some of the sources of possible contamination other than residual solvent that may be found in cans. Work carried out under the auspices of the A.S.B.C. Sub-Committee on Application of Gas–Liquid Chromatography to Analytical Problems in Brewing Chemistry (1974, 1975) show that consistent agreement between laboratories for a GLC method based on that of Colberg and Shapiro (1969) is not readily achieved. Bruchner *et al.* (1972) and Charalambous *et al.* (1973) describe the use of infrared reflectance and thermal analysis for the rapid identification of can linings and for the determination of the degree of cure. Their results, supplemented by data obtained by GLC using procedures described by Charalambous and Hardwick (1970, 1971), show that correlations exist between the information thus obtained and organoleptic evaluations of the beers concerned.

A relatively simple GLC technique for use in packaging quality control and similar laboratories is described by Garza and Bavisotto (1972) and some aspects of this method were adopted by the A.S.B.C. Sub-Committee when modifying the procedure of Colberg and Shapiro. The method gives excellent linear response and sensitivity for a number of solvents, including methylethyl ketone, methylisobutyl ketone, toluene, butanol, xylene, cyclohexanone and diacetone alcohol. Other solvents and mixtures thereof are known to be used in the manufacture of can bodies and ends; a similar GLC method for some of these, e.g. hexane and end "repair" lacquer, is useful for their detection, and has been used in the author's laboratory with success.

When considering the quality control of can bodies and ends, as with other packaging materials, emphasis must be placed on those aspects which may cause critical or major defects. These will vary from case to case and, frequently, unfortunately only become evident with experience with the product. More effort may be required at some periods on particular attributes than at others but the value of thorough visual examination of incoming samples cannot be too highly stressed nor can the value of close liaison between canner and manufacturer.

A check sheet for the examination of can bodies could include decoration, surface contamination, lining condition, metal exposure, flange condition, flange width, bottom end varnish and mechanical damage. Checks on ends might cover compound placement and condition, flange condition, solvent residues, and evaluation of the ring-pull and other opening devices.

The A.S.B.C. (1967) bath test, as devised for crown seal testing, can be used for the determination of gas retention of seamed cans and other abuse tests have been devised in various laboratories. An impact drop test, originally designed to test ecology ("pop-top") ends, is shown in Fig. 6. Cans are heated to various temperatures and then dropped vertically, seam-end first, onto a steel plate at the bottom of the apparatus.

Comparisons between types of ends are possible by noting the incidences of leaking cans obtained at standard temperatures.

3. Cartons

Standard methods for testing cartons, carton blanks and board are available from a number of sources and the extent of their use will depend on circumstances. Variations in moisture content can cause difficulties in gluing and departures from specification in respect to board weight, flap and other dimensions, scoring, etc. are obviously undesirable.

Equipment such as the Hinde and Dauche Crush Tester is available for the determination of flat crush resistance, an important parameter in carton performance. Gauges and templates can be used for physical dimensions.

Checks on the following have been found to be useful in control of cartons:

Basic weight of board—thickness of board
Scoring of board
Internal dimensions
Ply adhesion
Flap dimensions
Moisture
Flat crush resistance
Tape placement
Lithography

Not all the above checks are applicable always to all cartons or blanks; other checks could be necessary for control of new and differing types of pack.

FIG. 6. Impact tester for cans with ecology ends.

4. Crown Seals and other Closures

Purchase specifications, recommended by the brewing industry and containing details of testing methods, are available for crown seals and other closures. That of the U.S. Brewers Association (1972b) can be used as the basis for procedures for testing cork-lined and plastic-lined crown seals, pilfer-proof aluminium closures and convenience two-way crowns. The test methods stated and those considered desirable for further evaluation are given in Table 8.

Pope and Hulse (1970) describe procedures based on some of the U.S. Brewers Association methods and in addition give details of measurement of the weight and density of plastic (PVC) liners. The latter tests are of value in

Table 8. Crown seal test methods and references

Parameter	Method of reference
Internal pressure (instant pressure)	
cold	USBA (1972b)
hot	
Gas retention	USBA (1972b), A.S.B.C. (1967)
Dimensions:	
Height	Micrometer
Radius	Gauge
Inside diameter	Calipers
Outside diameter	Calipers
Thickness	Micrometer
Knee angle	Gauge (Pope and Hulse 1970)
Tinplate:	
Coating weight	ASTM A-623-68 (1968)
Base weight	ASTM A-623-68 (1968)
Temper—hardness	Rockwell 30 T scale
Lithography:	
Rust resistance	Empirical
Resistance to pasteurization	USBA (1972b)
Removal torque	Torque-test meter or similar
Liner (PVC) weight	Balance
Liner (PVC) density	Balance

the evaluation of crowns with flowed-in plastic liners as these crowns do not always have the margin of safety with regard to pressure retention found with cork-lined crowns.

Control of the weight and tensile strength of tin plate used in the manufacture of crowns is also important as is the conformance of the shell of the crown. For the latter, specification and measurement of the knee angle, as suggested by Pope and Hulse is useful.

Standard bottle necks, fabricated in stainless steel or glass, are essential for the evaluation of the performance of crowns and other closures as discussed in the U.S. Brewers Association specifications. Close collaboration between closure manufacturers, bottlers and suppliers of lining compounds has resulted in the evolution of practical testing procedures in a number of countries. Regular inter-laboratory checks should be carried out to ensure that comparable results are obtained on all testing equipment.

Experience has shown that if closures give instant (internal) pressure values significantly lower than pre-determined or specification values, poor performance in the plant and field may follow.

Abuse tests for closures are useful in some applications but attempts to standardize them have met with little success as shown by a report from the A.S.B.C. Sub-Committee on Evaluation of Packages and Packaging Materials (1972). However, many bottlers do have abuse procedures which give valuable information relative to performance of closures under the conditions encountered in their particular markets. For example, simple stacking tests involving placing pallets of full cartons four or five high for a long storage period will often show weaknesses in closures or other packaging materials. Single bottles, cartons or even pallets of bottles in cartons can be rocked or otherwise agitated in a manner to simulate transport conditions to highlight defects. Test loads can be sent to distant destinations and returned for detailed examination of the total package by means as described in section IV.B.2.

Measurement of the torque required to remove twist-off or convenience crowns is useful and several instruments are available for this purpose. In many plants, torque measurements are used on standard crowns although a simple apparatus can be constructed (see Fig. 7) to measure the force required to remove a standard lift-off crown under controlled conditions.

In the author's Company, it has been found that regular measurement of instant (internal) pressure at room temperature on steel necks is a most useful check. With the examination for lithographic faults and occasional checks on liner density and weight and knee angle of the shell, this procedure makes up a routine control procedure on advance samples of crowns. Sampling is usually carried out in conformance with a mutually agreed plan and very low sampling rates have been found to be effective, as mentioned by Harvey (1976).

Some manufacturers provide Referee Acceptance Sampling Schemes which incorporate inspection for both minor and major defects. A typical scheme is designed to accept consignments of crowns with 1% or less of major defects and 10% or less of minor defects. Close liaison between manufacturer and user ensures that agreed sampling and inspection methods are used and samples are provided well ahead of delivery. The acceptable quality limit (AQL) used in these and other schemes is subject to mutual agreement between parties.

Considerable importance is placed on the maintenance of optimum crimp diameters for the pack and plant concerned. Simple "go/no-go" gauges are used to provide on-line checks, which should be made at regular intervals. Test methods usually specify ranges of crimp diameters for certain determinations and these must be adhered to in order to obtain accurate results.

The resistance of crowns to the conditions occurring during pasteurization is of interest and an objective procedure for measuring this is given in the U.S. Brewers Association specifications. This involves immersing the crimped crowns in a weak (250 mg/l) solution of sodium hydroxide at 71 °C (160 °F) for 20 minutes after which they are examined for damage to lithography. A test for resistance to rusting is also of value.

FIG. 7. Simple device for evaluating sealing efficiency of lift-off crown seals.

5. Miscellaneous Materials

Many other packaging materials are not mentioned in the foregoing, and control of their quality can be vital in the packaging operation.

Adhesives, shrink-wrap film, cluster packs and trays and similar materials require evaluation and methods exist in most cases for testing. Modern adhesives, e.g. hot-melt types, should be checked for heat stability, compatability for mixing with other grades, density and softening point. An A.S.T.M. method E-28-67 is applicable to the latter.

PVA and dextrin adhesives require other checks and one that has been given attention is the determination of label removal conditions in order to achieve a reasonable degree of "ice-proofing" whilst retaining easy removal during bottle washing. Compatibility of adhesives with rubber and other components of labelling machines is also important.

Standard methods can be used for the evaluation of shrink-wrap film and other checks, when film is used for bottles, should include an evaluation of resistance to sunlight.

Many methods for the evaluation of packaging meterials evolve through discussion between supplier and user in solving mutual problems. Occasionally, standard methods have been prepared for other industries or other applications. Sometimes industry groups are set up to examine specific problems and from such examinations come tentative methods which are in turn evaluated by collaborative work.

6. Conclusion

The author is of the opinion that there is considerable scope for increased collaborative work, possibly on an international basis, in connection with the evaluation of packaging materials. It is to be hoped that, in spite of the difficulties involved, such work can eventually be undertaken on a basis similar to that now successfully employed by E.B.C., A.S.B.C. and others in connection with methods for the analysis of beer and organoleptic techniques.

The application of standardized suppliers' quality control systems, such as that outlined in Australian Standards 1821–1823 (1975), can be of great assistance in achieving improved quality control and quality assurance of packaging materials. Close liaison between supplier and user, as mentioned elsewhere, is essential as is the ability for the user, or his representative, to inspect the suppliers' manufacturing and control facilities.

ACKNOWLEDGEMENTS

The author's grateful thanks are due to his colleagues at The South Australian Brewing Company Limited, particularly to Messrs R. L. Taeuber, N. H. Pope and C. J. Hulse for help with the manuscript and illustrations and for valuable advice.

Varian Techtron Pty. Ltd. are thanked for permission to quote from their publication "Analytical Methods for Flame Spectroscopy" and to reproduce matter therefrom.

Drs. G. A. Howard and J. D. R. Mawer are thanked for permission to refer to an interim report, prepared for the E.B.C. Analysis Committee, on the measurement of dissolved oxygen in beer.

The encouragement and assistance of the late Dr. R. P. Hildebrand of Carlton and United Breweries Limited, Melbourne, and of Dr. J. R. Hudson,

Acting Director of the Brewing Research Foundation, Surrey, are gratefully acknowledged as is the typing work of Mrs. M. K. Ellis and Mrs. V. Engel.

Finally, the author thanks the Board of Directors of the South Australian Brewing Company Ltd., and, in particular, the Managing Director, Mr. L. C. Mills, for permission to contribute this Chapter.

REFERENCES

American Society for Testing Materials (1965). "Standard Methods of Test". The Society, Philadelphia.

American Society of Brewing Chemists (1975). "Methods of Analysis", 7th Revised Edition. A.S.B.C., St. Paul, Minn.

American Society of Brewing Chemists,

(1967). Report of the Subcommittee on Evaluation of Packages and Packaging Materials. Proc. 266.

(1971). Report of the Subcommittee on the Estimation of n-Heptyl p-Hydroxybenzoate. Proc. 343.

(1971). Report of the Subcommittee on Gallotannins in Beer. Proc. 348.

(1972). Report of the Subcommittee on the Application of Atomic Absorption Spectroscopy to Analytical Problems in Brewing Chemistry. Proc. 133.

(1972). Report of the Subcommittee on the Estimation of n-Heptyl p-Hydroxybenzoate. Proc. 163.

(1972). Report of the Subcommittee on Evaluation of Packages and Packaging Materials. Proc. 147.

(1973). Report of the Subcommittee on the Application of Atomic Absorption Spectroscopy to Analytical Problems in Brewing Chemistry. Proc. 160.

(1973). Report of the Subcommittee on Gallotannins in Beer. Proc. 176.

(1974). Report of the Subcommittee on the Application of Atomic Absorption Spectroscopy to Analytical Problems in Brewing Chemistry. Proc. 32.

(1975). Report of the Subcommittee on the Analysis of Dissolved Oxygen in Water, Wort and Beer, Proc. 93.

(1975). Report of the Subcommittee on Free Amino Nitrogen in Beer. Proc. 88.

(1976). Report of the Subcommittee on Coordination of New and Alternate Methods of Analysis. Journal, **34**, 92.

(1976). Report of the Subcommittee on Determination of Oxalate in Beer. Journal **34**, 111.

Amerine, M. A. and Ough, C. S. (1974). "Wine and Must Analysis". John Wiley, New York.

Amerine, M. A., Pangborn, R. M. and Roessler, E. B. (1965). "Principles of Sensory Evaluation of Food". Academic Press, New York and London.

Andrews, J. and Harrison, G. A. F. (1954). *J. Inst. Brew.* **60**, 133.

Andrews, J., Harrison, G. A. F. and Pierce, J. S. (1953). *J. Inst. Brew.* **59**, 293.

Andrews, J. and Lloyd, R. O. V. (1951). *J. Inst. Brew.* **57**, 268.

Andrews, J. and Stringer, W. J. (1953). *J. Inst. Brew.* **59**, 52.

Anonymous (1975). *Brewers' Digest* **50**, (8), 38.

Arkima, V. (1973). *J. Inst. Brew* **79**, 81.

Ashurst, P. R. (1963). *J. Inst. Brew.* **69**, 457.

Ashurst, P. R. and MacWilliam, I. C. (1963). *J. Inst. Brew.* **69**, 394.

Association of Official Analytical Chemists (1975). "Official and Tentative Methods of Analysis", 12th edition. Washington, D.C.

Ault, R. G. and Whitehouse, A. G. R. (1952). *J. Inst. Brew.* **58**, 136.

Baetz, R. A. and Kenner, C. T. (1975). *J. Agric. Food Chem.* **23**, 41.

Barrett, D. J. (1975). *CSIRO Food Res. Quart.* **35**, 68.

Barwald, G. and Prucha, J. (1971). *Brauwissenschaft* **24**, 397.

Baselt, F. C., Dayharsh, C. A. and Del Vecchio, H. W. (1954). *Proc. Am. Soc. Brew. Chem.* p. 141.

Bateson, J. B. and Leach, A. A. (1969). *Proc. E.B.C. Congr., Interlaken* p. 161.

Bayles, P. F., Brown, D. G. W. and Martin, P. A. (1968). *Proc. Am. Soc. Brew. Chem.* p. 21.

Belleau, G., Buday, A. Z. and Van Gheluwe, J. E. A. (1970). *Proc. Am. Soc. Brew. Chem.* p. 18.

Belleau, G. and Dadic, M. (1974). *Proc. Am. Soc. Brew. Chem.* p. 5.

Bengsston, K. (1953). *Wallerstein Lab. Commun.* **16**, 231.

Bennett, A. and Hudson, J. R. (1953). *J. Inst. Brew.* **59**, 137.

Bernstein, L. and Khan, A. (1973). *Proc. Am. Soc. Brew. Chem.* p. 30.

Bernstein, L. (1974). *Tech. Quart. Master Brewers Ass. Am.* **11**, 198.

Bicking, C. A. (1969). *Proc. Int. Conf. Qual. Control* p. 673.

Bishop, L. R. (1944). *J. Inst. Brew.* **50**, 244.

Bishop, L. R. (1972). *J. Inst. Brew.* **78**, 37.

Bishop, L. R. and Kloss, C. A. (1953). *J. Inst. Brew.* **59**, 213.

Bishop, L. R., Whitear, A. L. and Inman, W. R. (1975). *J. Inst. Brew.* **81**, 131.

Blom, J. (1937). *J. Inst. Brew.* **43**, 251.

Blom, J. (1957). *Proc. E.B.C. Congr., Copenhagen* p. 51.

Bowen, J. J. M. (1972). *Analyst* **97**, 1003.

Brandon, A. L. (1964). "Technicon International Symposium", Technicon Ardsley (Chauncey), N.Y.

Brandon, A. L. (1967). *Brewers' Digest* **42** (4), 96.

Brandon, A. L. (1968). *Proc. Am. Soc. Brew. Chem.* p. 10.

Brandon, A. L., Spence, L. R., Matthews, F. C., Palamand, S. R. and Hersch, P. A. (1972). *Tech. Quart. Master Brewers Ass. Am.* **9**, 105.

Breen, M. A. and Woodward, J. D. (1975). *J. Inst. Brew.* **81**, 307.

Brenner, M. W. and Laufer, L. (1972). *Proc. Am. Soc. Brew. Chem.* p. 98.

Brenner, M. W. and Khan, A. A. (1974). *J. Inst. Brew.* **80**, 54.

Brenner, M. W. and Khan, A. A. (1976). *J. Am. Soc. Brew. Chem.* **34**, 14.

Brenner, M. W., Blick, S. R., Frenkel, G. and Siebenberg, J. (1963). *Proc. E.B.C. Congr., Brussels* p. 233.

Brenner, M. W., Dayharsh, C. A. and Blenkinship, B. K. (1967). *Proc. Am. Soc. Brew. Chem.* p. 215.

Brenner, M. W., McCully, R. E. and Laufer, S. (1951). *Am. Brewer* **84**, 2, 39.

Brenner, M. W., Owades, J. L. and Golyzniak, R. (1953). *Proc. Am. Soc. Brew. Chem.* p. 83.

Brenner, M. W., Owades, J. L. and Golyzniak, R. (1954). *Proc. Am. Soc. Brew. Chem.* p. 81.

Brenner, M. W., Owades, J. L., Gutcho, M. and Golyzniak, R. (1954). *Proc. Am. Soc. Brew. Chem.* p. 88.

Brenner, M. W., Owades, J. L. and Fazio, T. (1955). *Proc. Am. Soc. Brew. Chem.* p. 125.

Brenner, M. W., Vigilante, C. and Owades, J. L. (1956). *Am. Brewer* **89**, 12, 40.

"British Pharmacopoeia" (1968). The Pharmaceutical Press, London, p. 1242.

British Standards Institution (1968). B.S. 4404 Method for the determination of arsenic (silver diethyldithlocarbamate procedure) (SBN : 580 00451 1).

Brobst, K. M. and Lott, C. E. (1965). *Cereal Chem.* **43**, 35.

Brown, D. G. W., Clapperton, J. F. and Dalgleish, C. E. (1974). *Proc. Am. Soc. Brew. Chem.* p. 1.

Bruckner, K. J., Charalambous, G. and Hardwick, W. A. (1972). *Tech. Quart., Master Brewers Ass. Am.* **9**, 47.

Buckee, G. K. (1972). *J. Inst. Brew.* **78**, 222.

Buckee, G. K. (1973). *J. Inst. Brew.* **79**, 261.

Buckee, G. K. (1974). *J. Inst. Brew.* **80**, 291.

Buckee, G. K. (1975). *J. Sci. Food Agric.* **26**, 557.

Buckee, G. K. and Hargit, R. (1976). *J. Inst. Brew.* **82**, 290.

Buckee, G. K. and Hickman, E. (1975). *J. Inst. Brew.* **81**, 399.

Buckee, G. K., Dolezil, L., Forrest, I. S. and Hickman, E. (1976). *J. Inst. Brew.* **82**, 209.

Buckee, G. K., Hickman, E. and Brown, D. G. W. (1974). *J. Inst. Brew.* **80**, 379.

Buday, A. Z., Belleau, G. and Van Gheluwe, G. (1972). *Proc. Am. Soc. Brew. Chem.* p. 56.

Burger, M. and Becker, K. (1949). *Proc. Am. Soc. Brew. Chem.* p. 102.

Byers, J. and Gray, P. P. (1953). *Wallerstein Lab. Commun.* **16**, 303.

Cairncross, S. E. and Sjostrom, L. B. (1950). *Food Technol.* **4**, 308.

Canales, A. M. and Cantu, R. G. (1974). *Tech. Quart., Master Brewers Ass. Am.* **11**, 17.

Canales, A. M., De Banchs, N. M. and Garzat, L. I. (1970). *Proc. Am. Soc. Brew. Chem.* p. 75.

Case, A. E. (1938). *J. Inst. Brew.* **44**, 362.

Challot, B., Blondot, P., Deymig, B. and Urion, E. (1967). *Proc. E.B.C. Congr., Madrid* p. 433.

Chapon, L. and Chemardin, M. (1967). *Proc. E.B.C. Congr., Madrid* p. 389.

Chapon, L., Louis, C. and Chapon, S. (1971). *Proc. E.B.C. Congr., Estoril* p. 307.

Charalambous, G. and Hardwick, W. A. (1970). *Tech. Quart., Master Brewers Ass. Am.* **7**, 55.

Charalambous, G. and Hardwick, W. A. (1971). *Tech. Quart., Master Brewers Ass. Am.* **8**, 21.

Charalambous, G. Bruckner, K. J. and Hardwick, W. A. (1973). *Tech. Quart., Master Brewers Ass. Am.*, **10**, 32.

Charalambous, G., Bruchner, K. J., Hardwick, W. A. and Linneloch, A. (1973). *Tech. Quart., Master Brewers Ass. Am.* **10**, 74.

Chemical Society (1975). Analytical Methods Committee. *Analyst* **100**, 54.

Clapperton, J. F. (1973a). *J. Inst. Brew.* **79**, 83.

Clapperton, J. F. (1973b). *J. Inst. Brew.* **79**, 495.

Clapperton, J. F. (1974). *J. Inst. Brew.* **80**, 164.

Clapperton, J. F., Dalgleish, C. E. and Meilgaard, M. C. (1976). *J. Inst. Brew.* **82**, 7.

Clark, L. C., Wolf, R., Granger, D. and Taylor, Z. (1953). *J. Applied Physiol.* **6**, 189.

Clark, R. V. B. (1942). *Wallerstein Lab. Commun.* **5**, 43.

Cloninger, M. R., Baldwin, R. E. and Krause, G. F. (1976). *J. Food Sci.* **41**, 1225.

Clydesdale, F. M. (1973). *Brewers' Digest* **48** (10), 46.

Colberg, K. H. and Shapiro, R. (1969). *Proc. Am. Soc. Brew. Chem.* p. 149.

Cooper, A. H., Hudson, J. R. and MacWilliam, I. C. (1961). *J. Inst. Brew.* **67**, 432.

Coote, N. and Kirsop, B. H. (1974). *J. Inst. Brew.* **80**, 474.

Curtis, N. S. (1966). *J. Inst. Brew.* **72**, 240.

Curtis, N. S. (1975). *J. Inst. Brew.* **81**, 391.

Cuzner, J., Marinelli, L. and Rehberger, A. J. (1970). *Proc. Am. Soc. Brew. Chem.* p. 102.
Cuzner, J., Bayne, P. D. and Rehberger, A. J. (1971). *Proc. Am. Soc. Brew. Chem.* p. 116.
Dadic, M. (1971). *Proc. Am. Soc. Brew. Chem.* p. 159.
Dadic, M. (1975). *Brewers' Digest* **50** (4), 54.
Dadic, M. (1976). *Brewers' Digest* **51** (4), 38.
Dadic, M. and Van Gheluwe, G. (1973). *Tech. Quart., Master Brewers Ass. Am.* **10**, 69.
Dallos, F. C., Lautenbach, A. F. and West, D. W. (1967). *Proc. Am. Soc. Brew. Chem.* p. 103.
Dawson, E. H., Brogdon, J. L. and McManus, S. (1963). *Food Technol.* **17** (9), 45; **17** (10), 39.
de Brune, P., Cremer, J., Dorrenboom, J. J. and White, J. H. M. (1974). *Tech. Quart., Master Brewers Ass. Am.* **11**, 286.
de Clerck, J. (1958). "A Textbook of Brewing", Vol. 2, p. 453. Chapman and Hall, London.
de Clerck, J. and de Djicker, G. (1957a). *Brauwelt* **97**, 700.
de Clerck, J. and de Djicker, G. (1957b) *Proc. E.B.C. Congr., Copenhagen* p. 43.
de Clerck, J. and Jerumanis, J. (1967). *Bull. Ass. Ec. Brass., Louvain* **63**, 137.
de Clerck, J. and Van Cauwenberge, H. (1957). *Wallerstein Lab. Commun.* **20**, 255.
Dellweg, H., John, M. and Trenel, G. (1970). *Proc. Am. Soc. Brew. Chem.* p. 154.
Drews, R., Barwald, G. and Niefind, H. J. (1969). *Proc. E.B.C. Congr., Interlaken* p. 419.
Einstein, M. A. (1974). *Tech. Quart., Master Brewers Ass. Am.* **11**, 94.
Eeckhaut, R. G. (1971). *Fermentatio* p. 7.
Enebo, L. (1957). *Proc. E.B.C. Congr., Copenhagen* p. 370.
Engan, S. (1971). *Brygmesteren* **28**, 191.
Engan, S. (1975). *Brygmesteren* **32**, 107.
European Brewery Convention (1975). "Analytica—E.B.C." 3rd edition. Schweizer Brauerei-Rundschau, Zurich.
European Brewery Convention: Analysis Committee (1976). *J. Inst. Brew.* **82**, 253.
European Brewery Convention.
(1968). Haze and Foam Group. *J. Inst. Brew.* **74**, 330.
(1970). Haze and Foam Group. *Tech. Quart., Master Brewers Ass.* **7**, 193.
(1975). Haze and Foam Group. *Proc. E.B.C. Congr., Nice* p. 715.
FAO/WHO Codex Alimentarious Commission (1969). "Sampling Plans for Prepackaged Foods (AQL 6.5)" Rome.
Feldman, F. J. and Purdy, W. C. (1965). *Anal. Chim. Acta* **33**, 273.
Fisher, A. (1972). *J. Inst. Brew.* **78**, 407.
Gales, P. W. (1976). *J. Am. Soc. Brew. Chem.* **34**, 123.
Gamache, L. D. (1968). *Proc. Am. Soc. Brew. Chem.* p. 120.
Gamer, L. S., Sanders, W. H. and Anderson, J. L., (1964). *Proc. Am. Soc. Brew. Chem.* p. 183.
Garza, A.C. and Bavisotto, V. S. (1972). *Proc. Am. Soc. Brew. Chem.* p. 104.
Gegiou, D. and Botsvali, M. (1975). *Analyst* **100**, 234.
Gjertsen, P. (1955). *Proc. E.B.C. Congr., Baden-Baden* p. 37.
Gjertsen, P., Undstrup, S. and Trolle, B. (1964). *Monats. Brau.* **17**, 232.
Glaser, M. A. (1971). *Tech. Quart., Master Brewers Ass. Am.* **8**, 160.
Glenister, P. R. (1974). *Proc. Am. Soc. Brew. Chem.* p. 11.
Glenister, P. R. (1975). "Beer Deposits—A Laboratory Guide and Pictorial Atlas." J. E. Siebel Sons Co., Chicago, Ill.
Goldberg, L. and Rydberg, U. (1966). *In* "Automation in Analytical Chemistry, 1965", p. 595. Technicon Symposia, Mediad Inc., New York.

Goodall, H. and Colquhoun, J. M. (1967). "Sensory Testing of Flavour and Aroma." The British Food Manufacturing Industries Research Association, Leatherhead, Surrey.

Gramshaw, J. W. (1969). *Tech. Quart., Master Brewers Ass. Am.* **6**, 239.

Gray, P. P. and Stone, I. (1939). *Wallerstein Lab. Commun.* **2**, 5.

Grigsby, J. H. and Palamand, S. R. (1976). *J. Am. Soc. Brew. Chem.* **34**, 49.

Gruss, R., Kleber, K. and Zurcher, C. (1975). *Monats. Brau.* **28**, 293.

Haas, G. J. and Fleischman, A. I. (1956). *Proc. Am. Soc. Brew. Chem.* p. 62.

Hall, R. D. (1956). *J. Inst. Brew.* **62**, 222.

Hansen, G. L. and Ramos, E. S. (1971). *Proc. Am. Soc. Brew. Chem.* p. 255.

Harold, F. V. and Szobolotzky, E. J. (1963). *J. Inst. Brew.* **69**, 253.

Harold, F. V., Hildebrand, R. P., Morieson, A. S. and Murray, P. J. (1961). *J. Inst. Brew.* **67**, 12.

Harold, F. V., Morieson, A. S. and Szobolotzky, E. J. (1962). *J. Inst. Brew.* **68**, 74.

Harris, G. and Ricketts, R. W. (1958). *J. Inst. Brew.* **65**, 331.

Harrison, G. A. F., Byrne, W. J. and Collins, E. (1965). *J. Inst. Brew.* **71**, 336.

Harvey, J. V. (1976). *Aust. Wine Brew. Spirit Rev.* **94**, 32.

Harvey, J. V. and Pope, N. H. (1962). *Proc. Conv. Aust. Sec. Inst. Brew.* p. 69.

Hashimoto, N. (1968). *Rep. Res. Lab. Kirin Brewing Co., Yokahama* **11**, 57.

Hashimoto, N. and Kuroiwa, Y. (1966). *Rep. Res. Lab. Kirin Brewing Co., Yokahama* **9**, 1.

Havlicek, J. and Samuelson, O. (1975). *J. Inst. Brew.* **81**, 466.

Heard, B. T. (1973). *J. Inst. Brew.* **79**, 371.

Helm, E. and Rickardt, O. C. (1936). *J. Inst. Brew.* **42**, 191.

Hemmens, W. F. (1975). *Proc. E.B.C. Congr., Nice* p. 439.

Hersch, P. A. (1973). *Am. Lab.* (August) p. 29.

Hildebrand, R. P. (1975). Private communication.

Hoff, J. T. and Herwig, W. C. (1976). *J. Am. Soc. Brew. Chem.* **34**, 1.

Hohn, K. and Issing, R. (1971). *Brauwissenschaft* **24**, 37.

Hough, J. S., Briggs, D. E. and Stevens, R. (1971). "Malting and Brewing Science". Chapman and Hall, London.

Howard, G. A. and Mawer, J. D. R. (1976). Private communication.

Hudson, J. R. (1959). *J. Inst. Brew.* **65**, 321.

Hudson, J. R. (1976). *Brewers Guardian* **105**, 41.

Hurst, R. E. (1974). *Analyst* **99**, 302.

Hurst, R. O. (1964). *Canad. J. Biochem.* **42**, 287.

Inoue, T. and Yamamoto, Y. (1970). *Rep. Res. Lab. Kirin Brewing Co., Yokahama*, **13**, 171.

Institute of Brewing (1971). "Recommended Methods of Analysis". *J. Inst. Brew.* **77**, 181.

Institute of Brewing.
   (1953). Analysis Committee. *J. Inst. Brew.* **59**, 136.
   (1971). Analysis Committee. *J. Inst. Brew.* **77**, 365.
   (1974). Analysis Committee. *J. Inst. Brew.* **80**, 486.
   (1975). Analysis Committee. *J. Inst. Brew.* **79**, 289.
   (1975a). Analysis Committee. *J. Inst. Brew.* **81**, 318.
   (1975b). Analysis Committee. *J. Inst. Brew.* **81**, 318.
   (1976). Analysis Committee. "Expression of Extracts in Metric Units" (private communication).

Jamieson, A. M. and Chen, E. C. H. (1972). *Proc. Am. Soc. Brew. Chem.* p. 92.

Jamieson, A. M. and MacKinnon, C. G. (1965). *Am. Brewer* **98**, 10, 37.
Jamieson, A. M. and Van Gheluwe, (1974). *Proc. Am. Soc. Brew. Chem.* p. 50.
Jansen, H. E. (1957). *J. Inst. Brew.* **63**, 204.
Jansen, H. E., Strating, J. and Westra, W. M. (1971). *J. Inst. Brew.* **77**, 154.
Jenkinson, P. and Compton, J. (1960). *Proc. Am Soc. Brew. Chem.* p. 73.
Jerumanis, J. (1971). *Bull. Ass. Anciens Etud. Brass., Louvain* **67**, 157.
Jones, M. A., Cope, R. and Rainbow, C. (1975). *Proc. E.B.C. Congr., Nice* p. 669.
Kaczor, J. (1968). *Proc. Am. Soc. Brew. Chem.* p. 29.
Katayama, H. and Horie, Y. (1971). *Rep. Res. Lab. Kirin Brewery Co., Yokahama.* **14**, 31.
Kavanagh, T. E., Steward, S. R., Hildebrand, R. P., Clarke, B. J. and Meeker, F. L. (1975). *J. Inst. Brew.* **81**, 322.
Kenigsberg, M. and Stone, I. (1955). *Anal. Chem.* **27**, 1339.
Kepner, R. E., Strating, J. and Weurman, C. (1963). *J. Inst. Brew.* **69**, 399.
Kijima, M. (1966) *Rep. Res. Lab. Kirin Brewery Co., Yokohama.* **9**, 57.
Kirkbright, G. F., Smith, A. M. and West, T. S. (1967). *Analyst* **92**, 411.
Kirkbright, G. F., Smith, A. M. and West, T. S. (1967). *Analyst* **91**, 411.
Kitabatake, K. and Amaha, M. (1968). *Bull. Brew. Sci., Tokyo* **14**, 17.
Klimovitz, R. J. (1972). *Tech. Quart., Master Brewers Ass. Am.* **9**, 63.
Klopper, W. J. (1954). *J. Inst. Brew.* **60**, 217.
Klopper, W. J. (1955). *Wallerstein Lab. Commun.* **18**, 123.
Klopper, W. J. (1972). *Int. Tijds. Brouw. Mout.* **31**, 158.
Klopper, W. J. (1973). *Proc. E.B.C. Congr., Salzburg* p. 363.
Klopper, W. J. (1974). *J. Inst. Brew.* **80**, 515.
Klopper, W. J., Tuning, B. and Vermier, H. A. (1975). *Proc. E.B.C. Congr., Nice* p. 659.
Klose, H. and Schmitt, E. (1972). *Brauwelt* **112**, 995.
Koike, K., Hashimoto, N., Kitami, H. and Okada, H. (1972). *Rep. Res. Lab. Kirin Brewery Co., Yokohama* **15**, 25.
Kowaka, M., Kohubo, E. and Kuroiwa, Y. (1971). *Rep. Res. Lab. Kirin Brewery Co., Yokohama* **14**, 61.
Larsen, B. A. and Sorensen, J. A. (1957). *Brygmesteren* **14**, 173.
Latimer, R. A., Glenister, P. R., Koepple, K. G. and Dallos, F. C. (1969). *Tech. Quart., Master Brewers Ass. Am.* **6**, 24.
Lawrence, W. C. (1964). *Wallerstein Lab. Commun.* **27**, 123.
Lawrence, W. C. (1968). *Proc. Conv. Aust. New Zealand Sect. Inst. Brew.* p. 11.
Leach, R. K., Kovesces, F. and Valyi, Q. (1974). *Proc. Am. Soc. Brew. Chem.* p. 58.
Lewis, M. J., Pangborn, R. M. and Tanna, L. A. S. (1974). *Tech. Quart., Master Brewers Ass. Am.* **11**, 83.
Lindsay, R. C., Withycombe, D. A. and Micketts, R. J. (1972). *Proc. Am. Soc. Brew. Chem.* p. 4.
Loisa, M., Nummi, M. and Daussant, J. (1971). *Brauwissenschaft* **24**, 366.
Lom, T. (1975). *Proc. Am. Soc. Brew. Chem.* p. 99.
Lundin, H. (1931). *Wschr. Brau.* **51**, 57.
McCowen, N. M., Palamand, S. R. and Hardwick, W. A. (1971). *Proc. Am. Soc. Brew. Chem.* p. 136.
MacFarlane, W. D. (1961). *J. Inst. Brew.* **67**, 502.
MacFarlane, W. D., Sword, P. F. and Blinoff, G. (1963). *Proc. E.B.C. Congr., Brussels* p. 174.
McGuinness, J. D., Laws, D. R. J., Eastwood, R. and Gardner, R. J. (1975). *J. Inst. Brew.* **81**, 237.

Mackereth, F. J. H. (1964). *J. Sci. Instrum.* **41**, 38.

MacPherson, J. K. and Buckee, G. K. (1974). *J. Inst. Brew.* **80**, 540.

Marinelli, L., Heckel, M. and Whitney, D. (1967). *Proc. Am. Soc. Brew. Chem.* p. 37.

Martin, R. J. (1971). *Brewers' Digest* **46**, (6), 44.

Meilgaard, M., Ayma, M. and Ruano, J. I. (1971). *Proc. Am. Soc. Brew. Chem.* p. 219.

Mercredy, J. M., Sonnemann, J. C. and Lenmann, S. J. (1975). *Brewers' Digest* **50** (6), 42.

Micketts, R. J. and Lindsay, R. C. (1974). *Tech. Quart., Master Brewers Ass. Am.* **11**, xix.

Miller, L. W. (1975). *Qual. Progress* **8**, 14.

Mitcheson, R. C. and Stowell, K. C. (1970). *J. Inst. Brew.* **76**, 335.

Moll, M., That, V. and Flayeaux, R. (1971). *Wallerstein Lab. Commun.* **34**, 115.

Moll, M., Flayeaux, R. and Lehaede, J. M. (1975a). *Indust. Aliment. Agricol.* **92**, 631.

Moll, M., Flayeaux, R. and Lehaede, J. M. (1975b). *Indust. Aliment. Agricol.* **92**, 635.

Monier-Williams, G. W. (1927). *Analyst* **52**, 415.

Mussche, R. (1974). *J. Inst. Brew.* **80**, 577.

National Health and Medical Research Council—Australia (1974). Food Standards Committee Decisions, March.

Ng, E. and Mocek, M. (1973). *J. Inst. Brew.* **79**, 165.

Nissen, B. H. and Ulbricht, E. J. (1950). *Proc. Am. Soc. Brew. Chem.* p. 9.

Otter, G. E. and Taylor, L. (1967). *J. Inst. Brew.* **73**, 570.

Otter, G. E. and Taylor, L. (1971). *J. Inst. Brew.* **77**, 467.

Otter, G. E. and Taylor, L. (1976). *J. Inst. Brew.* **82**, 264.

Otter, G. E., Silvester, D. J. and Taylor, L. (1972). *J. Inst. Brew.* **78**, 57.

Ough, C. S. (1976). *J. Agric. Food Chem.* **24**, 323.

Owades, J. L., Blick, S. R. and Owades, S. H. (1967). *Proc. Am. Soc. Brew. Chem.* p. 75.

Owades, J. L., Jakovac, J. and Vigilante, C. (1960). *Proc. Am. Soc. Brew. Chem.* p. 63.

Owades, J. L., Jakovac, J. A. and Vigilante, C. (1961). *Am. Brewer* **94**, 1, 23.

Owades, J. L. and Jakovac, J. A. (1963). *Proc. Am. Soc. Brew. Chem.* p. 22.

Owades, J. L., Rubin, G. and Brenner, M. W. (1958). *Proc. Am. Soc. Brew. Chem.* p. 66.

Owades, J. L., Rubin, G. and Brenner, M. W. (1959). *Proc. Am. Soc. Brew. Chem.* p. 66.

Palamand, S. R. (1974). *Tech. Quart., Master Brewers Ass. Am.* **11**, 90.

Parker, S. R. (1972). "Water Analysis by Atomic Absorption". Varian Techtron Pty. Ltd., Springvale, Australia.

Pessa, E. (1971). *Proc. E.B.C. Congr., Estoril* p. 333.

Pierce, F. D. and Brown, H. R. (1976). *Anal. Chem.* **48**, 693.

Pinnegar, M. A. (1966). *J. Inst. Brew.* **72**, 62.

Pinnegar, M. A. and Whitear, A. L. (1965). *J. Inst. Brew.* **71**, 398.

Pope, N. H. and Hulse, C. J. (1970). *Proc. Conv. Aust. New Zealand Sect. Inst. Brew.* p. 159.

Pope, N. H., Johns, H. and Allman, M. (1966). *Proc. Conv. Aust. Sect. Inst. Brew.* p. 95.

Postel, W. and Drawert, F. (1970). *Brauwissenschaft* **23**, 369.

Postel, W., Drawert, F. and Guvenc, U. (1972a). *Brauwissenschaft* **25**, 341.

Postel, W., Drawert, F. and Guvenc, U. (1972b). *Brauwissenschaft* **25**, 391.

Postel, W., Drawert, F. and Guvenc, U. (1973). *Brauwissenschaft* **26**, 46.

Postel, W., Drawert, F. and Guvenc, U. (1974). *Brauwissenschaft* **27**, 11.

Postel, W., Gorg, A. and Guvenc, U. (1976). *Brauwissenschaft* **29**, 132.

Powell, A. D. G. and Brown, I. H. (1962). *Proc. Conv. Aust. Sec. Inst. Brew.* p. 97.

Powell, A. D. G. and Brown, I. H. (1966). *J. Inst. Brew.* **72**, 261.

Prell, P. A. (1976). *Food Technol,* **30**, 11, 32.

Reynolds, C. L. (1972). *Tech. Quart., Master Brewers Ass. Am.* **9**, 158.

Rice, J. F., Pack, M. Y. and Helbert, J. R. (1973). *Proc. Am. Soc. Brew. Chem.* p. 31.
Richardson, P. J. and Mocek, M. (1971). *Proc. Am. Soc. Brew. Chem.* p. 128.
Richardson, P. J. and Mocek, M. (1973). *J. Inst. Brew.* **79**, 26.
Ricketts, J. and Coutts, M. W. (1951). *Am. Brewer* **84**, 8, 7.
Ricketts, J. and Coutts, M. W. (1951). *Am. Brewer* **84**, 9, 27.
Ricketts, J. and Coutts, M. W. (1951). *Am. Brewer* **84**, 10, 33.
Rigby, F. L. and Bethune, J. L. (1955). *J. Inst. Brew.* **61**, 325.
Robinson, A. J. (1976). *Brewer* **62**, 112.
Rohner, R. L. and Tompkins, J. R. (1970). *Proc. Am. Soc. Brew. Chem.* p. 111.
Rosculet, G. (1970). *Brewer's Digest* **45**, (4), 64.
Rosculet, G. (1971). *Brewers' Digest* **46** (6), 8.
Ross, S. and Clark, G. L. (1939). *Wallerstein Lab. Commun.* **6**, 46.
Rothchild, H. and Stone, I. M. (1938). *J. Inst. Brew.* **44**, 425.
Rowe, C. J. (1973). "Food Analysis by Atomic Absorption". Varian Techtron Pty. Ltd., Springvale, Australia.
Royston, M. G. (1971). *J. Inst. Brew.* **77**, 91.
Rudin, A. D. (1957). *J. Inst. Brew.* **63**, 506.
Saha, R. B., Middlekauf, J. E. and Hardwick, W. A. (1971). *Proc. Am. Soc. Brew. Chem.* p. 206.
Sainsbury, D. M. and Maw, G. A. (1967). *J. Inst. Brew.* **73**, 293.
Saletan, L. S. (1959). *Wallerstein Lab. Commun.* **22**, 125.
Saltzman, B. F. (1952). *Anal. Chem.* **24**, 106.
Sandra, P. and Verzele, M. (1975). *J. Inst. Brew.* **81**, 302.
Savage, D. J. and Thompson, C. C. (1970). *J. Inst. Brew.* **76**, 495.
Sawyer, R. and Dixon, E. J. (1968a). *Analyst* **93**, 669.
Sawyer, R. and Dixon, E. J. (1968b). *Analyst* **93**, 680.
Sawyer, R., Dixon, E. J. and Johnston, E. (1969). *Analyst* **94**, 1010.
Sawyer, R., Dixon, E. J., Lidzey, R. G. and Stockwell, P. B. (1970). *Analyst* **95**, 957.
Scherrer, A. (1972). *Wallerstein Lab. Commun.* **35**, 5.
Schreier, P., Drawert, F. and Junker, A. (1975). *Brauwissenschaft* **28**, 73.
Scruggs, C. E. and Baselt, F. C. (1955). *Wallerstein Lab. Commun.* **18**, 159.
Shah, S. K. (1975). *J. Inst. Brew.* **81**, 293.
Siegel, J. L., McRae, J. P. and Valyi, Z. (1974). *Proc. Am. Soc. Brew. Chem.* p. 60.
Singh, B. N. (1960). *Proc. Int. Conf. Qual. Control,* p. 677.
Slaughter, J. C. and Uvgard, A. R. A. (1971). *J. Inst. Brew.* **77**, 446.
Slaughter, J. C. and Uvgard, A. R. A. (1972). *J. Inst. Brew.* **78**, 322.
Smyly, D. S., Woodward, B. B. and Conrad, E. C. (1976). *J. A.O.A.C.* **59**, 14.
Sogawa, H. (1971). *Rep. Res. Lab. Kirin Brewing Co., Yokahama* **14**, 21.
Sogawa, H. (1972). *Rep. Res. Lab. Kirin Brewing Co., Yokahama* **15**, 17.
Soltoft, M. (1974). *J. Inst. Brew.* **80**, 570.
Somogyi, M. J. (1945). *J. Biol. Chem.* **160**, 61.
Somers, T. C. and Ziemelis, G. (1972). *J. Inst. Brew.* **78**, 233.
Spaeth, G., Niefind, H. J. and Martina, M. (1971). *Schweiz. Brau.-Rund.* **82**, 121.
Standards Association of Australia. (1975). Australian Standards 1821–1823 "Suppliers Quality Control Systems".
Steffer, P., Hammerling, A. and Beubler, A. (1970). *Nahrung* **14**, 599.
Steiner, K. (1971). *Schweiz. Brau.-Runds.* **82**, 117.
Steiner, K. (1972). *Schweiz. Brau.-Runds.* **83**, 193.
Steiner, K. and Lanzlinger, U. (1975). *Schweiz. Brau-Runds.* **86**, 84.
Stenroos, L. E., Siebert, K. J. and Meilgaard, M. (1976). *J. Am. Soc. Brew. Chem* **34**, 4.

Steward, S. R., Smith, J. L., Kavanagh, T. E., Hildebrand, R. P. and Clarke, B. J. (1974). *J. Inst. Brew.* **80**, 34.

St. Johnston, J. H. and Taylor, A. E. (1953). *J. Inst. Brew.* **59**, 141.

Stone, I. M. (1962). *Proc. Am. Soc. Brew. Chem.* p. 64.

Stone, I. M., Laschiver, C. and Saletan, L. T. (1968). *Proc. Am. Soc. Brew. Chem.* p. 125.

Stutler, J. R. and Dakin, P. E. (1963). *Proc. Am. Soc. Brew. Chem.* p. 26.

Stutzel, R. (1953). *Brau. Wiss. Beil.* **6**, 52.

Szarski, P. (1971). *Food Tech. Aust.* **23**, 216.

Szlavko, C. M. (1973a). *J. Inst. Brew.* **79**, 283.

Szlavko, C. M. (1973b). *J. Inst. Brew.* **79**, 450.

Takahashi, Y. and Sasaki, S. (1970). *Rep. Res. Lab. Kirin Brewing Co., Yokahama* **13**, 99.

Kanaka, M. (1960). *Talanta* **5**, 162.

Tanner, H. (1963). *Mitt. Geb. Lebens. Hyg.* **54**, 158.

ten Hoopen, H. J. G. (1973). *J. Inst. Brew.* **79**, 29.

Thompson, C. C. and Forward, E. (1969). *J. Inst. Brew.* **75**, 37.

Thorne, R. S. W. and Beckley, R. F. (1958). *J. Inst. Brew.* **64**, 38.

Thorne, R. S. W. and Nannestad, I. (1959). *J. Inst. Brew.* **65**, 175.

Thorne, R. S. W. and Nannestad, J. (1962). *J. Inst. Brew.* **68**, 257.

Thorne, R. S. W. and Svendsen, K. (1962). *J. Inst. Brew.* **68**, 57.

Thorne, R. S. W. and Svendsen, K. (1972). *J. Inst. Brew.* **78**, 154.

Trachman, H. (1969). *Wallerstein Lab. Commun.* **32**, 111.

Trachman, H. and Saletan, L. T. (1969). *Wallerstein Lab. Commun.* **32**, 199.

Trachman, H. and Saletan, L. T. (1971). *Proc. Am. Soc. Brew. Chem.* p. 171.

Trachman, H., Gantz, C. S. and Saletan, L. T. (1970). *Proc. Am. Soc. Brew. Chem.* p. 177.

Tressl, R., Holzer, M. and Neumann, L. (1975). *Monats. Brau.* **28**, 45.

Tripp, R. C., Timm, B., Lyer, M., Richardson, T. and Amundson, G. H. (1968). *Proc. Am. Soc. Brew. Chem.* p. 65.

Ulloa, H. G., Canales, A. M. and Zapata, B. D. (1975). *Proc. Am. Soc. Brew. Chem.* p. 167.

United States of America—Dept. of Defense (1950). "Military Standard 105A: Sampling Procedures and Tables for Inspection by Attributes". Washington.

United States Brewers Association, Inc. (1969). Beer and Ale Brewing Industry Can Purchase Specifications. Washington.

United States Brewers Association, Inc. (1972a). Recommended Brewing Industry Beer and Ale Bottle Purchase Specifications. Washington.

United States Brewers Association, Inc. (1972b). Brewing Industry Recommended Closure Purchase Specifications. Washington.

van Cauwenberge, H. and de Clerck, J. (1955). *Bull Ass. Anciens Etud. Brass., Louvain* **51**, 97.

Van Gent, P. K. and Kerrich, J. E. (1965). *Analyst* **90**, 335.

Varian Techtron Pty. Ltd., (1972). "Analytical Methods for Flame Spectroscopy". Varian Techtron Pty. Ltd., Springvale, Australia.

Wackerbrauer, K., Tesko, G., Todt, F. and Graff, M. (1975). *Proc. E.B.C. Congr., Nice,* p. 757.

Wainwright, R. (1973). *J. Inst. Brew.* **79**, 451.

Wang, P. S. and Sibert, K. J. (1974). *Tech. Quart., Master Brewers Ass. Am.* **11**, 110.

Webber, H. F. P., Taylor, L. and Marsh, A. S. (1955). *J. Inst. Brew.* **61**, 231.

Wehy, J. (1971). *Brauwissenschaft* **24**, 513.

Wehy, H. (1973). *Brauwelt* **113**, 555.

Weiner, J. P., Talph, D. J. and Taylor, L. (1975). *Proc. E.B.C. Congr., Nice* p. 565.

Weissler, H. E. and Eigel, J. A. (1967). *Proc. Am. Soc. Brew. Chem.* p. 206.

Whatling, H. J., Parfield, J. and Briggs, D. E. (1968). *J. Inst. Brew.* **74**, 525.

Whitear, A. L. (1974a). *J. Inst. Brew.* **80**, 514.

Whitear, A. L. (1974b). *J. Inst. Brew.* **80**, 376.

Williams, D. C. (1972). *Proc. Conv. Aust. New Zealand Sect. Inst. Brew.* p. 195.

Williams, R. S., Murray, D. W. and Quittenton, R. C. (1967). *Tech. Quart., Master Brewers Ass. Am.* **4**, 61.

Wohleb, R., Jennings, W. G. and Lewis, M. J. (1972). *Proc. Am. Soc. Brew. Chem.* p. 1.

Wood, S. A., Lloyd, R. O. V. and Whitear, A. L. (1968). *J. Inst. Brew.* **74**, 510.

Wren, J. J. (1971). *J. Inst. Brew.* **78**, 69.

Wren, J. J. (1976). *Brewers' Guardian* **105** (4), 86.

Young, R. A. (1971). *Tech. Quart., Master Brewers Ass. Am.* **8**, 137.

Zurcher, C. (1971). *Wallerstein Lab. Commun.* **34**, 199.

6. Flavour Stability of Packaged Beers

NAOKI HASHIMOTO

The Research Laboratories of Kirin Brewery Co. Ltd.,
Miyahara-Cho, Takasaki, Gumma Pref., Japan

When packaged beer is stored on the shelf it develops off-flavours which spoil its fresh flavour. These off-flavours are thought to result from oxidation processes in the beer and are generally referred to as an "oxidized flavour" or "stale flavour". Retarding development of this stale flavour represents one of the greatest challenges facing brewers today because the most important factor in the consumer's judgment of beer quality is flavour.

In this chapter attempts are made to follow the progress over the last 40 years in studies on the stale flavour and to provide those engaged in this field with information on the present state of the science and art of flavour stability so that they can apply this information to research and production. The subject is discussed under the following headings:

347

I. FLAVOUR CHANGES OCCURRING DURING STORAGE OF BOTTLED BEER

A. Progressive Phases of Flavour Deterioration

Packaged beer has a rather short shelf-life because beer undergoes slow and progressive deterioration which is manifested by deterioration in flavour, browning, and formation of hazes after the beer is in the market. Since a large element of the consumer's enjoyment of beer is the flavour, this flavour staling on storage of packaged beer is the most serious and perplexing trouble in the brewing industry. The increased use of bottled and canned beer has accentuated this problem.

It is generally agreed that staling involves a progression of flavour changes of beer during rather long storage. Drost *et al.* (1971b) first described the progressive phases of the flavour change, as follows:

Stage 1 Faint, sickly sweet smell, in which there is also a green note; taste is normal.

Stage 2 Heavier, sweet smell like raisins; this taste is sharply wry and acid; further, this taste remains equally strong in the next phases.

Stage 3 Heavy, sweet smell with a small, sharp top note, like honey in the comb.

Stage 4 Sharp, pungent smell, cardboard flavour, smell of leather.

Stage 5 Heavy, sweet smell, whisky-like, oxidized.

Meilgaard (1972) illustrated the staling process of a high-air bottled beer as shown in Fig. 1. The first sign of staling is a drop in overall flavour intensity, followed by a rise in intensity as stale flavours develop. A cardboard flavour begins to be detectable after 4 weeks at 33 °C, rises to a maximum after 8–12 weeks and then gives way to increasingly astringent, sweetish, woody and leathery flavours. The latter often reach a maximum after 6 to 9 months ordinary shelf storage. Many variations of this general scheme may be found. Sometimes, sulphury, musty, celery-like, phenolic and diacetyl off-flavours become detectable on staling. Descriptions of flavour changes at an early stage of development of the stale flavour often include words like "dull' or "lack of freshness". As the main changes during storage, Clapperton and Dalgliesh (1976) recognized an increase in sweet taste which coincides with the

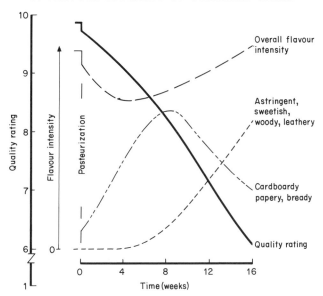

FIG. 1. Development of stale flavour with time on agitated storage at 33 °C. (From Meilgaard (1972).)

development of a toffee-like, burnt-sugar or caramel aroma and flavour. The development of these burnt and toffee-like notes are most readily discernible in lightly coloured beers. Beer staling is also accompanied by harsh after-bitter and astringent notes in the taste. With increase in time and temperature of storage, the desirable bitterness of the beer diminishes and an undesirable bitter aftertaste develops (Lewis *et al.* 1974). A bitter aftertaste increases significantly with the temperature of storage.

This recognition of a succession of flavours developing during storage leads to the idea that the different flavours are caused by changes in the qualitative and/or quantitative composition of flavour compounds. In all probability, several chemical processes take place simultaneously and, at a given time during staling, any one of the reactions may provide the dominant detrimental flavour component. The typical characters of stale or oxidized flavour are not easy to define, since they are progressive during storage and are due to a balance of many flavour contributions rather than one or a few key substances. Using trained panels, the author examined the profile of the typical deteriorated flavour developed in bottled beer stored with 2·5 ml of headspace air for two weeks at 30 °C. The main changes seemed to be as follows: lack of freshness, a stale or oxidized flavour, rough and harsh bitterness, lingering after-bitterness, an astringent taste and unbalance of individual flavour characters. Sometimes, a slight caramel flavour, off-flavour derived from hops, a mouldy flavour or a sulphury flavour developed.

In the international list of beer flavour terminology, which was recently recommended by a joint working group of the European Brewery Convention, American Society of Brewing Chemists, and Master Brewers Association of America (Clapperton *et al.* 1976), the terms "papery", "leathery", "ribes" and "mouldy" are selected as the most appropriate terms to describe the stale or oxidized flavour note of packaged beer. "Paper" is selected as the principal term to describe an initial stage of staling, bready (stale bread-crumb), cardboard, 2-trans-nonenal, old beer and oxidized beer. "Leathery" represents the notes of a later stage of staling, and is often used in conjunction with woody. "Ribes" is the preferred term for the blackcurrant-leaf-like taint which is also called "catty". It is found occasionally in old Yakima Cluster hops and in oxidized ales. At least for ales, ribes aroma is an earlier and a more reliable indicator of oxidative deterioration. Sometimes the terms earthy, musty, cabbagy-vegetable and sulphury were also used to describe the note represented by "ribes" (Clapperton and Dalgliesh 1976). "Mouldy" may be used as a general term to describe individual adjectives such as cellar-like, leaf-mould, woodsy, earthy and musty. Although the terms "stale" and "oxidized" should not be used because they refer to processes and do not specify the nature of the flavour impressions which are perceived, and they have widely different meanings with respect to other flavours and in other fields of flavour chemistry, these terms will be used for convenience in this review to describe overall impressions of the flavour of beer stored for a rather long time on the shelf and combinations of flavour components deriving from the deterioration common to all beers.

B. Flavour Stability

Although it is well known that the flavour of packaged beer deteriorates, quantitative data are still lacking on flavour stability as influenced by such conditions as the headspace air content, time and temperature of storage. This is mainly because the storage conditions prevailing in the market and the susceptibility of beer to flavour deterioration may vary from brewery to brewery or country to country. Furthermore, judgment of the maximum degree of flavour staling which brewers must permit in beer before it is used by consumers is a controversial issue. For example, the storage time required to reach a given staling level detectable by trained panellers is shown in relation to the amount of headspace air and storage temperature in Fig. 2. (Hashimoto 1976). Finished beers bottled with various levels of headspace air were stored for 100 days at two different temperatures. Flavour staling was greatly enhanced at temperatures above those encountered on refrigerated

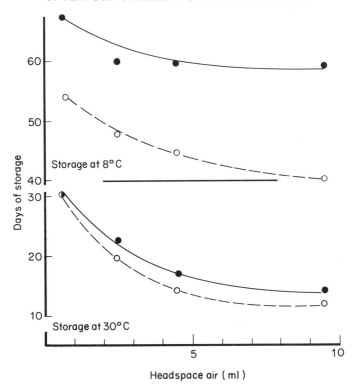

FIG. 2. Development of stale flavour in relation to staling of overall flavour: ●, time required for distinct staling of overall flavour; ○, time required for distinct development of stale flavour. Headspace air, ml/633 ml. (From Hashimoto (1976).)

storage. A distinct stale flavour developed after 40–55 days of storage at 8 °C and after 12–30 days at 30 °C in this case. Only minimal alteration in flavour occurred during six months' storage at 2–0 °C. It is fairly well established that a stale flavour can develop in beer with little or no air. Decreasing the air content reduces flavour staling, but it does not prevent it altogether. The harmful effect of a high storage temperature on flavour stability was found to be greater than that of headspace air.

Statistical analysis by Hashimoto et al. (1971) of the flavour pattern of beer showed that the stale flavour was the largest defect because it destroyed the harmonious balance of individual characters and thereby decreased the overall impression of beer flavour. The stale flavour which developed at temperatures of 30 °C or more, was especially detrimental, as seen in Fig. 2. In Fig. 3, the flavour stability of beer brewed on a pilot scale is shown in terms of the storage time required for a distinct overall impression of staling. In most

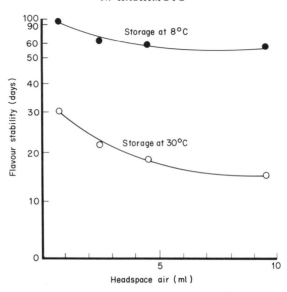

FIG. 3. Flavour stability of bottled beer. (From Hashimoto (1976).)

cases the clarity of the beer is not impaired, but the flavour deteriorates to a point where there is a typical stale note.

II. BRIEF HISTORY OF INVESTIGATION OF FLAVOUR STALING

A. Dissolved Oxygen and I.T.T.

It is perhaps pertinent to begin with more than 40 years of progress in studies on flavour staling of packaged beer. For almost a century, brewers and scientists serving the brewing industry have been aware of the adverse effect of oxidation on the flavour and shelf-life of finished beer. Reliable recognition of this essential cause of deterioration of beer on the shelf dates back to the studies of de Clerck who, in 1934, showed that the redox potential of beer decreased on storage. On the basis of this finding, intensive studies of this subject were made by many workers, notably Hartong (1934), Gray and Stone (1939a) and Van Laer (1940), and brewers recognized that deterioration of beer quality resulted from oxidative changes in the beer.

During the succeeding 30 years, efforts were made to exclude air and avoid metal pick-up during racking and filling (Emslander 1937, Helm 1939). In view of the technical difficulties in excluding air from bottled beer, chemical treatments such as addition of ascorbic acid or sulphites as antioxidants and use of glucose oxidase-catalase to remove oxygen from beer (Gray and Stone 1939b, Ohlmeyer 1957, Bethune and Rigby 1958, Reinke *et al.* 1963) found general acceptance. The indicator-time test (I.T.T.) developed by Gray and Stone (1939a) has been widely used for more than 30 years to measure the oxidation state of beer. This I.T.T. method is strictly a measure of reducing substances in beer, and is based on the time, in minutes, required for a given quantity of beer to effect 80% reduction in the colour of a given quantity of a standardized oxidation–reduction indicator (2,6-dichlorophenolindophenol). Interest was concentrated on the redox potential and the dissolved oxygen content of beer. It is impossible to refer to all the literature on this problem, but this had been thoroughly reviewed by a subcommittee on the "Oxidation State of Wort and Beer" of the American Society of Brewing Chemists (1965). As might be expected, the higher the temperature of storage, the faster is the oxygen pick-up in the headspace of the bottle by the constituents of beer, as seen in Fig. 4 (Van Gheluwe *et al.* 1970b), and the deterioration of the beer is greater when there is more air. Oxidation occurs mainly during the first day of contact.

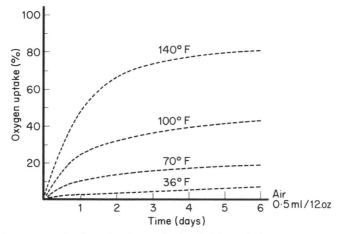

FIG. 4. Oxygen uptake from headspace by bottled beer during storage. (From Van Gheluwe *et al.* (1970b).)

B. Possible Participation of Polyphenols in the Oxidation

However, although brewers progressed along these lines, and their efforts resulted in processing improvements, they were not completely successful.

Staling continued even with a minimum air content of 0·1–0·3 ml per bottle. Excessive use of antioxidants was found to cause other off-flavours, such as a sulphury flavour and a reduced flavour on storage of the beer, whereas most of the glucose oxidase added was destroyed at the temperature of pasteurization. During this period of studies, the biochemical changes and complicated mechanisms involved in oxidative deterioration still remained obscure. Accordingly, in the early fifties, it became increasingly clear that more systematic studies were required.

The American brewing industry in particular has been demanding fundamental research on flavour stability. The problem of haze was no longer of serious importance, particularly with American-type light beers, as the clarity could be preserved by adsorption or enzyme treatment, so that interests became focused on flavour stability. In 1952, charter members of the American Society of Brewing Chemists, Barley and Malt Institute, Brewers Association of America, United States Brewers Association, Master Brewers Association of America and the Dominion Brewers Association created the Brewing Industries Research Institute for the purpose of conducting and coordinating industry-wide scientific research. The research project on flavour stability was regarded as the most urgent and most important as a whole and warranted financial support on that basis. The main result of this industry-sponsored research in the succeeding 15 years was the demonstration of the participation of polyphenols in the oxidative changes of finished beer (McFarlane 1970).

It has become increasingly evident that molecular oxygen does not take part directly in the process of oxidation in bottled beer. Hartong (1964) reported that bottled beer retains its fresh flavour as long as its colour remains unchanged. Brenner and Stern (1968) found that uptake of dissolved oxygen is more than would be expected from the reactions with added antioxidants such as bisulphite, dithionite and isoascorbate. They also suggested that the flavour changes are due to oxidation-initiated browning reactions. Even if sulphites do not actually serve as antioxidants, they are capable of inhibiting browning reactions by binding to carbonyl group. Van Gheluwe et al. (1970a) made extensive studies of oxygen uptake by beers with different air contents containing various amounts of added sulphite or sodium isoascorbate. These antioxidants did not react stoichiometrically with molecular oxygen and had less effect on oxygen uptake than expected. Since oxidation and reduction processes are generally defined in terms of electron migrations, concentration of attention on dissolved oxygen in beer, important as it undoubtedly is, has tended to obscure the mechanisms of beer oxidation, some of which may not involve the direct participation of oxygen. Headspace air, dissolved oxygen and I.T.T. together account for only about one-third of the observed variation in shelf-life stability (McFarlane 1970).

However, there have been very few experiments on the chemical changes accompanying beer oxidation (Lother 1936, Van Laer 1940, Hartong 1964, Chapon 1967, Brenner and Stern 1968). Extensive studies on the probable role of polyphenols in the oxidation of beer are due to the stimulating work of Owades and Jakovac (1966) and the hypothesis of McFarlane (1967). By introducing isotopic oxygen ^{18}O, into the headspace of bottled beer it was possible to study the fate of molecular oxygen during storage (Owades and Jakovac 1966). Results showed that about 65% of the polyphenol molecules incorporated ^{18}O. Incorporations by isohumulones and volatile carbonyls amounted to 5% and 30%, respectively. These results show that polyphenols are involved in reactions leading to the oxidation of beer. In fact, beers from which much of the polyphenol had been removed by treatment with nylon (Harris and Ricketts 1959) or Polyclar AT (McFarlane et al. 1963) were reported to have better flavour stability.

McFarlane (1967, 1968) advanced the hypothesis that the oxidative reactions resulting in formation of complexes of polyphenols and proteins as precursors of non-biological haze must also be included in any scheme of flavour staling. Let us touch upon the properties of polyphenols involved in the formation of haze. There is much evidence that protein–polyphenol complexes represent precursors of beer haze. Peptide bonds in proteins appear to combine with phenolic hydroxyl groups of polyphenols through a hydrogen-bond (Gustavson 1956). Polyphenols become more capable of combining with protein to form hazes after oxidative polymerization. For example, addition of a pure dimeric polyphenol to beer increased chill haze, whereas monomeric polyphenol had little affect. (Silbereisen and Kraffczyk 1968, Gramshaw 1967, 1969). From these findings, McFarlane (1970) suggested that the oxidation of polyphenols by molecular oxygen resulting in formation of haze complexes required the mediation of metal catalysts and enzymes and that components of an oxidase enzyme system containing copper in chill haze and readily oxidized polyphenols may act as powerful oxidation catalysts. Certainly, the complex is extremely unstable in the presence of molecular oxygen and has relatively high contents of iron (0·03–0·12%) and copper (0·02–0·16%) (Hudson 1955). Ascorbic acid can act as an antioxidant in protecting phenol compounds from oxidation.

Since then, special emphasis has been placed on the probable role of polyphenols in the oxidative deterioration of beer, but it is still uncertain how the polyphenols participate directly in the development of a stale flavour, as reviewed in the following section. Some polyphenols are also reported to act as antioxidants in beer (Van Gheluwe et al. 1970a, Dadic and Van Gheluwe 1971, Chen et al. 1972). Although McFarlane's hypothesis is not conclusive, it must be highly evaluated as it established another aspect, namely that flavour staling can be caused by biochemical oxidation in which molecular oxygen does not participate directly.

C. Volatile Aldehydes Responsible for Stale Flavour

Chemists have continued studies on the identification of volatile components responsible for the stale flavour. In earlier studies, Burger *et al.* (1954, 1959) claimed that the cardboard flavour was similar to that produced by the addition of 20–40 p.p.m. of acetaldehyde or 2 p.p.m. of furfural. Brenner *et al.* (1954b) observed that the odour of dimethyl disulphide at levels of a few p.p.b. in beer had a distinct resemblance to the papery note of highly oxidized beer. Ahrenst-Larsen and Hansen (1964) reported that development of a cardboard flavour was accompanied by increase in furfural. However, furfural is present in aged beer in concentration two or three orders of magnitude below its threshold.

Once gas chromatography had been introduced in this field, much relevant information about changes in the composition of volatile components of beer during shelf storage were obtained. It is now generally accepted that a stale or oxidized flavour is essentially due to the formation of volatile carbonyl compounds on storage. In particular, the detection of 2-*trans*-nonenal (Jamieson *et al.* 1970) which gives a cardboard flavour at a threshold level of less than 1 p.p.b., has led many investigators to isolate and identify other strongly flavoured aldehydes in stale beer. Results in the past decade are described in detail in the next section. Most recent research in this field has been focused on the pathways of formation of these volatile aldehydes and discrepant hypotheses have been proposed for the origin of these aldehydes. Recently, Hashimoto (Hashimoto 1976, Hashimoto and Eshima 1977) demonstrated conclusively that the aldehydes responsible for stale flavour mainly result from both melanoidin-mediated oxidation of higher alcohols and oxidative degradation of isohumulones in beer.

As reviewed above, all the really significant observations on flavour stability have been made in the past decade and information on this problem can be expected to accumulate rapidly in the future. Of course, the ultimate goal of research on flavour stability is to find the main cause of oxidized flavour and to learn how to prevent it and so extend the shelf-life of the product. This long-standing problem over the past 40 years should soon be settled if progress in this field continues at its present pace.

III. CHANGES IN THE LEVELS OF FLAVOUR COMPONENTS DURING STALING OF BEER

A. Changes in the Levels of Volatile Components

During storage of packaged beer, the concentrations of some flavour components may increase and some new compounds may be formed.

Although accurate information on these changes was necessary for elucidating flavour staling, little was forthcoming until 1963 because of difficulties associated with analysis of volatile compounds in beer. However, once gas chromatography had been introduced, a number of studies were made on changes in the composition of volatile components and on qualitative and quantitative differences in the compositions of beers with fresh and stale flavour. Ahrenst-Larsen and Hansen (1963) were the first to isolate components involved in flavour staling. Since then, much information about changes in the composition of volatile components during shelf storage has accumulated, particularly in the late 1960s. The following changes have been noted during staling of beer:

(1) Increase (deClerck and Delaunoy 1966, Zenz 1972, Stenroos 1973), decrease (Bavisotto and Roch 1959, 1960, Trachman and Saletan 1969, Engan 1970, 1972, Blockmans 1971) or no change (Bavisotto and Roch 1959, 1960, Trachman and Saletan 1969, Engan 1969, 1972, Wagner and Baron 1971, Hashimoto 1972, Stenroos 1973) in the concentrations of higher alcohols; increase in furfuryl alcohol (Trachman and Saletan 1969).

(2) Increase in volatile acetates (Ahrenst-Larsen and Hansen 1963, Arbogast *et al.* 1966, deClerck and Delaunoy 1966, Zenz 1972) and ethyl formate (Engan 1969); decrease in volatile acetates (Bavisotto and Roch 1959, 1960, Engan 1969–72, Blockmans 1971, Stenroos 1973), ethyl caproate and ethyl caprylate (Trachman and Saletan 1969, Stenroos 1973); no change in volatile acetates (Bavisotto and Roch 1959, 1960, Trachman and Saletan 1969, Wagner and Baron 1971, Hashimoto 1972, Stenroos 1973) and ethyl caproate (Trachman and Saletan 1969, Engan 1972).

(3) Increase in C_3 to C_{10} fatty acids (Trachman and Saletan 1969, Stenroos 1973); decrease in C_5 to C_{18} fatty acids (Trachman and Saletan 1969, Stenroos 1973).

(4) Increase in volatile aldehydes (Hartong 1964, Hashimoto 1966, 1972), acetaldehyde (Ahrenst-Larsen and Hansen 1963, Engan 1969, 1970, 1972, Steiner 1971, Wagner and Baron 1971, Zenz 1972), acetone (Ahrenst-Larsen and Hansen 1963, Hashimoto 1966), furfural (Ahrenst-Larsen and Hansen 1963, McDougal *et al.* 1963, Hashimoto 1972, Law and Lindsay 1972, Palamand *et al.* 1973, Drost *et al.* 1974, Brenner and Khan 1976, Davis and Palamand 1976) and 5-hydroxymethylfurfural (Ahrenst-Larsen and Hansen 1963; Hashimoto 1972, Palamand *et al.* 1973, Davis and Palamand 1976).

(5) Increase of diacetyl resulting from decarboxylation of 2-acetolactate (Arbogast *et al.* 1966, deClerck and Delaunoy 1966, Engan 1970, 1971); increase of dimethyl sulphide (Ahrenst-Larsen and Hansen 1963,

Table 1. Beer volatile components analysed after storage under various conditions (p.p.m.)†

Compound	Threshold (p.p.m.)	Initial	0 °C 30 Days	0 °C 60 Days	0 °C 90 Days	22 °C 30 Days	22 °C 60 Days	22 °C 90 Days	38 °C 30 Days	38 °C 60 Days	38 °C 90 Days
Normal air											
n-Propyl alcohol	50–800	10·5	10·6	10·4	10·3	10·8	10·3	10·1	11·3	11·3	11·0
Isobutyl alcohol	100–200	12·1	12·1	12·2	12·1	11·5	11·3	11·5	12·8	11·1	11·0
Isoamyl alcohol	50–100	60·5	60·5	61·0	61·5	62·8	60·4	60·4	64·8	67·9	67·3
Aliphatic alcohol total		83·1	83·2	83·6	83·9	85·1	82·0	82·0	88·9	90·3	89·3
Phenylethyl alcohol	75–120	21·0	21·0	21·4	21·4	20·4	20·5	20·5	19·5	21·8	21·6
Ethyl acetate	25–33	16·2	16·2	16·4	16·2	16·6	16·7	16·6	16·8	15·0	13·1
Isobutyl acetate	1–1·5	0·18	0·18	0·20	0·19	0·14	0·16	0·18	0·15	0·18	0·18
Isoamyl acetate	1–2·5	1·71	1·71	1·69	1·70	1·72	1·60	1·65	1·60	1·35	1·10
Banana ester total		1·89	1·89	1·89	1·89	1·86	1·76	1·83	1·80	1·53	1·28
Ethyl caproate	0·2–0·3	0·25	0·25	0·29	0·30	0·28	0·28	0·30	0·24	0·24	0·21
Ethyl caprylate	1–1·3	0·31	0·31	0·31	0·30	0·30	0·28	0·28	0·30	0·21	0·11
Apple ester total		0·56	0·56	0·60	0·60	0·58	0·56	0·58	0·54	0·45	0·32
Propionic	100	1·33	1·42	1·35	1·37	1·40	1·43	1·49	1·60	1·93	2·24
Isobutyric	200	0·74	0·74	0·76	0·76	0·78	0·79	0·80	0·85	0·95	0·96
Butyric	1	0·83	0·82	0·83	0·85	0·84	0·83	0·80	0·94	0·93	1·70
Isovaleric	8	0·46	0·46	0·51	0·46	0·53	0·58	0·70	1·01	1·08	1·17
Valeric	35	0·03	0·04	0·03	0·03	0·03	0·05	0·03	0·03	0·04	0·06
Caproic	5–10	1·25	1·26	1·25	1·25	1·26	1·29	1·33	1·28	1·28	1·33
Heptanoic		0·02	0·02	0·02	0·02	0·02	0·03	0·02	0·02	0·04	0·03
Caprylic	4–10	7·29	7·20	7·60	7·35	7·57	7·66	8·37	7·69	7·68	8·36
Nonanoic		0·05	0·05	0·04	0·05	0·05	0·04	0·04	0·06	0·05	0·08
Capric	10	3·18	3·17	3·18	3·21	3·17	3·15	3·22	3·25	3·16	2·77
Lauric		0·21	0·21	0·26	0·24	0·21	0·28	0·19	0·17	0·21	0·21
Myristic		0·13	0·13	0·13	0·13	0·14	0·14	0·14	0·14	0·14	0·10
Pentadecanoic		0·02	0·02	0·02	0·03	0·02	0·02	0·03	0·02	0·03	0·03
Palmitic		0·25	0·25	0·25	0·21	0·23	0·24	0·24	0·26	0·25	0·19
Heptadecanoic		0·03	0·03	0·03	0·03	0·03	0·03	0·02	0·03	0·03	0·03
Stearic		0·06	0·04	0·04	0·05	0·05	0·04	0·04	0·04	0·04	0·03
Oleic		0·17	0·21	0·20	0·18	0·16	0·15	0·14	0·15	0·14	0·07

High air

Propanol	50–800	10·7	11·0	10·9	11·1	11·5	11·2	11·9	10·8	11·1	11·3
Isobutyl alcohol	100–200	10·4	10·3	10·3	10·3	11·7	11·2	10·9	13·4	11·0	10·8
Isoamyl alcohol	50–100	62·0	64·2	64·4	65·5	66·3	67·9	70·3	67·2	69·2	69·8
Aliphatic alcohol total		83·1	85·5	85·6	86·9	89·5	90·3	93·1	91·4	91·3	91·9
Phenylethyl alcohol	75–120	21·3	22·5	22·5	22·8	21·3	23·0	23·2	18·9	22·0	24·4
Ethyl acetate	25–33	16·8	16·3	16·6	16·7	16·8	16·9	17·1	17·3	14·8	13·5
Isobutyl acetate	1–1·5	0·20	0·22	0·22	0·22	0·16	0·18	0·18	0·16	0·18	0·19
Isoamyl acetate	1–2·5	1·65	1·67	1·67	1·69	1·60	1·60	1·55	1·53	1·24	1·13
Banana ester total		1·85	1·89	1·89	1·91	1·76	1·78	1·73	1·69	1·42	1·32
Ethyl caproate	0·2–0·3	0·20	0·27	0·28	0·26	0·27	0·27	0·26	0·22	0·23	0·21
Ethyl caprylate	1–1·3	0·30	0·30	0·30	0·28	0·26	0·24	0·23	0·25	0·25	0·16
Apple ester total		0·50	0·57	0·58	0·54	0·53	0·51	0·49	0·47	0·48	0·37
Propionic		1·38	1·36	1·36	1·37	1·34	1·52	1·62	1·34	2·02	2·49
Isobutyric		0·78	0·86	0·76	0·74	0·79	0·84	0·89	0·59	0·90	0·92
Butyric		0·70	0·68	0·84	0·89	0·92	0·93	1·00	1·15	0·96	1·07
Isovaleric		0·48	0·43	0·50	0·60	0·87	0·97	1·13	1·14	1·07	1·40
Valeric		0·03	0·03	0·04	0·03	0·04	0·04	0·05	0·04	0·05	0·06
Caproic		1·32	1·39	1·30	1·29	1·37	1·39	1·39	1·51	1·53	1·55
Heptanoic		0·02	0·04	0·02	0·03	0·04	0·04	0·03	0·03	0·04	0·04
Caprylic		7·60	7·57	7·58	7·58	8·45	8·40	8·36	8·23	8·47	8·36
Nonanoic		0·05	0·05	0·04	0·05	0·06	0·05	0·06	0·07	0·07	0·06
Capric		3·31	3·30	3·63	3·61	3·50	3·60	3·20	3·54	2·91	2·80
Lauric		0·22	0·20	0·26	0·20	0·20	0·19	0·21	0·20	0·29	0·22
Myristic		0·14	0·14	0·14	0·13	0·13	0·13	0·13	0·09	0·08	0·12
Pentadecanoic		0·02	0·02	0·02	0·03	0·03	0·03	0·03	0·03	0·03	0·04
Palmitic		0·25	0·29	0·31	0·30	0·24	0·20	0·15	0·26	0·16	0·04
Heptadecanoic		0·03	0·05	0·03	0·03	0·05	0·05	0·06		0·05	0·06
Stearic		0·05	0·03	0·04	0·04	0·03	0·04	0·03	0·04	0·04	0·03
Oleic		0·21	0·14	0·19	0·18	0·11	0·10	0·10	0·04	0·05	0·06

† From Stenroos (1973).

deClerck and Delaunoy 1966, Engan 1971); decrease in sulphite and hydrogen sulphide (Hashimoto *et al.* 1968, Hashimoto 1972); increase in methional (Visser and Lindsay 1971b); increase (Bärwalt 1970, Engan 1970) or decrease (Engan 1972) in volatile phenols; decrease in hop oil components (Hashimoto 1970); and formation of isoprene (Zenz 1972).

The data on changes in the levels of volatile components, particularly of alcohols, esters and fatty acids, during storage seems to be conflicting, probably because of differences in the type of beer used, the storage temperature, the storage time, the level of headspace air, and the accuracy of analyses. Furthermore, the possible contribution of the changes to flavour staling must be discussed on the basis of the flavour thresholds for these volatile compounds. In extensive studies by Stenroos (1973), 12 oz. bottles of beer with 0·7 and 1·7 ml of air were stored at 0, 22 and 38 °C for 30, 60 and 90 days, and the effects of time, temperature and air on the levels of volatile compounds were examined statistically. Results suggested that increases in the levels of aliphatic alcohols were not connected with staling because none of these reached a threshold level. Ethyl acetate was found to be present at below the threshold level and to change only slightly. On storage at 38 °C, a significant decrease was found in isoamyl acetate, in the range of its threshold (see Table 1). Ethyl caproate was present at or slightly below its threshold and increased to above the threshold on storage at either 0 °C or 22 °C. Ethyl caprylate decreased with time under all storage conditions. Short-chain, C_3 to C_5, fatty acids, other than butyric acid, remained below their threshold levels. Butyric acid increased from below to above its threshold level. Fatty acids from C_6 to C_{10} were found to increase during storage, but not sufficiently to affect the flavour. The levels of longer-chain, C_{12} to C_{18}, fatty acids decreased, particularly with higher air contents and temperatures. Figure 5 (Hashimoto 1972) shows the changes in the levels of volatile components during storage at 50 °C. Under the conditions used, a characteristic oxidized flavour developed by the third day of storage. The levels of higher alcohols and esters remained fairly constant during storage. The changes in the levels of hydrogen sulphide, sulphur dioxide, furfural and 5-hydroxymethylfurfural were small in comparison with their threshold levels. The levels of many compounds changed during storage, but few of these compounds had effects on the flavour at the levels at which they were present.

B. Remarkable Increase of Volatile Aldehydes

The remarkable increase in the levels of volatile aldehydes seems to be parallel with development of the oxidized flavour, as seen in Fig. 6 (Hashimoto 1966, 1972). For evaluating the flavour of these volatile aldehydes formed in

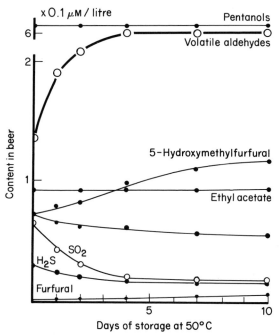

FIG. 5. Changes in the levels of flavour components during storage. Bottled beer containing 25 ml of headspace air was stored at 50 °C. The content of H_2S is shown in µmol/l. (From Hashimoto (1972).)

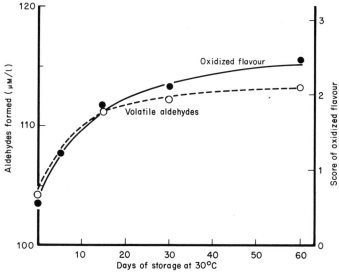

FIG. 6. Volatile aldehydes responsible for oxidized flavour. (From Hashimoto (1972).)

beer, carbonyl reagents were added to oxidized beer: approximately 50-ml portions of stored beer were poured into two glasses and then 2–20 drops of 1 M solutions of carbonyl reagents, such as 2,4-dinitrophenylhydrazine, hydroxylamine, sodium bisulphite and thiosemicarbazide, were added to one glass. The glasses were swirled and within a few minutes the oxidized beer treated with carbonyl reagent recovered its fresh flavour, differing from the off-flavour. The second glass served as a control. The disappearance of the oxidized flavour on adding 2,4-dinitrophenylhydrazine or other reagents capable of combining with carbonyl compounds in oxidized beer was also confirmed by Hartong (1964) and Wheeler et al. (1971).

This formation of volatile aldehydes was subsequently confirmed in relation to flavour staling by various investigators (Chang et al. 1970, Engan 1970, 1972, Pessa 1971, Steiner 1971, Wagner and Baron 1971, Wheeler et al. 1971, Chen et al. 1972, Lau and Lindsay 1972). Although all the saturated aldehydes with chain lengths of C_1 to C_9, and furfural and 5-hydroxymethylfurfural which were identified in beer appeared to be present in concentrations one or more orders below their thresholds, certain unsaturated aldehydes with 7 to 10 carbon atoms have flavour thresholds at or below 1 p.p.b. in beer, i.e. their flavours are 1 to 2 orders of magnitude stronger than that of the strongest flavoured thiols, as discussed in Vol. III, in the chapter "Beer Flavour" (Meilgaard and Moya 1970). The flavours of aldehydes are rarely pleasant, and they become worse with increase in chain length; 2-heptenal, 2-octenal and 2-nonenal have thresholds of less than 1 p.p.b. and unpleasant, cardboard-like flavours (Meilgaard 1975). The isolation of one of these aldehydes, 2-trans-nonenal, from a distillate of acidified beer by Jamieson and Van Gheluwe (1970) was described as a breakthrough in the identification of aldehydes responsible for stale flavour. The rise in concentration of 2-nonenal from 0·03 p.p.b. in fresh beer to 0·19 p.p.b. in stale beer (Wang and Siebert 1974a, 1974b) represents an increase of more than 0·1 p.p.b. of its threshold (Palamand and Hardwick 1969, Meilgaard and Moya 1970, Visser and Lindsay 1971a, Wang and Siebert 1974a, Meilgaard 1975). Forcing beer at 38 °C caused an increase to more than threshold level after 3–4 days, at which point the beer began to show a papery flavour. When beer was stored for 160 days at 0 °C, the estimated concentration of 2-nonenal remained well below its threshold and papery flavour did not increase (Wang and Siebert 1974a, 1974b).

Drost et al. (1971) stated that 2-nonenal does not have the typical flavour of stale beer, although a mixture of 1 p.p.b. each of 2-nonenal and 2-methyl-furfural, has a cardboardy flavour. This observation is to be expected, because in beer containing at least 340 volatile components (Hashimoto 1975), one compound is rarely capable of causing the overall impression of stale flavour. Further, as described in section I, we think that the cardboard flavour is only one of many flavour notes present in oxidized beer, such as papery, straw-like, bready, woody, leathery and other flavours, and that staling involves a progressive change in these flavour notes. Many changes may take place during storage and any one of these changes may provide the dominant flavour at a particular time. In view of the progression of flavour changes during staling, it is quite unlikely that 2-nonenal is responsible for more than the papery or cardboardy part of flavour deterioration. Moreover, significant flavour interactions, i.e. additive, synergistic or antagonistic, were observed between various aroma components found in beer (Meilgaard 1975).

Consequently, it is generally thought that volatile aldehydes or groups of these aldehydes formed in bottled beer during shelf storage are the main cause of the stale or oxidized flavour, at least as far as the aroma of stale beer is concerned. Off-flavoured aldehydes, such as 2-*trans*-nonenal (threshold in beer, 0·1 p.p.b.†) (Jamieson and Van Gheluwe 1970, Drost *et al.* 1971, Visser and Lindsay 1971a, Grigsby *et al.* 1972, Lau and Lindsay 1972, Wohleb *et al.* 1972, Markl and Palamand 1973, Palamand *et al.* 1973, Strating and Van Eerde 1973, Withycombe and Lindsay 1973, Drost *et al.* 1974, Wang and Siebert 1974a, 1974b), 2,4-hexadienal (800 p.p.b.) (Markl and Palamand 1973), 2-*trans*-6-*cis*-nonadienal (0·05 p.p.b.) (Visser and Lindsay 1971a, Markl and Palamand 1973), 2-*trans*-hexenal (600 p.p.b.) (Visser and Lindsay 1971a, Lau and Lindsay 1972, Markl and Palamand 1973), 4-heptenal (0·4 p.p.b.) (Markl and Palamand 1973), octanal (40 p.p.b.) (Trachman and Saletan 1969, Wheeler *et al.* 1971), nonanal (18 p.p.b.), decanal (6 p.p.b.) (Wheeler *et al.* 1971, Lau and Lindsay 1972), dodecanal (4 p.p.b.) (Wheeler *et al.* 1971) methional (250 p.p.b.) (Visser and Lindsay 1971b) and malonaldehyde, *p*-tolualdehyde and 6-methyl-5-heptene-2-one (Markl and Palamand 1973) have been detected in oxidized beer, and attempts to detect other aldehydes in oxidized beer are still in progress.

C. Changes in the Levels of Low-volatile Components

Other important staling compounds will probably be detected in beer when intensified studies are directed away from volatile aldehydes which now attract such great attention. Therefore, there are strong reasons to reserve conclusions on the causes of stale flavour until more complete information is available.

Changes in the levels of low-volatile components may be rather difficult to study, because for analysis of low-volatile or non-volatile compounds gas chromatography has serious drawbacks. A few other compounds have been reported to be present in oxidized beer. These are monoethyl succinate

† The flavour thresholds in beer of 239 volatiles including 56 aldehydes and 41 ketones were reported by Meilgaard (1975). For a fully up-to-date list, see Volume III.

(Palamand *et al.* 1973), 1-(2,3,6-trimethylphenyl)-1,3-butadiene 2,6,6-trimethyl-1-crotonyl-1,3-cyclohexadiene, ionones (Strating and Van Eerde 1973), *o*-aminoacetophenone and ethyl nicotinate (Palamand and Grigsby 1974). At a level of 1–2 p.p.m., monoethyl succinate was said to produce a straw-like flavour in beer. 1-(2,3,6-Trimethylphenyl)-1,3-butadiene has a strong leather/geranium odour and 2,6,6-trimethyl-1-crotonyl-1,3-cyclohexadiene has a lovely odour of black-currant. This compound and ionones are possibly formed by oxidation of carotenoids. *o*-Aminoacetophenone was found to produce a stale, grainy, waxy, and grape-like flavour at a level of 5 p.p.b. in beer. Ethyl nicotinate produces a grainy and papery flavour when added at a level of 2 p.p.m. to beer.

The possible roles of lactones and furanones in flavour staling also remain to be studied. Takahashi *et al.* (1976) isolated a lactone, 3-hydroxy-4,5-dimethyl-2(5H)-furanone, from saké stored for one month at 60 °C. This furanone, imparting a burnt flavour to saké, is believed to be formed by aldol condensation of α-ketobutyric acid with acetaldehyde. Since Hashimoto and Kuroiwa (1975) demonstrated that aldol condensation of aldehydes takes place under the mild conditions existing in beer during shelf storage, similar condensation or lactonization of unsaturated, hydroxy and keto acids in beer may explain the formation during storage of furanones and lactones. 2,5-Dimethyl-4-hydroxy-3(2H)-furanone was tentatively identified in oxidized beer (Palamand *et al.* 1973). This compound has a typical pineapple flavour and caramel-like flavour. The lactones found in beer are as follows; γ-butyrolactone (2 p.p.m.); γ-valerolactone (1·6 p.p.m.); δ-valerolactone (Spence *et al.* 1973); δ-isocaprolactone; γ-nonalactone (0·1–0·5 p.p.m.) (Drawert and Tressl 1972, Tressl and Renner 1975); γ-decalactone (5–20 p.p.b.) (Buttery *et al.* 1967, Tressl and Renner 1975); γ-octalactone (20–50 p.p.m.); γ-dodecalactone (5–20 p.p.b.); 4,4-dimethyl-2-buten-4-olid (50–100 p.p.b.); 4,4-dimethyl-4-butanolid (20–50 p.p.b.) (Tressl and Renner 1975). γ-Butyrolactone and γ-valerolactone give an estery, fruity, dull and harsh flavour at a level of 10 p.p.m. in beer (Spence *et al.* 1973).

It is well known that browning of beer takes place during storage. This browning is due entirely to the brown colour of melanoidins (Hashimoto and Koike 1971). Therefore, some of the many compounds formed by the amino-carbonyl browning reaction may be involved, to greater or lesser degree, in flavour staling, although the flavour potencies of individual compounds are still unknown. Of twelve furan derivatives which were reported to be present in beer (Tressl *et al.* 1975), furfural, 5-hydroxy-methylfurfural and furfuryl alcohol increased during storage, as described above. At least ten pyrazines, in a total concentration of 20 p.p.b., were detected in beer (Kosuge *et al.* 1971, Kavanagh *et al.* 1974). Maltol, 5-hydroxymaltol, 5-hydroxy-5,6-dihydromaltol, isomaltol, cycloten and

4-hydroxy-2,5-dimethyl-3(2H)-furanone must be examined because of their strong caramel-like flavours (Tressl *et al.* 1975). However, the conditions in ordinary staling of beer are not sufficiently drastic for the formation of these caramelization products to be of any importance.

D. Levels of Volatile Compounds during Pasteurization

An off-flavour is known to develop during tunnel pasteurization of bottled beer, and this is referred to as a pasteurization flavour. It was found that the formation of volatile aldehydes occurred during pasteurization as well as during storage on the shelf; and the formation of aldehydes was greater on increase in the air content of bottled beer (Hashimoto 1966). Increase in the level of acetaldehyde during pasteurization was confirmed by Szilvinyi and Püspök (1963), Arbogast *et al.* (1966), Basarova (1967) and Wheeler *et al.* (1971). Increase in hydrogen sulphide (Brenner *et al.* 1954b, Jansen 1964), furfural (Brenner and Khan 1976) and diacetyl (Shigematsu *et al.* 1964, Blockmans 1971) and little change in higher alcohols, esters, or fatty acids (Bavisotto and Roch 1960, Jenard 1960, Kepner *et al.* 1963, Drews and Riemann *et al.* 1967) were also found during pasteurization as well as during shelf storage.

Tunnel pasteurization may be considered as a sort of warm storage of bottle beer. Thus, formation of aldehydes on pasteurization may be essentially similar to the process on the shelf and it may be responsible for most of the flavour deterioration on pasteurization. Oxygen uptake in bottled beer was accelerated during pasteurization (Van Gheluwe *et al.* 1970a) and minimal pasteurization is recommended in the interest of flavour stability.

E. Oxidation of Polyphenols

In the past decade, attention has been concentrated on the deterioration of beer aroma. However, beer staling is also accompanied by development of harsh after-bitter and astringent notes in the taste. This change and the changes in the composition of such constituents as polyphenols and bitter acids during storage require study.

Polyphenols must be included in any scheme of flavour staling, as reviewed in section II, but phenolic compounds with a stale flavour have not yet been isolated from beer and it is still uncertain what the role of polyphenols is in the oxidation of beer flavour. Phenolic compounds in beer are classified into three main groups from the standpoint of their state of oxidation (Meilgaard 1974):

(1) monophenols: phenolic alcohols (5–10 p.p.m. in beer), phenolic acids (10–30 p.p.m.), phenolic amines and amino acids (10–20 p.p.m.);

(2) monomeric polyphenols: catechins (20–100 p.p.m.), anthocyanogens (40–100 p.p.m.), quercetins (more than 10 p.p.m.);

(3) oligomeric and polymeric polyphenols: hydrolysable (0–10 p.p.m.) and condensed (20–60 p.p.m.).

Among these phenolic compounds, increase in gallic acid, decrease in catechin (Charalambous *et al.* 1973) and oxidative conversion of ferulic acid (Dadic and Belleau 1975) were found to take place during storage. Dadic's study (1971) on the changes in anthocyanogen and catechin concentrations in beer indicated that some changes involving these constituents take place, and

Table 2. Flavour tests on oxidized polyphenols in beer†

Oxidized polyphenol added	Flavour threshold (p.p.m.)		Flavour description
	Reduced	Oxidized	
Quercetin	20	10	bitter, harsh
Kaempferol	50	50	—
Morin	10	50	—
Myricetin	10	10	winey, malty, papery, bitter, harsh, earthy
D-(+)-Catechin	20	10	bitter, harsh, bitter-sweet, astringent
Vanillic acid	20	10	harsh, bitter-sweet, sour, astringent, peppery, medicinal
Syringic acid	10	10	bitter, harsh, astringent, winey, malty
Protocatechuic acid	50	50	—
Gallic acid	50	10	bitter, harsh, astringent, dry, sour, sweet
Gentisic acid	20	10	bitter, astringent, dry, harsh
p-Hydroxybenzoic acid	20	10	bitter, harsh, astringent, acidic, vinegar
Ferulic acid	20	10	bitter-sweet, sour, vanilla, malty
Sinapic acid	20	10	bitter, astringent, harsh, sour, dry
Caffeic acid	20	10	bitter, harsh, sour, diacety
p-Coumaric acid	50	20	sour, dry, bitter, astringent, medicinal
trans-o-Coumaric acid	10	10	cinnamon, sweet, bitter-sweet, perfume, woody, dry
Chlorogenic acid	20	10	bitter, harsh, bitter-sweet, astringent

† From Dadic and Belleau (1973).

Hashimoto (1976) suggested the occurrence of polymerization of poly-hydroxyflavanes during storage of beer. Increase in molecular weight of polyphenols during storage was also observed by anion-exchange chromatography (Sogawa 1973).

Some phenolic amines and amino acids give a sharp, grainy astringency and bitter taste at a level of 20 p.p.m. in beer (Charalambous et al. 1972). Polyphenols are generally considered to be related to the harshness, bitterness and sometimes to the body of beer flavour (Verzele 1970, Hautke and Petricek 1971, Charalambous et al. 1972, Curtis and Clark 1960, Harris and Ricketts 1960). Kingstaad (1972) mentioned a possible influence of easily oxidizable phenolic monomers, such as phenolic acids, on beer flavour. The vanilla flavour, sometimes present in old beer, could be due to cinnamic acids. A current theory is that reduced monomeric polyphenols give body and freshness while oxidized polymeric polyphenols cause astringency and harshness. Bruckner et al. (1970) examined the effects of oxidized monophenols added to beer at levels of 30–50 p.p.m.; oxidized cinnamic acid imparted an aged taste and oxidized p-coumaric acid, a sharp, bitter taste. Oxidized gallic acid in particular caused strong astringency. In general, they caused increase in harshness or lingering bitterness which tended to dull the overall flavour impression of the beer, while in the reduced forms, they imparted a fresher taste. Quercitrin and catechin produced no marked changes. The harshness, bitterness and astringency of twelve phenolic acids and five monomeric polyphenols became more pronounced with simultaneous reduction of their thresholds when they were oxidized, as reported by Dadic and Belleau (1973). See Table 2.

Phenolic antioxidants, such as butylhydroxyanisol, dibutylhydroxytoluene and propyl gallate interfere with autoxidation primarily by transferring either a hydrogen atom or an electron to the chain-propagating species. However, a few of these antioxidants did not retard the development of stale flavour in beer (Hashimoto and Kuroiwa 1976). Exceptionally, Van Gheluwe et al. (1970) found that oxygen uptake was much faster in beers from which anthocyanogens have been partially removed, and Grigsby et al. (1974) reported that addition of dihydroquercetin effectively retarded the development of cardboardy character in the beer.

F. Oxidative Transformations of Hop Bitter Acids

Bitter acids of hops undergo oxidation during storage of hop cones and wort boiling. Most of the following bitter compounds hitherto identified, other than isohumulones, are regarded as the products of oxidative transformations of bitter acids: humulinones (Cook and Harris 1950); diisopentenyldihydroxy isohumulones (Ashurst and Elvidge 1966); dihydroxy humulones (Shaw and

Table 3. Bitterness of bitter acid derivatives found in beer[†]

Fraction	Sub-fraction[‡]	Major constituents of subfraction (peak no.)	Bitterness of subfraction		Intensity[§]
			Characteristics		
S-15	A	Unknown compounds	Sharp	⎫	5
	B	Shaw's compound (19)	Sharp	⎪	4
	C	Humulones (20)	Sharp	⎬ Sharp	5
		Lupdeps (22)	Sharp	⎪	
		Humulinic acids (24)	No bitter	⎪	
	D	Isohumulones (26)	No bitter	⎪	10
	E	Unknown compounds (28, 29)	Harsh	⎪	4
	F	Hulupones (30)	Sharp	⎭	5
	G	Lupdols (39)	Astringent	⎫	5
	H	Lupoxes b,c (44, 45)	Astringent	⎪	3
		Lupdoxes a,b (46, 47)	Astringent	⎪	
	I	Unknown compounds (54, 55, 56)	Astringent	⎪	2
	J	Ashurst's compound (58)	Astringent	⎪	2
S-3	K	Abeo-isohumulones (59, 60)	No bitter	⎬ Astringent	3
		Law's compound (61)	Astringent	⎪	
		Connet's compounds (62)	Astringent	⎪	
		Humulinones (63)	Astringent	⎪	
	L	Unknown compounds (64, 65)	Astringent	⎭	3
S-1	M	Lupoxes a	Harsh		1

† From Kowaka and Kokubo (1977).
‡ See Fig. 7.
§ Taking the intensity of isohumulones as 10.

Table 4. Constitutions of bitterness of fresh and oxidized beer†

Fraction	Sub-fraction‡	Bitterness contribution (%)				
		Fresh beer	Beer stored at 0 °C for 4 weeks	Beer stored at 50 °C 4 weeks	Beer brewed with slightly deteriorated hops	Beer brewed with very deteriorated hops
S-15	A	3·1	2·7	2·3	4·9	2·0
	B	0·5	0·4	0·5	0·5	0·7
	C	1·0 } 81·4	1·1 } 79·9	2·7 } 64·8	2·7 } 75·5	1·1 } 66·1
	D	68·0	65·6	48·1	55·9	50·1
	E	3·7	3·9	5·0	6·1	5·9
	F	5·1	5·2	5·4	5·4	6·3
S-3	G	4·8	5·0	6·5	4·0	5·0
	H	1·6	1·5	0·6	1·3	1·6
	I	2·0 } 15·4	2·1 } 16·2	5·5 } 25·2	1·8 } 18·4	2·7 } 24·6
	J	2·6	3·0	6·8	3·8	5·8
	K	3·1	3·1	4·0	4·5	6·2
	L	1·3	1·5	1·8	3·0	3·3
S-1	M	3·2	3·9	10·0	6·1	9·3
Bitterness units		29·0	28·0	24·0	27·5	29·0
Isohumulones content (mg/l)		25·9	25·2	15·5	20·3	17·6

† From Kowaka and Kokubo (1977).
‡ See Fig. 7 and Table 3.
§ Bitterness contribution (%) $= \dfrac{Y_i \times Z_i}{\sum_{i=A}^{M}(Y_i \times Z_i)} \times 100$;

where Y_i = intensity of bitterness, Z_i = content in beer.

Milles 1967); abeo-isohumulones (Verzele and Vanhoey 1967); dihydroxy-epoxyisohumulones (Connet and Elvidge 1968); seven oxidative products of isohumulones (Vanhoey *et al.* 1970); tricyclodehydroisohumulones (Laws and McGuiness 1974); hulupones (Spetsig *et al.* 1957, Brohult *et al.* 1959); 5-isopentenylhumulinic acids (Regan 1969); lupoxes *a* and *b* (Kokubo *et al.* 1971); lupoxes *c* (Kowaka *et al.* 1972); lupdoxes *a* (*Kokubo et al.* 1971); lupdoxes *b* (Kowaka *et al.* 1972); lupdeps and lupdols (Kowaka *et al.* 1973).

Very recently, on analysing at least 90 bitter compounds present in beer by silica-gel and ion-exchange chromatography, Kowaka and Kokubo (1977) found that the levels of isohumulones were low and the levels of the oxidation products described above were high, in beers brewed with deteriorated hops,

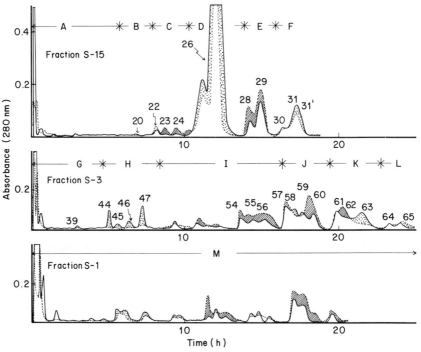

FIG. 7. Ion-exchange chromatograms of the bitter substances of fresh and oxidized beer. Continuous line: fraction S-15 (29 mg), fraction S-3 (20 mg) and fraction S-1 (15 mg) obtained from fresh beer (1 litre). Dotted line: fraction S-15 (20 mg), fraction S-3 (24 mg) and fraction S-1 (21 mg) obtained from oxidized beer (1 litre). The shaded and dotted areas in peaks indicate the increase and decrease, respectively in the quantities after storage for 4 months at 50 °C. Peak No.: 20 (humulones), 24 (humulinic acids), 26 (isohumulones), 58 (Ashurst's compound), 59, 60 (abeoisohumulones), 61 (Law's compound), 62 (Connet's compound), 63 (humulinones), 28, 29, 30, 31, 54, 55, 56, 57, 64, 65 (uncharacterized compounds). (From Kowaka and Kokubo (1977).)

or oxidized humulones and lupulones. Similar oxidative transformations of bitter acids took place in bottled beer during storage, as seen in Fig. 7. Isohumulones in beer decreased and were replaced by oxidation products during storage.

Oxidative deterioration affects the constitution of beer bitterness. Some of the oxidation products (Fraction S-15 shown in Table 3) are not as bitter as isohumulones, but they have sharp, lingering bitterness like isohumulones, while others (Fraction S-3 and S-1) have mild and astringent bitterness. As seen in Table 4, the bitterness of beer freshly brewed with fresh hops was characterized as sharp and lingering because the contribution of the former components accounted for 81 % of the total bitterness, while oxidized beer or beer brewed with very deteriorated hops had a dull and astringent bitterness because the contribution of the latter components was greater. A dilatory bitter taste seems to due to increase in subfraction I, J (Ashurst's compound), K (Law's compound, Connet's compound), L and M (lupoxes *a*) (Kowaka and Kokubo 1977).

IV. PATHWAYS OF FORMATION OF VOLATILE ALDEHYDES RESPONSIBLE FOR THE STALE FLAVOUR OF BEER

A. Reactions Involved in Formation of Volatile Aldehydes

Volatile aldehydes formed during shelf storage of packaged beer seem to be the main cause of a stale flavour. Consequently, most recent research on the stale flavour has been focused on pathways of formation of these volatile aldehydes. Discrepant hypotheses have been proposed for their formation and the following four routes of formation can be distinguished:

1. Amino-Carbonyl Reaction

The progressive browning occuring on storage of bottled beer is mainly caused by an amino carbonyl reaction (Hashimoto and Koike 1971). The amino carbonyl reaction involves a series of complicated reactions initiated by the formation of N-glycosides between reducing sugars and amino compounds and finally resulting in the formation of brown nitrogenous polymers named melanoidins. Two pathways of the amino-carbonyl reaction may be involved in the formation of volatile aldehydes in oxidized beer.

The first leads via Amadori rearrangement of N-glycosides to the formation of a series of unsaturated hexosones which, in turn, form melanoidins and/or furfural and substituted furfurals. Increase in the levels of furfural and 5-hydroxymethylfurfural, which however, do not exceed their flavour thresholds, is possibly attributed to this pathway. The second is Strecker degradation, by which dicarbonyl products of the first pathway react with α-amino acids to produce aldehydes of one less carbon atom than the amino acid. The possible role of Strecker degradation of amino acids in formation of a large number of short-chain carbonyls formed in oxidized beer was suggested by Chang et al. (1970), Wheeler et al. (1971) and Blockmans and Dujardin (1973).

Formation of formaldehyde from glycine, acetaldehyde from alanine and isobutyraldehyde from valine were demonstrated in a model solution of beer (Hashimoto and Kuroiwa 1975) and formation of isobutyraldehyde from valine and isovaleraldehyde from leucine, in beer (Blockmans et al. 1975). Methional was also detected in stale beer perhaps as the product of Strecker degradation of methionine, but the flavour given by methional alone is not regarded as similar to the stale flavour (Visser and Lindsay 1971b). The levels of amino acids, especially proline, in beer were reported to decrease during storage at 22 °C and 38 °C (Stenroos 1973).

Although the participations of these reactions in flavour deterioration are not necessarily excluded, it is unlikely that any of these saturated aldehydes and furfurals have low enough thresholds to be of importance as stale flavour compounds. Furthermore, it should also be noted that a typical oxidized flavour has never been detected in oxidized unfermented wort (Baker and Stollberg 1959, McFarlane 1967). Apparently, the essential precursors of the stale flavour in beer are neither amino acids nor sugars derived from wort.

2. Autoxidation of Unsaturated Fatty Acids

Another possible route of formation of aldehydes in aged beer is by autoxidation of unsaturated fatty acids, in particular, linoleic acid and linolenic acid. In milk, butter, vegetables, oils and many other foods, flavour staling is frequently caused by formation of various unsaturated carbonyl compounds of 6 to 12 carbon atoms, by autoxidation of unsaturated lipids. In the accepted free radical mechanism of autoxidation, a hydrogen atom is removed from the fatty acid molecule and the resulting radical reacts with molecular oxygen to form a peroxy radical, which in turn, removes a hydrogen atom from another molecule forming a hydroperoxide. The hydroperoxide is then polymerized or cleaved to lower aldehydes, fatty acids and other compounds. Table 5 is an excellent summary of present knowledge on the volatile carbonyls derived from unsaturated fatty acids (Badings 1970, Meilgaard 1972).

Detection of strongly flavoured aldehydes such as 2-trans-nonenal in aged beer strongly suggests that the autoxidation of unsaturated fatty acids, more than any other reaction, is operative during storage of beer (Meilgaard and Moya 1970, 1971, Meilgaard et al. 1971, Meilgaard 1972). Evidence was presented recently that a mixture of aldehydes including 2-*trans*-nonenal was directly formed by autoxidation of linoleic acid in a model solution of beer (Hashimoto and Kuroiwa 1975). Since the peroxidation occurs first at the α-carbon adjacent to a double bond of linoleic acid, n-pentanal may be formed by peroxidation at C_{14}, and n-hexanal and 2-*trans*-nonenal may result from peroxidation of C_{11} and C_8, respectively, followed by allyl rearrangement.

On the other hand, the participations of several enzymes in the chemical oxidation sequence of unsaturated fatty acids ultimately resulting in the formation of such aldehydes as 2-nonenal have been suggested, although conclusive proof for this is not yet available. Jamieson and Van Gheluwe (1970) reported that 5,9,13-triketoheptadec-14-en-4-ol isolated from beer is a precursor. Drost *et al.*. (1971a, b, 1974) reported that 9,12,13-trihydroxy-10-*trans*-octadecenoic acid and its isomer, 9,10,13-trihydroxy-11-*trans*-octadecenoic acid isolated from wort and beer gave a strong cardboardy flavour when added at 3 p.p.b. to beer during storage. These precursors are probably formed by enzymatic oxidation of linoleic acid in the mash, or perhaps even in the barley grain or during malting (Drost *et al.* 1971a, b, Graveland *et al.* 1972). These acids present at the levels of several p.p.m. were, however, reported to be too stable to break down in finished beer (Stenroos *et al.* 1976). Visser and Lindsay (1971a) noted a marked decrease in ethyl oleate, ethyl linoleate and ethyl linolenate during shelf storage of beer, and proposed probable reaction sequences for the formations of 2-*trans*-nonenal, 2-*trans*-6-*cis*-nonadienal and 2-*trans*-hexenal from ethyl esters of unsaturated fatty acids formed by fermentation (see Fig. 8). Enzymatic breakdown of phospholipids or glycerides by phospholipid or glyceride acyl hydrolases forming free fatty acids may also be operative. Colneleic acid and colnelenic acid derived from linoleic acid and linolenic acid by the actions of lipoxygenase and hydroperoxidase (Galliard *et al.* 1972, Galliard and Phillips 1973) were suggested to be precursors of 2-*trans*-nonenal and 2-*trans*-6-*cis*-nonadienal (Garza-Ulloa *et al.* 1976). However, to prove that this mechanism actually occurs in beer, it is necessary to demonstrate the presence in beer of lipoxygenase, hydroperoxidase, colneleic acid and colnelenic acid (Dominguez and Canales 1974).

Most lipids and long-chain fatty acids of beer are derived from raw materials: free fatty acids (0·5–5 p.p.m.) fatty acid esters (0·3 p.p.m.), free sterols (0·01–0·02 p.p.m.), sterol esters (0.01 p.p.m.), monoglycerides (0·1–0·3 p.p.m.), triglycerides (0·1–0·2 p.p.m.), phosphatides and glycolipids (less than 0·1 p.p.m.) (Meilgaard 1972). MacPherson and Buckee (1974) reported levels of 0·1–0·8 p.p.m. for oleic acid, 0·07–0·8 p.p.m. for linoleic acid and 0·02–0·1 p.p.m. for linolenic acid in seven lager beers, and these concentrations are well in excess of those required to form the trace amounts of volatile aldehydes found in aged beer. Witt and co-workers (1963, 1965, 1966, 1968, 1972) stated that the contents of lipids in beer reflect their levels in the

Table 5. Volatile carbonyl compounds identified in autoxidized unsaturated fatty acids†

Acid	Compounds identified	Quantity (p.p.m.)‡	Flavour threshold (p.p.b.)		Flavour in beer
			Paraffin oil	Beer	
C-18 : 1 oleic	n-heptanal	50	55	50–100	aldehyde, vinous, bitter
	n-octanal	320	40	40	orange peel, bitter, aldehyde
	n-nonanal	370	200	15–20	astringent, bitter, aldehyde
	n-decanal	80	700	5–7	bitter, aldehyde, orange peel
	2-trans-decenal	70	150	1	bitter, rancid, stale
	2-trans-undecenal	85	4200	(3)§	(bitter, rancid, fatty)
C-18 : 2 linoleic	n-pentanal	55	70	500	grass, banana, aldehyde
	n-hexanal	5100	80	300–400	bitter, vinous, aldehyde
	n-heptanal	50	see above		
	2-trans-heptenal	450	200	(0·5)	aldehyde, bitter, papery
	n-octanal	45	see above		
	1-octen-3-one	2	0·1		(metallic)
	2-cis-octenal	990			
	?-cis-octenal	25			
	2-trans-octenal	420	150	0·3–0·5	bitter, aldehyde, stale
	3-trans-nonenal	30			
	3-cis-nonenal	30			
	?-hydroxy-octenal	540			
	2-trans-nonenal	30	40	0·3	cardboard, oxidized
	2cis-decenal	20			
	2-trans-4-trans-nonadienal	30	460	0·5	oily, rancid, aldehyde
	2-trans-4-cis-decadienal	250		(50)	(sweet, aldehyde)
	2-trans-4-trans-decadienal	150	100	0·3	oily, aldehyde, deep-fried
	?-hydroxy-nonenal	1200			

C-18 : 3 linolenic				
1-penten-3-one	30	3		(sharp, fishy)
2-trans-butenal	10		8000	apple, green leaves, almond
2-trans-pentenal	35	1000		
2-cis-pentenal	45			(green leaves, paint)
n-hexanal	5	see above		
2-trans-hexenal	10	600	500–750	green leaves, bitter
3-trans-hexenal	15			
3-cis-hexenal	90		20	green leaves, fresh grass
2-trans-heptenal	5	see above		
2-trans-4-cis-heptadienal	320	40		
2-trans-4-trans-heptadienal	70	100		
2-cis-5-cis-octadienal	20			
3,5-octadien-2-one	30	300		(fatty, fruity)
2-cis-?-cis-nonadienal	30			
2-trans-6-cis-nonadienal	10	15	0·05	cucumber, green leaves
2-?-4-?-nonadienal	25			
2-?-4-?-7-?-decatrienal	55	38		(sliced beans)
2-?-4-?-7-?-decatrienal	30	24		(sliced beans)

† From Badings (1970) and Meilgaard (1972).
‡ In relation to the weight of acid autoxidized.
§ Thresholds and flavour descriptions given in brackets are estimates.

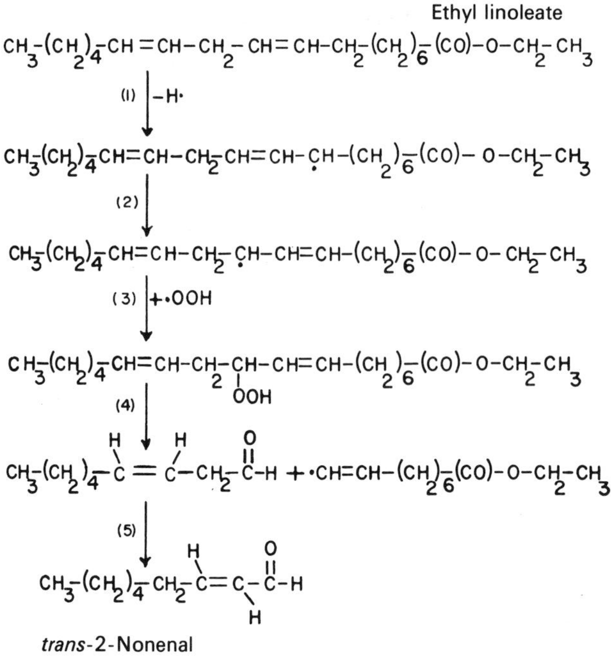

Ethyl linoleate

$$CH_3-(CH_2)_4-CH=CH-CH_2-CH=CH-CH_2-(CH_2)_6-(CO)-O-CH_2-CH_3$$

(1) $\downarrow$ $-H\cdot$

$$CH_3(CH_2)_4CH=CH-CH_2-CH=CH-\overset{\bullet}{C}H-(CH_2)_6-(CO)-O-CH_2-CH_3$$

(2) $\downarrow$

$$CH_3(CH_2)_4-CH=CH-CH_2-\overset{\bullet}{C}H-CH=CH-(CH_2)_6-(CO)-O-CH_2-CH_3$$

(3) $\downarrow$ $+\cdot OOH$

$$CH_3(CH_2)_4-CH=CH-CH_2-\underset{\underset{OOH}{|}}{CH}-CH=CH-(CH_2)_6-(CO)-O-CH_2-CH_3$$

(4) $\downarrow$

$$CH_3-(CH_2)_4-\overset{H}{\underset{}{C}}=\overset{H}{\underset{}{C}}-CH_2-\overset{O}{\overset{||}{C}}-H \;+\; \cdot CH=CH-(CH_2)_6(CO)-O-CH_2-CH_3$$

(5) $\downarrow$

$$CH_3-(CH_2)_4-CH_2-\overset{H}{\underset{}{C}}=\overset{}{\underset{H}{C}}-\overset{O}{\overset{||}{C}}-H$$

trans-2-Nonenal

FIG. 8. Possible route of formation of 2-trans-nonenal by autoxidation of ethyl linoleate. (From Visser and Lindsay (1971a).)

raw materials. Treating malt grist or malt with ethanol was shown to reduce the production of nonenal precursors during mashing (Dale et al. 1977). However, a wort made from pure malt germs which have high contents of linoleic acid and lipids did not develop a stronger stale flavour on heating than worts made from husk or aleurone-free endosperm (Meilgaard et al. 1971). Similarly, the flavour stability of a beer made using lipid-rich rice bran as an adjunct was not different from that of control beer (Hashimoto 1976). Furthermore, Hashimoto (1976) confirmed that development of a stale flavour in beer was not suppressed by addition of 200 p.p.m. of iso-butylhydroxytoluene (BHT), and antioxidant of fats and oils.

Although either enzymatic or free radical oxidation of unsaturated fatty acids may lead to the formation of volatile aldehydes in oxidized beer, staling is rarely retarded by reducing the level of a suspected unsaturated fatty acid in beer, as Meilgaard (1972) proposed: methods for doing this have been the use of raw materials containing smaller amounts of lipid, use of lipoxygenase inhibitors, clarification of lauter wort and efficient removal of hot and cold trub, which reduce carry over of lipids into beer, and inducing the yeast to take up unsaturated lipids during fermentation.

3. Melanoidin-Mediated Oxidation of Higher Alcohols

Volatile aldehydes may also be formed during storage by melanoidin-mediated oxidation of higher alcohols in beer. Hartong (1964) reported that bottled beer retains its fresh flavour ar long as its colour remains unchanged. Since marked browning of beer during storage is usually accompanied by an increase in the aldehyde concentration, it is very tempting to speculate that melanoidins causing browning may be involved in the formation of aldehydes in beer (Hashimoto and Koike 1971).

Hashimoto (1972) demonstrated the formation of volatile aldehydes through melanoidin-mediated oxidation of higher alcohols in beer. Many of the alcohols of beer can undergo oxidation to give the corresponding aldehydes, the oxidant being the carbonyl groups present in the melanoidins which are formed by the amino-carbonyl reaction during the boiling of wort and kilning of malt. It should be mentioned that molecular oxygen did not oxidize alcohol in the absence of melanoidins in beer. A specific mechanism has been proposed involving the transfer of hydrogen atoms or electrons from higher alcohols to reactive carbonyl groups of melanoidins with molecular weights of less than 1000, as seen in Fig. 9. Molecular oxygen did not oxidize

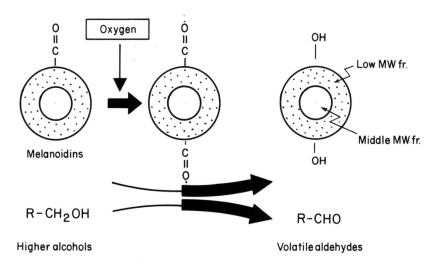

FIG. 9. Proposed mechanism of oxidation of higher alcohols by melanoidins in beer. (From Hashimoto (1972).)

alcohols directly in the absence of melanoidins, but accelerated the rate of oxidation of alcohols by melanoidins, probably because the melanoidins are transformed more easily in the presence of oxygen in such a way that the reactive carbonyl groups are involved in this electron-transfer system. It was shown that acetaldehyde, propanal, acetone, isobutanal, n-butanal, methyl-butanals and hexanal were all formed in this way during ageing (Hashimoto 1972). Similarly, phenylacetaldehyde was formed from phenylethyl alcohol (Pollock 1972). However, it should be mentioned that this reaction hardly explains the formation of unsaturated aldehydes with higher flavour potency.

This unexpected result may have a significant influence on the theories proposed to explain aldehyde formation in beer which does not involve direct participation of molecular oxygen. In the past, melanoidins have been considered to be important reducing agents in beer. This new role of melanoidins in the electron-transfer system of beer, revealed by Hashimoto, certainly represents part of the complicated mechanism of oxidation of beer. Baker and Stollberg (1959) found a large difference in the flavour stabilities of beers made with seven different yeasts. Because they failed to produce an oxidized flavour from wort, they advanced the hypothesis that precursors are formed by yeasts. The formation of aldehyde by melanoidin-mediated oxidation of higher alcohols seems to support this idea.

Contrary to this mechanism Chen et al. (1972) postulated that oxidation of alcohols may be a type of autoxidation initiated by a radical derived from an outside source, usually a peroxide or molecular oxygen. Pessa (1971) and Dadic et al. (1974) suggested that phenolic-mediated formation of volatile carbonyl compounds takes place in beer. Hashimoto also found that polyphenols, such as catechin, quercetin and dihydroquercetin, slightly oxidized higher alcohols to aldehydes in phosphate buffer at pH 4·2. In this case, hydrogen from the alcohol molecule may be taken up not by the carbonyl radical of melanoidins but by the phenoxy radical of poly-phenols. However, in a reaction system such as beer containing both melanoidins and polyphenols, the latter preferentially donate hydrogen to a melanoidin radical rather than accepting hydrogen from the alcohol, as demonstrated by Hashimoto and Kuroiwa (1975).

4. Oxidative Degradation of Isohumulones

Isohumulones undergo photodegradation forming several volatile com-pounds (Strating 1963/1964, Nakayama and Fly 1968, Zenz and Klaushofer 1970). One of these, 2-methyl-2-butene reacts with hydrogen sulphide to form 3-methyl-2-buten-1-thiol responsible for the sunstruck flavour of beer (Kuroiwa and Hashimoto 1961). Volatile compounds are also formed during boiling of hopped wort or storage of hops (Verzele 1967, Hartley and Fawcett 1968, De Mets and Verzele 1968, Palamand et al. 1969, Regan and Elvidge

1969, Green 1970a, b, Krüger and Neuman 1970a, b, Narziss and Forster 1971, 1972, Kuroiwa *et al.* 1973, Shimazu *et al.* 1975) probably by oxidative degradation of bitter substances.

Although formation of the volatile compounds from bitter substances in beer during shelf storage has only been confirmed in the case of isoprene (Zenz 1972, 1973a, b, 1974a, b), recently Hashimoto and Kuroiwa (1975) and Hashimoto and Eshima (1977) identified carbonyl compounds such as acetone, acetaldehyde, 2-methylpropanal, 3-methylbutan-2-one, 4-methylpentan-2-one, butenal, pentenal, hexenal and hexadienal as oxidative degradation products of isohumulones in a model beer system stored at 40 °C.

Isohumulones undergo oxidative degradation forming volatile aldehydes more easily than their derivatives, as shown in Table 6. The double bond or carbonyl group of the isohexenoyl side chain of isohumulones may be involved in this degradation. Moreover, this oxidation of isohumulones is completely suppressed by ascorbic acid and ferrous ions (Hashimoto 1976, 1979). Our finding that unhopped beer hardly ever develops a typical oxidized flavour on storage strongly suggests that this oxidative degradation of isohumulones plays an important role in flavour staling of beer.

Table 6. Volatile aldehydes formed by oxidative degradation of isohumulones and their derivatives[†][‡]

Bitter substance	Volatile aldehydes formed (μmol)
Isohumulones	5·8
Tetrahydroisohumulones	0·5
ρ-Isohumulones	0·1
Hulupones	2·9
Humulinic acids	0·1
Hard resins from hops	0·2

† From Hashimoto (1979).
‡ Thirty mg of sample were stored in 1 litre of 0·02 M phosphate buffer, pH 4·2, for 4 days at 50 °C.

5. Interaction of Reactions Involved in Formation of Volatile Aldehydes in Beer

As described above, amino acids, unsaturated fatty acids, higher alcohols and isohumulones are all thought to be precursors of the aldehydes formed in aged beer. As shown in Fig. 10, Hashimoto and Kuroiwa (1975), using a melanoidin solution of pH 4·2 as a model of beer, demonstrated that formation of volatile aldehydes in bottled beer is not due to a single reaction

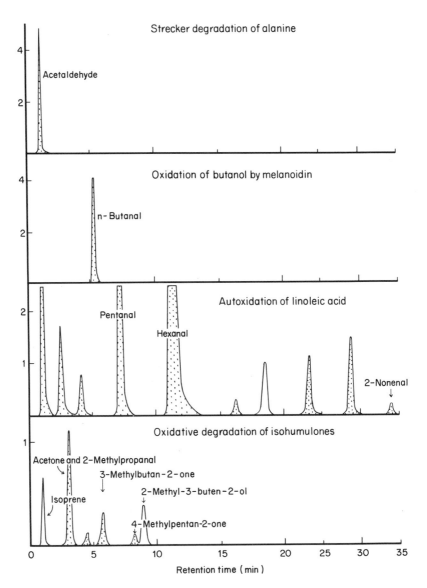

FIG. 10. Volatile aldehydes formed from amino acids, higher alcohols, unsaturated fatty acids and isohumulones. Twenty mmol of alanine, n-butanol, and linoleic acid and 50 mg of isohumulones were stored in 1 litre of a model beer system for 5 days at 50 °C. Dotted peaks: carbonyl compounds. (From Hashimoto and Kuroiwa (1975).)

such as Strecker degradation of amino acids, melanoidin-mediated oxidation of higher alcohols, autoxidation of fatty acids, or oxidative degradation of isohumulones, but to all these reactions simultaneously. A total of about 10 μmol per litre of volatile aldehydes was formed by these four routes, as seen in Fig. 11.

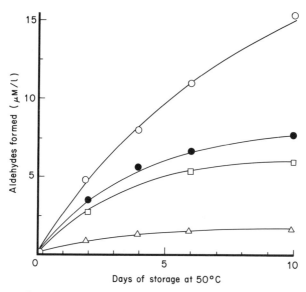

FIG. 11. Formation of volatile aldehydes from beer constituents during storage. A model beer system containing alanine (10 mmol), n-butanol(10 mmol), isohumulones (30 mg/l), or linoleic acid (1 mmol) was stored at 50 °C. ○, formed by Strecker degradation of alanine; ●, formed by oxidation of butanol with melanoidins; □, formed by oxidative degradation of isohumulones; △, formed by autoxidation of linoleic acid. (From Hashimoto and Kuroiwa (1975).)

Furthermore, it seems most unlikely that the oxidations of these precursors take place independently in bottled beer. As seen in Fig. 12 (Hashimoto and Kuroiwa 1975), the melanoidin-mediated oxidation of alcohol and amino acid increased with increase in the melanoidin concentration, whereas the oxidative degradation of isohumulones and autoxidation of fatty acid were suppressed by melanoidins. This antioxidative action of melanoidins may be due to their hydrogen donor property. On the other hand, as shown in Fig. 13 (Hashimoto and Kuroiwa 1975), isohumulones inhibited the oxidation of alcohol, the degradation of amino acids and the autoxidation of fatty acids. Perhaps, when phenolic compounds such as isohumulones and polyphenols in beer polymerize via their peroxides, the hydrogen liberated from them is

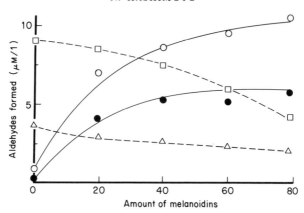

FIG. 12. Influence of melanoidins on aldehyde-forming reactions. Samples of solution containing sugars and glycine were boiled for 20, 40, 60 or 80 min. The resultant melanoidin solutions were stored with alanine (10 mmol), n-butanol (10 mmol), isohumulones (30 mg/l) or linoleic acid (1 mmol) for 4 days at 50 °C. ○, formed by Strecker degradation of alanine; ●, formed by oxidation of butanol with melanoidins; □, formed by oxidative degradation of isohumulones; △, formed by autoxidation of linoleic acid. (From Hashimoto and Kuroiwa (1975).)

transferred to the fatty acid radical and the carbonyl radical of melanoidins, and thereby stops autoxidation of fatty acids, melanoidin-mediated oxidation of higher alcohols and degradation of amino acids. Hashimoto and Kuroiwa (1975) found that isohumulones, like melanoidins, can oxidize higher alcohols to aldehydes. Hydrogen from the alcohol may be taken up not only by the carbonyl radical of melanoidins but also by the phenoxy radical of iso-humulones. However, in a reaction system such as beer containing both melanoidins and isohumulones, isohumulones preferentially donate hydrogen to a melanoidin radical rather than accepting hydrogen from the alcohol, as illustrated in Fig. 14. Therby, isohumulones inhibit the oxidation of higher alcohols with melanoidins. Moreover, molecular oxygen did not oxidize alcohol in the absence of melanoidins, but accelerated the rate of oxidation of isohumulones, fatty acids and higher alcohols by melanoidins and the degradation of amino acids, as will be described later.

6. Oxidative Decomposition and Aldol Condensation of Volatile Aldehydes Formed in Beer

Just as unsaturated fatty acids tend to undergo autoxidation in beer, so the unsaturated aldehydes formed by the four routes described above may also undergo secondary autoxidation on storage. For example, autoxidation of 2-trans-nonenal in the model beer system resulted in formation of n-pentanal,

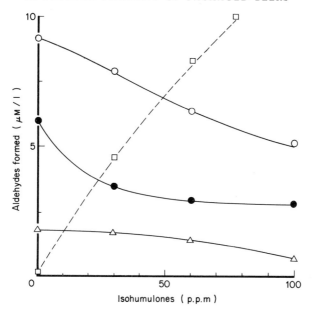

FIG. 13. Interaction of isohumulones with aldehyde-forming reactions. Alanine (10 mmol), n-butanol (10 mmol), or linoleic acid (1 mmol) was added to a model beer system containing various amounts of isohumulones, and stored for 4 days at 50 °C. Volatile aldehydes derived from isohumulones were determined as a control. ○, formed by Strecker degradation of alanine; ●, formed by oxidation of butanol with melanoidins; □, formed by oxidative degradation of isohumulones; △, formed by autoxidation of linoleic acid. (From Hashimoto and Kuroiwa (1975).)

n-hexanal, n-heptanal, n-octanal, and other compounds (Hashimoto and Kuroiwa 1975).

It is of great interest that aldol condensation of aldehydes takes place under the mild conditions existing in beer during shelf storage. Hashimoto and Kuroiwa (1975) found that 2-alkenals, such as 2-butenal, 2-pentyl-2-butenal and 2-*trans*-nonenal were formed by aldol condensation of acetaldehyde with acetaldehyde and/or with n-heptanal on storage of a model beer system containing 20 mmol of proline for 20 days at 50 °C. This condensation also took place in wort on storage at 50 °C. Similarly, 2-butenal, 2-ethyl-2-butenal, 2-*trans*-hexenal and 2-ethyl-2-hexenal were formed from acetaldehyde and n-butanal. Very little condensation occurred in the absence of amino acid: this amino acid may serve as a basic catalyst in this aldol condensation reaction of the aldehydes through the formation of imine intermediate, as shown in Scheme 1.

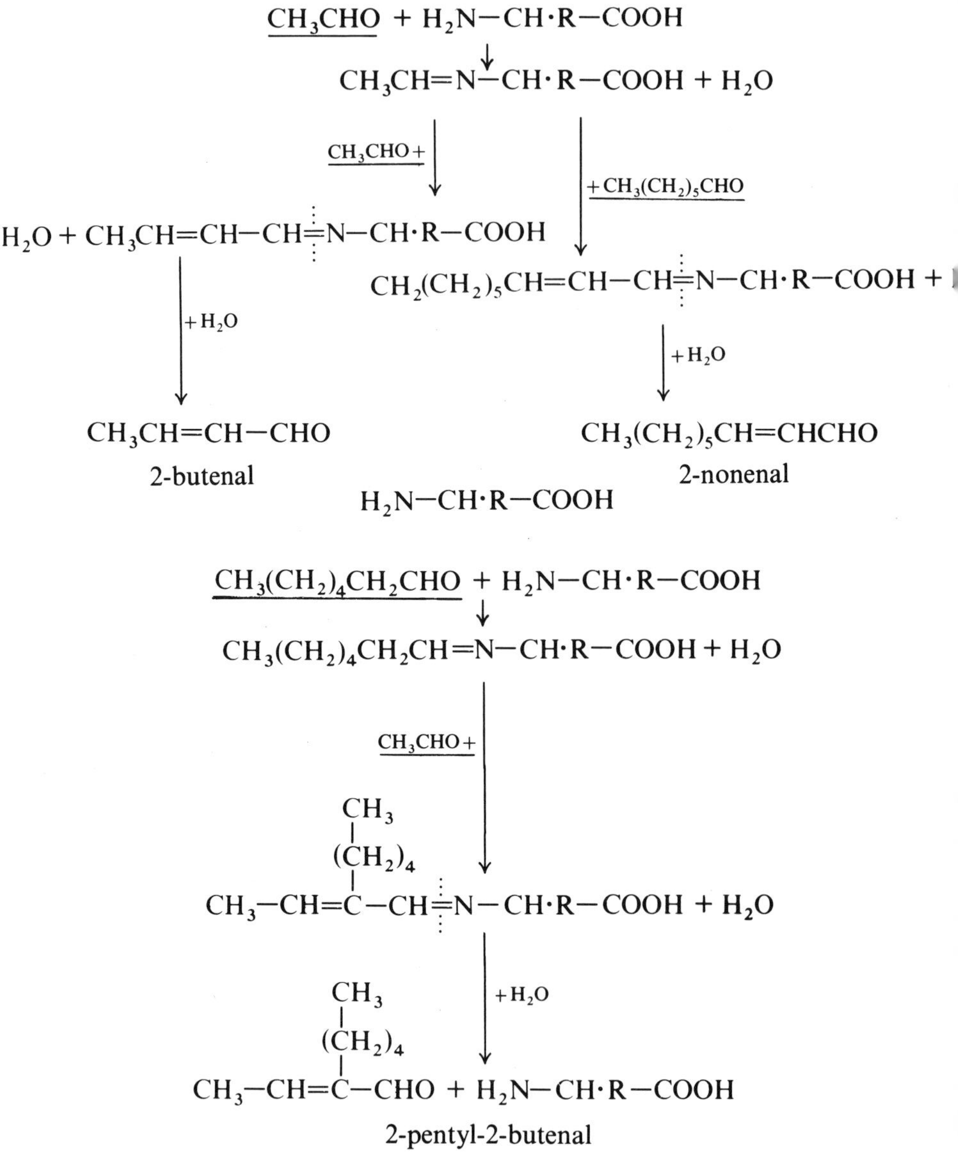

$$CH_3CHO + H_2N-CH \cdot R-COOH$$

$$\downarrow$$

$$CH_3CH=N-CH \cdot R-COOH + H_2O$$

$\xrightarrow{CH_3CHO+}$ (left branch) $\xrightarrow{+CH_3(CH_2)_5CHO}$ (right branch)

$$H_2O + CH_3CH=CH-CH\doteq N-CH \cdot R-COOH$$

$$CH_2(CH_2)_5CH=CH-CH\doteq N-CH \cdot R-COOH + \, |$$

$$\downarrow +H_2O \qquad\qquad\qquad\qquad\qquad \downarrow +H_2O$$

$$CH_3CH=CH-CHO \qquad\qquad CH_3(CH_2)_5CH=CHCHO$$

2-butenal $\qquad\qquad\qquad\qquad$ 2-nonenal

$$H_2N-CH \cdot R-COOH$$

$$CH_3(CH_2)_4CH_2CHO + H_2N-CH \cdot R-COOH$$

$$\downarrow$$

$$CH_3(CH_2)_4CH_2CH=N-CH \cdot R-COOH + H_2O$$

$\xrightarrow{CH_3CHO+}$

$$\begin{array}{c} CH_3 \\ | \\ (CH_2)_4 \\ | \\ CH_3-CH=C-CH\doteq N-CH \cdot R-COOH + H_2O \end{array}$$

$$\downarrow +H_2O$$

$$\begin{array}{c} CH_3 \\ | \\ (CH_2)_4 \\ | \\ CH_3-CH=C-CHO + H_2N-CH \cdot R-COOH \end{array}$$

2-pentyl-2-butenal

SCHEME 1.

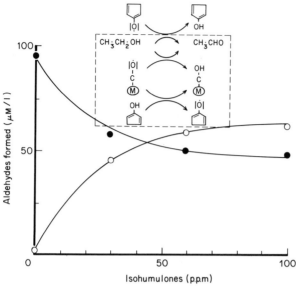

FIG. 14. Electron-transfer system between melanoidins and isohumulones. Various amounts of isohumulones and 4·5% ethanol were stored with or without melanoidins in 0·02 M phosphate buffer, pH 4·2 for 4 days at 50 °C. ●, with melanoidins; ○, without melanoidins; ⓜ, melanoidins; ⬠, isohumulones. (From Hashimoto and Kuroiwa (1975).)

From these findings, it seems likely that the alkenals or dienals found in oxidized beer may be derived not only from unsaturated lipid components but also from higher alcohols, amino acids or isohumulones in beer.

Based on these results, the complicated pathway illustrated in Fig. 15 was proposed as the mechanism of formation of volatile aldehydes during shelf storage of bottled beer (Hashimoto and Kuroiwa 1975). The carbonyl radicals of melanoids formed by an amino-carbonyl reaction in wort accept hydrogen atoms from higher alcohols with oxidation of the latter to the corresponding volatile aldehydes. The melanoidins also participate in Strecker degradation of amino acids in beer to yield aldehydes. On the other hand, the electron-donating activity of melanoidins suppresses the oxidative degradation of isohumulones and the autoxidation of fatty acids. Isohumulones, and perhaps polyphenols, donate electrons to melanoidin and to fatty acid radicals and thereby inhibit the melanoidin-mediated oxidation of higher alcohols, the degradation of amino acids and the radical-chain autoxidation of unsaturated fatty acids. Isohumulones themselves undergo oxidative degradation to volatile aldehydes. Thus, the reactions leading to formation of volatile

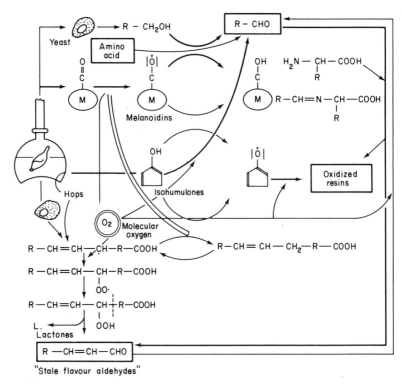

FIG. 15. Proposed pathways for formation of volatile aldehydes during shelf storage of bottled beer. Broad line: routes of formation of stale aldehydes (see p. 387); (M), melanoidins; isohumulones (and polyphenols), (O₂), molecular oxygen; L, lactones. (From Hashimoto and Kuroiwa (1975).)

aldehydes in beer are interrelated in a very complicated way. Furthermore, the unsaturated aldehydes resulting from these reactions undergo secondary oxidative decomposition to give shorter-chain aldehydes, and conversely, the saturated aldehydes are converted to longer-chain unsaturated aldehydes via aldol condensation in the presence of amino acid.

B. Pathways for Formation of Stale Aldehydes

A minor portion of the volatile aldehydes formed by these complicated pathways represent "stale flavour aldehydes" responsible for the stale or oxidized flavour developing in bottled beer. That is, although four kinds of

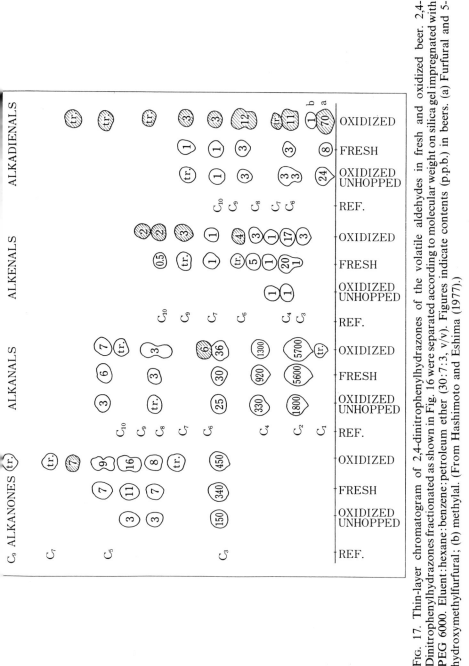

Fig. 17. Thin-layer chromatogram of 2,4-dinitrophenylhydrazones of the volatile aldehydes in fresh and oxidized beer. 2,4-Dinitrophenylhydrazones fractionated as shown in Fig. 16 were separated according to molecular weight on silica gel impregnated with PEG 6000. Eluent:hexane:benzene:petroleum ether (30:7:3, v/v). Figures indicate contents (p.p.b.) in beers. (a) Furfural and 5-hydroxymethylfurfural; (b) methylal. (From Hashimoto and Eshima (1977).)

carbon atoms which were marked out in this way have characteristic flavours and flavour thresholds in beer at 1 p.p.b. or less, their concentrations in oxidized beer are quite sufficient to be responsible for the stale flavour. When a mixture of aldehydes detected in oxidized beer was added to fresh beer, i.e. acetaldehyde at 6 p.p.m., acetone at 0·5 p.p.m., butanal at 0·5 p.p.m., 2-pentanone at 1·0 p.p.b., hexanal at 0·5 p.p.b., octanal at 0·5 p.p.b., nonanal at 0·5 p.p.b., 2-hexenal at 0·5 p.p.b., 2-heptenal at 0·5 p.p.b., 2-nonenal at 0·5 p.p.b., 2,4-hexadienal at 2·0 p.p.b., 2,4-heptadienal at 0·5 p.p.b., diacetyl at 1·0 p.p.b. and furfural at 12·0 p.p.b. as seen from Fig. 17, the beer was estimated by a taste panel to have a typical aroma of stale beer, with the exception that the sweetish caramel note was faint in treated beer (Hashimoto and Eshima 1977).

V. PREDICTION AND IMPROVEMENT OF FLAVOUR STABILITY OF BEER

A. Prediction of Flavour Stability

The ultimate goal of research on flavour stability is, of course, to find the main causes of the stale or oxidized flavour and to learn how to eliminate them and so extend the shelf-life of the product. With the foregoing background to the understanding of flavour staling, one's thoughts naturally turn to the question of what can be done in practice to eliminate the problem.

It is well known that beers vary in the extent of flavour staling on storage even when they are brewed under the same conditions. It is advisable to estimate the flavour stability of beer by tasting the stale flavour developed in sample beer stored under definite conditions. A possible test is as follows: freshly bottled beer is cooled to approximately 0 °C and opened. The bottle is then tapped to create foam and displace the air of the headspace and then 2 ml of air are introduced into the headspace under the foam using a syringe and the bottle is re-crowned. The bottle is then shaken 50 times and stored for 5–7 days at 40 °C, and then the stale flavour is tested by a taste panel, e.g. on a rating scale from grade 0 to grade 3:0, not perceptible; 1, faint; 2, distinct; 3, strong. Thus, the flavour stability of the product can be assessed without waiting several months for normal ageing to take place. A temperature of 40 °C is chosen because at higher temperature it may be more difficult to differentiate between different degrees of stronger staling.

However, objective and simple instrumental methods are needed for monitoring flavour staling in oxidized beer and for determining the susceptibility of beer to flavour staling. Determination of the trace amounts of several stale flavour compounds by instrumental analysis is very difficult. Consequently, the greatly increasing levels in oxidized beer of isoprene (Zenz

1973a, b) and furfurals (Grigsby and Palamand 1976, Brenner and Kahn 1976) have been employed as indices of the extent of beer staling. Colour and volatile aldehydes also increase during storage, but their changes are so small that their levels in oxidized beer would have to be compared with initial values for each lot of beer before shipping it out of the brewery. Although there is a correlation between increase in these compounds and decrease in taste panel scores, the levels of these compounds in beer are never above the flavour thresholds and so their changes are only a measure of incidental reactions taking place on storage.

Now that the main reactions involved in formation of a stale flavour have been elucidated, prediction of the flavour stability of beer should be attempted on the basis of the levels of precursors of stale compounds and the susceptibility of the precursors to oxidation. Moreover, to achieve quality control in the brewery, the susceptibility of products to flavour staling should be estimated by chemical analysis of freshly bottled beer and the results should promptly be applied to improving production and shipping. It is along this line that the following new index for prediction of flavour stability of beer was proposed by Hashimoto and co-workers.

To predict the flavour stability of beer, the levels of melanoidins, higher alcohols, and isohumulones should be measured, because these compounds are directly involved in the formation of stale aldehydes, as described in the preceding section. A fourth factor is the concentration of volatile esters in beer, because their flavour often masks the off-flavour developed in oxidized beer. Beer flavour results from a combination of the sensory impressions of a great number of different components present in beer and their interaction with each other. Stale aldehydes may contribute greatly to beer flavour because of their very characteristic aroma, while esters seem to be important in the building up of what may be called the background flavour of beer. Ales and stouts were believed to have greater resistance to sensory flavour changes on storage than do lagers. Probably there are no differences between the types of beer in the chemical changes they undergo, but the greater complexity of ale or stout flavours provides a masking effect (Clapperton and Dalgliesh 1976). When a mixture of ethyl acetate (2·5 p.p.m.), isoamyl acetate (0·5 p.p.m.), ethyl caproate (0·1 p.p.m.) and ethyl caprylate (0·25 p.p.m.) was added to oxidized beer, the stale flavour retained by the beer was estimated by a taste panel to be less perceptible under the sensory cover of the more intense flavour of these esters. When a beer was diluted with a half volume of carbonated water and then stored, the stale flavour developed in the diluted beer was stronger than that in the control. In the diluted beer, formation of stale aldehydes may be reduced by the decreased level of higher alcohols and isohumulones, but the estery flavour was attenuated so much that it did not mask the stale flavour because the levels of the esters were decreased to below their flavour thresholds

From multiple regression analysis of flavour staling in a pale lager beer, 66% of the stale flavour was defined as a function of variations in the levels of these four factors in the beers. Consequently, the correlation coefficient was as high as 0·6 to 0·8 between the sensory score of stale flavour developed in more than 50 beers stored for 7 days at 40 °C and the Flavour Stability Index (FSI) defined by the following equation:

$$(FSI) = 1·55 + 0·281 \times (\text{beer colour measured at 430 nm})$$
$$+ 0·207 \times (\text{isohumulones, p.p.m.}) + 0·0048$$
$$\times (\text{isoamyl alcohols, p.p.m.}) - 0·932 \text{ (isoamyl acetate, p.p.m.)}$$

Of course, the parameters must be determined in each brewery and in each type of beer. About 30 samples of freshly bottled beer, in which the colour, isohumulones, and volatile compounds are determined by routine methods are stored under definite conditions, e.g. with 2 ml of headspace air for 7 days at 40 °C. The stale flavour developed in the beer is then estimated by a trained panel by Quantitative Descriptive Analysis, e.g. on a 4-point rating scale. A linear 4-fold regression model is assumed to exist between the sensory score of stale flavour and the concentrations of the four components, and the parameters, i.e. partial regression coefficients, are estimated by computing the equation by the method of least squares. In the case of beers containing an antioxidant such as metabisulphite, the level of the additive should be involved as a variable in the equation. When any other component is found to be involved in flavour staling, the concentration of this component should be taken as a variable in multiple regression to increase the accuracy of the Flavour Stability Index. Unlike any other index yet presented, this index, FSI, has the merit that the flavour stability of the product beer can be predicted as soon as the beer is bottled, and the results can be used in controlling wort boiling, hopping or fermentation in the brewery.

B. Susceptibility of Beer to Flavour Staling

1. Alcohol-Oxidizing Activity of Melanoidins

Since the formation of stale aldehydes responsible for stale flavour is initiated by the oxidation of both higher alcohols and isohumulones, reduction in the levels of these precursors in beer should reduce the flavour staling of the resultant beer.

Hashimoto (1972, 1973) claimed that melanoidin-mediated oxidation of higher alcohols is inhibited by controlling the formation of melanoidins during wort boiling. The properties of melanoidins of beer vary with the conditions of the amino-carbonyl reaction taking place on wort boiling, under which the melanoidins are formed. The alcohol-oxidizing activity of mela-

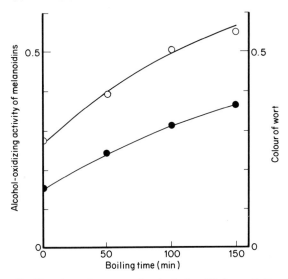

FIG. 18. Effect of boiling time of wort on the alcohol-oxidizing activity of melanoidins. Sweet wort was boiled and its colour and alcohol-oxidizing activity were measured at intervals. ○, alcohol-oxidizing activity of melanoidins; ●, colour of wort measured at 430 nm. (From Hashimoto (1973).)

noidins develops during the amino-carbonyl reaction on kettle boiling, as seen in Fig. 18. Therefore, prolonged boiling of wort results in an increased tendency to develop the alcohol-oxidizing activity of beer melanoidins.

Basic amino acids in wort tended to give melanoidins of darker colour, while neutral amino acids gave those with higher alcohol-oxidizing activity. Threonine constitutes about 82% of the total amino acids involved in melanoidin formation. The main sugars involved in the formation of the alcohol-oxidizing activity of melanoidins are maltose, glucose and fructose. The colour of melanoidins formed was proportional to the initial concentrations of amino acids and sugars, whereas the alcohol-oxidizing activity of the resultant melanoidins increased with the initial concentration of amino acids and decreased with that of the sugars, probably because such changes alter the ratio of amino acids to sugars in the formation of melanoidins. For this reason, the colour of boiled wort increased with the concentration of the wort boiled, but maximal activity of alcohol oxidation was obtained on boiling wort of nearly 15° Plato, as shown in Fig. 19 (Hashimoto 1973). When sweet wort is boiled at higher concentration, e.g. at 20° Plato, and then diluted to the desired concentration for pitching, the resulting beer should have melanoidins with normal colour intensity and with low activity to oxidize higher alcohols.

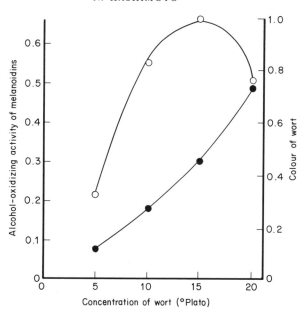

FIG. 19. Effect of concentration of wort during boiling on the properties of the resultant melanoidins. Samples of sweet wort of various concentrations were boiled for 30 min. ○, alcohol-oxidizing activity of melanoidins; ●, colour of wort measured at 430 nm. (From Hashimoto (1973).)

Molecular oxygen is not required for the amino-carbonyl reaction, so aeration of the wort has no appreciable effect on the properties of the melanoidins. The colour and alcohol-oxidizing activity of melanoidins increased more rapidly with increase in the pH of the wort. When wort was boiled in the presence of 50 to 200 p.p.m. of sodium bisulphite, the developments of colour and alcohol-oxidizing activity of the melanoidins were greatly inhibited. When sulphite was added after kettle boiling, it effectively suppressed the oxidizing activity and had no appreciable effect on the colour of the melanoidins.

However, the value of controlling the amino-carbonyl reaction during brewing to suppress the oxidation of higher alcohols in finished beer must be assessed in relation to other roles of the melanoidins in flavour, colour, head and haze formation in the beer. The melanoidin-mediated oxidation of alcohol in beer proceeded more rapidly at higher storage temperature, in the presence of air and at a lower pH value of beer, and was suppressed by the presence of 100 p.p.m. of bisulphite (Hashimoto 1972).

2. Levels and Composition of Bitter Substances

It is a foregone conclusion that the oxidative degradation of isohumulones to volatile aldehydes will be reduced by decreasing the levels of isohumulones themselves in finished beer. Reducing the hopping rate and using hops with a lower content of α-acid may result in improvement of the flavour stability of finished beer. Further, only minute amounts of volatile aldehydes were formed from oxidized isohumulones (Hashimoto 1979). Beers brewed with deteriorated hops contain larger amounts of oxidative products of isohumulones relative to isohumulones than beers brewed with fresh hops. Thus they have greater flavour stability than the latter, as shown in Table 9.

TABLE 9. Deterioration of α-acid of hops in relation to flavour stability of beer† ‡

Beer	Bitterness Units	Isohumulones (mg/l)	Stale flavour (%)
With fresh hops	22	20	100
With deteriorated hops (stored for 1 month)	24	17	104
With fresh hops	28	21	100
With deteriorated hops (stored for 5 months)	27	12	54
With fresh hops	26	20	100
With deteriorated hops (stored for 12 months)	21	4	65

† From Hashimoto (1979).

‡ Pairs of beers were brewed under similar conditions except for differences in the storage period of hops at 50 °C. The sensory intensity of the stale flavour is shown as a percentage of that of the parallel control.

Moreover, as seen in Table 6, isohumulones undergo oxidative degradation more easily than their derivatives, such as tetrahydroisohumulones and ρ-isohumulones because the double bond or carbonyl group of the isohexenoyl side chain of isohumulones is involved in this degradation (Hashimoto 1979). Thus use of tetra- (or hexa)-hydroisohumulones or ρ-isohumulones as bittering agents instead of isohumulones effectively suppressed the development of a stale flavour in beer, just as in the case of unhopped beer (Hashimoto 1979). Unlike isohumulones, the side-chains of these isohumulone derivatives do not undergo photochemical cleavage to form a 3-methyl-2-butenyl radical, and the resultant beers are also insensitive to the formation of sun-struck flavour (Kuroiwa and Hashimoto 1961, Koch et al. 1962, Bayne 1962, 1968, Hougen 1963, Kuroiwa et al. 1965, Worden and Todd 1971, Todd

TABLE 10. Isohumulones as precursors of
stale flavour† ‡

Bitter compound	Stale flavour§
Hopped beer	2·2
Isohumulones	1·8
Tetrahydroisohumulones	1·1
ρ-Isohumulones	1·1
Unhopped beer	1·0

† From Hashimoto (1979).
‡ Unhopped beer was stored with isohumulones
and their derivatives (25 p.p.m.) for 10 days at 40 °C.
§ Sensory score: 1; faint, 2; distinct, 3; strong.

et al. 1972). As seen in Table 7, the oxidative degradation of isohumulones in beer seems to be remarkably inhibited by the presence of 300 p.p.m. of sodium ascorbate.

3. Formation of Volatile Esters

It is commonly believed that, with the same grist and hops and essentially the same brewing process, the resulting beers may vary widely in the extent of flavour staling. On comparing a series of brewers yeasts, Baker and Stollberg (1959) found that the flavour stability of the beers depended on the strain of yeast used. This was probably due to variation in the formation of volatile esters masking the flavour arising from the stale aldehydes formed. About 34% of the variance in flavour stability of pale lager beer was explained by variation in the levels of ethyl acetate from 0·44 to 0·99 p.p.m., 32%, by variation of isohumulones from 24 to 34 p.p.m. and 12%, by variation of colour from 5·5 to 8·4 E.B.C. units (Hashimoto 1976).

The formations of higher alcohols and esters depend essentially on inherited characters of yeast strains and on factors affecting the metabolism of yeast. Selection of yeast strains may be some value in relation to the flavour stability of the resultant beer. Another chapter reviews works showing that ester formation depends upon the way the fermentation is conducted and on the physiological condition of the yeast. Generally, ester formation in brewing may be defined as a function of the amount of extract attenuated and the production of yeast mass during fermentation. Consequently, higher gravity wort, higher attenuation and a larger inoculum should be favourable for flavour stability of the resultant beer. In fact, beer with higher original gravity contains larger amounts of volatile esters than beer of normal original gravity and is comparatively insensitive to flavour staling. The production of beer with a given original gravity by fermenting wort of higher gravity and subsequently diluting the beer with water is a technique in commercial use in various countries, particularly in the United States. If not controlled, high-gravity brewing has a tendency to increase the level of esters in beer after dilution and hence the resistance to flavour staling.

4. Other Factors

Other than controlling the levels of melanoidins, isohumulones and volatile esters, various measures in brewhouse and fermentation had been believed to lead to significant differences in the susceptibilities of beers to flavour staling. MacFarlane's article entitled "Processing variables as they may affect the oxidation of beer" is an excellent review of these beliefs (MacFarlane 1967). However, it is very difficult, in the light of present knowledge, to obtain reliable evidence and explanation of these effects of processing variables on beer stability. Many of the variables seems to exert their main effect through a reduction of the tannin content of the beer. Only after further research on the possible participation of polyphenols in flavour staling will it be possible to develop more critical measures for determining the susceptibility of beer to staling. Removal of limited amounts of wort or beer polyphenols by polyamide resins may be of value.

A stale flavour develops more slowly on increase in the pH of beer (Meilgaard *et al.* 1971, Meilgaard and Moya 1971, Grigsby *et al.* 1972, Hashimoto 1976) probably because the oxidations of both higher alcohols and isohumulones to stale aldehydes are reduced at higher pH values (Hashimoto 1976). Generally, use of adjuncts results in a decrease of 0·2 or 0·3 unit in the pH value of beer.

C. Beer Handling for Retarding Flavour Staling

Mention was made above of some of the practical measures which, if adopted, could be expected to enhance the resistance of the beer to flavour staling. Certainly present knowledge of the mechanism of flavour staling may be of help in preventing staling. However, in the light of present knowledge, it seems impossible to eliminate completely flavour staling after prolonged storage of beer, because the main precursors of stale aldehydes such as melanoidins, higher alcohols, and isohumulones are present in concentrations 10 000 times more than the sub-microgram concentrations of their oxidation products required to produce severe flavour staling in beer. Moreover, these precursors are essential constituents of beer and their excessive removal has adverse effects on beer flavour itself. Then, ordinary techniques available for retarding oxidative deteriorations on storage come to attain a better usefulness in practice. These are listed below, and their effects in retarding flavour staling are compared in Fig. 2 and Table 7.

1. Rapid Consumption of the Product

Market quality control, including coding, rapid turnover, and checking warehouse inventories and rotation, makes it possible to sell the beer at the peak of its freshness.

2. Refrigerated Storage at Warehouses and Retail Outlets

Use of refrigeration generally slows down chemical process. On storage at below 10 °C, scarcely any flavour staling occurs, whereas at higher temperatures of 30 °C or more, staling becomes a serious problem.

3. Reducing Uptake of Air during Bottling

Oxidative reactions increase with the level of molecular oxygen in bottled beer, although these reactions later proceed in the absence of molecular oxygen. Most of the air in bottled beer is introduced during bottling, whereas the oxygen level in finished beer to be bottled is relatively small.

4. Addition of Antioxidants

Addition of such antioxidants as sulphite, bisulphite and ascorbic acid to finished beer is found to be effective. In particular a combination of antioxidants, e.g. 15 p.p.m. of potassium metabisulphite and 100 p.p.m. of sodium ascorbate may be recommended (Hashimoto 1976).

Since none of these improvements in brewing and handling are completely successful alone for preventing eventual development of a stale flavour, a combination of these conditions is recommended.

Controlling flavour staling in packaged beer represents a great challenge to brewers. Over the past 40 years, brewers have thought that control would be possible once the mechanism of staling was understood. Today, sufficient is known about the complicated mechanism of flavour staling to propose several processing variables to retard the staling. However, it is also realized that these practical measures for preventing flavour staling are limited because the staling seems to be linked to constituents essential for beer quality. Future studies will undoubtedly provide more information on the general mechanism of flavour staling, but this may be of no greater help in indicating practical means for enhancing the resistance of beer to flavour staling. Consequently, widespread use of market quality control, including especially storage of beer at the lowest practicable temperature, should be further adopted.

REFERENCES

Ahrenst-Larsen, B. and Hansen, H. L. (1963). *Brauwissenschaft* **16**, 1393.

American Society of Brewing Chemists, Report of the Subcommittee on Oxidation State of Beer (1967). *Proc. Am. Soc. Brew. Chem.* p. 276.

Arbogast, M., Maillard, A. Ch. and Urion, E. (1966). *Brass. Malt. Belg.* **16**, 48.

Ashurst, P. R. and Elvidge, J. A. (1966). *J. Chem. Soc.*, 675.

Badings, H. T. (1970). "Cold Storage Defects in Butter and Their Relation to Autoxidation of Unsaturated Fatty Acids". Thesis: University of Wageningen (Neth.).

Baker, D. L. and Stollberg, H. (1959). *Brewers' Digest* **34** (7), 46.

Bärwalt, G. (1970). *Monats. Brau.* **23**, 248.

Basarova, G. (1967). *Kvasný Prŭmsl* **13**, 26.

Bavisotto, V. S. and Roch, L. A. (1959). *Proc. Am. Soc. Brew. Chem.* p. 63.

Bavisotto, V. S. and Roch, L. A. (1960). *Proc. Am. Soc. Brew. Chem.* p' 101.

Bayne, P. D. (1968). U.S. Patent 3 418 135.

Bethune, J. L. and Rigby, F. L. (1958). *Proc. Am. Soc. Brew. Chem.* p. 62.

Blockmans, C. (1971). *Petit. J. Brass.* **79**, 107.

Blockmans, C. and Dujardin, C. (1973). *Bull. Ass. Anciens Eleves Inst. Ind. Ferment., Bruxelles* **16**, 83.

Blockmans, C., Devreux, A. and Masschelein, C. A. (1975). *Proc. E.B.C. Congr., Nice* p. 699.

Brenner, M. W. and Khan, A. A. (1976). *J. Am. Soc. Brew. Chem.* **34**, 14.

Brenner, M. W. and Stern, H. (1968). *Proc. 10th Conv. Aust. New Zealand Sec. Inst. Brew.* p. 89.

Brenner, M. W., Owades, J. L. and Golyzniak, R. (1954a). *Proc. Am. Soc. Brew. Chem.* p. 81.

Brenner, M. W., Owades, J. L., Gutcho, M. and Golyzniak, R. (1954b). *Proc. Am. Soc. Brew. Chem.* p. 88.

Brohult, S., Ryhage, R., Spetsig, L. O. and Stenhagen, E. (1959). *Proc. E.B.C. Congr., Rome* p. 121.

Bruckner, K. J., Charalambous, G. and Hardwick, W. A. (1970). *Tech. Quart., Master Brewers Ass. Am.* **7**, 228.

Burger, M. (1959). *Commun. Master Brewers Ass. Am.* **20** (7/8), 13.

Burger, M., Glenister, P. R. and Becker, K. (1969). *Proc. Am. Soc. Brew. Chem.* p. 72.

Buttery, R. G., Black, D. R., Lewis, H. J. and Ling, L. (1967). *J. Food Sci.* **32**, 414.

Chang, S., Tripp, R. C. and Richardson, T. (1970). *Tech. Quart., Master Brewers Ass. Am.* **7**, 198.

Chapon, L. (1967). *Bulletin De La Société Scientifique D'Hygiene Alimentaire L'Association Française des Technicients* **55**, 280.

Charalambous, G., Bruckner, K. J., Hardwick, W. A. and Weatherby, T. J. (1972). *Tech. Quart., Master Brewers Ass. Am.* **9**, 131.

Charalambous, G., Bruckner, K. J., Hardwick, W. A. and Linnebach, A. (1973). *Tech. Quart., Master Brewers Ass. Am.* **10**, 74.

Chen, E. Ch., Jamieson, A. M. and Dadic, M. (1972). *Tech. Quart., Master Brewers Ass. Am.* **9** (2), xxvi.

Clapperton, J. F. and Dalgliesh, C. E. (1976). *Eur. Brew. Conv., Haze and Foam Group Symposium, Berlin.*

Clapperton, J. F., Dalgliesh, C. E. and Meilgaard, M. C. (1976). *J. Inst. Brew.* **82**, 7.

Connet, B. E. and Elvidge, J. A. (1968). *J. Chem. Soc.*, 1193.

Cook, A. H. and Harris, G. (1950). *J. Chem. Soc.*, 1873.

Curtis, N. S. and Clark, N. G. (1960). *J. Inst. Brew.* **66**, 198.

Dadic, M. (1971). *Proc. Am. Soc. Brew. Chem.* p. 159.

Dadic, M. and Belleau, G. (1973). *Proc. Am. Soc. Brew. Chem.* p. 107.

Dadic, M. and Belleau, G. (1975). *Proc. Am. Soc. Brew. Chem.* **33**, 159.

Dadic, M. and Van Gheluwe, J. E. A. (1971). *Tech. Quart., Master Brewers Ass. Am.* **8**, 182.

Dadic, M., Van Gheluwe, J. E. A. and Valyi, Z. (1974). *Tech. Quart., Master Brewers Ass. Am.* **11**, 164.

Dale, A. R., Pollock, J. R. A., Moll, M. and That, V. (1977). *J. Inst. Brew.* **83**, 88.

Davis, D. P. and Palamand, S. R. (1976). *J. Am. Soc. Brew. Chem.* **34**, 55.

De Clerck, J. (1934). *J. Inst. Brew.* **40**, 407; *Bull. Ass. Anciens Etud. Brass., Louvain* **34**, 55, 78; *Wschr. Brau.* **51**, 196, 204, 213.

De Clerck, E. and Delaunoy, A. (1966). *Bull. Ass. Anciens Etud. Brass., Louvain* **62**, 1.

De Mets, M. and Verzele, M. (1968). *J. Inst. Brew.* **74**, 74.

Dominguez, X. A. and Canales, A. M. (1974). *Brewers' Digest* **49** (7), 40.

Drawert, F. and Tressl, R. (1972). *Tech. Quart., Master Brewers Ass. Am.* **9**, 72.

Drews, B. and Riemann, J. (1967). *Monats. Brau.* **20**, 254.

Drost, B. W., Van Eerde, P., Hockstra, S. and Strating, J. (1971a). *Tech. Quart., Master Brewers Ass. Am.* **8** (1), xv.

Drost, B. W., Van Eerde, P., Hockstra, S. and Strating, J. (1971b). *Proc. E.B.C. Congr., Estoril*, p. 451.

Drost, B. W., Duidam, J., Hockstra, S. and Strating, J. (1974). *Tech. Quart., Master Brewers Ass. Am.* **11**, 127.

Emslander, E. (1937). *Wschr. Brau.* **54**, 65.

Engan, S. (1969). *J. Inst. Brew.* **75**, 371.

Engan, S. (1970). *Brygmesteren* **27**, 123.

Engan, S. (1971). *Proc. E.B.C. Congr., Estoril*, p. 407.

Engan, S. (1972). *Brygmesteren* **29**, 313.

Galliard, T., Phillips, D. R. and Frost, D. J. (1972). *Chem. Phys. Lipids* **11**, 173.

Galliard, T. and Phillips, D. R. (1972). *Biochem. J.* **129**, 743.

Garza-Ulloa, H., Villarreal Garza, R. and Canales, A. M. (1976). *Brewers' Digest* **51** (4), 48.

Gramshaw, J. W. (1967). *J. Inst. Brew.* **73**, 455.

Gramshaw, J. W. (1969). *J. Inst. Brew.* **75**, 61.

Graveland, A., Pesman, L. and Van Eerde, P. (1972). *Tech. Quart., Master Brewers Ass. Am.* **9**, 98.

Gray, P. and Stone, I. (1939a). *Wallerstein Lab. Commun.* **3**, 5.

Gray, P. and Stone, I. (1939b). U.S. Patent 2 159 985.

Green, C. P. (1970a). *J. Inst. Brew.* **76**, 36.

Green, C. P. (1970b). *J. Inst. Brew.* **76**, 476.

Grigsby, J. H. and Palamand, S. R. (1976). *J. Am. Soc. Brew. Chem.* **34**, 49.

Grigsby, J. H., Palamand, S. R., Davis, D. P. and Hardwick, W. A., (1972). *Proc. Am. Soc. Brew. Chem.* p. 87.

Grigsby, J. H., Palamand, S. R. and Hardwick, W. A. (1974). *Proc. Am. Soc. Brew. Chem.* p. 64.

Gustavson, K. H. (1956). "The Chemistry of Tanning Process," p. 15. Academic Press, New York and London.

Harris, G. and Ricketts, R. W. (1959). *Proc. E.B.C. Congr., Rome*, p. 290.

Harris, G. and Ricketts, R. W. (1960). *J. Inst. Brew.* **66**, 313.

Hartley, R. D. and Fawcett, C. H. (1968). *Phytochemistry* **7**, 1395, 1641.

Hartong, B. D. (1934). *Wschr. Brau.* **52**, 409.

Hartong, B. D. (1964). *Monats. Brau.* **17**, 127.

Hashimoto, N. (1966). *Rep. Res. Lab. Kirin Brewing Co., Yokohama* **9**, 1.

Hashimoto, N. (1970). *Rep. Res. Lab. Kirin Brewing Co., Takasaki* **13**, 1.

Hashimoto, N. (1971). Doctorial thesis, Kyoto University.

Hashimoto, N. (1972). *J. Inst. Brew.* **78**, 43.

Hashimoto, N. (1973). *Rep Res. Lab. Kirin Brewing Co., Takasaki* **16**, 1.

Hashimoto, N. (1975) *Koryo* **112**, 23.

Hashimoto, N. (1976). *Rep. Res. Lab. Kirin Brewing Co., Takasaki* **19**, 1.

Hashimoto, N. (1979). *J. Inst. Brew.* **85**, 136.

Hashimoto, N. and Eshima, T. (1977). *J. Am. Soc. Brew. Chem.* **35**, 145.

Hashimoto, N. and Koike, K. (1971). *Rep. Res. Lab. Kirin Brewing Co., Takasaki* **14**, 1.

Hashimoto, N. and Kuroiwa, Y. (1975). *Proc. Am. Soc. Brew. Chem.* **33**, 104.

Hashimoto, N., Kuroiwa, Y. and Aramaki, K. (1968). *Rep. Res. Kirin Brewing Co., Takasaki* **11**, 43.

Hautke, P. and Petricek, D. (1971). *Monats. Brau.* **24**, 241.

Helm, M. (1939). *J. Inst. Brew.* **45**, 80.

Hougen, O. A. (1963). U.S. Patent 3 079 262.

Hudson, J. R. (1955). *J. Inst. Brew.* **61**, 127.

Jamieson, A. M. and Van Gheluwe, J. E. A. (1970). *Proc. Am. Soc. Brew. Chem.* p. 192.

Jansen, M. E. (1964). *J. Inst. Brew.* **70**, 401.

Jenard, H. (1960). *Brewers' Digest* **35** (4), 58.

Jerumanis, J. (1969). *Bull. Ass. Anciens Etud. Brass., Louvain* **65**, 169.

Kavanagh, T. E., Steward, S. R. and Clarke, B. J. (1974). *Proc. 13th Conv. Aust. New Zealand Sec. Inst. Brew.* p. 51.

Kepner, R. E., Strating, J. and Weurman, C. (1963). *J. Inst. Brew.* **69**, 399.

Koch, G. H., Herwig, W. C. and Kissel, T. L. (1962). U.S. Patent 3 044 879.

Kokubo, E., Kuroiwa, Y. and Kowaka, M. (1971). *Proc. Am. Soc. Brew. Chem.* p. 265.

Kosuge, T., Zenda, H., Tsuji, K., Yamamoto, T. and Narita, H. (1971). *Agric. Biol. Chem.* **35**, 693.

Kowaka, M. and Kokubo, E. (1977). *J. Am. Soc. Brew. Chem.* **35**, 16.

Kowaka, M., Kokubo, E. and Kuroiwa, Y. (1972). *Proc. Am. Soc. Brew. Chem.* p. 42.

Kowaka, M., Kokubo, E. and Kuroiwa, Y. (1973). *Proc. Am. Soc. Brew. Chem.* p. 66.

Kringstaad, H. (1972). *Brauwissenschaft* **25**, 272.

Krüger, E. and Neuman, L. (1970a). *Monats. Brau.* **23**, 117.

Krüger, E. and Neuman, L. (1970b). *Monats. Brau.* **23**, 269.

Kuroiwa, Y. and Hashimoto, N. (1961). *Proc. Am. Soc. Brew. Chem.* p. 28.

Kuroiwa, Y., Hashimoto, N., Hashimoto, H. and Nakagawa, K. (1965). Japan Patent 465 513.

Kuroiwa, Y., Kokubo, E. and Hashimoto, N. (1973). *Tech. Quart., Master Brewers Ass. Am.* **10**, 215.

Lau, V. K. and Lindsay, R. C. (1972). *Tech. Quart., Master Brewers Ass. Am.* **9** (1), xvii.

Laws, D. R. J. and McGuiness, J. D. (1974). *J. Inst. Brew.* **80**, 174.

Lewis, M. J., Pangborn, R. M. and Tanno, L. A. S. (1974). *Tech. Quart., Master Brewers Ass. Am.* **11**, 83.

Lother, A. (1936). *Wschr. Brau.* **53**, 305.

MacPherson, J. K. and Buckee, G. K. (1974). *J. Inst. Brew.* **80**, 540.

Markl, K. S. and Palamand, S. R. (1973). *Tech. Quart., Master Brewers Ass. Am.* **10**, 184.

McDougall, J., Shada, D. and Dakin, P. E. (1963). *Proc. Am. Soc. Brew. Chem.* p. 48.

McFarlane, W. D. (1967). *Tech. Quart., Master Brewers Ass. Am.* **4**, 239.

McFarlane, W. D. (1968). *Tech. Quart., Master Brewers Ass. Am.* **5**, 87.

McFarlane, W. D. (1970). "Industry-sponsored Research on Brewing", pp. 5–34. Brewing Industry Research Institute, Chicago, Ill.

McFarlane, W. D., Thompson, K. D. and Garratt, R. (1963). *Proc. Am. Soc. Brew. Chem.* p. 98.

Meilgaard, M. (1972). *Brewers' Digest* **47** (4), 48.

Meilgaard, M. (1974). *Tech. Quart., Master Brewers Ass. Am.* **11**, 118.

Meilgaard, M. (1975). *Tech. Quart., Master Brewers Ass. Am.* **12**, 107, 151.

Meilgaard, M. and Moya, E. (1970). *Tech. Quart., Master Brewers Ass. Am.* **7**, 135, 143.

Meilgaard, M. and Moya, E. (1971). *Tech. Quart., Master Brewers Ass. Am.* **8** (2), xvii.

Meilgaard, M., Moya, E., Ruano, J. I. and Ayma, M. (1971). *Proc. Am. Soc. Brew. Chem.* p. 219.

Nakayama, T. O. M. and Fly, W. H. (1968). *Proc. Am. Soc. Brew. Chem.* p. 198.

Narziss, L. and Forster, A. (1971). *Brauwissenschaft* **24**, 145.

Narziss, L. and Forster, A. (1972). *Brauwissenschaft* **25**, 8, 128, 239.

Ohlmeyer, D. W. (1957). *Food Tech.* **11**, 503.

Owades, J. L. and Jakovac, J. (1966). *Proc. Am. Soc. Brew. Chem.* p. 180.

Palamand, S. R. and Grigsby, J. H. (1974). *Brewers' Digest* **49** (9), 58.

Palamand, S. R. and Hardwick, W. A. (1969). *Tech. Quart., Master Brewers Ass. Am.* **6**, 117.

Palamand, S. R., Hardwick, W. A. and Cole, D. W. (1969). *Proc. Am. Soc. Brew. Chem.* p. 78.

Palamand, S. R., Grigsby, J. H., Davis, D. P. and Hardwick, W. A. (1973). *Proc. Am. Soc. Brew. Chem.* p. 132.

Perkins, E. G. and Witt, P. Jr. (1968). *Proc. Am. Soc. Brew. Chem.* p. 145.

Pessa, E. (1971). *Proc. E.B.C. Congr., Estoril* p. 333.

Pollock, J. R. A. (1972). *Proc. 12th Conv. Aust. New Zealand Sec. Inst. Brew.* p. 135.

Regan, J. P. (1969). *Proc. E.B.C. Congr., Interlaken* p. 471.

Regan, J. P. and Elvidge, J. A. (1969). *J. Inst. Brew.* **75**, 10.

Reinke, H. G., Hoag, L. E. and Kincaid, C. M. (1963). *Proc. Am. Soc. Brew. Chem.* p. 175.

Shaw, S. J. and Milles, A. K. (1967). *Proc. Am. Soc. Brew. Chem.* p. 45.

Shigematsu, N., Kitazawa, Y. and Yabuchi, Y. (1964). *Bull. Brewing Sci., Tokyo* **10**, 45.

Shimazu, T., Hashimoto, N. and Kuroiwa, Y. (1975). *Proc. Am. Soc. Brew. Chem.* **33**, 7.

Silbereisen, K. and Kraffczyk, F. (1968). *Tech. Quart., Master Brewers Ass. Am.* **5**, 135.

Sogawa, H. (1973). *Rep. Res. Lab. Kirin Brewing Co., Takasaki* **16**, 29.

Spence, L. R., Palamand, S. R. and Hardwick, W. A. (1973). *Tech. Quart., Master Brewers Ass. Am.* **10**, 127.

Spetsig, L. O., Steninger, M. and Brohult, S. (1957). *Proc. E.B.C. Congr., Copenhagen* p. 22.

Steiner, K. (1971). *Schweiz. Brau.-Runds.* **82**, 117.

Stenroos, L. E. (1973). *Proc. Am. Soc. Brew. Chem.* p. 50.

Stenroos, L. E., Wang, P., Siebert, K. and Meilgaard, M. (1976). *E.B.C. Haze and Foam Group Symposium, Berlin.*

Strating, J. (1963/1964). *Intern. Tijdsch. Brouw. Mout.* **23**, 97.

Strating, J. and Van Eerde, P. (1973). *J. Inst. Brew.* **79**, 414.

Szilvinyi, A. and Puspok, J. (1963). *Brauwissenschaft* **16**, 204.

Takahashi, K., Tadenuma, M. and Sato, S. (1976). *Agric. Biol. Chem.* **40**, 325.

Todd, P. H., Johnson, P. A. and Worden, L. R. (1972). *Tech. Quart. Master Brewers Ass. Am.* **9**, 31.

Trachman, H. and Saletan, L. T. (1969). *Proc. Am. Soc. Brew. Chem.* p. 19.

Tressl, R. and Renner, R. (1975). *Monats. Brau.* **28**, 195.

Tressl, R., Kossa, T. and Renner, R. (1975). *Proc. E.B.C. Congr., Nice* p. 737.

Tripp, R. C., Timm, B., Iyer, M., Richardson, T. and Amundson, C. H. (1968) *Proc. Am. Soc. Brew. Chem.* p. 65.

Van Laer, M. H. (1940). *Petit. J. Brasseur.* **48** (2057), 25.

Van Gheluwe, J. E. A., Jamieson, A. M. and Valyi, Z. (1970a). *Tech. Quart., Master Brewers Ass. Am.* **7**, 158.

Van Gheluwe, J. E. A., Valyi, Z. and Dadic, M. (1970b). *Brewers' Digest* **45** (11), 70.

Vanhoey, M., Vandewalle, M. and Verzele, M. (1970). *J. Inst. Brew.* **76**, 372.

Verzele, M. (1967). *Proc. E.B.C. Congr., Madrid* p. 77.

Verzele, M. (1970). *Fermentatio* **66**, 103.

Verzele, M. and Vanhoey, M. (1967). *J. Inst. Brew.* **74**, 451.

Visser, M. K. and Lindsay, R. C. (1971a). *Tech. Quart., Master Brewers Ass. Am.* **8**, 123.

Visser, M. K. and Lindsay, R. C. (1971b). *Proc. Am. Soc. Brew. Chem.* p. 230.

Wagner, B. and Baron, G. (1971a) *Monats. Brau.* **24**, 123.

Wagner, B. and Baron, G. (1971b). *Monats. Brau.* **24**, 225.

Wang, P. S. and Siebert, K. J. (1974a) *Proc. Am. Soc. Brew. Chem.* **32**, 47.

Wang, P. S. and Siebert, K. J. (1974b) *Tech. Quart., Master Brewers Ass. Am.* **11**, 110.

Wheeler, R. E., Pragnell, M. J. and Pierce, J. S. (1971). *Proc. E.B.C. Congr., Estoril* p. 423.

Withycombe, D. A. and Lindsay, R. C. (1973). *Tech. Quart., Master Brewers Ass. Am.* **10** (2), xix.

Witt, P. R. Jr. (1972). *Proc. Am. Soc. Brew. Chem.* p. 115.

Witt, P. R. Jr. and Burdick, A., II. (1963). *Proc. Am. Soc. Brew. Chem.* p. 104.

Witt, P. R. Jr. and Rineheimer, W. A. (1965). *Proc. Am. Soc. Brew. Chem.* p. 146.

Witt, P. R. Jr. and Sullivan, J. W. (1966). *Proc. Am. Soc. Brew.* p. 233.

Wohleb, R., Jennings, W. G. and Lewis, M. J. (1972). *Proc. Am. Soc. Brew. Chem.* p. 1.

Worden, L. R. and Todd, P. H. (1971). U.S. Patent 3 552 975.

Zenz, H. (1972). *Mitt. Versuchsst. Gärungsgew. Wien* **26**, 188.

Zenz, H. (1973a). *Mitt. Versuchsst. Gärungsgew. Wien* **27**, 183.

Zenz, H. (1973b). *Proc. E.B.C. Congr., Salzburg* p. 419.

Zenz, H. (1974a). *Mitt. Versuchsst. Gärungsgew. Wien* **28**, 85.

Zenz, H. (1974b). *Mitt. Versuchsst. Gärungsgew. Wien* **28**, 104.

Zenz, H. and Klaushofer, H. (1970). *Mitt. Versuchsst. Gärungsgew. Wien* **24**, 47.

7. Oxygen and Beer

LUCIEN CHAPON

Chaire de Biochimie II. UER Alimentation et Nutrition, Université de Nancy,
Boulevard des Aiguillettes, Nancy, France

In this chapter the aim has been more to summarize the present knowledge of the mechanisms controlling the oxidation of beer by molecular oxygen than to prepare a complete bibliographic review of all that has been published in this field. Those points are emphasized which seem to be indispensable to the understanding of phenomena related to oxidation and the results which one can consider to be fully established are pointed out. These points allow the reasons for the complexity of the problem to be identified with the objectives for future research. The study here presented is based on the research work carried out in the author's laboratory by sensitive original methods which have been developed and confirmed over twenty years.

I. INTRODUCTION

It has been recognized for a very long time (Pasteur 1876) that the oxygen of the air, even at low concentration, affects the organoleptic quality of beer in undesirable ways. Oxidation brings about most usually a change in flavour, a more or less pronounced browning and an early formation of hazes and sediments (Singruen 1940). The presence of air also favours the proliferation of infecting microorganisms or of yeast.

The first studies which can properly be described as scientific in this area of brewing followed from the application of the idea of redox potential to biological systems (Wurmser 1930). Here the pioneering works of de Clerck (1934a, b), Hartong (1934) and Mendlik (1934, 1935) should be cited as having illuminated the importance which should be attached to the elimination of oxygen after the end of fermentation.

Our understanding of this area, which has grown considerably in the last twenty years, still has significant lacunae as far as mechanisms are concerned because of: (1) the multiplicity of possible substrates for oxidation; (2) the diversity of redox reactions involved in ageing; (3) the very great complexity of the mechanisms of reduction of the molecule of oxygen.

The conditions prevailing in beer cause the oxidations to take place in it at very low rates which lend themselves poorly to direct experimental study. Innumerable attempts have been made to surmount this difficultly by replacing the natural oxidant, molecular oxygen, O_2, by a reactive agent, generally coloured, of which the changes in concentration can easily be followed as time goes on. Interesting though they are, these methods do not allow one to predict in a precise way how the beer will behave during ageing in the presence of limited amounts of oxygen, because the identity of behaviour of two substances towards an oxidizing agent does not necessarily mean that they will behave identically towards all others. Considerable differences may exist; of these we shall see several examples. Information obtained during the study of simple model solutions can be used to throw light on particular aspects of the oxidation mechanism of certain classes of reducing agents in beers, but when there is competition between several oxidizable constituents, the complexity increases to an extent greater than can readily be understood.

A. General Characteristics of Oxidation Reactions in Beers

The oxidations which take place in beer occur normally in a particular set of conditions which it is useful to underline at this point because they impose very strict limitations on the reactions and fix the lines of study. They are:

The beer contains, on average 4% of alcohol.

The pH lies between 3·9 and 4·7 (average 4·1).

The oxygen concentration is generally less than 1 mg/l.

The storage temperature is often the ambient temperature but it may vary from a few degrees above zero (in a refrigerator) to 40° or more in warehouses.

The rates of disappearance of oxygen and the rates of the many kinds of oxidation–reduction reactions which take place are always very slow. Shaking enhances the rate of consumption of oxygen.

The presence of light accelerates these reactions and may change their direction. Studies of the catalysis of the oxidation of beers must be carried out in the dark.

The oxidizable substrate consists of an extremely complex mixture of numerous substances, some of which, being present at very low concentrations, are not able to be analysed. Among the most abundant substances having reducing properties, one may mention polyphenols (100–200 mg/l), melanoidins and several reductones containing the grouping $-C(OH){=}C(OH)-$. Of these last it is very difficult to estimate the concentrations because of factors discussed later. Accessory additives may also be present, such as ascorbic acid (average 30 mg/l) and sulphurous acid or its salts (free sulphur dioxide often less than 10 mg/l). These substrates are not generally autoxidizable (they do not react directly with molecular oxygen, or only very slowly). Oxidation requires the intervention of catalysts which are essentially transition metals, iron and copper, either as simple ions, or complexes. The content of iron in total is normally less than 1 mg/l. The content of copper in all seldom exceeds 0·5 mg/l and is often much lower than that. In addition there exist, as we shall see, purely organic catalysts. Enzymic oxidation does not seem to take place in beer. Besides, the medium scarcely ever reaches its redox equilibrium; it evolves steadily, slowly it is true, but continuously.

B. The Experiments of Owades

The only direct analytical study undertaken to identify the transfer of oxygen to, and its distribution in, the various groups of substances present in beer during storage is that of Owades and Jakovac (1966), who used the stable isotope ^{18}O. Such studies require very special equipment and will be undertaken only rarely. Thus in order to analyse for this isotope when it is present in low concentration, it is essential to be able to use the technique of proton activation, which transforms heavy oxygen ^{18}O into a radioactive isotope of fluorine ^{18}F. Additionally, the separation of the substances and the counting of their activity must be carried out very quickly because the half-life of ^{18}F is only 1·88 hours.

The results obtained are very interesting and can be summarized as follows:

All the oxygen present in the headspace disappears.

The tannins undergo the greatest part of the oxidation.

The next most significant group of compounds which receive the labelled oxygen is that of the volatile carbonyl compounds.

Finally, the bitter substances undergo some oxidation.

The involvement of carbohydrate was not able to be proved.

If the oxidation which occurs is expressed as the percentage of the atoms of oxygen which have been fixed in each group of substances one obtains the following figures:

65% for tannins (assuming 320 to be the average molecular weight of monomeric tannins);

30% for carbonyl compounds;

only 5% for the bitter substances, which is negligible.

Finally, direct involvement of hydrogen with formation of $H_2^{18}O$ does not seem to be concerned in the reduction of molecular oxygen.

II. PRIMARY REDUCING AGENTS AND METHODS OF MEASURING THEM

A. Useful Oxidants

When one considers the phenomena of oxidation in beer, one must take into account the fact that the oxidant is the oxygen of the air, that is molecular oxygen, O_2, the solubility of which in beer is very similar to that in water, approximately 8 mg/l at ambient temperature under normal pressure.

When one considers the *reducing agents*, the problem is much less well defined. For instance, the concept of reducing sugar involves the use as oxidant of Fehling's solution or of ammoniacal silver nitrate (both of which are reagents with an alkaline reaction), but the sugars are not in any way involved in the direct fixation of oxygen under the conditions defined in the previous paragraph. On the other hand, the polyphenols, which reduce, with some vigour, Fehling's solution and ammoniacal silver nitrate, slowly reduce molecular oxygen.

It is not usually justified to use, in relation to oxidation by molecular oxygen, information drawn from experiments on the utilization of conventional chemical oxidizing reagents. However, these may be useful, although they may react simultaneously with several substances or with several groups of substances. Strong inorganic oxidizing agents such as potassium permanganate or iodine cannot be used directly with beer because they have no specificity. They react with far too many substances of which the majority do not react with molecular oxygen. Potassium permanganate has been used to measure the concentrations of tannins; but only after separation of these by adsorption. The simple considerations of the standard oxidation–reduction potential of conventional reagents are of only little predictive value and experimentation only allows one to make a satisfactory choice in relation to practical experiments, especially as regards the specificity of reactions having sufficiently short time scales.

B. 2,6-Dichlorophenolindophenol

The first reagent which gave rise to generally useful applications in brewing was 2,6-dichlorophenolindophenol (DCI), as studied by Hartong (1934). This reagent was reinvestigated several years later by Gray and Stone (1939a, b) who were able to devise an industrially usable method of measurement universally known as the Indicator Time Test (I.T.T.). The I.T.T. is the time in seconds required for 10 ml of beer to decolorize to the extent of 80% a known volume (0·25 ml) of a 0·01 N solution of DCI at 18 °C.

Since then the I.T.T. has been widely utilized, although the nature of the reducing agents which are affected by DCI is not clearly defined and although serious reservations have been expressed concerning the kinetics of its reduction (Case and Thompson 1961), as a result of which various authors have wished to improve the original procedure (Pierre 1938, Klopper 1955, Hartong *et al.* 1955).

DCI has been used in various electrometric (Chapon and Urion 1953) or colorimetric (de Clerck and Van Cauwenberge 1956, Reich and Rock 1960) methods with the aim of obtaining information on the reducing substances involved and above all to be able to discriminate between different types of reducing agents. In fact, hardly any other substance than ascorbic acid can be correctly measured by DCI in the presence of the natural reducing agents of beer (melanoidins, reductones and sulphites). In our opinion the best method consists of injecting the reagent (0·01 N solution) very slowly (1 ml/h) into beer (4 ml) in the actual cell of a recording colorimeter reading at a wavelength of 510 nm and continuously stirred. When ascorbic acid is present, DCI is reduced instantaneously upon its introduction into the cell. Its concentration begins to increase only when ascorbic acid is totally oxidized which is shown by the appearance of a weak rose colour. While the concentration of DCI remains very low in the medium it reacts only very slowly with the other reducing agents so that the possibility exists of examining precisely the end of the oxidation of the ascorbic acid.

A variation of this method, proposed by de Clerck (1956), attempts to use the differences in speed of reduction of DCI which exist between groups of reducing agents. *Immediate* reducing agents correspond to the amount of DCI reduced in less than 15 seconds (and consist largely of ascorbic acid together with part of the melanoidins), *rapid* reducing agents, which react between 15 seconds and 5 minutes (melanoidins and sulphites), and *slow* reducing agents, between 15 and 150 minutes (phenolic substances constitute the major part of the group). In fact, there is no clear frontier between the three groups defined in this way. There are overlaps, and the choice of time is arbitrary. Similar reservations can be made as regards the use of any other oxidizing agent. Methods based on kinetic data concerning the reduction of any particular oxidant added at the beginning of a reaction at relatively high concentration in a non-defined mixture cannot be exact for the following reasons:

(1) The concentrations of oxidizing and reducing agents both decrease simultaneously during the trial.
(2) The overall compositions differ between one beer and another, in particular the relative proportions of different reducing agents can vary substantially.
(3) Reducing agents of different types react simultaneously but with different rates.
(4) An individual pure substance (e.g. a polyphenol) may have complex oxidation kinetics.

When the oxidizing agent is highly coloured, when it is added from the start of the reaction at a relatively high concentration and when its reduction is followed colorimetrically, the sensitivity of the method for rapid reducing agents, which are present at low concentration, is necessarily low, as their concentration, obtained as the difference between two intense colours, is subject to substantial errors. On the other hand, if the oxidizing agent of which an excess is used is itself colourless or only weakly coloured and if the concentration is measured of a reduced coloured substance which is formed, the sensitivity and the reproducibility of the analysis may be much higher (as is the case, for instance, with the ferric iron complex of α,α'-dipyridyl).

C. Ferric Dipyridyl: Method of Chapon *et al.* (1971)

The freshly prepared reagent obtained by mixing a solution of α,α'-dipyridyl (3·9 ml of a solution prepared by dissolving dipyridyl (50 mg) in 0·1 N sulphuric acid (4 ml) and making to 50 ml volume with water) with a solution of ferric sulphate (0·1 ml of a solution prepared by mixing ferric alum (150 mg), concentrated sulphuric acid (0·2 ml) and water to 50 ml) is practically colourless. The addition to it of a small amount of reducing agent (0·1μ-equivalent per experiment, that is to say 50–100 μl of beer), which is negligible as compared with the concentration of the reagent, which can therefore be taken as constant, leads to the formation of the ferrous dipyridyl complex, which is intensely red and very stable. The concentration of ferrous dipyridyl can be followed during the reaction by reading the colour at 510 nm.

Study of the formation of ferrous dipyridyl shows that most of the polyphenolic compounds (other than the most simple ones) have complex oxidation kinetics. The rate of reaction, which is high at the beginning, declines progressively during several tens of minutes without any indication that a defined state of oxidation has been reached. This is what is always found with beer. Practical considerations make it necessary to set an arbitrary time for the reaction (3 minutes) at a defined temperature (25 °C) in order to obtain reproducible results. Substances may be characterized by the rates of the reaction under these conditions:

Instantaneous: ascorbic acid (2 equivalents per mole) and part of the reductones.
Steadily: melanoidins, sulphites, sulphydryl compounds.
Slowly: polyphenols, tannoids.
Without effect: alcohol, sugars, polysaccharides, proteins, bitter resins.

The behaviour of sulphite deserves to be discussed in some detail. The oxidation of sulphite by ferric dipyridyl takes about 10 minutes to reach a stable transmittance value. Ferrous dipyridyl thus formed is not only very far below the two equivalents expected but, additionally, the greater the amount of reducing substances provided by the sample, the higher is the difference (or the lower is the yield). Although it cannot be titrated in this way, it is easy to prevent sulphite from interfering in the titration of the other reducing agents: it suffices to add to the ferric dipyridyl in the cell of the colorimeter 100 μl of a solution of hydrogen peroxide (about 0·01 N) just prior to the addition of the sample. Hydrogen peroxide immediately oxidizes sulphite to sulphate without changing the course of oxidation of the other reducing agents by ferric dipyridyl.

The reducing power of beer lies between 0·5 milliequivalents per litre for pale, light, non stabilized beers and 3 milliequivalents per litre for dark, strong beers. For comparison it may be mentioned that a solution of ascorbic acid of concentration 30 mg/l has a reducing power of 0·3 milliequivalents per litre.

The reducing substances can be placed in appropriate categories by taking advantage of the practical possibilities of selective isolation of certain types of constituents. Indeed there is an excellent correlation between the concentration of tannoids adsorbed on insoluble polyvinylpyrrolidone (Polyclar AT = polyvinylpolypyrrolidone = PVPP) and the reducing power measured by the ferric dipyridyl method. Another possible way is to make a determination of reducing power prior to and after an ultrafiltration: this allows a distinction to be made between the reducing substances bound to nondialysable macromolecules and the small molecules which are freely dialysable. The utilization of a reagent like urea, able to break hydrogen bonds, allows further distinction to be made between loosely bonded phenolic substances (those which pass the ultrafiltration membrane) and tightly bound ones (those which are retained).

D. The α,α′-Diphenyl-β-picrylhydrazyl Radical

This reagent, which was used with beer by Owades and Zientara (1960), is intensely coloured. It has a redox potential significantly higher than that of dichlorophenolindophenol (1·2 V compared with 0·65 V). Its reactivity is very similar to that of ferric dipyridyl. It attacks the same substances with rates of reaction of the same order; however, sulphite is not oxidized. Its intense colour prevents its utilization in large excess, which complicates the kinetic measurements. The optical density at 520 nm is measured after exactly 5, 10 and 30 minutes. The results are expressed in milliequivalents/litre (0·4 to 0·8 after 5 minutes 0·6 to 1·1 after 30 minutes). The method of operation is more complicated than that with ferric dipyridyl. A comparative study (TEPRAL 1976) between the methods using this reagent and ferric dipyridyl, carried out on 34 samples of beer, gave an index of correlation $r = 0·866$.

E. Ferricyanide

When solutions containing certain reducing substances are heated with ferricyanide it is reduced to ferrocyanide which reacts with a ferric salt giving a colloidal solution of Prussian Blue of which the optical density is measured at a wavelength of 660–700 nm. The temperature, the duration of heating, and the pH determine the nature of the reducing agent which will have been attacked. At 100 °C and in alkaline medium, reducing sugars are oxidized. At 70° and pH 5 (Chapman and MacFarlane 1945) or at 50 °C at pH 6·6 (Crowe *et al.* 1948), certain reducing substances present in milk powder are attacked. Adachi (1958) applied the method to the constituents of malt wort. In all cases the colour increases with the time of reaction, approximately doubling between 15 and 80 minutes. No clear end point appears. It is necessary to fix an arbitary time for the reaction; this time is chosen to be relatively short, for example 15 minutes (for practical reasons). The values obtained by using this method (Karakus 1975) on 57 industrial malts were:

Reductones: 2·2 to 6·3 mg/100 g of dry matter.
Total reducing agents: 1·8 to 2·3 milliequivalents/100 g dry matter.
Total polyphenols: 50 to 103 mg/100 g dry matter.

F. Oxidations Catalysed by Peroxidase

The enzymic oxidation of numerous polyphenols by hydrogen peroxide together with peroxidase, which leads to a more or less intense brown coloration and to the formation of condensed products which precipitate proteins, affects only little the reducing power towards ferric dipyridyl (Chapon *et al.* 1971). One important result of this fact is that the measurement of reducing power, by whichever method, cannot reveal the degree of condensation reached by a solution of polyphenols during a preliminary oxidation.

The degree of browning and the formation of haze by the oxidation of beer in the presence of hydrogen peroxide and peroxidase gives certain information on its content of haze precursors, both polyphenolic and protein in nature. However, experience has not confirmed the hopes which have been held for this method as one suitable for predicting colloidal stability (Chapon *et al.* 1961, 1967a, b), although a variant combining the peroxidase oxidation of polyphenols with the measurement of their tanning power by means of cinchonine has been developed and used with satisfactory results (Thompson and Forward 1969).

III. MEASUREMENT OF THE REDOX CONDITIONS

Electrometric or colorimetric measurement of the oxidation–reduction state of a beer was introduced into brewing science by Mendlik (1934, 1935) and by de Clerck (1934a, b) and reviewed in many detailed papers in the brewing journals (Preece 1936, Laufer 1936). Initially attractive to the young theorists who saw in it the possibility of applying in practice fundamental conventional knowledge, this measurement soon proved to be difficult to use in routine fashion in a medium as complex as beer. It is useful to recall, for those not readily familiar with thermodynamic matters the reasons for the limitations of the method.

A. Oxidation–Reduction Equilibria

Classical thermodynamics allows it to be calculated that a redox system

$$Red \rightleftharpoons Ox + ne$$

consisting of oxidized form Ox and reduced form Red in aqueous solution is characterized by an electromotive force defined by:

$$E_H = E_0 + \frac{RT}{nF} 2 \cdot 303 \log \frac{[Ox]}{[Red]};$$

that is to say approximately

$$E_H = E_0 + \frac{0 \cdot 06}{n} \log \frac{[Ox]}{[Red]} \text{ at } 30 \,^{\circ}C,$$

in which E_H = potential in volts as compared with the standard hydrogen electrode; E_0 = half reduction potential, or standard redox potential of the system; R = universal gas constant; $1 \cdot 985$ cal mol^{-1} degree^{-1}; F = Faraday = 96 500 coulombs; T = absolute temperature; n = number of electrons transferred per reacting unit; [Ox] and [Red] = the activities of the species Ox and Red, which can generally be taken as being equal to the concentrations provided that the activity coefficients are similar, which is the case for non-electrolytes in dilute medium.

$$\frac{[Ox]}{[Red]} = \frac{\gamma(Ox)}{\gamma(Red)} \simeq \frac{(Ox)}{(Red)},$$

where ( ) = concentrations; γ = activity coefficient.

In certain cases one can measure this EMF directly by immersing in the solution an electrode of a noble metal (usually platinum) together with a reference electrode (for instance a calomel electrode). The system is maintained under an inert gas such as pure nitrogen. The EMF of the electrical system is measured by means of an electrometer of very high impedance (Wurmser 1930).

B. Limitations of Conventional Methods

The application of this method to beer gives misleading results because of the slowness with which platinum reaches a stable potential. In fact the medium does not conform with the thermodynamic conditions on which the theory relies.

For the measurement to have significant meaning in thermodynamic terms the system must be in equilibrium; must equilibrate rapidly with the electrode, that is to say, must be electroactive; must contain the constituents Ox and Red at relatively similar concentrations; must not be too dilute.

In beer, many oxidizable constituents are not electroactive and their concentration is low. Many systems exist together and are not necessarily in equilibrium one with the other. The presence of oxygen perturbs the measurement and must be eliminated, for instance by flushing the solution with pure nitrogen.

However, a platinum electrode reaches, after several hours, several days or several weeks, a stable value which is more or less reproducible for a beer in its reduced condition. In effect, the medium contains, at low concentration, intermediary electroactive substances of which we shall see that the main one is probably a complex containing iron. Clark (1923) suggested that the oxidation–reduction state be expressed in rH units:

$$rH = \log\frac{1}{[H_2]},$$

a relation which defines for the medium an imaginary pressure of hydrogen with which the electrode is in equilibrium. Assuming that two electrons are involved and that there is no loss of a proton in the pH region considered, rH is related to the potential by the relation

$$E_H = 30(rH - 2\,pH) \qquad \text{(in mV at 30 °C)}$$

The rH of a beer not containing oxygen falls from 16–18 to around 8–9 after several days, which corresponds to the decoloration of Methylene Blue.

C. Electroactive Substances

Wurmser (1930) showed that a non-electroactive system could effectively behave as an electroactive system in the presence of a low concentration of an electroactive intermediate. The classical example is the system formed by a substrate of a dehydrase, its oxidation product, the enzyme, and Methylene Blue as intermediate. Even when the oxygen has been completely eliminated by entrainment, the platinum electrode retains the memory of it during several tens of minutes. The simultaneous utilization of the platinum electrode and of a non-polarizable electrode (a dropping mercury electrode used as a redox electrode which responds instantly to the elimination of dissolved oxygen) shows this phenomenon well. It should however be underlined that the mercury potential is itself influenced by the presence of anions which are adsorbed at the mercury–solution interface, forming a double layer, and in consequence the dropping mercury electrode does not always measure the redox potential.

Although, because of the slowness of its response, the platinum electrode is unsatisfactory for a practical measurement of the redox condition of beer, it allows, when used in fundamental research, the illustration of the role of iron complexes in the catalysis of oxidation by molecular oxygen (see section III. D).

In wines, which are relatively rich in content of the metallic ions iron and copper, simple analytical methods (using ferrocyanide or thiocyanate) can be used to find the oxidation state of the iron (Ribéreau-Gayon 1933). The iron is converted rapidly into the trivalent condition when the wine comes into contact with air. Later, after removal of the air, it is slowly reduced to the ferrous condition. The ferric form is in fact one of the essential oxidizing reagents. The presence of organic substances capable of forming complexes with iron alters the potential of the ferrous–ferric system and thus modifies its ability to catalyse the oxidation of different oxidizable substrates. As certain of those systems are electroactive, the platinum electrode measures in fact the variations which are produced in the redox condition of the system by the effect of reducing agents or oxidizing agents which are not electroactive.

In beers, in which the concentrations of metallic ions are much lower, the proof is much more difficult but potentiometric studies lead to similar conclusions to those which have been deduced from the study of wines.

D. Ions and Complexes

The two common metals iron and copper, which are present normally in trace amounts in beer, easily give complexes with numerous organic substances, for instance those which contain carboxylic acid, hydroxy, amino and sulphydryl groups. If the stability of the complex with the metal in its maximum oxidation state is greater than that in which the metal is in its minimum oxidation state there is a movement of the oxidoreduction potential towards lower levels since the concentration of the free oxidized form becomes lower. For instance, ethylenediaminetetracetate (EDTA) lowers the potential of the ferrous–ferric system by nearly 300 mV because the stability of the ferric EDTA complex is greater than that of the ferrous EDTA complex. (If EDTA is represented by YH_4, and the metal by M, the reaction constants $K_{My} = [MY]/[M][Y]$ are respectively $\log K_Y Fe^{III} = 25 \cdot 1$; $\log K^Y Fe^{II} = 14 \cdot 33$ (as indicated by Jander 1956). In the presence of EDTA, ferrous iron becomes titratable by dichlorophenolindophenol and the titration can be followed by electrometry because the system remains electroactive at concentrations of the order 1 mg/l (Urion et al. 1957). On the other hand, if the complex of the metal in its minimum oxidation state is more stable than the corresponding complex with the maximum oxidation state, there is a shift of the redox potential towards higher levels. For instance, α,α'-dipyridyl (and other reagents of the same group which have a greater affinity for the ferrous form than for the ferric form) raises the potential.

Experience shows (Urion *et al.* 1957) that, if one adds to beer which is totally free of traces of oxygen a few milligrams per litre of ferrous iron (in the form of Mohr's salt) and one adds slowly potassium permanganate while measuring the potential with a platinum electrode, one obtains a sigmoid curve shifted towards a lower level by some tens of millivolts compared with that which one would obtain by adding the same amount of iron in acetate buffer. Further, ferrous iron in solution in beer is oxidized by air more rapidly than when dissolved in an acetate buffer of the same pH. This is proof that iron exists in beer in complex forms. The remaining ferrous iron can easily be measured in the following manner. First of all, the oxygen is removed from the beer by entrainment with pure nitrogen. EDTA is then added and the ferrous iron measured by the slow addition (1 to 2 ml/h) of 0.1 N dichlorophenol-indophenol while measuring the potential of the platinum electrode. The height of the S-curve gives directly the concentration of ferrous iron. This method is not applicable to the original content of the iron in the beer, as its concentration is too low and it may, additionally, be bound in complexes which are not electroactive.

It is found that the ferric complex which is formed *rapidly* during contact with air is *slowly* reduced by the reducing agents of beer during prolonged storage in the total absence of oxygen. The slow fall of the potential of the platinum electrode, which takes place steadily during the storage of beer after elimination of the oxygen with which it had been in contact, reflects essentially the slowness with which the ion complex system becomes equilibrated with the medium.

Among the various substances of beer to which the role of complexing agents can be attributed, it appears that oxalate takes first place. Oxalate is normally present in beer in concentrations from 12 to 28 mg/l according to the kind of beer (Brenner 1957), and is therefore present in amount fully sufficient to complex not only the iron normally present in beer but also the few milligrams per litre which may be added to exaggerate the phenomenon. In the presence of oxalate, in acetate buffer (pH 4), iron gives an electrometric titration curve having a value for half reduction in the region normally found for iron in solution in beer.

Other organic acids in model solutions (or in beer) do not show unambiguous phenomena. Although they give coloured complexes with ferric ion, polyphenols and tannoids do not change substantially the potential of the ferric–ferrous system (the complexes are not electroactive).

To summarize, complexing agents which have a greater affinity for the ferric forms tend to increase, in general, the oxidizability by oxygen. Those which have a higher affinity for the ferrous form reduce it. No practical solution seems to be in sight for inactivating the iron normally present in beer.

As it is bound in certain natural complexes, in particular ferroporphyrins: haemin, cytochrome c, peroxidase, and catalase, iron may not be determined by colorimetric methods based on the formation of a coloured complex (α,α'-dipyridyl, o-phenanthroline, ferrozine (Canales $et\ al.$ 1975)) or by catalytic methods using the oxidizing property of the complex Fe/EDTA. It may therefore participate in electron transport in a way totally different from that of iron which is less strongly bound.

It is accordingly necessary to use care in any attempt to establish correlations between catalytic activity and iron because of the existence of different types of complex of which the activities are not necessarily identical. For instance, a knowledge of the content of total iron as measured by atomic absorption spectrometry (Frey $et\ al.$ 1966) is not sufficient.

E. Metastable Systems

A simple experiment illustrates in remarkable fashion the influence which the existence of intermediate electron carriers may have on the rate of fixation of oxygen (Moll 1977). An aqueous solution of ascorbic acid ($0 \cdot 1$ N) is treated with iron/EDTA in catalytic amount, $0 \cdot 5$ mg/l, and stirred under air at ambient temperature and in the dark. It is found that the rate of uptake of oxygen as measured by a respirometer is slow. However, when traces of Methylene Blue are added, the rate of absorption increases by three to fourfold whereas, in the absence of iron/EDTA, a similar addition has no effect. It is well known in biochemistry that two systems of dehydrogenases can be coupled and reach a true equilibrium only if a common coenzyme (e.g., NAD, NADP, cytochrome b) is present. $In\ vitro,$ Methylene Blue can replace the coenzyme (Green 1940).

The experiment described above shows that, for non-enzymatic conditions, reactions of the same type may be involved and that the presence or absence of a suitable intermediate, truly a co-factor, can influence substantially the speed with which the system evolves. Beer contains constituents of which the behaviour recalls that of Methylene Blue. They play the role of intermediates in the transfer of electrons between ascorbic acid and oxygen without themselves being capable of reducing oxygen. It may be thought that this results from redox systems (Q/QH_2) of which the normal potential is in the neighbourhood of those of A/AH_2 and of the catalyst X/XH_2 (Q/QH_2 represents a quinone/hydroquinone hypothetical system):

$$AH_2 \ \overset{Q}{\underset{QH_2}{\diagdown\diagup}} \ A \qquad \overset{XH_2}{\underset{X}{\diagdown\diagup}} \qquad \overset{O_2}{\underset{H_2O_2}{\diagdown\diagup}}$$

In very dilute medium, the rates are necessarily low, so that the presence of such intermediates takes on particular importance. They reduce to some extent the chemical sluggishness and have an action comparable with that of the electroactive intermediates involved in the exchange of electrons between a redox system and an electrode. They reduce the extent of the metastable domain, which consequently increases the reaction rate and therefore diminishes the stability of beer, stability being defined as the time required for the beer to reach an arbitrarily defined level of transformation, under defined conditions.

IV. THE OXIDATIC REACTION

We shall use the terms *oxidatic* and *peroxidatic* to characterize reactions having some analogy with oxidations catalysed respectively by oxidases and peroxidases but mediated by catalysts which are non-enzymic in nature. The terms *oxidasic* and *peroxidasic* will be used only for enzymic reactions (Chapon and Chapon 1978).

Experience shows that the addition to beer of some milligrams per litre of copper ions increases substantially the rate of fixation of oxygen. Copper is an excellent catalyst of the oxidation of ascorbic acid (AH_2) (Kellie and Zilva 1935, Mack and Kertesz 1936, Siffert 1946, Barron *et al.* 1936), so that solutions of ascorbic acid buffered to pH 4 can be used as models to study details of the catalysis by copper.

The study of catalysts which are involved in the reduction of oxygen in conditions of concentration and of pH comparable with those which exist in beers has led to a very sensitive method known as "the Methylene Blue colorimetric method", as developed in the author's laboratory (Chapon *et al.* 1957, 1958a, 1959a, b, 1960, Chapon and Chapon 1962, Genty-Aimé 1961). The method and principles will now be discussed in order that the nature of the information it gives and its limits can be understood.

A. Methylene Blue Colorimetric Method

A solution of ascorbic acid (0·025 N), prepared in an inert atmosphere buffered to pH 4·1 by sodium hydroxide, decolorizes a solution of Methylene Blue ($8·3 \times 10^{-4}$ M). The rate of decoloration is strongly accelerated by light and also takes place in the dark; it is total in every case. The base solution thus prepared will be referred to as solution S in what follows. It recolorizes only very slightly when saturated with air if the reagents are very pure, and fixes oxygen very slowly (1·6 μl/100 ml/min) by autoxidation.

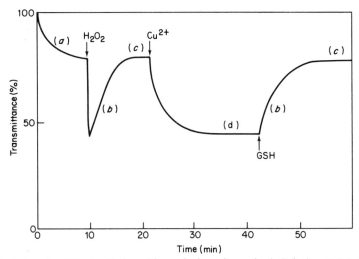

FIG. 1. Principle of the Methylene Blue colorimetric method. Solution S (Methylene Blue (MB) + Ascorbic acid (AH$_2$)) is colourless under nitrogen. When saturated with air in the cuvette of the colorimeter, it undergoes a slight autoxidation. The transmittance reaches a stable value within 10 minutes (*a*). If solution S contains peroxidase, the addition of H$_2$O$_2$ immediately releases MB which afterwards is slowly reduced by the ascorbic acid in great excess. The transmittance returns to the starting value (*c*). The addition of copper ions provokes the formation of MB at a constant rate. A dynamic steady state occurs between formation and decolouration of MB. An unchanging transmittance value (*d*) is the sign of a stable oxidation rate. The greater the concentration of catalyst, the lower the plateau. The addition of glutathione (GSH) complexes the copper ions. The transmittance returns to the initial value (*c*). A quinone which releases MB immediately gives the same response as H$_2$O$_2$, but the reaction occurs even without peroxidase. A stable organic catalyst gives the same type of response as copper ions but its activity is not affected by GSH.

The addition of catalytic amounts of copper (a few ng per 5 ml of solution S) brings about the expected increase in the rate of fixation of oxygen with appearance of a blue coloration stable during several tens of minutes which is the more intense as the concentration of copper is higher. The intensity of the colour which can be measured directly by colorimetry at 660 nm, in weak light, is related directly to the rate of oxidation and allows qualitative and quantitative study to be made of factors which influence it. The activity can be expressed by the increase of the concentration of Methylene Blue which results from the addition of a known quantity of catalyst.

We can provisionally represent the reactions which are involved by the scheme:

$$
\text{AH}_2 \underset{\text{A}}{\overset{\text{Methylene Blue}}{\bigtimes}} \underset{\text{2Cu}^{++}}{\overset{2\text{H}^+ \;\; \text{2Cu}^+}{\bigtimes}} \underset{\text{H}_2\text{O}_2}{\overset{\text{O}_2}{\bigtimes}} \qquad \textbf{(I)}
$$

In the system, Methylene Blue/leuco-Methylene Blue represents an intermediate acting between the copper ions and the ascorbic acid. Precise measurements have shown that more than 92% of the electrons are carried by the intermediate Methylene Blue despite the very unfavourable ratio between the molar concentrations (Methylene Blue/ascorbic acid = 1/300). As the reduction of Methylene Blue formed is comparatively slow under the conditions used, its equilibrium concentration represents approximately sixty times the weight of the copper which has caused it to be formed, which explains the extreme sensitivity of the solution towards copper. The specific activity of copper (moles of oxygen consumed/min/atom of copper) is of the order of 13·6.

Hydrogen peroxide, which is relatively stable under the experimental conditions, accumulates in the solution and may reach concentrations of the order of some milligrams per litre. The concentration depends on the rate of oxidation and grows with it (Chapon and Chapon 1962). In the presence of peroxidase (from horseradish) hydrogen peroxide is rapidly decomposed and it is again leuco-Methylene Blue which plays the role of preferential hydrogen donor, in such a way that for the same rate of consumption of oxygen the rate of formation of Methylene Blue in the presence of peroxidase is double that shown in Scheme (1). This scheme may therefore be completed as shown in Scheme (II) which indicates the possible formation of two molecules of Methylene Blue for one of oxygen consumed: one during the oxidatic stage (*a*) and one during the so-called peroxidasic phase (*b*).

The hydrogen peroxide can be removed also by sulphite (50–100 μg per test) and in this case Methylene Blue is formed only during the oxidatic stage (*a*). The reaction that replaces the peroxidasic step (*b*) in the equation (II) may be written:

$$H_2O_2 \diagdown \diagup SO_2$$
$$\text{spontaneous}$$
$$H_2O \diagup \diagdown SO_3$$
$$(c)$$

Finally, numerous substances which do not necessarily have the character of reducing agents, as defined in section II, can be involved in oxidation coupled with that of ascorbic acid, under certain conditions. The reaction is represented by Scheme (II) (d) which now replaces (b) in Scheme (II).

$$H_2O_2 \diagdown \diagup RH_2$$
$$\text{catalyst having} \qquad (d)$$
$$\text{peroxidatic activity}$$
$$2H_2O \diagup \diagdown R$$

In contrast with the oxidation of sulphite, which consumes almost all of the hydrogen peroxide formed during the oxidatic step (*a*), the oxidation of a substrate such as RH_2 might involve only a fraction of the hydrogen peroxide which is formed. Colour reactions do not allow distinction of the part which is due to coupling of a substance RH_2 because the oxidation of reduced Methylene Blue during the peroxidatic stage is carried out under conditions of concentration imposed by the colorimetric method and these conditions cannot be altered without changing the relative proportions of the reaction steps. The importance of coupled oxidation of substrates of which the oxidized form has a particularly low threshold for sensorial perception can be realized in relation to the part it plays in the loss of organoleptic qualities of the beer as related to the effects of oxidation. These reactions are at present little understood, for the problem is difficult. One particular aspect of it will be studied later.

As will be seen in what follows, a variety of substances may have actions similar to that of copper in Schemes (I) and (II). These are catalysts in the strict sense if their specific activity is high. The colorimetric method then permits study to be made of the catalytic activity of a complex medium towards the oxidation of ascorbic acid. Judicious use of inhibitors allows allocation of overall activity to different catalysts present.

B. Metal Ion Catalysts

1. Copper and its Complexes

On account of its high sensitivity towards copper ions, the colorimetric method can be applied to the study of catalytic activity due to these ions either in model solutions or directly in beer, in samples having volumes of the order of 0·1–0·2 ml (Chapon *et al.* 1959c). It allows it to be shown that copper ions can be readily complexed by sulphydryl compounds in general, such as glutathione, cysteine, diethyl dithiocarbamate, thiourea, or thioglycollic acid, by EDTA or nitrilotriacetic acid in very low concentration (50–100 µg per test), and lose their activity.

The copper present in beer occurs partly in complexes having no oxidatic activity in ascorbic acid solution. Oxygen of the air destroys a part of the complex, liberating copper ions, and the catalytic activity thus increases progressively with residence time in the presence of air (Chapon *et al.* 1959c).

In the presence of *o*-phenanthroline, copper which is bound in complexes with glutathione and cysteine is displaced and exhibits an activity similar to that of free copper ions, while the copper/diethyl dithiocarbamate complex is not changed. However, the latter is fairly rapidly oxidized by air with the reappearance of oxidatic activity.

The use of reagents such as glutathione, diethyl dithiocarbamate, *o*-phenanthroline and dipyridyl allows one to obtain an idea of the partition of the copper between free ions, labile complexes, and stable complexes and to follow the variations in these different categories with regard to the effects of oxidation. By analogy with what happens in model solutions, it may be concluded that the fraction of the activity of beer which disappears following the addition of glutathione (100 µg per test) is due to free copper ions only. Iron ions at comparable concentrations are inactive in solution S. There is nevertheless a "residual activity" which is not sensitive to sulphydryl inhibitors and which can be attributed at least partly to organic substances formed during coupled oxidation of certain polyphenols (see section IV.C), and in the amino-carbonyl reaction (Maillard reaction).

2. Iron and its Complexes

As compared with copper ions, iron ions, interacting with ascorbic acid under the conditions of the colorimetric technique described, have an oxidatic activity about 1000 times weaker than that of copper ions. This ratio is not constant and depends on the level of concentration used.

On the other hand, iron ions have a significant peroxidatic activity. In oxidations catalysed by iron ions, hydrogen peroxide never reaches a high concentration (Chapon *et al.* 1960). Addition of EDTA, which gives a very stable complex with trivalent ions, substantially activates the oxidatic activity of iron and inhibits its peroxidatic activity. It is for this reason that solution S, to which EDTA has been added, which will be named solution C in what follows, allows estimates to be made of the free iron and of that which is bound in complexes having lower stability than that of the EDTA/iron complex. The sensitivity of solution C to iron ions is about 100 times greater than that of solution S (Chapon et al. 1959b). The specific activity of the EDTA/iron complex = 2·5; that of iron ions = 0·02. Under these conditions copper is totally inhibited. The activity which is measured includes in addition to that of iron the "residual activity" as defined in section IV.B1.

If the ferric form is the effective oxidizing agent for a primary substrate it may be expected that the EDTA/ferric complex will be a weak oxidant, that is to say will only oxidize reducing agents which are said to be "energetic", of low redox potential. The complex ferric/oxalate will be more active and free iron ions still more so. The ferric dipyridyl complex is an energetic oxidant of which the properties have been put to successful use (section II.C).

On the other hand, if the ease with which molecular oxygen oxidizes ferrous complexes is compared, then they can be listed in the inverse order:

$$EDTA > nitrilotriacetic\ acid > oxalate > Fe^{2+} > dipyridyl;$$

the latter complex is not oxidized by oxygen. Thus the activity of iron depends strictly on the composition of the medium with regard to substances capable of complexing it. However, it would be dangerous to limit consideration of the problem to the redox potentials of the catalyst and the substrate and to hope to draw useful information concerning the kinetics of the reaction. This aspect of the problem will be discussed later (section IV.E).

3. Porphyrins

The presence of coproporphyrins in very low concentration (0–60 μg/l) in beer was reported by McFarlane (1959, McFarlane and Blashke 1959). This substance arises from the oxidative transformation of porphyrinogen arising itself from the metabolism of the yeast. Porphyrinogen is stabilized by the presence of ascorbic acid; it partially disappears during pasteurisation while coproporphyrin is relatively more stable. A high concentration of copro-porphyrin in packaged beer can arise, according to McFarlane, only as a result of oxidation during storage. It is not known to what extent these substances can act as catalysts in the oxidation of oxidizable constituents of beers. However, they have been detected in haze substance, probably combined with protein, and the question would be worth further study. In relation to these results, it is interesting to consider a little known aspect of a very widespread ferroporphyrin, haemin, the prosthetic group of numerous enzymes involved in oxidation or involved in electron transport. Haemin does not exist in the free state in beer. The colorimetric method describes some of its particular oxidatic properties which are worthy of brief discussion here as they can clarify certain aspects of the oxidation of beers. Haemin, dissolved in a very dilute solution of sodium hyroxide under an atmosphere of pure nitrogen (doubly distilled water 500 ml, sodium hydroxide 30–40 mg), possesses a high but fugitive oxidatic activity towards solution S (Marchetti 1963, Chapon and Chapon 1977). The colour maximum is reached after two minutes. The changes in transmittance are shown in Fig. 2, from which it can be calculated that, at the point of maximum concentration of Methylene Blue, about 75% of the haemin has already been destroyed in the reaction which it catalyses.

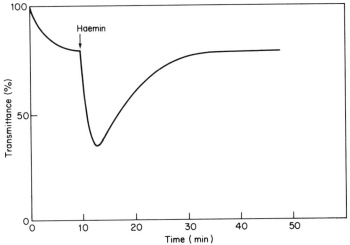

FIG. 2. Haemin is an outstanding example of an unstable catalyst. The oxidatic activity, initially very high, disappears very quickly (from Chapon *et al.* (1977)).

The initial sensitivity is again above that of free copper ions (specific activity 246 calculated from the equilibrium value, corresponding to 25% of the haemin used). Its rapid destruction is probably the reason why haemin has been considered not to have oxidatic activity towards ascorbic acid (Barron *et al.* 1936).

The iron in ferroporphyrin is not sensitive to the action of EDTA, as shown by the fact that haemin produces the same concentration of Methylene Blue in presence of EDTA (solution C, very sensitive to catalysis by iron ions) as in its absence (solution S). Glutathione is inactive. In the products arising from the oxidation of haemin, iron, though having no oxidatic activity, remains sequestered as regards EDTA or reagents of the dipyridyl group. Catalase, peroxidase, haem enzymes, and cytochrome *c* have no oxidatic activity towards ascorbic acid under the conditions of the colorimetric method.

C. Organic Catalysts

1. Naphthoquinones

5-Hydroxynaphthoquinone (juglone), which has not been detected in beer, may nevertheless be taken as a model to test the hypothesis that a purely organic quinone/hydroquinone couple can function as a true oxidatic catalyst. Such couples having high specific activity are rare. A few microlitres of a solution of juglone (1 mg) in 70% ethanol (100 ml) shows, in solutions S and C, an oxidatic activity which is high and which is not inhibited by sulphydryl compounds at the level of those which are effective in complexing copper (Stenger 1961). However, the addition of relatively high concentrations of cysteine (0·6 mg in the test) increases the response to the colour reaction at the same time as it renders juglone relatively unstable. After reaching a maximum the activity diminishes significantly as shown in Fig. 3. The strongest

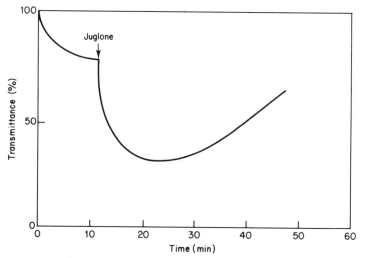

Fig. 3. Juglone (in presence of cysteine) is an example of an organic catalyst of which the oxidatic activity disappears during its action, but much more slowly than that of haemin (from Chapon *et al.* (1977).

activation is obtained when 0·6 mg of cysteine is used per test and in these conditions the specific activity is approximately 3·7. The reason for such behaviour is not as yet known. EDTA does not affect the activity. Another naphthoquinone, flaviolin (2,5,7-trihydroxy-1,4-naphthoquinone) also possesses a high specific oxidatic activity insensitive to cysteine and stable over prolonged periods of time.

2. Polyphenols

The oxidation by air of catechin in aqueous solution at pH 4, coupled to that of ascorbic acid or to that of dihydroxyfumaric acid, in the presence of copper or of iron or of the complexes of iron with nitrilotriacetic acid or EDTA leads to the appearance of a stable oxidatic activity which is insensitive to the inhibitors of the reactivity of copper (Chapon and Chapon 1977). It should be emphasized that neither spontaneous oxidation of catechin in aqueous solution nor its oxidation by hydrogen peroxide in the absence of metals nor its oxidation by hydrogen peroxide in presence of peroxidase give rise to the substantial oxidatic activity.

The substances involved with oxidatic activity are extractable by ethyl acetate from the medium. After chromatography several times on Sephadex LH 20 columns, with methanol as an eluent, only two fractions display oxidatic activity. They can be isolated in very minute amounts. Their migration speed is slightly lower than that of catechin. The first one (X_1) is blue; it has been crystallized from cold methanol. The slower one (X_2) is olive green; it also has recently been obtained in pure form. Both are fairly stable in ethyl acetate. They lose their activity during several weeks in methanol and more quickly in water even under nitrogen. They are destroyed in a few seconds in alkaline medium and on oxidation with hydrogen peroxide and peroxidase. Both are reversible electroactive systems of which the E_0 has been estimated in a dynamic way (see Fig. 6). Work is in progress to elucidate the structure of these interesting substances (Chapon and Chapon 1978, 1980).

Catechin is always present in beers, in concentrations up to 10 mg/l. It is present both in malt and the hops. It is a component of numerous anthocyanogens of which some at least (for instance procyanidin B3), by coupled oxidations, give rise to a stable oxidatic reaction.

This behaviour may be suggested as an explanation of the increase in the residual activity of the beer which takes place when the beer is oxidized by air. Thus the autocatalytic pattern of ascorbic acid oxidation while dissolved in certain beers saturated with air may be interpreted as due in part to the liberation of increasing quantities of copper ions, and in part by the formation of catalysts resulting from the coupled oxidation of certain polyphenols of which catechin may be regarded as a model (Chapon and Chapon 1977). However, it seems that the formation of such catalysts is still insufficient to account for the autocatalytic course of the oxidation of ascorbic acid in presence of catechin and iron ions (Chapon and Chapon 1979).

3. Isoalloxazines

The presence of these substances in beer is chiefly due to the metabolism of yeasts. Neither riboflavine, which exists in beer at concentrations between 0·3 and 1·3 mg/l (Hopkins and Wiener 1944, 1945, Scriban 1970) nor its derivatives riboflavine-5-phosphate or flavine-adenine-dinucleotide which occur in numerous enzyme systems (flavoproteins), have real oxidatic activity against solutions of ascorbic acid. However, by simple exposure to daylight, dilute aqueous solutions (0·001 N) of riboflavine and its 5-phosphate rapidly acquire an oxidatic activity observable during the first hours with the aid of the colorimetric method (Moll 1977). In the rigorous absence of oxygen and under strong illumination (100 watts at 10 cm distance during several hours) the oxidatic activity increases more rapidly, reaches a level which is twice as high as in the presence of air, and begins to fall after 10 hours.

The product responsible for this effect, which is yellow with green fluorescence and has an ultraviolet spectrum scarcely different from that of riboflavine or its 5-phosphate, has been identified as formylmethylflavine (De Kok et al. 1971, Fall and Petering 1956). It is rapidly destroyed by light in the presence of air. It shows, in relation to ascorbic acid, a strong oxidatic activity which is stable in the dark (the specific activity is of the order of 5·5). As with the other catalysts mentioned, it can bring about coupled oxidation of catechin, with the appearance of substances which have oxidatic functions.

4. Melanoidins

It is well known that the brown solutions obtained by the Maillard reaction during malt curing and wort boiling have, in relation to dichlorophenol-indophenol, ferric dipyridyl and diphenylpicrylhydrazyl, reducing properties falling into the three categories designated as immediate, rapid and slow reducing agents. These solutions undergo very slow oxidation in the air and are sensitive to catalysis in this respect by metal ions but much less so than ascorbic acid. The colorimetric method allows it to be shown that certain of the non-dialysable constituents which are present have the properties of oxidatic catalysts and that they are not sensitive to the classical inhibitors of metals (Chapon and Chapon 1979). Their activity on ascorbic acid solutions buffered to pH 4–5 can be confirmed by manometric means. As in the case of catalysis by the iron/EDTA complex, the rate of fixation of oxygen increases substantially in the presence of Methylene Blue.

D. Catalytic Power of Haze Substances

It is well established that mineral elements are involved in the formation of reversible and irreversible hazes in beers (Hudson 1955, Chapon 1965). According to Hudson (1959), between 20 and 70% of the total metal ions present in beer are associated with haze and if one takes account of the weights involved it is possible to draw the conclusions that the concentration of ions is between 5000 and 50 000 times greater in the haze than in the beer.

Certain metallic ions of which the solutions are readily hydrolysed at the pH of beer provide effective centres of condensation for haze precursors. Tin

(Sn^{2+}) is from this point of view the most dangerous element. Ferric ions induce, immediately upon their addition to beer, a haze which disappears slowly (Silbereisen and Wittman 1957), whereas at the same concentration ferrous ions are inactive.

However it seems logical to consider two types of metal ions:
  (1) those which, like tin, have no apparent role in the phenomena of oxidation; and
  (2) those which, like iron, are oxidation catalysts.

The fact that copper and iron are concentrated in hazes suggests that these metals are already preferentially associated, in beer, with certain haze precursors (Gorinstein 1974). It is tempting to think that the substances involved are more especially sensitive to oxygen (for instance tannins) and that the phenomena of oxidation appear in more intense fashion in the particles already formed as a result of the high local concentration of catalysts. Such oxidation would facilitate condensation towards the formation of irreversible haze by the establishment of covalent linkages and the growth of the particles. Thus could be explained, at least as a hypothesis, the fact that the formation of oxidation haze shows in most cases an autocatalytic trend. The fraction of cold haze which is soluble in a solution of polyvinylpyrrolidone of molecular weight 12 000 or 24 000 undergoes oxidation in air, becoming brown, while its original clear solution gives rise to permanent haze just as a beer would do under these conditions. As shown by Baker et al. (1960), manometric studies of the consumption of oxygen by beer show always the existence of an induction period followed by a rapid increase in the rate of absorption until a more or less stable level is reached. It is not proven that as a result of their association with polyphenols or proteins metallic ions can be activated in a way comparable with that which results from their incorporation into metalloenzymes but it cannot be excluded that the local concentration thus realized would be favourable to the formation of oxidation products, themselves having activity like that of those formed during the oxidation of catechin (see section IV.C2).

However this may be, the autocatalytic course of oxidation of beers, at least when they are saturated with oxygen, is a general fact which is well established. Several factors may be involved as contributors to it and it is not easy to specify at present the exact part which should be attributed to each of them.

E. Kinetics of Oxygen Absorption

The rate at which oxygen oxidizes the reducing substances of a beer is governed by manifold factors. The relationship between redox potentials and oxidation kinetics has been studied recently (Chapon and Chapon 1979).

For a substance like X/XH_2 in Scheme (I) or (II) (Section IV) to be a catalyst for the oxidation of ascorbic acid two conditions must be fulfilled:

(1) The reduced form XH_2 must be rapidly oxidized by molecular oxygen.

(2) the oxidized form X must be rapidly reduced by the oxidizable substrate.

These kinetic conditions are not necessarily simultaneously fulfilled and cannot be deduced from simple consideration of the standard redox potentials of the systems involved. The redox potentials only express a thermodynamic possibility for the reaction to occur.

Theoretical treatment leads one to attribute an essential role to the difference of the redox potentials (E_{02} for the catalyst E_{01} for the oxidizable substrate). The values E_{02} and E_{01} are in that case the potentials of half reduction of the systems, measured in the specific conditions of the reaction studied. Fig. 4 illustrates the main results if the concentration of oxygen is kept constant. For the same initial rate, that is when the catalysts studied are used in such amounts that the rate constant is the same for all the trials, the rate of oxidation of the substrate AH_2 obeys kinetics of variable order, from first order for $E_{02} - E_{01}$ largely positive to second order for $E_{02} = E_{01}$ and to third order and beyond for $E_{02} - E_{01}$ largely negative.

The detection of substances endowed with oxidatic activity by means of the colorimetric method, corresponds to the initial conditions of Fig. 4. On account of the very high sensitivity of the method, the rates of oxidation are

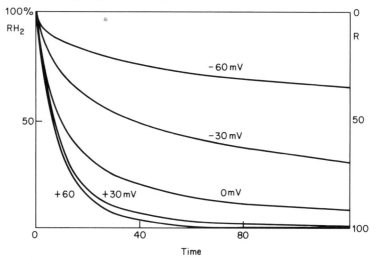

FIG. 4. Theoretical curves of disappearance of substrate (RH_2) versus time in dependence on the difference $E_{02} - E_{01}$ of the redox potential of the catalyst and substrate. The rate constants, hence the initial activity, are the same for all cases. (From Chapon et al. (1979b)).

always extremely low, hence the concentration of the dehydroascorbic acid formed during an experiment is absolutely negligible. The specific activities mentioned for the different catalysts correspond to the initial rates. From the foregoing it can be seen that the equality of initial activities for different catalysts does not necessarily imply identity for the entire course of the reactions. It can hence be understood why the manometric method, which measures the oxygen consumption until an advanced stage of substrate oxidations has been reached, gives results which sometimes differ by a very large amount from what would be expected from the results of the colorimetric method.

Now, if we consider as a supplementary condition that the amount of oxygen available is limited, as is always the case in practice, the spreading of the curves is still broader than shown in Fig. 4. In the particular case, when the amount of available oxygen exactly corresponds to what is necessary to oxidize AH_2 and when, besides, $E_{02} = E_{01}$, the kinetics are third order.

Now if the system A/AH_2 is no longer reversible, as is the case when A is not stable (dehydroascorbic acid), if it is not electroactive (SO_3^{2-}/SO_4^{2-}) or if the catalyst disappears with time (some organic catalysts), kinetics are modified towards the cases of Fig. 4, in a way difficult to predict. The broad range of E_0 covered by iron complexes, together with the diversity of their properties, can explain to a large extent the diversity of kinetics observed.

Figure 5 gives the half reduction potentials (measured at pH 4 by a dynamic method) of various redox systems (catalysts, substrates and inactive substances) effectively involved in beers or used in model trials. But the analysis of the actual phenomena is still more complicated. In fact, a peroxidatic step, in which hydrogen peroxide formed in the oxidatic step intervenes, also contributes to the overall mechanism. This step has its own catalysts and its own laws which are reviewed in the next section.

V. PEROXIDATIC ACTIVITY

A. Secondary Substrates for Oxidation; Coupled Oxidation

We have described as primary substances for oxidation those substances which can play a role similar to that played by ascorbic acid in the reactions discussed. They are capable of reducing the oxidized form of the catalyst which can be considered in fact as the real oxidant in the oxidatic stage. The catalyst is transformed to the reduced condition, and in this form it brings about in its turn the reduction of molecular oxygen. The interested reader will find very well documented recent reviews on this important problem in the books "Molecular mechanisms of oxygen activation" (Hayaishi 1974) and "Biotechnology" (Rehm 1977). The mechanisms for the reduction of molecular oxygen may be summarized as follows;

(1) A one-electron mechanism leading to a perhydroxyl radical O_2H (or $\cdot O_2H$).

$$O_2 + H^+ + 1e \longrightarrow \cdot O_2H$$

or its conjugated base the superoxide anion O_2^-, ($pK_a 4\cdot 88 \pm 0\cdot 1$);

(2) A two-electron mechanism, leading to the formation of hydrogen peroxide.

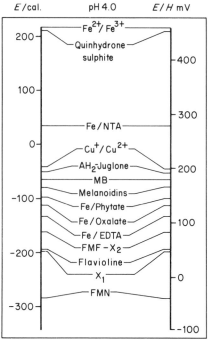

FIG. 5. Redox potentials of different systems (catalysts, substrates and other substances) determined by a dynamic method which consists of slowly injecting dichlorophenolindophenol (or potassium permanganate for the higher values) into the solution previously brought to its reduced state by dithionite. The potentials of a platinum electrode are recorded. The chosen value for E_0 corresponds to the half-wave potential.

X_1 and X_2 are the catalysts formed on coupled oxidation of catechin, FMF is formylethylflavin, a photolysis product of riboflavine 5-phosphate. Considering these values and Fig. 5, one sees the very broad range of variation of the kinetics which can be found, even if the amount of catalyst is taken so as to give the same initial oxidation rate in all the trials. The wide range covered by the iron complexes must be emphasized. (From Chapon et al. (1979b)).

$$O_2 + 2H^+ + 2e \longrightarrow H_2O_2$$

It should be noted that in neither of these two mechanisms is the O—O link in molecular oxygen broken.

In acid medium the perhydroxyl radical is unstable and undergoes spontaneous dismutation (maximum rate at pH 4·8);

$$2 \cdot O_2H \longrightarrow H_2O_2 + O_2$$

Whatever be the mechanism, hydrogen peroxide is formed and this is in fact the product which is observed. Important differences result according to the conditions which are used. When ascorbic acid in pure solution is oxidized by air, hydrogen peroxide is formed and its concentration steadily increases in the medium. The maximum concentration which is reached increases with the concentration of the catalyst in the case of copper or in the case of the ferric/EDTA complex; it decreases, on the other hand, when the catalyst is iron ions (Chapon et al. 1960). We have further shown that if ascorbic acid dissolved in beer is oxidized by air, the presence of free hydrogen peroxide cannot normally be detected (Chapon et al. 1959) and that, additionally, the quantity of oxygen consumed by the oxidation of one mole of ascorbic acid approaches one mole of molecular oxygen (Urion et al. 1956). While one atom of oxygen oxidizes ascorbic acid, the other atom oxidizes another substance (RH_2) present in the medium. This is the phenomenon of coupled oxidation (or induced oxidation) which can be indicated overall schematically as:

ascorbic acid $+ RH_2 + O_2 \longrightarrow$ dehydroascorbic acid $+ R + 2H_2O$

and is a very general phenomenon discovered towards the end of the last century by Schönbein as cited by Wurmser (1930). The substances symbolized by RH_2 are the secondary oxidation substrates. They may have various structures. It is not necessary that they should show reducing properties comparable with those of primary reducing agents as defined above. In fact, the number of substances which can play the role of secondary substrates more or less effectively is very large. Their effectiveness varies according to their nature, their concentration in the medium and the presence of catalysts. For instance, alcohol is oxidized to acetaldehyde and isopropyl alcohol to acetone (Urion et al. 1956). Now, when hydrogen peroxide is added to beer at low concentrations (some milligrams per litre), it appears to be relatively stable. Its disappearance takes, normally, several hours and often more than a day. The rate of disappearance depends both on the presence of primary oxidizable substrates and of catalysts having peroxidatic functions. These simple experiments show that the active form of oxygen is not hydrogen peroxide but an activated form of molecular oxygen. The participation of the

free radical ·OH is certain. That of the perhydroxyl radical, of which the
existence is ephemeral and the reactivity low, has not been shown but it cannot
be definitively excluded. The existence of "complex forms of oxygen" as
intermediary oxidizing agents has been postulated, but remains hypothetical
(Staudinger et al. 1956). The specific peroxidatic activity of beer may be
studied by following at the same time the disappearance of hydrogen peroxide
injected into the beer as well as that of ascorbic acid which has been added in
known concentration. It is found that different samples show substantial
differences, as a function of the concentration and the nature of catalysts.
Here, iron and its complexes play an essential role.

B. Model Systems

Because of the complexity of the composition of beer, the study of the
participation of different classes of secondary substrates is extremely difficult.
Utilization of simplified model mixtures allows the problem to be made less
complex and to bring into it solid facts in relation to several precise points.

Polyphenols are implicated in the formation of oxidation hazes. For
instance, catechin in dilute aqueous solution is slightly autoxidizable by air
with formation of tannoids of progressively increasing degrees of condensation which, in concentrations as low as a few milligrams per litre, induce
directly a chill haze in beer (Chapon et al. 1975). Such autoxidation is slow and
requires from several days to several weeks. It is accelerated by the presence of
traces of iron or copper. In addition, catechin is a secondary substrate for
coupled oxidation of ascorbic acid (Chapon and Chapon 1977). In this case
the condensation reactions occur more rapidly. They may already be observed
after some hours and continue in spite of the presence of an excess of reducing
agent which cannot, in this particular case, where oxygen is freely available,
exercise any protective role except where the concentration is relatively high.
Indeed, the violet coloration and related phenomena of condensation only
occur when about half of the ascorbic acid has been oxidized. From the
tannoids there are formed, in this case in small quantities, substances having
oxidatic properties identical with those of substances which are formed by
autoxidation and which cause the kinetics of the oxidation to show autocatalytic effects. Some substances formed on coupled oxidation seem to play
the part of intermediate electron carriers similar to that of MB (section III.E)
and contribute to the autocatalytic kinetics exemplified in Fig. 6.

This shows a typical case where a reducing agent can bring about oxidations
which are more rapid than those which would occur in its absence. Such a
duality of effects allows it to be understood why there are in the literature so
many contradictory reports relating to usefulness of ascorbic acid and of
reducing agents in general (e.g. reductones or melanoidins) as regards the

stability of beers. The euphoria which followed the first publications of Gray and Stone (1939a, b, 1948) on the use of L-ascorbic acid (Vitamin C) or of its isomer D-ascorbic acid (or isoascorbic acid), which has no vitamin activity, was followed by a certain degree of scepticism and the use of ascorbic acid was in many cases abandoned. In fact the results which are obtained depend on the availability of oxygen and one cannot expect that any protection will be provided if the oxygen content of the beer is excessive and if there is not a sufficient excess of ascorbic acid.

In a ternary mixture comprising 5×10^{-3} M ascorbic acid, 5×10^{-3} M catechin and 0–5% ethanol, it is easily shown that the oxidation of catechin is considerably inhibited (Chapon and Chapon 1977) (See Fig. 7).

The yellow coloration which the solution acquires on the one hand and the content of titratable tannoids on the other, are, additionally, less intense when there is more alcohol. It can be established that with an identical concentration of catalyst the rate of oxidation, as estimated by the amount of acid which has disappeared in a given time, diminishes as the content of alcohol increases. More research is needed in order to be able to explain this last point,

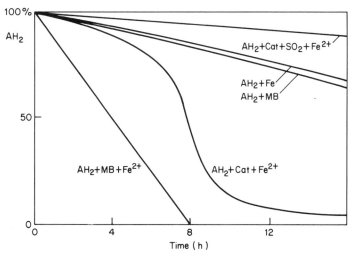

FIG. 6. Disappearance of ascorbic acid during the oxidation in air of solutions buffered at pH 4·1 with various oxidizing systems.

Methylene Blue has no oxidatic activity.
Iron ions are weak oxidatic catalysts.
The mixture ($MB + Fe^{2+}$) is very efficient.
On coupled oxidation, catechin leads to substances which produce a huge enhancement of the oxidation rate.
On suppressing the peroxidatic step, SO_2 not only suppresses the autocatalytic behaviour but slows down the oxidation of ascorbic acid.
(From Chapon et al. (1979b)).

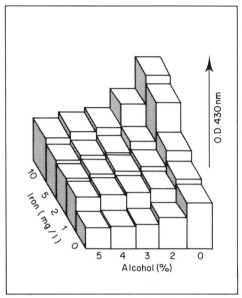

FIG. 7. Ethanol slows down the oxidation of catechin by air, coupled with that of ascorbic acid, for all concentrations of iron. The intensity of the yellow colour is taken here as a measure of the extent of oxidation of catechin (from Chapon (1977)).

because it is not easy to see how, in Scheme (**II**), the peroxidatic phase can influence the reduction of oxygen. In the presence of a mixture of ions of iron and copper, the protection given by alcohol is weaker.

C. Study of the Peroxidatic Stage

The so-called peroxidatic stage of the oxidation can be studied independently of the oxidatic phase by slowly injecting a solution of hydrogen peroxide into a solution of ascorbic acid and of the presumed substrate RH_2, in the presence of variable amounts of different catalysts. The reaction mixture is kept under nitrogen and the residual ascorbic acid is measured together with the hydrogen peroxide. The methods elaborated in our laboratory, allowed us to study the mechanisms of this important reaction (Chapon and Chapon 1979).

At least in certain cases (mixtures of ascorbic acid, catechin, iron) the results are qualitatively very similar to those arising when the oxidant is oxygen.

The system comprising a reducing agent (ascorbic acid or dihydroxyfumaric acid), hydrogen peroxide and a metal ion or complex produces hydroxyl radicals $\cdot OH$ according to the following scheme

$$H_2O_2 + Fe^{2+} \longrightarrow Fe^{3+} + OH^- + \cdot OH \quad \text{(Fenton's reaction)}$$

If iron exists only at a catalytic level, this reaction cannot go on unless a primary reducing agent able to reduce the ferric ions to the ferrous state is present. Ascorbic acid plays this role very efficiently

$$Fe^{3+} + \tfrac{1}{2}AH_2 \longrightarrow Fe^{2+} + \tfrac{1}{2}A + H^+$$

Unlike the radical $\cdot O_2H$, the hydroxyl radical $\cdot OH$ is extremely reactive and able to attack very many organic substrates. The types of reaction which it brings about are: removal of hydrogen; hydroxylation of aromatic rings; breakage of covalent bonds.

A metal catalyst may function both in the oxidatic stage and in the peroxidatic stage or have a marked preference for one or the other. Thus copper ions and ferric/EDTA have activity which is essentially oxidatic; iron ion and above all the iron nitrilotriacetic acid complex have an activity which is principally peroxidatic (Chapon et al. 1960). Mixtures of iron and copper show synergistic effects like those which have often been noted (Ribéreau-Gayon 1933, Dekker and Dickinson 1940) without their cause being clearly understood. A mixture of iron with a deficit of EDTA may thus be at the same time effective in both oxidatic and peroxidatic stages. Thus it may be explained that in the systems known as Udenfriend and Hamilton systems (see Hayaishi 1974), in which mixtures of ascorbic acid, iron, EDTA, oxygen and an aromatic substrate were used, the yield of hydroxylated derivatives varied qualitatively and quantitatively with the ratio of iron to EDTA (Cier and Nofre 1959).

It would certainly be wrong to consider that the peroxidatic stage, as it is shown in scheme (II), is the only possible route for coupling of oxidation. The participation of the $\cdot O_2H$ radical is not definitely excluded and one would classify as active oxygen any complex form of oxygen which is partially reduced and of which the activity is responsible for coupled oxidation without considering its nature (Staudinger et al. 1965).

D. Protective Substances

One defines a protective substance as any compound which prevents active oxygen reacting with so-called dangerous substances, that is to say those of which the oxidation would lead to an alteration in the quality of beer. Some reducing agents might be typical reducing substances of the type of which the oxidized form is "inoffensive" and which would exert their action as well on the oxidatic stage as on the peroxidatic stage. Others, such as alcohol, can be oxidized only by active oxygen. Others again can orient the oxidation reactions towards particular substrates and thus have in fact the dual characteristics of inhibitors for certain types of reaction and activators for others.

1. Reducing Agents

(a) Ascorbic acid, with the reservations made above, falls into this category. If oxygen is present in a limited amount, ascorbic acid incontestably exerts a protective action on beer. The same may be true of melanoidins, to which the exceptional flavour stability of dark beers has been attributed. However, at the present time none of the trials we devised allowed us either to demonstrate the occurrence of such a protection or to exclude it. Melanoidins do not slow down (as ethanol does) the condensation of catechin on coupling with ascorbic acid oxidation. They do not act (as glutathione does) as a trap for free radicals and do not stop the chain reactions which bring about the oxidation of many ethanol molecules by H_2O_2 in presence of ascorbic acid and iron ions (Chapon et al. 1979). They cannot replace ascorbic acid in the reduction of ferric ions to allow Fenton's reaction to go on. They combine with oxygen extremely slowly although they contain constituents which react instantaneously with dichlorophenol or ferric dipyridyl. It is not excluded that phenolic substances may play a comparable role. Certain traditional German and Czechoslovakian breweries consider in fact that the good organoleptic stability of beers of Pilsen type may be attributed to their relatively high concentrations of phenolic compounds (Kretschmer 1971, Mostek 1968). Exact experimental data are not sufficiently available to build a coherent theory on these lines. In the conditions of actual knowledge today, the protection could occur above all at the level of the peroxidatic stage, the polyphenols involved thus playing the role of radical scavengers. The nature of the protective substances, their concentration and their mechanism of action remain to be precisely defined.

(b) The mode of action of sulphur dioxide and sulphites involves a different mechanism. At the pH of beer, free sulphur dioxide is oxidized only very slowly by oxygen. It is only a weak reducing agent towards dichlorophenol-indophenol, ferric dipyridyl and diphenylpicrylhydrazyl radical. On the other hand, it is instantaneously oxidized by hydrogen peroxide, even if the concentrations of the reagents are very low. For this reason it is an excellent substrate for coupled oxidation (Kielhöfer and Würdig 1958–1960), providing an effective and cheap protection. The colorimetric method shows clearly that sulphur dioxide suppresses the peroxidatic step by combining preferentially with the hydrogen peroxide which is formed (perhaps with $\cdot O_2H$) and also decreases the rate of turnover of the catalyst in the oxidatic phase.

In proportion to the concentration of sulphur dioxide, browning of the solutions is delayed for phenolic derivatives such as catechins and barley tannins. It effectively inhibits oxidative condensations. Its use in wine-making at levels approaching 400 mg/l of total sulphur dioxide (though this would be unsuitable for beer because of effects on flavour) provides not only anti-oxidant properties but a considerable antiseptic effect.

(c) The role of alcohol as a secondary oxidation substrate has been discussed in section V.A. It should be emphasized here that this is the organic compound of which the concentration is by far the highest in beer and that in model solutions its effects on catalysis by iron ions is already considerable at 1% concentration. It must be pointed out, however, that, according to the results of recent work (Chapon and Chapon 1979) ethanol is not capable of providing a general protection against oxidation by ·OH free radicals. For instance the anthocyanins of red wine are very quickly decolorized by injection of hydrogen peroxide if (i) a small concentration of ascorbic acid is added and (ii) the reaction is carried out under pure nitrogen. In the presence of air the oxidative destruction of the anthocyanins is minimized or even prevented. It must be concluded that one has to be very careful in transferring to beers the information gained from the study of model systems. There appear to be present in beers substances which are preferentially oxidized as are the anthocyanins of red wine, even when they are present at very small concentrations. As our understanding of those matters increases we realize better the extreme complexity of the problem of oxidation by molecular oxygen.

2. Inhibitors

As has been shown in the previous section, EDTA inhibits copper and suppresses the peroxidatic activity of iron but increases its oxidatic activity. The inhibition of the peroxidatic characteristics may explain the effective protection which the EDTA exerts in relation to certain categories of substrates. It has even been proposed to add EDTA to beer (Gray and Stone 1960a, b) up to a maximum concentration of 25 mg/l, in order to minimize the unwanted effects of oxidation (Anon 1961). In fact, Blockmans et al. (1975) have shown that in its presence aminoacids no longer give rise to corresponding aldehydes by coupled oxidation. On the contrary, nitrilotriacetic acid, which increases the peroxidatic characteristics of iron ions, may favour the oxidation of plentiful substrates such as ethanol and protect, at least partially, the easily polymerizable polyphenols or other substrates, the oxidation of which gives rise to off-flavours.

But do there exist in beer natural substances which are able to play a role comparable with that played by the complexing agents described above in the model solutions? The only partial answer we have today is given by the surprising behaviour of oxalate in model systems (Chapon and Chapon 1979). At low concentrations (less than 20 mg/l) oxalate enhances the peroxidatic characteristics of iron, while at higher concentrations it inhibits them.

VI. PHOTOOXIDATION

A. General Characteristics; Photosensitizers

The visible light absorbed by beer (blue and violet) exerts a rapid and substantial effect on certain of its constituents. The light is absorbed by, among others, brown substances (melanoidins and polyphenolic derivatives) and fluorescent substances (including riboflavine, which plays a well known role as photosensitizer) (Hand and Greisen 1942). It suffices to say that the mechanisms involved are essentially free-radical. On the one hand light accelerates the redox reactions which take place even in the dark (Urion *et al.* 1957). On the other hand, it brings about photolytic reactions which have a strong unpleasant effect on the organoleptic properties of beer (sun-struck flavour; Gray and Stone 1948, Gray *et al.* 1941).

When one studies the catalytic effect of a beer on the oxidation of ascorbic acid by measuring the course of fixation of aerial oxygen with time, by manometric methods, or indeed by measuring from time to time the concentration of residual ascorbic acid, it is found that even in diffuse light the rate of oxidation is definitely greater than in total darkness. When the intensity of the light is high the rate may be increased several fold.

As a general rule, light may be more important for the rate of oxidation of beer substrates than metallic ion catalysts. This fact should not be lost sight of in the taking of analytical samples and their transport prior to analysis for any factor related to the phenomena of oxidation. The formation of sulphydryl compounds leads to the disappearance of the catalytic activity of copper. This reappears following subsequent exposure of beer to the air.

Although sulphydryl compounds are present in beer only at very low concentrations (of the order of 50 µg/l) (Sandegren 1949) and cannot, consequently, affect the measurement of primary reducing agents, they have great practical importance by reason of their extremely low flavour threshold. The effect of sunlight on beer is easily shown by potentiometry: the platinum electrode indicates immediately a fall in the redox potential corresponding to the rapid disappearance of electroactive oxidized forms; the dropping mercury electrode shows a similar trend.

B. Photolysis and its Results

1. Model Systems

As is well known, ascorbic acid slowly reduces Methylene Blue in darkness. If the mixture is exposed to strong light, the reaction proceeds very quickly. A method of measurement of ascorbic acid, based on this reaction, has been proposed (Martini and Bonsignore 1934). Besides, the molecule of Methylene Blue also undergoes photolysis with the formation of sulphydryl compounds, the presence of which can be detected by the inhibitory effect which they exert on the oxidatic activity of copper ions (Chapon *et al.* 1958). This is why base solutions S and C should be stored in total darkness.

Riboflavine and riboflavine-5-phosphate undergo photolytic degradation, with the appearance of reducing power arising from the rupture of the ribityl side chain (Hölmstrom and Oster 1961). In pure aqueous solution and in the absence of oxygen, reduction of the isoalloxazine ring occurs. A platinum electrode dipped into a completely deaerated dilute solution of riboflavin (5 mg/100 ml, for example), shows a fall in redox potential of which the rate depends on the intensity of light. Stable in the dark, the potential falls by several millivolts per minute in the artificial light of the laboratory. In more complex media, the reduction may be transferred to certain reducible substances, for instance, Methylene Blue or ferric complexes. Free radical reactions initiated by photosensitizers are involved in the formation of sulphydryl compounds. In the presence of air, oxygen is itself reduced to hydrogen peroxide which may under certain conditions appear in the free state in the medium.

2. Beers

The intensity of sun-struck flavour is influenced to a large extent by the oxygen content of the beer, including dissolved oxygen and oxygen in the headspace. It is more intense if the liquid is of low oxygen concentration as in this case certain sulphydryl compounds such as hydrogen sulphide or mercaptans may accumulate, as has been shown by Gray and Stone (1948, Gray *et al.* 1941). On the other hand, in the presence of oxygen these malodorous substances are not formed or are oxidized to substances much less dangerous for odour. The nature of the principal substance responsible for sun-struck flavour was elucidated by Obata and Horitso (1959), Kuroiwa and Hashimoto (1961), Hashimoto *et al.* (1963) and Hashimoto and Kuroiwa (1966); it is 3-methyl-2-butene-1-thiol. This mercaptan arises from the reaction between hydrogen sulphide formed by photolysis of sulphur compounds present in the proteins and the radical 3-methyl-2-butenyl, itself formed as a result of photolytic cleavage of the 4-methyl-3-pentenoyl group of the isohumulones.

VII. MEASUREMENT OF DISSOLVED OXYGEN IN BEER

Innumerable researches have been devoted to this problem in the most diverse fields. The subject was recently reviewed by Hitchmann (1978). Four different principles have been used as a basis for measuring the quantity of oxygen dissolved in beer. The method which is selected is chosen in relation to the objective of the test, its ease of application, the cost of the equipment, the time required and the degree of precision required of the measurement.

A. Volumetric Methods

For routine control, volumetric measurements are sufficient. The Zahm–Nagel apparatus, in which the total amount of gas present in the beer is removed by entrainment with carbon dioxide and the latter is then absorbed in an alkaline solution, is well known. The result is expressed as air, as the true concentration of oxygen in the entrained mixture of gases cannot be effectively determined. The methods of Larsen and Sørensen (1957) as modified by Kipphan (1964) are based on these principles. Their precision is not high. It depends on temperature and the results can be falsified if beer carried over with the carbon dioxide comes into contact with the concentrated potash which absorbs the carbon dioxide.

B. Colorimetric Methods

The colorimetric method using indigo carmine (sodium indigodisulphonate) depends on the oxidation of the leuco-derivative of the coloured compound by the oxygen contained in the samples (Rothchild and Stone 1938, de Clerck and Heindryckx 1962, Jerumanis 1971). The leuco-derivative is prepared as required by the reduction of indigosulphonate by the exactly necessary quantity of sodium dithionite and handled under a layer of paraffin oil. The method lends itself well to measurements made in solutions having little colour. It requires only a standard colorimeter but demands careful working. Its sensitivity is limited.

C. Chromatographic Methods

The gas chromatographic method was introduced to brewing work for the first time by Bethune and Rigby (1958). Since then, several variants have been proposed. They allow nitrogen and oxygen to be determined simultaneously. Though these methods are excellent for comparative work in research laboratories, they have not been used in industrial practice, probably because of the cost of chromatographs and of the technical work which their use demands.

D. Electrometric Methods

Electrochemical methods can be used for continuous or discontinuous measurement. They give a direct and rapid indication of the quantity of oxygen present in beer and their use is widespread. These are certainly the methods of choice. There are various forms of the equipment. All are based on the electrochemical reduction of the molecular oxygen which, by diffusion from the medium being studied, reaches a negatively polarized electrode. The oxygen reacts with electrons, forming water:

$$O_2 + 4e + 4H^+ \longrightarrow 2H_2O$$

The current which results from the reaction, under well-defined conditions, is a linear function of the oxygen concentration (or of its partial pressure). Calibration is easy and the measurement requires only a few seconds. On this principle are based: classical polarography (dropping mercury electrode which is difficult to use in a brewery), various pieces of equipment as developed by Tödt (1952) and a more recent American version (Galloway et al. 1967).

Systems using the principle of the membrane electrode of Clark et al. (1953), in various forms, have found a large field of application. The polarized electrode, which is of small dimensions, is separated from the medium under study by a thin membrane (Teflon or polyethylene) which is permeable to gas but impermeable to the major part of the dissolved substances. This membrane protects the electrode itself from unwanted interference. One must take care that the liquid layer in contact with the membrane is constantly renewed in order to avoid a local reduction in the concentration of oxygen which would limit the diffusion to the polarized electrode where the electrochemical reduction takes place.

The latest version of the Tödt apparatus uses a potentiostatic arrangement to supply the polarized electrode. It has digital read-out and internal calibration. The region in which it makes measurement is from 0·00 to 9·99 mg of oxygen per litre. The apparatus is robust, selective and adapted for continuous measurement at a flow rate of 5–10 l/h but can also be used for measuring the oxygen content of beer in the bottle. Wackerbauer et al. (1975) have made detailed study of factors which can affect the precision of the measurements.

E. Limitations

The sensitivity of electrochemical measurements of oxygen, further increased by the utilization of membranes, is a very attractive aspect of these methods. Interference by most dissolved substances is thus minimized if not totally eliminated. The main interfering substance appears to be carbon dioxide which intervenes by affecting the pH. According to Wackerbauer et al. (1975), sulphur dioxide at concentrations up to 50 mg/l does not interfere.

As for the oxidized forms of oxygen carriers remaining in beer after removal of dissolved oxygen by entrainment, they are necessarily present at low concentration. In the colorimetric method using indigosulphonate, they can cause, as a result of the oxidation of a small quantity of the leuco-derivative, the appearance of a small amount of coloured material which would be attributed to oxygen. In practice this leads to no problems. On the other hand, for the study of the mechanisms of oxidation, the discrimination between molecular oxygen and oxygen bound to an electron carrier presents considerable interest. A variant of the Methylene Blue colorimetric methods, using an inert atmosphere, allows the existence of such combinations to be established (Chapon *et al.* 1977).

Sulphydryl compounds are present in concentrations too small to affect significantly the measurement of oxygen. Besides, they disappear totally in the presence of air and are detectable only in beers which have been reduced or irradiated.

VIII. EFFECTS OF RAW MATERIALS AND PROCESSING METHODS ON THE CONCENTRATION OF REDUCING SUBSTANCES IN BEER

The primary reducing substances of natural origin, over which it is possible to exert control during processing without resorting to the use of artificial reducing agents, are the polyphenols, the melanoidins and the reductones.

A. Polyphenols

These arise from both the barley and the hops.

1. Barley

As well as simple polyphenols and phenolic compounds, there are present in barley condensed products having fairly strong tanning properties, the tannoids. Although the formation of solutions of the former can be considered as simple dissolution, for the tannoids it is governed essentially by adsorption equilibria in which the insoluble proteins of the grist play an essential role (Chapon and Chemardin 1964, Jacobsen and Lie 1974, Jacobsen *et al.* 1974). It is therefore not the total quantity of polyphenol, such as one can measure in the laboratory by using extraction solvents such as dimethylformamide, *N*-methylpyrrolidone or acetone/water (Jerumanis 1969) which alone influences the composition of the extract. These equilibria depend on:

the temperature (an increase in temperature increases the amount of extraction);

the absolute quantity of insoluble protein, in the role of adsorbent (the more insoluble proteins present, the less efficient the extraction);

the relationship between the volume of the solution and the amount of insoluble matter (the more dilute the mash the more the extraction tends to become complete);

the concentration of soluble protein in the extract (an increase in this parameter favours extraction);

oxidation (in the presence of air the extraction of tannoids is substantially reduced, as enzymic oxidation leads to condensation, following which they are adsorbed more strongly on the insoluble proteins of the spent grains) (Chapon and Chemardin 1964).

The concentration of polyphenols in barley is a varietal character. However, the degree of variation arising from varietal causes is less than which is induced by environmental factors (Jacobsen and Lie 1974, Chapon *et al.* 1969). It may be said that within a single variety:

the content of tannoids varies inversely with the concentration of protein;

barleys rich in tannoids are more easy to malt than barleys poor in tannoids.

Malting ripe barleys, the densities of which at 20 °C (according to Hartong and Kretschmer 1970) are lower than 1·31 and of which the water absorption power is higher than 47·5%, generally possess high tannoid contents. Although the differences in tannoid contents are much more significant than those of the contents of the polyphenols, the total concentration of tannoids and polyphenols in barleys is nevertheless interesting to consider. A very significant positive correlation exists between extractable tannoids and total polyphenols (Chapon and Kretschmer 1970).

2. Malt

The total concentration of polyphenolic substances of the grain changes only slightly during malting. There is indeed a slight loss during steeping, but while the grain stucture is intact the polyphenols are protected from the action of the oxidases. Starting from a given barley and in conformity with what has just been said, a strong modification of proteins during malting favours the extraction of tannoids (Chapon and Kretschmer 1970).

After a malting process which has been well carried out, the quantity of tannoids extractable by water is approximately double that which can be extracted from the original barleys under the same conditions, except that in the case of the malts of the Munich type, where the kilning leads to a substantial drop in the quantity extractable. It seems also to depend on the barley composition, because we found in certain years that the increase was lower than two-fold.

The factors which govern the extraction of tannoids from the grist of barley or malt in the laboratory play a comparable role in the preparation of wort in the brewhouse. Increased proteolysis during mashing favours extraction. This is especially what occurs with a stand at 45 °C associated with a lactic acidification of the mash.

In consequence, malts which are low in protein content and well modified (those which one considers as good malts) give, other things being equal, worts which contain higher concentrations of tannoids than are obtained from malts which have higher contents of protein and are less well modified (Bellmer 1976).

This may appear to be a paradox if one considers, as is often done, that the tannoids or polyphenols are the principal substances leading to a colloidal instability of beers as a result of their ability to condense with one another and to unite with proteins to produce haze. However, a logical interpretation can be advanced in this area if one considers the fact that the degree of simplification of the soluble protein of the extract increases at the same time as the content of the tannoid rises (Chapon et al. 1969). It is an experimental fact that the content of "sensitive proteins", that is to say those which are the first to be precipitated following the additions of tannins at low concentrations, varies in the inverse sense to the content of the tannoids. The proteotannic equilibrium thus assures compensation of the pernicious effect which an excess of the one or the other of the components would have on the colloidal stability of beer (Steiner 1965, 1966).

Basing his views on years of observation in the brewery and on results of micromalting, Kretschmer (1963) (see also Chapon and Kretschmer 1964, 1969) supports the idea that a barley giving a cold water extract which is rich in substances reducing ammoniacal silver nitrate is easy to malt and provides a malt which should not pose any problem during mashing. Although this method gives results which are reproducible only with difficulty, the trend is indisputable and the result may be interpreted to a large extent by the high positive correlation which exists between the reducing power ("Reduktonkraft") of cold water extract prepared without particular precautions and the content of the tannoids as determined by polyvinyl-pyrrolidone on extracts prepared whether in an inert atmosphere or in the presence of reducing agents such as ascorbic acid (Chapon and Chermardin 1964) or of inhibitors such as hydrazine (Chapon et al. 1959). A relatively anaerobic malting process does not appear to lead to an increased production of reducing substances in the sense described. The extraction of tannoids is only increased by enhanced proteolysis.

The utilization of unmalted grain, of which the contribution of reducing power to the extract is slight in comparison with that of malt, leads, as a result of dilution, to a reduction of the concentration of the polyphenols in wort.

Intense aeration during mashing and saccharification reduces the tannoid concentration of the wort for the reasons discussed in section VIII.A. According to de Clerck and Van Cauwenberge (1956), brewing in the absence of air has damaging consequences as regards the clarification of wort and the quality of the finished product. Recent investigations by Narziss (1979) seem to support the reverse conclusion. The explanation of this apparent discrepancy may lie in the fact that the trials described by de Clerck were conducted in the laboratory with strict exclusion of air from the very start of mashing in, while those of Narziss are limited to the effect of a more or less prolonged contact of air (or oxygen) with a wort produced in an industrial brewery. The rigorous control of oxidation at every stage of brewing is in practice far beyond the capability of existing techniques. Mashing by the infusion method together with a quick inactivation of oxidases in the first runnings and spargings reduce the loss of tannoids.

3. Hops

Hops contain, according to the variety and the origin, between 5% and 10% of polyphenolic substances. These polyphenols are more condensed than those of malts. They are nevertheless easily soluble in water and their extraction by boiling water from a hop grist is practically complete, because the cones do not contain any substantial amount of insoluble protein able to retain by adsorption a significant fraction of the tannins, as is the case for barley. By reason of their high tanning power, hop polyphenols contribute to the precipitation of the most easily precipitable nitrogenous fraction of wort; albumin and globulin disappear in part due to the combined effect of heat and of tannins. Boiling thus leads to a reduction of the tannoid content of wort in such a way that the substances with the highest tanning power are eliminated in the coagulum, the hot break and the cold break. It should be underlined here that the worts which are least rich in sensitive proteins retain to the greatest extent the tannoids arising from the hops, so that there exists a positive correlation between malt tannoids and tannoids of hopped beer, but this correlation is indirect in nature and is due to variations in the concentrations of proteins which can be precipitated by the tannins (Chapon et al. 1969, 1976).

The reducing power due to the polyphenols (slow reducing agents of de Clerck) increases with the hop rate. It is necessary to take into account in this context not only the quantity of bitter substances which a hop may provide and on which the hopping rate is calculated, but also its content of polyphenol. The ratio of polyphenols to α-acids may vary considerably. A recent study (Chapon et al. 1976) gave extreme value of 0·3 to 2 (the use of extract which contains only bitter substances makes no contribution to the reducing power of worts). Hop tannin concentrates, obtained by hot water extraction of hop cones following extraction of the bitter substances with organic solvents, contain oxidized and polymerized polyphenols which make only a small contribution to the precipitation of proteins and to the reducing power of worts. They are considered to be responsible for an astringent and unpleasant bitterness (Kretschmer 1975).

The use of formaldehyde (Macey *et al*. 1964), which leads to the removal of a complementary fraction of phenolic substances in an insoluble protein/polyphenol/formaldehyde complex, diminishes the reducing power slightly.

The oxidation of hot wort, which favours the formation of protein break by increasing the tanning power of polyphenols without affecting the colour (Schild and Huymann 1951), has been strongly discussed. Our knowledge of the fundamental processes is insufficient to define at which stages oxidation is beneficial and beyond which limits it becomes troublesome (Narziss, 1979).

B. Melanoidins; Reductones

In the brewing literature, reductones and melanoidins are almost always associated (de Clerck and Van Cauwenberge 1956), but reductones have never been isolated from beers (Reich and Rock 1960, Mostek 1968).

The so-called Maillard reaction causes the non-enzymic formation of brown substances having reducing properties: the melanoidins. These substances are formed during the heating of mixtures of sugars and amino acids during the kilning of malt, especially during curing, and during wort boiling. They consist of extremely complex mixtures of substances, the molecular weights of which cover a large range from simple compounds up to condensed non-dialysable material; and it is not possible by analytical means to resolve these mixtures into pure individuals of defined structures. 3-Deoxy-D-glucosone has recently been identified in worts (Hashimoto and Kuroiwa 1975). Its concentration increases in parallel with the development of colour during wort boiling and its presence is considered to be a proof of the occurrence of the Strecker reaction.

The contribution of pale malts to the reducing power of the extract, apart from that which is due to polyphenolic substances, is very small (0·2 meq./100 g). On the other hand, coloured malts (caramel malts, brown malts, and especially malts of Munich type) can confer a significant reducing power on wort, of the order of 1 meq./100 g of malt (Chapon *et al*. 1969). No natural means is known which allows the reducing power of the wort to be increased without a parallel increase in its colour and, in the preparation of pale beers, this type of reaction is scarcely acceptable.

The increase in colour during boiling thus has several origins. The first of importance is the Maillard reaction, the second the oxidation of phenolic substances, and the third the caramelization of sugars.

The melanoidins have been suggested as being responsible for the oxidation of alcohols with the formation of aldehydes (Hashimoto and Kuroiwa 1975, Hashimoto 1972, Hashimoto and Koiké 1971). From the foregoing (section IV.C.4) it does not seem that this reaction could be interpreted as an oxidation coupled to that of melanoidins. It is not proved that the last substances can act as primary substrates. Their oxidatic activity, recently discovered (Chapon *et al.* 1979), might play a part in such phenomena. In the absence of oxygen, the mechanism is unclear.

C. Fermentation

During fermentation, contrary to a widely held view, the reducing power of the medium does not increase (Gray and Stone 1939). It may even have a tendency to decrease slightly following the disappearance of the fraction of the tannoids which is adsorbed partly on the yeast, and partly on proteins rendered insoluble as a result of the fall of the pH. The reducing role of the yeast seems to be limited to the almost complete removal of dissolved oxygen and to the production of traces of sulphydryl compounds. The rH falls towards 8 to 9 but, as the medium is essentially unbuffered from the redox point of view, very little oxygen suffices to cause the rH to increase again towards 15 to 16, the normal value for beers at packaging.

D. Filtration and Stabilization

The more drastic the stabilization procedures, the greater is the degree of removal of reducing substances. This is especially true for the treatment by specific adsorbants of polyphenols (nylon, or Polyclar AT = polyvinyl polypyrrolidone). Filtration, which is always accompanied by adsorption of macromolecular aggregates (protein/tannin associations with lower solubility at low temperatures), leads to a small decrease of the tannoid content of beers. As pointed out earlier, the relative decrease in tannoids is always greater than that of reducing substances. Excessive stabilization can lead to deterioration of organoleptic quality (Synge 1975, Kretschmer 1975).

IX. REDUCING AGENTS AND STABILITY

In the light of the arguments developed in the preceding paragraphs, it is quite clear that one cannot be exact in defining the way in which actual analytical data should be interpreted in order to draw a conclusion as to what should be the composition of beer which will meet traditional criteria of quality and stability.

Maintaining the beer in the reduced condition would appear to be sensible in this case. But can this be reached purely by providing a high concentration of reducing substances and, if the answer is yes, then which? Beers having high indicator time test values have often shown a better stability than others which may have been richer in reducing substances (Curtis and Clark 1959).

One point appears certain but it is necessay to emphasize it as it has been so overlooked; the first step to take consists in systematically eliminating all sources of air which may contact the beer from the first moment at which the beer no longer contains yeast. If this is not done, all other steps will probably be no more than palliatives. The use of the artificial reducing agents ascorbic acid and sulphites, or a combination of the two, can be effective; nevertheless the role played by SO_2 is far from having the simplicity which seems to result from the mechanisms proposed in section V.D.1.

Fear of the appearance of sun-struck flavour in reduced beers is, it would seem, misplaced. One can always take steps to protect the beverage from light; besides, if the beer is not in a sufficiently reduced state the sun-struck flavour may perhaps not appear but other unwanted flavours will take its place, together with a loss of colloidal stability resulting from accelerated oxidation.

If it appears to be well established that oxidation alone can explain only the 30–40% loss of colloidal stability which is observed (McFarlane 1970), there remains a certain parallel between lack of colloidal stability and lack of flavour stability.

Much remains to be done on the study of coupled oxidations in complex media. If this article encourages new research in this area in order to obtain better knowledge of the relationships between oxygen and beer, the author will have achieved his end.

Acknowledgements

The author thanks most sincerely the French brewing industry for the material help and the interest which it has never ceased to show in his work. He greatly thanks his devoted collaborators, in particular his wife as Maître Assistant, and Mme Bayeul, Technical Assistant, for their valuable help.

REFERENCES

Adachi, S. (1958). *J. Agric. Chem. Soc. Japan.* **32**, 313.
Anon. (1961). *Federal Register.* July 13, 6271.
Baker, D. L., Kinsman, G. H. and Hellmann, N. N. (1960). *Proc. Ann. Meet. Am. Soc. Brew. Chem.* p. 146.
Barron, E. S. G., De Meio, R. H. and Klemperer, F. (1936). *J. Biol. Chem.* **112**, 625.
Bellmer, H. G. (1976). *Brauwelt* **116**(24), 789.

Bethune, J. L. and Rigby, F.L. (1958). *J. Inst. Brew.* **64**, 170.

Blockmans, C., Devreux, A. and Masschelein, C. A. (1975). *Proc. E.B.C. Congr., Nice* p. 699.

Brenner, M. W. (1951). *Proc. E.B.C. Congr., Copenhagen* p. 349.

Canales, A. M., Garza Ulloa, H. and Zapata, B. D. (1975). *Proc. Ann. Meet. Am. Soc. Brew. Chem.* p. 172.

Case, A. C. and Thompson, E. H. (1961). *J. Inst. Brew.* **67**, 513.

Chapman, R. A. and MacFarlane, W. D. (1945). *Canad. J. Res.* **23**, 91.

Chapon, L. (1965). *J. Inst. Brew.* **61**, 127.

Chapon, L. and Chapon, S. (1962). *Bull. Soc. Chim. France*, 1416.

Chapon, L. and Chapon, S. (1977). *Proc. E.B.C. Congr., Amsterdam* p. 661.

Chapon, L. and Chapon, S. (1979a). *Proc. Ann. Meet. Am. Soc. Brew. Chem.* **2**, 96.

Chapon, L. and Chapon, S. (1979b). *Proc. E.B.C. Congr., Berlin* p. 341.

Chapon, S. and Chapon, L. (1978). *Bull. Liaison Groupe Polyphénols, Narbonne.* No. 8, 295.

Chapon, S. and Chapon, L. (1980). *Bull. Liaison Groupe Polyphénols, Narbonne,* No. 10 (in press).

Chapon, L. and Chemardin, M. (1964). *Proc. Ann. Meet. Am. Soc. Brew. Chem.* 244.

Chapon, L. and Kretschmer, K. F. (1964). *Monats. Brau.* **17**, 279.

Chapon, L. and Kretschmer, K. F. (1969). *Monats. Brau.* **22**, 110.

Chapon, L. and Kretschmer, K. F. (1970). *Brauwelt,* **110**(22), 395.

Chapon, L. and Urion, E. (1953). *Proc. Ann. Meet. Am. Soc. Brew. Chem.* p. 78.

Chapon, L., Chapon, S. and Bourzeix, M. (1980). Unpublished.

Chapon, L. Chapon, S. and Urion, E. (1957). *Bull. Soc. Chim. France,* 794.

Chapon, L. Chapon, S. and Urion, E. (1959b). *Bull. Soc. Chim. France* 856.

Chapon, L. Chapon, S. and Urion, E. (1959c). *Proc. E.B.C. Congr., Rome* p. 322.

Chapon, L. Chapon, S., Aimé, N. and Urion, E. (1958a). *Bull. Soc. Chim. France* 157.

Chapon, L., Chapon, S., Aimé, N. and Urion, E. (1959b). *Bull. Soc. Chim. France* 1366.

Chapon, L., Chapon, S., Genty-Amié, N. and Urion, E. (1959a). *Bull. Soc. Chim. France* 81.

Chapon, L., Chapon, S., Chemardin, M. and Kretschmer, K. F. (1969). *Proc. E.B.C. Congr., Interlaken* p. 73.

Chapon, L., Chapon, S., Seyer, R. and Louis, C. (1975). *Proc. E.B.C. Congr., Nice* p. 423.

Chapon, L., Chollot, B. and Urion, E. (1961). *Proc. E.B.C. Congr., Vienna* p. 319, 334.

Chapon, L., Louis, C. and Chapon, S. (1971). *Proc. E.B.C. Congr., Estoril* p. 307.

Chapon, S., Chapon, L. and Urion, E. (1960). *Bull. Soc. Chim. France* 2012.

Chapon, L., Louis, C., Chapon, S., Moll, M. and Kretschmer, K. F. (1976). *5th Intern. Fermentation Symposium Berlin,* 383; *Monats. Brauerei* (1977). **30**, (12) 541.

Chollot, B., Blondot, P., Deymié, B. and Urion, E. (1967b). *Proc. E.B.C. Congr., Madrid* p. 433.

Chollot, B., Thomalla, M. and Urion, E. (1967a). *Proc. E.B.C. Congr., Madrid,* 423.

Cier, A. and Nofre, C. (1959). *Bull. Soc. Chim. France* 1523.

Clark, L. C., Wolf, R., Granger, D. and Taylor, Z. (1953). *J. Appl. Physiol.* **6**, 189.

Crowe, L. K., Jenness, R. and Coulter, S. T. (1948). *J. Dairy Sci.* **31**, 595.

Curtis, N. S. and Clark, A. G. (1959). *Brewers' Guild J.* **45**, 186.

De Clerck, J. (1934a). *Bull. Assoc. Ec. Brass, Louvain* **34**, 55, 78.

De Clerck, J. (1934b). *J. Inst. Brew.* **40**, 407.

De Clerck, J. and Heindryckx, W. (1962). *Bull. Assoc. Ec. Brass., Louvain* **58**, 151.

De Clerck, J. and van Cauwenberge, H. (1956). *Bull. Assoc. Ec. Brass., Louvain* **52**, 1, 61.

De Kok, A., Veeger, C. and Hemmerich, P. (1971). *In* "Flavins and Flavoproteins" (Kamin, H. ed.). University Park Press, Baltimore; Butterworth, London.

Dekker, A. O. and Dickinson, R. G. (1940). *J. Am. Chem. Soc.* **62**, 2165.

Fall, H. H. and Petering, H. G. (1956). *J. Am. Chem. Soc.* **78**, 377.

Frey, S. W., De Witt, W. G. and Bellamy, B. R. (1966). *Proc. Ann. Meet. Am. Soc. Brew. Chem.* p. 172.

Galloway, H. M., Raabe, E. A. and Bates, W. (1967). *Proc. Ann. Meet. Am. Soc. Brew. Chem.* p. 79.

Genty-Aimé, N. (1961). Contribution à l'étude de l'oxydation de l'acide ascorbique par l'oxygene moléculaire en présence de bleu de Méthylène. Thèse, Sciences Nancy.

Gorinstein, S. (1974). *J. Food Sci.* **39**(5), 953.

Gray, P. P. (1960b). *Wallerstein Lab. Commun.* **23** (82), 181.

Gray, P. P. and Stone, I. (1960A). *Proc. Ann. Meet. Am. Soc. Brew. Chem.* p. 166.

Gray, P. P. and Stone, I. (1936b). *J. Inst. Brew.* **45**, 253, 443.

Gray, P. P. and Stone, I. (1939a). *Wallerstein Lab. Commun.* **5**, 5.

Gray, P. P., Stone, I. and Rothchild, H. (1941). *Wallerstein Lab. Commun.* **4** (11), 29.

Gray, P. P. and Stone, I. (1948). Bottle Beer Quality. A 10 Year Research Record, p. 101.

Green, D. E. (1940). "Mechanisms of Biological Oxidations." Cambridge University Press, Cambridge.

Hand, B. D. and Greisen, E. C. (1942). *J. Am. Chem, Soc.* **64**, 358.

Hartong, B. D. (1934). *Wschr. Brau.* **51**, 409.

Hartong, B. D., Klopper, W. J., Mendlik, F., Oppenoorth, W. F., Van Veldhuizen, H. and Weisenborn, J. G. (1955–1956). *Int. Tidjds. Brou. Mout.* 161.

Hashimoto, N. (1972). *J. Inst. Brew.* **78**, 43.

Hashimoto, N. and Koike, K. (1971). *Rep. Res. Lab. Kirin Brewing Co., Yokohama* **14**, 1.

Hashimoto, N. and Kuroiwa, Y. (1966). *Proc. Ann. Meet. Am. Soc. Brew. Chem.* p. 181.

Hashimoto, N. and Kuroiwa, Y. (1975). *Rep. Res. Lab. Kirin Brewing Co., Yokohama* **18**, 1.

Hashimoto, N., Kokubo E. and Nakagawa, K. (1963). *Proc. Ann. Meet. Am. Soc. Brew. Chem.* p. 21.

Hayaishi, O. (1974). "Molecular Mechanisms of Oxygen Activation". Academic Press, New York and London.

Hitchmann, M. L. (1978). "Measurement of dissolved oxygen", Wiley and Orbisphere Laboratories.

Holstrom, B. and Oster, G. (1961). *J. Am. Chem. Soc.* p. 83.

Hopkins, R. H. and Wiener, S. (1944A). *J. Inst. Brew.* **50**, 124.

Hopkins, R. H. and Wiener, S. (1944b). *J. Inst. Brew.* **51**, 34.

Hudson, J. R. (1955). *J. Inst. Brew.* **71**, 299.

Hudson, J. R. (1959). *J. Inst. Brew.* **65**, 321.

Jacobsen, T. and Lie, S. (1974). *Tech. Quart., Master Brewers Ass. Am.* **11** (2), 155.

Jacobsen, T. Lie, S. and Chapon, L. (1974). *Tech. Quart., Master Brewers Ass. Am.* **11** (4), 255.

Jander, G. (1956). Neuere Massanalytische Methoden, 397. F. Enke Verlag, Stuttgart (Komplexometrische Titrationsmethoden, G. Schwarzenbach and W. Schneider).

Jérumanis, J. (1969). *Bull. Assoc. Ec. Brass., Louvain* **65**, 169.

Jérumanis, J. (1971). *Bull. Assoc. Ec. Brass., Louvain* **67**, 157.

Karakus, M. (1975). Thèse Docteur, Ingénieur. Université de Nancy.

Kellie, A. E. and Zilva, S. S. (1935). *Biochem. J.* **29**, 1028.

Kielhöfer, E. and Würdig, G. (1958). *Weinberg und Keller* **5**, 644.

Kielhöfer, E. and Würdig, G. (1959). *Weinberg und Keller* **6**, 21.

Kielhöfer, E. and Würdig, G. (1960). *Weinwissenschaft* **15**, 103.

Kipphan, H., Herrmann, J. A., Karacas, C. and Latuszek, J. (1964). *Brauwissens.* **17**, 336.

Klopper, W. J. (1955–1956). *Int. Tidjds. Brou. Mout.* 161.

Kretschmer, K. F. (1963). *Brauwelt.* **103**, 335.

Kretschmer, K. F. (1970). *Brauwelt.* **110**, 1705.

Kretschmer, K. F. (1971). *Brauwelt.* **111** (89), 1975.

Kretschmer, K. F. (1975). *Brauwelt.* **115**, 1049, 1111.

Kuroiwa, Y. and Hashimoto, N. (1961). *Proc. Ann. Meet. Am. Soc. Brew. Chem.,* 28.

Larsen, B. A. and Sørensen, J. E. (1957). *Brygmesteren,* **14**, 173.

Laufer, S. (1936). *Am. Brewer* **69** (1), 15, 24.

MacFarlane, W. D. (1959). *Proc. Ann. Meet. Am. Soc. Brew. Chem.,* p. 81.

MacFarlane, W. D. (1970). Industry Sponsored Research on Brewing. Brewing Industry Research Institute, Chicago, Ill.

MacFarlane, W. D. and Blashke, E. (1959). *J. Inst. Brewing* **65**, 266.

Macey, A., Stowell, K. C. and White, H. B. (1964). *Proc. Ann. Meet. Am. Soc. Brew. Chem.* p. 22.

Mack, G. L. and Kertesz, Z. I. (1936). *Food Res.* **1**, 377.

Marchetti, J. (1963). Dipl. Etudes Supérieures, Nancy.

Martini, E. and Bonsignore, A. (1934). *Biochem. Z.* **273**, 170.

Mendlik, F. (1934). *Wchr. Brau,* **51**, 305.

Mendlik, F. (1935). *Wchr. Brau.* **52**, 417.

Moll, N. (1977). Thèse de Specialité, Nancy.

Mostek, J. (1968). *Brauwissenschaft* **21** (7), 253.

Obata, Y. and Horitsu, H. (1959). *Bull. Agric. Chem. Soc. Japan* **23**, 3, 186.

Owades, J. L. and Jacovac, J. (1966). *Proc. Ann. Meet. Am. Soc. Brew. Chem.* p. 180.

Owades, J. L. and Zientara, F. (1960). *Proc. Ann. Meet. Am. Soc. Brew. Chem.* p. 68.

Pasteur, L. (1876). Etudes sur la bière. Oeuvres de Pasteur T. V. Masson, Ed. Paris (1928).

Pierre, L. (1938). *Brasseur Francais* **2**, 536.

Preece, I. A. (1936). *J. Inst. Brew.* **75**, 37.

Rehm, H. J. (1977). "Biotechnology" Band 81 No. 1670–1692. Verlag Chemie–Weinheim, New York.

Reich, H. and Rock, R. M. (1960). *Proc. Ann. Meet. Am Soc. Brew. Chem.* p. 78.

Ribéreau–Gayon, J. (1933). Contribution à l'étude des Oxidations et Réductions dans les vins, Delmas, Ed. Bordeaux, 2nd ed.

Rothchild, H. and Stone, I. (1938). *J. Inst. Brew.* **44**, 425.

Sandegren, E. (1949). *Proc. E. B. Congr., Lucerne* p. 78.

Schild, E. and Huymann, M. V. (1951). *Brauwissenschaft* 1.

Scriban, R. (1970). *Ann. Nutr. Alim.* **24**, B 377.

Sieffert, L. Z. (1946). *Vitaminforschung* **17**, 52.

Silbereisen, K. and Wittmann, G. (1957). *Proc. E.B.C. Congr., Copenhagen* p. 263.

Singruen, E. (1940). *Wallerstein Lab. Commun.* **3**, 75.

Staudinger, H., Kerekjarto, B., Ullrich, H. and Zubrzycki, Z. (1965). *In* "Oxidases and Related Compounds" (King, T. E., Mason, H. S. and Morrison, K., Eds), p. 815. Wiley, New York.

Steiner, K. (1965). *Proc. E.B.C. Congr., Stockholm* p. 260.

Steiner, K. (1966). *Schweiz. Brau–Runds.* **77**, 403.

Stenger, C. (1961). Dipl. Etudes Supérieures, Nancy.

Stone, I. (1960). Wallerstein Lab. Commun. **23**, 191.

Synge, R. L. M. (1975). *Pl. Fds. Hum. Nutr.* **24** (3, 4), 337.

T.E.P.R.A.L. Internal report cited by Moll (1976).

Thompson, C. C. and Forward, E. (1969). *J. Inst. Brew.* **75**, 37.

Tödt, F. Woldt, G. and Koch, R. (1952). *Brau. Wiss. Beil.* **5**, 87.

Urion, E., Chapon, L., Chapon, S. and Metche, M. (1957). *Proc. E.B.C. Congr., Copenhagen* p. 281.

Urion, E., Chapon, L., Chapon, S. and Metche, M. (1956). *Bull. Soc. Chim. Biol.* **38**, 1217.

Wackerbauer, K., Teske, G., Tödt, F. and Graff, M. (1975). *Proc. E.B.C. Congr., Nice,* 757.

Wurmser, R. (1930). "Oxydations et Réductions". Presses Universitaires de France.

8. Gushing in Beer

M. AMAHA and K. KITABATAKE

Central Research Laboratories, Asahi Breweries, Limited, Ohta-ku, Tokyo, Japan

I. INTRODUCTION

Gushing or overfoaming in beer is an undesirable phenomenon which is naturally regarded with disfavour by the consumer and which may negatively affect the sales of beer. It is safe to assume that there is probably no brewery that has not suffered from this unpleasant problem.

Since the early works on gushing by Windisch (1923a, b) and Lüers (1924), a great number of papers dealing with the incidence, factors, causes, and remedies of gushing have been presented by authors from European countries, North America, United Kingdom, and Japan, indicating that the gushing in beer has been and still is a problem of world-wide importance to the brewing industry.

Excellent literature surveys have already been presented by Helm and Richardt (1938), Beattie (1951), Brenner (1957), Thorne and Helm (1957),

Gjertsen *et al.* (1963), Thorne (1964), Gjertsen (1967) and , more recently, by Gardner (1973) and Kieninger (1976).

Despite the many research works dealing with gushing, its real cause has not yet been clearly elucidated and methods of anticipating, preventing and curing gushing have yet to be established. During the last 15 years, however, important progress has been achieved in research on gushing, particularly on the nature of the factors causing or affecting gushing. It is expected that substantial understanding of the nature of gushing inducers and suppressants will naturally lead to a complete solution of this traditionally important problem of the brewing industry.

II. THE PHENOMENON OF GUSHING

A. Definition

In its usual sense the term gushing is used to describe the overfoaming of beer occurring when packaged beer is opened. Normally, when a bottle or a can of beer is opened its carbon dioxide is released slowly, though the beer usually contains 4–5 g carbon dioxide per litre, i.e. it is supersaturated to the extent of 150% to 200% with respect to carbon dioxide. In the case of gushing beer, a sudden release of carbon dioxide takes place at the instant the container is opened, creating a vast number of very minute bubbles throughout the beer volume which expand and ascend very quickly, resulting in a bursting stream of foamy beer that flows out of the container. In severe cases, more than half the content may be lost, occasionally showing a continuous spurt 2–10 cm high. This violent gushing action usually ceases after a few seconds.

According to Vogel (1949), beer showing gushing can be divided into three classes, e.g. mishandled beer, wild beer, and gushing beer. Most package beers show gushing if they are subjected to rough treatment (agitation) before or during opening of the container. This is naturally classified as mishandled beer. Overcarbonated beer or beer with excessive air content which overfoams on opening is termed wild beer. Both of these conditions can be readily corrected. The term gushing thus designates beer that overfoams excessively and which cannot be classified as mishandled or wild.

The gushing phenomenon which we mainly deal with in this section is the unpredictable, almost explosive liberation of carbon dioxide which causes violent overfoaming when a container of beer is gently opened.

The gushing problem is not confined to beers. Cider gushing is also well known and wildness in soft drinks is not uncommon.

B. Outbreaks of Gushing and its Typing

Gushing in beer appears to have been a traditional problem since the bottling of beer began in the middle of the 16th century in Great Britain (Beattie 1951). Incidents of gushing in the brewing industry may be classified into two types; sporadic or transitory and epidemic or serious. Sporadic gushing is limited to a certain brewery and may be cured rather easily by correcting some mistakes in the production process. Epidemic gushing occurs in much wider area affecting several breweries at the same time; it appears to be attributable to some abnormality in the season's malt.

Examples of incidents of epidemic gushing described in the literature are listed in Table 1. In 1938, Helm and Richardt (1938) stated that gushing

TABLE 1. Outbreaks of epidemic gushing described in the literature

Area	Year	Suspected cause	Reference
Northern Europe	1922	Malt	Helm and Richardt (1938)
	1927	Malt	
	1955	Malt	Gjertsen *et al.* (1963)
England	1950	Malt	Beattie (1951)
U.S.A.	1948–1949	Malt	Gray and Stone (1956)
	1955	Malt	
Japan	1936–1937	Malt (?)	Nakamura (1954)
	1957	Malt	Shimamoto *et al.* (1962)
	1958	Malt	Munekata *et al.* (1961)
Australia	1948	Malt and ageing	Harvey (1955)
	1952		

appears periodically, and the epidemics have occurred in Denmark, Norway, Holland, South America and the U.S. The authors were convinced that the primary cause of gushing could be traced to the barley years and variety. In fact, a severe incident of gushing in 1955 in some breweries of northwestern Europe was confirmed to be due to local barley of the 1954 harvest which had deteriorated owing to the exceptionally unfavourable conditions during harvesting (Gjertsen *et al.* 1963). Though its cause was not clearly explained at the time, the widespread occurrence of gushing in several breweries has been noted in the U.S. and England in 1948–1949 and 1950, respectively. In Japan, outbreaks of gushing in some breweries were noticed in 1936–1937 and 1957–1958, and some particular malts from certain local barley lots were found to be responsible (Nakamura 1954, Munekata *et al.* 1961, Shimamoto *et al.* 1962).

Munekata *et al.* (1961) made careful observation of the gushing phenomenon for several years in their breweries, and proposed dividing gushing into two types; "summer-type" gushing and "winter-type" gushing. Summer-type gushing occurred only when bottled beer was shaken or stored at high temperatures above 25 °C up to 45 °C. No gushing was observed when the bottles were shaken or stored at 0 °C prior to opening at 20 °C. On the contrary, winter-type gushing occurred only after shaking or storing the bottles at cold temperatures. The latter type of gushing appears to be an important problem in countries such as the U.S. and Japan where packaged beer is often drunk, after being chi'led, at cold temperatures (Gray and Stone 1956, Brenner 1957).

In Australia, a seasonally cyclic occurrence of gushing in bottled beer was reported by Harvey (1955), who systematically examined the frequency of the incidence of gushing using the bottled beer samples kept for 2, 4 and 6 months for shelf-life tests. His observations showed that the maximum tendency of gushing occurred after keeping bottled beer samples for 3–4 months at 20 °C. Typical results are shown in Table 2. It will be seen that in general the incidence of gushing is lowest in the early summer and that the majority of the

TABLE 2. Cyclic incidence of gushing in bottled beer in Australia, 1949–1954 (Harvey, 1955)

Month of Bottling	Percentage of gushing beer in bottled beer samples after keeping for 4 months					
	1949	1950	1951	1952	1953	1954
Jan	7·1	Nil	9·5	10·4	Nil	Nil
Feb	12·5	4·3	5·3	11·9	0·8	1·5
Mar	4·4	5·6	12·3	15·5	5·2	0·9
Apr	5·6	20·0	11·1	19·4	3·6	2·2
May	1·4	26·0	5·4	12·1	2·9	1·2
Jun	Nil	12·1	6·7	8·9	1·9	Nil
Jul	1·2	11·0	2·7	4·0	Nil	1·2
Aug	Nil	2·9	8·5	8·8	Nil	Nil
Sep	1·1	3·2	4·2	2·7	Nil	Nil
Oct	9·3	2·5	4·2	0·8	Nil	Nil
Nov	1·1	0·8	Nil	0·9	Nil	Nil
Dec	Nil	11·5	9·8	Nil	Nil	Nil

All samples were stored horizontally at approximately 20 °C for 4 months, and on the day of examination they were stood upright for one hour before opening. A sample which overfoamed to such an extent that one inch or more of beer was lost from a 26 oz. bottle was defined as gushing beer.

peaks have occurred in the autumn through the six years, 1949–1954. This type of gushing, which we may tentatively call "aged beer gushing", has also been recently noticed to occur mostly in autumn in beers in the Japanese market. It is well known that the packaged beer rarely shows gushing just after bottling and pasteurization but the gushing tendency increases with time, reaches a peak after 2–10 weeks, and then gradually decreases (Windisch 1923b, Helm and Richardt 1938, Gray and Stone 1949).

From the point of view of the causes of gushing, the research group of Carlsberg (Gjertsen *et al.* 1963) proposed to divide the gushing of beer into two types, namely (1) "primary gushing" which occurs periodically and appears to be related to the quality of malt, and (2) "secondary gushing" which is due to faults during beer production or to the incorrect treatment of bottled beer.

Evidence to show that the primary gushing associated with the malt quality is most probably caused by growth of microorganisms, either before threshing (field fungi) or during storage (storage fungi) or during malting, has been presented by Gjertsen *et al.* (1965), Amaha *et al.* (1973) and Gyllang and Martinson (1976a, b) as will be described later in detail.

Incidences of secondary gushing, which is due to certain particular causes other than malt quality, have been reported by many investigators. Some typical examples are shown in Table 3. Incidence of gushing due to the use of

TABLE 3. Incidences of secondary gushing due to particular causes other than malt quality

Country	Suspected cause	Reference
Denmark	Iron (5 and 25 mg/l)	Nielsen (1932)
U.S.A.	Heavy metals	Gray and Stone (1956)
U.S.A.	Calcium oxalate	Burger and Becker (1949)
U.S.A.	Microcrystals of calcium oxalate	Brenner (1957a, b)
U.S.A.	Internal surface of weathered bottle	Burger *et al.* (1956)
England	Nickel chelate of isohumulones	Rudin and Hudson (1958)
Holland	Hydrogen formed from aluminium spot	Ferdinandus *et al.* (1962)
Germany	Detergent for bottle washing	Dacks and Nitschke (1977)

certain kinds of isomerized hop extracts has been reported in recent years (Whitear and Button 1971, Schur and Pfenniger 1971, Laws and McGuinness 1972), and the methods of remedying this type of gushing have been presented (Humphrey 1969, Gardner *et al.* 1973).

III. MEASUREMENT OF GUSHING

Since gushing in beer is a physical phenomenon which is very susceptible to variations in physical and chemical conditions, it is extremely important to standardize the methods of estimating the gushing tendency of packaged beers. Naturally, laboratory methods of measuring gushing potential should aim at achieving some correspondence with practical experience. However, because of the diversity of conditions to which beer is subjected in commercial practice, there is no accepted standard method for estimating gushing. The basic factors that should be standardized in the measurement of gushing are: (1) duration and temperature of storing of packaged beer samples prior to the gushing test; (2) intensity and duration of agitation (shaking) before opening; (3) length of rest time before opening; and (4) the temperature at opening. The effects of some of these basic factors on the gushing tendency have been well established in an early work by Helm and Richardt (1938).

Various laboratory test methods proposed by several different groups for the measurement of the gushing potential of packaged beers are shown in Table 4, and the detailed procedures of some typical methods are as described below.

1. Shaking methods

The original "shaking method" proposed by Thorne and Helm (1957) is as follows. The beer bottles are placed on a rotary shaker and shaken (33 revolutions per min) for 24 h at 20 °C about a line at right angles to their axis. The bottles are rested standing for 1 h and then opened at 20 °C. The volume of beer that overflows out of the bottles is determined as the measure of gushing potential. They use ten bottles of each beer sample in order to obtain a reliable mean value.

Gray and Stone (1956a) developed two cold treatment methods which simulate the conditions of commercial practice in the U.S.A., where beers are consumed cold and may be held very cold for variable time periods before being consumed. In the first method, which they call the rapid shake test, a series of bottles is held at −2 °C for 24 h and then attempered to 20 °C for 1 h. The bottles are then shaken 30 times in 15 sec by hand, and opened after standing for 15–120 sec. This test was suggested as a quick means of assessing the potentiality for gushing of the sample. In their second method, the extended cold storage test, the test samples are held at −2 °C for varying time periods (2–18 weeks), then attempered to 25 °C for 1 h before opening.

Brenner (1957a) developed an accelerated gushing test using a vibrating cold box, to cope with the commercial gushing complaints in North America. In his method, bottles (or cans) are placed at 30 ° ±2 °F for 2 to 3 days in the vibrating box, attempered to 20 °C (cans to 10 °C) and then shaken for 15 sec on a laboratory shaker and opened after resting for 30 sec. Beer packages which do not overfoam more than 10 ml in this accelerated test are considered commmercially acceptable.

TABLE 4. Laboratory test methods for estimating gushing potential of packaged beers

	Preliminary treatment	Rest	Additional acceleration
Shaking method of Thorne and Helm (1957)	Shake on a rotary shaker (33 r.p.m.) at 20 °C for 24 h	Rest for 1 h at 20 °C before opening	—
Cold treatment methods by Gray and Stone (1956a)	(a) *Rapid shake test:* Store at −2 °C for 24 h	Rest for 1 h at 20 °C	Shake 30 times in 15 sec by hand, rest standing for 15–120 sec and open
	(b) *Extended cold storage test:* store at −2 °C for 2–18 weeks	Rest for 1 h at 25 °C, and open	—
Vibrating cold box test by Brenner (1957a)	Place on a vibrating cold box at 30° ±2 °F for 2–3 days	Attemperate to 20 °C (cans 10 °C)	Shake for 15 sec on a laboratory shaker, rest for 30 sec, and open
Inversion test by Gjertsen et al. (1963)	(a) *Mild test:* Store at 20 °C for 5, 10, 20 and 30 days. Invert slowly 3 times in 10 sec	Rest for 30 sec and open	—
	(b) *Severe test:* Shake at 20 °C for 5 and 10 days	Rest for 10 min	Three inversions in 10 sec, and rest 30 sec before opening
"Summer-type" and "Winter-type" tests by Munekata et al. (1961a)	(a) *Summer-type gushing test:* Shake at 37 °C for 6 h and then keep bottles horizontally lying at 20 °C for 3, 15 and 30 days	—	Invert gently 3 times in 10 sec, and rest for 40 sec, and open
	(b) *Winter-type gushing test:* Store at 0 °C for various periods until the clouding of beer begins. Place on a shaking machine and shake at 30 °C for 3 h	Rest for 3 min and open	

2. Inversion test methods

The original "inversion test" by Nielsen (1932), in which a beer bottle is gently rotated (360°) three times during a definite time (10 sec) and then opened after a resting time of 30–60 sec, is very easy and useful as a preliminary test for assessing the gushing potential of any beer sample.

Gjertsen *et al.* (1963) extended this original method to obtain more reproducible results for their studies on the gushing potential of weathered barley, and proposed two inversion tests. In the mild test, the bottles are kept lying at rest at 20 °C for 5, 10, 20 and 30 days respectively, then gently rotated three times, left for 30 sec and opened. In the severe test, the bottles are shaken horizontally in a lying position in a rocking cupboard at 20 °C for 5 and 10 days. Then the bottles are left at rest for 10 min, rotated three times and again left standing for 30 sec before opening. It is stated that the degree of gushing measured by the mild test corresponds to that occurring on the market, while the severe test gives a more sensitive determination of the gushing tendency. The gushing figures of less than 50 ml in the severe test indicate that no gushing will occur on the market, while figures over 100 ml are regarded as a warning of gushing tendency under specifically unfavourable conditions.

3. "Summer-type" and "Winter-type" tests

Munekata *et al.* (1961), who have found two different types of gushing in the Japanese beer market, namely "summer-type" gushing and "winter-type" gushing, reported different test methods for each type. Details of the procedures (Munekata 1976, personal communication) are shown in Table 4.

All the test methods described above are often modified to some extent by some workers, according to the objectives of their experiments. Laws and McGuinness (1972) selected a box shaking method for their study on the gushing potential of isomerized hop extracts. In their method, the materials to be tested are added to the ice-cold beer bottles. The bottles are recrowned and shaken for 18 h in a box shaker (stroke 1·4 cm, 270 strokes per min) for 18 h. Then the bottles are removed from the shaker and left to stand for 30 min before removing the crown. In the authors' laboratory, a rapid shaking method has been adopted for studies on gushing-inducing factors produced by moulds (Amaha *et al.* 1973). Depending on what type of gushing the brewer encountered, it is essential to select one or two test methods that should afford a good measure of the possibility of outbreaks of gushing on the market.

IV. PHYSICAL FACTORS AFFECTING GUSHING

A. Theoretical Consideration of the Gushing Phenomenon

Normal beers contain about 4–5 g CO_2 per litre which corresponds to 172–216% saturation at 10 °C and 237–296% saturation at 20 °C with respect to the carbon dioxide solubility, i.e. beer is supersaturated. It would not therefore, be strange to assume that the beer which overflows on opening (releasing of the overpressure) is normal and that the beer which is quiet on opening is abnormal. However, practical experiences show that most carbonated beverages, including beer, wine and soft drinks, are quiet on opening, if the packages are opened gently without agitation.

1. Krause's Nuclei Hypothesis

In a classic paper by Krause (1936) on the stability of supersaturated carbon dioxide solution (in particular, beer), it has been theoretically shown that carbon dioxide solutions up to 250% supersaturation should be stable, according to the equilibrium theories developed by Ostwald and Gibbs. Thus, Krause proposed that bubble formation in beer is contingent upon either an abnormally high degree of supersaturation or the presence of non-moistened particles, and that the bubbles formed on opening a bottle of beer must have developed from "dry spots" on the walls or on particles hovering in the beer. Such particles may be formed during shaking of the bottle, the material for the particle being furnished from substances adsorbed to the bubbles yielded by the shaking. Krause concluded that in gushing beer a great number of nuclei, which act as centres for the release of CO_2 bubbles, are formed when gas bubbles, whose surface contains surface active substances, are shaken or whipped into the beer. In a closed bottle, such bubbles are unstable and are forced to redissolve under the prevalent pressure in the bottle. This causes the concentration of the surface active substances and finally they form colloidal micelles which may then act as nuclei or "dry spots" for the sudden release of CO_2 when the excess pressure is removed at the opening of the bottle.

The validity of Krause's nuclei hypothesis was later proved by Schmith (1952) who conducted some experiments using a model solution of carbon dioxide (0·42% CO_2) in water. In his experiments, the addition of small quantities of colloidal ferric oxide or aluminium hydroxide (1·4–2·3 mg per 335 ml) could cause spontaneous release of CO_2 in the supersaturated solution after shaking the bottle in a hopping-cupboard for four days. In the control bottle, which stood at rest for four days, the added colloids had no effect. The same author further found that in the bottles which were completely filled (without leaving any neckspace), the added colloid did not show any effect, substantiating Krause's hypothesis that the existence of a boundary between the liquid and gaseous phases is an essential condition for the formation of the nuclei.

A more modern mathematical treatment of growth and decay of gas bubbles in liquids has been presented by Keller (1964), who also showed that a supersaturated solution is stable against bubble formation since all sufficiently small bubbles (with the initial radius R_0 smaller than an equilibrium radius R_e)

will dissolve. He states that only when there are nuclei which can produce sufficiently large bubbles, do growing bubbles occur in carbonated water.

Thus, Krause's nuclei hypothesis has been regarded by many investigators as providing the most reliable basis for understanding the gushing phenomenon (Curtis and Martindale 1961, Thorne 1964, Gjertsen 1967, Gardner 1973).

2. The Nature of Nuclei in Gas Release

As described above, gushing may be regarded as a purely physical phenomenon caused by the presence of "nuclei" which trigger the spontaneous release of carbon dioxide as the solution becomes supersaturated when overpressure is released on opening the package. There is a diversity of opinion, however, as to the nature of the "nuclei". It has been postulated (Beattie 1951, Brenner 1957b) that these "nuclei" include (1) microbubbles formed from undissolved gases when the beer is agitated; (2) irregular surfaces on the container wall; (3) glass fragments caused by weathering of the bottles; (4) dusts from crown closures, including lacquer dust; (5) cells of yeast, mould or bacteria; (6) diatomaceous earth; (7) microcrystals of calcium oxalate; (8) precipitated heavy metal-protein complexes; (9) high levels of dissolved air or nitrogen; (10) colloidal substances resulting from some inherent properties of malt.

Most of the above listed "nuclei" (except the last one) can be rather easily eliminated by normalizing the production processes in the brewery; thus, sporadic gushing due to these "nuclei" factors can be corrected. It is also true that the presence in bottled beer of some solid particles as listed above does not necessarily cause gushing (Curtis and Martindale 1961).

On the other hand, in the cases of epidemic gushing, the true nature of gushing-inducing nuclei remains to be clarified. The true gushing-inducing nuclei appear to develop from nuclei precursors normally existing in beer, the quantity of nuclei precursors present in different beers varying considerably. These precursors develop into fully developed nuclei through various conditions such as oxidation, cold or warm temperatures, and the presence of certain heavy metals, as has been pointed out by Gray and Stone (1956a).

Gardner (1973), who recently gave an elaborate discussion on the mechanism of gushing in beer, postulated the following three possible types of nuclei which would facilitate gas release from solutions. Type I, solid hydrophobic particles; Type II, gas residues sorbed on a solid support; and Type III, stabilized microbubbles. The latter two types actually consist of embryonic bubbles and can be referred to as bubble nuclei. Hydrophobic nuclei might be expected to lead to an increase in the ease of bubble formation. A hydrophobic surface may trap the embryonic bubbles, though they may not be themselves nuclei for gas release (Gardner 1973). In fact, it has often been observed that gushing beer after shaking contains a great number of rather stable microbubbles that remain suspended in the beer for many minutes and act as nuclei for gushing (Brenner 1957a, Curtis and Martindale 1961, Gjertsen 1967). The observation that fully filled bottles never gush (Schmith 1952, Helm and Richardt 1938, Curtis and Martindale 1961) and the commercial experience that bottles kept and carried in an upright position show far less gushing than do bottles kept in a horizontal position appear to indicate the necessity for gushing of gas bubbles introduced into the beer from neck space air. Thus, bubble nuclei as the cause of gushing have been suggested by a number of investigators (Curtis and Martindale 1961, Guggenberger and Kleber 1963, Gjertsen 1967). Gardner (1973) concluded that embryonic gas bubbles are the most likely type of nuclei to occur in gushing beer. However, an important question still remains, namely why such bubble nuclei are formed only in gushing beer and not in normal beer.

B. Physical Factors Affecting Gushing

1. Agitation

The importance of agitation, i.e. mechanical disturbance of beer, in inducing gushing has long been known, as is reflected in the fact that many gushing tests involve vigorous shaking. Both the intensity of shaking and the

TABLE 5. Effect of agitation on the gushing activity of a beer to which a gushing-inducing factor (NGF) from *Nigrospora* sp. was added†

Agitation	Rest time before opening	Gushing (ml from 340 ml bottles)
None	—	0
3 times inversion in 30 sec	30 sec	0, 0, 0, 0
5 min rotation	5 min	trace
15 min rotation	5 min	5
30 min rotation	5 min	10
60 min rotation	5 min	15, 15, 20, 35
60 min rotation	17 h	0, 0, 0, 0
60 min rotation + 17 h rest and then 3 times inversion in 30 sec	30 sec	60, 80, 60, 70

† Each bottle containing 0·06 p.p.m. of NGF was pasteurized at 60 °C for 20 min.

duration of shaking time are factors affecting the gushing potential of beer. In the case of a gushing beer in Denmark, Helm and Richardt (1938) obtained a maximum gushing tendency after shaking 10–20 days at 20 °C. Table 5 illustrates the effects of agitation on the gushing of a beer to which a purified preparation (NGF) of the gushing-inducing factor from *Nigrospora* sp. No. 207 (Amaha *et al.* 1973) was artificially added. When the pasteurized beer containing 0·06 p.p.m. of NGF was subjected to an inversion test (three times inversion in 30 sec and a 30 sec rest before opening) there was no gushing. When the same bottles were agitated by placing them on a rotating machine (20 r.p.m.) for 5 to 60 min, the gushing activity was found to increase with increasing the length of shaking time. In the case of 60 min agitation, the gushing activity disappeared after 17 h rest, but it was recovered in a more severe form when the bottles were subjected to a three times inversion test. Table 6 also shows the effects of agitation and rest time on the gushing potential of a beer experimentally brewed with a gushing malt.

The prone position of bottles during shaking is also an important factor to be noted. As mentioned, in commercial practice it is well known that beer bottles which are transported standing exhibit much less gushing than those transported prone (Gray and Stone 1949). Laboratory tests also proved that beer bottles shaken standing vertically exhibit the least tendency of gushing while the bottles shaken in a lying position parallel to the direction of shaking showed the largest tendency of gushing (Helm and Richardt 1938). As has been described previously, bottles fully filled with beer or carbonated water do not show any gushing.

2. Temperature

(a) *Storage temperature of beer prior to agitation*

It is known that the lower the storage temperature of bottled beer before shaking, the larger the tendency to gush. For example, Helm and Richardt (1938) found that when the same beer samples were kept at 2 °C, 12 °C and 20 °C for 2 weeks, and then shaken at 20 °C, the amount of overfoaming on opening was 91, 76 and 55 ml, respectively. With American beers it has been confirmed that gushing tendency is evoked by storing the packaged beers at low temperature (28–32 °F) for 1–4 weeks (Gray and Stone 1949, Brenner 1957a). However, Munekata *et al.* (1961) found that in their summer-type gushing, which was due to certain particular lots of malt, gushing occurred only when bottled beer was stored or shaken at temperatures higher than 25 °C; no gushing occurred at lower temperatures.

(b) *Temperature at which the bottled beer is agitated*

According to Helm and Richardt (1938), beer bottles shaken at 8 °C showed a smaller amount of gushing than those shaken at 20 °C. On the contrary, Brenner (1957a) found that the gushing tendency of American commercial beers was aggravated by placing the packaged beer in a vibrating cold box at 30 ° ±2 °F. In the case of the winter-type gushing of Munekata *et al.* (1961), gushing occurred only when the beer bottles were shaken or stored at lower temperatures (0 °C) but not at higher temperatures. Thus, it appears that the effects of temperature are often entirely different in different types of gushing.

(c) *Temperature at opening of package after agitation*

This is an important factor influencing the gushing tendency. It is generally known that the higher the temperature of beer at the instant of opening the package, the more intense the gushing. As an example, Helm and Richardt (1938) showed that when the bottles of the same gushing beer were opened at 12 °, 20 ° and 30 °C the overfoaming values were 25, 87 and 147 ml, respectively.

3. Shape and Size of Containers

The shape and size of containers profoundly affect the gushing tendency of beer. In the authors' laboratory, Hayashi (1971) compared the gushing potential of beer when filled in five different types of bottles. As shown in Table 6, in general, the larger the capacity of the container (more exactly the deeper the beer layer at standing position) the greater was the gushing tendency. It was also noticed that the bottles having square shoulders gave much more gushing than those having sloping shoulders.

The shape of package also affects the temperature–gushing relationship. In his accelerated tests (Table 4), Brenner (1957a) investigated the effect of several opening temperatures (0 °–45 °C) on gushing activity using almost 400 beer samples packaged in four different types of container. The maximum gushing activity occurred at a different opening temperature in each type of packages; the "average" temperatures of maximum activity being 6 °C for 12-oz. Flat-top cans, 10 °C for 12-oz. Cone-top cans, 17 °C for 32-oz. Steinie bottles and 37 °C for 12-oz. Export bottles.

There are probably several variables operating in the effects of the shape of packages; the volume of headspace, the depth of beer layer in which bubble nuclei are formed, the nozzle or inverted funnel effect of bottles, etc.

4. Carbon Dioxide Content

In an old study on a gushing beer, Windisch (1923a) ascribed the cause of gushing to the abnormally high content of carbon dioxide which was 0·48%. Nielsen (1932) examined the effect of the carbon dioxide content on gushing and found that gushing could not be due to a too high content of carbon dioxide. Blom (1934) found with a gushing beer that the gushing values were gradually increasing with increasing carbon dioxide content of beer. In practice it is also known that the gushing tendency of a beer can be reduced to some extent by reducing its carbon dioxide content, though it is impossible to

TABLE 6. Effects of shape and size of bottles on the gushing potential of a beer experimentally brewed with a gushing malt†

Agitation and rest before opening	Large bottles (633 ml) with square shoulders	Large bottles (633 ml) with sloping shoulders	Middle-size bottles (500 ml) with sloping shoulders	Small bottles (334 ml) with square shoulders	Small bottles (334 ml) with sloping shoulders
3 h rotation and then rest for 10 min	50 ml	24 ml	12 ml	8 ml	4 ml
24 h rotation and then rest for 10 min	245 ml	220 ml	120 ml	90 ml	78 ml
72 h rotation and then rest for 72 h	42 ml	60 ml	40 ml	22 ml	10 ml

† **Depths of beer layer in each bottle are:** large bottles, 21·9 cm; middle-size bottles, 19·0 cm; small bottles with square shoulders, 18·1 cm; small bottles with sloping shoulders (steinie), 14·0 cm.

abolish the gushing character of beer by such a procedure (Helm and Richardt 1938).

5. Neckspace Air

As described repeatedly, bottles completely filled with beer do not show gushing under condition of agitation where the normally filled bottles show a distinct gushing (Schmith 1952, Thorne and Helm 1957, Curtis and Martindale 1961). On the other hand, it has often been observed that the larger the neckspace air the more intense the gushing of beer (Gray and Stone 1949, Brenner 1957a). In these and some other aspects it appears that criteria which favour gushing also favour haze formation. Thus, oxidation of beer, resulting from air in the neckspace, has been postulated as a cause of gushing by several authors (Windisch 1923b, Gray and Stone 1956a). However, it is not easy to distinguish between the chemical effect of oxidation and the physical effect of air as an activator of "nuclei" or as the microbubbles *per se*.

The kind of headspace gas in the bottle also affects the gushing potential of beer. Helm and Richardt (1938), who replaced the neckspace gas with air,

TABLE 7. Effects of the kind of neckspace gas on the gushing potential of a beer prepared with gushing malt S†‡

Atmospheric gas in neckspace	Duration of shaking at 25 °C			Gas pressure after 72 h (kg/cm^2/20 °C)
	24 h	48 h	72 h	
CO_2	272 ml	308 ml	316 ml	2·12
O_2	122	278	298	2·38
H_2	94	205	235	2·64
N_2	14	58	94	2·72
Air	16	75	133	2·66

† Beer was filled in 633 ml bottles. Neckspace gas was replaced by CO_2, O_2, H_2, N_2 or air by blowing each gas into neckspace for 30 sec prior to crowning.

‡ After shaking on a rotating machine (20 r.p.m.) at 25 °C for 24–72 h, gushing potential was determined by an inversion test, i.e. 3 times inversion in 10 sec and then 30 sec rest before opening. The figures show an average value of gushing in duplicate runs.

CO_2, N_2, H_2 or O_2, found that the effects of individual gases were different between the two samples of gushing beer. In the authors' laboratory, Hayashi (1971) examined the effects of five different atmospheric gases in neckspace on the gushing potential of a beer that was experimentally brewed with a gushing malt. As can be seen in Table 7, carbon dioxide gave the highest gushing potential, followed by oxygen, hydrogen, air, and nitrogen, throughout the whole period of agitation from 24–72 h. The reason why such big differences in the gushing potential should result from the replaced neckspace gases has not yet been explained.

V. GUSHING INDUCERS AND THEIR ORIGINS

A. Malt as the Cause of Gushing

As shown in Table 1, most of the epidemics of gushing encountered in the past 50 years are believed to be due to some defects in the malt quality (Nielsen 1932, Helm and Richardt 1938, Gray and Stone 1956a). In fact it was found by many investigators that certain particular lots of malt could regularly give rise to a beer with a distinct gushing tendency (Nakamura 1954, Munekata *et al.* 1961, Curtis *et al.* 1961, Gjertsen *et al.* 1963).

Lüers (1924) had earlier expressed the idea that malt protein and their degradation products in beer might play a role in gushing. Nielsen (1932) reported that the content of formol-titratable nitrogen in gushing beer was abnormally low. On the other hand, Nakamura (1954), who conducted detailed analyses of a gushing malt and a normal malt, found an abnormally high proteolytic activity in the former and suggested that the enhanced proteolysis could be a cause of gushing in beer. Most other authors, however, could not find any definite differences in the analyses of nitrogenous components between gushing beer and normal beer.

To investigate the direct relationship between gushing and malt quality, intensive research efforts were initiated in the U.S.A. and Denmark with regard to the epidemics of gushing which occurred with barley harvested in 1948 and 1954, respectively. Both of these barley years were characterized by exceptionally wet and rainy weather during the ripening and harvest periods. At the Barley Improvement Conference, Burkhart (1952) reported that the new American Barley variety Moore of the 1950 harvest, which was more subject to damage by weathering, had produced gushing in many experimental brews. Dickson and Burkhart (1956) and Burkhart *et al.* (1960), who carried out an extensive work on the quality evaluation of hybrid barley selection by use of a micro-malting and a micro-brewery, provided further evidence to show that barley samples which are more or less severely weathered are prone to give rise to gushing in beer. A similar observation has also been made in the E.B.C. trials of several barley varieties in 1958, and the Carlsberg Research Group (Gjertsen *et al.* 1963) confirmed that the severe gushing in 1955 was caused by Danish barley of 1954 which was harvested in rainy weather and stored in silos with high contents of moisture. Gjertsen *et al.* (1963) further found that a gushing-inducing substance could be extracted by hot ethanol from gushing malt of the 1954 harvest. Thus, a direct relationship between gushing in beer and "weathered barley" became very apparent, at the same time suggesting an involvement of microorganisms as a cause of gushing.

B. Involvement of Microorganisms in Gushing

During growth and ripening, and also during harvesting and storage, barley grains are normally contaminated with a considerable variety of soil microorganisms including bacteria, yeasts and moulds. It is therefore natural to assume that the deterioration of weathered barley is largely due to its microflora. Extensive studies on the mycoflora of barley grains have been conducted by Tuite and Christensen (1955) and Kotheimer and Christensen (1961) in the U.S.A., by Flannigan (1970) in Great Britain, by Lund *et al.* (1971) in Denmark, and by Amaha *et al.* (1973) in Japan. From these studies it is generally known that barley grains are initially contaminated with the "field fungi" such as *Alternaria, Fusarium, Helminthosporium, Stemphylium* and *Cladosporium,* but during storage of barley the "storage fungi" such as *Aspergillus, Penicillium* and *Rhizopus,* become predominant, with the type depending on the moisture contents.

Clear proof showing that gushing is caused by microorganisms growing on barley grains was first presented by Prentice and Sloey (1960) and Sloey and Prentice (1962), who added cultures of 97 isolates of microorganisms (mostly isolated from barley grains) to the steep water in their micro-malting tests. The resulting malt samples were analysed and examined by micro-brewing. Their results showed that several strains of *Fusarium* and a strain of *Aspergillus* could cause changes in the analytical values, such as increases in wort nitrogen, increases in α-amylase and diastatic power, and decreased gas-stability (i.e. gushing) in beer. Following these works, Gjertsen *et al.* (1965) confirmed in much larger experimental malting tests that inoculation of several *Fusarium* cultures onto barley grains during steeping could yield gushing malts. However, since the addition to the mash of mycelial extract or culture filtrate of *Fusarium* failed to show gushing in beer, these authors were inclined to conclude that gushing is not caused by the *Fusarium* itself but is a result of an interaction between *Fusarium* and the germinating barley.

In 1973, Amaha *et al.* (1973) succeeded in proving that certain gushing-inducing substances are produced by several mould strains in a liquid culture medium. They first isolated 48 strains of mould from 28 samples of weathered barley of the 1970 and 1972 harvests in Japan. The isolated strains were then cultivated in a modified Richard's solution containing NH_4Cl (5·28 g), KH_2PO_4 (5 g), $MgSO_4$ (1·22 g), $FeCl_3.6H_2O$ (12 mg), sucrose (30 g) and Difco's yeast extract (2 g) per litre of water. After growing for 5–6 days at 25 °C, filtrate of the cultures was taken and concentrated to one-tenth of its original volume. Aliquots (2–5 ml) of the concentrates were then added to bottles containing 340 ml of normal beer for the gushing tests. The results revealed that eleven mould isolates, belonging to *Alternaria, Stemphylium,*

TABLE 8. Gushing-inducing potentials of culture filtrates of mould strains isolated from barley grains (from Amaha *et al.* (1973))

Moulds	Strain number	Gushing from 340 ml bottle†		
		Run 1 (ml)	Run 2 (ml)	Average (ml)
(1) Field fungi				
Alternaria spp.	109	25	40	32
	206	5	5	5
	304	6	0	3
	4004	0	0	0
Stemphylium sp.	103	145	140	142
Cladosporium spp.	4014	0	0	0
	7004	0	0	0
Helminthosporium spp.	306	0	0	0
	404	0	0	0
Fusarium spp.	112	4	5	4
	301	30	0	15
	4012	5	5	5
F. Graminearum‡	IFO 4474	180	180	180
Nigrospora sp.	207	190	180	185
(2) Storage fungi				
Aspergillus glaucus	409	90	50	70
group	4001	30	20	25
	6005	0	0	0
	6013	40	70	55
A. oryzae-flavus	104	0	0	0
group	107	5	5	5
	4007	0	0	0
Other *Aspergillus* spp.	106	5	5	5
	307	75	65	70
	407	0	0	0
Penicillium spp.	4002	0	0	0
	4016	10	10	10
	7001	180	170	175
Rhizopus spp.	4003	0	0	0
	6010	0	0	0

† Gushing was determined by a rapid-shake test.
‡ An authentic strain from the Culture Collection of the Institute of Fermentation, Osaka.

Fusarium, Aspergillus, Penicillium, Nigrospora and a type culture of *Fusarium graminearum* are capable of producing certain gushing-inducing factor(s) in the culture medium (Table 8). Attempts were then made to isolate and identify the gushing-inducing factors from the culture media of the three most active strains, *Nigrospora* sp. No. 207, *Stemphylium* sp. No. 103, and *Fusarium graminearum* IFO-4474, as will be described in the following section.

More recently, Gyllang and Martinson (1976a, b) investigated the myco-flora of gushing malts in North Europe and found that the gushing malts contained a high proportion of grains contaminated by storage fungi such as *Aspergillus, Penicillium* and *Rhizopus*. It has also been proved that the two dominant species, *Aspergillus fumigatus* and *Aspergillus amstelodami* could cause gushing in beer when they were added to the steeping water.

C. Gushing Inducers produced by Moulds

1. Isolation and Purification of the Gushing Factor produced by *Nigrospora* sp. No. 207

The gushing-inducing factor produced by *Nigrospora* sp. No. 207 has been isolated in a pure form from the liquid culture medium (Amaha *et al.* 1973). The optimal cultural conditions for the production of the gushing factor by this strain have been previously determined using a modified Richard's solution as the basal medium (Kitabatake and Amaha 1974). The addition of yeast extract (0·2%) was essential for the maximal production of gushing factor.

After growing in the modified Richard's solution for five days at 25 °C under aerobic condition, the culture medium was filtered to remove mycelial cells. To the filtrates, ammonium sulphate was added to give a saturation of 60%. The precipitates were collected and extracted with a small amount of 80% aqueous methanol. The methanol extract was then fractionated by successive solvent treatments with n-butanol, ethyl ether and acetone to separate the gushing factor from foreign materials. The crude preparation thus obtained was then dissolved in a small amount of 80% methanol and chromatographed on a column of Sephadex LH-20. Gushing-active fractions of eluates were collected, concentrated and lyophilized. The lyophilized powder was then dissolved in a small amount of 8 M urea and applied to a column of Sephadex G-100 equilibrated with 8 M urea. The active fractions were pooled and dialyzed against distilled water. The dialysed gushing factor was applied onto a column of DEAE-Sephadex A-25 previously equilibrated with 0·01 M Tris buffer, pH 8.0. The active fraction that was eluted with 0·1 M NaCl was then extracted with n-butanol after adjusting the pH to 2·0. The butanol extracts were transferred to 80% methanol and finally rechromatographed on a column of Sephadex LH-20. The fractions corresponding to the first peak were collected and lyophilized to obtain a white powder. This purified preparation gave only one spot when developed on thin-layer plates of silica gel G or Avicel SF with three different solvent systems, and also gave a single band on disc electrophoresis. Yield of the purified preparation was 30–50 mg from one litre of culture filtrate. The gushing-inducing activity of this purified preparation was extremely high, causing vigorous gushing when added to a normal beer at a concentration as low as 0·05 p.p.m. (Amaha *et al.* 1973).

When barley was artificially infected with this *Nigrospora* strain, the resulting malt gave a beer of strong gushing tendency. Attempts were then made to isolate and identify the gushing factor from the *Nigrospora*-infected barley, and Kitabatake and Amaha (1976) isolated the two gushing factors of similar nature in a pure form through the same purification procedures as described above. One of the newly isolated factors (B-II) appeared to be identical to the *Nigrospora* gushing factor (NGF) which had been previously isolated from the liquid culture medium. The second factor was found to be somewhat different from NGF in several aspects, such as the lower content of aspartic acid, the mobility on disc electrophoresis, and the gushing activity.

2. Chemical Nature of the *Nigrospora* Gushing Factor

The purified preparation of *Nigrospora* gushing factor (NGF) is soluble in water, aqueous methanol and ethanol and water-saturated butanol, but is insoluble in acetone, ether and chloroform. It gives a positive colour with ninhydrin and Cu-Folin reagents, but shows no sugar reaction when tested with anthrone. These facts, together with the specific absorption in the IR spectrum, suggested that NGF must be a polypeptide of rather hydrophobic nature.

Amino acid analyses of the acid hydrolysates revealed that NGF is composed of 14 kinds of amino acids and ammonia. Table 9 shows the amino acid composition of the *Nigrospora* gushing factor isolated from liquid culture (NGF) and those (B-I and B-II) isolated from the artificially infected barley grains (Kitabatake and Amaha 1976). It will be seen that all these gushing factors are characterized in common by: (1) the lack of the four residues, methionine, histidine, tyrosine, and tryptophan; (2) a relatively higher proportion of hydrophobic residues, such as proline, alanine, leucine and valine; and (3) the high content (about 10%) of half-cystine residues. The only difference found was the relatively lower content of aspartic acid in B-I. The molecular weight of NGF was estimated as 16 500 based on the elution position in gel filtration.

Some physicochemical properties of NGF are summarized in Table 10. NGF is stable at room temperature for over 12 months. It is also stable against heat in the pH range of 4–8. When NGF or the powder of the *Nigrospora*-infected barley was added to the mash tun, the finished beer showed a distinct gushing tendency, indicating that the gushing factor of *Nigrospora* can survive through the whole process of brewing, including kettle boiling (Kitabatake and Amaha 1976). NGF is resistant to digestion with chill-proofing enzymes,

TABLE 9. Amino acid composition of *Nigrospora* gushing factors obtained from the culture filtrate (NGF) and from artificially infected barley (B-I and B-II)

Amino acid	Amino acid residue (g/100 g protein)		
	NGF	B-I	B-II
Aspartic acid	13·2	9·4	12·0
Threonine	8·7	8·1	8·3
Serine	3·3	3·2	3·4
Glutamic acid	6·8	11·2	11·5
Proline	10·6	12·5	12·9
Glycine	4·4	4·1	4·2
Alanine	10·8	9·8	9·9
Half-cystine	9·8	9·5	9·9
Valine	7·0	6·6	6·6
Methionine	0	0	0
Isoleucine	2·8	2·9	2·8
Leucine	11·0	11·1	10·7
Tryosine	0	0	0
Phenylalanine	5·5	7·1	5·8
Tryptophan	0	0	0
Lysine	3·1	3·2	2·8
Histidine	0	0	0
Arginine	3·7	3·7	3·5
Amide-NH_3	(2·2)	(2·3)	(2·5)

TABLE 10. Physico-chemical properties of *Nigrospora* gushing factor (NGF)

Molecular weight	16 500 by gel filtration
Isoelectric point	4·0
Sedimentation coefficient	$s_{20w} = 1·23$ S
Optical density at 280 nm	$E_{1\,cm}^{1\%} = 1·2$ (in 80% aqueous methanol)
Polarity index	33%
Surface tension	64·5 dyne/cm (0·01% aqueous solution)
Heat stability	Survive 2 h heating at 100 °C in buffer solutions of pH 4–8

such as papain, ficin and bromelin, though it is digested with Pronase, pepsin, trypsin or thermolysin (Amaha *et al.* 1973).

If we estimate the polarity of the NGF molecule from the amino acid composition following the method of Capaldi and Vanderkooi (1972), NGF is found to have a polarity index of approximately 33%, an exceptionally low value as the water-soluble protein, i.e. NGF, is a fairly hydrophobic protein. It is well known that proteins of such hydrophobic nature have a tendency to aggregate in aqueous solution through intermolecular interactions between thc hydrophobic regions (Haurowitz 1963, Morrisett *et al.* 1975). These facts appear to support the hypothesis that hydrophobic regions of a proteinous molecule would play a role as the "dry spots" or nuclei in releasing carbon dioxide from beer (Krause 1936, Gardner 1973).

The effect of NGF on the surface viscosity of beer is shown in Table 11. The addition of NGF (0·3–1·0 mg) to beer brings about a large increase in surface

TABLE 11. Effect of *Nigrospora* gushing factor (NGF) on the surface viscosity of beer† (from Kitabatake (1974))

NGF added (p.p.m.)	Surface viscosity (g/sec)		
	Time (min) after pouring the beer samples		
	5	15	30
0	0·0128	0·0164	0·0624
0·3	0·0169	0·0459	0·1203
1·0	0·0267	0·1280	0·7477

† The surface viscosity of degassed beer was measured with an oscillating-disc surface viscosimeter (Kyowa-Kagaku, Type SVR-SP1).

viscosity. That the increase in surface viscosity of beer correlates quantitatively with gushing has been reported by Gardner (1972).

3. Chemical Modifications of *Nigrospora* Gushing Factor (NGF)

In order to explore the structural properties of NGF molecule responsible for the gushing activity as well as to have an insight into the mechanism of gushing in beer, some chemical modifications of the NGF protein were carried out by Kitabatake and Amaha (1977). The effects of chemical modifications on the gushing activity of NGF are summarized in Table 12. Cleavage of disulphide bonds of NGF, either oxidative or reductive, caused complete inactivation of the gushing activity, indicating that the disulphide bonds are essential for exhibiting the activity. Modifications of amino groups of NGF with maleic anhydride or *O*-methylisourea did not affect the gushing activity, whereas their modification with trinitrobenzene sulphonate (TNBS) reduced the activity to some extent. Modification of arginine-guanidino groups with phenylglyoxal markedly reduced the gushing activity. On the other hand, when the free carboxyl groups of NGF were modified by methylation or by amide formation, the gushing activity was drastically reduced, implying that the acidic groups of NGF molecule are important. From these results, it appears that both the maintenance of definite molecular conformation and the maintenance of certain surface charges are essential for the NGF protein to exhibit its gushing-inducing activity.

TABLE 12. Effects of chemical modifications on the gushing activity of *Nigrospora* gushing factor (NGF)†

Groups modified	Total number of group in NGF	Modifications	Inactivation of gushing factor
Disulphide bonds	8	Oxidation with performic acid	+
		Reduction with 2-mercaptoethanol	+
		Reduction with sodium borohydride	+
Amino groups	4–5	Maleylation with maleic anhydride	−
		Trinitrobenzene sulfonation with TNBS	±
		Guanidination with O-methylisourea	−
Free carboxyl groups	6–7	Methylation with methanolic HCl	+
		Amide formation with a water-soluble carbodiimide and nucleophiles	+
Guanidino groups	4	Modification with phenylglyoxal	+

† From Kitabatake and Amaha (1977).

4. Gushing Factors produced by *Stemphylium* and *Fusarium*

The gushing-inducing factor produced by *Stemphylium* sp. No. 103 has been isolated in a pure form from the liquid culture medium (Amaha *et al.* 1973). The purified preparation was able to induce gushing at a concentration of 4 p.p.m. when added to a normal beer. The *Stemphylium* gushing factor is soluble in water, but insoluble in methyl and ethyl alcohols, ether and acetone. Chemical analyses of acid hydrolysates of this factor revealed that it is composed of 85% glucosamine and 10% peptide. The gushing activity was destroyed by incubation with pepsin, pronase or chitinase. Thus, the *Stemphylium* gushing factor is a peptidoglycan. When heated at 100 °C for 2 h in 0·1 M acetate buffer solutions of pH 4–6, the gushing factor retained about 50% of its activity, suggesting that this factor would survive kettle boiling at least partially.

Despite the earlier findings that growth of several *Fusarium* strains on germinating barley grains gave rise to a malt of strong gushing tendency (Prentice and Sloey 1960, Gjertsen *et al.* 1965), attempts to isolate and identify the *Fusarium* gushing factors are still uncompleted. When a strain of *Fusarium graminearum* (IFO 4474) was grown in a modified Richard's solution, a considerable amount of gushing-inducing substances was produced in the medium (Amaha *et al.* 1973). By solvent fractionation, the gushing-inducing factors were divided into two fractions; one soluble and one insoluble in methanol. The methanol-insoluble fraction was highly purified through column chromatography on DEAE-Sephadex and Sephadex G-50. The results of chemical and enzymatic analyses showed that this methanol-insoluble fraction is also a peptide-containing substance.

D. Gushing Inducers from Hops

In the early 1970s, when isomerized hop extracts for direct addition to beer became commercially available, the use of isomerized extract as partial or whole replacement of the hop grist sometimes caused gushing in beer (Whitear and Button 1971, Schur and Pfenninger 1971). This stimulated a search for the gushing inducers in the isomerized extracts and led to an important discovery that both gushing promoting factors and suppressing factors are present in the hop grist (Carrington *et al.* 1972, Laws and McGuinness 1972, Sandra *et al.* 1973, Gardner *et al.* 1973).

Laws and McGuinness (1972) found that there are two types of gushing promoting factor in isomerized hop extracts. One type was dehydrated humulinic acid which could induce gushing in commercial beers at concentrations of 5–25 p.p.m. However, dehydrated humulinic acid was not a normal constituent in isomerized hop extracts, though it was present in a particular

TABLE 13. Gushing promoting or suppressing actions of hop resin components. (Summarized from Carrington *et al.* (1972), and partly from Laws and McGuinness (1972))

	Gushing promotion†	Gushing suppression†
Trans-isohumulone	−	
Cis-isohumulone	−	
Trans-isocohumulone	−	
Cis-isocohumulone	−	
Trans-allo-isohumulone	−	
ρ-Isohumulone A_1	−	
Humulinic acid	−	
Dehydrated humulinic acid‡	+ +	
Tetrahydro-*trans*-isohumulone	+ +	
Hexahydro-*trans*-isohumulone	+ +	
Spiro-isohumulones	+ +	
Oxidation products (Abeo-isohumulones)‡	+ +	
α-Acids	−	+ ∼ + +‡
β-Acids	−	+
Cohulupone	−	+
Lupuloxinic acid	−	+

† Symbols: + +, strong action; +, weak to moderate action; −, no action.
‡ Data from Laws and McGuinness (1972).

extract to the extent of 5%. The other type of gushing promoter was therefore sought by fractionating the hop extracts by thin-layer chromatography, and oxidation products of humulone and/or isohumulone, which are similar to abeo-iso-α-acids, were found to provoke gushing in beers at a concentration of 5 p.p.m. The content of oxidation products in six commercial isomerized extracts varied from 2·6 to 8·8%, and, in general, the higher the quantity of oxidation products in an extract the greater was its tendency to promote gushing.

On the other hand, Carrington *et al.* (1972) examined the gushing promoting and the suppressing effects of a variety of hop resin components and their derivatives, using highly purified preparations. Among the 16 compounds tested, the following three hydrogenated or cyclized derivatives of isohumulone were found to be strong gushing promoters: tetrahydro-*trans*-isohumulone, hexahydro-*trans*-isohumulone and spiro-isohumulones. The other hop components showed no action or a rather weak to moderate suppressing action on gushing.

The gushing-promoting action and the gushing-suppressing action of individual hop resin components are summarized in Table 13.

E. Other Gushing Inducing Factors

1. Metallic ions

It has been known for many years that some heavy metals cause gushing in beer. Nielsen (1932) reported two cases of gushing caused by iron in concentrations of 5 and 25 p.p.m. respectively. In 1949, Gray and Stone (1949) confirmed that the addition of 1 p.p.m. of iron to commercial beer increased the gushing tendency of various beers. Gray and Stone (1956a) further conducted an extensive study on the gushing-inducing potentials of a variety of metallic ions, using both a rapid shake method and an extended cold storage test for the detection of gushing potential. Among the nineteen heavy metals which were found active in inducing gushing in beer in quantities of few p.p.m., tin, titanium, uranium, yttrium, lanthanum, bismuth, nickel, iron and molybdenum were the most active, in decreasing order of effectiveness. Addition of small amounts of the chelating agent EDTA was found to suppress the development of gushing caused by the presence of traces of iron and other active metals, except titanium and uranium.

Rudin and Hudson (1958) found that nickel or iron at concentrations of 2–5 p.p.m. (as sulphate) cause gushing in hopped beer, but not in unhopped beer. The nickel chelate of isohumulone and to a lesser degree the corresponding compound of iron could provoke gushing in unhopped beer. Guggenberger and Kleber (1963), who discussed mechanism of the development of gushing in beer, proposed that formation of ferric carbonate on the surface of "gas nuclei" has practical significance in producing the condition for gushing.

Although some isolated instances of sporadic gushing may rightly be attributed to iron, the concentrations of iron or nickel which have been found to be effective in inducing gushing are much higher than those usually found in normal beer from modern breweries.

2. Calcium Oxalate Crystals

Burger and Becker (1949) found that beer which had a latent tendency toward eventual precipitation of calcium oxalate gave violent gushing after shaking. Existence of a consistent correlation between gushing and oxalate content has been confirmed by Burger et al. (1965) and Brenner (1957a, b). The latter author suggested that microcrystals of calcium oxalate may act as "nuclei" in causing gushing. In his observations, gushing could be induced by the creation of conditions favourable to precipitation of calcium oxalate, and the gushing activity of beer could be reduced or removed by subjecting beer to condition which would solubilize or remove insoluble oxalate. It would be worthy of noting here that high air content of packaged beer definitely aggravated the gushing potential of beer containing microcrystalline oxalates (Brenner 1957a).

3. Other Factors

A few other factors have also been reported as the cause of sporadic gushing in beer. Ferdinandus et al. (1962) reported an instance of gushing which was caused by the combined presence of dissolved hydrogen and nitrogen in the beer. In this particular case, the hydrogen originated from the action of beer on the aluminium spot in the crown cork in bottles stored in a horizontal position.

Another cause of sporadic gushing which has sometimes been encountered both in beers and in other carbonated beverages is roughness of the internal surface of the bottles. Burger et al. (1956) reported a case of gushing which was due to badly weathered bottles. Passage through the bottle washer did not eliminate the gushing trouble.

Improper cleaning or rinsing of the bottles may also provoke gushing, as a considerable number of dry spots which become evolving centres of carbon dioxide gas remain attached to the internal surface of bottles. In fact, Dacks and Nitschke (1977) have recently reported a case of sporadic gushing which is associated with the use of a certain kind of bottle-washing detergent. They observed by means of membrane filtration that insoluble condensation particles of microscopic size were present in the detergent and these were not readily removed from the bottle by ordinary rinsing procedures.

VI. ANTI-GUSHING FACTORS

It has been earlier known that gushing of beer can be suppressed or promoted by hop substances and their derivatives. Munekata *et al.* (1961), using a gushing malt and several different kinds of hops, demonstrated that the gushing tendency of beer was greatly influenced by the variety of hops. As shown in Table 14, the gushing values of beer varied widely from 0 to 349 ml,

TABLE 14. Effects of the kinds of hops on the gushing potential of beer brewed with a gushing malt, BT. (Munekata *et al.* 1961)

Kinds of hops	Gushing[†] from 630 ml bottle (ml)	Tannin in beer (p.p.m.)	Iso-α-acids in beer (p.p.m.)	Ratios Tannin/iso-α-acids
G-57	349	248	17·2	14·4
PG-58	347	225	24·7	9·1
G-58	300	250	20·0	12·5
T-57	97	186	29·2	6·3
Z-58	85	214	30·6	6·7
D-58	0	227	39·9	5·7
Non-hop	113	165	0	$\leqslant$

† Gushing values determined by the summer-type gushing test.

depending on the kinds of hops used. Analyses of the six hops and the final beers indicated that the ratios of tannin to α-acids (or iso-α-acids in beer) were roughly proportional to the gushing activities of beers, suggesting a possible gushing-suppressing effect of α-acids (and iso-α-acids) and a gushing-promoting effect of polyphenols. Curtis *et al.* (1961) also showed that the hop rate could be an important factor in controlling gushing and that the gushing-suppressing effects of hops varied with the variety of hops used.

In a later publication, Munekata *et al.* (1965) further showed that purified preparations of α-acids, iso-α-acids and certain other products from α- and β-acids including hulupone were effective in suppressing the summer-type gushing of beers. A more recent work by Laws and McGuinness (1972), who investigated the origin of gushing factors in isomerized hop extracts, confirmed that addition of 5 p.p.m. of humulone almost completely suppressed the gushing potential of a commercial beer which gushed severely. Humulone was also very effective in suppressing gushing caused by the addition of dehydrated humulinic acid to beer. Cohulupone was also shown to be a gushing-suppressor, though its effect was less than that of humulone (cf. Table 13).

In connection with the gushing potential of isomerized hop extracts, Carrington *et al.* (1972) reported an interesting observation that C_{16} to C_{20}

unsaturated acids such as palmitoleic, oleic, linoleic, and linolenic acids were all active in suppressing gushing caused by added promoter (from isomerized hop extract), while the saturated fatty acids such as palmitic and stearic acids acted as mild gushing promoters in non-gushing beers. A mixture of fatty acids extracted from hops, which consisted of palmitic acid (23%), linoleic acid (26%) and linolenic acid (51%) were also found to be as effective as the most active single acids in suppressing gushing.

On the other hand, Gardner *et al.* (1973) found that hop oil has a very strong gushing-suppressing effect even at levels as low as 1 p.p.m. Among the various hop oil components, caryophyllene was particularly effective and this hydrocarbon compound appeared to be more effective than linoleic acid in suppressing gushing when compared at 2 p.p.m. Anti-gushing factors such as hop oil and fatty acids appear to be generally effective in suppressing various types of gushing: not only natural gushing but also those types of gushing caused by the addition of such inducers as nickel, dehydrated humulinic acid, abeo-isohumulones, and the *Nigrospora* gushing factor (Carrington *et al.* 1972, Gardner *et al.* 1973, Kitabatake 1974). The anti-gushing effects of several fatty acids and surfactants against gushing induction by the *Nigrospora* gushing factor (NGF) are shown in Table 15. Oleic acid and

TABLE 15. Anti-gushing effects of fatty acids and surfactants against the gushing induction by *Nigrospora* gushing factor (0·1 p.p.m.) (from Kitabatake (1974))

Addition	Quantities added (mg/340 ml)	Foam† stability	Clarity of beer	Gushing (ml/340 ml)
None (control)	−	+	clear	130
Myristic acid	3	−	opal‡	0
Palmitic acid	3	−	opal	86
Oleic acid	0·5	−	opal	0
Monostearin	5	−	opal	0
Lauryl alcohol	5	−	opal	0
Lecithin	0·5	−	opal	0
Lysolecithin	2	+	clear	0
Sodium lauryl sulphate	5	±	opal	0

† +, Good; −, bad.   ‡ Opalescent.

lecithin are found to be very effective in inhibiting the gushing caused by NGF (0·1 p.p.m.). The addition of these effective compounds (except lysolecithin) to beer, however, impairs both the foam stability and the clarity of beer.

From the recent findings of the gushing inducers and the suppressors as described in this and the preceding sections, it is now quite clear that the beer contains both gushing promoters and gushing suppressors, and thus the gushing potential of a beer is determined by the balance of promoters and inhibitors.

VII. PROCESS VARIABLES AFFECTING GUSHING

From the practical point of view of preventing gushing, it is important to know how the gushing of beer is affected by the raw materials and the process of brewing and bottling.

A. Malt and the Malting Process

Selection of raw materials, i.e. of barley, malt and hops, is the most reliable and effective means for preventing the occurrence of gushing in beer. As it is quite evident that severe epidemics of gushing have been closely associated with weathered barley, the use of discoloured barley grains for malting should be avoided by preliminary inspection. Obviously, gushing in beer which is due to faulty malt is related to the deterioration of barley and malt by microorganisms through the whole periods from growth of barley to the end of malting process. Although certain barley varieties have been reported to be peculiarly prone to cause gushing in beer (Burkhart 1952, Dickson and Burkhart 1956), the defect may be explained by their susceptibility to damage by weathering (Gjertsen 1967). Excessive moisture during ripening, harvest and post harvest storage naturally favours the growth of microorganisms on the barley grains. As it has been recently shown that besides the field fungi the storage fungi such as *Aspergillus* and *Penicillium* could cause gushing in beer (Amaha *et al.* 1973, Gyllang and Martinson 1976a, b), it is important to ensure that malting plant is carefully cleaned. High temperatures during the germination period will also favour growth of moulds such as *Aspergillus amstelodami* and *Aspergillus fumigatus* which have been known to cause gushing (Gyllang and Martinson 1976a, b). The addition of formaldehyde (0·14%) to the steep water has been found to prevent gushing in beers brewed from *Fusarium*-infected grains (Gjertsen *et al.* 1965).

B. Hops and Hopping

It has been generally known that the higher the hop rate the smaller the gushing potential of a beer (Curtis *et al.* 1961, Munekata *et al.* 1961, Gjertsen *et al.* 1963). As described in the previous sections, hops contain both anti-gushing factors and promoting factors, and the gushing-suppressing effect of hops differs widely depending on the variety (see Table 14). Hence, selection of "good quality" hops with regard to the anti-gushing potential should aid in preventing or suppressing gushing of beer. The effect of combining the various qualities of malt and hop has been examined by Curtis *et al.* (1961). Their results demonstrated that if the hops are rich in anti-gushing substances, quiet beer can be brewed from malt of strong gushing tendency even when the hop rate is low. Conversely if the hops are relatively poor in anti-gushing substances but the malt is rich in gushing substances, gushing beer will be obtained if the hop rate falls below a critical value.

Since hop oil is a very potent gushing suppressor, the addition of trace amounts of hop oil, or dry hopping, can be another means to cure gushing.

C. The Brewing Process

Nakamura (1954) reported that quiet beer could be brewed from gushing malts by modifying the mashing process so as to restrict proteolysis. Munekata et al. (1961), however, found that modifications of the mashing process had no remarkable effect on the summer-type gushing, which was due to certain defective malts. Yeast strains and the conditions of fermentation did not have any distinct influence upon the gushing of finished beers (Munekata et al. 1961).

The gushing potential of beer changes during the brewing process. Curtis et al. (1961), who determined gushing potentials of unhopped wort, hopped wort and the bottled beer of four brews each of brown ale and pale ale, found that unhopped worts could show gushing when carbonated, while hopped worts were quiet with the exception of one brew for brown ale. The only brown ale which gushed at the hopped wort stage gave the highest gushing potential figure of all the bottled beers. Two brown ales which showed no gushing potential at the hopped wort stage gushed in bottle, indicating that an increase in gushing potential occurs between the hopped wort and the final beer. Munekata et al. (1961), working with a lager-type beer, also found that the gushing potential increased greatly with fermentation and lagering. Thus, the prediction of gushing potential of beer at the stages of either unhopped wort or hopped wort appears, unfortunately, to be impossible. In the authors' laboratory a rapidly fermented beer from Congress wort has been temporarily used for detecting the gushing potentials of malt.

In connection with the sporadic occurrence of gushing which was regarded as due to the presence of microcrystals of calcium oxalate, Brenner (1957b) recommended the addition of calcium ions to the mash liquor for precipitation of the oxalate. Markedly improved stability against the cold-type gushing is obtained when the molar ratio of calcium to oxalate exceeds ten to one. However, the summer-type gushing which is associated with the use of defective malts is not corrected by calcium enrichment (Munekata et al. 1961, Curtis et al. 1961).

Some means for stabilizing beer against haze affect the gushing tendency of beer. Cooling and filtration of wort or beer may favour the removal of anti-gushing factors such as α-acids, higher fatty acids and phospholopids. The influence of proteolytic enzyme preparations on the gushing tendency of beer from abnormal malts has been investigated by Helm and Richardt (1938).

When added to beer before pasteurization, pepsin could decrease the gushing tendency at levels of 0·2 to 1·0 g per hectolitre, while papain enhanced or evoked the gushing tendency at concentrations of 0·06 g to 0·2 g per hectolitre. Treatments of gushing beer with adsorbents may in some cases be useful for reducing gushing potentials. It has been reported that the use of charcoal (0·5%), fuller's earth (1%), Tansul (1%), kaolin (1%), activated alumina (1%) and bleaching earth (0·2%) were effective in this respect (Curtis and Martindale 1961, Gjertsen et al. 1963). Treatment of gushing beers with nylon powder is also effective in reducing the severity of gushing (Munekata et al. 1961, Hudson 1962). However, the practical use of most of the above adsorbents for the treatment of gushing beer is limited, as they may often impair the flavour and head retention of the beer. The most practical measure to correct gushing beer is the appropriate blending of gushing beer with normal beer (Gjertsen 1967).

Because of the diversity in the cause and type of gushing in beer, it must be said that a specific precaution may be effectively applied only to the specific cause of gushing. To establish the remedies for any type of gushing, accumulation of more knowledge on the cause and mechanisms of gushing is desirable.

REFERENCES

Amaha, M., Kitabatake, K., Nakagawa, A., Yoshida, J. and Harada, T. (1973). *Proc. E.B.C. Congr., Salzburg* pp. 381–398.

Beattie, G. B. (1951). *Wallerstein Lab. Commun.* **14**, 81–99.

Blom, J. (1934). Beretning om det 6. skandinaviske Brygmesterkursus i Kobenhavn, p. 109.

Brenner, M. W. (1957a). *Proc. Ann. Meet. Am. Soc. Brew. Chem.* pp. 5–21.

Brenner, M. W. (1957b). *Proc. E.B.C. Congr., Copenhagen* pp. 349–362.

Burger, M. and Becker, K. (1949). *Proc. Ann. Meet. Am. Soc. Brew. Chem.* pp. 102–115.

Burger, M., Glenister, P. R. and Becker, K. (1956). *Proc. Ann. Meet. Am. Soc. Brew. Chem.* pp. 169–178.

Burkhart, B. A. (1952). *Barley Improvement Conference* p. 11.

Burkhart, B. A., Otis, O. J. and Dickson, A. D. (1960). *Proc. Ann. Meet. Am. Soc. Brew. Chem.* pp. 123–128.

Capaldi, R. A. and Vanderkooi, G. (1972). *Proc. Nat. Acad. Sci., U.S.A.* **69**, 930–932.

Carrington, R., Collett, R. C., Dunkin, I. R. and Halek, G. (1972). *J. Inst. Brew.* **78**, 243–254.

Curtis, N. S. and Martindale, L. (1961). *J. Inst. Brew.* **67**, 417–421.

Curtis, N. S., Ogie, P. J. and Carpenter, P. M. (1961). *J. Inst. Brew.* **67**, 422–427.

Dacks, E. and Nitschke, R. (1977). *Brauwelt* **117**, 129–131.

Dickson, A. D. and Burkhart, B. A. (1956). *Proc. Ann. Meet. Am. Soc. Brew. Chem.* pp. 143–155.

Ferdinandus, A., Gombert, J. and Jansen, H. E. (1962). *J. Inst. Brew.* **68**, 250–253.

Flannigan, B. (1970). *Trans. Br. Mycol. Soc.* **55**, 267–276.

Gardner, R. J. (1972). *J. Inst. Brew.* **78**, 391–399.
Gardner, R. J. (1973). *J. Inst. Brew.* **79**, 275–283.
Gardner, R. J., Laws, D. R. J. and McGuinness, J. D. (1973). *J. Inst. Brew.* **79**, 209–211.
Gjertsen, P. (1967). *Brewers' Digest* **42** (5), 80–84.
Gjertsen, P., Trolle, B. and Andersen, K. (1963). *Proc. E.B.C. Congr., Brussels* pp. 320–341.
Gjertsen, P., Trolle, B. and Andersen, K. (1965). *Proc. E.B.C. Congr., Stockholm* pp. 428–438.
Gray, P. P. and Stone, I. (1949). *Proc. Ann. Meet. Am. Soc. Brew. Chem.* pp. 127–139.
Gray, P. P. and Stone, I. (1956a). *Proc. Ann. Meet. Am. Soc. Brew. Chem.* pp. 83–108.
Gray, P. P. and Stone, I. (1956b). *Wallerstein Lab. Commun.* **19**, 335–339.
Guggenberger, J. and Kleber, W. (1963). *Proc. E.B.C. Congr., Brussels* pp. 299–317.
Gyllang, H., and Martinson, E. (1976a). *J. Inst. Brew.* **82**, 182–183.
Gyllang, H. and Martinson, E. (1976b). *J. Inst. Brew.* **82**, 350–352.
Harvey, J. V. (1955). *Proc. 3rd Conv. Inst. Brewing Australia and New Zealand Section* pp. 10–16.
Haurowitz, F. (1963). "The Chemistry and Function of Proteins", pp. 149–154. Academic Press, New York and London.
Hayashi, H. (1971). *Annual Report of Research Laboratories of Asahi Breweries Ltd.* **9**, 91–108.
Helm, E., and Richardt, O. C. (1938). *Wschr. Brau.* **55**, 89–94.
Hudson, J. R. (1962). *J. Inst. Brew.* **68**, 460–466.
Humphrey, A. M. (1969). West German Patent 2 050 968 (and U.S. Patent 3 870 810 11 March 1975).
Keller, J. B. (1964). *In* "Cavitation in Real Liquids" (R. Davies ed.), pp. 19–29, Elsevier, Amsterdam.
Kieninger, H. (1976). *Brauwelt* **116**, 1600–1603, 1633–1636.
Kitabatake, K. (1974). "Studies on the Gushing Inducing Substances produced by Moulds", Doctoral thesis, University of Tokyo.
Kitabatake, K. and Amaha, M. (1974). *Bull. Brewing Sci., Tokyo* **20**, 1–8.
Kitabatake, K. and Amaha, M. (1976). *Bull. Brewing Sci., Tokyo* **22**, 9–19.
Kitabatake, K. and Amaha, M. (1977). *Agric. Biol. Chem.* **41**(6), 1011–1019.
Kotheimer, J. B. and Christensen, C. M. (1961). *Wallerstein Lab. Commun.* **24**, 1–7.
Krause, B. (1936). *Svenska Bryggareforen. Manadsbl.* **51**, 221–236.
Laws, D. R. J. and McGuinness, J. D. (1972). *J. Inst. Brew.* **78**, 302–308.
Lüers, H. (1924). *Wschr. Brau.* **41**, 49–50.
Lund, A., Pedersen, H. and Sigsgaard, J. (1971). *J. Sci. Food Agric.* **22**, 458–463.
Morrisett, J. D., Jackson, R. L. and Gotto, A. M. Jr. (1975). *Ann. Rev. Biochem.* **44**, 183–207.
Munekata, H., Honjo, T., Koshino, S. and Hosaka, M. (1961). *Bull. Brewing Sci., Tokyo* **6**, 1–11.
Munekata, H., Koshino, S. and Yada, H. (1965). *Bull. Brewing Sci., Tokyo* **11**, 25–31.
Nakamura, H. (1954). *J. Inst. Brew.* **60**, 420–427.
Nielsen, J. (1932). Beretning om det 5. skandinaviske Brygmesterkursus i Kobenhavn, p. 83 (cited by Gjertsen *et al.* 1963).
Prentice, N. and Sloey, W. (1960). *Proc. Ann. Meet. Am. Soc. Brew. Chem.* pp. 28–33.
Rudin, A. D. and Hudson, J. B. (1958). *J. Inst. Brew.* **64**, 317–318.
Sandra, P., Claus, H. and Verzde, M. (1973). *J. Inst. Brew.* **79**, 142–147.
Schmith, T. (1952). *Acta Chem. Scand.* **6**, 223–237.

Schur, F. and Pfenninger, H. B. (1971). *Proc. E.B.C. Congr., Estoril* pp. 107–114.

Shimamoto, M., Kitazawa, Y. and Hayashi, H. (1962). Report of the Suita Laboratory: *Brew. Sci. Res. Institute, Tokyo* **4**, 83–92.

Sloey, W. and Prentice, N. (1962). *Proc. Ann. Meet. Am. Soc. Brew. Chem.* pp. 24–29.

Thorne, R. S. W. (1964). *Brewers' Digest* **39** (6), 50–52, 65.

Thorne, R. S. W. and Helm, E. (1957). *J. Inst. Brew.* **63**, 415–435.

Tuite, J. F. and Christensen, C. M. (1955). *Cereal Chem.* **32**, 1–11.

Vogel, E. H. Jr. (1949). Commun. Master Brewers Ass. Am. **10**, 6–7.

Whitear, A. L. and Button, A. H. (1971). *Proc. E.B.C. Congr., Estoril* pp. 129–141.

Windisch, W. (1923a). *Wschr. Brau.* **40**, 70–71.

Windisch, W. (1923b). *Wschr. Brau.* **40**, 121–123.

9. Beer Spoilage Microorganisms

C. RAINBOW

Burton upon Trent, Staffordshire, England

I. INTRODUCTION

A. Spoilage as a Function of Beer Composition

Compared with many foodstuffs, beer is resistant to microbial spoilage because of its relatively low nutritional status, its content of products of yeast metabolism, its adverse values of pH and redox potential and its content of hop bitter substances (Rainbow 1958, 1971).

The first three factors reflect the vital activities of yeast, which abstracts from worts nutrients of low molecular weight of all classes (carbohydrates, nitrogen compounds, salts, growth factors, other quantitatively minor nutrilites and free oxygen), replacing them with metabolic products (ethanol, CO_2, higher alcohols, esters, organic acids) less suitable as microbial nutrients. Simultaneously, reducing conditions are established and the pH

491

TABLE 1. Qualitative composition of wort and beer (after Rainbow (1971))

	Wort	Beer
Assimilable by yeast	Maltotriose, maltose, sucrose, glucose, fructose; small quantities of other hexoses and pentoses; Amino acids, small peptides; Mineral salts; Growth factors, purines, pyrimidines and their derivatives	Present in concentrations substantially diminished according to extent of yeast growth and fermentation
	Organic acids	Fate not known, but some excreted by yeast
Not assimilable by yeast	Maltodextrins, β-glucans; Degraded proteins, polypeptides; Polyphenols; Hop bittering substances	Remain in beer
	Higher fatty acids	Largely removed during brewing
Fermentation products	Absent, except low concentrations present in malt	Ethanol, CO_2, fusel alcohols, esters, glycerol, acetate, lactate, pyruvate, lower (C_4 to C_{12}) fatty acids

value falls, contingent on the absorption by yeast of amino acids and small peptides and the excretion by it of organic acids. In addition, hop bitter substances make a small contribution to the components of beer which discourage microbial growth (Table 1). Not surprisingly, therefore, beer spoilage is confined to a few species of bacteria and yeasts. Time was, when wooden casks were common as beer containers, that moulds caused spoilage indirectly when, having grown on the walls of empty casks, a mustiness ("caskiness") was imparted to the beer racked into them (Brown 1916). Moulds are not otherwise beer spoilers.

Ability to grow at about pH 4·0 may be the most critical factor determining which microbial species can grow in and therefore spoil beer. On this criterion, most saprophytic yeasts might present themselves as having beer spoilage properties. However, since spoilage is confined to relatively few species, other factors, such as type of metabolism (fermentative or oxidative) and the presence of metabolic products of the culture yeast, must exert decisive roles. It seems unlikely that the nutritive status of beer would be critical because, despite its depleted nutrient content, beer almost invariably contains residual fermentable sugars (often enhanced by added "priming") and other nutrients. This, coupled with its simple nutritional requirements and great biosynthetic abilities (Rainbow 1970) indicates that, having gained access to beer, a potential spoilage yeast would find adequate nutrients in most, if not all, beers.

The effect of pH in restricting the number of bacterial species as beer spoilers is even greater. Indeed, if we consider spoilage as a result of their growth in beer, as distinct from wort, only certain lactic rods and cocci, the acetic acid bacteria and certain zymomonads need be considered. Most beers are likely to contain all the constituents required for the nutrition of both genera (*Acetobacter* and *Acetomonas* or *Gluconobacter*) of acetic acid bacteria (Rainbow 1966), but the presence of free oxygen is critical. With beer spoilage lactic acid bacteria, the nutritional status of the beer is important in determining its proneness to spoilage and beer lacking any one of the amino acids or growth factors to which lactic acid bacteria are nutritionally exacting (Moore and Rainbow 1955) would be proof against spoilage by them. Hop bittering substances, known to have an inhibiting effect on Gram-positive bacteria, may also discourage lactic acid bacteria, but their effect may be rather small in modern lightly hopped beers.

B. Factors Affecting the Nutritional Status of Beer

The nutritional status of beer is related to the vital activity of yeast during fermentation. Thus, the greater the yeast growth and the more vigorous the fermentation, the greater the nutritional demands made by the yeast on its substrate (wort) and the more depleted in nutrients is the resultant beer. Conversely, factors causing poor attenuation will make beers more prone to microbial spoilage because of their greater residual content of microbial nutrients. Such factors include early flocculation of yeast and defective fermentations, no matter how caused.

Beer composition, and therefore proneness to spoilage, is also affected by wort composition. For example, worts with high contents of yeast-assimilable nitrogen may yield beers containing excessive amounts of residual nitrogen compounds, potentially dangerous as microbial nutrients. Conversely, if yeast-assimilable nitrogen is relatively deficient, attenuation could be restricted by insufficient yeast reproduction, yielding beers which, if low in microbial nitrogenous nutrients, contain a balance of fermentable sugar available to spoilage yeasts. Malt nitrogen modification and the balance of carbohydrate to nitrogen in wort are therefore relevant to the microbial spoilage of beer.

The nutritional status of beer may be raised by contributions, particularly of amino acids and growth factors, from yeast cell contents, if (a) yeast is not removed promptly and sufficiently at the end of primary fermentation, circumstances which may be aggravated when the yeast is physiologically enfeebled as a result of defective fermentations; and (b) conditions prevail in which "shock excretion" can occur (Lewis and Phaff 1963, 1964, 1965).

II. SPOILAGE BY BACTERIA

A. Lactic Acid Bacteria

1. Historical

The lactic spoilage of alcoholic drinks occupied the attention of Pasteur (1866) and, by 1871, the great British brewing scientist, H. T. Brown, with the benefit of some years of practical brewing experience, knew the life history and effects of the lactic rods then causing serious spoilage of the Burton stock beers, brewed during the cool months and stored for sale during the warm months, after brewing had ceased. He also recognized the organisms responsible for other types of spoilage and developed his method of "forcing" beers to predict their microbiological stability (see Brown 1916). Indeed, when Pasteur's "Études sur la Bière" appeared in 1876, he was in advance of the practice it advocated. Armstrong (1937) said that Brown ". . . did for brewing what Lister . . . did for surgery: both by way of practice had arrived at results coincident with those of the great French observer."

Pasteur (1876) described his lactic spoilage rods as "bacilles des bières tournées" and van Laer (1892) named them *Saccharobacillus pastorianus*. The subject then lay neglected until Shimwell (1935a) described laboratory experiments and brewery work on problems of spoilage by lactic rods. He concluded that the production of acidity in beer by *S. pastorianus* was promoted by residual fermentable carbohydrate: it was independent of the concentration of residual nitrogen and degree of attenuation, which did not represent the quality of the residual extract. He confirmed the progressive inhibition of acid formation in beer as the hop rate increased and referred to Brown's suggestion for the removal of *Saccharobacillus* from pitching yeast by passing it through successive fermentations in wort containing 0·1% tartaric acid. Shimwell (1935b) published the first detailed account of the cultural characteristics of the bacterium and, while reviewing earlier work (Shimwell 1936b), urged the correctness of the generic name *Lactobacillus* rather than *Saccharobacillus*. Shimwell's important work covering the entire field of brewing bacteriology is summarized in his own series of articles (Shimwell 1947b, 1948b, c, 1949).

2. Classification

In the family *Lactobacteriaceae,* beer spoilage species are found in the genera *Lactobacillus* (lactic rods) and *Pediococcus* (lactic cocci). However, references to beer lactobacilli were confined to *Lactobacillus* (then *Saccharobacillus*) *pastorianus*, until Shimwell (1941) reported a strain of short rods growing faster than *L. pastorianus* in acidified beer, a strain causing ropiness and other strains producing diacetyl. His short rods may have been *L. brevis*, strains of which were isolated by Kulka and studied by Moore and Rainbow (1955). In Bergey's Manual, Rogosa (1974) now lists the species *brevis*, *buchneri*, *fermentum* (heterofermentative) and *leichmanii* and *plantarum* (homofermentative), whose ecology and properties befit them for spoilage. To these may be added *L. casei* (homofermentative), recently reported by Eschenbecher (1969) as spoiling (presumably lager) beer.

The heterofermenters produce chiefly lactic and acetic acids, ethanol and CO_2 from glucose, and mannitol from fructose (Breed *et al.* 1957). Typically, they ferment L-arabinose, but differ in optimum temperature and in ability to ferment di- and tri-saccharides. Thus, *L. buchneri* has the same temperature optimum (ca. 30 °C) as *L. brevis*, but differs from it in fermenting melezitose and in growth factor requirements. *L. fermentum* differs from these species in not usually fermenting arabinose and in having an optimum of 35–40 °C, or higher.

Spoilage lactic cocci have been known in brewing since 1880 as "sarcinae", because their tetrads of cells were mistaken for the cubical packets of eight cells typical of true sarcinae. Shimwell and Kirkpatrick (1939) first showed that brewer's "sarcina" was a lactic coccus. From a comparison of beer "sarcinae" obtained from various beers of different countries, they concluded that ". . . 'beer sarcinae' or 'beer pediococci' are neither sarcinae, 'pediococci' nor micrococci, but morphologically, culturally and physiologically belong to . . . the genus *Streptococcus*". They ascribed the characteristic honey-like odour of "sarcina-sick" beer to the formation of diacetyl by the beer cocci and believed that their cocci from English ales belonged to the same species (*Strept. damnosus*) as numerous strains isolated in 1904–6 from European beers by Claussen and called by him *P. damnosus* or *P. perniciosus*. The situation at this stage was summarized by Shimwell (1941).

Shimwell's view that "brewer's sarcina" is a streptococcus is not currently accepted in Bergey's Manual. Pederson *et al.* (1954) readily distinguished pediococci, isolated from sources other than beer, from *Streptococcus*, *Micrococcus* and *Sarcina* by their tetrad grouping and by their relatively high production of optically inactive lactic acid and urged that they be considered as a separate genus *Pediococcus* (Balcke 1884), classified with *Diplococcus*, *Streptococcus* and *Leuconostoc* in the tribe *Streptococcaceae*, family *Lactobacteriaceae*.

As now described in Bergey's Manual (Kitahara 1974), the genus *Pediococcus* is based on a taxonomic study by Nakagawa and Kitahara (1959). Five species are recognized: *cerevisiae*, *acidilactici*, *pentosaceus*, *halophilus* and *urinae-equi*. Of these, strains of *P. cerevisiae* are the beer spoilers: *P. acidilactici* fails to grow in hopped wort or beer, *P. pentosaceus* is also sensitive to hop antiseptics and the other species do not grow at pH 5·0 or lower. However, the possibility remains that *P. pentosaceus* could spoil beer if it acquired a tolerance to hop antiseptics, especially in the environment of modern lightly hopped beers.

In considering beer spoilage by lactic cocci, we are therefore chiefly concerned with the type species *P. cerevisiae,* with which *P. damnosus* Claussen, its varieties *salicinaceus* Mees and *diastaticus* (Andrews and Gilliland 1952), *P. perniciosus* Claussen and *P. mevalovorus* (Kitahara and Nakagawa 1958) are regarded as synonymous. This view will be adopted for present purposes, although it is at variance with that of Clausen and his co-workers. After comparing eleven pediococci isolated from Norwegian brewery products with one strain each of *P. cerevisiae* and *P. acidilactici* respectively from the NCTC and NCIB collections, Solberg and Clausen (1973a) deemed it more correct to classify pediococci from brewery products as *P. damnosus,* since they had certain biochemical and physiological properties different from those described for *P. cerevisiae* and *P. acidilactici* in Bergey's Manual. Agglutination studies with the same strains (Clausen *et al.* 1975) support this opinion. The strains showed 100% mutual serological binding capacity, consistent with the biochemical and physiological homology Solberg and Clausen (1973a) had reported. They concluded that the genus *Pediococcus* should consist of the four species *cerevisiae, damnosus, parvulus* and *halophilus,* in accordance with the serology of the pediococci as reported by Coster and White (1964). Günther and White (1961), Kerbaugh and Evans (1968) and Garvie (1974) also consider brewery pediococci fit the description of *P. damnosus* Claussen, whereas *P. cerevisiae* has features not specific to it.

3. Types of Lactic Beer Spoilage

(a) *Lactobacilli*

That lactic acid bacteria remain potentially the most dangerous of beer spoilage bacteria may be ascribed to their microaerophilic nature, their relative indifference to free oxygen and their acquisition of appreciable tolerance to hop antiseptics (Shimwell 1936b), to ethanol concentrations up to about 6% (Shimwell 1935a) and to low pH values. Spoilage by heterofermentative species is probably more common than that by homofermenters.

Beer spoilage by lactobacilli is characterized by a "silky" turbidity accompanied by acid, "dirty" (acetoin) or "buttery" (diacetyl) off-flavours. Less frequently, "ropiness" is symptomatic, but this type of spoilage is more commonly caused by pediococci or by acetic acid bacteria (see (c) below).

(b) *Pediococci*

The pediococcal spoilage of beer is characterized by acid formation and the so-called "sarcina sickness" or "sarcina odour" for which diacetyl is known to be responsible, while some capsule-forming strains produce "ropiness" (see below). As homofermenters, pediococci form no other acid than lactic.

Pediococci prefer a lower temperature for growth (optimum 25 °C) than do lactobacilli: they may therefore be less deterred by low storage and conditioning temperatures than are lactobacilli.

(c) *Ropiness*

For convenience, beer ropiness will be discussed here, since the phenomenon is most commonly caused by pediococci. However, as has already been mentioned, lactobacilli are sometimes responsible, while rope formation by certain acetic acid bacteria was once not uncommon in cask beers to which air had gained access.

Early work on ropiness was reported by Baker *et al.* (1912) who described rope formation by *Bacterium aceti viscosum* (now *Acetobacter viscosum*), but some time elapsed before Shimwell (1936c, 1947a, 1948a) showed that ropiness could be produced by representatives of either gram-negative acetic acid bacteria or gram-positive lactic cocci. His first paper described *Acetobacter capsulatum,* comparing it with *B. aceti viscosum* and showing by staining that, in wort and beer, and only in the presence of oxygen, the organism produced gelatinous capsules, which coalesced to a slimy zoogloeal mass responsible for the rope phenomenon, the capsular material being so voluminous that relatively few cells might produce ropiness without much attendant turbidity.

However, Shimwell (1948a) recognized that ropiness was more commonly caused by cocci, two strains of which, named by him as *Streptococcus damnosus,* produced the symptoms of "sarcina sickness" (turbidity, sediment, slight acidity and diacetyl odour) and, in the absence of free oxygen and/or presence of CO_2, the typical ropy slime, physically demonstrable under the microscope by staining. Later, Kulka *et al.* (1949) isolated from ropy beer *Streptococcus mucilaginosus* (sp. nov.), which produced small, not voluminous capsules and was distinct from other beer spoilage cocci in rendering beer viscous under aerobic as well as anaerobic conditions and in producing neither diacetyl nor acetoin. Both this strain and that of Shimwell are now treated in Bergey's Manual as strains of *P. cerevisiae* (Kitahara 1974).

A list of the characters by which Shimwell distinguished acetic and pediococcal rope is summarized in Table 2. Of particular interest is that, while predisposition of beers to rope formation by acetic acid bacteria depends on the presence of polysaccharide dextrins (Shimwell 1947a), that by pediococci

TABLE 2. Distinguishing features of acetic and pediococcal ropiness (after Rainbow (1971))

Criterion	Acetic "rope"	Pediococcal "rope"
Causative organism	Gram-negative; catalase-positive	Gram-positive; catalase-negative
pH	Acid tolerant	Progressively inhibited as pH falls
Oxygen	Oxygen required	"Rope" associated with absence of oxygen and/or presence of carbon dioxide
Nutrition	Not exacting	Exacting
Carbohydrates	Dextrin primer required; predisposition determined during mashing	Fermentable sugar required
Beer qualities	Attenuation, priming and yeast not factors in predisposition, except when poor attenuation is associated with high dextrin	Poor attenuation, priming and weak or highly flocculent yeast cause predisposition
Hop bitters	Do not inhibit	Sensitive, but strains may have acquired tolerance
Ethanol	Above 6% (v/v) not tolerated	Tolerant; "rope" produced in strong beers

requires the presence of fermentable sugars (Shimwell 1948a). The two types of capsular substances thus seem to have different biochemical origins. Structural studies on the pediococcal rope substance from beer seem to be lacking, but it may resemble that produced by a "streptococcus", isolated by Barker *et al.* (1955) from a ropy wine, which produced slime from sucrose, but not from maltose or glucose. The slime substance ($[\alpha]_D^{20} + 194$ ° in N NaOH) was an α-1,6-linked glucan (dextran), yielding isomaltose and isomaltotriose on partial hydrolysis.

The slime substance of *Acetobacter capsulatum* also seems to resemble structurally that formed by the wine pediococcus: it had a similar $[\alpha]_D^{20}$ of $+196$ ° in N NaOH and it was a glucan consisting essentially of α-1,6-linked chains, of average chain length about 13, branched through positions 1 and 4 (Barker *et al.* 1958). However, if the two rope substances are indeed chemically similar, Shimwell's observations on the different saccharides predisposing beer to ropiness suggest that different enzyme systems are concerned in the two cases. Possibly, a glycosyl acceptor ("primer"), analogous to the maltodextrins in amylose biosynthesis catalysed by phosphorylase, is essential for the biosynthesis of capsular polysaccharide by *A. capsulatum*, a view supported by Hehre and Hamilton (1949), who synthesized a polysaccharide from amylodextrins with a cell-free extract of this organism.

4. Nutrition and Metabolism

(a) *Lactobacilli*

Members of the genus *Lactobacillus* are nutritionally fastidious, being incapable of synthesizing a number of amino acids, some growth factors of the vitamin B complex and purine and pyrimidine bases. Because of these exacting requirements, lactobacilli, especially some homofermentative species like *L. casei* associated with the environment of the dairy, and *L. plantarum* (*L. arabinosus*) were applied for the microbiological assay of amino acids and growth factors, the first reported assay being that devised by Snell and Strong (1939) for riboflavin.

(*i*) *General nutrition*. These complex nutritional requirements extend to heterofermentative lactobacilli, including beer spoilage strains. Russell *et al.* (1954) reported the vitamin requirements of 34 strains and Moore and Rainbow (1955) the vitamin, purine, pyrimidine and amino acid requirements of four strains (two of them identified as *L. brevis* and the others also probably this species) isolated from the contaminant flora of ale yeasts. For growth, all four strains needed exogenous supplies of (a) at least three growth factors from pantothenate, nicotinate, riboflavin and pteroylglutamate, thiamin and biotin being stimulatory; (b) at least one purine and one pyrimidine; and (c) between 11 and 17 amino acids.

(ii) *Carbohydrate metabolism*. The beer spoilage lactobacilli, *L. brevis*, *L. buchneri*, *L. fermentum*, *L. leichmanii* and *L. plantarum* produce acid from glucose, fructose, maltose and (except *L. brevis*) sucrose, while all but *leichmanii* and *fermentum* produce acid from L-arabinose (Breed *et al.* 1957). For their heterofermenters, Moore and Rainbow (1955) found that (a) maltose, fructose and a mixture of glucose and L-arabinose promoted better growth than did glucose alone; (b) growth on maltose was better than on any other single carbohydrate; and (c) rate of growth on pentoses appeared to depend on a chemical change occurring in the medium when sterilization by heat was carried out with the pentose in admixture with the other constituents of the medium, growth being slower in the same medium containing pentose which had been sterilized separately. This chemical change may involve the isomerization of aldopentose to ketopentose, a step sparing the organism the necessity to produce enzymes to effect it. Indeed, it is known that the isomerases, kinases and epimerases required to transform pentoses to xylulose 5-phosphate, intermediate in their fermentation by other (not beer spoilage) hetero-lactobacilli, are inducible (Burma and Horecker 1958). The fermentation of one molecule of pentose to one molecule each of acetic and lactic acids is given schematically in Fig. 1. The formation from L-arabinose of

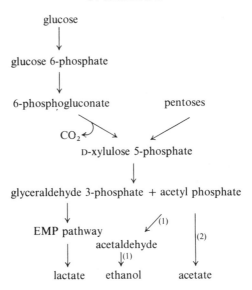

FIG. 1. Heterolactic fermentation of glucose (HMP pathway) and pentoses. From acetyl phosphate, reaction sequence (1) is followed with glucose and (2) with pentose as substrate.

considerable volatile and non-volatile acid in a 1 : 1 ratio (Moore and Rainbow 1955) suggests that pentose fermentation by brewery hetero-lactobacilli also proceeds by this pathway.

The heterolactic fermentation of glucose yields one molecule each of lactic acid, ethanol and CO_2. The mechanism (Fig. 1), which does not involve the complete Embden-Meyerhof-Parnas (EMP) fermentation pathway, depicts the pathway as elucidated for the heterofermentative lactic coccus *Leuconostoc mesenteroides* and for *Lactobacillus pentoaceticus*. In other lactobacilli, like *L. brevis,* a second type of fermentation:

$$\tfrac{3}{2} \text{ glucose} \longrightarrow 2 \text{ glycerol} + \text{acetic acid} + CO_2$$

is superimposed on the first to about 20–30% of the glucose utilized (Wood 1961). This seems to be so for the brewery strains examined by Moore and Rainbow, which, while producing predomidantly non-volatile acid, also produced appreciable volatile acid during growth on malt wort or on glucose-containing synthetic medium.

Moore and Rainbow's strains grew well on fructose, transforming it to mannitol. This is consistent with Wood's (1961) statement that the fermen-tation balances of *L. brevis* approximate to the equation:

$$3 \text{ fructose} \longrightarrow 2 \text{ mannitol} + \text{lactic acid} + \text{acetic acid} + CO_2$$

As strains of *L. brevis,* the brewery lactobacilli described by Moore and Rainbow (1955) fitted the pattern of carbohydrate utilization just described. However, their observation that all their strains grew more rapidly and extensively on maltose than on glucose or other single carbohydrates indicated that these strains metabolized maltose by a process, the initial steps of which did not involve hydrolysis by maltase.

This point was studied by Wood and Rainbow (1961), who showed that, during growth on maltose, glucose accumulated in the medium. For further work, they selected a brewery lactobacillus (strain L1), remarkable in that it did not grow at pH values exceeding 5·2 and, more particularly, in that it grew readily only on maltose of many carbohydrates tested. It thus appeared to be uniquely suitable for the study of maltose metabolism. Cell-free extracts of L1 possessed neither detectable maltase nor maltose kinase activity and, since L1 failed to grow on glucose, they presumably lacked glucokinase activity. However, in the presence of inorganic orthophosphate, they catalysed the phosphorolytic cleavage of maltose to free glucose and a glucose phosphate, which was identified as β-glucose 1-phosphate. The enzyme also catalysed the synthesis of maltose, with concurrent release of inorganic phosphate, from β-glucose 1-phosphate and glucose. α-Glucose 1-phosphate would not replace the β-anomer in this reaction. Cell extracts of Moore and Rainbow's strains of *L. brevis* and another untyped brewery lactobacillus (L2) also contained maltose phosphorylase.

All these brewery lactobacilli therefore appeared either to lack (L1 and L2) or to possess only weak glucokinase activity (L3, L4, L5 and L6), but they contained an enzyme, maltose phosphorylase, catalysing the reversible reaction:

The enzyme (maltose phosphorylase, maltose : orthophosphate glucosyl transferase, E.C.2.4.1.8) is remarkable in that the glucosyl group it transfers from the α-1,4-linked maltose molecule to inorganic phosphate undergoes simultaneous inversion to the β-configuration. It is therefore specific for α-D-glucose in one direction of the reaction and β-D-glucose residues in the other and is quite distinct from the more widely distributed α-glucan phosphorylase (E.C.2.4.1.1), catalysing the phosphorolytic cleavage of starch and glycogen to α-D-glucose 1-phosphate. Previously, maltose phosphorylase had been observed only in *Neisseria meningitidis* (Fitting and Doudoroff 1952), the causative coccus of meningitis in man, but other species of *Neisseria* have now been shown to possess the enzyme (Schieger and Schramm 1961, Ben-Zvi and Schramm 1961). These gram-negative bacteria do not seem to be taxonomically closely related to the lactobacilli. However, like the strains of *L. brevis* possessing maltose phosphorylase, their ability to utilize carbohydrates other than maltose and glucose is restricted.

Commenting on the surprising "preference" shown by beer lactobacilli for maltose over glucose, Wood and Rainbow (1961) suggest that their maltose phosphorylase system may have been developed in response to prolonged culture in the presence of maltose in beer. Whether maltotriose, almost always present in substantial amounts in beer, serves as a substrate for the enzyme is not yet known: nor has the problem been resolved of the subsequent stage of metabolism of β-glucose 1-phosphate by these lactobacilli. Possibly the transformation proceeds first through glucose 6-phosphate, which can enter the pathway of heterolactic fermentation (Fig. 1).

That Wood and Rainbow's findings may be widely relevant to beer lactobacilli is indicated by the work of Inoue and Yamamoto (1965), who isolated from malt and young Japanese beer a strain of *L. pastorianus* "belonging to the *L. brevis* group", which grew better on maltose than on glucose medium and cleaved maltose by phosphorolysis to β-glucose 1-phosphate and glucose. Cell extracts of the organism also contained a phosphoglucomutase by which β-glucose 1-phosphate was transphosphorylated to glucose 6-phosphate.

(iii) *Nitrogen metabolism.* Both the homo- and heterofermentative lactobacilli are auxotrophic for many amino acids. Their ability to interconvert amino acids is therefore not extensive. However, one interesting feature of amino acid metabolism was revealed by Moore and Rainbow (1955). Rate of growth and final growth of two strains (L3 and L4) of *L. brevis* in a casein hydrolysate–growth factors–salts medium containing glucose as sole major source of energy was much stimulated by supplementing the medium with relatively large concentrations of L-arginine (2 mg/ml). Washed suspensions of these strains converted L-arginine to citrulline, ornithine and ammonia, no urea being detected as a product of this transformation. That arginine did not stimulate growth when glucose + L-arabinose (a more satisfactory energy source than glucose alone) was provided led Moore and Rainbow (1955) to believe that arginine exerted its stimulatory effect by providing *L. brevis* with a source of energy as ATP generated by the cleavage of arginine. Evidence for the following reaction sequence was obtained by Rainbow (1965, 1975):

(1) *Catalysed by arginine deiminase* (L-arginine iminohydrolase, 3.5.3.6.):

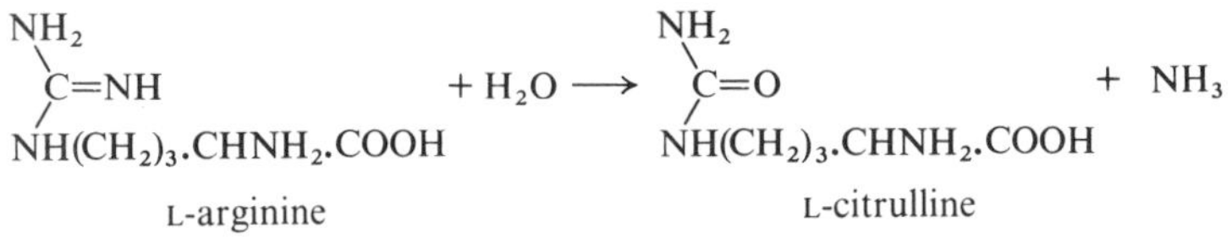

$$
\begin{array}{c}
NH_2 \\
\diagdown \\
C{=}NH \\
\diagup \\
NH(CH_2)_3.CHNH_2.COOH
\end{array}
\quad + H_2O \longrightarrow \quad
\begin{array}{c}
NH_2 \\
\diagdown \\
C{=}O \\
\diagup \\
NH(CH_2)_3.CHNH_2.COOH
\end{array}
\quad + NH_3
$$

$$\text{L-arginine} \qquad\qquad \text{L-citrulline}$$

(2) *Catalysed by ornithine carbamoyltransferase* (carbamoylphosphate: L-ornithine carbamoyltransferase, 2.1.3.3):

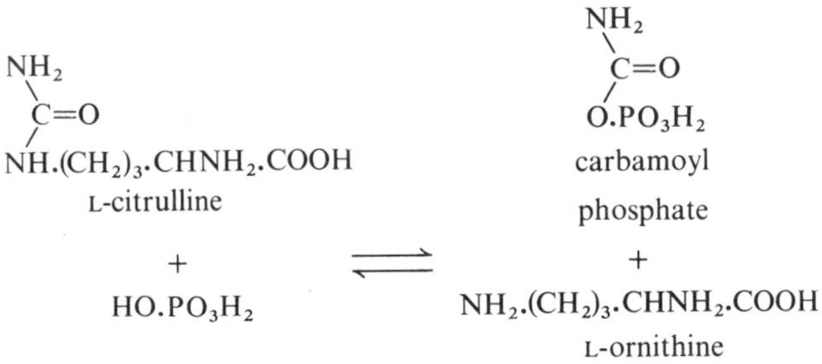

$$
\begin{array}{c}
NH_2 \\
\diagdown \\
C{=}O \\
\diagup \\
NH.(CH_2)_3.CHNH_2.COOH \\
\text{L-citrulline}
\end{array}
\qquad
\begin{array}{c}
NH_2 \\
\diagdown \\
C{=}O \\
\diagup \\
O.PO_3H_2 \\
\text{carbamoyl} \\
\text{phosphate}
\end{array}
$$

$$
\begin{array}{ccc}
+ & \rightleftharpoons & + \\
HO.PO_3H_2 & & NH_2.(CH_2)_3.CHNH_2.COOH \\
& & \text{L-ornithine}
\end{array}
$$

(3) *Catalysed by carbamate kinase* (ATP: carbamate phosphotransferase, 2.7.2.2):

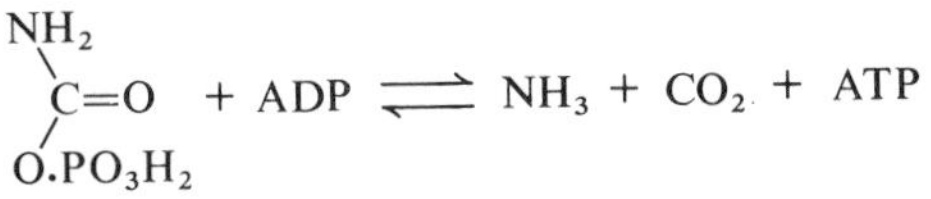

$$
\begin{array}{c}
NH_2 \\
\diagdown \\
C{=}O \\
\diagup \\
O.PO_3H_2
\end{array}
\quad + ADP \rightleftharpoons NH_3 + CO_2 + ATP
$$

In parallel experiments, Rainbow (1975) did not detect this unusual system in the homofermentative *L. arabinosus,* in *Acetobacter rancens* or in *Saccharomyces cerevisiae,* but it has been reported in the lactic coccus *Streptococcus faecalis* (Knivett 1954).

(b) *Pediococci*

There is much less information on the nutrition and metabolism of beer pediococci than on beer lactobacilli, possibly because their study has been discouraged by their slowness of growth and difficulty of cultivation, including a preference for anaerobic conditions (Solberg and Clausen 1973a) and by lack of interest in this field of bacteriology.

(i) *Nutrition*. Beer pediococci may be even more nutritionally fastidious than beer lactobacilli, since Solberg and Clausen (1973a) had to devise special malt-tomato juice media to overcome the difficulties they experienced in cultivating them. All the strains of *P. cerevisiae* examined by Nakagawa and Kitahara (1959) had essential requirements for niacin, biotin, purine and pyrimidine bases and a peptide-like substance, while riboflavin, pyridoxin and, for some strains, ascorbate or thioglycollate were stimulatory. The amino acid requirements of *P. cerevisiae* seem not to have been reported, but they may be as complex as those of *P. pentosaceus,* which requires 16 of them, as well as niacin, leucovorin, pantothenate and, for a few strains, riboflavin: methionine, lysine, biotin and pyridoxin are stimulatory and requirements for organic bases vary with strain (Jensen and Seeley 1954). Solberg and Clausen (1973b), for 11 strains of brewery pediococci, also report essential requirements for biotin, pantothenate and riboflavin, while pyridoxin stimulated most strains and was essential for one and a component in Tween 80 was essential for 8 strains. No strain required folate, *p*-aminobenzoate, cyanocobalamin, thiamin or niacin. *P. cerevisiae* also requires CO_2 for growth (Weinfurtner *et al.* 1955, Nakagawa and Kitahara 1959), while free O_2 inhibits it (Weinfurtner 1957). Another pediococcus, isolated by Kitahara and Nakagawa (1958), had an unusual requirement for mevalonate. These workers regarded the strain as *P. mevalovorus* sp. nov., but Kitahara (1974) in Bergey's Manual classifies it as a strain of *P. cerevisiae.*

One point of distinction between *P. cerevisiae* and *P. pentosaceus* lies in the former's tolerance to hop antiseptics, which persists after maintenance in unhopped media (Nakagawa and Kitahara 1959). Nevertheless, hop antiseptics may induce the formation of giant cells in *P. cerevisiae* (Nakagawa and Kitahara 1962).

The difficulties workers have found in cultivating beer pediococci, together with the unusual requirements (a peptide-like substance, mevalonate, Tween 80 constituents) of some strains, indicates that they may be even more fastidious than beer lactobacilli and that they may require yet other growth factors, such as those reported by Sakaguchi (1960, 1962) to be required by *P. halophilus* (*P. soyae*). One of these was a peptide present in casein hydrolysate and another was identified as glycine-betaine, replaceable by carnitine. Yet another is the β-glucoside of D-pantothenic acid, a substance 8–10 times as active as D-pantothenic acid in promoting the growth of a pediococcus newly isolated from beer (Eto and Nakagawa 1974). It also supported the growth of *Leuconostoc* and other pediococci, but not that of four lactobacilli tested.

(ii) *Metabolism*. The beer pediococci are homofermenters, producing DL-lactic acid (the L-form usually predominating) from glucose, with traces of other products, but no gas (Kitahara 1974). Acid is produced by *P. cerevisiae* from glucose, fructose, mannose, maltose and sometimes from galactose and salicin, but not from pentoses, lactose, sucrose, α-methyl glucoside, mannitol, sorbitol nor (except for the strain isolated by Andrews and Gilliland 1952) starch.

Beer pediococci also produce acetylmethylcarbinol (acetoin) and diacetyl. Although they are quantitatively minor products, they are important because of their adverse effects on beer flavour. Nakagawa and Kitahara (1959) found that *P. cerevisiae* produced 10–70 p.p.m. of acetoin and 2–5% of this amount of diacetyl.

Beer pediococci are gram-positive, anaerobic or microaerophilic and usually catalase-negative, but they may possess some catalase activity from an enzyme which is not a metallo(haem)-porphyrin (Dolin 1961).

Detailed knowledge of the metabolism of beer pediococci is lacking. It may be a reasonable assumption that carbohydrate is metabolized by the EMP pathway, but experimental proof is not available. Neither are there reports of their nitrogen metabolism. It would be interesting to know whether they transform arginine by the arginine deiminase system which operates in heterofermentative beer lactobacilli and in the lactic coccus, *Streptococcus faecalis* (Knivett 1954).

B. Acetic Acid Bacteria

1. Historical

Persoon (1822) made the first biological study of the film which forms on the surface of alcoholic liquids undergoing acetification: but, while recognizing its vegetable nature and naming it *Mycoderma,* he failed to associate its presence with the formation of acidity. Kützing (1837) first isolated acetic acid bacteria, but he regarded them as algae and called them *Ulvina aceti.* That acetification was brought about by the living cells composing the films at the surface of acetifying liquids was finally established by Pasteur (1864) in his "Mémoir sur la Fermentation Acétique", which forms part of his "Études sur le Vinaigre" (1868). Pasteur described the organism, adopting Persoon's name *Mycoderma aceti* for it and showed that it absorbed oxygen from the air and produced acetic acid during its growth on media containing ethanol. Hansen (1879) showed that there were several species of acetic acid bacteria responsible for acetification and he isolated from sour beer three organisms, which he named *Bacterium aceti, B. pasteurianum* and *B. kützingianum,* differing in form and behaviour during growth on beer. He also observed the striking morphological changes, sometimes referred to as pleomorphism or "involution forms", promoted in cells of acetic acid bacteria by changes in temperature.

A second great group of biochemical activities of acetic acid bacteria, albeit not important in beer spoilage, are those involving the oxidation of primary and secondary alcohol groups. For example, glucose is oxidized to gluconic and 2- and 5-oxogluconic acids, glycerol to dihydroxyacetone and sorbitol to sorbose (for reviews, see Asai (1968), Rainbow (1961, 1966)). The oxidation of glucose to gluconate was reported by Boutroux (1880) and by A. J. Brown (1885, 1886, 1887) working with *B. aceti* and *B. xylinum,* while Bertrand (1896, 1898) isolated from the fermenting juice of mountain ash berries "sorbose bacteria", which oxidized sorbitol to sorbose.

2. Classification

The distinctive property of acetic acid bacteria in oxidizing ethanol to acetic acid at neutral acid pH values led to earlier generic names (*Mycoderma, Ulvina, Bacterium,* etc.). being discarded in favour of *Acetobacter,* first used by Beijerinck (1898). However, there is now good reason to recognize two genera of acetic acid bacteria based on their ability to "over-oxidize" acetic acid to CO_2 and water. Pasteur (1864, 1868) recognized this power in some species, but it is lacking in others, especially those which are potent in oxidizing glucose, gluconate, glycerol, sorbitol and other alcohols, glycols and poly-alcohols. The dichotomy of types of acetic acid bacteria was recognized by Vaughn (1942) and Frateur (1950), who did not, however, accord generic distinction to the acetate-oxidizers as compared with the non-acetate-oxidizers, which lacked this property.

TABLE 3. Comparison of *Acetobacter* with *Gluconobacter* (*Acetomonas*) (after Rainbow (1966))†

Acetobacter spp.	*Gluconobacter* spp.
1. Oxidize ethanol to acetate	Oxidize ethanol to acetate
2. "Over-oxidize" acetate and lactate to carbon dioxide and water	Do not "over-oxidize" acetate or lactate
3. If motile, peritrichous flagella	If motile, polar flagella
4. Simple growth requirements; grow well on lactate ("lactaphiles")	Grow well on glucose ("glycophiles") but not lactate; require exogenous growth factors and *Glu, Asp, Pro,* or $NH_3 + OG$ for growth
5. Transaminate $Glu \rightleftharpoons Asp$	Transaminate feebly or not at all
6. Decarboxylate *Asp* to α-alanine	Usually lack aspartic β-decarboxylase
7. Cells contain all enzymes of the tricarboxylic acid cycle	Isocitrate dehydrogenase absent; most other enzymes feebly developed
8. Some strains ketogenic	All strains strongly ketogenic

† *Glu* = glutamate; *Asp* = aspartate; *Pro* = proline; OG = 2-oxoglutarate.

Leifson (1954) proposed generic distinction between morphologically distinct groups comprising species with (a) peritrichous flagella or non-flagellated species with similar physiology (genus *Acetobacter*); and (b) polar flagella and non-flagellated species with similar physiology (genus *Acetomonas*). Strains in type (a) oxidized acetate and lactate to CO_2 and water (cf. Vaughn's Group I), while those of type (b) did not (Vaughn's Group II, non-acetate oxidizers). Other work on flagellation by Shimwell (1958) and Asai and Shoda (1958) confirmed Leifson's view, although the Japanese workers prefer to *Acetomonas* the generic name *Gluconobacter*, adopted by them in 1935 in recognition of the marked ability of members of the genus to form gluconate from glucose.

Nutritional and biochemical studies by Rainbow and Mitson (1953), Brown and Rainbow (1956), Cooksey and Rainbow (1962) and Williams and Rainbow (1964) also support this division into *Acetobacter* and *Acetomonas*, which correspond to their "lactaphilic" and "glycophilic" acetic acid bacteria respectively (see section II. B.4).

These points are discussed in detail by Asai (1968) and summarized by Rainbow (1961, 1966), from whose later review Table 3 is derived.

As section II.B.3 will describe, many acetic acid bacteria isolated from beer and pitching yeast in the period 1936–39 were accorded specific rank. However, de Ley and Frateur (1974) recognize only three species of the genus *Acetobacter* (*aceti, pasteurianum* and *peroxydans*), based on Frateur's (1950) three groups, and only one species of *Gluconobacter* (*G. oxydans*), other previous species being relegated to sub-specific rank. These authors prefer the name *Gluconobacter* Asai to *Acetomonas* Leifson.

3. Types of Acetic Beer Spoilage

Acetic beer spoilage is characterized by acetification without gas formation, accompanied by the formation of a film and a ring on the vessel at the surface of the liquid. Other symptoms may include rope formation (Shimwell 1936c, Comrie, 1939, Walker and Tosic 1945) and turbidity (Cosbie *et al.* 1942, 1943, Tosic and Walker 1944), while Kulka and Walker (1946b), in describing the influence of 14 strains on the condition and flavour of beer, reported bitter, unpleasant and "strange" flavours, even when the beers were not sour. Perhaps the oxidation by the bacteria of polyalcohols, such as that of glycerol to dihydroxyacetone, could account for these flavours.

Comparative aspects of rope formation by acetic acid bacteria have already been discussed (section II.A.3(c)) and only a few comments will be added here. Capsule formation occurred in all the 14 strains examined by Kulka and Walker (1946a), who suggested it might be characteristic of all acetic acid bacteria and later (1948) demonstrated, by positive staining, capsule formation in a strain which gave a non-viscid type of growth. Ropiness and other types of beer spoilage by acetic acid bacteria were reviewed by Shimwell (1948b).

The extent of spoilage of beer by acetic acid bacteria depends on the strain (Tosic and Walker 1943, Kulka *et al.* 1948, Walker and Kulka 1949) and on the alcohol content of the beer, since the bacteria are progressively inhibited by increasing ethanol concentrations and, beyond 6%, completely so (Shimwell 1936c, Comrie 1939). Control of acetic beer spoilage cannot be exerted through hop antiseptic substances, to which the gram-negative acetic acid bacteria are tolerant. However, they are obligate aerobes (catalase-positive), and prevention of access of air to beer at all stages of processing after fermentation and during dispense offers the readiest means of control. The low incidence of acetic spoilage of modern beers is ascribable to this factor, to improved hygiene in breweries and to the application of pure culture yeasts, which eliminated the bacteria from pitching yeasts, from which they were readily isolatable, especially from ale yeasts (Kulka *et al.* 1946, 1948). Shimwell (1960) regarded the acetomonads as the more dangerous beer spoilers.

4. Nutrition and Metabolism

(a) *General*

It has been known since Hoyer's work in 1898 that some acetic acid bacteria would grow on a simple defined medium (Hoyer's medium), consisting of ethanol, ammonium sulphate and mineral salts. The ability of some of them to utilize ammonium salts as sole source of nitrogen for growth has been confirmed by Frateur (1950), Rao and Stokes (1953), Rainbow and Mitson, (1953) and Hall *et al.* (1953, 1956). However, not all strains grow on these simple media and Rainbow and Mitson (1953) and Brown and Rainbow (1956) were able to distinguish "lactaphilic" and "glycophilic" strains according to their nutritional requirements. Members of the former group grew well on a simple defined lactate–ammonia–salts medium, while the glycophiles grew well when glucose, but not lactate, was supplied as main source of carbon and energy and glutamate, aspartate or proline as the source of nitrogen. Growing on glucose, the glycophiles also required exogenous supplies of niacin, pantothenate and, in one case, *p*-aminobenzoate. With ammonium salts as sole source of nitrogen in glucose–salts–growth factors medium, the glycophilic strains failed to grow unless an organic acid of the tricarboxylic acid (TCA) cycle, of which 2-oxoglutarate was particularly effective, was also provided.

Cooksey and Rainbow (1962) traced these nutritional distinctions to the metabolic level by showing that cell extracts of lactaphiles effected reversible transamination between glutamate and aspartate:

$$
\begin{array}{cc}
\begin{array}{c} CH_2CH_2COOH \\ | \\ CHNH_2COOH \\ \textit{glutamate} \end{array} & + & \begin{array}{c} CH_2COOH \\ | \\ CO.COOH \\ \textit{oxaloacetate} \end{array}
\end{array}
$$

$$\Updownarrow$$

$$
\begin{array}{cc}
\begin{array}{c} CH_2CH_2COOH \\ | \\ CO.COOH \\ \textit{2-oxoglutarate} \end{array} & + & \begin{array}{c} CH_2COOH \\ | \\ CHNH_2COOH \\ \textit{aspartate} \end{array}
\end{array}
$$

In glycophiles, this ability was only feebly or not developed. The same paper reported the ability, unusual in aerobes, of lactaphiles to β-decarboxylate L-aspartate to α-alanine:

$$
\begin{array}{c} CH_2COOH \\ | \\ CHNH_2COOH \\ \textit{aspartate} \end{array} \longrightarrow \begin{array}{c} CH_3 \\ | \\ CHNH_2COOH \\ \textit{α-alanine} \end{array} + CO_2
$$

With one exception, glycophiles lacked this ability.

Cooksey and Rainbow suggested that the abilities of lactophiles to transaminate and to oxidize acids of the TCA cycle were related metabolic phenomena, the biosynthesis of the key amino acids glutamate and aspartate taking place by transamination from the corresponding oxo-acids generated in the cycle. Observations that there is indeed a fundamental metabolic difference between the genera *Acetobacter* (lactaphilic, acetate-oxidizing) and *Gluconobacter* (glycophilic, non-acetate-oxidizing) support this view. King and Cheldelin (1952) and Stouthamer (1959) reported that non-acetate-oxidizing strains lacked an operative TCA cycle, a conclusion confirmed by Williams and Rainbow (1964), who examined cell extracts of five lactaphiles and five glycophiles for the activities of seven enzymes catalysing the reactions of the cycle. They showed that all the glycophilic extracts lacked both NAD^+- and $NADP^+$-linked isocitrate dehydrogenases, while the lactaphilic extracts possessed the $NADP^+$ enzyme (E.C. 1.1.1.42) and also detectable activity of the NAD^+ enzyme. Further, the glycophiles had only feeble citrate synthase, aconitate hydratase, fumarate hydratase and L-malate dehydrogenase activities, although their 2-oxoglutarate dehydrogenase and succinic dehydrogenase activities were comparable with those in lactaphilic extracts. The acetate-oxidizers thus possess the enzymic equipment to operate the TCA cycle and so generate 2-oxoglutarate, from ammonia and which glutamate can be synthesized. By contrast, the non-acetate-oxidizers cannot thus generate 2-oxoglutarate and must rely on preformed supplies of it (or other TCA cycle acids) before glutamate can be synthesized.

(b) *Oxidations by acetic acid bacteria*

Characteristically these bacteria oxidize primary or secondary alcohol groups in a variety of aliphatic alcohols, glycols and such polyalcohols as have the *cis* arrangement of two secondary alcohol groups adjacent to a primary alcohol group (Bertrand's rule, 1904). Thus, configuration (*a*) is oxidizable as shown, but the *trans* configuration (*b*) is not:

$$
\begin{array}{ccc}
\underset{\underset{\text{OH OH}}{|\ \ |}}{\overset{\overset{\text{H H}}{|\ \ |}}{\text{R}-\text{C}-\text{C}-\text{CH}_2\text{OH}}} \rightarrow
\underset{\underset{\text{OH}}{|}}{\overset{\overset{\text{H O}}{|\ \ ||}}{\text{R}-\text{C}-\text{C}-\text{CH}_2\text{OH}}} &
&
\underset{\underset{\text{H OH}}{|\ \ |}}{\overset{\overset{\text{OH H}}{|\ \ |}}{\text{R}-\text{C}-\text{C}-\text{CH}_2\text{OH}}}
\\
(a) & & (b)
\end{array}
$$

In some cases, a terminal —CHOH · CH$_3$ group in a polyol behaves as an elongated —CH$_2$OH group, since L-fucitol is oxidized to L-fuco-4-ketose (Richtmeyer *et al.* 1950). Ketogenic activities on glycols and polyols are particularly characteristic of strains of *Gluconobacter* and have been applied in industry to prepare dihydroxyacetone from glycerol and sorbose (an intermediate in the synthesis of ascorbic acid) from sorbitol.

Another important oxidation, particulary associated with gluconobacters, is that by which the reducing group of aldohexoses is oxidized to carboxyl. Thus, D-glucose is converted, without phosphorylation, to D-gluconate, which may be further attacked, still without cleavage of the 6-C chain, form D-2- or D-5-oxogluconate:

$$
\underset{\underset{\text{OH OH H \ \ OH}}{|\ \ |\ \ |\ \ |}}{\overset{\overset{\text{H H OH H}}{|\ \ |\ \ |\ \ |}}{\text{CH}_2\text{OH}-\text{C}-\text{C}-\text{C}-\text{C}-\text{CHO}}} \rightarrow
\underset{\underset{\text{OH OH H \ \ OH}}{|\ \ |\ \ |\ \ |}}{\overset{\overset{\text{H H OH H}}{|\ \ |\ \ |\ \ |}}{\text{CH}_2\text{OH}-\text{C}-\text{C}-\text{C}-\text{C}-\text{COOH}}}
$$

D-*glucose* D-*gluconic acid*

$$
\underset{\underset{\text{OH OH H \ \ O}}{|\ \ |\ \ |\ \ ||}}{\overset{\overset{\text{H H OH}}{|\ \ |\ \ |}}{\text{CH}_2\text{OH}-\text{C}-\text{C}-\text{C}-\text{C}-\text{COOH}}}
\qquad
\underset{\underset{\text{O \ \ OH H \ \ OH}}{||\ \ |\ \ |\ \ |}}{\overset{\overset{\text{H OH H}}{|\ \ |\ \ |}}{\text{CH}_2\text{OH}-\text{C}-\text{C}-\text{C}-\text{C}-\text{COOH}}}
$$

D-2-*oxogluconic acid* D-5-*oxogluconic acid*

Washed cell suspensions of *G. oxydans* oxidize glucose to all three of these acids, some 2-oxogluconate being further oxidized to D-arabonate and CO$_2$ (Fewster 1958):

$$
\underset{\underset{\text{OH OH H \ \ O}}{|\ \ |\ \ |\ \ ||}}{\overset{\overset{\text{H H OH}}{|\ \ |\ \ |}}{\text{CH}_2\text{OH}-\text{C}-\text{C}-\text{C}-\text{C}-\text{COOH}}} \rightarrow
\underset{\underset{\text{OH OH H}}{|\ \ |\ \ |}}{\overset{\overset{\text{H H OH}}{|\ \ |\ \ |}}{\text{CH}_2\text{OH}-\text{C}-\text{C}-\text{C}-\text{COOH}}} + \text{CO}_2
$$

D-2-*oxogluconic acid* D-*arabonic acid*

King and Cheldelin (1957) prepared a particulate enzyme fraction from *G. oxydans* containing a glucose oxidase catalysing gluconolactone formation from glucose, but the direct oxidation of glucose to 2-oxogluconate may occur simultaneously with glucose metabolism via the hexosemonophosphate (HMP) pathway (Kitos *et al.* 1958). It seems that acetic acid bacteria metabolize glucose (a) through the HMP pathway; and (b) by oxidation to gluconate and oxogluconates. When (a) is impossible (i.e. when the appropriate kinase is lacking) glucose is either not attacked, or it is oxidized to metabolic "dead-end" products like gluconate and oxogluconates.

Stouthamer (1959) found no evidence that the glycolytic (EMP) pathway operated in acetic acid bacteria, while de Ley (1961) showed that, at best, only a few of them contained a weak glycolytic system. The main dissimilative pathway of carbon metabolism in *Acetobacter* and *Gluconobacter* may be the HMP pathway.

The oxidative transformations described in this section are of doubtful importance in beer spoilage, except, as has already been suggested, they may contribute to the foreign, but not acid, flavours found in some beers infected with acetic acid bacteria. Further information on the oxidative activities of these bacteria may be sought in the reviews by Prescott and Dunn (1959), Hall (1963) and Asai (1968) and in shorter reviews by Rainbow (1961, 1966).

(c) *Oxidation of ethanol*

In beer spoilage, the chief biochemical activity of acetic acid bacteria is that of oxidizing ethanol to acetic acid, an activity which endows them with their chief industrial importance as the agents of vinegar production, but renders them beer spoilage organisms.

Henneberg (1897) showed that ethanol was oxidized by acetic acid bacteria through acetaldehyde as intermediate, the oxidation of the latter proceeding by an oxidation–reduction dismutation (Neuberg and Windisch 1925):

(1) $CH_3CH_2OH \xrightarrow{-2H} CH_3CHO$

(2) $CH_3CHO + CH_3CHO + H_2O \longrightarrow CH_3COOH + CH_3CH_2OH$

the ethanol regenerated in reaction (2) being then subject to oxidation in reaction (1). Under aerobic conditions, both reactions were presumed to proceed together, until all ethanol had been converted to acetic acid.

However, the weak dismutative abilities of some strains led Wieland and Bertho (1928) to suggest that acetaldehyde might be oxidized by a dehydrogenase:

$$CH_3CHO + H_2O \xrightarrow{-2H} CH_3COOH$$

so that the oxidation of ethanol to acetaldehyde is catalysed by alcohol dehydrogenase and that of acetaldehyde by aldehyde dehydrogenase (Asai 1968).

Evidence that both enzymes exist came from Lutwak-Mann (1938), who found the alcohol dehydrogenase of his *Acetobacter suboxydans* (now *G. oxydans*) was NAD-linked. This was confirmed by King and Cheldelin (1954), whose enzyme failed to act on acetaldehyde. Conversely, their purified aldehyde dehydrogenase did not attack ethanol: it attacked propionaldehyde and n-butyraldehyde and required NADP as coenzyme, NAD being only one-quarter as effective as NADP. However, possibly both NADP- and NAD-dependent aldehyde dehydrogenases were present, as demonstrated for *A. aceti* by Rao and Gunsalus (1955), although their *A. suboxydans* contained only the NADP-linked enzyme. The unusual acetate-oxidizing species *Acetobacter peroxydans* (catalase-negative and produces no acid from glucose) also appears to contain distinct dehydrogenases for alcohol and acetaldehyde, since the oxidation of ethanol to acetaldehyde, but not that of the latter to acetic acid, was inhibited by 10^{-3} M arsenite, both oxidations being dependent on NADP but not NAD (Tanenbaum 1956). This finding disagrees with that of Atkinson (1956), whose alcohol dehydrogenase of *A. peroxydans* was NAD-linked. Kida and Asai (unpublished work, quoted by Asai (1968)) found that the alcohol and acetaldehyde dehydrogenases of *A. dioxyacetonicus* (probably a subspecies of the acetate-oxidizing *A aceti*) were both NADP-dependent. NADP-dependency has also been reported for a species of *Acetobacter* (acetate-oxidizing) used for preparing Japanese vinegar (Nakayama 1960). Nakayama (1961a, b) also demonstrated an acetaldehyde dehydrogenase and a new alcohol dehydrogenase in an acetobacter, both broadly specific. The new alcohol dehydrogenase was an alcohol-cytochrome-553 reductase, having an absorption spectrum like that of cytochrome *c*. Nakayama considers that, during oxidation of ethanol by this enzyme, electrons are passed to the haem iron of cytochrome-553 and the acetaldehyde is oxidized either by an enzyme for which cytochrome-553 is an electron acceptor, or by one which is NADP-linked.

It therefore seems that NAD- and NADP-dependent and coenzyme-independent alcohol and aldehyde dehydrogenases exist in various acetic acid bacteria and that, in some strains at least, more than one enzyme may be responsible for either stage of the oxidation. Consistent with this is Prieur's (1957) finding that NAD-independent and NAD-dependent systems were involved in ethanol oxidation by *A. aceti* subspecies *xylinum,* operating optimally at pH 5·7 and pH 8 respectively.

As strict aerobes, cytochromes are concerned in the electron transport system, with molecular oxygen as terminal acceptor. Both Tanenbaum (1956) and Nakayama (1959) thought that the terminal oxidation of ethanol involved a cytochrome oxidase. Reference has already been made to the latter's work on alcohol-cytochrome-553 reductase.

(d) *Oxidations of other alcohols*

Acetic acid bacteria oxidize alcohols other than ethanol, but less readily. Thus, n-propyl, n-butyl, n-amyl and n-hexyl alcohols, but not methanol, are oxidized at rates which diminish in order of length of carbon chain, while the oxidation is generally weaker in the order primary → secondary → tertiary alcohols. The broad specificities of the new alcohol dehydrogenase (alcohol-cytochrome-553 reductase) and aldehydrogenase (Nakayama 1959, 1960, 1961b) are consistent with the ability of the acetic acid bacteria to oxidize many alcohols and aldehydes. Among the latter are propionaldehyde, n-butyraldehyde, isovaleraldehyde, benzaldehyde and furfuraldehyde.

(e) *Pigment formation*

Many strains of *Gluconobacter,* but only one acetobacter (*A. aceti* subspecies *liquefaciens*) produce γ-pyrone and water-soluble brown pigments from glucose. The following pathway for γ-pyrone formation and the evidence for it is given by Asai (1968):

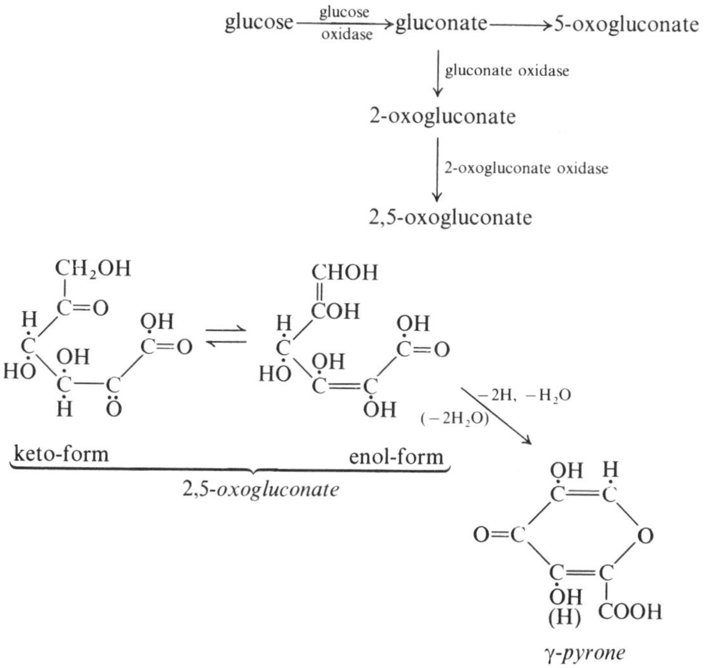

glucose $\xrightarrow[\text{oxidase}]{\text{glucose}}$ gluconate $\longrightarrow$ 5-oxogluconate

$\downarrow$ gluconate oxidase

2-oxogluconate

$\downarrow$ 2-oxogluconate oxidase

2,5-oxogluconate

keto-form   enol-form

2,5-*oxogluconate*

γ-*pyrone*

The formation of brown pigments occurs by a mechanism not yet understood, but it is related to γ-pyrone production.

C. *Zymomonas Anaerobia*

1. Isolation, Spoilage Symptoms and Classification

Shimwell (1937) first isolated this bacterium from densely turbid ale with an unpleasant odour and flavour. Because he could not allocate this gram-negative, motile, plump rod, which tended to aggregate into rosette-like clusters in older cultures, to any bacterial genus, he proposed it as a new species *Achromobacter anaerobium*. He considered it ". . . by far the most malignant beer disease bacterium yet recorded, because of very rapid development under anaerobic conditions in highly hopped beer of low pH". Indeed, while reporting the isolation of a non-motile variety (var. *immobilis*), Shimwell (1948c) stated it was fortunate that the organism appeared not to occur commonly. Comrie (1939) also isolated the organism from ale, reporting properties consistent with those given by Shimwell.

His misgivings concerning the classification of *A. anaerobium* led Shimwell (1950) to create, in the family *Pseudomonadaceae*, a new genus *Saccharomonas*, to include bacteria causing a substantially quantitative fermentation of glucose to ethanol and CO_2, such as *S. anaerobia* (*A. anaerobium*), *Termobacterium mobile* Lindner and the bacterium isolated from pulque, *Pseudomonas lindneri* Kluyver and Hoppenbrouwers. However, the bacterium has now been removed from the *Pseudomonadaceae* and assigned to the genus *Zymomonas* as *Z. anaerobia* (Shimwell) Kluyver as a genus of gram-negative, facultative anaerobic rod, containing one other species, *Z. mobilis* (Carr 1974). While *Z. mobilis* is common in fermenting plant juices in tropical countries, *Z. anaerobia* is the beer spoiler, and *Z. anaerobia* var. *pomaceae* is the "cider sickness' organism, spoiling sweet ciders and perries (Millis 1956).

2. Nutrition and Metabolism

Belaïch and Senez (1965) performed the first nutritional studies on zymomonads, finding that *Z. mobilis* grew on an amino acid mixture, but less effectively on ammonium salts in glucose medium supplemented with pantothenate. However, the nutrition of the beer spoilage species *Z. anaerobia* differs appreciably (Bexon and Dawes 1970). Thus, although both species utilize only a few energy sources, the beer spoilers are more restricted, utilizing only glucose and fructose, but not sucrose, maltose, lactose, gluconate, glycerol or pyruvate. The utilization of sucrose by *Z. mobilis* in a peptone-yeast extract medium serves to distinguish it from *Z. anaerobia*. The requirement of the latter for added biotin and lipoate and its greater exactingness for amino acids are other points of difference. *Z. anaerobia* grew much less well on ammonium chloride as sole source of nitrogen: when presented with single amino acids, it grew best on arginine, tryptophan, cystine and glutamate, but to obtain maximum growth in defined medium, a mixture of 21 amino acids had to be provided. In hopped beer, *Z. anaerobia* grows over the range pH < 3·4 to > 7·5, although its activity is diminished at pH 3·6 (Shimwell 1937). It is inhibited by ethanol concentrations exceeding 7% (v/v), completely so at 8% (Comrie 1939).

Z. anaerobia ferments glucose substantially to ethanol and CO_2 (Shimwell 1937, 1948c, Comrie 1939). According to Shimwell (1937), some acetaldehyde was formed and the cultures acquired a stench, for which H_2S was partly responsible. Acetylmethylcarbinol and diacetyl were not detected. *Z. anaerobia* is facultatively aerobic, both aerobically and anaerobically grown cells containing cytochromes, which differed from those of *Z. mobilis*: it fermented 1 mole of glucose almost quantitatively to 1·8 moles of ethanol and 1·9 moles of CO_2, a little acetaldehyde also being formed (McGill *et al.* 1965). Fructose yielded 1·5 moles each of ethanol and CO_2 per mole, rather more acetaldehyde being obtained than from glucose, together with glycerol and a little of a substance behaving like hydroxypyruvic aldehyde. Experiments with [1-^{14}C]glucose indicated that *Z. anaerobia*, like *Z. mobilis* (Ribbons and Dawes 1961), fermented glucose by the Entner–Doudoroff route:

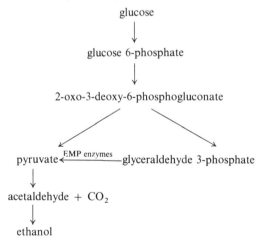

D. Wort Bacteria

The so-called wort bacteria (Lindner's termobacteria) are commonly members of the *coli-aerogenes* group of the family *Enterobacteriaceae*. They include species in the genera *Enterobacter*, *Klebsiella*, *Citrobacter*, *Arizona*,

Hafnia and *Escherichia* and sometimes members of the families *Pseudomonodaceae* and *Achromobacteriaceae* (Eschenbecher and Ellenrieder 1975). They are gram-negative, hop-tolerant and, although incapable of growth in normal beers, may cause off-flavours arising from their activities in wort before fermentation, or under the special circumstances discussed below. The wort bacteria were reviewed by Priest *et al.* (1974).

1. The *coli-aerogenes* Group

The group is typified by *Escherichia coli* and *Enterobacter* (lately *Aerobacter* or *Klebsiella*) *aerogenes,* transmitted to wort from the air or from infected brewing plant. If their activities on wort are allowed to become appreciable, they may transfer to beer undesirable flavours, not removed by yeast fermentation, variously described as celery-like, parsnip-like, mushroom-like, smoky or mouldy (Shimwell 1948c, Helm, 1949, Weinfurtner *et al.* 1962, Thorwest, 1965). Further, the indole-positive *Esch. coli* has also been blamed for phenolic ("medicinal") flavours (Helm 1949) and fermentations contaminated with enterobacteria yielded beers with increased contents of phenols (Bernstein *et al.* 1968). Enterobacteria may also promote diacetyl and acetoin formation by yeast (Weinfurtner *et al.* 1962), perhaps by stimulating yeast to produce 2-acetolactate, the thermolabile precursor of diacetyl (Priest and Hough 1974).

Unless cooled wort is allowed to stand for long periods, spoilage of beer by wort bacteria is unlikely to occur in normally brewed beers (Shimwell 1948c). However, in very weak beers, especially those with pH values exceeding 5·0 and receiving short lagering times, their activities may be sufficient to cause spoilage. Such conditions occurred in Europe during World Wars I and II, when *Pseudomonas* and *Escherichia* types were reported as beer spoilers (Chevalier 1946).

No attempt will be made here to review the nutrition and metabolism of bacteria of the *coli-aerogenes* group, which have been extensively studied in non-brewing contexts: in the brewing context, reference may be made to Priest and Hough (1974).

2. The Common Rod Bacterium of Brewer's Yeast

(a) *Classification and properties*

This organism, once often spoken of as the "short fat rods of pitching yeast", has been long known as an inhabitant of brewers' pitching yeasts in Britain and America, although seemingly not in Europe (Shimwell 1948c). Shimwell (1936a) described its isolation from brewer's yeast, its morphology and cultural and physiological characteristics. It is a gram-negative, highly pleomorphic rod, tolerant of hop antiseptics and concentrations of ethanol up to 6% (v/v). On malt wort, it produced hydrogen, carbon dioxide (but see 2(d) below), ethanol and volatile and non-volatile acids, causing a pronounced fruity, parsnip-like odour and flavour. It grew most rapidly in unhopped wort at pH 5·0: as pH values increased to pH 9·0, so did the length of the rods, but it failed to grow and produce acid when the pH fell to about 4·4.

At this time, Shimwell could not classify the bacterium and called it Bacterium Y. However, Shimwell and Grimes (1936), having extended its description, tentatively proposed to classify it as *Flavobacterium proteum* (later *F. proteus*) sp. nov., despite its producing little or none of the yellow pigment characteristic of the genus. They described it as plump rods with rounded ends, normally 0·8–1·2 μm × 1·5–4 μm, but highly pleomorphic in neutral or slightly alkaline medium: it was non-motile, producing neither spores nor capsules, facultatively anaerobic, not proteolytic and it reduced nitrate to nitrite. It produced acid and gas from maltose and glucose, a trace of acid, but no gas, from sucrose, neither acid nor gas from lactose and no acetylmethylcarbinol from glucose (Voges-Proskauer negative).

Shimwell (1948c) commented on "the rather negative grounds (for its classification) that it appeared to differ from other members of that genus (*Flavobacterium*) less than from those of any other", considering it a misnomer, although he could not decide "to what bacteriological group to allocate this curious bacterium". Ultimately, Shimwell (1963, 1964) proposed to create a new genus *Obesumbacterium*, in which *O. proteus* was the sole species, in order to accommodate it. Nevertheless, the taxonomic position of *O. proteus* remains uncertain: Weeks (1974), in Bergey's Manual, lists it as an alternative name to *F. proteus* under *Flavobacterium species incertae sedis*, the whole genus being, like *Zymomonas*, one of the genera of gram-negative, facultatively anaerobic rods of uncertain affiliation. This position will presumably not have taken consideration of the work of Priest *et al.* (1973), who, on the basis of conventional physiological and biochemical criteria and studies of its DNA composition, find a close relationship with *Hafnia alvei* (family *Enterobacteriaceae*) and propose that *O. proteus* should be reclassified as *Hafnia protea* comb. *nov.* In what follows, the name *H. protea* will be used.

(b) *Beer spoilage by* H. protea

It has long been believed that *H. protea* is harmless in brewing (e.g. see Brown 1916) and, since the proportion of its cells to those of brewer's yeast remained fairly constant from pitching to pitching (Shimwell 1936a), that the bacterium reproduces during primary fermentation to the same extent as do the cells of pitching yeast. Strandskov *et al.* (1953) observed that, after introducing a pure culture into the brewery, the contamination of successive yeast crops with *H. protea* progressively increased to a maximum during 9–10 fermentations and then remained steady, the curve of bacterial population against time during fermentation having a similar shape to that of yeast in suspension. After 48 h of fermentation, no further bacterial growth occurred, probably because of the fall in pH. There is also evidence that metabolic differences between yeast strains and the composition of wort influence the development of *H. protea* (Strandskov and Bockelmann 1956).

While it seems that *H. protea* is indeed relatively harmless as a beer spoiler, some qualification is necessary. Firstly, like the *coli-aerogenes* wort bacteria, if *H. protea* is allowed to proliferate appreciably in wort before pitching, the resultant beer may have the fruity, parsnip-like odour and flavour characteristic of its growth in wort. Secondly, this organism can develop in beers with abnormally high pH values (>4.5). Thirdly, it may affect beer flavour directly by producing strain-independent increases in levels of n-propanol, isobutanol, isopentanol, 2,3-butanediol and 2-acetolactate and strain-dependent increases in levels of dimethyl sulphide and dimethyl disulphide (Priest and Hough 1974); and indirectly by interaction with yeast strain, some of which suffer some inhibition by *H. protea,* so that fermentation is retarded, the pH of the beers being 0.1–0.3 units higher than normal, despite the racking gravity being unaffected (Strandskov and Bockelmann 1957).

(c) *Nutrition*

Strandskov and Bockelmann (1955) first studied the nutritional requirements of *H. protea*. Their minimal growth medium contained glucose, salts, eight specific amino acids (of which glutamate and arginine were the most important), uracil and adenine, but no vitamins were required. Glucose supported better growth than any other carbohydrate tested. The results of Thomas *et al.* (1972) were similar: in defined media, arginine plus either glutamate or aspartate supported growth, which was enhanced by additional amino acids, but not by biotin, folate, inositol, nicotinate, pyridoxin, riboflavin or thiamine, and only slightly by a mixture of these growth factors. In a peptone–water medium, *H. protea* grew well on glucose, fructose, mannose, galactose or maltose, but poorly and produced no acid on lactose, sucrose, raffinose, xylose or arabinose. In defined glucose medium, the optimum for growth was pH 7.3.

(d) *Metabolism*

Acetic, formic, 2-oxoglutaric, pyruvic and succinic acids are products of fermentation by *H. protea* growing in defined medium: in brewer's wort, they include acetoin, ethanol, lactic acid, fusel alcohols, some volatile acids and dimethyl sulphide, but not diacetyl (Thomas *et al.* 1972). Unlike Shimwell (1936a), these workers failed to detect hydrogen or other gas production from glucose or maltose. Experiments by Thomas *et al.* on the oxygen uptake of washed cell suspensions indicated that *H. protea* synthesized a terminal electron transfer chain, repressed by anaerobiosis, and a glucose oxidase complex. Cytochrome *b*, but not *a* or *c*, was detected in the cells and radio-respirometric measurements indicated that the EMP pathway was not solely responsible for the metabolism of glucose. Certain enzymes involved in the EMP, HMP and TCA pathways were demonstrated in cells grown aerobically and anaerobically. Those concerned with the EMP and HMP pathways were most active in the latter cells and were repressed by glucose, while lactic dehydrogenase and the enzymes of the TCA cycle were most active in aerobically grown bacteria.

During growth on brewer's wort, the concentrations of wort arginine, lysine, ammonia, aspartate, serine, tyrosine and leucine decreased, while those of several other amino acids, notably alanine, histidine, methionine and valine, increased. By contrast, during growth in defined arginine–glutamate medium, rapid glutamate utilization was paralleled by rapid accumulation of ammonia and slower utilization of arginine coincided with an accumulation of urea (Thomas *et al.* 1972).

H. protea, like other enterobacteria, thus seems to be metabolically versatile, dissimilating sugars by more than one pathway, the relative contributions of which are determined by conditions of aerobiosis or anaerobiosis. There are inconsistencies in reports of gas production, but these may reflect different experimental conditions, or even strains with different enzymic ability to decompose formate into carbon dioxide and hydrogen. *H. protea* shows nutritional exactingness towards certain amino acids, especially arginine and glutamate, the metabolism of the former being indicative that an urea cycle operates.

III. SPOILAGE BY YEASTS

A. What are "Wild" Yeasts?

In brewing, any yeast having a property significantly different from the culture yeast may, in the broadest sense, be considered to be a "wild" yeast and potentially a beer spoilage yeast. Gilliland (1967) defined a wild yeast as "any yeast not deliberately used and under full control". Thus, he includes harmless as well as harmful yeasts, the former conforming to this definition as indicative of process imperfections.

Clearly, yeasts which differ generically or specifically from the brewery culture strain, whether *Saccharomyces cerevisiae* in ale breweries or *Sacch. uvarum* (*Sacch. carlsbergensis*) in lager breweries, may be spoilage yeasts. Less obviously, strains of *Sacch. cerevisiae* may cause spoilage in lager breweries and those of *Sacch. uvarum* may do so in ale breweries. Still less obviously, strains of the same culture species, other than the specific strain applied in a particular brewery, can behave as spoilage yeasts (Bunker 1961). Thus, in a brewery relying on a flocculent strain, a non-flocculent strain of the same species may so change the pattern of attenuation and yeast separation as to create spoilage symptoms (Curtis and Wenham 1958). Conversely, a contaminant flocculating strain may adversely affect fermentations with a non-flocculent yeast. This contingency is best countered by introducing a fresh pure culture into the brewery. In ale breweries, fractional selection of the pitching may be effective, if less immediately so.

B. Taxonomic Status

Names given by authors to their isolates of yeasts reflect contemporary taxonomic views and new knowledge has often shown these names to be unsuitable or erroneous. Since authors' nomenclature will be used in what follows, some attempt to relate such names to those adopted in the most modern and authoritative work on yeast taxonomy (Lodder 1970) is necessary (Table 4).

Beer-spoiling wild yeasts comprise both ascosporogenous and anascosporogenous species. According to A. Hansen (1948), those wild yeasts of E. C. Hansen which must be considered in the brewery are: (a) sporogenous *Saccharomyces* species (*pastorianus, intermedius, validus, ellipsoideus, turbidans*); (b) the film-forming sporogenous species *Pichia membranaefaciens* and *Hansenula anomala* and the asporogenous *Mycoderma cerevisiae;* and (c) certain *Torulopsis* spp. (asporogenous).

All the species in (a) and *Sacch. willianus* are now regarded as synonymous with *Sacch. cerevisiae* (van der Walt 1970) and it is remarkable that, among so many yeasts sufficiently closely related to be classifiable within the same species, there are differences great enough to render some strains suitable for beer production, while others are not and are, indeed, beer spoilers. One such difference is undoubtedly that of response to isinglass finings, in ale breweries, an important property depending on the net surface charge carried by yeast cells (Wiles 1951, Rudin 1958), but not a property applied for taxonomy. Other differences may involve the ability of different species to produce those quantitatively minor fermentation products which affect beer flavour and aroma.

The position of the asporogenous yeasts in groups (b) and (c) above is more complex. These small yeasts, once commonly called "torula yeasts" (the generic name *Torula* has long since been discarded) probably represent stabilized haploid strains of sporogenous species. Indeed, in some cases, where sexual phenomena have been observed, a species has had to be transferred to a sporogenous genus. Thus, species of *Candida* have been found to constitute haploid mating types of ascosporogenous species (van Uden and Buckley

TABLE 4. Obsolete names of brewery wild yeasts and their modern equivalents†

Obsolete name	Modern name (Lodder 1970)
Br. dublinensis	*Br. anomalus*
Br. schanderlii	*Br. intermedius*
C. krusei var. *vanlaeriana*	*P. membranaefaciens*
C. mycoderma	*P. membranaefaciens; C. valida; C. vini*
C. pelliculosa	Imperfect form of *H. anomala*
C. robusta	Imperfect form of *Sacch. cerevisiae*
E. anomalus	*H. anomala*
Kl. brevis	*Kl. apiculata*
Kl. lindneri	*Kl. apiculata*
Monilia spp	*Candida* spp
Mycocandida spp	*Candida* spp
Mycoderma cerevisiae	*C. vini*
Mycoderma cerevisiae var. *pulverulentum*	*H. anomala*
Mycoderma vanlaeriana	*P. membranaefaciens*
P. alcoholophila	*P. membranaefaciens*
P. belgica	*P. membranaefaciens*
Pseudosaccharomyces apiculatus	*Kl. apiculata*
Rh. glutinis (some strains)	*Cr. infirmo-miniatus*
Rh. infirmo-miniatus	*Cr. infirmo-miniatus*
Rh. mucilaginosa	*Rh. rubra*
Sacch. acetaethylicus	*H. anomala*
Sacch. anomalus	*H. anomala*
Sacch. apiculata	*Kl. apiculata*
Sacch. carlsbergensis	*Sacch. uvarum*
Sacch. ellipsoideus	*Sacch. cerevisiae*
Sacch. intermedius	*Sacch. cerevisiae*
Sacch. membranaefaciens	*P. membranaefaciens*
Sacch. oviformis	*Sacch. bayanus*
Sacch. pastorianus	*Sacch. cerevisiae*
Sacch. saturnus	*H. anomala*
Sacch. turbidans	*Sacch. cerevisiae*
Sacch. validus	*Sacch. cerevisiae*
Sacch. willianus	*Sacch. cerevisiae*
T. famata	*T. candida*
T. kefyr	*C. kefyr*
T. mogii	Imperfect form of *Sacch. rouxii*
Willia anomala	*H. anomala*

† *Br.* = *Brettanomyces; C.* = *Candida; Cr.* = *Cryptococcus; E.* = *Endomyces; H.* = *Hansenula; Kl.* = *Kloeckera; P.* = *Pichia; Rh.* = *Rhodotorula; Sacch.* = *Saccharomyces; T.* = *Torulopsis.* Yeasts not listed above are mentioned in the text by their correct names according to Lodder (1970).

1970). For example, *C. pelliculosa* is recognized as the imperfect (haploid) form of *H. anomala, C. valida* as that of *P. membranaefaciens* and *T. mogii* as that of *Sacch. rouxii*. In other cases, genera have been eliminated and their erstwhile species placed more appropriately in other genera. Thus, *Mycoderma cerevisiae* has become *C. vini*.

The wild yeasts already named do not comprehend all those reported as beer spoilers: others will be mentioned in section III.C.

In what follows, the abbreviations used for the names of accepted genera will be those listed by Lodder (1970).

C. Wild Yeasts as Beer Spoilers

1. General

Following work in the 1870s on the lactic spoilage of beer, H. T. Brown turned his attention to the turbidities ("frets") caused in beer, especially that to which oxygen had gained access, by the development of "secondary yeasts". Reminiscing, Brown (1916) describes how his "forcing test" for detecting bacterial infection in beer and for predicting the behaviour of beer in cask was less successful as regards "frets", adding ". . . perhaps . . . secondary 'frets' of this nature are today responsible for more brewing troubles than those due to bacterial infection."

Great impetus was given to the study of wild yeasts by the work of E. C. Hansen, subsequent to his appointment in 1878 to the Carlsberg Laboratory. As Brown found in ale breweries, so Hansen found that wild yeasts were common beer-spoiling contaminants in lager breweries. Hansen devised methods of isolating pure yeast cultures and showed how they might be applied to eliminate bacterial and wild yeast spoilage of beer. Pasteur is quoted (A. Hansen 1948) as writing: "Hansen was the first to realize that beer yeast should be pure, and that not only with regard to microbes and disease ferments in the narrow sense, but also that it should be free from cells of wild yeast."

Since Brown and Hansen, there have been many descriptions of beer spoilage by wild yeasts and the subject has been reviewed by Wiles (1954, 1961) and Gilliland (1961). Unpasteurized draught (cask) beers, such as still constitute a sizeable proportion of the output of British breweries, are especially prone to such spoilage, taking the form of unfinable turbidity ("frets") and/or off-flavours and, in some cases, acidity, loss of alcohol or excessive attenuation. Baker et al. (1929), reporting on hazes produced by Saccharomyces spp., Mycoderma cerevisiae and white and pink "torulae" (the latter presumably species of Rhodotorula), described flavours produced by these contaminants as dry, rough, washy, mawkish, thin, bitter, fruity, sour or sharp. Wiles (1950, 1954, 1961) and Hemmons (1954, 1955) surveyed draught ales, while Brady (1958) studied top fermentation pitching yeasts from 13 breweries. Hemmons (1954) isolated from mild, bitter and pale ales, as served to the consumer, 41 Saccharomyces, 41 Pichia and 36 asporogenous types. He noted the widespread occurrence of two film-forming species of Pichia (especially P. membranaefaciens) and Candida (especially C. mycoderma) in draught ales, while 30% of the draught bitters and pale ales were infected with *Sacch. carlsbergensis*. He divided these yeasts into those (a) fining with isinglass finings when grown under aerobic or micro-aerophilic conditions; (b) fining only when grown under micro-aerophilic conditions; and (c) failing to fine when grown under either conditions (Hemmons 1955). *Sacch. carlsbergensis, Sacch. oviformis, Kloeckera, Torulopsis* and *Rhodotorula* belonged to group (c). Hemmons considered that finings tended to reduce infection with *Pichia* spp. and certain *Candida* spp., because the micro-aerophilic conditions prevailing at the time of fining favour a satisfactory fining reaction.

Off-flavours may be imparted to beers as a result of abnormal formation of C_4 to C_{10} fatty acids by wild yeasts. While these acids arise during normal primary fermentation (Jones *et al.* 1975), experimental beers produced from three contaminant wild *Saccharomyces* spp and *Brettanomyces anomalus* contained much more isobutyrate and isovalerate, but less caproate and caprylate, than those produced by brewing strains of *Sacch. uvarum* (Arkima 1973).

2. Origin and Extent of Infection

According to Wiles (1954), ale pitching yeasts may be infected with one wild cell per 5000 culture cells, brewery plant being by far the greatest source of infection, and he considers the belief that spoilage yeasts flourish in beer because of their simple nutritional requirements is erroneous, some of them having specific and complex requirements. In an examination of pitching yeasts from 13 breweries, Brady (1958) found that, in most cases, they contained about one wild cell per 10^6 culture cells. She noted the presence of species of *Pichia, Hansenula* and *Debaryomyces* and of asporogenous genera, many of the wild yeasts belonging to genera previously found in pitching yeast and spoiled beer, while others had not been recorded. In this work, isolations were made by plating on lysine medium (Walters and Thiselton 1953), so that certain wild yeasts, including *Saccharomyces* spp., would be disregarded.

Applying the sensitive and specific immunofluorescence technique, Richards (1968) found the pattern of infection of pitching yeasts with wild *Saccharomyces* (often the chief cause of trade returns of non-fining beer) bore little relation to the level of infection with other wild yeasts or bacteria. Once a *Saccharomyces* infection was established, its level, although variable, never fell lower than that detectable by the technique, so that they seem to be more persistent contaminants than other wild yeasts or bacteria and provide a better indication of contamination than do bacteria or lysine-utilizing yeasts. Richards also showed that, after a series of batch fermentations, pitching yeasts normally became contaminated with wild yeasts and bacteria, the level of wild *Saccharomyces* spp. being usually less than 10 per 10^6 brewing cells and, while arbitrary standards of infection must be established, he suggests that pitching yeasts should be rejected when the level of infection exceeds 10 wild *Saccharomyces* per 10^6 brewing cells.

Concentrations even as low as one cell of *Sacch. cerevisiae* var. *turbidans* per 160×10^6 brewing cells were reported to produce a detectable haze in beer (Ellison and Doran 1961). This non-finable yeast could be controlled by introducing into the brewery, at intervals of 3–4 days, fresh pure culture yeast blends, when, after fairly long periods of brewing, the concentration of non-fining yeast was considerably reduced.

3. Development during Fermentation

In laboratory fermentations, aerated by shaking, *P. membranaefaciens, C. mycoderma* and *T. colliculosa* competed successfully with a brewing strain of *Sacch. cerevisiae*. However, under simulated brewing conditions with flocculent and non-flocculent strains of top and bottom yeasts, they failed to establish substantial populations in pitching yeast or in green beer, except with flocculent top yeast, when the wild yeasts multiplied steadily throughout the fermentation (Brady and Hough 1961). According to Bourgeois (1969), the growth of wild yeasts during primary (presumably lager) fermentation is suppressed, but it might resume soon after removal of the primary yeast by flocculation or filtration.

4. Sporogenous Spoilage Yeasts

(a) Saccharomyces *spp.*

Strains of *Sacch. carlsbergensis* are prominent among the yeasts causing turbidity of draught ales in the trade according to Wiles (1949), but he also isolated *Sacch. cerevisiae* (including var. *turbidans*), *P. belgica, P. alcoholophila* and asporogenous species (see below) from spoiled draught beers (Wiles 1950). His strains of *carlsbergensis* and *cerevisiae* grew rapidly in beer to produce a non-finable haze.

Wiles (1954) lists strains of *Sacch. cerevisiae* and *Sacch. carlsbergensis* as producing haze and "fret", *Sacch. willianus* as producing haze and fermentation in primed beer, *Sacch. diastaticus* as causing "super-attenuation" (see below) and *P. membranaefaciens* as causing films. He states that *H. anomala* may cause spoilage, but no yeasts with the characters of *Sacch. pastorianus* and *Sacch. cerevisiae* had been detected. Contrary to the view then commonly held, he therefore did not believe that the species *pastorianus* and *cerevisiae* var. *ellipsoideus* were responsible for most wild yeast infections of British beers, for which he blamed strains of *Sacch. carlsbergensis,* while maintaining (Wiles 1956, 1961) that many beer-spoiling strains, like *pastorianus* and *cerevisiae* var. *ellipsoideus,* are so closely related to culture yeasts that they may be regarded as troublesome strains of *Sacch. cerevisiae* (top yeast) or

Sacch. carlsbergensis (bottom yeast), differing from them in temperature optimum, flocculence, finability, or ability to use some special beer constituent. This view anticipated the tendencies of modern taxonomy and is shared by Windisch (1962a, b), who states that the most dangerous beer spoilage yeasts are closely related to brewing yeasts, from which they might even arise by mutation. As evidence, he cites his finding that 20 isolates of *Sacch. pastorianus* were homothallic, despite the less frequent cocurrence of homothallic than of heterothallic yeasts, and that, since brewery yeasts are often aneuploid, such complex cells may mutate and behave as wild yeasts.

Micro-electrophoretic experiments by Wiles (1951) showed that, in the presence of finings, finable and non-finable yeasts migrated at pH 4·1 to the cathode, indicating that, when coated by the finings, the yeasts were positively charged. This coating was permanent (not removed by washing with buffer) with negatively charged yeasts, whereas the coating of finings on non-finable yeasts was readily washed from the cell surface, which he therefore regarded as different from that of the finable yeasts in lacking a charge. Reference has already been made to Hemmons' (1955) work on the effect of conditions of aerobiosis on the fining process (III.C,l).

"Super-attenuation" is a type of beer spoilage caused by *Sacch. diastaticus,* first isolated by Andrews and Gilliland (1952) as a contaminant of wort and later from brewer's yeast and old beer. Besides the mono-, di- and tri-saccharides fermented by brewer's yeast, *Sacch. diastaticus* secretes a glucamylase (Hopkins 1955) enabling it to ferment starch and dextrins and so to attack the residual dextrins of beer, causing naturally conditioned beers to attenuate excessively. Gilliland (1954) described the morphological, physiological and genetic characters of this yeast, of which flocculent and non-flocculent varieties exist. It has been isolated from Irish, English and American beers and justified as a separate species (Gilliland 1966).

(b) Hansenula, Pichia *and other sporogenous species*

Hansen (1904) allotted to the genus *Willia* the species previously called *Sacc. anomalus* and *Sacch. saturnus.* The present classification as *Hansenula* for this strongly fermentative genus, members of which form hat-shaped ascospores, assimilate nitrate and produce unusually large amounts of esters, is due to Sydow and Sydow (1919). Of the 25 species listed by Wickerham (1970), *H. anomala* is the most commonly associated with beer spoilage, although *H. subpelliculosa* was isolated from pitching yeast by Brady (1958). Formerly, *Hansenula* appeared under names such as *Sacch. anomalus, Sacch. acetaethylicus, C. pelliculosa, Endomyces anomalus, Mycoderma cerevisiae, Willia anomala* and several specific names in *Monilia* and *Mycocandida.* Its non-sporulating (haploid) strains correspond to *C. pelliculosa* (Wickerham 1970).

Under aerobic conditions, *H. anomala* forms pellicles, but the formation of much ethyl acetate is symptomatic of its spoilage.

It is noteworthy that "killer" yeast strains occurred the most frequently within the genus *Hansenula* (see section III.D), 12 such strains being detected in the 29 strains tested by Philliskirk and Young (1975).

The genus *Pichia* was also established by Hansen (1904). Of the 35 species listed by Kreger-van Rij (1970), only the type species, *P. membranaefaciens,* is stated to have been isolated from beer. This yeast is considered to be the perfect form of *C. valida.* Discarded synonyms include *Sacch. membranaefaciens, Willia belgica, Mycoderma vanlaeriana, C. krusei* var. *vanlaeriana* and other specific names in the genera *Saccharomyces, Endomyces, Hansenula, Zygosaccharomyces* and in *Pichia* itself (e.g. *alcoholophila* and *belgica*). It differs from species of *Hansenula* in failing to assimilate nitrate and from *H. anomala* in particular in fermenting glucose weakly, or not at all, and in not fermenting sucrose and maltose. Because it is an aerobic organism able to assimilate ethanol, its beer spoilage symptoms may include loss of alcohol as well as the formation of films and hazes. The latter may be finable (see section III.C.l).

Hemmons (1954) made 41 isolates of *P. membranaefaciens, P. fermentans* and other species from 41 English draught beers. *Pichia* spp. were found in 75% of the beers examined, *P. membranaefaciens* being the commonest. Earlier reports of *Pichia* spp. in spoiled beers include those of Wiles (1950), who isolated *membranaefaciens* from 22 turbid draught beers, and Walker and Wiles (1952), while Brady (1958) found this species as a contaminant of ale pitching yeast. Wiles (1961) regards *P. membranaefaciens, C. krusei* and *C. mycoderma* as non-fastidious, film-forming yeasts found in beer to which oxygen has gained access.

Reports of other sporogenous yeasts associated with beer spoilage are comparatively few. Three strains of *Hanseniaspora valbyensis* were found in draught beers by Hemmons (1955) and Brady (1958) isolated one strain of *Debaryomyces hansenii* from pitching yeast. However, these genera may be more common in beer than a survey of brewing literature indicates: *H' spora uvarum* is ubiquitous in nature and it and *H' spora valbyensis* may be overlooked under the cloak of their imperfect form, *Kloeckera apiculata* (Phaff 1970).

5. Asporogenous Spoilage Yeasts

(a) Candida *spp.*

Many species of *Candida* are now recognized as the imperfect forms of other genera (see section III.B), especially *Hansenula* and *Pichia*. However, some of these haploid forms are so stable that the sexual phenomena by which their perfect (sporogenous) forms are revealed have not yet been observed. It is therefore practical to discuss beer spoilage ascribed to *Candida* spp. as such, the question whether a candida isolated in the brewery is really the haploid form of a sporogenous yeast being largely of academic importance.

Among the asporogenous yeasts, *Candida* spp. are probably the commonest spoilers, or potential spoilers, of beer. Of the 81 species listed by van Uden and Buckley (1970), *C. guilliermondii, C. ingens, C. intermedia, C. lambica, C. mesenterica, C. sake, C. valida* and *C. vini* are indicated as having been found in beer. Other specific names used by authors mentioned below have now been rejected by Lodder's monograph in favour of one or other of these eight species. Many earlier reports of beer spoilage by *Mycoderma* spp. (Baker *et al.* 1929, Cosbie *et al.* 1941) should now perhaps be attributed to *Candida* spp. following the elimination of the genus *Mycoderma* from modern yeast classification and the allocation of mycodermae of brewing significance (including *C. mycoderma*) to the species *C. valida* and *C. vini* (van Uden and Buckley 1970).

Of 118 yeasts isolated by Hemmons (1954, 1955) from draught beers at point of sale, 20 were *C. mycoderma, C. robusta* or other *Candida* spp. Wiles (1950) found *Mycoderma cerevisiae* in 22 turbid draught beers and 13 of 16 isolates of film-forming yeasts isolated by Walker and Wiles (1952) from draught ales and pressed yeast proved to be *C. mycoderma*. This species occurred commonly in British pitching yeasts, 9 out of 13 samples of which contained *Candida* spp. (Brady 1958). Species of the genus are also probably contaminants in lager breweries.

Being film-forming aerobic yeasts, *Candida* spp. are likely spoilers of draught beers to which air has gained access following a period of dispense. They may also reduce beer pH values from 4·15 to 3·05 (Walker and Wiles 1952) and contribute to the general, non-finable haze of turbid ales (Wiles 1950). Of the species isolated from beer, *ingens, mesenterica, valida* and *vini* do not ferment, but their ability to assimilate ethanol may cause its loss from infected beers.

(b) Brettanomyces *spp.*

Gilliland (1961) drew attention to the role of this species in developing condition and flavour in certain high-gravity and lambic beers, as well as to their spoilage action on beers of lower gravities. Clausen (1904) first reported the role of *Brettanomyces* in the secondary fermentation and the creation of the characteristic flavour of English stock beers. Shimwell (1938) mentions a species causing a "fret" and, writing under the pseudonym "Brettanomyces" (1952, 1959), he described the production by *Brettanomyces* of turbidity and a mawkish "nose" in beers of original gravity lower than 1060°. However, Wiles (1953) considered that *Br. bruxellensis* was rarely detected in beer and unlikely to spoil it. Perhaps this opinion reflects experiences with beers weaker than the stock ales with which earlier workers were concerned. The technological importance of this genus is less than of yore, especially in Britain, when stock ales and naturally conditioned bottled beers were produced in large quantities.

Gilliland (1961) isolated 44 strains of *Brettanomyces* from naturally conditioned beers with off-flavours. All these strains produced off-flavours added in pure culture to beer. He classified them as *Br. bruxellensis, Br. schanderlii* and a species later named *Br. dublinensis* sp. nov. (Gilliland 1962). Van der Walt (1970) now regards the latter as *Br. anomalus* and *Br. schanderlii* as *Br. intermedius*.

(c) Kloeckera *spp.*

The type species *apiculata* has the greatest brewing significance. Its earlier names (*Sacch. apiculatus, Pseudosaccharomyces apiculatus, Kl. brevis, Kl. lindneri*) are now regarded as synonyms of this species. As isolated by Wiles (1950, 1954) from turbid beers, *Kl. brevis* grew rapidly in beer, producing an unfinable haze. Hemmons (1954, 1955) isolated 7 strains of *apiculata* and one of *africana* from 8 of 41 ales sampled in trade. According to Wiles (1961), *Kl. apiculata* may not occur as the sole spoilage organism, being often found, growing at low temperatures when glucose is present, in draught ales turbid with *Sacch. carlsbergensis* or *Sacch. cerevisiae*. Consistent with this, Phaff (1970) states that *Kl. apiculata* ferments glucose, but not other diagnostic test sugars.

(d) Cryptococcus *and* Rhodotorula *spp.*

Members of these genera receive comparatively rare mention as beer spoilers. Wiles (1950) makes no mention of them in his work on spoiled draught beers and among Hemmons' (1954, 1955) 118 isolates from draught ales only three were "pink yeasts" (strains of *Rh. glutinis* and *Rh. minuta*) and there were no cryptococci. Brady (1958) found *Rh. mucilaginosa* (Phaff and Ahearne 1970) in the pitching yeasts from 4 out of 13 ale breweries and *Cr. albidus* in only one sample. Both genera are mentioned by Bourgeois (1969) in connection with lager beer spoilage. *Cr. infirmo-miniatus,* a species once believed to be *Rh. glutinis* or *Rh. infirmo-miniatus* because it produces a pink pigment, has been isolated from beer bottle cleaning equipment (Phaff and Ahearne 1970), but this is not proof that it possesses spoilage properties.

(e) Torulopsis *spp.*

Like *Cryptococcus* and *Rhodotorula, Torulopsis* seems not often to be associated with beer spoilage. In the pitching yeasts of 13 ale breweries, *T. colliculosa* was a contaminant in six, *T. inconspicua* in four, *T. famata* in two and *T. sake* in one. Species also occur as wild yeasts in lager brewing (Bourgeois 1969). *T. famata* has now been transferred to the species *T. candida* and *T. sake* excluded from the genus and placed in *Candida sake* (van Uden and Vedal-Leiria 1970). Among his 118 isolates of yeasts from draught beers, Hemmons (1954) found only *T. famata*.

Reports of the spoilage symptoms caused by *Torulopsis* species are also few: they do not react to finings (Hemmons 1955), but *T. candida* and *T. inconspicua* may be especially dangerous when air gains access to beer, both species having a predominantly assimilative, but only weakly fermentative or non-fermentative metabolism (see section III.C.6).

6. Nutrition and Metabolism

The nutritional requirements of wild *Saccharomyces* spp. seem to resemble those of brewer's yeasts, which have great biosynthetic abilities and therefore simple nutritional requirements. Many ale yeasts can synthesize their cell substance from glucose, ammonia, appropriate salts and trace elements, if D-biotin and sometimes also D-pantothenate and/or *meso*-inositol are provided (Rainbow 1970). However, there seem to be brewing strains independent of preformed vitamins, since van der Walt (1970) records that growth of *Sacch. cerevisiae* and *Sacch. uvarum* in vitamin-free medium is "variable". As sole major sources of nitrogen, brewing yeasts can utilize ammonium salts and many individual amino acids, of which lysine is an important exception. This inability to use lysine has been applied to detect wild yeasts, such as *Pichia, Hansenula, Torulopsis, Candida, Brettanomyces* and *Kloeckera*, all of which grow on it, in brewery cultures (Walters and Thiselton 1953).

Both sporogenous and asporogenous spoilage yeasts thus seem to have simple nutritional requirements, ranging from those growing on glucose–ammonia–salts medium without added growth factors to those requiring the latter: none of them appears to need preformed amino acids (van der Walt 1970). A few species (e.g. *H. anomala, C. valida, Br. anomalus, Cr. infirmo-miniatus*) also grow on nitrate as source of nitrogen.

The fermentative and assimilative abilities of spoilage yeasts towards carbohydrates and other major carbon and energy sources provide the main metabolic interest, especially for diagnostic purposes. Some spoilage yeasts with an oxidative (aerobic) metabolism (*C. ingens, C. vini, C. mesenterica, Cr. albidus, Cr. infirmo-miniatus, Rh. rubra, T. candida* and *T. inconspicua*) do not ferment, or, like *Deb. hansenii, P. membranaefaciens* and *C. valida*, only weakly so. All others ferment glucose, vary in ability to ferment other sugars from *Saccharomyces* and *Brettanomyces* spp. which ferment a range of mono- and di-saccharides, to *C. lambica* and *Kl. apiculata*, which ferment only glucose. Ability to ferment starch and maltodextrins is restricted to *Sacch. diastaticus*, lactose to Br. anomalus and melibiose to *Sacch. uvarum* and some strains of *C. guilliermondii* (Table 5).

The assimilative abilities of beer spoilage yeasts are summarized in Table 6.

TABLE 5. Fermentative abilities of some spoilage yeasts (data from Lodder (1970))†

	Glucose	Galactose	Sucrose	Maltose	C'biose	Trehalose	Lactose	Melibiose	S/starch
Sporogenous spp.									
Deb. hansenii	w or –	w or –	w or –	w or –	–	–	–	–	–
H'spora uvarum	+	–	–	–	+ or –	–	–	–	–
valbyensis	+	–	–	–	+ or –	–	–	–	–
Hansenula anomala	+	(+)	+	+	–	–	–	–	–
P. membranaefaciens	w or –	–	–	–	–	–	–	–	–
Sacch. bayanus	+	–	+	+	–	+ or –	–	–	–
cerevisiae	+	+	+	+	–	+ or –	–	–	–
diastaticus	+	+	+	+	–	+	–	–	+
uvarum	+	+	+	+	–	+ or –	–	+	–
Asporogenous spp.									
Br. anomalus	+	+	+	w or –	+	w or –	+	–	–
bruxelliensis	+	+	+	+	+	+	–	–	–
intermedius	+	+	+	+	+	+	–	–	–
C. guilliermondii	+	+ or w	+ or w	–	–	+ or w	–	+ or –	–
ingens	–	–	–	–	–	–	–	–	–
intermedia	+	+	+	+ or w	–	+, w or –	–	–	–
lambica	+	+	+	+	–	–	–	–	–
mesenterica	–	–	–	–	–	–	–	–	–
sake	+ or w	+, w or –	+, w or –	+, w or –	–	+, w or –	–	–	–
valida	w or –	–	–	–	–	–	–	–	–
vini	–	–	–	–	–	–	–	–	–
Cr. albidus and infirmo-miniatus	–	–	–	–	–	–	–	–	–
Kl. apiculata	+	–	–	–	–	–	–	–	–
Rh. rubra	–	–	–	–	–	–	–	–	–
T. candida	–	–	–	–	–	–	–	–	–
T. colliculosa	+	–	+	+	–	+	–	–	–
T. inconspicua	–	–	–	–	–	–	–	–	–

† + = fermented; (+) = usually fermented; w = weakly fermented; – = not fermented; c'biose = cellobiose; S/starch = soluble starch.

Table 6. Assimilative abilities of some spoilage yeasts (data from Lodder (1970))[†]

	Galactose	Sucrose	Maltose	Cellobiose	Trehalose	Lactose	Melibiose	Soluble starch	Pentoses	Polyols	α-Me glucoside	Salicin	Ethanol	Glycerol	Nitrate	Vitamins
Sporogenous spp.																
Deb. hansenii	+	+	+	+	+	±	+	+	+	+	+	+	+	+	−	+
H'spora uvarum and valbyensis	−	−	−	+	−	−	−	+	−	−	−	+	−	−	+	±
H. anomala	±	+	+	+	+	−	−	+	±	−	+	+	+	+	+	−
P. membranaefaciens	−	−	−	−	±	−	−	−	±	−	±	−	+	±	+	±
Sacch. bayanus	+	+	+	−	±	−	−	−	±(x)	±	±	−	+	±	−	±
cerevisiae	+	+	+	−	±	−	−	−	±(r)	±	±	−	±	±	−	+
diastaticus	+	+	+	−	+	−	−	+	−	+	+	−	+	+	−	+
uvarum	+	+	+	−	+	−	+	−	−	±	±	−	+	±	−	+
Asporogenous spp.																
Br. anomalus	+	+	+	−	+	+	−	−	−	±(s)	±	+	+	+	+	+
bruxelliensis	−	+	+	−	+	−	−	−	±(r)	±(s)	+	−	+	+	±	+
intermedius	+	+	+	+	+	−	−	w/−	±(r)	±(s)	+	+	±	+	±	+
C. guilliermondii	+	+	−	+	+	−	+	+	+	+	+	+	+	+	−	+
ingens	+	+	−	−	+	−	−	+	+(x)	+	+	+	+	+	−	+
intermedia	+	+	+	+	+	−	−	−	+(x)	+	−	+	±	+	−	+
lambica	−	+	+	+	+	−	−	−	+(r)	−	+	+	+	+	−	+
mesenterica	−	+	+	+	+	−	−	−	±	+	+	+	+	+	−	−
sake	+	+	+	+	+	+	−	−	+(x)	+	+	+	+	+	−	+
valida	−	+	+	+	+	±	−	−	−	+	−	+	+	+	+	+
vini	−	+	+	−	−	−	−	−	−	+	−	+	+	±	−	+
Cr. albidus	+	+	+	+	+	+	−	−	−	+(i)	+	+	−	−	−	−
infirmo-miniatus	w	+	−	+	±	±	−	−	−	+(i)	−	+	w/−	−	−	+
Kl. apiculata	−	−	−	−	−	−	−	−	−	−	−	−	−	−	−	+
Rh. rubra	±	+	+	±	+	±	−	−	+	+	+	+	±	±	−	+
T. candida	+	+	+	+	+	±	±	−	±	±	±	±	+	±	−	+
colliculosa	−	+	+	−	+	−	−	−	−	+	+	−	+	+	−	−
inconspicua	−	−	−	−	−	−	−	−	−	−	+	−	+	+	−	+

† All species assimilate glucose. + = assimilated; w = weakly assimilated; ± = assimilated by some strains; − = not assimilated. In vitamins column, + = exogenous supplies required. x = xylose; r = ribose; s = sorbitol; i = inositol.

Again, they range from the restricted ones of *Hanseniaspora* spp., *P. membranaefaciens, C. vini, C. lambica, Kl. apiculata* and *T. inconspicua* to the more extensive abilities of *Saccharomyces* spp., *Deb. hansenii, Candida* spp. other than *lambica,* two of the three listed species of *Brettanomyces* and *T. candida.* Of unique diagnostic interest is the ability of *Cr. albidus* and *Cr. infirmo-miniatus* to assimilate inositol.

D. Killer Yeasts

The discovery by Bevan and Makower (1963) of strains of yeast ("killer yeasts") which kill other sensitive strains adds another aspect to considerations of beer spoilage. The killer factor appears to be a glycoprotein secreted by the killer cells (Woods and Bevan 1968, Bussey 1972). Evidence that brewery fermentations can be infected with killer strains, which caused the death of culture yeast and transmitted a phenolic flavour to beer, was first presented by Maule and Thomas (1973), who isolated flocculent and non-flocculent strains, lethal to ale and lager yeasts, from production-scale stirred continuous fermenters. The killer factor was highly active at pH 3·8–4·2 and, when infection reached 2%, the concentration of the factor created an advantage in continuous operation such that the proportion of killer yeast rose, the brewing yeast was rapidly killed and the beer acquired a "herbal" or "phenolic" off-flavour. The killer strains had the characteristics of *Sacch. cerevisiae,* but differed from the brewing strain in being able to ferment further, in having a small cell size, in antigenic reaction and in being pleomorphic in mixed culture. Commenting on the lack of reported incidence of killer yeasts in industry, Maule and Thomas suggest that, in most fermentation systems, killer yeasts would be less favoured than in the continuous system with which they were working.

In experiments in which mixtures of killer and sensitive strains of *Sacch. cerevisiae* were tested in batch and continuous fermentations, Young and Philliskirk (1975) found that the rate and extent of killing was greatest at 15–20 °C, being reduced more than 50% at 27 °C. In batch culture, the lethal effect increased as the proportion of killer strain was increased, up to the highest level tested (10%), while 0·001% was ineffective even in continuous fermentation. Aeration was not a critical factor, but killer strains soon became dominant in aerated continuous culture, indicating that the killer factor, rather than high growth rate, exerted the selective pressure favouring the killer strains.

Of 28 genera surveyed by Philliskirk and Young (1975), species of 7 genera possessed killing activity against *Sacch. cerevisiae,* the highest incidence occurring in *Hansenula* and the lowest in *Saccharomyces.* Killer strains were found in other genera (*Pichia, Candida, Torulopsis*) of possible brewery significance, but not among 58 strains of lager yeast. There were 28 killer strains of *Saccharomyces,* but 27 of these were laboratory strains, the high incidence of killer activity among which was traced to inbreeding from one or other of two killer *cerevisiae* strains. The other 11 strains comprised *Sacch. cerevisiae* (three ale brewing, Maule and Thomas strain, "American yeast foam", a baking, a sherry and a thermophilic strain) and a strain each of *diastaticus, capensis* and *uvarum.*

Kreil *et al.* (1976) found no killer yeasts among 230 strains from a Munich yeast collection, although all 24 test strains of *Sacch. cerevisiae* (top yeast) were sensitive to killer factor, as were all five baker's and 10 out of 11 wine yeasts examined. By 3-litre-fermentations of Munich pale wort with five different bottom yeasts contaminated with 0–30% of killer yeast cells, these workers showed that, even with 3% of killer yeast, the rate of fermentation, fall in pH, yeast count and concentrations of volatile esters and alcohols were less, while that of aldehyde was greater, than in the absence of killer yeast, the finished beers having estery and fruity off-flavours. They suggest that, in some cases, killer yeast contaminants may be responsible for defects in commercial brewery fermentations.

IV. DETECTION, ENUMERATION AND IDENTIFICATION

A. General

The difficulties in detecting contaminants on brewery samples are that we are usually seeking a few cells, either in an overwhelming background of culture cells (e.g. in pitching yeasts and beers at stages before filtration); or in high dilution in beers ready for packaging. In addition, with wild yeasts, their appearance so resembles culture yeast as to be indistinguishable from it under the microscope. Conventional methods of detecting microbial contaminants have been reviewed by Ault and Newton (1971).

B. Bacteria

Direct microscopic counts may suffice for preliminary examination, but they are likely to be inaccurate and uninformative about types present and their viability. In examining yeast samples, it is sometimes helpful to effect a partial separation of bacteria, if necessary after dilution, by brief centrifuging, before the supernatant is examined under the microscope, directly or after concentrating the organisms by membrane filtration. While detection may be rendered easier thereby, enumeration remains difficult and imprecise and identification of bacterial types is unsure.

Applications of differential media offer more fruitful approaches to problems of detecting and enumerating bacteria. From a study of comparative growth rates of a beer lactobacillus in wort, beer and a beer solids–maltose–yeast extract medium, Dean (1957) selected the latter at pH 5·0–6·2 and 20–25 °C as best for detecting lactobacilli; and yeasts could be suppressed by including 2 mg of actidione per litre of medium. This antibiotic was applied for this purpose by Green and Gray (1950). Williamson (1959) developed three solid selective media for the rapid independent estimation by plate counts of cell numbers of acetic acid bacteria, lactobacilli and *Hafnia protea* in British top yeasts. Medium A (selective for acetic acid bacteria) contained beer solids, ethanol (4% v/v), yeast extract and actidione (10 µg/ml) at pH 4·2; medium L (selective for lactobacilli) contained maltose, unhopped beer solids, yeast extract, casein hydrolysate, liver extract, actidione (10 µg/ml) and polymyxin (10 µg/ml) at pH 6·5, incubation being under carbon dioxide; and "deep liver" agar (selective for *H. protea*), a medium described by Haynes *et al.* (1955), supplemented with actidione (10µg ml). In all cases, plates were incubated for 4–6 days at 30°. Ault and Woodward (1965) detected and estimated viable lactobacilli in 30–36 h by incubation at 30° in an unhopped beer–gelatin medium containing 10 µg of actidione per ml by direct microscopic examination in the counting chamber of a haemocytometer slide.

An application of differential media to detect pediococci was that of Janesch (1957), who examined vaseline-sealed preparations in starch-turbid beer. Nakagawa (1964) used a semi-solid medium of yeast extract, mannose (or salicin), sodium acetate, ascorbic acid and actidione to detect pediococci in beer and Emeis (1962) applied Wallerstein Laboratories differential (WLD) medium, containing glucose, yeast extract, pancreatic casein digest and actidione, but later (1969) recommended another special medium for the purpose.

Of the conventional procedures, the use of differential media, sometimes coupled with centrifugation or membrane filtration, remains the most useful and frequently applied to detect and enumerate brewery bacteria. However, care must be taken that the composition of the medium meets the nutritional requirements of all the bacteria sought. Thus, a medium for detecting lactobacilli which lacks maltose and whose reaction exceeds pH 5·2, cannot detect the lactobacillus (strain L1) of Wood and Rainbow (1961), while one lacking mevalonate cannot detect *Pediococcus cerevisiae* var. *mevalovorus*. To counter the problem of the time required for bacteria to grow, several rapid methods have been devised: consideration of these is deferred to section IV.D.

C. Wild Yeasts

The difficulties of distinguishing wild from culture yeasts under the microscope render yeast infections the greatest problem of detection, enumeration, identification, control and treatment in brewing microbiology.

Ault and Newton (1971) list the characteristics for the practical differentiation of wild from culture yeasts as: (a) microscopic appearance; (b) heat resistance; (c) sporulation; (d) ability to ferment certain sugars; (e) ability to grown on selective media; and (f) serological properties. Campbell (1971b) has reviewed methods, including serological techniques, of detecting and identifying yeasts.

1. Classical Methods

The resistance to heat of vegetative cells of different yeasts has been applied for their differentiation. Culture yeasts in aqueous suspension are killed by heating to 53° for 10 min, whereas species of *Torulopsis, Hansenula, Pichia, Candida,* some haze-forming strains of *Saccharomyces* and *Sacch. diasticus* are not (Ault 1954).

E. C. Hansen first used sporulation tests to differentiate yeasts, early formation of ascospores on plaster of Paris, Gorodkowa's agar or acetate agar indicating the presence of wild yeasts. However, the method is time-consuming, insensitive and scarcely amenable for enumeration purposes and it fails to detect asporogenous species. Lund and Thygesen (1957) applied sporulation to detect wild *Saccharomyces* after differentially destroying brewing yeasts by heat. When samples contaminated with *Sacch. ellipsoideus, Sacch. pastorianus* and *P. membranaefaciens* were heated at 50° for 20 min, only 0·05–0·6% of the brewing cells survived as compared with 11–89% of the wild yeasts. Enrichment cultures were then prepared and sporulated on acetate medium. By this combined technique of heat treatment and sporulation, one cell of *ellipsoideus* could be detected among $0·5 \times 10^6$ culture cells.

Campbell and Thompson (1970) measured low levels of *Saccharomyces* contaminants in beers and wines by a method based on the presumptive coliform test. This technique would not, however, lend itself to the detection of small numbers of contaminants when many culture cells were present.

2. Selective Media

These have long been used to detect wild yeasts. Beer itself is such a medium and has been applied since about 1880, when H. T. Brown devised the "forcing" test, in which the test beer is incubated at elevated temperatures to promote the proliferation of spoilage microorganisms. Brown (1916) himself recognized the shortcomings of the method in detecting spoilage yeasts. The detection of wild yeasts by inoculating samples into wort acidified with tartaric acid is essentially the same technique. However, Hoffmann (1955) found that 1% or 1·5% of the acid was insufficient to suppress the growth of large numbers of culture cells, while 2% inhibited both culture and wild cells, no wild cells being detectable in either case. Windisch (1955) also found the technique unsatisfactory, because wild *Saccharomyces* spp. were no more tolerant of tartrate concentrations exceeding 2% than were most brewer's or distiller's yeasts, although several strains of *Candida, Sacch. ellipsoideus and Sacch. exiguus* tolerated more than 3%.

Selective media containing L-lysine as major source of nitrogen (Walters and Thiselton 1953) continue to find routine application in brewery laboratories, but it has the disadvantage of not detecting spoilage *Saccharomyces* spp., which resemble *Sacch. cerevisiae* and *Sacch. uvarum* in not utilizing this amino acid as sole source of nitrogen. Kato (1967) sought to overcome this difficulty by applying a second differential medium, containing 20 μg of crystal violet per ml, on which wild yeasts, including *Sacch. pastorianus, cerevisiae* var. *ellipsoideus* and *diastaticus,* grew but culture yeasts did not. Scherrer *et al.* (1969) confirmed that all wild yeasts could be detected and counted by the joint use of these media.

Hall (1971) differentiated wild yeasts (including *Saccharomyces* spp.) from culture *Sacch. cerevisiae* by observations of the form, colour and rate of growth of their colonies growing on WLN agar. This medium, applied by Czarnecki and van Engel (1959) to distinguish respiration-deficient from normal culture yeasts, is identical with WLD medium (see section IV.B), except that actidione is omitted. Ale yeasts failed to reduce the bromocresol green in this medium, giving dark or medium green colonies, while wild yeasts gave pale green, bluish or white colonies. Hall could detect one wild cell in about 10^6 culture cells with WLN agar.

The glucose–malt extract–peptone–yeast extract differential medium (SDM) of Brenner *et al.* (1970) contained fuchsin–sulphite mixture to inhibit the growth of brewer's top and bottom yeasts, while permitting that of *Sacch. diastaticus, Sacch. cerevisiae* var. *ellipsoideus, H. anomala* and *C. tropicalis.* Using this medium, Brenner and Hsu (1971) surveyed 63 breweries on four continents, finding a fairly uniform level of contamination in that 14% of yeasts were contaminated at a probably significant level (0·01%). The genera found were *Saccharomyces* (81%), *Candida* (8%), *Hansenula* (3% and unidentified genera (8%). According to Seidel (1973), the differentiation of culture from wild yeasts on SDM was as good as on crystal violet or lysine agar, but certain strains, described as dangerous wild yeasts, of *P. membranaefaciens, T. candida* and *Sacch. pastorianus* grew on SDM. He considered that crystal violet and lysine agar were better for routine tests, because they differentiated between wild *Saccharomyces* and other wild yeasts. However, after comparative tests with pure cultures of *Sacch. uvarum, Sacch.*

diastaticus and *C. utilis* on SDM, crystal violet and lysine agars, Seidel and Lofflmann (1975) decided that crystal violet medium was unsuitable for routine testing because it permitted the growth of culture yeast when in admixture with *Sacch. diastaticus,* although not on its own.

To detect wild yeast in brewing yeast, Lin (1973) recommends plating about 2×10^5 cells on SDM and incubating at 30 °C for 4–5 days. Culture ale and lager yeasts themselves gave small colonies, from which the large ones of *Sacch. cerevisiae* var. *ellipsoideus* and *C. mycoderma* were easily distinguishable, but colonies of *C. tropicalis, T. kefyr* and *Sacch. fermentati* resembled those of culture yeasts. Since most yeasts thus detected were lysine-negative, SDM is useful for detecting them (Lin 1974a).

Lin (1974b) devised a medium, containing glucose, malt extract, yeast extract, phosphate, ammonium chloride, crystal violet and fuchsin–sulphite mixture, which prevented the growth of ale and lager yeasts, but supported that of 15 test wild yeasts, excepting the lysine-positive *Sacch. fermentati* and *T. kefyr*. Distinct colonies were visible after 5 days at 30 °C.

Lin (1975a) classified five differential media into group I (lysine and actidione media) suitable to detect wild yeasts other than those in the genus *Saccharomyces,* more species and a higher proportion being detected by the lysine medium; and group II comprising media suitable for detecting wild *Saccharomyces* spp. (crystal violet, SDM and Lin's medium). Lin preferred his medium and recommended that it and lysine medium be employed together to detect wild yeasts in the brewery.

When membrane filtration is applied to concentrate organisms in samples containing few cells, Lin (1975b) showed that caution must be exercised. He found that detection of wild yeasts was difficult with cellulosic membranes because they counteracted inhibition of all lager and some wild yeasts on actidione, crystal violet or Lin's medium, but a polycarbonate filter did not. The behaviour of ale yeasts was not affected by the type of membrane and most wild yeasts in low concentrations in liquid samples were readily detected by the polycarbonate filter used in conjunction with lysine or Lin's medium.

The different sensitivities of yeasts to inhibition by actidione were applied by Harris and Watson (1968) to differentiate strains of brewing yeast on hopped wort agar containing a critical concentration of actidione (0·06 μg/ml), while brewing and wild yeasts were distinguishable with 0·16 μg of actidione per ml.

3. Serological Methods

By virtue of the antigenic macromolecular polysaccharides situated at, or near, the yeast cell surface and the qualitative differences in some of them according to genus, species and even strain of yeast, immunological reactions can be applied for the highly specific, sensitive and rapid detection and enumeration of wild yeasts.

Immunological sera are usually prepared by intravenous injections of saline suspensions of pure cultures of yeasts into rabbits in increasing doses over a period of about two months: blood is then withdrawn, the globulin antibody fraction is precipitated from it by half-saturation with ammonium sulphate and then submitted to "cross-absorption" to produce an antiserum, which combines specifically with cells of the same species as that injected. Cross-absorption is performed to remove from the serum antibodies common to several species or strains. Thus, in the present context, a serum prepared against a wild yeast would be treated with cells of the culture yeast, leaving an antiserum reacting only with the antigens of the wild yeast. The cross-absorption technique is described by Campbell and Allan (1964). Antisera thus prepared are usually applied to detect and enumerate wild yeasts by the techniques of immunofluorescent microscopy, or slide agglutination.

(a) *Immunofluorescent (IMF) microscopy*

In this technique, antisera are cross-absorbed and chemically coupled to fluorescein isothiocyanate to yield fluorescent antibodies, which attach themselves to the appropriate yeast, cells of which thus fluoresce in ultraviolet light and are readily seen and counted under a fluorescence microscope. The technique was applied to baker's yeast by Kunz and Klaushofer (1959). Details of the method recommended by the Institute of Brewing are given by Pierce (1973).

Using two sera, carefully cross-absorbed with a brewing *Sacch. cerevisiae,* Richards and Cowland (1967) detected all brewery contaminants of the genus *Saccharomyces* and, with a controlled cross-absorption procedure with a carefully selected brewing strain, they distinguished also some wild strains of *cerevisiae* itself. To detect wild *Saccharomyces* in lager yeasts, Richards (1969) had to apply two sera combinations absorbed by two different strains of *Sacch. uvarum,* representing the serological subgroups I and II, which correspond, in general, with the two antigenically distinct groups found by Campbell and Allan (1964) (see section IV.C.3(b)).

Richards (1972) found that, while all 15 strains representing 7 species of *Saccharomyces* were antigenically distinct by immunofluorescence, the sero-types showed a continuous spectrum of antigenic properties. He therefore rejects serological properties as a useful taxonomic feature, but regards them as valuable for the rapid detection of contaminants.

The IMF reactions of antisera against *Sacch. diastaticus, Sacch. uvarum* and *Sacch. cerevisiae* var. *ellipsoideus* were tested by Haikara and Mäkinen (1972) with 10 *carlsbergensis* and 35 wild yeast strains. No distinction could be made until the sera were cross-absorbed with a *carlsbergensis* strain, when 22 of the wild yeasts, including 14 *Saccharomyces* yeasts, were detectable. From experiments with 61 pure culture wild and 93 pitching yeasts, Haikara and Enari (1975) concluded that the IMF technique was more sensitive, quicker and revealed more genera than methods depending on selective media. They prepared antisera for *Sacch. diastaticus, uvarum, cerevisiae* var. *ellipsoideus, pastorianus* and *C. guilliermondii* and, except the latter (where it was unnecessary), cross-absorbed them with a *carlsbergensis* brewing strain. The *C. guilliermondii* serum was the most effective, revealing 61% of the wild yeasts, some of which were not detected by other sera. Applied to serial brewery re-pitchings, the IMF technique showed that wild yeast counts, when referred to the number of viable cells of brewing yeasts, increased in proportion to the number of pitchings.

(b) *Slide agglutination tests*

Essentially, these tests consist in mixing a loopful of serum with one of yeast suspension on a microscope slide and observing for agglutination (clumping) of cells indicative of a positive reaction. In their application to yeasts in general and to yeasts of brewing significance in particular, Campbell and his co-workers have been pre-eminent, while Kocková-Kratochvílová and Sandula (1963) applied a modification of the method, based on a two-stage diffusion in agar. In practice, slide agglutination tests are less suitable for enumeration work than is immunofluorescence.

By these tests, Campbell and Allan (1964) demonstrated two antigenic groups among 19 strains of *Sacch. cerevisiae* corresponding to the morphological subdivisions *cerevisiae* and *cerevisiae* var. *ellipsoideus.* All 12 strains of *cerevisiae* possessed three distinct antigens, only one of which was carried by the seven strains of the variant, which had an additional antigen absent from *cerevisiae.* Since the antigenic structure of *cerevisiae,* but not of its *ellipsoideus* variant, differed from those of several other *Saccharomyces* species tested, a method for the serological identification of *Sacch. cerevisiae* presented itself. However, agglutination tests with six specific antisera applied to 46 species of yeasts in 12 genera showed less obvious differences, several genera containing no antigenically distinct species and being antigenically identical with other genera (Campbell, 1971a). Nevertheless, brewing strains of *Saccharomyces* were distinguishable from most of the species tested and could readily be detected by IMF microscopy. Campbell (1972a) described a simplified scheme for identifying yeasts, after isolating them on normal or selective media, or by membrane filtration. The isolates are cultured and the cultures tested serologically and morphologically, colonies of the same species having the same appearance and cells of the same species the same morphology and serological properties.

By agglutination tests, Campbell and Brudzynski (1966) showed that there appear to be two antigenically distinct groups of *Sacch. uvarum* (*carlsbergensis*), although they were neither morphologically nor physiologically distinct. They prepared a serum which agglutinated three *uvarum* strains, but not cells of ten other *Saccharomyces* spp., while nine other *uvarum* strains, *diastaticus* and *cerevisiae* var. *ellipsoideus* were serologically identical.

Campbell (1967) showed that *Sacch. cerevisiae* and *Sacch. rouxii* were antigenically unique and distinguishable by agglutination from all other *Saccharomyces*. However, flocculent and non-flocculent yeasts of the same species, despite the different proportions of mannan in their cell walls, were antigenically identical and fining properties and antigenic grouping did not correlate. Serological differences depended on cell-wall polysaccharides, which could be extracted and reacted with antibody, whereas cell-wall protein components reacted only feebly, if at all.

(c) *Serology and yeast classification*

Sufficient has already been said to indicate that serology has applications in yeast classification. In this field, too, Campbell has made important contributions, following earlier demonstrations by agglutination tests of differences between species of *Saccharomyces, Hansenula, Candida* and *Torulopsis* by Tsuchiya *et al.* (1957, 1961) and between species of *Saccharomyces* by Sandula *et al.* (1964).

Campbell (1967) identified, in *Saccharomyces* spp. seven antigens in individual species in different combinations of one, two or three. By cross-absorption, he prepared diagnostic sera, by which *uvarum* strains could be divided into the antigenic groups I and II already mentioned (section III.C.3(a)). Group II strains *diastaticus* and *ellipsoideus* all had the same antigenic structure. Having prepared nine diagnostic sera from six *Saccharomyces* spp., after cross-absorption with five different *Saccharomyces* spp., Campbell (1969) allocated strains to four groups (A–D) according to reaction with four "primary" sera, which identified some species, but only distinguished groups of others, some of which could be distinguished by reaction with five "secondary" diagnostic sera. Campbell (1970) found that classification of 28 *Saccharomyces* spp. by serology was compatible with that based on 9 standard morphological and 35 standard physiological tests and 4 tests of fining properties. From computer analyses of these tests, he distinguished ten groups which agreed well with their serological groupings. He concluded that, by a rapid slide agglutination test with his sera A, B, C and D, an isolate of the genus *Saccharomyces* could be placed in its appropriate taxonomic group; for more precise identification, his "secondary" sera 1, 2 and 5 must also be applied.

From a similar study of 47 species from 13 genera (including *Saccharomyces*), Campbell (1971c) concluded that, while most groups were antigenically homogeneous, serology alone did not serve to distinguish taxonomic groups. For the rapid identification of the species he tested, Campbell presented a key based on properties of agglutination (or IMF) with six sera, anaerobic growth, cell morphology, formation of pseudomycelium and growth on synthetic medium with lysine or nitrate as sole source of nitrogen.

When he applied numerical analysis to 15 morphological and 43 physiological characters to the genera *Saccharomyces* and *Kluyveromyces*, Campbell (1972b) found that, on the basis of 90% matching of the various characters, 23 groups of *Saccharomyces* differed sufficiently to warrant species differentiation and four main subgroups (70% matching of characters) were distinguished: *cerevisiae, exiguus, florentinus* and *rouxii*. The *Kluyveromyces* spp. were so closely related to those of *Saccharomyces* that he proposed they be included in the latter genus. Following a study in which he fed to a computer the results of assimilation and fermentation tests, serological properties, growth in 8% and 10% ethanol, anaerobic growth and the clearing of chalk and tributyrin agars (each species being defined by 58 characters), Campbell (1973a) proposed a system allowing identification of the combined genus *Saccharomyces + Kluyveromyces*, in which equal value was attached to all tests. However, the system provided no short cuts to identification, because all 58 tests had to be done to identify species: for rapid identification, he preferred serological reactions and morphology.

After applying the same numerical analysis to examine the relationship between *Hansenula, Pichia, Debaryomyces*, seven other sporogenous genera and *Brettanomyces*, Campbell (1973b) has made several proposals for their reclassification, which await general acceptance.

D. New Methods of Detection

In modern breweries, there are special problems of microbiological quality control associated with the detection of a few living cells in large volumes of beer being presented to high-speed packaging lines. Such contamination might arise from imperfections of plant hygiene, filtration or pasteurization, its introduction during the process of packaging, or from imperfectly sterilized containers and filling equipment. Essentially, the problems are those of rapid detection of cells in high dilution.

Harrison *et al.* (1974) reviewed methods of rapid detection under four headings: those depending on (a) biochemical characteristics; (b) changes in the medium contingent on growth or metabolism of cells; (c) physical properties; and (d) staining. Among (a) are methods measuring the light produced when luminol is activated by haem compounds and when luciferin emits flashes of light under the influence of luciferase and ATP; or measurement of the NAD-activated reduction of tetrazolium salts to coloured formazans; or, again, measurement of the acids or fluorescent compounds produced on hydrolysis of certain esters. In all these cases, the living cell provides the haem compound, ATP, NAD or esterase on which the respective reaction depends. Under (b), they list changes of pH or conductance, evolution of ^{14}C-labelled carbon dioxide, uptake of radioactive substrate, or the detection of volatile metabolic products by gas chromatography. Under (c), are listed gravimetry, silting index, cell counting and turbidity; and under (d), direct staining of individual cells or micro-colonies and their microscopic examination and the collection of cells on a transparent tape, followed by staining and electronic scanning. These authors developed a method in which organisms were inoculated into a glucose–yeast extract–Tween 80 medium and changes in pH were followed. In their system, significant changes of pH were caused by *Saccharomyces cerevisiae* or *Lactobacillus fermentum* in 30 h and by *Acetobacter rancens* or *Zymomonas anaerobia* in 40 h: the time required for detection diminishing with greater inocula, so that gross contamination would be detected in 0·5–6 h.

Portno and Molzahn (1977) point out two inadequacies of methods of microbiological control as applied to beer during packaging: (i) the "biological time" between sampling and obtaining results is too great to allow corrective action to be taken and despatch prevented when beer does not attain the necessary microbiological standard; and (ii) with batch or in-line sampling of supposedly sterile beers, neither the time nor the period of duration of infection can be established. They consider that methods in which conventional techniques are accelerated are of limited value; they require 16–24 h and only detect relatively high levels of contamination. Such methods are those which depend on membrane filtration and direct examination of the micro-colonies developed after incubation on agar medium (Middlekauff *et al.* 1967) or on filter paper soaked in saffranin (Richards 1970).

Rapid detection of contaminants by radio-tracer techniques are of two kinds. That described by Bourgeois *et al.* (1973) depends on the assimilation of ^{14}C by cells separated on membrane filters and incubated at 28 °C for 9–24 h on a synthetic medium containing ^{14}C-lysine. With *Sacch. uvarum,* 10 cells/membrane were detected in 9 h and 1 cell/membrane in 24 h. The second method depends on the evolution of labelled carbon dioxide, usually by the fermentation of ^{14}C-glucose. In the hands of Harrison *et al.* (1974), 10–100 cells of *Sacch. cerevisiae* per ml were detected in 15 h, or 10^4 cells/ml in 4 h, but about 36 h of incubation were necessary to detect 10^4 zymomonads per ml. That the method detected neither *Acetobacter rancens* nor *Lactobacillus fermentum* is to be expected, since these bacteria produce no or comparatively little carbon dioxide from glucose, but it might be successful with them if labelled calcium carbonate ($Ca^{14}CO_3$) were included in the incubation medium. Box and Ferguson (1975) enhanced the sensitivity of the method with an improved, more complex incubation medium and by aspirating the evolved ^{14}C-labelled carbon dioxide through a "cold finger" to remove water vapour into the scintillation counting fluid. In experiments with an ale yeast, they detected 25 cells in 8 h and fewer than 5 cells in 24 h.

Neither of these radio-tracer techniques is rapid and sensitive enough for the quality control applications envisaged by Portno and Molzahn (1977), who describe a method based on the hydrolysis of fluorescein diacetate by the esterase activity of contaminating cells (Paton and Jones 1975). They collected their commercial beer samples in sodium acetate solution (to give a final concentration of 0·5%), this salt acting to promote esterase activity as a necessary preliminary to the reliable assessment of contamination. The contaminants, after collection on a black membrane filter, were treated *in situ* with fluorescein diacetate at pH 7·2 for 15 min, washed, counterstained with rhodamine B at pH 7·6, again washed and the filter then scanned with a special microscope with incident blue light (420 nm). Living cells of yeasts and bacteria present in the sample are revealed by their green-yellow fluorescence, while dead cells (which rapidly lose their esterase activity) appear pink-brown. The procedure takes 20 min plus the time taken to scan, which may vary from 10 sec, for heavily contaminated samples, to the 15 min required to scan the whole membrane when no cells are present. One viable yeast cell is readily identifiable, bacterial cells less so, unless present in large numbers. Unless viable counts were very low, agreement between results obtained by the method and those by conventional plate counts were good. The same paper describes equipment performing automatic, continuous, microbiological sampling of beer on strips of sterile, cloth-reinforced membrane filter. The device enables a continuous record to be made of the microbiological state of beer passing a sample point and, used in conjunction with the fluorescence method of detection, allows continuous detection of contaminants rapidly enough to eliminate the inadequacies of methods of microbiological quality control as stated by Portno and Molzahn.

V. CONCLUSIONS

That losses of beer from microbiological spoilage are less serious than of yore is largely the result of improved brewery hygiene and the pasteurization or sterile filtration of beer. Concerning the former, not only have brewery cleaning techniques improved, but so also has the related matter of design of plant and equipment, both in the brewery and at point-of-sale. Concerning the latter, the high proportion of pasteurized packaged beer must be noted. Indeed, it can be said that prevention is the keynote of the control of microbial beer spoilage and it seems logical to predict that, by further and improved applications of hygienic practices in the brewery and at the sales outlet, it will become a rare occurrence.

Control of spoilage is also conceivable through nutritional or metabolic factors. Thus, avoidance of access of air to finished beer is perhaps the most important factor determining the comparative rareness of acetic spoilage in unpasteurized beers, while the effects of vigorous yeast growth and fermentation in removing essential nutrients, coupled with the prevention of leakage of yeast cell contents into beer, undoubtedly discourage the growth of lactic acid bacteria. However, the attainment of an absolute deficiency of one or more nutrilites in beer may rarely be attainable (and, for wild yeasts and acetic acid bacteria, even impossible) and likely to be incompatible with the type of beer being brewed. The other possibility, of using inhibitors or preservatives outside the range of "natural" beer components to prevent microbial proliferation in beer, is undesirable on aesthetic grounds and unworthy of consideration when more attractive preventive alternatives are available.

Finally, the possibility of biological control of beer spoilage microorganisms merits brief speculation. Are there highly specific phages which might be applied unobjectionably to control the bacteria concerned? Equally, are there specific parasites which might control wild yeasts? None have yet been found. Does the phenomenon of killer yeasts hold any key to the biological control of wild yeasts?

It seems to the present writer that the preventive approach through improvements in hygiene and plant and equipment design is the only unequivocally desirable method of control of microbial beer spoilage: indeed, it could attain such a state of excellance that pasteurization, with its attendant high energy consumption and product flavour changes, could be eliminated.

REFERENCES

Andrews, J. and Gilliland, R. B. (1952). *J. Inst. Brew.* **58**, 189.

Arkima, V. (1973). *Proc. E.B.C. Congr., Salzburg* p. 309.

Armstrong, H. E. (1937). *J. Inst. Brew.* **43**, 375.

Asai, T. (1968). "Acetic Acid Bacteria, Classification and Biochemical Activities". University of Tokyo Press, Tokyo.

Asai, T. and Shoda, K. (1958). *J. Gen. Appl. Microbiol.* **4**, 289.

Atkinson, D. E. (1956). *J. Bact.* **72**, 195.

Ault, R. G. (1954). *Brewers' Guild J.* **40**, 391.

Ault, R. G. and Newton, R. (1971). *In* "Modern Brewing Technology" (W. P. K. Findlay, ed.), p. 164. Macmillan, London.

Ault, R. G. and Woodward, J. D. (1965). *J. Inst. Brew.* **71**, 36.

Baker, J. L., Day, F. E. and Hulton, H. F. E. (1912). *J. Inst. Brew.* **18**, 651.

Baker, J. L., Ward, T. J. and Hulton, H. F. E. (1929). *J. Inst. Brew.* **35**, 458.

Balcke, J. (1884). *Wschr. Brau.* **1**, 181.

Barker, S. A., Pautard, F., Siddiqui, I. R. and Stacey, M. (1955). *Chem. Ind.* p. 1450.
Barker, S. A., Bourne, E. J., Bruce, G. T. and Stacey, M. (1958). *J. Chem. Soc.* p. 4414.
Beijerinck, M. W. (1898). *Cent. Bakt.* **4**, 209, 214.
Belaïch, J.-P. and Senez, J. C. (1965). *J. Bact.* **89**, 1195.
Ben-Zvi, R. and Schramm, M. (1961). *J. Biol. Chem.* **236**, 2186.
Bernstein, L., Blenkinship, B. K. and Brenner, M. W. (1968). *Proc. Ann. Meet. Am. Soc. Brew. Chem.* p. 150.
Bertrand, G. (1896). *C. R. Séan. Acad. Sci.* **122**, 900.
Bertrand. G. (1898). *Ann. Inst. Pasteur* **12**, 385.
Bertrand, G. (1904). *Ann. Chim. Phys.* **3** (8), 181, 195, 227.
Bevan, E. A. and Makower, M. (1963). *Proc. 11th Congress of Genetics* **1**, 202.
Bexon, J. and Dawes, E. A. (1970). *J. Gen. Microbiol.* **60**, 421.
Bourgeois, C. (1969). *Biotechnique* p. 2.
Bourgeois, C., Mafort, P. and Thouvenot, D. (1973). *Proc. E.B.C., Salzburg* p. 219.
Boutroux, L. (1880). *C. R. Séan. Acad. Sci.* **91**, 236.
Box, T. C. and Ferguson, B. (1975). *Proc. Ann. Meet. Am. Soc. Brew. Chem.* p. 133.
Brady, B. L. (1958). *J. Inst. Brew.* **64**, 304.
Brady, B. L. and Hough, J. S. (1961). *J. Inst. Brew.* **67**, 438.
Breed, R. S., Murray, E. G. D. and Smith, N. R. (1957). "Bergey's Manual of Determinative Bacteriology", 7th edition, p. 541. The Williams & Wilkins Co., Baltimore.
Brenner, M. W. and Hsu, W. P. (1971). *Tech. Quart., Master Brewers Ass. Am.* **8**, 45.
Brenner, M. W., Karpiscak, M., Stern, H. and Hsu, W. P. (1970). *Proc. Ann. Meet. Am. Soc. Brew. Chem.* p. 79.
Brown, A. J. (1885). *J. Chem. Soc.* **49**, 172.
Brown, A. J. (1886). *J. Chem. Soc.* **50**, 463.
Brown, A. J. (1887). *J. Chem. Soc.* **51**, 638.
Brown, G. D. and Rainbow, C. (1956). *J. Gen. Microbiol.* **15**, 61.
Brown, H. T. (1916). *J. Inst. Brew.* **22**, 265, 327.
Bunker, H. J. (1961). *In* "Progress in Industrial Microbiology" (D. J. D. Hockenhull, ed.), Vol. 3, p. 27. Heywood and Co., London.
Burma, D. P. and Horecker, B. L. (1958). *J. Biol. Chem.* **231**, 1039, 1053.
Bussey, H. (1972). *Nature, London.* **235**, 73.
Campbell, I. (1967). *Proc. E.B.C. Congr., Madrid* p. 145.
Campbell, I. (1969). *J. Appl. Bact.* **31**, 515.
Campbell, I. (1970). *J. Gen. Microbiol.* **63**, 189.
Campbell, I. (1971a). *J. Appl. Bact.* **34**, 237.
Campbell, I. (1971b). *Tech. Quart., Master Brewers Ass. Am.* **8**, 129.
Campbell, I. (1971c). *J. Gen. Microbiol.* **67**, 223.
Campbell, I. (1972a). *J. Inst. Brew.* **78**, 225.
Campbell, I. (1972b). *J. Gen Microbiol.* **73**, 279.
Campbell, I. (1973a). *J. Gen. Microbiol.* **77**, 127.
Campbell, I. (1973b). *J. Gen. Microbiol.* **77**, 427.
Campbell, I. and Allan, A. M. (1964). *J. Inst. Brew.* **70**, 316.
Campbell, I. and Brudzynski, A. (1966). *J. Inst. Brew.* **72**, 556.
Campbell, I. and Thompson, J. W. (1970). *J. Inst. Brew.* **75**, 465.
Carr, J. G. (1974). *In* "Bergey's Manual of Determinative Bacteriology" (R. E. Buchanan and N. E. Gibbons, eds), 8th edition, p. 353. The Williams and Wilkins Co., Baltimore.
Chevalier, M. (1946). *Petit J. Brass.* **54**, 186.

Claussen, N. H. (1904). *J. Inst. Brew.* **10**, 308.

Clausen, O. G., Hegna, I. K. and Solberg, O. (1975). *J. Inst. Brew.* **81**, 440.

Comrie, A. A. D. (1939). *J. Inst. Brew.* **45**, 342.

Cooksey, K. E. and Rainbow, C. (1962). *J. Gen Microbiol.* **27**, 135.

Cosbie, A. J. C., Tosic, J. and Walker, T. K. (1941). *J. Inst. Brew.* **47**, 382.

Cosbie, A. J. C., Tosic, J. and Walker, T. K. (1942). *J. Inst. Brew.* **48**, 82.

Cosbie, A. J. C., Tosic, J. and Walker, T. K. (1943). *J. Inst. Brew.* **49**, 88.

Coster, E. and White, H. (1964). *J. Gen Microbiol.* **37**, 15.

Curtis, N. S. and Wenham, S. (1958). *J. Inst. Brew.* **64**, 421.

Czarnecki, H. T. and van Engel, E. L. (1959). *Brewers' Digest* **34** (3), 52.

Dean, R. T. (1957). *J. Inst. Brew.* **63**, 36.

De Ley, J. (1961). *J. Gen. Microbiol.* **24**, 31.

De Ley, J. and Frateur, J. (1974). *In* "Bergey's Manual of Determinative Bacteriology" (R. E. Buchanan and N. E. Gibbons, eds), 8th edition, pp. 251, 276. The Williams and Wilkins Co., Baltimore.

Dolin, M. J. (1961). *In* "The Bacteria" (I. C. Gunsalus and R. Y. Stanier eds), Vol. II, pp. 342–343. Academic Press, New York and London.

Ellison, J. and Doran, A. H. (1961). *Proc. E.B.C. Congr., Vienna* p. 224.

Emeis, C. C. (1962). *Brewer's Digest* **37** (12), 32.

Emeis, C. C. (1969). *Monats. Brau.* **22**, 8.

Eschenbecher, F. (1969). *Brauwissenschaft* **22**, 14.

Eschenbecher, F. and Ellenrieder, M. (1975). *Proc. E.B.C. Congr., Nice* p. 497.

Eto, M. and Nakagawa, A. (1975). *J. Inst. Brew.* **81**, 232.

Fewster, J. A. (1958). *Biochem. J.* **69**, 582.

Fitting, C. and Doudoroff, M. (1952). *J. Biol. Chem.* **199**, 153.

Frateur, J. (1950). *La Cellule* **53**, 287.

Garvie, E. J. (1974). *Int. J. Systematic Bact.* **24**, 301.

Gilliland, R. B. (1954). *Wallerstein Lab. Commun.* **17**, 165.

Gilliland, R. B. (1961). *J. Inst. Brew.* **67**, 257.

Gilliland, R. B. (1962). *J. Inst. Brew.* **68**, 51.

Gilliland, R. B. (1966). *J. Inst. Brew.* **72**, 271.

Gilliland, R. B. (1967). *Brewers' Guardian* (Dec.), p. 37.

Green, S. R. and Gray, P. P. (1950). *Wallerstein Lab. Commun.* **13**, 357.

Günther, H. L. and White, H. (1961). *J. Gen. Microbiol.* **26**, 199.

Haikara, A. and Enari, T.-M. (1975). *Proc. E.B.C. Congr., Nice* p. 363.

Haikara, A. and Mäkinen, V. (1972). *Brauwissenschaft* **25**, 266.

Hall, A. N. (1963). *In* "Biochemistry of Industrial Micro-organisms" (C. Rainbow and A. H. Rose eds), pp. 607–621. Academic Press, New York and London.

Hall, A. N., Thomas, G. A., Tiwari, K. S. and Walker, T. K. (1953). *Arch. Biochim. Biophys.* **46**, 485.

Hall, A. N., Husain, I., Tiwara, K. S. and Walker, T. K. (1956). *J. Appl. Bact.* **19**, 31.

Hall, J. F. (1971). *J. Inst. Brew.* **77**, 513.

Hansen, A. (1948). "Jørgensen's Micro-organisms and Fermentation", pp. 22, 264, 280, 342. Charles Griffin, London.

Hansen, E. C. (1879). *C. R. Trav. Lab., Carlsberg* **1**, 49, 96.

Hansen, E. C. (1904). *Zentr. Bakteriol. Parasitenk.,* Abt. II, **12**, 259.

Harris, J. O. and Watson, W. (1968). *J. Inst. Brew.* **74**, 286.

Harrison, J., Webb, T. J. B. and Martin, P. A. (1974). *J. Inst. Brew.* **80**, 390.

Haynes, W. C., Wickerham, L. J. and Hesseltine, C. W. (1955). *J. appl. Microbiol.* **3**, 361.

Hehre, E. J. Hamilton, D. M. (1949). *Proc. Soc. Exp. Biol., N.Y.* **71**, 336.
Helm, E. (1949). *Schweiz. Brau.-Runds., Congress Sondernummer* p. 7.
Hemmons, L. M. (1954). *J. Inst. Brew.* **60**, 288.
Hemmons, L. M. (1955). *J. Inst. Brew.* **61**, 376.
Henneberg, W. (1897). *Cent. Bakt.* **3**, 933.
Hoffmann, U. (1955). *Brauwelt* p. 1397.
Hopkins, R. H. (1955). *Proc. E.B.C. Congr., Baden-Baden* p. 52.
Inoue, T. and Yamomoto, Y. (1965). *Rep. Res. Lab. Kirin Brewing Co., Yokohama* **8**, 33.
Janesch, I. (1957). *Brauerei* **11**, 718.
Jensen, E. M. and Seeley, H. W. (1954). *J. Bact.* **67**, 486.
Jones, M. O., Cope, R. and Rainbow, C. (1975). *Proc. E.B.C. Congr., Nice* p. 669.
Kato, S. (1967). *Bull. Brew. Sci., Tokyo* **13**, 19.
Kerbaugh, M. A. and Evans, J. B. (1968). *Appl. Microbiol.* **16**, 519.
King, T. E. and Cheldelin, V. H. (1952). *J. Biol. Chem.* **198**, 127; 131.
King, T. E. and Cheldelin, V. H. (1954). *Biochem. Biophys. Acta* **14**, 108.
King, T. E. and Cheldelin, V. H. (1957). *J. Biol. Chem.* **224**, 579.
Kitahara, K. (1974). *In* "Bergey's Manual of Determinative Bacteriology" (R. E. Buchanan and N. E. Gibbons eds), 8th edition, pp. 513–515. The Williams and Wilkins Co., Baltimore.
Kitahara, K. and Nakagawa, A. (1958). *J. Gen. Appl. Microbiol.* **4**, 21.
Kitos, P. A., Wang, C. H., Mohler, B. A., King, T. E. and Cheldelin, V. H. (1958). *J. Biol. Chem.* **233**, 1295.
Knivett, V. A. (1954). *Biochem. J.* **56**, 602, 606.
Kocková-Kratochvílová, A. and Sandula, J. (1963). *Kvasný průmysl* **9**, 181.
Kreger-van Rij, N. J. W. (1970). *In* "The Yeasts" (J. Lodder, ed), p. 445. North-Holland, Amsterdam and London.
Kreil, J., Kieninger, H. and Teuber, M. (1976). *Brauwissenschaft* **29**, 102.
Kulka, D. and Walker, T. K. (1946a). *J. Inst. Brew.* **52**, 129.
Kulka, D. and Walker, T. K. (1946b). *J. Inst. Brew.* **52**, 283.
Kulka, D. and Walker, T. K. (1948). *J. Inst. Brew.* **54**, 148.
Kulka, D., Tosic, J. and Walker, T. K. (1946). *J. Inst. Brew.* **52**, 132.
Kulka, D., Tosic, J. and Walker, T. K. (1948). *J. Inst. Brew.* **54**, 126.
Kulka, D., Cosbie, A. J. C. and Walker, T. K. (1949). *J. Inst. Brew.* **55**, 315.
Kunz, C. and Klaushofer, H. (1959). *Mitt. Versuchsst. Gärungsgew. Wein* **13**, 51.
Kützing, F. T. (1837). *J. Prakt. Chem.* **11**, 385.
Leifson, E. (1954). *Antonie van Leeuwenhoek* **20**, 109.
Lewis, M. J. and Phaff, H. J. (1963). *Proc. Ann. Meet. Am. Soc. Brew. Chem.* pp. 123, 144.
Lewis, M. J. and Phaff, H. J. (1964). *J. Bact.* **87**, 1389.
Lewis, M. J. and Phaff, H. J. (1965). *J. Bact.* **89**, 960.
Lin, Y. (1973). *Brewer's Digest* **48** (5), 60.
Lin, Y. (1974a). *Brewers' Digest* **49** (3), 38.
Lin, Y. (1974b). *Proc. Ann. Meet. Am. Soc. Brew. Chem.* **32**, 69.
Lin, Y. (1975a). *J. Inst. Brew.* **81**, 410.
Lin, Y. (1975b). *Proc. Ann. Meet. Am. Soc. Brew. Chem.* **33**, 124.
Lodder, J. (1970). "The Yeasts". North-Holland, Amsterdam and London.
Lund, A. and Thygesen, P. (1957). *Proc. E.B.C. Congr., Copenhagen* p. 241.
Lutwak-Mann, C. (1938). *Biochem. J.* **32**, 1364.
Maule, A. P. and Thomas, P. D. (1973). *J. Inst. Brew.* **79**, 137.

McGill, D. J., Dawes, E. A. and Ribbons, D. W. (1965). *Biochem. J.* **97**, 44P.
Middlekauff, J. E., Shewey, D. R. and Bono, A. W. (1967). *Proc. Ann. Meet. Am. Soc. Brew. Chem.* p. 187.
Millis, N. F. (1956). *J. Gen. Microbiol.* **15**, 521.
Moore, W. B. and Rainbow, C. (1955). *J. Gen. Microbiol.* **13**, 190.
Nakagawa, A. (1964). *Bull. Brew. Sci., Tokyo* **10**, 7.
Nakagawa, A. and Kitahara, K. (1959). *J. Gen. Appl. Microbiol.* **5**, 95.
Nakagawa, A. and Kitahara, K. (1962). *J. Gen. Appl. Microbiol.* **8**, 142.
Nakayama, T. (1959). *J. Biochem.* **46**, 1217.
Nakayama, T. (1960). *J. Biochem.* **48**, 813.
Nakayama, T. (1961a). *J. Biochem.* **49**, 158.
Nakayama, T. (1961b). *J. Biochem.* **49**, 240.
Neuberg, C. and Windisch, F. (1925). *Biochem. Z.* **166**, 454.
Pasteur, L. (1864). *Ann. Sci. École Norm. Sup., Paris* **1**, 113.
Pasteur, L. (1866). "Études sur le Vin" Masson, Paris.
Pasteur, L. (1868). "Études sur le Vinaigre" Through "Oevres de Pasteur" (P. Vallery-Radot, ed.) Vol. III. Masson, Paris (1924).
Pasteur, L. (1876). "Études sur la Bière" Gauthier-Villars, Paris.
Paton, A. M. and Jones, S. M. (1975). *J. Appl. Bact.* **38**, 199.
Pederson, C. S., Albury, M. N. and Breed, R. T. (1954). *Wallerstein Lab. Commun.* **17**, 1.
Persoon, C. H. (1822). *Mycologia Europea* **1**, 96.
Phaff, H. J. (1970). In "The Yeasts" (J. Lodder, ed.) pp. 209, 1146. North-Holland, Amsterdam and London.
Phaff, H. J. and Ahearne, D. G. (1970). In "The Yeasts" (J. Lodder, ed.), p. 1215 *et seq.* North-Holland, Amsterdam and London.
Philliskirk, G. and Young, T. W. (1975). *Antonie van Leeuwenhoek* **41**, 147.
Pierce, J. S. (1973). *J. Inst. Brew.* **79**, 134.
Portno, A. D. and Molzahn, S. W. (1977). *Brewers' Digest* **52**, 44.
Prescott, S. C. and Dunn, C. G. (1959). "Industrial Microbiology", 3rd edition, p. 428. McGraw-Hill, New York and London.
Priest, F. G. and Hough, J. S. (1974). *J. Inst. Brew.* **80**, 370.
Priest, F. G., Cole, J. A. and Hough, J. S. (1973). *J. Gen. Microbiol.* **75**, 295.
Priest, F. G., Cowbourne, M. A. and Hough, J. S. (1974). *J. Inst. Brew.* **80**, 342.
Prieur, P. (1957). *C. R. Séan. Acad. Sci.* **244**, 253.
Rainbow, C. (1958). *J. Inst. Brew.* **64**, 135.
Rainbow, C. (1961). In "Progress in Industrial Microbiology" (D. J. D. Hockenhull, ed.), Vol. 3, p. 43. Heywood and Co., London.
Rainbow, C. (1965). *Brewers' Digest* **40** (2), 50.
Rainbow, C. (1966). *Wallerstein Lab. Commun.* **29**, 5.
Rainbow, C. (1970). In "The Yeasts" (A. H. Rose and J. S. Harrison, eds), Vol. III, pp. 147–224. Academic Press, New York and London.
Rainbow, C. (1971). *Process Biochem.* **6** (4), 15.
Rainbow, C. (1975). In "Lactic Acid Bacteria in Beverages and Food" (J. G. Carr, C. V. Cutting and G. C. Whiting, eds), p, 149. Academic Press, London and New York.
Rainbow, C. and Mitson, G. W. (1953). *J. Gen. Microbiol.* **9**, 371.
Rao, M. R. R. and Gunsalus, I. C. (1955). *Fed. Proc.* **14**, 267.
Rao, M. R. R. and Stokes, J. L. (1953). *J. Bact.* **65**, 405.
Ribbons, D. W. and Dawes, E. A. (1961). *Biochem. J.* **81**, 3P.
Richards, M. (1968). *J. Inst. Brew.* **74**, 433.

Richards, M. (1969). *J. Inst. Brew.* **75**, 476.
Richards, M. (1970). *Wallerstein Lab. Commun.* **33**, 97.
Richards, M. (1972). *Antonie van Leeuwenhoek* **38**, 177.
Richards, M. and Cowland, T. W. (1967). *J. Inst. Brew.* **73**, 552.
Richtmeyer, N. K., Stewart, L. C. and Hudson, C. S. (1950). *J. Am. Chem. Soc.* **72**, 4934.
Rogosa, M. (1974). *In* "Bergey's Manual of Determinative Bacteriology" (R. E. Buchanan and N. E. Gibbons, eds), 8th edition, p. 576. The Williams and Wilkins Co., Baltimore.
Rudin, A. D. (1958). *J. Inst. Brew.* **64**, 392.
Russell, C., Bhandari, R. R. and Walker, T. K. (1954). *J. Gen. Microbiol.* **10**, 371.
Sakaguchi, K. (1960). *Bull. Agric. Chem. Soc. Japan* **26**, 638.
Sakaguchi, K. (1962). *Rep. Noda Inst. Sci. Res., Japan* **6**, 13.
Sandula, J., Kocková-Kratochvílová, A. and Zameknikova, M. (1964). *Brauwissenschaft* **17**, 130.
Scherrer, A., Sommer, A. and Pfenninger, H. (1969). *Brauwissenschaft* **22**, 191; 273.
Schieger, Z. and Schramm, M. (1961). *J. Biol. Chem.* **236**, 2183.
Seidl, H. (1973). *Brauwissenschaft* **26**, 179.
Seidl, H. and Lofflmann, W. (1975). *Brauwissenschaft* **28**, 39.
Shimwell, J. L. (1935a). *J. Inst. Brew.* **41**, 245.
Shimwell, J. L. (1935b). *J. Inst. Brew.* **41**, 481.
Shimwell, J. L. (1936a). *J. Inst. Brew.* **42**, 119.
Shimwell, J. L. (1936b). *J. Inst. Brew.* **42**, 452.
Shimwell, J. L. (1936c). *J. Inst. Brew.* **42**, 585.
Shimwell, J. L. (1937). *J. Inst. Brew.* **43**, 507.
Shimwell, J. L. (1938). *J. Inst. Brew.* **44**, 563.
Shimwell, J. L. (1941). *Wallerstein Lab. Commun.* **4**, 41.
Shimwell, J. L. (1947a). *J. Inst. Brew.* **53**, 280.
Shimwell, J. L. (1947b). *Wallerstein Lab. Commun.* **10**, 29, 119, 195.
Shimwell, J. L. (1948a). *J. Inst. Brew.* **54**, 237.
Shimwell, J. L. (1948b). *Wallerstein Lab. Commun.* **11**, 27.
Shimwell, J. L. (1948c). *Wallerstein Lab. Commun.* **11**, 135.
Shimwell, J. L. (1949). *Wallerstein Lab. Commun.* **12**, 71, 187, 267, 349.
Shimwell, J. L. (1950). *J. Inst. Brew.* **56**, 179.
Shimwell, J. L. (1952). *Brewers' J.* **88**, 209.
Shimwell, J. L. (1958). *Antonie van Leeuwenhoek* **24**, 187.
Shimwell, J. L. (1959). *Brewers' J.* **95**, 41.
Shimwell, J. L. (1960). *Brewers' Digest* **35** (7), 38.
Shimwell, J. L. (1963). *Brewers' J.* **99**, 759.
Shimwell, J. L. (1964). *J. Inst. Brew.* **70**, 247.
Shimwell, J. L. and Grimes, M. (1936). *J. Inst. Brew.* **42**, 348.
Shimwell, J. L. and Kirkpatrick, W. F. (1939). *J. Inst. Brew.* **45**, 137.
Snell, E. E. and Strong, F. M. (1939). *Ind. Eng. Chem., Anal. Edn.* **11**, 346.
Solberg, O. and Clausen, O. G. (1973a). *J. Inst. Brew.* **79**, 227.
Solberg, O. and Clausen, O. G. (1973b). *J. Inst. Brew.* **79**, 231.
Stouthamer, A. H. (1959). *Antonie van Leeuwenhoek* **25**, 241.
Strandskov, F. B. and Bockelmann, J. B. (1955). *Wallerstein Lab. Commun.* **18**, 275.
Strandskov, F. B. and Bockelmann, J. B. (1956). *Wallerstein Lab. Commun.* **19**, 313.
Strandskov, F. B. and Bockelmann, J. B. (1957). *Proc. Ann. Meet. Am. Soc. Brew. Chem.* p. 94.

Strandskov, F. B., Baker, H. W. and Bockelmann, J. B. (1953). *Wallerstein Lab. Commun.* **16**, 261.

Sydow, H. and Sydow, P. (1919). *Ann. Mycol.* **17**, 33.

Tanenbaum, S. W. (1956). *Biochim. Biophys. Acta* **21**, 335, 343.

Thomas, M., Cole, J. A. and Hough, J. S. (1972). *J. Inst. Brew.* **78**, 332.

Thorwest, A. (1965). *Brauwelt* **105**, 845.

Tosic, J. and Walker, T. K. (1943). *J. Inst. Brew.* **49**, 276.

Tosic, J. and Walker, T. K. (1944). *J. Inst. Brew.* **50**, 296.

Tsuchiya, T., Fukazawa, Y., Hayashi, S., Amemiya, S. and Sano, Y. (1957). *Japan J. Microbiol.* **1**, 205.

Tsuchiya, T., Fukagawa, Y. and Yamase, Y. (1961). *Japan J. Microbiol.* **5**, 417.

Van der Walt, J. P. (1970). *In* "The Yeasts" (J. Lodder, ed.), pp. 34, 555, 863. North-Holland, Amsterdam and London.

Van Laer, H. (1892). *Académie Royale de Belgique,* **47**, 1.

Van Uden, N. and Buckley, H. (1970). *In* "The Yeasts" (J. Lodder, ed.), pp. 893, 1067, 1073. North-Holland, Amsterdam and London.

Van Uden, N. and Vidal-Leiria, M. (1970). *In* "The Yeasts" (J. Lodder, ed.), p. 1235. North-Holland, Amsterdam and London.

Vaughn, R. H. (1942). *Wallerstein Lab. Commun.* **5**, 5.

Walker, T. K. and Kulka, D. (1949). *Wallerstein Lab. Commun.* **12**, 7.

Walker, T. K. and Tosic, J. (1945). *J. Inst. Brew.* **51**, 245.

Walker, T. K. and Wiles, A. E. (1952). *J. Inst. Brew.* **58**, 140.

Walters, L. S. and Thiselton, M. R. (1953). *J. Inst. Brew.* **59**, 401.

Weeks, O. B. (1974). *In* "Bergey's Manual of Determinative Bacteriology" (R. E. Buchanan and N. E. Gibbons, eds), 8th edition, pp. 357, 363. The Williams and Wilkins Co., Baltimore.

Weinfurtner, F. (1957). *Brauwissenschaft* p. 127.

Weinfurtner, F., Uhl, A. and Pöhlmann, R. (1955). *Brauwissenschaft* pp. 166, 192.

Weinfurtner, F., Eschenbecher, F. and Thoss, G. (1962). *Brauwelt* p. 1485.

Wickerham, L. J. (1970). *In* "The Yeasts" (J. Lodder, ed.), p. 226. North-Holland, Amsterdam and London.

Wieland, H. and Bertho, A. (1928). *Liebig's Ann.* **467**, 95.

Wiles, A. E. (1949). *J. Inst. Brew.* **55**, 165, 172.

Wiles, A. E. (1950). *J. Inst. Brew.* **56**, 183.

Wiles, A. E. (1951). *Proc. E.B.C. Congr., Brighton* p. 84.

Wiles, A. E. (1953). *J. Inst. Brew.* **59**, 265.

Wiles, A. E. (1954). *Wallerstein Lab. Commun.* **17**, 259.

Wiles, A. E. (1956). *Brewers' Guild J.* **42**, 459.

Wiles, A. E. (1956). *Brewers' Digest* **36** (1), 40.

Williams, P. J. le B. and Rainbow, C. (1964). *J. Gen. Microbiol.* **35**, 237.

Williamson, D. H. (1959). *J. Inst. Brew.* **65**, 154.

Windisch, S. (1955). *Proc. E.B.C. Congr., Baden-Baden* p. 69.

Windisch, S. (1962a). *Schweiz. Brau.-Runds.* **73**, 2.

Windisch, S. (1962b). *Colloques sur les Levures, Nancy* p. 61.

Wood, B. J. B. and Rainbow, C. (1961). *Biochem. J.* **78**, 204.

Wood, W. A. (1961). *In* "The Bacteria" (I. C. Gunsalus and R. Y. Stanier, eds), p. 59 *et seq.* Academic Press, New York and London.

Woods, D. R. and Bevan, E. A. (1968). *J. Gen. Microbiol.* **51**, 115.

Young, T. W. and Philliskirk, G. (1975). *Proc. E.B.C. Congr., Nice* p. 333.

10. Brewery and Malthouse Effluents and their Management

J. D. G. ARMITT

Castlemaine Perkins, Brisbane, Australia

The malting and brewing industries throughout the world generally have recognized their responsibilities towards the environment. Both industries consume large volumes of water, discharging the vast majority as liquid effluents. The quality of the effluent discharged is primarily a function of the standard of house-keeping adopted and the conditions and charges imposed by the controlling authority. Conversely, the conditions imposed by the authority depend to a very large extent on the siting of the malthouse and/or brewery, the size of operation and the volume and quality of effluent discharged.

1. GENERAL CHARACTERISTICS OF MALTING AND BREWERY EFFLUENTS

The general characteristics of malting and brewing effluents can be described in relatively simple terms of oxygen demand expressed as biochemical oxygen demand (BOD) or chemical oxygen demand (COD), suspended solids (SS), pH, temperature and flow parameters. Methods for the determination of these parameters along with an explanation of oxygen demand are given in section III.

Liquid effluents from maltings and breweries are characterized by a high organic loading arising principally from dissolved carbohydrates and, in the case of breweries, alcohol from beer wastes, and a varying content of suspended solids depending on the efficiency of internal house-keeping. The efficiency of the operation as measured in terms of load should not be related solely to the concentration of pollutants in the waste stream as there can be enormous variations in the use of water resulting in wide ratios per unit of production.

A. Malting Effluents

Under normal circumstances steep liquor and excess water from the germination stage are the only liquid wastes that should arise in malting apart from tank and floor washings. Steep liquor has a high oxygen demand and it may contain a high concentration of suspended solids if the grain is dusty and/or dirty.

Simpson (1967b) showed that the BOD of composite samples from five different malting plants ranged from 390 mg/l to 1860 mg/l. These figures were accompanied by a corresponding wide range of water usage but yielded quite consistent BOD loadings (Table 1).

A low water usage figure of 0·48 m³/tonne quoted by Lines (1966) was probably achieved by spraying and recirculating the steep water (Reynolds *et al.* 1966, Anon 1975a) over the grain. Isaac (1966) quotes figures of 1·4 to 1·8 m³/tonne of barley and refers to continuous immersion steeping as using up to four times these quantities. The Royal Commission on sewage in the early part of this century considered that 2·4 to 3 m³ water would be used normally for every tonne of barley (see Jackson and Lines 1972). A more

TABLE 1. BOD_5 content and water usage in five different maltings†

BOD load	Malting plant					
	A	B	C	D	E	$\bar{x}$
BOD_5 (mg/l)	390	825	540	1470	1860	—
Water usage (m^3/tonne)	11·3	4·7	7·1	2·3	2·3	5·5
BOD_5 load (kg/tonne)	4·46	3·93	3·75	3·39	4·29	3·93

† From Simpson (1967b).

recent study has compared malt and beer quality with the volume of steep water used over the range 0·72–2·40 m^3/tonne barley corresponding with an effluent discharge range of zero to 1·68 m^3/tonne barley (Sommer 1977).

Simpson analysed the various steep waters from malting plant E for nitrogenous substances as well as BOD_5 content and found that effluent quality improved with each successive steeping (Table 2). This was also the experience of a Canadian study (Brown 1967).

TABLE 2. Typical analyses of steep water from malting plant E†

Source of effluent	BOD_5 (mg/l)	Org-N (mg/l)	NH_2-N (mg/l)	Available N (mg/l)	BOD_5 : N‡
1st Steep	2800	132	32	98	29
2nd Steep	2250	75	17	54	42
3rd Steep	1900	64	16	48	40
4th Steep	490	12	2	8	61
Composite sample	1860	71	17	52	36

† From Simpson (1967b).
‡ Ratio of BOD_5 to available nitrogen.

Brown (1967) reported BOD levels of 300 to 1800 mg/l ($\bar{x} = 500$ mg/l), suspended solids of 50 to 250 mg/l ($\bar{x} = 95$ mg/l) and a pH of 5·5 to 7·0 ($\bar{x} = 6·5$) in combined malting effluent. The pH values of drainings discharged from successive steepings were all within the range of 5·0–5·5. The quality of washings from the germinating drums varied with the proportion of hulls in the samples.

B. Brewery Effluents

Brewery effluents are more complex than those from maltings because of the various stages of the process producing different types of discharge. The brewing process can be regarded as a number of batch operations each contributing to varying degrees to the total effluent of the brewery (Fig. 1).

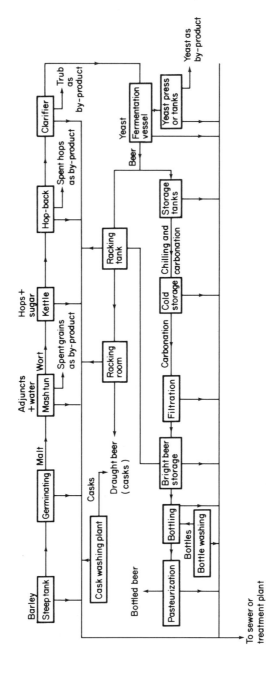

FIG. 1. Process flow diagram of malting and brewing operations showing major sources of effluent discharges.

The principal constituents of the individual waste streams emanating from the brewing process are shown in Table 3.

TABLE 3. Characteristic constituents of brewery wastes†

Source	Operation	Principal constituents
Steep tank‡	draining	cellulose, other carbo-hydrates, protein
Mash tun	rinsing	cellulose, other carbo-hydrates, polypeptides
Lauter tun	last runnings and washings	cellulose, other carbo-hydrates, polypeptides, some spent grain
Grain presses and holding bins	pressing and draining	cellulose, other carbo-hydrates, protein, polypeptides, some spent grain
Kettle	rinsing	wort, trub
Hop strainer	rinsing (spent hops treated as solid waste or mixed with spent grains)	wort, trub
Hot wort tank	trub discharge and rinsing	wort, trub (hot break)
Fermenters	rinsing	beer, yeast and trub (cold break) residues, detergent, sanitizer
Lager/storage tanks	rinsing	beer, yeast, haze particle (protein-polyphenol-carbohydrate complexes), detergent, sanitizer
Filters	blow-down, rinsing	beer, yeast, diatomaceous earth, haze residues
Bottle washer	washing and discharge	caustic soda, labels, glue, beer residues
Bottling	filling, crowning, pasteurizing	beer
Racking area	keg washing, filling	beer, beer residues, detergent
Miscellaneous	degreasing, boiler blow-down, conveyer lubrication, floor maintenance	lubricants, boiler additives, detergents, polishes etc.

† From Ault (1969), Lones (1968), Meyer (1973), Ramsay (1971).
‡ Wet milling of malt.

The liquid phase of brewery effluents therefore contains mainly carbo-hydrates, proteins, peptides, amino acids, polyphenols, ethanol and sodium hydroxide, while the solids consist principally of cellulose, protein–tannin–carbohydrate complexes, silica and yeast cells. Detergents and sanitizers, in addition to sodium hydroxide, will be present but generally concentrations of these other substances are so low that no difficulties will be experienced with their discharge and treatment. As breweries inevitably reduce the proportion of water used in production through economic necessity, these compounds will assume greater importance. Toxic substances such as heavy metals, organic solvents, etc., are not normally present in waste water from breweries.

The organic nature of brewery effluents makes them relatively simple to characterize and in most cases an almost complete description of effluent quality for all intents and purposes can be couched in terms of:

(1) Organic load, expressed as oxygen demand (BOD, COD, etc.)
(2) Suspended solids
(3) pH and Temperature
(4) Hydrological parameters

1. Organic Load

The total oxygen demand of brewery effluent is a function of both its concentration and the volume discharged. There are many references in the literature that quote the "strength" of the effluent; there are few that relate effluent quality to a basic unit of production. However, numerous references indicate a BOD content of around 1000 mg/l (Table 7).

Drainings, residues and leakages of wort and beer during manufacturing and processing operations, together with the over-fob discharged from beer racking and packaging lines, constitute almost the entire organic loading of brewery wastes. The oxygen demand of wort and beer will vary according to the concentration of extract in the original wort (Chapman and O'Callaghan 1977), although reported data are at variance (Table 4).

TABLE 4. Oxygen demand (BOD or COD) of wort and beer

Concentration of extract (SG)	Oxygen demand (mg/l)		Refs.
	Wort	Beer	
1·045	100 000(†)	90 000(†)	Lones (1968)
1·053	96 000(‡)	—	Prins (1967)
1·048	—	77 000(‡)	Prins (1967)
	—	63 000(†)	Isaac and Anderson (1973)
	—	50 000(†)	Isaac and Anderson (1973)
1·043	130 000(†)	100 000(†)	Armitt (1975)
Amber ale		51 000(†)	Isaac (1966)
Brown ale		69 000(†)	Isaac (1966)

† BOD measurements.
‡ COD measurements.

Assuming that beer has a BOD_5 of 100 000 mg/l, 570 ml of discarded beer imposes an oxygen demand equivalent to the daily domestic sewage discharge from one person (Sidwick *et al.* 1973).

Depending on the content and nature of suspended solids in the effluent, recovery of spent process material, e.g. corn, malt and hops, yeast and liquid residues draining from storage tanks as well as diatomaceous earth from filters reduced the organic and suspended solids loadings by approximately 50% in one study (von Lossberg and Yorgiadis 1973). Kühbeck *et al.* (1971) determined the BOD values of solid wastes from four breweries and found that on average, waste yeast accounted for 66·6%, the total trub for 32·1% and kieselguhr and yeast residues for only 1·3% of the total BOD demand. A survey conducted by the Joint Development Committee (1973) of the Institute of Brewing and the Allied Brewery Traders Association revealed that yeast was the main contaminant present.

In the above three studies, inclusion of wort and beer residues with the solid material would probably be responsible for the majority of the organic loading. It is assumed therefore that the figure of 165 000 mg/l for the BOD content of liquid yeast (1973) is the effect of a contribution from entrained beer residues as well as the direct effect of autolysed and intact yeast cells. If a large percentage of the yeast cells are in state of autolysis the autolysate would add very significantly to the oxygen demand because of the nature of the cell plasma and other cell constituents (Wysocki 1972, Wysocki and Glöckner 1972).

TABLE 5. Effect of removal of suspended solids on BOD_5 content of brewhouse and cellar wastes†

Type of suspended solids present by inspection‡	BOD_5 (mg/l)		BOD_5 reduction (%)
	Centrifuged	Control	
Spent hops and trub	3960	4810	18
Spent hops and kieselguhr filter sludge	6510	7650	15
Spent hops	2170	2830	23
Kieselguhr filter sludge	1230	1510	12

† From Armitt (1975).
‡ Collected from brewhouse and cellar drainage system.

Recovery of intact yeast by centrifugation or filtration results in only a marginal improvement of BOD demand (Anon 1975, Beeckmans and Edeline 1957). The author (1975) showed that centrifugation (15 000 g/20 min) of samples of brewhouse and cellar wastes produced only a moderate improvement in oxygen demand (Table 5).

These figures indicate that it is the entrained wort and beer that contributes to the high oxygen demand of these solid wastes and that the solids themselves are rather stable in a five day BOD test.

Beer losses and therefore organic loads from the bottling hall occur primarily as a result of the start-up and shut-down procedures of the bottle and can fillers, from bottle breakage and fobbing prior to crowning. Meyer (1973) measured beer losses of 1·0–1·2% from bottling lines and 2·5% from can lines giving an overall loss of 1·4%. Armitt (1975) assumed that all of the organic loading in the effluent from the bottling halls was due to beer and calculated the estimated losses from BOD_5 data of 1·67% for refillable 740 ml bottles and 1·9% for non-refillable 370 ml bottles.

2. Suspended Solids

Any of the solid matter listed in Table 3 can contribute to the suspended solids (SS) content of a brewery effluent. Again depending on procedural and house-keeping practices operating within commercial breweries, the chief sources of SS will be spent grains and hops, trub, yeast, diatomaceous earth and label pulp (Ehmann 1968).

Simpson (1967b) showed that the SS content in effluent from seven English breweries ranged between 200 mg/l and 660 mg/l, which covers the range of results from other surveys viz Australia (Armitt *et al.* 1972) (327 mg/l), U.S.A. (Lewis 1969, Schneider 1950) (200–602 mg/l) and the U.K. (Ault 1969, Isaac and Anderson 1973) (313–323 mg/l). The literature (Joint Development Committee 1973) also quotes figures for SS concentration up to 1000 mg/l and as low as 30 mg/l, the latter figure probably being the result of treatment.

The natural variations in the SS content of brewery effluent is covered in more detail in section IV.

3. pH and Temperature

Literature references to aspects of pH and temperature of brewery effluents are limited (Table 7).

The Australian study (Armitt 1975) showed that the mean pH values of discharges from the 370 ml non-refillable bottle, the 370 ml can line and the brewhouse, cellaring and racking departments were 7·7, 7·5 and 7·7 respectively. Wide variations (see section IV) in pH were observed in effluent from the brewhouse and cellar areas due presumably to the discharge of alkaline detergents. Effluent discharged from the 740 ml refillable bottle line showed a high mean pH of 10·8, the result of carry-over of caustic soda from the bottle washer.

Brewery effluents contain both acid (wort of pH 5·0–5·5 and beer of pH 3·5–4·5) and alkaline (bottle washer and other detergents and "boiler blow-down") components. Admixture of effluents from the product end with those from the bottle washer will result, without acid dosing, in discharges that are definitely alkaline, the final pH of mixed effluent depending on the relative proportion of beer lost in the filling operation. Mixed brewery effluent, as a result of its content of wort and beer, has some buffering capacity, which precludes estimation of the mean pH from the flow and pH data.

Appreciable quantities of low-grade heat energy are discharged in brewery effluent, the loss arising from all processing departments of the brewery, viz. water used for cooling, keg and bottle washing and tunnel pasteurization. Temperature characteristics have not been included in the surveys of most workers. The Australian study (Armitt 1975) showed that the temperature of effluent from the Racking Department reached as high as 75·6 °C, coinciding with the discharge of the cask washer at the close of the operations for the day. The temperature characteristics of effluent discharged from the production areas are shown in Table 6.

TABLE 6. Temperature characteristics of brewery effluent†

	Temperature (°C)	
Production area	$\bar{x}$	Range
Brewhouse and cellars + rack	45·0	26·7–75·6
740 ml bottle line	38·3	27·8–45·6
370 ml bottle line	37·8	26·7–54·4
Can pasteurizer	35·6	26·7–53·3
Combined effluent	40·0	—

† From Armitt (1975) and Armitt *et al.* (1972).

Note: (1) Minima of temperature ranges approximate the mean temperature of mains water.
(2) Mean temperature (40 °C) of combined effluent is a weighted average over a 24-hour period.

4. Hydrological Parameters

As would be expected, there are considerable variations between breweries in the ratio of water consumed or alternatively in the ratio of effluent to beer produced. There could be several contributing factors for the wide variation of 4–33 as quoted in the literature (Table 7), Abson and Johnson (1964) being sufficiently bold to indicate that the ratio varies between countries. Factors such as the following influence water management within the brewery:
(1) Cost of water to the brewery. Some breweries are fortunate enough to have their own supplies, with minimum effect on the overall brewing costs.

(2) Effluent treatment.

(3) Conditions and charging system governing the discharge of effluent to the sewer.

(4) Type of product; especially in relation to the proportion of beer racked into kegs compared with that packaged into bottles and cans.

Breweries designed for bulk production in tankers or kegs will generally use less water per unit of production than those designed for packaging into bottles and cans.

Bidwell (1975a), in a research study on costs, claimed that new breweries used less water per unit of production than older breweries but also expressed doubt on the quality of some of the data. Simpson (1967b) and Ault (1969) calculated ratios for 7 to 10 English breweries, this information being used for comparison in the Australian study (1975). The latter study reported the following effluent to production ratios for the various production departments:

Bottle line (refillable bottle: bottle washing, filling and pasteurizing)   9·2

Bottle line (non-refillable bottle: new glass, rinsing only, filling and pasteurizing)   4·1

Brewhouse and cellars + rack   1·7

Total brewery effluent   7·05

C. Summary

As indicated throughout this section, breweries vary widely in the quality of effluent produced. Table 7 provides a ready summary of the available literature concerning the quality of mixed brewery effluent.

TABLE 7. Summary of reported quality characteristics of brewery effluent

Quality parameter	Quoted measurement	Country	Reference
BOD_5 (mg/l)	786 ($\bar{x}$ of 10 breweries) ($R = 349$–1200)	U.K.	(a)
	850	U.S.A.	(b)
	500–1000	U.K.	(c)
	1000 ($R = 690$–2230)	Germany	(d)
	420–1200	U.S.A.	(c)
	600	Germany	(c)
	600–1400	Czechoslovakia	(c)
	620 (no bottling)	U.K.	(c)
	400 (bottling only)	U.K.	(c)
	1750	U.S.A.	(e)
	847	U.S.A.	(f)

(*continued p. 561*)

TABLE 7. (*cont.*)

Quality parameter	Quoted measurement	Country	Reference
	400–1200	U.K.	(g)
	1100 ± 200 (COD)	Sweden	(h)
	1631	U.S.A.	(i)
	952	Australia	(j)
	445	U.S.A.	(k)
	948	U.K. (mainly)	(l)
	1305	U.K.	(l)
	1000–1500	U.S.S.R.	(m)
	1529	Finland	(n)
	806 (COD = 1133)	Netherlands	(o)
	800–1000	Japan	(p)
	825	U.S.A.	(q)
	1622	U.S.A.	(q)
kg/hl (i.e. kg BOD$_5$/hl of prod.)	0·75 ($\bar{x}$ of 10 breweries) ($R = 0·32–1·51$)	U.K.	(a)
	0·95	U.S.A.	(e)
	0·63	Australia	(j)
	0·59 (large breweries)	U.K.	(l)
	0·63 (med. and small breweries)	U.K.	(l)
	0·45 (COD)	Sweden	(h)
Suspended solids (mg/l)	750	U.S.A.	(b)
	575 (no bottling)	U.K.	(c)
	290 (bottling only)	U.K.	(c)
	723	U.S.A.	(e)
	200–400	U.K.	(g)
	451 ($\bar{x}$ of 7 breweries) ($R = 200–660$)	U.K.	(r)
	602	U.S.A.	(i)
	327	Australia	(j)
	200	U.S.A.	(k)
	418	U.K. (mainly)	(l)
	367	U.K.	(l)
	93	U.S.A.	(f)
	350–450	Japan	(p)
	762	Finland	(n)
	280	U.S.A.	(q)
	772 (industry mean)	U.S.A.	(q)
kg/hl (i.e. kg SS/hl of prod.)	0·39	U.S.A.	(e)
	0·17	Sweden	(h)
	0·40 ($\bar{x}$ of 7 breweries) ($R = 0·17–0·65$)	U.K.	(r)
	0·22	Australia	(j)
	0·39 (large breweries)	U.K.	(l)
	0·29 (med. and small breweries)	U.K.	(l)

(*continued p. 562*)

TABLE 7 (*cont.*)

Quality parameter	Quoted measurement	Country	Reference
pH	8·0	U.S.A.	(b)
	5·9 (no bottling)	U.K.	(c)
	11·0 (bottling only)	U.K.	(c)
	8·0	U.S.A.	(e)
	4·1–8·5 (R of $\bar{x}$ pH's of 25 breweries)	U.K.	(s)
	10·8 (bottling only with bottle washing)	Australia	(j)
	7·7 (bottling only with no bottle washing)	Australia	(j)
	7·7 (brewhouse, cellars + rack)	Australia	(j)
	6·0–6·5	Germany	(d)
	4·5–11·5	Japan	(p)
Temperature (°C)	30–40	Sweden	(h)
	13–49 (R of $\bar{x}$ temp. of 26 breweries)	U.K.	(s)
	40	Australia	(j)
Hydrological (hl/hl), i.e. hl of effluent discharged/hl of beer	8–12	U.K.	(c)
	9–13	U.S.A.	(c)
	33	Germany	(c)
	10–20	Czechoslovakia	(c)
	15	Germany	(d)
	9–13	U.K.	(g)
	4·0	Sweden	(h)
	7·0	Australia	(j)
	9·9 ($\bar{x}$ of 7 breweries) ($R = 4·5$–$23·0$)	U.K.	(r)
	9·5	U.S.A.	(k)
	8·4	Japan	(p)
	4·2	U.S.A.	(q)
	10·0 (industry mean)	U.S.A.	(q)

(a) Walker (1972); (b) Brown (1967); (c) Abson and Johnson (1964); (d) Koehler (1968); (e) McWhorter and Zielinski (1974); (f) O'Rourke and Tomlinson (1963); (g) Lines (1966); (h) Meyer (1973); (i) Lewis (1969); (j) Armitt *et al.* (1972); (k) Schneider (1950); (l) Bidwell (1975b); (m) Botuk *et al.* (1973); (n) Willvonseder (1978); (o) Klijnhout (1977); (p) Sasahara (1977); (q) Bays (1978); (r) Simpson (1967b); (s) Joint Development Committee (1973).

II. REQUIREMENTS OF CONTROL AUTHORITIES

As demands on the finite volume of water available to man for domestic, industrial and recreational use increase, there is a growing need to improve the quality of effluent discharges. This is reflected in the requirements and standards enforced by government agencies and local authorities.

A. Water Pollution Control in the U.K.

A close working relationship between industry, represented by the Confederation of British Industry (CBI), and the British Government on environmental matters in the U.K. is part of a tradition extending over many decades. This has been described as "a relationship sometimes castigated by those who distrust its essentially reasonable and evolutionary approach as excessively cosy. But in terms of achievement it has much to commend it" (Felgate 1972).

This statement sums up the policy behind water pollution control in the U.K. The Control of Pollution Act 1974 (1975; see also Cockburn 1977) extends the evolutionary approach a stage further by applying the previous methods of water pollution control to virtually all inland and coastal waters. Therefore, whereas control was previously applied in a general sense only to non-tidal inland water and certain tidal waters (based in salinity levels), the new Act will apply to all other relevant waters including specified underground water, tidal stretches of rivers and coastal water.

Preceding the introduction of Water Pollution Control Act 1974 there had been a major reorganization of the water industry under the Water Act 1973, an Act which allowed for the management of water, sewage and trade effluents to pass from a local to a regional basis. This meant that in England and Wales, as from April 1974, after a lengthy period of local control in which the water services were administered by some 1600 separate bodies (Kershaw 1976) covering 100 water boards, 50 local authorities, 7 committees and 30 water companies, responsibility for the supply of water and treatment of sewage and trade effluents was distributed to 10 new Regional Water Authorities (RWA). Nine of the RWAs are based in England and one in Wales. In addition to their basic responsibilities of water supply and sewage treatment, the RWAs have control over land drainage, fisheries and water used for recreational pursuits—a total water management approach.

For a review of the position as it affected breweries prior to 1974, the reader is referred to papers by Tidswell (1965), Ault (1969), Simpson (1967a, 1967b), Miles and Southgate (1971), Elliott (1971) and Lewin (1970).

As far as the malting and brewing industries are concerned, the reorganization also means that control of, and charging for, trade effluent disposal to sewers have moved from a local to a regional authority, and that the costs of sewage treatment are likely to be calculated on the average cost of treating sewage over the region. The discharge of effluents, treated or untreated, will still require the consent of, and will be subjected to, the conditions imposed by the respective water authority.

The consent procedure has been and still is fundamental to the control of water pollution in the U.K. Applications for consent to discharge to watercourses must be made to the RWA concerned and they must contain information about the point source of discharge, the composition, nature and temperature of the effluent, the highest rate of discharge and the maximum daily quantity.

Prescriptive rights under the Public Health (Drainage of Trade Premises) Act, 1937 allowed breweries, along with other manufacturers with legal discharges prior to 1937, lawful exemptions and low effluent charges under more recent legislation (Ault 1969, Miles and Southgate 1971, Lewin 1970). However, under the Control of Pollution Act 1974 (1975), directions can be made to vary the conditions laid down in a consent or previous direction and to subject all discharges previously exempted to the full requirements of existing controls.

Guidelines issued by a joint CBI/RWA Working Party (Confederation of British Industry 1976) set out recommendations for the control and charging of trade effluents by RWAs, e.g.

  (i) Positive measurement of the volume of trade effluent discharged is generally required.
 (ii) The oxidation charge should be based on COD (Chemical Oxygen Demand) as measured by acidified dichromate.
(iii) The cost of treatment and disposal of secondary sludges arising from biological oxidation should be allocated to the oxidation load of the effluent.
 (iv) There should be no charge for toxic constituents as their concentrations should be so limited by the consent conditions as to render the waste capable of satisfactory treatment and disposal by the RWA.
  (v) Trade effluents should be charged on the following type of formula using average flow conditions:

$$C = R + V + \frac{O(t)}{O(s)} B + \frac{S(t)}{S(s)} S$$

where C = total charge per cubic metre of trade effluent; R = reception and conveyance charge per cubic metre; V = volumetric and primary treatment cost per cubic metre; $O(t)$ = concentration of COD (in mg/l) of the trade effluent after one hour quiescent settlement at pH 7; $O(s)$ = concentration of COD (in mg/l) of settled sewage; B = biological oxidation cost per cubic metre of settled sewage; $S(t)$ = concentration of suspended solids (in mg/l) of the trade effluent at pH 7; $S(s)$ = concentration of suspended solids (in mg/l) of crude sewage; S = treatment and disposal costs of primary sludges per cubic metre of sewage.

Further guidelines are set out for determining unit costs for R, V, B and S.

A notable feature of this formula is that the oxygen demand of both the trade effluent and the mixed sewage is determined by COD. For the purposes of charging, a COS/BOD_5 ratio of 2 will be taken as being equivalent to the oxygen demand as determined by the BOD test. This ratio, calculated on domestic sewage, assumes that for all trade effluent with a COD/BOD_5 ratio of less than two, the biological cost of treatment will be more than that as determined by the BOD_5 method. Indications are that mixed malting and brewery effluents should possess ratios of 1·3–2, with the concentration of suspended solids influencing the actual ratio. (Brown 1967, McKee and Pincince 1974, Schumann 1967, Wysocki 1973, Klijnhout 1977, Sasahara 1977).

The COD method was selected as a replacement for the BOD_5 procedure on the grounds of its quickness, cheapness and its capability to be automated. Because of the relatively poor sensitivity of the COD test, oxygen demand of treated effluents and river water is likely to be assessed ultimately by TOC (total organic carbon) analysis.

There is interest by industry in how the frequency of sampling may best be related to the magnitude of discharge so as to give a fair estimate of average conditions; guidelines on this most important aspect can be expected in the future.

B. Water Pollution Control in the U.S.A.

Secondary treatment of domestic and industrial effluents within the U.S. is comparatively new (Imsande 1975). Following World War II only some of the states possessed sewage treatment facilities. Congress provided some appropriation to the states in the 1950s but with the small amount of funds available only small communities were able to benefit.

The Federal Water Pollution Control Administration Act passed in 1956 and with amendments in 1961, 1965 and 1966 formed the basis for up-grading federal activities in water pollution control (O'Leary 1969). A scale of increased grants commensurate with development of state programmes based on enforceable quality standards was used as an incentive for states to meet the cost of establishing and maintaining adequate pollution control programmes. This Act and the amendments did comparatively little towards alleviating the problem and in response to the environmental movement of the late 1960s the Senate overwhelmingly but perhaps with lack of conviction (Sellinger 1972) voted for a complete change of policy and goals to meet the growing concern for the environment. The remodelled legislation included the introduction of the Federal Water Pollution Control Act Amendment of 1972 (1972). Two of the major conditions of this new Act were (a) that every point source of pollution should have a permit, and (b) that municipal sewage treatment plants should have secondary treatment (U.S. Environmental Protection Agency 1976).

The system of limitations and permits provided by this Act and exercised through the "national pollutant discharge elimination scheme" (NPDES) by the Environmental Protection Agency (EPA) required that all industry discharging wastes into navigable waters to achieve by 1 July 1977 the "best practicable control technology currently available" (BPCTCA). This tech- nology represents the average of the best existing waste treatment perform- ance within each of 70 different categories of industry (Josephson 1975). Some concept of how the EPA could administer this aspect of the legislation within the brewing industry was provided by Sellinger (1972). The Act also provided that by 1 July 1983 the "best available technology economically achievable" (BATEA) must be in force. This latter technology will be based on the very best control and treatment measures that have been developed or are capable of being developed within the appropriate industrial category. Guidelines for wastewater management in the beverage industry were issued by the EPA in 1977 (Joyce and Scaief 1977). All new plants upon commencement of operations must have the "best available demonstrated control technology" (BADCT). As put by the EPA, "this system of controls and limitations is designed to help America to two great goals"; firstly by July 1983, water that is clean enough for swimming, boating and protection of fish, shell-fish and wildlife; secondly by 1985 no further discharges of pollutants into the nation's waters (U.S. Environmental Protection Agency 1976).

A national commission on water quality set up by Congress to review the programme and progress of the 1972 legislation, reported, in 1976, that the 1977–1982 programme was feasible but recommended that the 1985 goal be delayed for at least 5 years on economic grounds. The Council on Environmental Quality estimated that manufacturing industry in the U.S. could expect to spend $90 billion on water pollution control in the 10 years 1972–1981 (Fri 1974). This burden of cost and the resulting inflationary pressures were mainly responsible for the 1977 amendments to the 1972 Act. These amendments now set the deadline for installation of "best conventional technology" (BCT), in place of BATEA for the treatment of conventional pollutants within the food industry at 1 July, 1984 (Josephson 1978a, Anon 1978f). In addition, the EPA is required to apply a test of "reasonableness" before it strengthened effluent standards for industry that has already met the 1977 BPCTCA standard (Anon 1978d).

The brewing industry, as a result of the volume and strength of its effluent, is feeling the impact of the new legislation because most breweries in the United States are located in cities and discharge their effluent to public sewers (McKee and Pincince 1974, Imsande 1975, Fri 1974). Under the new legislation, federal grants for sewage treatment plants are payable only after the sewage authority has adopted or decided to adopt a system of charging to assure that each recipient of waste treatment services pays a proportionate share of the costs of operation and maintenance (McKee and Pincince 1974). The latter authors have estimated that the annual effluent surcharges for a hypothetical brewery in Los Angeles County with a capacity of one million barrels per year could increase from $70 000 to more than $500 000 based on the new guidelines. Breweries, together with industry generally, will certainly completely reappraise their housekeeping and effluent control in the light of these figures and of the EPA's encouragement for municipal authorities to continue to treat industrial effluent (Sellinger 1972).

C. Water Pollution Control in Western Europe and Australia

Legislation for the protection of the environment in Western Europe and Australia, as in many other countries, is comparatively recent; controls in most instances are exercised on a provincial rather than a national basis. In 1969, Sweden introduced the Law of Environmental Protection. The requirements pertaining to breweries under this Law are confined to those under construction or renovation and applies to both air pollution control and noise control as well as to water management (Meyer 1973). The proposed and current legislation in effect within the nine member states of the European Economic Community (EEC) has been briefly reviewed by Klijnhout (1977) who also compared the costs of waste discharges per hectolitre of beer produced for five of the EEC countries.

Directives from the Commission of the European Communities (CEC) will compel member countries of the EEC who have not organized towards comprehensive environmental control to adopt programmes within a specified time. The monitoring networks measuring air and water quality in Italy (Gatti and Lee-Frampton 1976) are the first steps towards such a programme in that country. More stringent controls are being imposed on both industrial and domestic effluents in West Germany (Miller 1977, Anon 1974, Kuntze 1976) with increased emphasis on the control of suspended solids (Koller 1974, Mändl and Koller 1974) although the introduction of federal legislation has been delayed until 1981 (Klijnhout 1977).

Up to 1970 there was a complete lack of comprehensive legislation for the control of water pollution in Australia, such controls as did exist being fragmented through the many state and local government instrumentalities. Constitutionally, the main responsibility for the environment over the greater part of Australia lies with the states, while the Commonwealth adopts a coordinating and advisory role (Howson 1972). Four of the five Commonwealth statutes dealing with water pollution are concerned with the Australian coastline and its surrounding waters.

Since 1970 five of the six Australian states have introduced new legislation governing the discharge of liquid wastes and bringing the responsibility for the control of water pollution under one single authority. New South Wales and Queensland introduced Clean Waters Acts in 1970 and 1971 respectively while Victoria, Western Australia (Montgomery 1972) and Tasmania introduced Environment Protection Acts in 1970, 1971 and 1973 respectively. South Australia has not introduced any new legislation with respect to water pollution control, which probably reflects the cohesion of existing legislation in that State as reported by the Senate Select Committee (Senate Select Committee on Water Pollution (Australia) 1970). Licensing of industrial discharges under specified conditions is fundamental to all the Acts (Mailer 1976).

D. Effluent Quality Limitations

1. To Sewers

No across-the-board standards can be applied to the discharge of malting and brewing effluents. In the past, however, the so-called 30:20 Royal Commission Standard gained both univeral and international application irrespective of the degree of dilution, aeration capacity, or the intended use of the effluent water after treatment. The setting of such a standard is ascribed to the 1912 Report of the Royal Commission on Sewage Disposal. Roberts (1974) draws attention to the fact that the standard was never intended to be a universal one and concludes that the Commissioners were remarkably well informed and far more flexible than the frequent out-of-context references to their work might imply.

Any system designed to protect water quality and the aquatic environment is dependent on a number of fundamental factors including: capacity and ability of sewage treatment to cope with the pollutants; ratio of volume of treated sewage to volume and flow rate of the receiving water; concentrations of pollutants in the receiving water; flow pattern of untreated sewage to the treatment plant.

As far as malting and brewing effluents are concerned the major quality limitations imposed by the sewerage authorities are outlined below.

(a) pH

The pH of malting and brewing effluents is normally limited to the range 6·0–10·0 although there are instances of lower pH (Ramsay 1971, Le Seelleur 1971, Beeckmans et al. 1953), and of pH as high as 10·5 (Ramsay 1971, Le Seelleur 1971) being acceptable. Control is designed to prevent corrosion within sewers and the sewage treatment plant.

(b) *Temperature*

Consents, agreements, permits and licences usually limit the temperature of brewery effluent to about 40 °C with the actual limit being slightly higher (Brown 1939) or lower depending on the volume of discharge and whether the brewery is located in a temperate or warm climate.

(c) *Oxygen demand*

Limitations imposed on malting and brewing effluents by the controlling authorities with respect to oxygen demand are probably indicative of the size or capacity of the sewage treatment plant. Limitations expressed in terms of permanganate value (PV), biochemical oxygen demand (BOD), McGowan strength, chemical oxygen demand (COD) or total organic carbon (TOC) are often necessary to avoid overloading of the biochemical purification process in the case of small or overtaxed treatment plants. Where size and capacity are adequate, there are often no limitations imposed on oxygen demand. Therefore, as a general rule, where limitations are applied on BOD_5, acceptable concentrations range between 250 mg/l and 10 000 mg/l depending on circumstances.

(d) *Suspended solids*

Limitations on the content of suspended solids are necessary to prevent blockages in sewers and to alleviate sludge disposal problems at the sewage treatment plant. The slight abrasive action provided by a low concentration of acceptable suspended solids is considered useful as it tends to keep sewer pipes free of bacterial and fungal growths. Size and rate sedimentation of the solids are important factors to be considered by the receiving authority. In the case of brewery effluents, the discharge of suspended solids occurs infrequently (see Section IV) and therefore it is important to limit the effect of peak discharges in the mixed effluent leaving the brewery.

As in the case of oxygen demand, local circumstances determine the maximum limit. For reasons similar to those mentioned above under ideal conditions an upper limit of 2000–3000 mg/l might be tolerable although this range far exceeds the 800–1000 mg/l mentioned by Lewin (1970). Where treatment capacity is limited, the upper permitted concentrations may be as low as 200 mg/l.

Charges for removal of both oxygen demand and suspended solids can be calculated on a basis of either the actual concentration contained within the effluent or that which is in excess of the standard permitted concentration. Sewerage authorities working on a Mogden formula (Simpson 1967a) or one of its modifications take into account the cost of unit operations for conveying and removal of pollutants. Those authorities imposing surcharges above an acceptable standard obviously cost on unrealistically high charges for conveying and unrealistically low charges for treatment.

(e) *Oil and grease*

It is usual to limit the content of oil and grease in trade effluent to 100–200 mg/l. Malting and brewing effluents may normally be expected to meet such a standard under normal operations.

(f) *Dissolved solids*

Some natural waters high in sulphate content may cause problems in sewerage systems (Walker 1965). Limitations as low as 300 mg/l sulphate have been imposed on some industrial effluents in areas surrounding the Rhine, presumably to control salt concentrations generally in that river. Values of sulphate up to 800 mg/l are not unusual in Burton-on-Trent well water (Walker 1965, Rudin 1976). Breweries in which caustic soda in bottle rinse water is neutralized by means of sulphuric acid contribute to the content of sulphate in the effluent.

Local circumstances therefore determine the limitations applied on sulphates as well as other substances that are commonly discharged in brewery effluent such as synthetic detergents, chain lubricants and sanitizing agents.

2. To Watercourses

Where breweries are treating effluent on site, the limitations imposed on the treated effluent with respect to oxygen demand and suspended solids are generally very stringent and are determined by local circumstances. In the case of pH and temperature the limits imposed are generally determined by the conditions prevailing within the stream or river and these could well vary between summer and winter.

Instrumentation is generally essential for measuring flow data in relation to modern consent or permit conditions. The extent of instrumentation required for monitoring quality aspects depends largely on the fate of effluent (to sewer or watercourse following treatment), effluent variability and local circumstances. Two useful publications are available from the U.S. Environmental Protection Agency on the subjects of design criteria for reliability and monitoring industrial waste water.

As with all statistical data, the precision and accuracy of the methods used to obtain the data must be taken into account. Where consents and permits limit the discharge of pollutants and where control authorities do not realize the inherent inaccuracies of data measurement, it is important to evaluate analytical precision and accuracy in order to establish the real quality of the discharge (Russel and Tiede 1978). This applies principally to discharges of treated effluent to water-courses.

III. MEASUREMENT OF FLOW AND QUALITY CHARACTERISTICS

Whether the fate of effluents is to be sent to the sewer or treated on-site the first step in their management is definition of their physical, chemical and biological characteristics. While a comprehensive analysis of the mixed effluent will determine quantitatively the acceptability of effluent for discharge or treatment it does little to offer suggestions for prevention of waste at the numerous point sources of discharge within the brewery. Ideally, therefore, measurement of flow and quality characteristics is best performed on each waste stream as it leaves the production process. However, the possibility of analysing effectively the effluents from unit processes depends entirely on the design of the drainage network.

In mixed brewery effluent the important characteristics to be determined can be described generally as follows (Simpson 1967b):

(i) *Hydraulic factors.* Maximum, average and peak hourly flow rates under maximum production conditions are perhaps more important to the manager of the sewage treatment plant than quality considerations.

(ii) *"Conventional" treatment factors.* Oxygen demand and suspended solids content: Maximum, minimum and peak rates of discharge under maximum production conditions are again the important considerations.

(iii) *Chemical factors.* pH, alkalinity and toxic substances are important factors because of their effect on biological treatment and also, in the case of acids and alkalis, the effect on concrete sewers. Under normal circumstances toxicity of brewery effluent should not be a problem.

A. Measurement of Hydraulic Factors

1. Metering

One cannot begin to quantify brewery effluent without a good knowledge of the flow characteristics. Soroko (1973) presented a short review of most types of flow sensing devices in use to-day for the management of waste-water. The various meters for closed full pipe, partial full pipe, and open channels are discussed as well as recent developments in flow metering devices including ultra-sonic flow meters. Table 8 summarizes the main characteristics of open-channel and full pipe flow sensors. It is not the purpose of this chapter to consider the various flow meters available as this has been concisely reviewed by Soroko.

TABLE 8. Comparison table: flow sensors†

	Flow range	System per cent accuracy	Scale character	Cost	Upstream requirements	Head or pressure loss	Installation consideration
Open channel							
Parshall flume	15·1	7	3/2	Med to high	Slope for free fall fixed dimension per size	Low	Flume walls must be clean
Triangular weir	50·1	6	5/2	Med	Slope for free fall Low velocity at weir box	High	Clean out ports
Rectangular weir	15·1	4	3/2	Med	Slope for free fall Low velocity at weir box	Med	Clean out port
Full pipe							
Venturi tube	4·1	2	Sq. Rt.	High	10D straight run	Low	Purge recommended
Flow tube	4·1	2	Sq. Rt.	Med.	10–20 straight run	Low	Purge recommended
Concentric orifice	4·1	2	Sq. Rt.	Low	10–30 straight run	High	Purge recommended
Pilot tube	4·1	10	Sq. Rt.	Low	20–30 straight run	None	Purge recommeded
Magnetic meter	20·1	0·5	Linear	Med. to High	None	None	Power required: integral range change available

† From Soroko (1973).

2. Recording

Recording is an essential part of metering. A visual record provides a check on the operation of the flow meter in addition to yielding information about flow patterns. The circular chart recorder can be used to perform the functions of integration and transmission in addition to recording. Electric, electronic and pneumatic analog signals can be transmitted from the point of measurement. Some devices transmitting pulsed signals are able to be used as remote integrators and registers. When so obtained, the data can be processed by computer (Barrett 1974). The use of a computer is most valuable in carrying out surveys on effluents. Many control authorities insist on metering and recording of flow data and where computers are available for processing operational data within the malthouse or brewery, it is generally useful to use them to process all data associated with flow and quality aspects of effluent (Barrett 1974).

3. Sampling

This is an essential part of any effluent measuring system. Samples can either be (i) discrete as in grab samples, or (ii) composited. Automatic sampling (Reiter and Sobel 1973) may remove the drudgery of manual sampling particularly in inaccessible drainage channels (Raynes 1977) and allow more samples to be taken; it does not remove, however, the responsibility of collecting a sample which is a meaningful aliquot of the volume discharged (Murray 1977). Automatic samplers vary in their degree of sophistication. The following basic requirements, must be met if automatic samplers are to yield accurate information:

(i) The sample must be representative of the effluent being measured; this may not be the problem of the sampler as much as the characteristics of the sample point and the flow past this point.
(ii) The sampler must remain free of blockages.
(iii) Refrigeration of the sample in warm environments is essential. For COD determinations, chemical preservatives may be used to prevent natural biodegradation of the sample.
(iv) The sampling must be proportional to the flow where samples are composited.

One point to consider with composite sampling is its effect in diluting out the occasional peak discharge. A compromise must be made here between frequency of sampling and the number of samples forming a composite bulk. As an example of the effect of very frequent sampling and a high degree of compositing, we may consider the following hypothetical results representing the occasional discharge of an effluent with a very high suspended solids content.

Suspended solids content (mg/l)
Discrete analysis: 90, 30, 70, 3400, 60, 50, 10, 40, 120, 80, 40, 30
Composite sampling $\bar{x} = 335$
Analysis in composites of four:

$$90, 30, 70, 3400 \quad 60, 50, 10, 40 \quad 120, 80, 40, 30$$
$$\bar{x} = 898 \qquad\qquad \bar{x} = 40 \qquad\qquad \bar{x} = 68$$
$$\text{Overall } \bar{x} = 335$$

Both methods of sampling and analysis possess a mean solids concentration of 335 mg/l but even a composite of four samples has attenuated the influence of the occasional peak discharge. Clearly then, the degree of compositing should be limited if effects of peak discharges are to be noticed.

Any metering facility complete with integration can be used to activate an automatic sampler, the simplest being a system that transmits a pulsed electronic signal (Soroko 1973, Thompson 1976, Raynes 1977). A number of signal pulses can then be used to activate a contact closure attached to an automatic sampler to provide proportional flow sampling. Where sample composition is being carried out with this type of automatic sampler, the prime requirement of the sampler is to deliver the pre-determined volume. A check on the volumes of effluent in the sample bottles will determine if sampling is being carried out correctly.

A variety of electronic and clockwork controllers for proportional and interval-sampling respectively are available for the automatic collection of effluent samples. Some of the apparatus commercially available has been reviewed by Lewin and Latten (1973).

Proportional compositing of samples collected by fixed-interval timers must be carried out manually. An event marker would be required to indicate the times of sampling so that the respective flow rates can be determined.

B. Determination of Conventional Treatment Factors

1. Oxygen Demand

The oxygen demand of an effluent, simply quoted, is the quantity of oxygen, expressed in mg/litre, required to oxidize the organic components within the sample to essentially carbon dioxide and water. In aquatic environments, natural microorganisms within the water grow and consume dissolved oxygen when unstable effluents are discharged, thereby depriving higher forms of life, including fish, of essential oxygen. The amount of oxidation required is dependent on, among other factors, the type of effluent involved, for example it has been stated that the biodegradation of domestic sewage is relatively constant at 70% in five days, whereas industrial discharges vary from 25% to 95% in the same period (Le Blanc 1974).

There is no absolute method for determining under any conditions the actual oxygen demand of a mixed sample when it is discharged to the environment. Classically, the most accepted method for the determination of the biochemical oxygen demand (BOD) was that proposed by the British Royal Commission on Sewage Disposal. In 1913, in their eighth report, the Commision proposed that the weight of oxygen required for the biochemical oxidation of organic material over a period of five days at 65 °F (18·3 °C) be taken as a measure of the quality of water. The temperature of 65 °F was the maximum stream temperature expected in the U.K. during summer months. In addition, the Commission recommended that, to minimize errors, the incubation period for the BOD test should be standardized at five days. Interestingly, five days was the maximum period considered for any British river to flow from its source to the sea.

The currently recognized standard method and procedures of the American Public Health Association (APHA), American Water Works Association (AWWA) and the Water Pollution Control Federation (WPCF) for the determination of BOD_5 states that the five day incubation be controlled at 20 °C $\pm$ 1 °C (American Public Health Association 1975).

Today, principally because of the time required to carry out BOD_5 analyses, chemical and instrumental methods are replacing the biochemical ones. Earlier chemical methods were based on oxidation of the sample with acidified potassium permanganate to yield a result known as the permanganate value (PV) (Walker 1971) or McGowan strength which related PV with ammoniacal and organic nitrogen (Fish 1973). These methods have been largely replaced by others using acidified potassium dichromate. Results of the latter method are commonly expressed as the chemical oxygen demand (COD) or dichromate value (DV). The additions of catalysts to the digest have been reported (Moore et al. 1951, Dobbs and Williams 1963) as well as automation of the method (Snaddon et al. 1973).

Instrumental techniques now exist for the measurement of total organic carbon (TOC) and total oxygen demand (TOD) within three minutes (Bond 1974). The TOC analyser method as described by Hall et al. (1963) measures the carbon dioxide produced from the catalytic decomposition of organic substances present in the effluent sample, the carbon dioxide being measured by infrared spectrophotometry.

In the case of the TOD method, oxygen-free nitrogen is fed into a zirconia oxygen-dosing cell where, by application of an electric potential to the cell wall, oxygen is transported from outside the cell to dose the nitrogen to a predetermined concentration. After injection of the sample of effluent into the gas stream, the mixture is combusted at 900 °C. A second zirconia cell is then used to restore the oxygen level to the original concentration thereby giving the oxygen demand or the TOD of the sample (Bond 1974).

The advantages of TOC and TOD analyses in giving rapid results are offset by the high initial equipment costs and this can be expected to act as a deterrent to smaller dischargers to use these methods. However, the instrumental methods will be attractive to the control authorities and it is likely that some authorities will adopt these as official methods for determining the oxygen demand of treated and untreated effluents within the near future.

Numerous modifications to standard methods for the determination of BOD and COD have been suggested over the years. Le Blanc (1974) has reviewed the rapid BOD test methods while Baker-Munton (1963) described a simple dichromate COD measurement using colour discs to correlate BOD values for malting effluent. The measured colour change bore a definite relationship to the BOD_5 measurements, so that, by comparing the colour with standard colour discs, a direct measurement of the BOD_5 was obtained. Fairly consistent correlations between BOD and TOD and between BOD and COD have been quoted for domestic sewage but such is not the case with industrial effluents (Ford 1968a, 1968b, Delcommune 1971) because of the variation in effluent composition. Hence these correlations are satisfactory while composition of the effluent does not change (Gaudy 1972) and one can see how it may be applied to malting effluent where the majority of the organic content originates from one point in the process—the steeping water. However, the variations in effluent quality which are characteristic of brewery discharges may well lead to modification of the correlations with changes in composition.

There has been considerable interest also in simplifying the rather tedious procedure of the standard COD method by shortening the digestion period or lowering the digestion temperature. Results have shown that equivalent readings are possible only for effluent samples that are very readily oxidizable and consequently these modified procedures suffer the same disadvantages of imprecision as attempts to correlate different methods.

Micro- semi-automated analyses for COD incorporating the reliability of the standard digestion procedure (American Public Health Association 1975) with reportedly increased sensitivity and with the precision of an automated procedure (based on the spectrophotometric measurement of Cr^{III}) have been recently published (Jirka and Carter 1975, Pitt et al. 1973).

Catroux and Morfaux (1972) determined BOD_5 by carrying out COD determinations at the beginning and end of the five-day incubation. The basis of their work was expressed as

$$BOD_5 = COD_0 - COD_5$$

where $COD_0 =$ COD value of the seeded effluent at the start of the test and $COD_5 =$ COD value of the seeded effluent after incubation for five days. The authors concluded that the use of this technique obviated the need to dilute the sample and it was possible to use increased seeding rates.

An assessment of the BOD by accounting for all materials entering and leaving the malthouse or the brewery, as suggested by Søltoft (1967), may give a more reliable estimate than a poorly organized analytical survey but it is unconvincing to a control authority as an indicator of the strength and composition of an effluent. Furthermore, such an approach yields no information whatsoever concerning other quality parameters such as suspended solids, pH and temperature, nor anything about the important variations in flow and quality.

The method finally selected for determination of oxygen demand depends to a very large extent on the purpose of carrying out the analysis. If it is to pinpoint the major sources of BOD waste within the malthouse or brewery any of the methods mentioned above will yield meaningful results. However if the purpose is to measure the mixed effluent as it discharges into a local authority sewer it makes very good sense to adhere to the methods and procedure as laid down by the local authority. Deviations from the official, if not standard, method must weaken the case of the discharger when negotiating on effluent charges and surcharges.

The methods and procedures described in the following pages are based on the standard methods of the APHA, AWWA and the WPCF (American Public Health Association 1975).

2. Determination of Biochemical Oxygen Demand (BOD$_5$)

Apparatus

Incubation bottles. 250–300 ml capacity with groundglass stoppers fitted with water seal. If special BOD bottles with flared mouths are not available, suitable water seals can be made by fitting 5 cm lengths of rubber hosing.

Incubator. Air incubator or water bath thermostatically controlled at 20 °C ± 1 °C and capable of excluding all light.

Reagents

Distilled water. Water used for preparation of solutions and dilution water must be of the highest quality, distilled from a block tin or an all-glass still. It must contain less than 0·01 mg/l copper, and be free of chlorine, chloramines, caustic alkalinity, organic material or acids.

Phosphate buffer solution. Dissolve 8·5 g potassium dihydrogen phosphate, KH_2PO_4, 21·75 g dipotassium hydrogen phosphate, K_2HPO_4, 33·4 g disodium hydrogen phosphate heptahydrate, $Na_2HPO_4.7H_2O$ and 1·7 g ammonium chloride, NH_4Cl, in about 500 ml distilled water and dilute to 1 litre. The pH of this buffer should be 7·2 without further adjustment.

Magnesium sulphate solution. Dissolve 22·5 g $MgSO_4.7H_2O$ in distilled water and dilute to 1 litre.

Calcium chloride solution. Dissolve 27·5 g anhydrous $CaCl_2$ in distilled water and dilute to 1 litre.

Ferric chloride solution. Dissolve 0·25 g $FeCl_3.6H_2O$ in distilled water and dilute to 1 litre.

Acid and alkali solutions, 1 N. For neutralization of effluent samples.

Sodium sulphite solution, 0·025 N. Dissolve 1·575 g anhydrous Na_2SO_3 in 1 litre distilled water. This solution is not stable and therefore should be prepared daily.

Seeding material. The selection of the proper seeding material is an important factor in the BOD determination. With malting and brewery effluents a satisfactory seed may be obtained by using the supernatant liquor from domestic sewage which has been stored at 20 °C for 24–36 hours.

Procedure

Preparation of dilution water. Aerate the distilled water until it is saturated with dissolved oxygen. The distilled water used should be as near 20 °C as possible and of the highest purity. Place the desired volume of distilled water in a suitable bottle and add 1 ml each of phosphate buffer, magnesium sulphate, calcium chloride and ferric chloride solutions for each litre of water.

Seeding. Seed the dilution water, but only past experience can determine the actual amount of seed to be added (0·05% used in the Australian study (Armitt 1975, Armitt *et al.* 1972)). Seeded dilution water should be used the day it is prepared.

Neutralization. Neutralize samples containing caustic alkalinity or acid to about pH 7·0 with 1N H_2SO_4 or NaOH. The pH of the seeded dilution water should not be changed by the preparation of the lowest dilution of sample. Chlorine residues can be neutralized with the appropriate quantity of sodium sulphite solution.

Dilution technique. Make several dilutions of the prepared sample so as to obtain 40 to 70% depletion of oxygen. Experience again is the best guide

(In the Australian survey (Armitt 1975, Armitt *et al.* 1972) sample concentrations ranged mainly between 0·1% and 1·0%.)

(a) Carefully siphon the standard, seeded dilution water into a graduated cylinder of 1 to 2 litre capacity, filling the cylinder half full without entrainment of air. Add the quantity of carefully mixed sample to make the desired dilution and dilute to the appropriate level with dilution water. Mix well, avoiding entrainment of air. Siphon the mixed dilution into two BOD bottles, one for incubation and the other for determination of the initial dissolved oxygen in the mixture; stopper tightly, provide a water seal and incubate for 5 days at 20 °C. Prepare succeeding dilutions of lower concentrations in the same manner, or by adding dilution water to the unused portion of the preceding dilution.

(b) The dilution technique may be greatly simplified by measuring suitable amounts directly into bottles of known capacity with a large-tip volumetric pipette and filling the bottle with just sufficient dilution water so that the stopper can be inserted without leaving air bubbles.

Determination of dissolved oxygen

The method outlined below is based on the standard method (American Public Health Association 1975) for the determination of dissolved oxygen, which uses the azide modification of the iodometric procedure. Other methods such as instrumental analyzers may be used for measuring the dissolved oxygen content of BOD_5 samples; but if results are to be compared with those obtained by the control authorities it is recommended that the official method of the authority concerned be used.

Reagents

Manganese sulphate solution. Dissolve 480 g $MnSO_4.4H_2O$ in distilled water, filter and dilute to 1 litre. This solution should liberate not more than a trace of iodine when added to an acidified solution of potassium iodide.

Alkali-iodide-azide reagent. Dissolve 500 g sodium hydroxide, NaOH, and 135 g sodium iodide, NaI, in distilled water and dilute to 1 litre. (Alternatively 700 g potassium hydroxide, KOH, and 150 g potassium iodide, KI, may be used. The sodium and potassium salts can be interchanged.) To this solution add 10 g sodium azide, NaN_3, dissolved in 40 ml distilled water. This reagent should not give a colour with starch when diluted and acidified.

Sulphuric acid. Concentrated of approximately 36 N.

Starch solution. Prepare an emulsion of 5–6 g soluble starch in a beaker or a mortar with a small amount of distilled water. Pour this emulsion into 1 litre of boiling water, bring to boil for a few minutes and let settle overnight. Use the clear supernatant. This solution may be preserved with 1·25 g salicylic acid per litre or by the addition of a few drops of toluene.

Sodium thiosulphate stock solution. Dissolve 24·82 g $Na_2S_2O_3.5H_2O$ in boiled and cooled distilled water and dilute to 1 litre. Preserve by adding 5 ml chloroform or 1 g NaOH per litre.

Standard sodium thiosulphate titrant, 0·025 N. Prepare the standard solution either by diluting 250 ml sodium thiosulphate stock solution to 1 litre or by dissolving 6·205 g $Na_2S_2O_3.5H_2O$ in freshly boiled and cooled distilled water and diluting to 1 litre. Preserve by adding 5 ml chloroform or 0·4 g NaOH per litre. One millilitre of standard sodium thiosulphate solution, exactly 0·0250 N, is equivalent to 0·200 mg dissolved oxygen. Standardize with potassium biniodate.

Standard potassium biniodate solution, 0·025 N. A stock solution equivalent in strength to 0·1 N thiosulphate solution contains 3·249 g/l $KH(IO_3)_2$. The biniodate solution equivalent to the 0·025 N thiosulphate contains 0·8124 g/l $KH(IO_3)_2$ and may be prepared by diluting 250 ml stock solution to 1 litre. Standardize the biniodate solution by the following procedure. Dissolve approximately 2 g KI, free from iodate, in an Erlenmeyer flask with 100 to 150 ml distilled water; add 10 ml of 1 in 10 H_2SO_4, followed by exactly 20 ml standard biniodate solution. Dilute to 200 ml and titrate the liberated iodine with the thiosulphate titrant, adding starch toward the end of the titration, when a pale straw colour is reached. Exactly 20 ml 0·025 N thiosulphate should be required when the solutions are of equal strength. It is convenient to adjust the thiosulphate solution to exactly 0·0250 N.

Procedure

To the sample contained in a 250–300 ml bottle add 2 ml manganese sulphate solution followed by 2 ml alkali-iodide-azide reagent, well below the surface of the liquid; stopper with care to exclude air bubbles and mix by inverting the bottle several times. When the precipitate settles, leaving a clear supernatant above the manganese hydroxide floc, shake again. When settling has produced at least 100 ml clear supernatant, carefully remove stopper and immediately add 2 ml concentrated H_2SO_4 by allowing the acid to run down the neck of the bottle, restopper and mix by gentle inversion until dissolution is complete. Ensure that the iodine is uniformly distributed throughout the bottle before decanting the amount needed for titration. This should correspond to 200 ml of the original sample after correction for the loss of sample by displacement with the reagents. Therefore, when a total of 4 ml

(2 ml each) of the manganese sulphate and alkali-iodide-azide are added to a 300 ml bottle, the volume taken for titration should be $200 \times 300/(300-4) = 203$ ml. Titrate with 0·025 N thiosulphate solution to a pale straw colour, add 1 to 2 ml freshly prepared starch solution and continue the titration to the first disappearance of the blue colour.

Calculations

Dissolved oxygen (D.O.) content in sample:

1 ml 0·025 N sodium thiosulphate = 0·2 mg D.O. contained in 200 ml sample.

Therefore 0·2 mg D.O. in 200 ml = 1 mg/l

i.e. No. ml 0·025 N sodium = mg/l D.O.

thiosulphate titrant

Expression of BOD$_5$:

$$BOD_5 \text{ (mg/l)} = \frac{(D_1 - D_2) - (B_1 - B_2)f}{P}$$

where D_1 = D.O. content of diluted sample at zero time; D_2 = D.O. content of diluted sample after incubation for 5 days; B_1 = D.O. content of seed control at zero time; B_2 = D.O. content of seed control after incubation for 5 days; f = ratio of seed in sample to seed in control; P = decimal fraction of sample used.

3. Determination of Chemical Oxygen Demand (COD)

General Discussion

The sample is refluxed with known amounts of potassium dichromate and sulphuric acid. The excess dichromate is titrated with ferrous ammonium sulphate. The amount of oxidizable organic matter, measured as oxygen equivalent is proportional to the potassium dichromate consumed. The method can be used to determine COD values of 50 mg/l or greater using concentrated dichromate. With dilute dichromate, values below 10 mg/l are less accurate. If there is to be a delay before analysis, the sample may be preserved by acidification with sulphuric acid. For samples containing high COD values initial dilutions should be carried out in volumetric flasks to reduce the inherent error in measuring small sample volumes.

Apparatus

Reflux apparatus. This apparatus consists of 500 ml or 250 ml Erlenmeyer flasks with ground-glass 20/40 neck and 300 mm jacket Liebig, West or equivalent condensers with 20/40 ground-glass joint and a hot plate with sufficient power to produce at least 1·4 watts/cm^2 of heating surface, or equivalent, to ensure an adequate boiling of the contents of the refluxing flask.

Reagents

Standard potassium dichromate solution, 0·250 N. Dissolve 12·259 g $K_2Cr_2O_7$ primary standard grade, previously dried at 103 °C for 2 h, in distilled water and dilute to 1 litre. Nitrite nitrogen significantly interferes with the COD test but this should not be a problem in malting and brewing effluents. Where nitrites are present, consult the standard method (American Public Health Association 1975) for correction with sulphamic acid.

Sulphuric acid reagent. Concentrated H_2SO_4 containing 22 g silver sulphate, Ag_2SO_4, per 4 kg bottle (1 to 2 days required for dissolution).

Standard ferrous ammonium sulphate titrant, 0·10 N. Dissolve 39 g analytical grade $Fe(NH_4)_2(SO_4)_2.6H_2O$ in distilled water, add 20 ml concentrated H_2SO_4, cool and dilute to 1 litre. This solution must be standardized daily against the standard potassium dichromate solution.

To standardize, dilute 10 ml standard potassium dichromate solution to about 100 ml. Add 30 ml concentrated H_2SO_4 and allow to cool. Titrate with the ferrous ammonium sulphate titrant, using 2 or 3 drops of ferroin indicator:

$$\text{Normality} = \frac{\text{ml } K_2Cr_2O_7 \times 0.25}{\text{ml } Fe(NH_4)_2(SO_4)_2}$$

Ferroin indicator solution. Dissolve 1·485 g 1,10 phenanthroline monohydrate, together with 0·695 g $FeSO_4.7H_2O$ in water and dilute to 100 ml.

Mercuric sulphate. Analytical grade crystals.

Procedure

Place 50 ml sample or a smaller aliquot diluted to 50 ml in the 500 ml refluxing flask. Add 1 g $HgSO_4$ using a reagent spoon, several boiling chips and 5 ml H_2SO_4 very slowly with mixing to dissolve the $HgSO_4$. Cool while mixing to avoid possible loss of volatile materials in the sample. Add 25 ml 0·250 N $K_2Cr_2O_7$ solution and again mix. Attach the flask to the condenser and start the cooling water. Add the remaining H_2SO_4 (70 ml) through the open end of the condenser. Continue swirling and mixing while the acid is being added. (*Caution: The reflux mixture must be thoroughly mixed before heat is applied. If this is not done, local heating occurs in the bottom of the flask and the mixture may be blown out of the condenser.*)

The use of 1 g $HgSO_4$ is sufficient to complex 100 mg chloride (2000 mg/l). If a slight precipitate develops it does not adversely affect the determination.

Reflux the mixture for 2 h. A shorter reflux period may be used for particular effluents if it has been found to give the maximum COD. Cool and then wash down the condenser with distilled water. Dilute the mixture with distilled water to about twice its volume, cool to room temperature and titrate the excess dichromate with standard ferrous ammonium sulphate, using 2 to 3 drops of ferroin indicator. Although the quantity of indicator is not critical it should not vary between samples even when analysed at different times. The colour change is sharp, going from blue-green to reddish-brown, and should be taken as the end-point although the blue-green colour may reappear within minutes. Reflux in the same manner a blank consisting of distilled water, equal in volume to that of the sample, together with the reagents.

Samples ranging from 10 ml to 50 ml may be used, providing the volumes, weights and normalities of the reagents are adjusted accordingly.

An alternative procedure for dilute samples is given in the standard methods (American Public Health Association 1975).

Calculation

$$\text{COD (mg/l)} = \frac{(a-b)\,N \times 8000}{\text{ml sample}}$$

where COD = chemical oxygen demand from dichromate; a = ml $Fe(NH_4)_2(SO_4)_2$ used for blank; b = ml $Fe(NH_4)_2(SO_4)_2$ used for sample; N = normality of $Fe(NH_4)_2(SO_4)_2$.

4. Determination of Suspended Solids

The precision of this determination varies directly with the concentration of suspended solids in the sample. There is no satisfactory procedure for obtaining the accuracy of the method on wastewater samples because the true concentration of suspended solids is unknown.

Apparatus

Glass fibre filter discs, e.g. Gelman type A, Whatman GF/C or equivalent. Water vacuum pump or suction apparatus. Air oven capable of maintaining temperature of $104\,^{\circ} \pm 1\,^{\circ}C$.

Procedure

Measure out a 100 ml aliquot of the well mixed sample, collected for determination of oxygen demand, in a volumetric flask or wide-tip pipette. If large particles are present, measure the sample in a 100 ml measuring cylinder, transfer to the volumetric flask and adjust to the mark with a wide-tip pipette. Filter the sample through a glass fibre filter using suction. With suction still applied wash the filter with three successive 20 ml portions of distilled water.

Dry the filter and residue at 104 °C for one hour and allow it to cool to room temperature in a desiccator prior to weighing.

Calculation

Total suspended solids (mg/l) = mg suspended solids × 10.

5. Determination of pH and Temperature
General Discussion

The possibility exists in most breweries for the water or local authorities to exercise controls on pH and temperature of brewery effluent. Where controls are required management should look to prevention rather than the cure of the situation. The latter approach entails continuous monitoring for pH and temperature with accompanying alarm and control systems. When surveys are being conducted continuous measurement and recording of effluent will provide meaningful data within a very short time. Temperature and pH probes can be mounted either directly in the effluent stream or, for ease of service and maintenance, in a separate flow cell complete with small pump mounted adjacent to the point of discharge to the sewer. There are numerous commercial instruments available for the continuous measurement and recording of pH and temperature.

Apparatus

pH. pH meter and recorder fitted with a glass electrode—preferably a combined glass electrode—automatic temperature compensation, and continuous recording facilities.

Temperature. Temperature recorder fitted with a mercury capillary tube.

Procedure

pH. The assembly should be checked over the temperature range expected with two standard buffers, usually at pH 9·18 and 4·01, making any necessary adjustments. The electrodes should be rinsed and immersed in water or salt solution according to the manufacturer's directions until used.

Install the pH recorder in the discharge line and note the sensitivity of the recorder to changes of pH within the effluent. It may be necessary to check the standarization of the recorder once or twice daily. During these checks note the sensitivity of the electrodes as they are susceptible to accumulation of deposits from the effluent. The proper care of the electrodes includes:

(a) Removing any film from the electrodes with the proper solvent or a mild detergent, using soft tissue and exercising care to wipe away all the film.

(b) Repeated rinsing with distilled water and wiping with soft tissue to remove all solvent or detergent.

(c) Where sensitivity is poor, restoring the glass electrode by immersing in 2% hydrochloric acid for 2 hours or more, then rinsing thoroughly with distilled water.

(d) Ensuring that the calomel electrode contains saturated potassium chloride, KCl.

Temperature. The temperature recorder should be checked against a precision thermometer certified by the National Bureau of Standards or equivalent prior to installation and occasionally thereafter (e.g. 2–3 week intervals).

IV. FLUCTUATIONS IN FLOW AND QUALITY CHARACTERISTICS

Comprehensive data on the fluctuations that occur within effluents from individual malt houses and breweries are somewhat limited. This is due mainly to compositing of samples in surveys that have been reported, thereby removing some evidence of the fluctuating nature of effluent quality. Compositing was not extensive in the survey carried out by O'Rourke and Tomlinson (1963) and they were able to demonstrate the wide hourly variations in flow rate, BOD/COD suspended solids and pH.

The variations that exist in daily composite samples collected over one week have been reported by Walker (1972) and Thiel and Du Toit (1965). Walker also provided a comparison of oxygen demand (expressed as PV, BOD_5 and COD), suspended solids and pH at 15-minute intervals over a five-hour period on samples taken automatically from a British brewery but excluding the bottling hall. A graphical representation of the variations in BOD, suspended solids, pH and flow was presented by Lones (1973) but with an imprecise timescale.

In the Australian study (Armitt 1975, Armitt *et al.* 1972) flow and quality characteristics were measured for approximately three weeks at each of four discharge points representing the following production areas:

Sample Point No. 1: brewhouse, fermentation and storage cellars; racking department.

Sample Point No. 2: 740 ml "Quart" bottle lines (washers, fillers and pasteurizer); can filler.

Sample Point No. 3: can pasteurizer; 740 ml bottle packaging area (labellers, carton packers, palletizer).

Sample Point No. 4: 370 ml "Pint" bottle line (rinser, fillers, pasteurizer and packaging area).

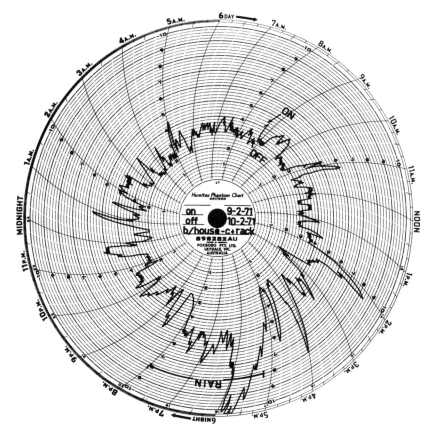

FIG. 2. A copy of an actual recording showing variations in flow of effluent from the brewhouse and cellars plus rack areas (sample point no. 1) during a 24-hour period.

Because production on the can line was both discontinuous and small by comparison with the 740 ml bottle lines, there was almost a complete isolation of the latter for this study.

As reported by other workers (Isaac 1966, Isaac and Anderson 1973, O'Rourke and Tomlinson 1963) the greatest fluctuations in flow and quality parameters occurred in the effluent from the brewhouse and cellars plus racking area. A copy of an actual flow chart from this area is shown in Fig. 2. The majority of peak discharges are less than 30 min in duration and are due mainly to the release of tank washings, last runnings, etc. The effects of these peak discharges from this area are attenuated when results for a period are averaged and when this effluent is combined with that from the bottling halls, the latter, by comparison, being constantly large (Fig. 3).

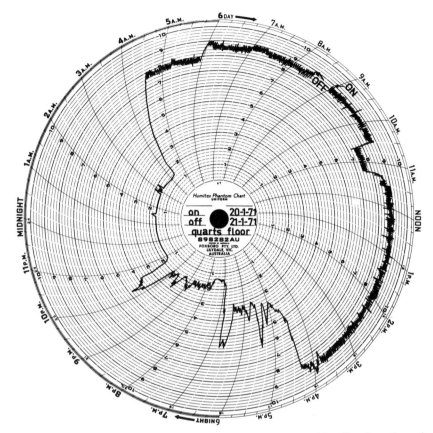

FIG. 3. Daily recordings of the flow of effluent from the 740 ml bottling lines (sample point no. 2) were consistently of the type indicated by this graph. Note that the reduction in effluent flow during the lunch period between 10.30 a.m. and 11.30 a.m. is reflected in the combined profile for the total brewery discharge (see Fig. 5).

Flow patterns representing the average of approximately three weeks recording for each of the four sampling points are shown in Fig. 4; Fig. 5 shows the pattern when the four graphs are combined to produce an average pattern for the whole brewery. The latter is almost a large template of the flow from the bottling hall (Fig. 3) because of this area's contribution to the overall flow.

Recordings of flow were analysed also for non-production periods (weekends and holidays) and it is significant that under these conditions effluent flows were on the average almost 10% of the daily maximum flow for production periods. Running taps and hoses were mainly responsible for this discharge; this fact illustrates one area of potential saving. The increase in flow

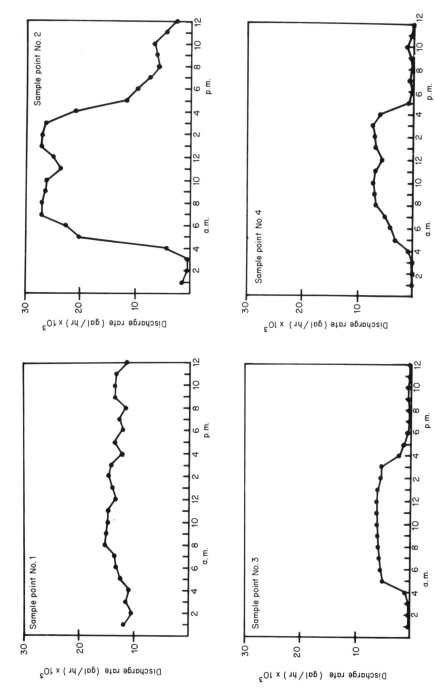

FIG. 4. *Daily average* flow pattern for each of the brewery's four sampling points: production periods.

between 11 p.m. and midnight on non-production days arises because of the commencement of operations for the week at 10.30 p.m. on Sunday evenings.

Flow rates measured at 15-min intervals were computed to produce a daily frequency distribution analysis as a function of the overall maximum flow rate recorded for each sampling point. The frequency distributions show the fluctuations in the daily average (Fig. 6) and the daily maximum (Fig. 7) flow rates as a percentage of the overall maximum rate. Perhaps the most significant observation from Fig. 6 is that because sample points No. 1 and No. 2 discharged on the average more than 80% of the total brewery effluent the average daily flow from the brewery was always more than 70% of the overall maximum rate.

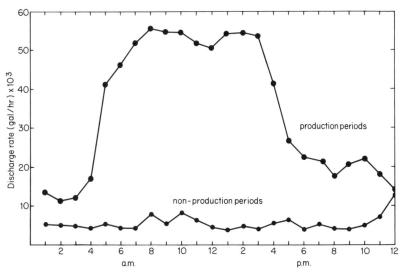

FIG. 5. *Average daily* flow profile for total brewery effluent produced by combining average flows from each sample point: production and non-production periods.

Fluctuations in the average hourly discharge of suspended solids from the brewhouse and cellars and racking areas are shown in Fig. 8 which represents the results of 467 analyses expressed on a time basis. The numerous peaks shown on the graph bear no real significance to the time of day but represent the influence of sporadic discharges of highly concentrated wastes in spite of the fact that 15 to 20 samples were used to calculate each hourly mean. Suspended solids levels as high as 21 530 mg/l were obtained in individual samples (Table 9).

BOD$_5$ data for the same comparison as the above was not possible because samples were composites of 3–4 samples. Nevertheless BOD$_5$ results as high as

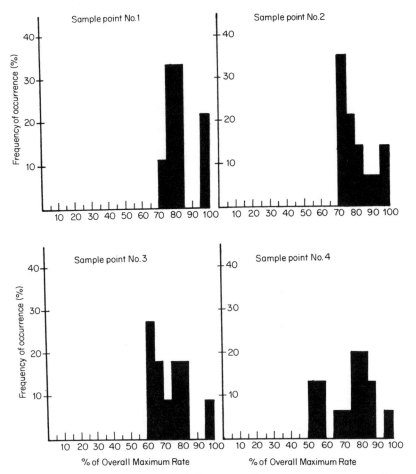

FIG. 6. Frequency distribution of *daily average* flow rate as percentage of *overall maximum* rate for each of the four sampling points: production periods.

7800 mg/l were obtained from the brewhouse and cellars plus racking sample point and as high as 870 mg/l from the bottling halls (Table 9).

Continuous recording of pH at the four sampling points (Fig. 9) again revealed that effluent from the brewhouse and cellars plus racking area showed the greatest fluctuations. Readings sampled from the chart recordings at 15-min intervals produced the information shown in Table 9 which exemplifies the variable pH produced largely as a result of discharges of beer, last runnings and detergent and caustic soda solutions. The 740 ml bottling hall constantly produced effluent in the pH range of 10 to 12, due to the discharge of sodium hydroxide from the bottle washer. The 370 ml bottling

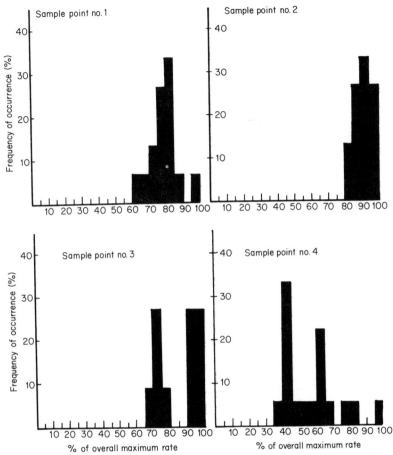

FIG. 7. Frequency distribution of *daily maximum* flow rates as percentages of *overall maximum* rates for each of the four sampling points: production periods.

line filling new non-refillable bottles, which require a water rinse only, discharged the majority of its effluent in the pH range 7 to 8.

Temperature profiles (Fig. 10) of effluent discharged from the four sampling points showed once more the variability that is characteristic of effluent from the brewhouse and cellars plus racking areas. The weighted mean temperature of effluent from this area was 45 °C compared with the calculated brewery mean of 40 °C (Table 9).

Fluctuations of the parameters measured in this survey and mentioned in this section are summarized in Table 9. The range of values given for BOD_5 and suspended solids includes those samples collected at night following cessation of packaging operations.

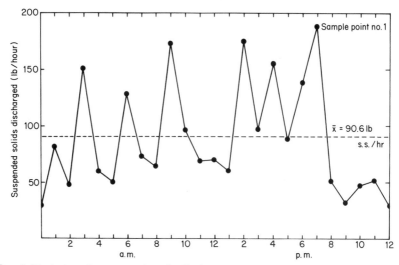

FIG. 8. Variations in average hourly discharge of suspended solids from brewhouse and cellars plus rack areas (sample point no. 1).

TABLE 9. Fluctuations in flow and quality characteristics of effluent from brewery production areas†

Production area→	Brewhouse cellars + racking	740 ml Bottle line	370 ml Bottle line	Total
BOD$_5$ (mg/l)				
Weighted $\bar{x}$	2099	199	479	952
Range	19–7800	5–845	0–870	—
kg BOD$_5$/hl beer	B/H&C 0·46	0·18	0·19	0·63
	Rack 0·15			
Suspended solids (mg/l)				
Weighted $\bar{x}$	697	113	16	327
Range	2–21530	2–3472	1–42	—
kg SS/hl beer	0·17	0·10	0·007	0·22
pH				
$\bar{x}$ pH	7·7	10·8	7·7	—
Range	4·6–12·2	5·8–12·8	6·0–9·0	—
Temperature (°C)				
Weighted $\bar{x}$	45	38·3	37·8	40
Range	26·7–75·6	27·8–45·6	26·7–54·4	—
Flow ratio				
effluent/beer	1·7	9·2	4·1	7·0
	Rack 5·5			

† From Armitt (1975) and Armitt *et al.* (1972).

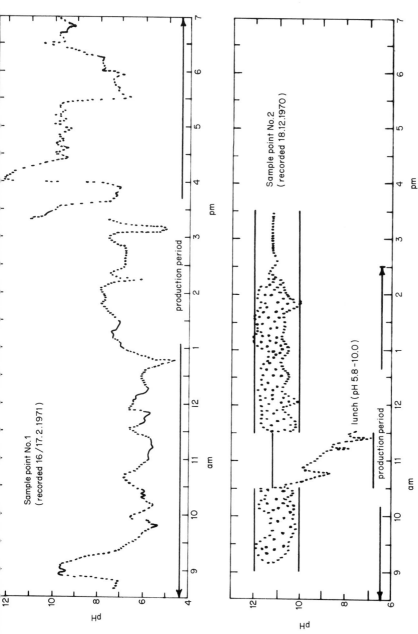

FIG. 9 (*a*). pH profiles of effluent discharged from the brewhouse and cellars plus rack areas (sample point no. 1) and from the 740 ml bottling lines (sample point no. 2).

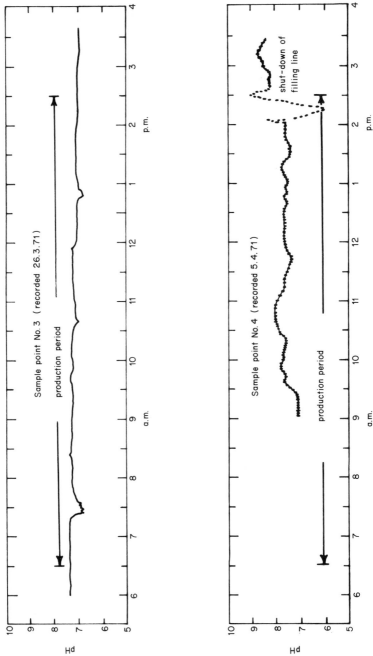

Fig. 9 (b). pH profiles of effluent from the can pasteurizer (sample point no. 3) and from the 370 ml bottling line (sample point no. 4).

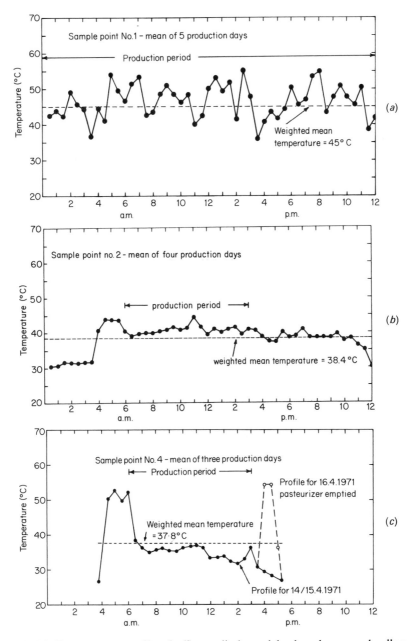

FIG. 10. (*a*) Temperature profile of effluent discharged by brewhouse and cellars plus rack areas (sample point no. 1). (*b*) Temperature profile of effluent discharged by 740 ml bottling lines (washers, fillers, pasteurizer) and can filler (sample point no. 2). (*c*) Temperature profile of effluent discharged by 370 ml bottling lines (rinsers, fillers and pasteurizer) and packaging areas (sample point no. 4).

A. Summary

Fluctuations in the flow and quality of mixed brewery effluent reflects the variations occurring in the respective discharges from the unit process areas. Under normal conditions the bottling and racking halls produce large quantities of effluent which tends to be more consistent in quality except for the periods coinciding with the beginning and end of operations. The brewhouse and cellar areas undoubtedly are the sources of the majority of fluctuations in both flow and quality characteristics.

V. TREATMENT OF MALTING AND BREWING EFFLUENTS

A. Criteria for Selection of a Treatment Plant

The majority of the literature available on malting and brewing effluents is associated with aspects of treatment either as a result of specific experiences (Lewis 1969, Schneider 1950, McWhorter and Zielinski 1974, Anon 1967a, Love et al. 1973, Sidwick 1975, Janssen 1976, Klijnhout 1977, Sasahara 1977, Campbell 1977) or in papers dealing with the subject in a general manner (Simpson 1967b, Ault 1969, Lones 1968, Isaac 1966, 1969, 1976). Our knowledge of the state of the art is therefore obtained mainly from breweries and maltings which have established on-site treatment or from engineering consultants who have designed and built such plants. However it is expected that more complete treatises will become available in the future.

In the past the low charges for water and sewage-treatment were a disincentive for maltings and breweries to consider on-site treatment where this alternative existed. It has been argued recently that with the present escalation of these charges the economics could favour total treatment on site (Brown 1967, Grimshaw 1975). In 1968 the breakeven point for a brewery to operate its own activated sludge treatment plant was considered to be one million gallons of effluent per week, a figure which was based on an effluent/production ratio of 6 : 1 (Stebbing 1968). However, others (Lones 1973, Sidwick 1975, Franke 1963) have concluded that on-site treatment would probably result in higher costs and should be considered only as a last resort. The reasons for this attitude include the following factors:

Value of the area of land occupied by the treatment plant.

Cost and difficulty of developing and maintaining effluent treatment technology, which requires engineering, chemical and, possibly, microbiological supervision.

The constant requirement to produce effluent to a high standard, the controlling authority possessing in most cases the right to halt production if standards are not met.

Problems associated with sludge disposal—with 0·3 to 0·4 kg of sludge generated per kg of BOD, the amount of solids and sludge to be removed from a brewery producing 5000 m^3 of effluent daily is in the order of 2·7 to 3·2 tonnes.

Risks of mist and odour nuisances from treatment plant.

The economics of treating any effluent are associated with the scale of the operation and, when the treatment is carried out by the sewage authority, the advantages of scale are maximized as the volume is increased by mixing in domestic sewage and other industrial effluents (Anand *et al.* 1977). Cost reduction programmes within the malt-house or brewery are better directed towards prevention, recovery and utilization of wastes (Joint Development Committee 1973, Lones 1973, Crane and Zievers 1974, McDonald 1974c, Willvonseder 1978). Capital costs associated with centrifuges, presses etc., to remove the effluent load could reap rewards greater than any gained by effluent treatment and without involving the brewery or the maltings in sewage management (Wysocki and Glockner 1972, Wysocki 1972, Craine and Zievers 1974, Berck 1973).

Maltings and breweries in certain locations, e.g. large establishments in country areas, have no alternative but to treat their own effluent. For on-site treatment numerous authors (Joint Development Committee 1973, Mackay 1972, Lones 1977) have summarized adequately the criteria for selection of an effluent treatment plant, viz.

It should be capable of producing a final effluent of the required BOD and solids content.

It should be as simple as possible to run and maintain.

It should be free of infections and odours.

It should be economically viable.

It should be compact and unobtrusive.

B. Factors Affecting Biological Treatment of Malting and Brewing Effluents

Malting and brewing effluents were once considered difficult to treat by conventional processes (Ault 1969, Grimshaw 1975, Newton *et al.* 1962), there existing a belief that the only satisfactory method of disposal and treatment was by addition to domestic sewage. However, the experience now available shows that, given the correct conditions, malting and brewing effluents can be treated successfully to meet very stringent standards (McWhorter and Zielinski 1974, Sidwick and Gurney 1975, Anon 1975c, Pettet 1964, Eckenfelder 1959, Klijnhout 1977, Sasahara 1977). The operating conditions for efficient treatment of brewery effluent have been found to differ from those of municipal sewage in having a higher concentration of mixed liquor suspended solids (MLSS), a lower BOD : MLSS ratio, and requiring a longer aeration period and a higher aeration rate (Sasahara 1977). The earlier beliefs indicating the necessity of mixing the effluents with domestic sewage were due to the lack of complete understanding of the biological requisites for the degradation of such effluents and the problems experienced with treatment at Burton upon Trent (Miles and Southgate 1971, Walker 1965). Here high concentrations of sulphate (Walker 1965, Rudin 1976), up to 800 mg/l in the well water used for brewing, contributed very significantly to the septic and corrosive conditions within the sewers and the over-loaded sewage treatment plant.

For effective and rapid biological oxidation of organic matter there is a nutritional BOD : nitrogen : phosphorus requirement of about 100 : 6 : 1 (Simpson 1967b, Isaac and Anderson 1973), this ratio varying with temperature (Helmers 1952) and the type of treatment plant (Simpson 1967b, Ault 1969). A ratio commonly adopted for wastes to be treated by the activated sludge process is a BOD : N : P of 100 : 5 : 1 which advances to 150 : 5 : 1 for biological filter plants (Miles and Southgate 1971) to allow for the effect of nutrients released from the autolysed biomass. In general, malting and brewing effluents have a BOD : N ratio much greater than 17, whereas the ratio in domestic sewage is much less than 17 and therefore one can appreciate the advantages of mixing such effluents with sewage.

Because of sporadic discharges of strong malting and brewing effluents with varying nutritional content (O'Rourke and Tomlinson 1963), the nutritional balance within the treatment plant can be controlled largely by provision of a suitably-sized retention tank. Such a tank acts as a mixing vessel as well as balancing the flow to the treatment plant (Blenkinship 1976).

The activity and efficiency of a treatment plant is influenced greatly by pH and the literature reports that a pH within the range of 6–9 (Ault 1969, Lones 1977, Eckenfelder 1959, Sanders 1973) is desirable, although optimum conditions may be reached within a narrower range. Grimshaw (1975) states that the pH optimum lies between 7 and 8 while Sidwick and Gurney (1975) report that malting effluent was treated significantly better than a 30 : 20 standard by holding the pH of the mixed liquor steady at about 7·5. At the Pabst Brewery (McWhorter and Zielinski 1974), concentrated sulphuric acid was pumped automatically into an aerated grit chamber when the pH exceeded 8·5, reaching a maximum feed rate at 9·5. Neutralization of alkaline effluents with boiler flue gas has been proposed in a German paper (Schwarzimuller 1977).

Caustic solutions present, overall, the biggest problem to a treatment plant (Lom 1977). With proper control of alkaline effluents from other areas of the brewery's operations, the continual discharge from the bottle washers may be manageable without causing great problems in the treatment plant, provided it is well mixed with other effluents. Caustic discharges from the brewhouse and cellar operations, from the water softener and from boiler "blow-down" should be collected and dosed automatically or metered at a controlled rate to the main effluent stream (McWhorter and Zielinski 1974). Final protection of the treatment plant against sudden or accidental discharges of caustic soda solutions could be provided by a pH monitoring unit attached to an acid or carbon dioxide dosing device (Naecker and Goettsche 1973, Grunert and Hermes 1972, Anon 1972, Hoffman 1973, Lange 1972, Lom 1977).

In addition to the temperature, nutritional and pH aspects the efficiency of treatment is dependent upon the concentration of bacterial sludge or microflora contained within the effluent as in the case of suspended growth systems or contained on the support media of fixed growth systems. The different types of biological filters constructed of solid and plastic supports handle organic loads at rates which are functions of the surface area of the supports (Isaac and Anderson 1973, Isaac 1969, Chipperfield 1967, Askew 1969). In activated sludge treatment, some of the bacterial sludge from the secondary settling tank is returned to the aeration tank for admixture with fresh effluent so as to maintain a suspended solids concentration of 2000 to 3000 mg/l (Ault 1969, McWhorter and Zielinski 1974). Concentrations of mixed liquor suspended solids up to 10 000 mg/l have been used in recent applications for very efficient treatment of brewery effluent (BOD = 3·4 mg/l; BOD removal = 99·6%) by the activated sludge process (Sasahara 1977).

Obviously, as the organic load of an effluent increases the efficiency of treatment must also increase so as to maintain the final effluent within the standards required. For instance, if an effluent has a BOD loading of 1000 mg/l and is treated with 98% efficiency, the treated effluent contains an organic load equal to

$$\frac{2}{100} \times \frac{1000}{1} \text{mg/l} = 20 \text{ mg/l}.$$

If the concentration of BOD in the raw effluent increases to an average of 2500 mg/l, the efficiency of the plant must improve to

$$\frac{2480}{2500} \times \frac{100}{1} = 99 \cdot 2\%$$

to maintain the same concentration of BOD in the treated effluent. This improvement in efficiency entails increased costs as additional treatment must be provided.

It is not the intention of this chapter to detail the technology of design of waste treatment plants. For specifications of plants that are apparently performing satisfactorily the reader is referred to the specific texts (Isaac and

Anderson 1973, McWhorter and Zielinski 1974, Isaac 1976, Sidwick and Gurney 1975).

Summary

The removal of the organic load from an effluent by biological processes involves a reaction, the kinetics of which, including its rate and efficiency, are affected by the following conditions: temperature; nutrient level; pH; concentration of bacterial sludge; concentration of organic load in the untreated effluent; flow balancing; load balancing; duration of treatment.

C. Biological Oxidation Methods of Treatment

In the treatment of industrial effluents generally, there has been a trend recently towards the introduction of new methods for on-site treatment as well as more intelligent application of well established practices. This has been due in part to an increasing emphasis on the recovery of effluents and the re-cycling of water. Thus, the number of available physicochemical (Dureau 1978, Dietrich 1978, Naito et al. 1974) and biological options (Borne 1976a, b, Dureau 1978) has increased.

A consideration of the thermodynamic inputs shows that the biological methods of waste-water treatment are most acceptable environmentally, ecologically and in most cases economically. Mühleck (1972) reported that the cost advantage of biological methods of waste-water treatment was four to one. In biological systems of effluent treatment, much of the free energy of a chemical reaction can be stored as biochemical bond energy and can thus be used in the synthesis of other compounds required for cell maintenance and growth. The concept of maximizing the available energy with a concomitant decrease in system entropy has attracted world-wide attention and it is conceivable that in the near future the systems selected for pollution control will be selected on the basis that they should cause the lowest possible increase in entropy (Westermann 1971).

When systems are developed and accepted in which the large cell mass which is generated by oxidation treatment methods is used economically instead of presenting expensive problems arising from its disposal, on-site treatment of industrial effluents will gain appeal. Should this happen the effluents of the malting and brewing industries could become valuable substrates for producing cell biomass.

Dissolved organic matter contained in liquid effluents can be completely converted to the stable end products, carbon dioxide and water, by utilizing a rapid process of enforced oxygenation in the presence of a high concentration of bacterial cells or by a slower natural process utilizing a combination of anaerobic and aerobic processes. Anaerobiosis results in a slower rate of decomposition, produces a smaller deposit of sludge, generates methane and hydrogen sulphide and consequently is best suited for the treatment of concentrated wastes with BODs in excess of 10 000 mg/l. Because the volumes of effluent discharged by breweries are large, their anaerobic treatment requires a large space and is generally not practicable.

The biological oxidation of malting and brewing effluents can be expressed simply as the result of two basic reactions (Lones 1977) which overall summarize a myriad of complex biochemical reactions:

(i) *Assimilation*:
$$\text{Organic matter} + O_2 + NH_3 + \text{bacteria} \longrightarrow \text{new cells} + CO_2 + H_2O$$

(ii) *Auto-oxidation*:
$$\text{Cells} + O_2 \longrightarrow CO_2 + H_2O + NH_3$$

The factors that were discussed in the previous section control the above oxidation processes. The overall mechanism for this conversion is summarized in Fig. 11. Removal of ammonia from the treated effluent can be achieved either by raising the solution pH and stripping the ammonia with air or bacteriologically by aerobic nitrification of ammonia to nitrates followed by anaerobic reduction of nitrate to nitrogen gas (Shell and Burns 1973).

The stages of treatment that contribute to oxidation of effluent have been listed (Joint Development Committee 1973, Lones 1977) as: flow balancing; screening; nutrients and pH; primary settlement; oxidation; secondary settlement; final polishing; sludge disposal.

No lengthy discussion will be given here on the various stages of biological oxidation of malting and brewing effluents. A general review of the characteristics of the system, currently being used for the treatment of trade effluents in general will present a more useful view of the types of systems that are available. Dureau (1978) classified three main systems for the biological oxidation of trade effluents:

(1) *Land-intensive systems*
    (a) Lagoons
    (b) Spray and flood irrigation
(2) *Suspended growth systems*
    (a) Activated sludge
    (b) Activated sludge variations
    (c) Aerated lagoons
    (d) Oxygen-rich systems
(3) *Fixed growth systems*
    (a) Trickling filters
    (b) Plastic packed towers
    (c) Biodiscs

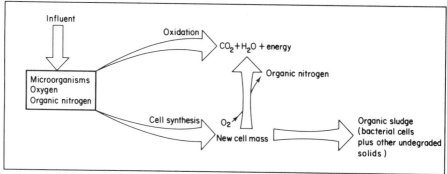

FIG. 11. Mechanism for biological oxidation of malting and brewing effluents.

1. Land-intensive Systems

(a) Lagoons

The advantages of lagoons are their low capital and running costs, simplicity of operation and their ability to produce a reasonably stable effluent. Cases have been reported where this system is used for the treatment of fermentation wastes (Tooloose *et al.* 1962) and as a polishing lagoon in the treatment of brewery wastes (McWhorter and Zielinski 1974).

For complete treatment the normal system consists of a primary anaerobic basin (3–6 m deep) followed by oxidation in aerobic lagoons, shallow enough (0·5–1·5 m) to permit sunlight to penetrate to the bottom of the lagoon, thus allowing the production of oxygen through photosynthesis by green algae.

If properly designed, the combination of anaerobic and aerobic lagoons can achieve an overall removal of 90–95% BOD when treating strong processing wastes from the food industry. Effective solids removal is essential prior to the introduction of the effluent to the aerobic pond in order to prevent the deposition of sludge. Sludge deposition is the reason that a single aerobic treatment is difficult to control where a lagoon system is used.

(b) Spray and flood irrigation

This system should not be confused with farm irrigation. Purification is achieved by the action of soil microflora. A grassy ground cover provides a protective habitat for the soil microorganisms and a vast surface area for adsorption of organic impurities. Suitable grasses are those which are water tolerant, grow abundantly and form a turf. No examples of treating malting and brewing effluents by this means are known to the author.

2. Suspended Growth Systems

A flow diagram depicting the stages of biological oxidation of malting and brewing effluents by suspended growth systems is shown in Fig. 12. A

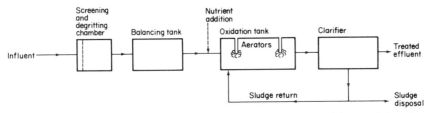

FIG. 12. Flow diagram for activated sludge treatment of malting and brewing effluents.

characteristic of these systems is the maintenance of bacterial sludge concentrations in the oxidation tank by returning a portion of the settled sludge collected from the clarifier. Many methods are used to control the suspended growth process with the result that a general review of the literature will lead to a confusing number of terms.

The three parameters in widest application for both design and operation are: food to microorganisms ratio (F/M); quantity of either mixed liquor suspended solids (MLSS) or mixed liquor volatile suspended solids (MLVSS); solids retention time (SRT). Harbold (1976) compared these parameters and concluded that the active mass of solids (MLSS) in the aeration tanks is the parameter to be preferred because its relation to other variables is theoretically sound and measuring it requires a minimum of laboratory work. The concentration of MLSS in the aeration tank is controlled by the amount of sludge returned from the clarifier.

(a) Activated sludge

For wastes containing appreciable organic loads and where effluent of high quality is desired, activated sludge provides the most successful method of treatment, and is the method most widely used for the treatment of domestic sewage and industrial effluents.

A completely mixed activated sludge process, in which the influent and return activated sludge are evenly distributed throughout the oxidation tank, provides an excellent buffer against load, temperature and toxic "shocks" and therefore it can withstand more successfully the problems of "sludge bulking" which were common in some of the earlier plants. This condition, in which the sludge has poor settling characteristics (Lones 1977), has been shown to be due to deficiency of nutrients. The most common methods of oxygenating the waste liquor are the blowing of compressed air into the tank through coarse or fine bubble diffusers and by the use of mechanical aerators which "beat" air into the liquor.

Activated sludge treatment plants are used to treat on-site the effluents from breweries in the U.S.A. (Lewis 1969, McWhorter and Zielinski 1974,

McDonald 1973), the U.K. (Isaac 1976), France (Heyden and Kanow 1975), Germany (Lippmann 1975), Canada (Love *et al.* 1973), Italy (Heller and Fuchs 1974) and Japan (Sasahara *et al.* 1974a, Sasahara 1977). As Isaac (1969, 1976) pointed out, though it is unusual for the standard activated sludge process to be used for the treatment of malting effluents there is no fundamental reason why it cannot be used for this class of effluent. Perhaps the difficulties associated with variations in flow to the oxidation tanks and the necessity of providing aerobic conditions within the balancing tank are the main reasons for lack of application in this area (Isaac 1969). Simple methods are available for monitoring and controlling activated sludge systems to ensure optimum operating conditions (Thibault and Tracy 1978).

(b) *Activated sludge variations*

There are a number of variations to the standard activated sludge process, the principal ones being as follows.

(i) *Extended Aeration.* This process utilizes a low organic loading and as a result it has a high capability to accept shock organic loadings with minimal production of solids and minimal effect on performance efficiency.

The United States Environmental Agency (EPA) has selected extended aeration as the "Best Available Technology Economically Achievable" (BATEA) for a number of food processing industries (Dureau 1978). It is favoured for the treatment of food wastes because:

Highly sophisticated operating techniques are not required.

It has relatively low capital costs, although operating costs are higher due to the greater volume of air required.

Substantial short term overloads in flow and strength cause only slight reductions in efficiency.

Solids disposal problems are minimized by well stabilized conditions of the sludge and its easy drying properties.

There are no problems arising from flies, mosquitos or odours.

Malting waste is being treated by this system in an Irish installation using four surface aerators (Sidwich and Gurney 1975).

(ii) *Pasveer ditch.* A modification of the activated sludge and extended aeration processes with lower capital and operating costs was developed by Dr. Pasveer of the Netherlands. The oxidation ditch is a closed circuit, lined or unlined, shallow, elliptical channel (1–1·5 m deep), of trapezoidal cross section with one or more horizontal aerators which also impart motion to the oxidizing liquor. The loading parameters are similar to other extended aeration processes. Power consumption is low and in larger plants the horizontal rotor can be replaced by a mechanical aerator with the ditches being arranged in the form of a carousel.

The use of this process has been applied in the treatment of both malting (Anon 1967a, b) and brewing (Anon 1975c, Klijnhout 1977) effluents with efficiencies up to 99·7% for removal of BOD (Anon 1967a, Klijnhout 1977). The capital cost in 1967 was claimed to be about one-half to one-third lower than the conventional activated sludge system (Anon 1967b).

(iii) *Bardenpho process.* This South African development removes, in addition to 95% of the BOD, 90% of the nitrogen and 70–95% of the phosphorus without the use of chemicals (Dureau 1978, Barnard 1975). In this process, the raw effluent is first mixed with underflow from the final clarifier for a short period in an anaerobic basin. During this stage the phosphorus is fixed in the sludge and thereby removed from the system. The liquor passes to the second zone for denitrification, which is achieved by the addition of fully nitrified liquor and then agitating the mass without aeration. This is followed by the main aeration, in a chamber in which the nitrogen and BOD in the raw influent are oxidized and the contents recycled. Some of the mixed liquor passes to the fourth stage (agitation with aeration) where the remaining nitrates are denitrified. A final short aeration releases the nitrogen gas and prepares the mixed liquor for settlement in the final clarifier.

(iv) *I.C.I. Deep Shaft Process.* In a comparatively recent development, the Deep-Shaft Process (Anon 1978c, Bolton 1978), an oxidation column 0·5–10 metres in diameter and from 50 to 150 metres deep is used. The process, apart from the mechanics, is similar to other suspended growth systems; the wastewater is screened, degritted and then mixed with recycled sludge and fed into a central shaft.

Compressed air is added to provide the oxygen and drive the liquor down the shaft. The deep shaft provides pressures of 5 to 15 atmospheres, thereby permitting a 5 to 15 fold increase in the solubility of oxygen and this, combined with higher temperatures, ensures faster utilization of oxygen and more complete oxidation. Space requirements are minimal and the cost is claimed to be at least 20% less than more conventional systems (Dureau 1978). These claims have been justified in the results of a pilot study carried out by a Canadian brewery (Knudsen 1978). Further savings in space and cost requirements are claimed for the recently patented PROST (pressure-recycling oxidation sewage treatment) system (Othmer 1977).

(c) *Aerated lagoons*

An aerated lagoon is a basin (2–3 m deep) in which the wastewater is treated on a flow-through basis, oxygen being supplied by surface aerators mounted on pontoons. Depending on the degree of mixing, lagoons are classified as either aerobic or aerobic-anaerobic. In an aerobic lagoon it is essential to maintain both the incoming and biological solids in a state of complete suspension. If the solids removed by the clarifier are then returned to the lagoon the process is similar to the conventional activated sludge system.

In aerobic-anaerobic lagoons aeration is incomplete and some of the incoming suspended solids together with the cellular solids formed settle to the bottom of the lagoon. Anaerobiosis develops in the sludge with further decomposition and stabilization of the effluent. For optimum treatment there is an optimum retention time; if the retention time is too long, bacterial cells will autolyse and thus release nutrients for autoxidation. Because the level of solids maintained in the lagoon is low (usually less than 500 mg/l), temperature variations have a profound effect on the rate of BOD removal.

(d) Oxygen-rich systems

In this process pure oxygen is injected into the wastewater in closed, stirred reaction vessels. Features of this system are (i) low retention time (1·5–3 hr), (ii) high MLSS concentration (5000–8000 mg/l) and (iii) high dissolved oxygen content (80–100 mg/l) (Dureau 1978, Shaw 1975).

Oxygen-activated sludge systems have been spectacularly successful (Dureau 1978). Pilot plant investigations with brewery effluent were conducted at Purdue University in 1972 (Jewell et al. 1973, Anon 1978e) and the introduction in 1976 of a 20 000 m³/day expansion at a municipal sewage treatment plant, using this method, demonstrated that it was capable of dealing with problems caused by the receipt of a greater proportion of brewery discharge in the effluents to be treated (Anon 1978e). Injection of pure oxygen into public sewer mains has been used for the pre-treatment of mixed sewage in certain situations (Boon et al. 1977) and for upgrading treatment at overtaxed treatment plants, thereby delaying the need to provide increased treatment capacity (Fallwell 1974). Other major advantages claimed for this system include the formation of smaller amounts of sludge and ability to adjust to shock loadings (Fallwell 1974).

3. Fixed Growth Systems

In fixed growth systems bacterial and other microbial growths are contained on inert media of stones, clinker, plastic, etc., while the effluent "filters" or gravitates through the reactor. An outline of a flow process suitable for treatment of malting and brewing effluents is shown in Fig. 13.

(a) Trickling filters

One of the oldest methods of biological treatment of sewage and other organic wastes is the so-called percolating or trickling filter. The reactor

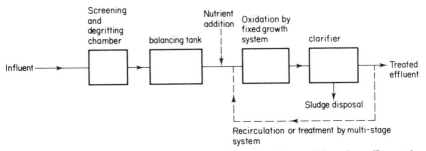

FIG. 13. Flow diagram for biological oxidation of malting and brewing effluents by fixed growth systems.

consists of a bed (1–2 m deep) of graded inert material, such as clinker, broken rock or gravel on the surface of which develops a slimy biomass containing a balanced community of bacteria, fungi, protozoa, worms and fly larvae. Greater depths have been used for treatment of malting wastes especially where the climate demands that the filter be enclosed (Isaac and Anderson 1973, Isaac 1969) although it has been more recently stated that trickling filters become impracticable at heights more than 2·5 m (Sidwick and Preston 1976).

Hydraulically powered rotating arms distribute the raw influent over the reactor bed. As the biomass increases in thickness, anaerobiosis develops in the layers closest to the graded fill, producing gas and loosening the slime which sloughs off and is discharged from the filter. The amount of biomass present is a function of the BOD loading and in the case of strong wastes it can grow so fast that it blocks the voids in the filter causing "ponding" (Sidwick 1975, McDonald 1973).

This system has been used widely to treat malting and brewery effluents (Schneider 1950, McWhorter and Zielinski 1974, Uhl and Hancke 1969) but it is now largely out-dated for treating sewage and industrial wastes in general. For full treatment of the waste, BOD loadings are of the order of 0·10–0·15 kg/m^3/day. Higher loadings (0·2–0·3 kg/m^3/day) are achieved with alternating double filtration (two filters and two final clarifiers) (Isaac and Anderson 1973, Sidwick 1975, Lones 1977, Borne 1976b).

(b) *Plastic packed towers*

During the late 1950s and early 1960s plastic products made from polyvinylchloride (PVC), polystyrene and polypropylene with the trade names of "Flocor", "Cloisonyle", "Surfpac", "Biopac" (Joint Development Committee 1973, Chipperfield 1967, McDonald 1973) and "Koroseal" (Dureau 1978) were developed. These products were lightweight (density of PVC = 16–18 kg/m^3), rigid filter media and when mounted in a tower are now referred to as high-rate biofilters (Lones 1977, Askew 1969, McDonald 1973).

The plastic medium was designed with:

high voidage (94–98%) (Sasahara *et al*. 1974) to eliminate clogging and assist ventilation;

a large specific surface (85–90 m^2/m^3) to ensure maximum efficiency of contact between the biomass and the effluent;

a high mechanical strength to permit the building of treatment systems in the form of towers, 3–12 m high, occupying a relatively small amount of ground space.

For very strong wastes typical of the malting and brewing industries, plastic packed towers provide excellent roughing treatment, removing up to 70% of the BOD at very high loadings (2–3 kg BOD/m^3/day) which is about 10 times the loading of trickling filters (Lones 1977, Dureau 1978). The ability of the plastic media to handle high-load conditions without problems of clogging is associated with the high void volume.

While, in the majority of cases, biofilters are used either for partial treatment prior to treatment by one of the suspended growth methods (McWhorter and Zielinski 1974, McDonald 1973, 1974, Cottrel 1975, Gaeng 1974, Sasahara *et al*. 1974b), or as a pre-treatment prior to discharge to the sewer (Walker 1972, Grimshaw 1975, Sanders 1973, Chipperfield 1967, McDonald 1973) or as treatment of a selected waste containing very high concentrations of organic matter, multi-stage systems are in operation providing over 95% removal of BOD (Grimshaw 1975, McDonald 1973, Gaeng 1974, Campbell 1977). They have been used also for the recovery of water of sufficiently high quality for re-use in the food industry (Askew 1969).

(c) *Biodiscs*

In this system the effluent to be treated remains stationary while the fixed biomass attached to thin parallel discs spaced about 2 cm apart rotates slowly (0·5–1·5 r.p.m.) by means of a shaft supported just above the surface of the waste. The discs have a high specific surface of 40 m^2/m^3 (Dureau 1978). In a triple-stage process, brewery waste in the U.S.S.R. with a BOD of 1000–1500 mg/l was treated to 98·5% purification by this means (Botuk *et al*. 1973, 1975). The rotating disc units are also suitable for partial treatment of strong wastes (Sidwick 1974). These rotary biological contactors are chosen for compactness, appearance and for trouble-free and silent operation (Borne 1976b).

D. Selection of an Effluent Treatment Process

Standard systems for treatment of sewage and industrial effluents include a primary clarifier to remove the majority of suspended solids prior to biological oxidation (Isaac 1969). In the case of malting and brewing effluents, which can contain significant quantities of suspended solids, prevention is better than cure. Good housekeeping will minimize the ingress of barley and malt grains, rootlets and spent grains to the drainage system and suitable screens can be used to recover such solids from floor drainage if accidental loss should occur. Systems capable of screening solids as small as 20 μm have found application in the brewing industry for straining spent liquor (Anon 1978b). Yeast and filter solids are also best controlled upstream by recovery procedures (Hawley 1973) (see section VII). Therefore there should be no particular need to provide a primary settling tank where malting and brewing effluents are treated on-site. Screening, degritting (to remove broken glass, crown seals, etc.), pH control, addition of nutrients, and, depending on the system of treatment to be used, flow to a balancing tank should be the total pre-treatment required prior to biological oxidation.

E. Pretreatment

In situations requiring a reduction of BOD, such as sewer discharges, to satisfy a consent or a permit condition or prior to treatment on-site, it is useful to isolate very concentrated effluents, for separate treatment in a small plant. A pilot study at one U.S. brewery showed that spent grain press liquor containing 1·5–2·0% dissolved solids and 13 000–15 000 mg/l of COD could be oxidized with 90% efficiency very rapidly by circulation through a closely packed biological column using fully aerated conditions (Middlekauff *et al.* 1968). Plastic-packed towers or activated sludge plants are most appropriate for this purpose if properly managed so as to achieve the desired results without the problems which may arise in an inefficiently operated plant (Lones 1977). In a renewal of interest in anaerobic treatment processes, it has been suggested that strong liquid wastes (above 1500 mg/l BOD) in addition to solids and sludges could be treated successfully by these means (Scammell 1975). The results of pilot plant trials (Lovan and Foree 1972) with brewery spent-grain liquor (3100–14 000 mg/l BOD) were similar to those obtained by oxidative degradation of the same waste (Middlekauff *et al.* 1968).

Flow balancing, pH, nutrients, sludge removal and all other factors associated with full-scale treatment are also of paramount importance for trouble-free operation of pre-treatment plants (Anon 1978a). The hazards of poisoning, fire, explosion and oxygen-depletion arising from treatment and pre-treatment of brewery effluent have been highlighted; particularly the dangers presented by the release of hydrogen sulphide at high concentrations (Wren 1978).

F. Post Treatment

A waste treatment plant at one U.S. brewery (McWhorter and Zielinski 1974, McDonald 1973) employs a multi-stage process consisting of screening, degritting, primary clarification, high-rate biofiltration, activated sludge treatment, final clarification, effluent polishing lagoon (4 hectare capacity), aerobic sludge digestion, sludge lagoons and sludge irrigation. The purpose of the effluent polishing lagoon is to provide a buffer between the treatment plant and the receiving stream so that the latter will not be affected by temporary discharges of poor quality effluent. While such a facility was considered a necessary part of this design it must be remembered that any of the suspended or fixed growth systems discussed are capable of yielding high-quality effluent provided the design parameters are correct.

The consistent production of high-quality effluents from treatment plants coupled with the high cost of water will lead in the future to interest in tertiary treatment and recycling of such effluents. Tertiary treatment includes passage through activated carbon (Bailey 1975, Anon 1977b) and finally sterilization with chlorine or ozone, the advantages of the latter being indicated by its short half-life of 20 min and the absence of reaction products like chlorophenols and chloroamines (McLain 1973). Chlorination is already, in some countries a necessary requirement of consent conditions pertaining to the discharge of treated brewery effluent to natural waterways (Anon 1976e). Sand filtration has found application in the food industry for polishing effluent prior to re-use (Cottrell 1975).

G. Cost of Effluent Treatment

It is very difficult to present meaningful data on capital costs associated with the treatment of malting and brewery effluents in general, as the recorded and reported costs on civil engineering projects rarely have a common basis. Also the unit cost may or may not include ancillaries. Costs may be depressed or exaggerated by local conditions and demands. Sidwick and Preston (1976), however, have reviewed the cost of treating effluents to varying standards by activated sludge and fixed growth systems. Capital costs of plants, mostly installed by their firm, were adjusted to August 1975 levels. Regression analyses were computed and their results have been further summarised by Joslin (1974). Neither capital costs of land and sludge treatment nor operating costs are included in the comparison. Therefore significant cost areas which are vital in making a decision on the type of treatment plant to install are unavailable: e.g. operating costs for sludge treatment and disposal can be as high as 50% of the total operating costs (Lippmann 1975, Scammell 1975). These and other deficiencies are evident in a recent Dutch report on costs of effluent treatment (Klijnhout 1977).

In September 1976 Janssen (1976) estimated the capital cost at approximately \$1800/kg of BOD entering the plant and operating costs at 18–22 c/kg BOD. Sidwick updated once in 1974 and again in 1975 the capital and operating costs presented in 1972 by Isaac and Anderson who used the basis of a 1966 study (Isaac 1966) to compare effluent treatment plants at three breweries in the U.K. In a model exercise Le Seelleur (1971) calculated separately the capital and operating costs for a brewery producing 1000 U.S. barrels per day. Annual operating costs for effluent treatment at a small German brewery were less than 4% of the investment cost (Erling *et al.* 1977).

In the absence of sufficient data for a cost comparison between biological filters composed of conventional and synthetic support media, experience has shown that installations using conventional media are least expensive in capital cost when the filter influent is of a strength and nature similar to domestic sewage. However, at feed liquor strengths of greater than 300 mg/l BOD, synthetic support media become increasingly less expensive and in the case of strong malting and brewing effluents the balance favours synthetic support media. In many instances, where land costs are a critical consideration, filters using synthetic support media, with which construction is possible to a height of 12 m, have obvious advantages over trickling filters, which become impracticable at heights greater than 2·5 m (Sidwick and Preston 1976).

The progressive stages of decision-making involved in an overall programme to provide water and effluent treatment plants has been outlined by Gaffney (1974) with particular reference to the escalation of costs between the tendering stage and completion of the work. The same author has listed some of the potential faults of the consultancy practice and while these are probably more applicable to the public sector, private management must take cognizance of them as far as cost containment is concerned. Lindsey (1974), at the same symposium, outlined the importance of involving the contractor in the initial study.

As far as costs involved for reception and treatment of wastes by a sewage authority are concerned, past literature has cited the vagaries in costing between authorities both in the U.K. (Ault 1969, Abson and Johnson 1964, Sidwick 1974) and the U.S. (Cannon and Draeger 1968, Janssen 1976) including lawful exemptions under prescriptive rights (Ault 1969, Miles and Southgate 1971, Lewin 1970). Transport costs associated with removal of unwanted solids from the malthouse or brewery can be appreciable and it is vital that solid material be as dry as possible. Current developments in new pressure-leaf filters indicates that it is feasible to dewater to 50–55% solids (Craine and Zievers 1974). These British and U.S. experiences summarize the changing policies of water management authorities throughout the world, and industry in general will increasingly be meeting the actual cost of sewage treatment (Dart 1975) so that increasing costs are generally to be expected (Ismande 1975, Janssen 1976).

Whether malting and brewing effluents are disposed of by delivery to the sewer or by treatment on site, treatment and disposal are costly items and these costs increase with increasing strength and volume. The minimization of waste is therefore basic to waste control. Spillage must be reduced to a minimum; smooth operation of bottle, can and keg filling lines must be ensured to avoid excessive over-fobbing; tanks must be emptied completely before opening to drain; waste beer must not be wasted to drain; spoilt batches of material must not be flushed to drain. The importance of good house-keeping practices (see section VII.E.) is stressed as the most direct and most effective means of reducing costs for both sewage disposal and treatment on-site.

H. New Methods of Effluent Utilization and Treatment

As a result of the more stringent controls being placed on sewage and industrial effluents throughout the world there has been much interest recently in the development of new and improved techniques in waste treatment and utilization. There is no doubt that modifications and improvements to existing biological methods of treatment, with emphasis on energy inputs, capital and operating cost, and reaction times will find ready application. The use of upgraded techniques within the malting and brewing industries has probably already commenced. The use of oxygen in conventional and deep shaft systems (see section V. C) could find application where treatment is necessary and where land is at a premium (Fallwell 1974).

Developers of vertical column reactors containing a fluidized medium such as sand (Anon 1976c) or highly porous rigid silica (Anon 1976a) for maintaining steady-state biomass concentrations of 10 000 to 40 000 mg/l of volatile suspended solids have claimed (i) loading rates 20 times that of suspended growth systems and 5 times that of pure-oxygen systems and (ii) much reduced times for BOD removal, nitrification and denitrification (Anon 1976c). Capital savings of 20–30% and a 49% reduction in construction time with comparable operating costs to conventional plants are also claimed. This system has reached a commercial scale with the installation of a 100 000 m^3/day plant in the U.S. (Anon 1976b).

"Polishing" of slightly polluted process water and tertiary treatment of effluent from on-site treatment is anticipated to be increasingly used as recycling becomes more attractive and acceptable, technologically as well as economically (McDonald 1974b), despite the fact that the cost of tertiary treatment in large scale plants is about 40% of the total operating costs (Anand et al. 1977). The advantages and disadvantages of granular media filtration, and activated carbon adsorption, for removal of residual suspended solids and soluble organic material, respectively, have been reviewed by Shell and Burns (1973). Activated carbon (Batchelor 1977) has a further potential use, in the removal of hypochlorite used for the sterilization of final effluent, necessary because of the concern for the effect of the reaction products such as chlorophenols and chloroamines on the aquatic enviroment (McLain 1973), and because of their effects on flavour. The use of magnetic polymers and physicochemical methods may find application in water purification (Raper 1976).

An alternative to the technique using chlorination followed by activated carbon adsorption treatment for the tertiary treatment of effluents is treatment with activated carbon followed by ozonization: in the future, the latter could find application for the production of potable water from treated effluents (McLain 1973). Although more expensive than chlorine, bromine chloride is claimed to be safer (lower vapour pressure), reduces retention time, has a higher solubility and has greater efficacy in killing bacteria and viruses (Anon 1979). Reverse osmosis and ultrafiltration membrane processes used singly or in combination are two techniques that could provide suitable alternatives to the above if and when the economics become feasible (Berck 1973, Cruver 1973, Diefenbaugh 1976).

Recovery process, designed to retrieve suspended solids (Button et al. 1977) and strong liquors from unit operations in preference to discharging effluents, may produce by-products which can serve as useful substrates for a range of microorganisms as well as saving on the cost of effluent treatment. Brewery spent grain liquor shows a 96% reduction in BOD when used for the growth of Aspergillus niger (Hang et al. 1975). Growth of other fungi (Zdybiewska 1963) including mushrooms (Shannon and Stevenson 1975) on the liquors recovered from spent grain, trub and fermentation sludge has been reported. Further information on the fermentation of pollutants and the production of single-cell protein from strong organic waste-water is available (McLoughlin 1972, Tomlinson 1976). Reverse osmosis and ultrafiltration membrane processes also have application in recovery processes by concentrating suspended and dissolved solids (Cruver 1973, Diefenbaugh 1976). Ultrafiltration has been successful in one brewery since 1977 for treatment, recovery and reuse of caustic soda from bottle washing effluent (Schneider 1978).

VI. TREATMENT AND DISPOSAL OF SLUDGES

The solids contained in untreated waste, together with the bacterial sludges produced by the treatment processes, constitute perhaps the most difficult area of waste treatment. The costs of their disposal amount to as much as 50% of the total operating cost in an aerobic system (Scammell 1975). The major problem of sludges is concerned with the water content and the difficulties of removing this water (Borne 1976b). Solids concentration in sludges produced by activated sludge treatment is as little as 1% (Anon 1976e) but can be increased to 4 to 5% solids by centrifugation (Woolcock 1975) or an air-flotation process in conjunction with coagulants such as cationic poly-electrolytes, lime and ferric chloride (Lewis 1969, Anon 1976e, Dlouhy and Dahlstrom 1969). Japanese experience with sludges produced by activated sludge treatment of brewery effluents show a solids concentration of 10 to 12% (Sasahara 1977). This study also showed that one tonne of dried sludge was produced for every 4000 hl of beer brewed. The effluent contained a BOD content of 800 to 1000 mg/l and a total BOD load of 26 000 tonnes annually. Vacuum filtration will increase the solids content to 15 to 20% (Anon 1976e) while modern improvements in pressure leaf filters are said to make them capable of producing a cake containing 50 to 55% solids (Craine and Zievers 1974). A mechanical belt press, which can be mounted on a mobile trailer, is said to be capable of dewatering sludges with 2·5 to 5·0% solids, to a product having 18 to 20% solids content (Josephson 1978b). Anaerobic digestion of primary solids and sludges produces only 10 to 20% of the sludge produced by a high-rate aerobic process (Scammell 1975) (0·3–0·4 kg sludge/kg BOD removed (Lones 1977); and the sludge produced is more easily dewatered (Ault 1969).

Anaerobic treatment of sewage solids and sludges has been used tradition-ally in the past mainly as an adjunct to treatment by the trickling filter, and has found application at several U.S. breweries (Schneider 1950, Lewis 1969) as early as 1950. In one such installation (Schneider 1950) the methane gas produced by anaerobic digestion of solids and sludge, collected from the primary and secondary clarifiers, respectively, was burned and used to produce hot water which was then circulated through the digester to heat the contents and consequently accelerate anaerobiosis.

Anaerobiosis was used previously for the digestion of sewage sludge with little fundamental understanding of the biochemical mechanisms involved and of the effects of inhibitory substances on such mechanisms. Chlorinated hydrocarbons and heavy metals were found to be a common cause of digestion failure in the U.K. (Borne 1975) while synthetic detergent exerted a bacteriostatic effect (Lewin 1970).

In view of their potential to provide a useable source of energy (methane), and of the improved understanding of the biological mechanisms involved and of the existence of better process controls (Barber and Dale 1978) for increasing the efficiency of sludge digestion, new studies have been made of the application of anaerobic digestion to industrial wastes (liquid wastes as well as sludges) (Borne 1976b). Scammell (1975) sets out a comparison of the efficiencies of the aerobic and anaerobic processes:

In the oxidation of one kilogram of glucose in an aerated treatment plant approximately 15 722 kJ of energy is utilized as heat or for cell growth. In anaerobiosis the one kilogram of glucose produces approximately 550 litres of methane with a calorific value of 13 300 kJ thus showing 85% utilization of the available energy.

This advantage of anaerobiosis exists while no attempt is made to utilize the sludge from the oxidative process; further costs are incurred in disposing of this sludge. If and when processes are developed to utilise both the cell mass (as is, or the respective protein or other fractions) and the carbon dioxide then the advantage of anaerobiosis would be less pronounced. Approximately 45% of the total free energy available in biological oxidative processes is contained as chemical-bond energy in adenosine triphosphate (ATP) (Klotz 1967).

In the anaerobic process more than 80% of the BOD is removed as a mixture of approximately 70% methane and 30% carbon dioxide (Lewin 1970). The overall mechanism can be considered as having two main stages (Scammell 1975):

(i) Enzymic transformation of complex materials to simple fatty acids—mainly acetic, propionic and butyric, plus hydrogen, carbon dioxide, ammonia and salts.

(ii) Production of methane and further carbon dioxide from the enzymic transformation of fatty acids.

The key overall processes of conversion can be represented by:

$$CH_3COOH \longrightarrow CH_4 + CO_2$$
$$CO_2 + 8H \longrightarrow CH_4 + 2H_2O$$

To carry out the digestion, provision is made to accomodate sludge for 21 to 30 days at a constant temperature (27–35 °C) with adequate mixing (Lewin 1970).

In addition to the production of methane gas, which can be used either in gas engine generators or in heating equipment, the advantages of the anaerobic process are seen in the greatly reduced amount of sludge to be removed, much less offensive odour of the sludge and its easier dewatering (Ault 1969).

The capital cost of the improved anaerobic technology is comparable to conventional aerobic methods while running costs are negligible, if not eliminated, due to the offsetting value of the production and utilization of methane gas. Problems that might be encountered in the liquid effluent discharge from the digester include the objectionable odours of sulphides and it may be necessary to instal gas scrubbers (Lovan and Foree 1972) or activated carbon adsorption treatment (Shell and Burns 1973) to control this nuisance.

Irrespective of the type of waste treatment used, sludge disposal will be a necessary and important part of effluent management. The alternatives available are: land disposal, as slurry, filter cake, dry powder or compost (Borne 1976b); sludge filtration followed by incineration; sludge concentration followed by incorporation into animal feed.

The traditional method for disposal of sewage sludge in the U.K. has been by spray irrigation (Cottrell 1975). Land disposal will have limited potential and attraction for maltings and breweries because of the lack of suitable land and the continual need to dispose of the sludge. Both spray irrigation (McWhorter and Zielinski 1974) and road transport to an agricultural area (Lewis 1969) have been used by U.S. breweries to dispose of liquid and filtered sludges respectively. Sewage sludges in a wet or dried condition have been used as fertilizers (Anon 1977c, Sasahara 1977). Incineration of the filtered material is practicable (McDonald 1974a) but the high moisture content means that a support fuel will be necessary in most cases. While interest in this method existed in the early 1970s and continues as far as sewage sludges are concerned, the current trend in the brewing industry is towards utilization of the sludge in animal feedstuffs. In a new \$4·5 million sludge treatment programme, one U.S. brewery (Anon 1976e, Bays 1977) will convert sludge generated by 12 activated sludge treatment plants to a high-protein supplement for incorporation into an animal-feed-stuff. The sludge is to be dried by multi-effect evaporation. It is anticipated that 0·5–1·0 tonne of dried sludge will be produced each day. Sludge from high rate biofilters has been evaluated at another U.S. brewery as an additive to animal feed-stuff (Cottrell 1975).

VII. COMPREHENSIVE APPROACH TO EFFLUENT MANAGEMENT

A. Basic Philosophy

The management of malting and brewing effluents cannot be viewed in isolation without including other aspects of the impact of the industries on the environment. These relate mainly to air (smokestack and odour emissions) and noise emissions. Treatment of one pollution source could contribute to the problems of another, e.g. treatment of effluent on site may be successful in providing effluent of a satisfactory quality but the risk of odour and noise problems to the surrounding community may make the proposal totally unacceptable. The result of the ever-tightening standards and interlocking environmental pressures has been to increase drastically the working costs of environmental control (Gastou 1975). As indicated in the various sections of this chapter the fundamental natures of malting and brewing effluents are responsible for the majority of these increased environmental costs.

A comprehensive approach to effluent management may be set out as follows:

Obtain, study and assess the immediate requirements of the statutory bodies concerned with effluent disposal and treatment.

Seek and obtain, where available, the guidelines for future controls including air and noise emissions.

Survey malting and brewing effluent streams to identify and quantify:
    (i) processes producing "strong" effluents;
    (ii) processes producing unpolluted or only slightly-polluted effluents.

Based on above factors assess the costs of:
    (i) disposal direct to sewer,
    (ii) pre-treatment and then disposal to sewer,
    (iii) collection of strong pollutants for transport or utilization,
    (iv) re-use and recycling.

Investigate good housekeeping practices in relation to effluent control and water usage.

Continuously update effluent data with respect to requirements, charges and working costs.

The cost structure for effluent control is related directly to the statutes governing effluent disposal. The decision of control authorities that industry must ultimately meet the actual cost of effluent conveyance and treatment (Dart 1975) has already led to huge increases in charges (Imsande 1975, Janssen 1976, Askew 1975, 1976). As a result of this there may be an advantage for some maltings and breweries in building their own treatment plants. A decision on such matters should be delayed until exhaustive studies of present treatment costs and their future projections have been completed and every effort has been made to contain and minimize waste (Lones 1973, Franke 1963). As indicated in section V, large maltings and breweries established in country areas may have no alternative but to go into the sewerage business.

No matter what the final decision is, it is essential to be fully aware of present and proposed statutes governing effluent discharges. As a result of the escalating costs of sewage disposal and treatment brought about by the imposition of more stringent standards placed on both raw and treated effluents and by the desire of control authorities to pass on the "true" costs of effluent treatment, maltings and breweries will recognize the financial rewards to be gained from the comprehensive approach (Mailer 1976, Bidwell 1975d, Bays 1978). In effect, the increased charges and costs will make this an area to which more attention will be given. In future, the nature, amounts and characteristics of effluent may then change drastically. In fact when effluent ratios of 5 : 1 or less are discussed, this is evidence that effective control has begun (Meyer 1973, Bays 1978). This ratio is, of course affected by the proportion of beer produced in kegs, in returnable bottles and in non-returnable containers.

The total approach to effluent management generally results in a more efficient process with associated savings in wort and beer as well as achieving a reduction in water charges and costs in waste treatment. Reducing the waste load by one half can reduce the operating cost by half and the capital cost by 30% in the case of treatment on-site (Bays 1978).

B. Assessment of Statutes

To assess the requirement of the control authority, it is necessary to obtain detailed information of the conditions and charges imposed on effluents discharged to receiving waters as well as those discharged to the sewerage system. It is essential to be conversant with the methods of sampling and analysis which are used by the controlling authority. Because of the wide variations that can occur in composition of malting and brewing effluents, excessive charges will result from inefficient sampling by the authority. This situation could be corrected by (i) preventing the discharge of strong effluents, or (ii) thorough mixing of effluents or (iii) demonstration to the authority concerned that sampling is inadequate and unjust to both parties. A cost study will show definite advantages for a waste reduction programme but it will be necessary to determine whether it is more beneficial to collect and transport strong wastes to a disposal site or to "bleed" strong wastes from the collection vessel at a more constant rate into the main effluent stream.

Where discharges are regulated by a permit system it is important to understand the accuracy and precision of analytical data obtained by the controlling authority. Consequently there is a need for the brewery or malt-house to: (i) determine and state the limits on its ability to measure effluent data; (ii) use these limits to set internal performance standards for pollution control and (iii) attempt to gain recognition in current and future permit negotiations of the magnitude of the uncertainties in making measurements (Russell and Tiede 1978).

Well organised control authorities are in a position to give guidelines on future control measures and possibly the charges to be imposed. Where environmental programmes, including the control of water pollution, have been instigated only comparatively recently, it is unlikely that the authorities will be of assistance in this regard due to their lack of experience and management in this field.

The management policy and sewerage charges will be influenced primarily by the existing capacity of the sewer and sewerage treatment plant and its ability to receive and process industrial effluents. The wise brewery and malthouse managers will consult with the controlling authority on the future policy of the authority to provide increased treatment capacity because such information is vital in organizing the water re-use and recycling programme which is destined to become part of future operations.

C. Management of "Strong" Effluents

Once the effluent survey has pinpointed those areas which discharge wastes with high organic loads and suspended solids, proper consideration can be given to their management. There are three avenues to be explored: prevention and reduction; recycling; collection and disposal.

It is obvious that if the effluent load can be substantially reduced by preventing the entry of wort, beer and suspended solids to the waste stream in the first place then some of the problem is removed entirely. There is evidence to show that good housekeeping practices have been responsible for a 75% decrease in effluent loading (Janssen 1976); another brewery regards "waste as merely a resource out of place" (Anon 1976e). Control by prevention has many advantages over recovery processes based solely on effluent *per se* (Wysocki 1973).

Recycling of brewhouse effluents is another way of reducing the problem and there are examples where this has progressed beyond the experimental stage. One American brewery recovers the liquor from pressed spent grain and recycles it to the brewhouse (Coors and Jangaard 1975). This process has led to a 1% increase in brewhouse yield and in addition has reduced brewing water requirements by 5% and the evaporation load of the spent grain driers by 14%. Wort composition is unaffected as are the flavour profile and chill stability of the final beer provided the liquor is handled sanitarily and processed quickly following separation from the spent grains. The solids removed from the liquor by centrifugation have been assessed for inclusion with hamburger meat, biscuits and bread (Finley *et al.* 1976).

Recycling of the last runnings and that of the kettle break (trub) to the mash tun following collection in hot wort receivers and whirlpool separators is carried out quite extensively (Lewis 1976). The admixture of spent diatomaceous earth, yeast and tank bottoms with the mash has been carried out on an experimental basis (Lewis 1976). Incorporation of diatomaceous earth with the spent grains must be controlled accurately to avoid feeding problems with animals (Burnett 1976) and to meet legal requirements as in the U.S.A. where regulations limit the level in animal feed as an inert carrier or an anti-caking agent to 2% of the total ration (Anon 1977a). Addition of autolysed yeast and other brewhouse effluents to spent grains has been responsible for a 50% increase in revenue from sales of wet and dried grains (Hawley 1973).

Concentrated effluents containing appreciable amounts of wort and beer pose more difficult problems than ones containing a high concentration of solids. Over-fob from the bottling, canning and racking operations and rinsings from fermenter, storage and bright beer tanks and used kegs could be collected and tankered to a disposal-treatment facility located either on site or away from the brewery. Concentration by vacuum distillation followed by spray drying of the concentrate for admixture to stock feed is a feasible proposition (Janssen 1976), as is alcohol recovery from waste beer (Wysocki 1973).

It is most important to recognize that effluents are more manageable while they remain in a concentrated condition when the mechanics of satisfactorily and economically handling them are more favourable than if they were allowed to join the main effluent stream.

D. Re-use and Recycling of Effluent

In this discussion a differentiation has to be made between recycling of brewhouse effluents as discussed above and re-use and recycling of effluents in general. Bidwell's (1975c) definition will be used to describe "re-use" as the use of the same water in an operation while the term "recycling" is used where the effluent from a number of operations is cleaned and the water used again, but not necessarily in the same operation. There are many potential and interesting areas of exploitation but whether such things as the possible use of alkaline rinsing liquors from bottle washers in steeping barley for malting purposes (Litzenburger 1978) will actually be used only time and much experimentation will tell.

The increasing costs of water and wastewater will lead to more critical attention being paid to re-use and recycling in the next few years than ever before (Askew 1975, Anon 1976d, Judell 1972, Möbius 1973). Industry in general has been rather slow to organize its thinking on re-use and recycling (Appleyard and Shaw 1974) and it has taken the very sudden and very recent cost increases of water and treatment of effluent to provide the necessary incentive (Sasahara et al. 1974, Josephson 1977, Symposium Report 1974).

Breweries have and should have no hesitation concerning the re-use of water which is handled within a closed system and the recycling of water from wort cooling operations as a feed stock for hot liquor within the brewhouse is perhaps the best illustration. The same would apply to the re-use/recycling of water from flash pasteurizers and other heating and cooling operations that are carried out under closed or semi-closed systems. However breweries, like most food factories, are cautious about the effects of the use of slightly polluted water such as is discharged from bottle and can pasteurizers. Such water could be cooled in evaporative towers, reused during the day and utilized at the end of the day for floor-washing. Purification of this water by treatment with activated carbon (Batchelor 1977) or magnetic polymers (Raper 1976) followed by chemical sterilization should render it suitable for any purpose within the brewery.

E. Housekeeping

Paramount in any comprehensive approach to water conservation (Koelle 1977) and effluent management is the application of good housekeeping practices and all that has been said in this section with regard to effluent control could be summarized under this heading. The use of water and the discharge of effluent is largely an attitude of mind and it is this attitude that must be changed if any real lasting effects are to be realized.

The efficiency of housekeeping is portrayed in the quantity of effluent as well as its quality. Once facilities are available for measuring flow and taking representative samples the opportunity exists for monitoring the losses of beer and caustic soda by direct analytical measurement of alcohol and alkalinity respectively. Wort losses are more difficult to determine accurately by analysis of the carbohydrate content in effluent because one has to take into account the carbohydrate contributions from waste beer and last runnings. Alcohol analysis by gas chromatography and alkalinity measurement by acid neutralization to the end point of phenolphthalein were used to quantitate hourly discharges of beer and sodium hydroxide in effluent samples collected by an automatic sampler over a 24-hourly period at the author's brewery (Healy and Armitt 1978).

Acknowledgement

Many of the literature references used in the preparation of this chapter were obtained from the library of the Brewing Research Foundation, England during a study period made possible by The Winston Churchill Memorial Trust, Australia and the author's employers, Castlemaine Perkins, Queensland. The assistance of all three establishments is gratefully acknowledged.

REFERENCES

Abson, J. W. and Johnson, A. R. (1964). Int. Bottler and Packer **38** (5), 85.
American Public Health Association (1975). "Standard Methods for the Examination of Water and Wastewater", 14th edn. Amer. Public Health Assn., Washington D.C.
Anand, A. S., Albertson, O. E. and Fox, R. D. (1977). *Effluent and Water Treatment J.* **17** (2), 67.
Anon. (1967a). *Brewers' J.* **103** (1224), 63.
Anon. (1967b). *Int. Brewing and Distilling* **1** (6), 24.
Anon. (1972). *Brauwelt* **112** (70), 1418.
Anon. (1974). *Brauer Malzer* **54** (22), 1037.
Anon. (1975a). *Brauwelt* **115** (50), 1667.
Anon. (1975b). *Brew. Distilling Int.* **5** (12), 24.
Anon. (1975c). *Brewers' Guardian,* **104** (5), 66.
Anon. (1976a). *Chem. Eng.* **83** (16), 57.
Anon. (1976b). *Chem. Eng.* **83** (19), 99.
Anon. (1976c). *Chem. Eng.* **83** (23), 87.
Anon. (1976d). *Int. Brewing and Distilling* **6** (10), 3.

Anon. (1976e). *Modern Brewery Age* **27** (22), MS14.
Anon. (1977a). *Brewers' Digest* **52** (12), 53.
Anon. (1977b). *Env. Sci. and Technol.* **11** (9), 854.
Anon. (1977c). *Env. Sci. and Technol.* **11** (3), 223.
Anon. (1978a). *Brew. Distilling Int.* **8** (5), 26.
Anon. (1978b). *Brew. Distilling Int.* **8** (5), 29.
Anon. (1978c). *Effluent and Water Treatment J.* **18** (1), 33.
Anon. (1978d). *Env. Sci. and Technol.* **12** (2), 129.
Anon. (1978e). *Env. Sci. and Technol.* **12** (3), 250.
Anon. (1978f). *Env. Sci. and Technol.* **12** (10), 1115.
Anon. (1979). *Chem. Eng.* **86** (1), 103.
Appleyard, C. J. and Shaw, M. G. (1974). *Chem. Ind.* (6), 240.
Armitt, J. D. G. (1975). M.Sc. Thesis Univ. Queensland.
Armitt, J. D. G., Dargusch, W. and Healy, P. (1972). *Wallerstein Lab. Commun.* **35**, 203.
Askew, M. W. (1969). Reprint from *Effluent and Water Treatment J.* (Oct./Nov.).
Askew, M. W. (1975). *Process Biochem.* **10** (1), 5.
Askew, M. W. (1976). *J. Inst. Brew.* **82**, 319.
Ault, R. G. (1969). *Chem. Ind.* (4), 87.
Bailey, C. (1975). *Process Eng.* (Feb.) 116.
Baker-Munton, M. H. (1973). *Proc. E.B.C. Congr., Brussels* p. 497.
Barber, N. R. and Dale, C. W. (1978). *Chem. Eng.* **85** (16), 147.
Barnard, J. L. (1975). *Water Res.* **9**, 485.
Barrett, P. (1974). *Tech. Quart., Master Brewers Ass. Am.* **11** (1), 43.
Batchelor, J. S. (1977). *Effluent and Water Treatment J.* **17** (4), 175.
Bays, J. (1978). *Brewers' Guardian* **107** (11), 37.
Bays, J. D. (1977). *Tech. Quart., Master Brewers Ass. Am.* **14** (1), 47.
Beeckmans, I. *et al.* (1953). *Bull. Centre Belge Et. Document. Eaux* (*Liege*) No. 21,164, (via *Chem. Abst.* **47**, 12749g.
Beeckmans, I. and Edeline F. (1957). *Bull. Centr. Belge Et. Eaux Document.* (*Liege*), No. 35, 18.
Berck, B. (1973). *Tech. Quart., Master Brewers Ass. Am.* **10** (1), 56.
Bidwell, R. (1975a). *Brewing Trade Rev.* **90** (1061), 19.
Bidwell, R. (1975b). *Brewing Trade Rev.* **90** (1062), 69.
Bidwell, R. (1975c). *Brewing Trade Rev.* **90** (1063), 112.
Bidwell, R. (1975d). *Brewing Trade Rev.* **90** (1064), 166.
Blenkinship, B. K. (1976). *Proc. 14th Conv. Inst. Brew. Austr. and New Zealand Sect. Melbourne* p. 141.
Bolton, D. H. (1978). *Brew. Distilling Int.* **8** (5), 32.
Bond, A. (1974). *Process. Eng.* (Dec.) p. 65.
Boon, A. G., Skellett, C. F., Newcombe, S., Jones, J. G. and Forster, C. F. (1977). "Water Pollution Control", **76**, Part 1. Inst. Water Pollution Control, U.K.
Borne, B. J. (1976a). *Effluent and Water Treatment J.* **16** (9), 455; **16** (10), 523.
Borne, B. J. (1976b). *Effluent and Water Treatment J.* **16** (10), 523.
Borne, J. (1975). *Chem. Ind.* (1) 13.
Botuk, B. O., Dimitrevskii, N. G., Vasilenko, Yu. P. and Kryzhanovskii, L. K. (1973). *Ferment. Spirit. Prom.* (3). 22 (via *Chem. Abstr., * **79** (4), 23294 u).
Botuk, B. O., Dimitrevskii, N. G., Fortuchenko, L. A., Vasilenko, Yu. P. and Kryzhanovskii, L. K. (1975). *Vodosnabzh. Sanit. Tech.* (1), 13 (via *Chem. Abst.* **83**, 84329p.)

Brown, B. M. (1939). *J. Inst. Brew.* **45**, 551.

Brown, W. F. (1967). *Proc. Ann. Meet. Am. Soc. Brew. Chem.* p. 98.

Burnett, F. R. (1976). *Proc. 14th Conv. Inst. Brewing Austr. and New Zealand Sect. Melbourne* p. 148.

Button, A. H., Stacey, A. J. and Taylor, B. (1977). *Proc. E.B.C. Congr., Amsterdam* p. 377.

Campbell, W. (1977). *Process Biochem.* **12** (6), 6.

Cannon, J. P. and Draeger, F. J. (1968). *Tech. Quart., Master Brewers Ass. Am.* **5** (4), 239.

Catroux, G. and Morfaux, J. N. (1972). *Austr. Chem. Process. Eng.* (Dec.), 14.

Chapman, J. and O'Callaghan, J. R. (1977). *The Brewer* **63** (June), 209.

Chipperfield, P. N. J. (1967). *Effluent and Water Treatment Convention,* (via *Effluent and Water Treatment J.*).

Cockburn, A. G. (1977). *Brewers' Guardian* **106** (1), 25.

Confederation of British Industry (1976)."Trade Effluent Discharged to the Sewer— Recommended Guidelines for Control and Charging".

Control of Pollution Act 1974. (1975). Chapter 40. HMSO, London.

Coors, J. H. and Jangaard, N. O. (1975). *Proc. E.B.C. Congr., Nice* p. 311.

Cottrell, W. R. T. (1975). *Process Eng.* (Feb.), 120.

Craine, R. W. and Zievers, J. F. (1974). *Tech. Quart., Master Brewers Ass. Am.* **11** (1), 47.

Cruver, J. E. (1975). *Water and Sewage Works J.* **120** (10), 74.

Dart, M. C. (1975). *Chem Ind.* (1), 9.

Delcommune, Th. (1971). *Bull. Ass. Etud. Brass., Louvain* **67**, No. 2 and 3.

Diefenbaugh, J. E. (1976). *Cereal Foods World* **21** (4), 159.

Dietrich, K. R. (1978). *Monats. Brau.,* **31** (2), 47.

Dlouhy, P. E. and Dahlstrom, D. A. (1969). *Tech. Quart., Master Brewers Ass. Am.* **6** (1), 14.

Dobbs, R. A. and Williams, R. T. (1963). *Anal. Chem.* **35**, 1064.

Dureau, M. B. (1978). *Food Technol. Austr.* **30** (11), 436.

Eckenfelder, W. W. (1959). *Paper Ontario Industrial Waste Conf.* **6**, 195.

Ehmann, F. E. (1968). *Tech. Quart., Master Brewers Ass. Am.* **5** (1), 78.

Elliott, S. (1971). *Brewers' Guardian* **100** (11), 37.

Erling, F., Gregor, C. H. and Neubert, O. (1977). *Brauwelt* **117** (32), 1080.

Fallwell, W. F. (1974). *Chem. Eng. News* **52** (28), 7.

Federal Water Pollution Control Act Amendment of 1972 (1972). U.S. Public Law 92–500, 92 Congress, 18 Oct. 1972.

Felgate, E. (1972). CBI Review, "Industry and Pollution", p. 27.

Finley, J. W., Walker, C. E. and Hautala, E. (1976). *J. Sci. Food Agric.* **27** (7), 655.

Fish, H. (1973). *Effluent and Water Treatment J.* **13** (5), 279.

Ford, L. D. (1968a). *Proc. 23rd Ind. Waste Conf. Purdue Univ., W. Lafayette, Indiana, U.S.A.*

Ford, L. D. (1968b). Public Works, **99**, 89.

Franke, G. (1963). *Brauwissenschaft* **16** (7), 282.

Fri, R. W. (1974). *Brewers' Digest* **49** (4), 18.

Gaeng, F. E., (1974). *Brauwelt* **114** (69), 1471.

Gaffney, M. P. (1974). *Process Biochem.* **9** (1), 7.

Gastou, P. (1975). *Proc. E.B.C. Congr., Nice* p. 625.

Gatti, L. and Lee-Frampton, J. (1976). *Env. Sci. Technol.* **10** (12), 1092.

Gaudy, A. F. (1972). *J. Water Pollut. Control Fed.* **44** (6), 1044.

Grimshaw, C. (1975). *Brew. Distilling Int.* **5** (4), 31.

Grunert, K. and Hermes, B. (1972). *Brauwelt* **112** (70), 1419.

Hall, C. E. van, Safranko, J. and Stenger, V. A. (1963). *Anal. Chem.* **35** (3), 315.

Hang, Y. D., Splittstoesser, D. F. and Woodams, E. E. (1975). *Appl. Microbiol.* **30** (5), 879.

Harbold, H. S. (1976). *Chem. Eng.* **83** (26), 157.

Hawley, J. S. (1973). *Tech. Quart., Master Brewers Ass. Am.* **10** (1), 1.

Healy, P. and Armitt, J. D. G. (1978). Unpublished.

Heller, R. and Fuchs, F. (1974). *Brauwelt* **114** (60), 1268.

Helmers, E. N. *et al.* (1952). *Sewage and Industrial Wastes* **24**, 496.

Heyden, W. and Kanow, P. (1975). *Brauwelt* **115** (42), 1398.

Hoffman, S. (1973). *Brauwelt* **113** (46), 995.

Howson, P. (1972). "Commonwealth Policy and Achievements on the Australian Environment", 24 May 1972.

Imsande, R. R. (1976). *Tech. Quart., Master Brewers Ass. Am.* **12**(4), 253.

Isaac, P. C. G. (1969). *Brewers' Guild J.* **52** (623), 441.

Isaac, P. C. G. (1975). *Process Biochem.* **12** (2), 17.

Isaac, P. C. G. (1976). *Effluent and Water Treatment J.* **9** (11), 597.

Isaac, P. C. G. and Anderson, G. K. (1973). *J. Inst. Brew.* **79**, 154.

Jackson, C. J. and Lines, G. T. (1972). *Pure Appl. Chem.* **29** (1–3), 381.

Janssen, W. C. (1976). *Brauwelt* **116** (39), 1235.

Jewell, W. J., Eckenfelder, W. W. and Cavalier, M. E. (1973). *Purdue Univ. Eng. Bull. Ext. Ser.* No. 140, Pt. 1, 487, via *Chem. Abst.* **80**, 63563h.

Jirka, A. M. and Carter, M. J. (1975). *Anal. Chem.* **47** (8), 1397.

Joint Develop. Cttee (1973). *Brewing Trade Rev.,* **88** (1039), 99.

Josephson, J. (1975). *Env. Sci. Technol.* **9** (10), 908.

Josephson, J. (1977). *Env. Sci. Technol.* **11** (2), 126.

Josephson, J. (1978a). *Env. Sci Technol.* **12** (9), 1002.

Josephson, J. (1978b). *Env. Sci. Technol.* **12** (12), 1244.

Joslin, J. R. (1974). *Process Biochem.* **9** (1), 10.

Joyce, M. E. and Scaief, J. F. (1977). U.S. Environ, Prot. Agency Off. Res. Dev., (Rep.) E.P.A., 1977, EPA–600/2–77–048.

Judell, T. L. (1972). *Proc. 12th Conv. Inst. Brewing Austr. and New Zealand Sect. Perth* p. 69.

Kershaw, M. A. (1976). *Process Biochem.* **12** (2), 37.

Kessler, H. (1972). *Brauwelt* **112** (36), 723.

Klijnhout, A. F. (1977). *Proc. E.B.C. Congr., Amsterdam* p. 325.

Klotz, I. M. (1967). "Energy Changes in Biochemical Reactions". Associated Press, New York, London.

Knudsen, F. B. (1978). *Brewers' Digest* **53** (5), 46.

Koehler, R. (1968). *Wasser. Luft Betr.* **12** (6), 343 (via *Chem. Abstr.,* **69** (20), 80007v.)

Koelle, R. N. (1977). *Tech. Quart., Master Brewers Ass. Am.* **14** (4), 244.

Koller, A. (1974). *Brauwelt* **114** (54), 1167.

Kühbeck, G., Petschik, F. and Koller, A. (1971). *Brauwelt* **111** (49), 1023.

Kuntze, R. E. (1976). *Monats. Brau.* **29** (3), 98.

Lange, P. (1972). *Brauwelt* **112** (67), 1367.

Le Blanc, P. J. (1974). *J. Water Pollut. Contr. Fed.* **46** (9), 2202.

Le Seelleur, L. A. (1971). *Tech. Quart., Master Brewers Ass. Am.* **8** (1), 52.

Lewin, V. H. (1970). *Process Biochem.* **5** (6), 53.

Lewin, V. H. and Latten, A. (1973). *Process Biochem* **8** (6), 15.

Lewis, H. V. (1969). *Am. Brewer* **102** (7/8), 9.
Lewis, M. J. (1976). *Process Biochem.* **11** (3), 4.
Lindsey, S. E. J. (1974). *Process Biochem.* **9** (1), 12.
Lines, G. (1966). *J. Inst. Brew.* **72**, 11.
Lippmann, P. (1975). *Brauwelt* **115** (10), 269.
Litzenburger, K. (1978). *Brauwelt* **118** (26), 932.
Lom, T. (1977). *Tech. Quart., Master Brewers Ass. Am.* **14** (1), 50.
Lones, D. P. (1968). *Brewers' Guild J.* **54** (650), 628.
Lones, D. P. (1973). *The Brewer* **59** (703), 223.
Lones, D. P. (1977). *Brewers' Guardian* (Feb.), 21.
Lossberg, L. G. von and Yorgiadis, S. (1973). *Eng. Bull. Purdue Univ. Eng. Ext.,* No. 140 (pt. 1), 578 (*Chem. Abst.,* **80**, 63567n).
Lovan, C. R. and Foree, E. G. (1972). *Brewers' Digest* **47** (2), 66.
Love, L. S., Guilluame, F. and Weihs, H. (1973). *Tech. Quart., Master Brewers Ass. Am.* **10** (3), 134.
Lund, H. F. (1971). "Industrial Pollution Control Handbook". McGraw-Hill, New York.
Mackay, C. (1972). *Brewing Rev.* **87** (1033), 267.
Mailer, J. A. B. (1976). *Proc. 14th Conv. Inst. Brew. Austr. and New Zealand Sect. Melbourne* p. 137.
Mändl, B. and Koller, A. (1974). *Brauwissenschaft* **27** (10), 265.
McDonald, D. (1974a). *Brew. Distilling Int.* **4** (8), 20.
McDonald, D. (1974b). *Brew. Distilling Int.* **4** (10), 48.
McDonald, D. (1974c). *Brew. Distilling Int.* **4** (11), 46.
McDonald, D. P. (1973). *Int. Brewing and Distilling* **3** (6), 12.
McKee, J. E. and Pincince, A. B. (1974). *Tech. Quart., Master Brewers Ass. Am.* **11** (1), 35.
McLain, L. (1973). *Process Eng.* (Feb.), 104.
McLoughlin, A. J. (1972). *Process Biochem.* **7** (1), 27.
McWhorter, T. R. and Zielinski, R. J. (1974). *The Brewer* **60** (719), 485.
Meyer, H. (1973). *Proc. E.B.C. Congr., Salzburg* p. 429.
Middlekauff, J. E., Shewey, D. R. and Boyce, W. H. (1968). *Proc. Ann. Meet. Am. Soc. Brew. Chem.* p. 42.
Miles, G. D. and Southgate, B. A. (1971). "Modern Brewing Technology", (Findlay, W. P. K. ed.). Macmillan, London.
Miller, S. S. (1977). *Env. Sci. Technol.* **11** (2), 134.
Möbius, C. H. (1973). *Brauwelt* **113** (87), 1862.
Montgomery, D. D. (1972). *Proc. 12th Conv. Inst. Brewing Austr. and New Zealand Sect. Perth* p. 65.
Moore, W. A., Ludzack, F. J. and Ruchhoft, C. C. (1951). *Anal. Chem.* **23**, 1297.
Mühleck, H. (1972). "Water Management—Basic Issues", p. 443. O.E.C.D., Paris.
Murray, R. S. (1977). *Effluent and Water Treatment J.* **17** (4), 187.
Naecker, J. and Goettsche, R. (1973). *Int. Brewing and Distilling* **3** (3), 23.
Naito, S., Ohtaki, A. and Onozuka, T. (1974). Japanese Patent 744670 "Treatment of Waste Water from Brewery" (via *Chem. Abst.* **84**, 1846423).
Newton, D., Keinath, H. L. and Hillis, L. S. (1962). *Purdue Univ. Eng. Bull. Ext. Ser.* No. 109, 332.
O'Leary, L. B. (1969). *Tech. Quart., Master Brewers Ass. Am.* **6** (1), 11.
O'Rourke, J. T. and Tomlinson, H. D. (1963). *Am. Brewer* **96** (1), 27.
Othmer, D. F. (1977). *Chem. Eng.* **84** (13), 117.

Pettet, A. E. J. (1964). *J. Inst. Brew.* **70**, 474.
Pitt, W. W., Katz, S. and Thacker, L. H. (1973). A.I.Ch.E. Symp. Ser. 1973, **79** (129), 1 (via *Chem. Abst.* **79**, 34977v.)
Prins, H. (1967). *Proc. E.B.C. Congr., Madrid* p. 131.
Ramsay, T. G. (1971). *Tech. Quart., Master Brewers Ass. Am.* **8** (3), 152.
Raper, W. G. C. (1976). *Proc. 14th Conv. Inst. Brewing Austr. and New Zealand Sect. Melbourne,* p. 145.
Raynes, S. H. (1977). *Proc. E.B.C. Congr., Amsterdam* p. 335.
Reiter, W. M. and Sobel, R. (1973). *Chem. Eng. Deskbook* 18 June, 59.
Reynolds, T., Button, A. H. and MacWilliam, I. C. (1966). *J. Inst. Brew.* **72**, 282.
Roberts, F. W. (1974). *Chem. in Brit.* **10** (6), 215.
Royal Commission on Sewage Disposal (1912). 8th Report, London, H.M.S.O., (via *The Surveyor,* 12th and 19th Oct., 1968).
Rudin, A. D. (1976). *Brewers' Guardian* **105** (12), 30.
Russell, D. L. and Tiede, J. J. (1978). *Chem. Eng.* **85** (22), 115.
Sanders, K. G. (1973). *Brewers' Guardian* **102** (8), 37.
Sasahara, T. (1977). *Proc. E.B.C. Congr, Amsterdam* p. 313.
Sasahara, T., Ara, T. and Kitamura, Y. (1974a). *Rep. Res. Lab. Kirin Brewing Co., Yokohama* (17), 39.
Sasahara, T., Ara, T. and Kitamura, Y. (1974b). *Rep. Res. Lab. Kirin Brewing Co., Yokohama,* (17), 51.
Scammell, G. W. (1975). *Process Biochem.* **10** (8), 34.
Schneider, K. (1978). *Brauwelt* **118** (6), 163.
Schneider, R. (1950). Sewage and Industrial Wastes **22** (10), 1307.
Schumann, G. (1967). *Monats. Brau* **20** (12), 416.
Schwarzimuller, A. (1977). *Brau. Industrie* **62** (Aug.), 863.
Sellinger, F. J. (1972). *Brewers Digest* **47** (3), 36.
Senate Select Committee on Water Pollution (Australia) (1970).
Shannon, L. J. and Stevenson, K. E. (1975). *J. Food Sci.* **40** (4), 826.
Shaw, R. G. (1975). Waste Management, Control, Recovery, Reuse Int. Ed. 1974 Australian Waste Conf. (publ. 1975), 117 (via *Chem. Abst.,* **84** (18), 126328r.)
Shell, G. L. and Burns, D. E. (1973). *Effluent and Water Treatment J.* **13** (4), 203.
Sidwick, J. M. (1974). *Effluent and Water Treatment J.* **14** (9), 491.
Sidwick, J. M. (1975). *Int. Bottler and Packer* **75** (1), 43.
Sidwick, J. M. and Gurney, V. C. (1975). *Effluent and Water Treatment J.* **15** (2), 69.
Sidwick, J. M. and Preston, J. R. (1976). *Effluent and Water Treatment J.* **16** (5), 238.
Sidwick, J. M., Watson, J. D. and Watson, D. M. (1973). *Int. Bottler and Packer* **47** (11), 64.
Simpson, J. R. (1967a). *Brewers' J.* (Aug.), 33.
Simpson, J. R. (1967b). *Brewers' J.* (Sept.), 32.
Snaddon, X. V. M., Mayo, S. A. and Cope, J. (1973). *Process Biochem.* **8** (9), 15.
Søltoft, M. (1967). *J. Inst. Brewing* **73**, 393.
Sommer, G. (1977). *Proc. Ann. Meet. Am. Soc. Brew. Chem.* **35** (1), 9.
Soroko, O. (1973). *Tech. Quart., Master Brewers Ass. Am.* **10** (3), 139.
Stebbing, P. J. (1968). *J. Inst. Brew.* **74**, 4.
Symposium Report. (1974). *Process Biochem.* **9** (2), 26.
Thibault, G. T. and Tracy, K. D. (1978). *Chem. Eng.* **85** (20), 155.
Thiel, P. G. and Toit, P. J. du (1965). *J. Inst. Brew.* **71**, 509.
Thompson, R. G. (1976). *Chem. Eng.* **83** (13), 151.
Tidswell, M. A. (1965). *Brewers' Guild J.* **51** (605), 122.

Tomlinson, E. J. (1976). *Water Res.* **10** (5), 413.

Tooloose, D. L. *et al.* (1962). *Purdue Univ. Eng. Bull. Ext. Ser.* No. 112, 758 (via *Chem. Abst.,* **60**, 5192a.)

U.S. Environment Protection Agency. "Monitoring Industrial Wastewater". Handbook 6002, Technology Transfer, Washington D.C.

U.S. Environmental Protection Agency (1974). "Design Criteria for Mechanical, Electrical and Component Reliability", E.P.A. 430–99–74–001, U.S. Govt. Printing Office, Washington, D.C.

U.S. Environmental Protection Agency (1976). "No Small Task", June.

Uhl, A. and Hancke, K. (1969). *Brauwissenschaft* **22** (5), 208.

Walker, J. F. (1965). *Brewing Trade Rev.* (Aug.) (79), 488.

Walker, J. F. (1971). *Brewers' Guardian* **100** (11), 33.

Walker, J. F. (1972). *Water Pollution Manual,* 174.

Westermann, D. H. (1971). *Tech. Quart., Master Brewers Ass. Am.* **8** (4), 207.

Willvonseder, G. (1978). *Brew. Distilling Int.* **8** (5), 37.

Woolcock, R. J. (1975). *Filtration and Separation* **12** (2), 174.

Wren, J. J. (1978). *J. Inst. Brew.* **84**, 310.

Wysocki, G. (1972). *Brauwelt* **112** (75), 1544.

Wysocki, G. (1973). *Int. Brewing and Distilling* **3** (2), 19.

Wysocki, G. and Glockner, H. (1972). *Brewers' Digest* **47** (1), 86.

Zdybiewska, M. (1963). *Zesz. Nauk. Politech. Slaska, Inst. Sanit.* **5**, 27 (via *Chem. Abst.* **67**, 20598n.)

Subject Index

629